MicroTimes named Ed Krol one of 1993's top 100 industry leaders and unsung heroes. About *The Whole Internet* they wrote, "The book against which all subsequent Internet guides are measured. Krol's work has emerged as an indispensable reference to beginners and seasoned travelers alike as they venture out on the data highway."

The Whole Internet User's Guide & Catalog "is an encyclopedic compendium of all the places to explore, the short-cuts to get there, the reasons to linger, the treasures you might find, and the tools to make this free world-wide service worthwhile."
—*Kevin Kelly, WIRED*

"For the Internet novice with limited computer experience, the best introduction is Ed Krol's *The Whole Internet User's Guide & Catalog.*"
—*The New York Times*

"*The Whole Internet User's Guide & Catalog* will probably become the Internet user's bible because it provides comprehensive, easy instructions for those who want to get the most from this valuable electronic tool."
—*David J. Buerger, Editor, Communications Week*

"*The Whole Internet User's Guide & Catalog* is currently THE definitive user guide to the Internet, and it frankly has no rivals. A simple recommendation—if you are interested in the Internet, buy it."
—*Jack Rickard, Editor, Boardwatch Magazine*

"*The Whole Internet User's Guide & Catalog* is the single best book on what's out there in the global electronic village. It does for the free Internet what Alfred Glossbrenner's books did for fee-based online databases. It's the first compendium on the world's largest computer network."
—*Greg Goode, Syndicated News Service*

"I recommend *The Whole Internet User's Guide & Catalog* very highly. Although there are many other competing works out there, this one covers almost everything anyone could want to know, is well written for both the novice and the experienced user, and is available now at a very reasonable price. All who are reading this review should have a copy on their desk, and a copy in their public, academic, or special library for reference by other potential users."
—*Dan Lester, Associate University Librarian, Boise State University*

"This is the kind of book that you get several extra copies of to give away when someone asks you 'What's Internet?' or to staff or colleagues when you want to give them the hint that they could be more effective in their work if they used Internet."
—*Anthony M. Rutkowski, SprintLink*

"In a word, it is a *must* for all Internet sites as a complement to much of the resource material and guides you would already have accumulated."
—*Dr. Ian Hoyle, Senior Research Scientist, BHP Research-Melbourne Laboratories*

"There is a new book out called *The Whole Internet* by Ed Krol. I highly recommend this book to anyone interested in learning more about the Internet."
—*Scott Yanoff, the "Yanoff list," Inet Services*

"I wasn't sure that an 'old hand' like me would learn much from an overview guidebook targeted at mere users, but there are whole chapters in here on subjects I've been meaning to find out about, such as gopher, wais, and www."
—*Steve Summit, Grizzled Internet Vet*

"Krol's style throughout the book is a breezy conversational style that is designed to not intimidate users but rather, make them feel at ease as they explore a potentially complex area."
—*Naor Wallach, Newsbytes News Network*

"*The Whole Internet User's Guide & Catalog*, published by O'Reilly & Associates and prepared by Ed Krol, covers the basic utilities used to access the network and then guides the reader through Internet's 'databases of databases'. The book also covers how to find software and how to deal with network problems and other troublesome issues."
—*UNIX Review*

"You can imagine that on Friday (the day I received *The Whole Internet*), the moment I laid it down, someone else was snapping it up. I had to guard it with my life! I think that pretty much speaks for itself."
—*Phil Draughon, Sr. Analyst, Distributed Systems, ACNS Networking*

"If you read just one technical manual this year, let it be *The Whole Internet User's Guide & Catalog*. Author Ed Krol, a University of Illinois computer administrator, has written a surprisingly clear and much-needed guide to services available on the world's largest and fastest-growing computer network."
—*Beppi Crosariol, Financial Times of Canada*

THE WHOLE INTERNET

USER'S GUIDE & CATALOG

SECOND EDITION

ED KROL

O'REILLY & ASSOCIATES, INC.
103 MORRIS STREET, SUITE A
SEBASTOPOL CA 95472
(800) 998-9938 • (707) 829-0515
EMAIL: *nuts@ora.com* OR *uunet!ora!nuts*

The Whole Internet User's Guide & Catalog
by Ed Krol

Editor: Mike Loukides

Production Editor: Ellen Siever

Printing History:

September 1992:	First Edition.
November 1992:	Minor corrections.
February 1993:	Minor corrections.
May 1993:	Minor corrections.
July 1993:	Minor corrections.
November 1993:	Minor corrections. Updated Resource Catalog.
April 1994:	Second Edition.

This book is printed on acid-free paper with 50% recycled content, 10-15% post-consumer waste.
O'Reilly & Associates is committed to using paper with the highest recycled content available
consistent with high quality.

ISBN: 1-56592-063-5

TABLE OF CONTENTS

PREFACE _____ xix

    Audience   xxi
    Approaching This Book   xxii
    Conventions   xxiii
    Acknowledgments   xxiii

CHAPTER ONE

WHAT IS THIS BOOK ABOUT? _____ 1

    Something for Everyone   2
    What You Will Learn   3
        What If I Don't Know UNIX?   5
    What You Need   6
    What an Internet Connection Means   7
        Getting Connected?   9
    How This Book Is Organized   10

CHAPTER TWO

WHAT IS THE INTERNET? _____ 13

    What Makes Up the Internet?   15
    Who Governs the Internet?   16
    Who Pays for It?   17
    What Does This Mean for Me?   17
    What Does the Future Hold?   18
        New Standard Protocols   18
        International Connections   18
        Commercialization   19
        Privatization   19

CHAPTER THREE

HOW THE INTERNET WORKS _____23

Moving Bits From One Place to Another   23
    Packet Switched Networks   24
    The Internet Protocol (IP)   24
    The Transmission Control Protocol (TCP)   27
    Other Transmission Protocols   28
Making the Network Friendly   29
    Applications   29
    The Domain Name System   30
        The Domain System Structure   30
        Domain Name Lookup   32
        Domain Name System Hints   33

CHAPTER FOUR

WHAT'S ALLOWED ON THE INTERNET?_____35

Legal Implications   35
    Research, Education, and the Federal Dollar   36
    Commercial Use   37
    Export Laws   37
    Property Rights   38
Politics and the Internet   39
Network Ethics   40
    Individualism   40
    Protecting the Internet   41
Ethics and the Private Commercial Internet   42
Security Consciousness   43
    Passwords   45
    Importing Software   46
    Misconfigured Software   47

System Software Flaws 47

What If My Computer Is Violated? 47

CHAPTER FIVE

REMOTE LOGIN _____ 49

Simple TELNET 50

What's Really Going On 51

TELNET Command Mode 52

Non-standard TELNET Servers 55

 TELNET to Non-standard Ports 56

 Mimicking Alternate Clients 58

TELNETting to IBM Mainframes 58

CHAPTER SIX

MOVING FILES: FTP _____ 65

Getting Started With FTP 66

 Common Problems 68

 Browsing on a Remote Machine 69

 Directories in FTP 73

 ASCII and Binary Transfers 74

 Transferring Multiple Files 77

 FTP Command Summary 79

Anonymous FTP 81

Handling Large Files and Groups of Files 83

 Compressed Files 83

 Moving a Whole Directory 85

  Shell archives 88

  Other archival utilities 89

Special Notes on Various Systems 89

 Target: Digital Equipment VMS Systems 90

 Target: MS-DOS Systems 93

 Target: IBM VM Systems 94

Target: Macintosh   96
Last Words: Some Practical Advice   97

CHAPTER SEVEN

ELECTRONIC MAIL   101

When Is Electronic Mail Useful?   101
Hints for Writing Electronic Mail   104
How Electronic Mail Works   105
   It's All in the Address   106
Acquiring Electronic Mail Addresses   110
Choosing an Email Package   110
The UNIX Mail Program   111
   Reading Your Mail   112
   Sending Messages   114
A Shopping List of Features   115
   Universally Supported Features   115
      Aliasing   116
      Folders   116
      Forwarding   117
      Inclusion of Text Files 119
      Mailing Lists   119
      Reply   120
   Commonly Supported Features   121
      Carbon copies   121
      Blind carbon copies   122
      Signature files   122
   Unusual and Non-standard Features   123
      Attaching documents   123
      Notification of receipt 123
      Notification of reading 123
      Message cancel   123
Sending Binary Data as ASCII   124
MIME: Multi-purpose Internet Mail Extensions   126
   What MIME Does   127
   Pine: A MIME Example   129
When Electronic Mail Gets Returned   132
   Unknown Hosts   133

Unknown Recipients 135
Mail Can't Be Delivered 136
Failures Involving Multiple Recipients 137
Last Ditch Help 137
Mail Lists and Reflectors 138
Dropping Your Subscription 140
Moderators and List Etiquette 142
File Retrieval Using Electronic Mail 143
Internet-style Servers 143
Listserv-style Requests 144
Listserv file retrieval commands 144
Majordomo file retrieval 145
Almanac file retrieval 145
The FTPmail Application Gateway 146
Other FTPmail Servers 147
FTPmail to IEUnet 148
BITFTP 148
Taking a Break 148

CHAPTER EIGHT

NETWORK NEWS_____151

Newsgroups and News System Organization 153
Getting Started 157
Setting Up nn 158
Reading News 160
What Is a News Item? 160
Using a Newsreader 160
Steering a Newsreader 163
Saving News Articles 165
Controlling What You Read 166
Subscribing and unsubscribing 166
Killing and auto-selecting items 167
Catching Up 169
rot13 170
Posting Articles 171
Adding to an Existing Discussion 171
Starting a New Discussion 173
Replying via Email 175

Other Hints and Conventions   175
Summary of nn Commands and Features   176
   Command-line Options   177
   Some Selection Mode Commands   178
   Some Reading Mode Commands   179
A Philosophically Different Newsreader: tin   180
   Following Up and Posting   184
   Quitting tin   185

CHAPTER NINE

FINDING FILES _____ 187

How Archie Works   188
Contacting Archie   189
Using Archie With Telnet   191
   Searching by Filename   192
   Controlling Filename Matching   195
   Controlling a Search Geographically   196
   Searching the Descriptive Index   198
   Other Archie Commands   199
   Archie Configuration Variables   200
Using Archie by Electronic Mail   201
Archie Using a Client   203
Post-processing Archie Output   204
Archie Under the X Window System   205

CHAPTER TEN

FINDING SOMEONE _____ 209

Why Isn't There a Single Internet Directory?   210
   Mobile Users   210
   Standards   211
   Security and Privacy   211
CSO Directories   212
Finding a User on a Specific System   212
   Finger as a general information server   214
   When finger fails   215
Whois   215

The USENET User List   219
X.500 Directory Services   221
    Native X.500   221
    X.500 access   223
Knowbot Information Service   227
Netfind   229

CHAPTER ELEVEN

TUNNELING THROUGH THE INTERNET: GOPHER _____233

The Internet Gopher   234
    Finding a Gopher Client   236
    How Gopher Works   238
Finding Internet Resources   238
    Looking at Text Files   240
    Moving to Other Servers   242
    Index Searches   244
    Searching for Things in Menus   247
        Basic Veronica   247
        Advanced Veronica   250
        Jughead—the searcher you never see   251
    White-pages Servers   251
        Gopher index white-pages searches   252
        CSO directory searches   252
    FTP Through Gopher   256
    Using Telnet Through Gopher   259
Remembering Where You Are With Bookmarks   261
    Pointing to Another Server   263
Gopher Development   263
    Other Gopher Clients   264
    A Last Word   264

CHAPTER TWELVE

SEARCHING INDEXED DATABASES: WAIS _____265

How WAIS Works   266
Getting Access   268
    Formulating a WAIS Search   269

Finding a library	270
Asking your question	273
Refining a Search	275
When Searches Don't Go as Planned	276
Public WAIS Clients	277
Adding Sources	282
New Sources That Aren't in the Directory-of-Servers	283
Building Your Own Sources	285

CHAPTER THIRTEEN

THE WORLD WIDE WEB _____ 287

Getting Started	289
The Web and Gopher	291
Navigating the Web With www	293
Navigating the Web With xmosaic	294
Getting Started	295
Searching Through a Document	300
Saving and Printing Files	300
Advanced Navigation	302
Using the hotlist	302
Window history	304
Working with multiple windows	304
Making Annotations	305
Working With Other Services	306
Searchable Indexes	306
Gopher and FTP Servers	308
Using TELNET Servers	310
Using WAIS Servers	310
The WAIS Directory of Servers	313
Reading Network News	314
Going Outside the Web	314
Opening other resources	315
Uniform Resource Locators	315
Setting Up Your Own Home Page	317
Hints for Mosaic Users	318
Cancelling	318
Minimizing Delays While Loading Images	318
Getting the Big Picture—or the Big Sound	319

Keyboard Shortcuts	320
When Things Go Wrong	321
Where the Web is Going	321
Other Kinds of Documents	321
Making Your Own Links	321
Creating Hypertext Documents	322
How Can I Help?	322

CHAPTER FOURTEEN

OTHER APPLICATIONS_____325

The R Commands	325
Security and Validation	326
Remote Login	327
Escape sequences	329
Moving Files	329
Distributing Files	331
X Windows	333
Disk and File Sharing	335
Time Services	337
FAX Over the Internet	338
Conversations With Others	339
Talking	340
Chats	341
Ytalk	342
Internet Relay Chat	342
Games	346
The Uncategorizable: MUDs	347
Audio and Video	349
Robotic Librarians	350

CHAPTER FIFTEEN

DEALING WITH PROBLEMS _____351

The Ground Rules	352
Gather Baseline Information	354
The Battleplan	355
Know the Hours of Operation	355

Read the Error Message 356
Did You Change Anything? 358
Try a Different Destination 358
Try Your Neighbor's System 359
Try to Reach a Local System 359
Look Around Your Office 359
Check Your Local Connection 360
Dial-up connections 361
LAN, PPP, or SLIP connections 362
Some Consolation 362
Talking to Operations Personnel 363
Dealing With Coaxial Ethernets 363
Token Ring Notes 365

RESOURCES ON THE INTERNET _____369

Stalking the Wild Resource 370
Friends 370
Network News and Mailing Lists 370
Archie 371
Gopher 371
WAIS 372
The World Wide Web 372
A Few Special Resources 372
The InterNIC 372
Registration Services 373
Database Services 373
Information Services 374
U.S. Government Resources 374
The Global Network Navigator 376
Domain Name Lookup 377
How We Did It 378
What Is a Resource? 379
Accuracy and Permissions 379

Using the Catalog   380
The Whole Internet Catalog   383

APPENDIX A

GETTING CONNECTED TO THE INTERNET   457

Grades of Service   458
    Dedicated Internet Access   458
    SLIP and PPP   459
    ISDN Access   460
    Dial-up Access   460
    UUCP Access   461
    Access Via Other Networks   462
    Telephone Connections   462
Service Providers   462
    POPs and 800 Numbers   463
    There's No Such Thing as a Cheap Lunch   464
    Internet Coops   464
    Regional Versus National   465
    The Providers Themselves   467

APPENDIX B

INTERNATIONAL NETWORK CONNECTIVITY   489

Summary of International Connectivity   489
Country Codes and Connectivity   489

APPENDIX C

ACCEPTABLE USE   495

The NSFNET Backbone Services Acceptable Use Policy   495

APPENDIX D

A UNIX PRIMER   497

Logging In   497
Command Basics   498
    How Commands Look   498

Essential Commands	499
Standard Input and Output	501
Directory Structure	502
Legal Filenames	503
Filename Wildcards	503
Other Books	504

GLOSSARY _____ 505

TECHNICAL INDEX _____ 517

CATALOG INDEX _____ 531

FIGURES

CHAPTER ONE: WHAT IS THIS BOOK ABOUT?   *1*

1-1   A true Internet connection   *8*
1-2   A dial-up Internet connection   *8*

CHAPTER THREE: HOW THE INTERNET WORKS   *23*

3-1   Internet hardware   *25*
3-2   IP envelopes   *25*
3-3   TCP packet encapsulation   *28*
3-4   Domain authority   *31*

CHAPTER SIX: MOVING FILES: FTP   *65*

6-1   Moving many files   *86*

CHAPTER SEVEN: ELECTRONIC MAIL   *101*

7-1   Local mail reflectors   *142*

CHAPTER EIGHT: NETWORK NEWS   *151*

8-1   User's view of the news system   *153*
8-2   Implementation of the news system   *155*

CHAPTER NINE: FINDING FILES   *187*

9-1   How Archie works   *189*
9-2   Initial xarchie screen   *205*
9-3   xarchie search results   *206*

CHAPTER TEN: FINDING SOMEONE   *209*

10-1   Phone book structure   *222*
10-2   X.500 tree structure   *223*

CHAPTER TWELVE: SEARCHING INDEXED DATABASES: WAIS   *265*

12-1   Main window   *269*
12-2   Directory-of-servers query   *271*
12-3   Selecting a source   *271*
12-4   Results of directory search   *272*
12-5   Result of behavior problems search   *274*

12-6   Article you retrieved   274
12-7   Feedback search setup   275
12-8   Source maintenance window   285

CHAPTER THIRTEEN: THE WORLD WIDE WEB   287
13-1   NCSA Mosaic home page   291
13-2   NCSA Mosaic home page   296
13-3   Global Network Navigator home page   298
13-4   The Whole Internet Catalog subject index   299
13-5   Search through current document window   300
13-6   Save document window   301
13-7   Print document window   302
13-8   Mosaic Navigate menu   303
13-9   Mosaic Hotlist window   303
13-10   Creating an annotation   305
13-11   Searchable indexes   307
13-12   Mosaic viewing an FTP archive   308
13-13   Opening a resource   315
13-14   NCSA Mosaic options menu   319

CHAPTER FIFTEEN: DEALING WITH PROBLEMS   351
15-1   The Internet cloud   352
15-2   Network schematic   354
15-3   Typical thick Ethernet   364
15-4   Thin Ethernet—tap and terminator   364

APPENDIX B: INTERNATIONAL NETWORK CONNECTIVITY   489
B-1   International connectivity summary   490

TABLES

CHAPTER THREE: HOW THE INTERNET WORKS   *23*
3-1   *Original High-level Domains*   *32*

CHAPTER SIX: MOVING FILES: FTP   *65*
6-1   *Common File Types and Modes*   *76*
6-2   *Common Compression Programs*   *84*

CHAPTER SEVEN: ELECTRONIC MAIL   *101*
7-1   *Comparison of Communication Techniques*   *102*
7-2   *Addressing Users of Other Networks*   *107*
7-3   *Subscribing to Mailing Lists*   *141*
7-4   *FTPmail and BITFTP servers*   *148*

CHAPTER EIGHT: NETWORK NEWS   *151*
8-1   *Common Distribution Keywords*   *174*

CHAPTER NINE: FINDING FILES   *187*
9-1   *Available Archie Servers*   *190*

CHAPTER TEN: FINDING SOMEONE   *209*
10-1   *Public Netfind Access Sites*   *230*

CHAPTER ELEVEN: TUNNELING THROUGH THE INTERNET: GOPHER   *233*
11-1   *Public Gopher Access Sites*   *237*

CHAPTER TWELVE: SEARCHING INDEXED DATABASES: WAIS   *265*
12-1   *Public WAIS Servers*   *277*
12-2   *Waisindex Input Formats*   *285*

CHAPTER THIRTEEN: THE WORLD WIDE WEB   *287*
13-1   *Common Mosaic Icons*   *309*

CHAPTER FIFTEEN: DEALING WITH PROBLEMS   *351*
1   *Accessing The InterNIC*   *374*
2   *Almanac Servers*   *375*

APPENDIX A: GETTING CONNECTED TO THE INTERNET   457

A-1   Telephone Line Options   *462*
A-2   Nationwide and International Service Providers   *467*
A-3   Regional Service Providers   *473*

APPENDIX B: INTERNATIONAL NETWORK CONNECTIVITY   489

B-1   Key to Connectivity Table   *490*

PREFACE

Audience
Approaching This Book
Conventions
Acknowledgments

This is a book about the Internet, the world's largest computer network. It's aimed at the "garden variety" computer user: not the expert or the computer afficionado, just someone who has a job to get done. To those of us who have been using the Internet for a long time, a lot of what we discuss has become commonplace. But to get a sense for what the Internet is, and why this book is important, we need to take a few steps back.

Ten or twelve years ago, a minor revolution occurred when personal computers became common. Within a few years everyone had a computer at home, or in the office. And, to be honest, most people thought that was adequate: a little help doing budget planning, a nice word processor for writing letters, and we were satisfied. Some visionaries talked about computers as information appliances: you could use your home or office computer to connect to the national news services, get stock reports, do library searches, even read professional journals or literary classics—but, at the time, these were far-reaching ideas.

Well, time has passed since computers first moved from behind the "glass wall" into our offices and homes. In those dozen or so years, another revolution, arguably more important than the first, has taken place. And that revolution was computer networking. Personal computers are great, but computers become something special when they're connected to each other.

With the Internet, networking has come of age. The information resources that visionaries talked about in the early 80's are not just research topics that a few advanced thinkers can play with in a lab—they're real-life realities that you can tap into from your home. Once you're connected to the Internet, you have instant access to an almost indescribable wealth of information. You have to pay for some of it, sure—but most of it is available for free. Through electronic mail and bulletin boards (called *newsgroups* in Internet-lingo), you can use a different kind of resource: a worldwide supply of knowledgeable people, some of whom are certain to share your interests, no matter how obscure. It's easy to find a discussion group on almost any topic, or to find people interested in forming a new discussion group. While free advice is often worth what you pay for it, there are also lots of well-informed experts who are more than willing to be helpful.

In the 18 months since the first edition appeared, the Internet has become an even richer place. There are more people, partly because of the Clinton Administration's talk of an Information Superhighway. Now, everyone wants to get on; you can read about the Internet in *Time*, watch news items about it on your local TV station; you even see some advertisements giving electronic mail addresses. There are also more (and better) resources: there's a whole world of multimedia resources, including museums, exhibitions, art galleries, and shopping malls, that didn't exist two years ago. Even the visionaries would be astonished by what we've achieved.

Well, then, where do you start? Getting a handle on the Internet is a lot like grabbing a handful of Jello—the more firm you think your grasp is, the more oozes down your arm. You don't need to deal with Jello in this manner to eat it, you just need the right tool: a spoon. And you need to dig in and start eating. The same is true of the Internet. You don't need to be an expert in telephone lines, data communications, and network protocols for it to be useful. And no amount of gushing about the Net's limitless resources will make the Internet useful. You just need to know how to use some tools and to start working with them.

As for uses, we've got millions of them. They range from the scholarly (you can read works analyzing Dante's *Divine Comedy*); to the useful (you can look at agricultural market reports); to the recreational (you can get ski reports for Aspen); to the humorous ("How do I cook Jello?"). It is also an amazing tool for collaboration: working with other people on your own *magnum opus*.

In a sense, the existence of this book is a tribute to the power and usefulness of the Internet. Mike Loukides, the editor, and I met via electronic mail. Network users were clamoring to get me to update a help guide I wrote a long time ago, "The Hitchhiker's Guide to the Internet." I was about to volunteer when Mike sent me an electronic mail message and asked "How about doing it as a book?" This spurred a number of messages about outlines and time frames until both were finalized. The legalities and contracts were handled by the Postal Service; electronic contracts were too commercial for the Internet at the time, and are still too high-tech for courts to deal with. And we were on our way.

Shortly thereafter, I was shipped macro libraries to use in production, and began shipping chapters to Mike, all by email. He would annotate, change, and ship them back to me by the same means. Occasionally, we would trade file directories, screen images, and illustrations. Except for the final review copies and illustrations, everything was handled via the Internet. The whole process was accomplished with less than ten telephone calls.

Think for a minute about what this means. Traditional Post Office service between Illinois (where I live) and Connecticut (where Mike lives) takes three days. If you want to pay extra, you can use a courier service and cut the time down to one day. But I can ship the entire book to Mike over the Internet in a few minutes.

I also gathered the information in the *Resource Catalog* without having to leave home. I watched newsgroups, followed email discussions, and used various tools to acquire the information for the catalog, all of which are explained in the book. Before including any of the resources, I verified that they really existed by reaching out across the network and touching them.

It was almost a year before I finally met some of the amazingly professional people, who helped through my first book at O'Reilly & Associates, in person. It's always an interesting experience to finally meet network acquaintances, and in this case it was even more interesting, since I had spent thousands of hours with them electronically.

Audience

This book is intended for anyone who wants access to the Internet's tremendous resources. It's a book for professionals, certainly, but not computer professionals. It's designed for those who want to use the network, but who don't want to become a professional networker in order to use it. If you're a biologist, or a librarian, or a lawyer, or a clergyman, or a high school teacher, or _____ (fill in your profession here), there's a lot of material and data available that will help you do your job. At the same time, you'll probably find recent Supreme Court opinions or chromosome maps much more interesting than the network itself. You want to use the network as a tool; you don't want to make the network your life. If this description fits you, you need this book. It will get you started and point you towards some interesting resources. If, after this, you find that networking becomes your life—well, that's your decision. The Internet has a way of becoming habit forming.

Although I've based our examples on UNIX, this book does not assume that you're a UNIX user. We had to choose some common ground; UNIX systems are prevalent on the Internet, so it was a logical choice. However, the same utilities are available for virtually any operating system; and, with minor variations, you'll find that they work the same way. If you're using DOS, a Macintosh, VAX/VMS, or some other kind of computer, please pardon the UNIX bias—but you really shouldn't find it a problem.

Very specifically: while writing this book, my model audience was a new graduate student in a non-technical discipline (i.e., not computer science or any form of engineering) who needed to use the Internet to do research. Of course, this presumes an audience ranging from Italian scholars to sociologists to physicists, with a correspondingly wide range of computer experience. I do assume that you're computer literate—if you weren't you probably wouldn't even be looking at this book—and that you are familiar with *some* computer and its operating system, but not necessarily UNIX.

This book is also intended for the experienced network administrator: the one whose job it is to keep a company's or campus's networks working reasonably well. No, you're not supposed to read it; you probably know everything in here already. (Maybe not, though. Check out the chapter on the World Wide Web—Mosaic is one of the newest and most exciting ways of finding Internet information.) If you have this job, you probably spend most of your time answering the same fifty questions. When a new crop of students or employees arrives, you might not get any work done for weeks. With any luck, this book answers most of their questions. From the beginning, we were trying to write a book that would answer as many questions as possible. If you are a network administrator, this book is intended for you—so you can give it away, or post a note on your door saying, "Go to the bookstore, buy this book, and read it before bugging me!"

As with all Nutshell handbooks, O'Reilly & Associates is interested in hearing from readers. If you have any comments or suggestions, please send them to nuts@ora.com. (If you don't know what this means, read Chapter 7, *Electronic Mail.*)

Approaching This Book

Of course, there are many ways to approach the Internet; likewise, there are many ways to read this book. Here are a few suggestions. If you:

Are completely new to the Internet
> Start at the beginning and read to the end. You might want to pay particular attention to the *Resource Catalog*, which tells you what you'll find, and Appendix A, *Getting Connected to the Internet*, which tells you how to get connected. You'll also find Chapter 13, which discusses the World Wide Web, of interest; this chapter includes a discussion of the Mosaic browser, which is the most user-friendly Internet tool now available. But, basically, you ought to read the entire book. If you want, you can skim Chapters 3 and 4, which explain how the Internet works and what's allowed; but please revisit these later.

Are familiar with the Internet, but not a user
> Skip to Chapter 5; in this chapter, we start discussing the basic utilities that you use on the Internet.

Are an experienced Internet user
> Skip to Chapter 9. Chapters 9 through 13 discuss the newest tools to come on the scene: Archie, some newer "white pages" services, Gopher, WAIS, and the World Wide Web. Even if you've been around for a while, you may want to brush up on these. If you're not familiar with these tools, you really should be.

Have used the Internet casually
> Read the first four chapters to get the background you may have missed; and then scan the Table of Contents for chapters whose topics are unfa-

miliar to you. If you do this, read the chapters in order, because many of the newer facilities (Chapter 9 and above), build on each other.

Want to get connected to the Internet
> Look at Appendix A, which discusses various ways of getting a connection.

Want to know what's available before committing yourself
> Look at the *Resource Catalog*.

Are only interested in electronic mail and network news
> Read Chapters 7 and 8, which discuss the email and news services. But—please, read the rest of the book, too. You don't know what you're missing.

Conventions

In this book, we use the following conventions:

- Command names are printed in **bold**; for example, **telnet** or **archie**.
- Names of services or protocols are printed in uppercase or with the initial letter capitalized; for example, TELNET or Archie.
- Input typed literally by the user is printed in **bold**; for example, **get host-table.txt**.
- Internet names and addresses are printed in **bold**; for example, **ora.com**.
- Menu titles and options are printed in bold.
- Filenames are printed in *italic*; for example, */etc/hosts*.
- Names of the USENET newsgroups are printed in *italic*; for example, *rec.music.folk*.
- "Variables"—placeholders that the reader will replace with an actual value—are printed in *italic*. For example, in the command **ftp** *hostname*, you must substitute the name of a computer on the Internet for *hostname*.
- Within examples, output from the computer is printed in `constant width` type.
- Within examples, text typed literally by the user is printed in **`constant bold`** type.
- Within examples, variables are printed in `constant italic` type.
- Within examples, explanatory comments are often placed in *italic* type.

Acknowledgments

A whole host of people helped with this book. First and foremost is my wife Margaret. Without her support and help, it never would have come to pass. She read and corrected most of it, searched Gopher for resources, and tried things to see if my explanations really were sufficient for a computer professional to use the Internet. Also, she took over enough of the running of our home to give me time to devote to the project.

Next comes my daughter Molly, who did without me in many ways for the better part of a year while I was writing. (This is Molly's second experience with computing fame—she was the toddler with a penchant for emergency-off switches, after whom "Molly-guards" are named in the "Hackers Dictionary.")

Then there is Mike Loukides, the editor, project leader, confidence-builder, and cheerleader, who dragged me, sometimes kicking and screaming, to the finish line. In the beginning, Mike helped me to think through just what the book needed to contain, and then made sure that everything made it in. Near the end, when Tim O'Reilly asked us to beef up the coverage of a couple of topics, Mike did most of the restructuring and wrote a significant part of the new material.

Next are all the people at the University of Illinois who helped. George Badger, the head of the Computing and Communications Service Office, for the support I needed with the project. Beth Scheid for picking up some pieces of my real job while I was preoccupied with book-related problems. The real technical people, who answered some bizarre questions and made some of the examples possible: Charley Kline, Paul Pomes, Greg German, Lynn Ward, Albert Cheng, Sandy Seehusen, Bob Booth, Randy Cotton, Allan Tuchman, Bob Foertsch, Mona Heath, and Ed Kubaitis. The faculty of the Graduate School of Library Science was also involved, especially Greg Newby, who had a number of suggestions about how to approach the searching tools of the Internet.

Two people were my test audience: Lisa German, a recent library science graduate, and Pat King, a then-neophyte system administrator. They knew little about the Internet when they began reading the book as it was written, chapter by chapter. They pointed out all the things that were used before explained or were just plain explained too technically. Lisa also spent many hours visiting most of the notable anonymous FTP servers on the Internet searching for resources. It's pretty amazing what someone with a knowledge of common cataloging words and phrases can do with Archie,* but I guess that's what librarians are trained to do.

A large group of people read the book, or just pieces of it, checking for technical errors, inconsistencies, and "useful stuff that I left out." These included Eric Pearce, Robin Peek, Jerry Peek, Mitch Wright, Rick Adams, Tim Berners-Lee, Susan Calcari, Deborah Schaffer, Peter Deutsch, Alan Emtage, Chris Schulte, Martyne Hallgren, and Jim Williams. The book would not be anywhere near as useful without their help.

The interior design of the book, which is a departure from O'Reilly & Associates' previous books, was sparked by a comment of Dale Dougherty's. He thought it a shame that the standard dry "technical book" interior didn't live up to the whimsical promise of Edie Freedman's cover. Tim O'Reilly picked up on that comment,

---

*A file search tool explained in Chapter 9, *Finding Software*.

and insisted on a redesign to make the book and catalog more accessible to a non-technical audience. Edie actually developed the design (with her usual flair) and selected all of the illustrations for both the chapter dividers and the catalog. Her design work was not just something that happened after the book was done, but an integral part of how it turned out. The design was then implemented in **troff** by Lenny Muellner, something no sane person should be asked to do. It included the illustrations of Chris Reilley and the text copy-edited by Rosanne Wagger, who corrected more typos than I thought existed. Together this crew turned a rough manuscript into a work of art.

For the second edition, Ellen Siever did a wonderful job of crash-editing, in addition to pulling together the list of service providers in Appendix A; Jennifer Niederst and John Labovitz created the print rendition of the *Resource Catalog* (from the online catalog for GNN), using software developed by Terry Allen. Clairemarie Fisher O'Leary copyedited the *Resource Catalog* and assisted with production, Kismet McDonough performed the final production quality-control edit, Chris Tong updated the index, and Linda Mui verified the resources in the *Resource Catalog* under a lot of time pressure.

Finally, I'd like to thank the people at Yoyodyne Software Systems, especially John McMahon and John Vance Stuart whose domain I invaded.

CHAPTER ONE

WHAT IS THIS BOOK ABOUT?

Something for Everyone
What You Will Learn
What You Need
What an Internet Connection Means
How This Book Is Organized

In the early 1900's, if you wanted to tinker with horseless carriages, you fell in with other tinkerers and learned by doing. There were no books about automobiles, no schools for would-be mechanics, no James Martin courses. The market was too small for these training aids. In addition, there were good reasons to fall in with a group of experts: early cars were so unreliable that they could hardly be called transportation. When your car broke down, you needed to fix it yourself, or have some good friends who could come to the rescue. You fiddled and asked questions of others. Soon you could answer questions for a novice. Eventually, you might become a highly regarded mechanic (in computing, called a "guru"). When you got to this level, your car might actually be useful transportation, not just an expensive hobby.

Eight years ago, the Internet was in much the same state. The network only had a few thousand users. All of its users either had ready access to experts, or were experts themselves. And they needed expertise—the network was slow and unreliable. Its major purpose was not to do anything useful, but to help people learn how to build and use networks.

In the past eight years, the number of Internet users has increased a thousand-fold; and thousands of new users are being added daily. These people use the network for their daily work and play. They demand reliability, and don't want to be mechanics. They want to be chemists, librarians, meteorologists, kindergarten teachers . . . , who happen to use the network. So now they demand documentation—something to read on the train to work to improve their job skills. They are computer-literate, but not network-literate. This book is about network literacy.

Something for Everyone

The usefulness of the Internet parallels the history of computing, with a lag of about ten years. About ten years ago, personal computers brought computing from the realm of technical gurus to the general public: "the rest of us," as Apple said in their advertisements. The Internet is currently making the same transition.

As with personal computers (or, for that matter, automobiles), the Internet made the transition from an expert's plaything to an everyday tool through a "feedback loop." The network started to become easier to use—in part because the tools were better, in part because it was faster and more reliable. Of the people who were previously scared away from the Internet, the more venturesome started to use it. These new users created a demand for new resources and better tools. The old tools were improved, and new tools were developed to access new resources, making the network easier to use. Now another group of people started finding the Internet useful. The process repeated itself; and it's still repeating itself.

Whatever their sophistication, Internet users are, as a whole, looking for one thing: information. They find information from two general classes of sources: people and computers. It's easy to forget about the Internet's "people" resources, but they're just as important (if not more so) as the computers that are available. Far from being a machine-dominated wasteland, where antisocial misfits sporting pocket protectors flail away at keyboards, the Internet is a friendly place to meet people just like yourself. You're a potential network user if you are:

- A science teacher who needs to remain current and develop curricula
- A Unitarian-Universalist minister in a town of fundamentalists, looking for some spiritual camaraderie
- A criminal lawyer who needs to discuss a case with someone who has a particular kind of legal expertise
- An eighth grader looking for others whose parents don't understand real music

And so on. For all of these people, the Internet provides a way of meeting others in the same boat. It's possible—in fact, it's usually easy—to find an electronic discussion group on almost any topic, or to start a new discussion group if one doesn't already exist.

The Internet also provides these people with access to computer resources. The science teacher can access a NASA-funded computer that provides information—past, present, and future—about space science and the space program. The minister can find the Bible, the Koran, and the Torah, waiting to be searched for selected passages. The lawyer can find timely transcriptions of U.S. Supreme Court opinions in Project Hermes.* The eighth grader can discuss musical lyrics with other eighth graders, or can appear to be an expert among adults. After all, he is the only one who understands the lyrics.

---

*See "Supreme Court Decisions" in the Law section of the Resource Catalog.

This is just the beginning. Sure, you will still find a lot of things about computer internals and the network itself, but this is quickly being eclipsed by information about non-computer related fields. A large part of this book is a catalog of information sources you can access through the Internet. In creating this catalog, we picked as broad a range of sources as possible, to show that the Net really does have something for everyone. If we cataloged every resource on the Internet, the book would be huge—and most of it would be telling you about different software repositories. While we cover our share of software repositories, anyone can find software (if you can't, this book will show you how). What's harder is finding the other gems half-buried in the muck. Since one person's gem is another's muck, we grouped the catalog by subject.

The nice thing about all this is that you play on your terms. When trying something new in person, you're likely to be plagued by doubts. You hear about a bridge gathering at the community center, and think "Am I good enough?", "Am I too good?", "Will my ex-wife be there?" On the network, you can:

- Devote as much or as little time as you like

- Become casual acquaintances or fast friends with someone

- Observe discussions or take part

- Walk away from anything you find objectionable, or fight every wrong

If you like, you can make your collected works of poetry available to anyone who would like to read them. There is very little risk, so you might as well try.

What You Will Learn

Just as there is no one use for the network, there is also no one way to use the network. If you learn everything in this book, you will become a competent network user. You will know how to access every common thing on the network, and you'll know how to get the software needed to do the uncommon things. But it will still be only one way. There are different software packages and philosophies of use which you may like better—there is nothing wrong with them.

Many people view the Internet as the Interstate Highway System for information. You can drive cross-country in a Porsche, a pick-up truck, or a Yugo—they all get you there. (Well, maybe not the Yugo.) This book takes you on a tour in a 1985 Chevy Impala. A Chevy may not be as sexy or fast as a Porsche, but it does offer you a comfortable ride to your destination. Also, you won't get stuck in Outback, Montana because the one mechanic in town has never seen a metric wrench.

In particular, here's what we will cover:

- How to log on to other computers on the Internet (**telnet**). Many computers are "publicly available" for various kinds of work. Some of these computers allow anyone to use them; for some, you have to arrange for an account in advance. Some of these computers can be used for "general purpose" work; others provide some special service, like access to a library catalog or a database.

- How to move files from one computer to another (**ftp**). There are many public archives scattered around the network, providing files that are free for the taking. Many of these archives provide source code for various computer programs, but other archives hold recipes, short stories, demographic information, and so on. You name it, you can probably find it (or something reasonably close).

- How to send electronic mail to other people who use the Internet. The Internet provides worldwide electronic mail delivery.

- How to read and participate in group discussions (USENET news). There are discussion groups for topics ranging from the obscure to the bizarre to the practical.

- How to locate various network resources, ranging from people to software to general databases ("white pages," **archie**, **gopher**, WAIS, World-Wide Web). One of the Internet's problems is that it's too rich; there are so many resources available, it's hard to find what you want, or to remember later where you found it. A few years ago, the network was like a library without a catalog. The "cataloging" tools are just now being put into place. We'll tell you how to use some new and exciting tools (and some older, less-exciting tools) to locate almost anything you might possibly want, ranging from people and software to sociological abstracts and fruit-fly stocks.

With these tools, you'll have the network at your fingertips. There is one problem, though. There are many different versions of all of these tools. I had to pick one configuration to discuss in this book. I typically chose basic, keyboard-oriented UNIX software for the examples. I did this for a couple of reasons. First, people who are going to have the most trouble dealing with the network probably have the least sophisticated computer setup. They are more likely to have a PC with two floppy drives than a high-end computer with a graphics monitor and a mouse. With the software I'm discussing, a lower-end computer will work fine. Second, when you start using the Internet, you may not be connected to it directly. You may access the network by using a modem to "dial up" a computer that is connected. Most of the time, that computer will be running UNIX; it's a fact of Internet life. Well, under those conditions you either are using a real terminal (like a Digital Equipment VT100) or some emulation program, like Procomm, Versaterm, or Kermit, that makes the fanciest computer act like a VT100 terminal. In either case, you are stuck with characters and commands.

For the most part, what you can do on the Internet is defined by the network itself, not by the software you run on your computer to gain access. Using a mouse and pull-down menus may make the network easier to use, but it really doesn't let you do anything you couldn't do with a character-oriented display and keyboard. So, by making this choice, we're not limiting what you can do. Nor are we limiting the book. If you go out and buy some mouse-based software, you'll find that all the concepts in this book are still applicable. You'll just be pushing buttons rather than typing commands.

What If I Don't Know UNIX?

It doesn't matter if you don't know UNIX. The Internet is not UNIX. There are two parts to using the network: running programs on your computer to access the Internet and using those programs to do things across the network. For a PC/DOS user, the program that lets you connect to another system for an interactive terminal session is no different from any other PC/DOS program. The program's name is **telnet**, so you type:

```
A: telnet
```

This looks just like starting WordPerfect or Lotus. The same is true for any other brand of computer.

For your edification, let me show you the comparable UNIX command:

```
% telnet
```

Still think you need to know UNIX?

Once you get the program running, it will look just like every other program you run on your computer: if you normally use commands, it will have commands; if you use pull-down menus, it will have menus. Regardless of how you work, the things you can do will be the same. Think about how the network works (a subject we'll discuss more in Chapter 3). Cooperating computers send precisely defined messages back and forth. These messages only allow certain things to happen. If those messages allow something to happen, it can. If they don't, it can't. It doesn't matter whether your computer is a PC, a Macintosh, a VAX, or a UNIX workstation;* the messages it sends to other Internet computers are the same.

So, the examples in this book were all done on UNIX systems—it shouldn't matter. The commands you use may be slightly different, to make them more like a "normal" command on your computer system, but when and why you use which command will remain the same. If an example shows that you start the **ftp** program (you use this to move files), connect to a file archive on some computer, and retrieve a certain file; then on a PC/DOS computer, you need to do those same steps in the same order. If you know how to run standard software on a computer, and if you read this book, you should be able to use the Internet.

At times, you may find that this discussion briefly descends into UNIX details, like "uses the PAGER environment variable." I tried to be very explicit in explaining examples, and this is the price I paid. If you're not interested in UNIX, skip the details, but look at the explanation of what's going on. If the UNIX version of the program has to deal with some condition, like the screen filling up, the PC/DOS or Macintosh program will have to do it, too. They will do it in a manner that is

---

*This is not strictly true. The programs may be limited by what a particular computer's operating system may allow. Or the software for your computer may be an older (or newer) version than the corresponding program on another computer.

"normal": i.e., the way PC/DOS or a Macintosh handles similar events in other programs. So, you might even be able to guess what you should do in an emergency.

What You Need

You need three things to explore and use the Internet: a desire for information, the ability to use a computer, and access to the Internet. Desire for information is the most important. That's what the Internet offers: the information you want, when you want it—not "details at noon, six and ten, stay tuned." Without that desire, this book's contents won't impress you. If I say, "Let's check the agricultural markets, the special nutritional requirements of AIDS sufferers, ski conditions, and home beer recipes," and you reply, "So what?" then you're not ready. If your response is, "Wow," then the Internet is for you.

You use the Internet with a computer. You don't have to be a computer scientist to use it. You do need to be able to operate one, run existing programs, and understand what files are. Some computer jargon might help, but mostly you need a couple of very basic buzzwords:

bit The smallest unit of information. A bit can have the value 1 or the value 0. Everything in computing is based on collecting hunks of bits together, manipulating them, and moving them from place to place. For example, it takes eight bits to represent a standard alphabetic character.

K A suffix meaning "about 1000," derived from the Greek kilo. For example, 8.6K characters means 8600 characters. In computing, K may refer to 1000 or 1024 depending on the context, but who cares? For our purposes, "about 1000" is good enough.

click A verb meaning "to select something with a mouse." Sliding a mouse around on the desk moves an arrow on the screen. Programs that use a mouse frequently display simulated "push-buttons" on the screen. You activate those buttons by positioning the arrow on the button you want to push, and pressing the button on the mouse. This is commonly called "clicking" that button.

If I did my job in writing this book, you will learn what you need to know along the way. How's that for going out on a limb?

Finally, you need an Internet connection. This book is oriented towards someone who has a connection and needs to know how to use it. That connection can take a variety of flavors, ranging from a full connection via a local area network (*LAN*), to a timesharing account on another computer using a terminal emulation package. If you already have a connection, you can skip the next section. If you don't have a connection, Appendix A discusses how to get one.

What an Internet Connection Means

If you ask someone, "Are you connected to the Internet?" you might get some strange answers. The question has a good, precise answer, but that's not what many people think about. For many people, the question, "Are you connected" is similar to the question "Do you shop at J.C. Penney's?" Shopping at J.C. Penney's means different things to different people. To some, Penney's is a store at the mall; to others, it is a catalog. Whether the answer to the question is "yes" or "no" probably depends on whether the respondent has been able to get what he or she wanted at Penney's, not the means by which the purchases were made. The same is true of Internet connections. If I ask, "Are you connected?", the question you are likely to hear is, "Can I do the Internet things I want to do from my terminal?" For example, many people who only use electronic mail think they are connected to the Internet when, in fact, they aren't. Before you get started, it's important to know what a connection means. Once you know that, you can figure out whether or not you already have one; if you don't have one, you can determine what kind of connection service you want to buy and how much you should pay.

The Internet offers a wide range of services. We've already seen a partial list of these services: electronic mail, bulletin boards, file transfer, remote login, index programs, and so on. To get the complete set of services, you must have a TCP/IP-style connection (treat this as a buzzword right now—we'll get to what it means in a while). A TCP/IP connection to the Internet is like a Vulcan mind meld on *Star Trek*. Your computer is part of the network: your computer knows how to contact every computer service on the Internet, though it may need some special software to use some of them. Anything which can happen between networked computers can occur. For example, if you want a file, you can move it directly to your workstation, as in Figure 1-1.

If you are only interested in some limited services, you don't necessarily need a full connection to the Internet. That is: you can beg, borrow, or buy an account on a computer that is connected to the Internet. Then you can use a terminal emulator to dial in from your computer to the Internet machine; log in; read mail, fetch files, and do whatever you want (Figure 1-2). In this situation it's fair to say, "I have access to the Internet" or, "I have an Internet connection" because you can do anything the Internet will allow you to do—on the remote machine.*

However, you can't say, "My home computer is connected to the Internet," because it isn't. What's the difference? Well, once you've dialed in to your remote system, you can read and write electronic mail. But you can't send or receive electronic mail from your home system directly; you have to log in to some remote access point first. If you want to save an important mail message, you can save it on the remote system. But you can't save it on your own computer's disk directly; you'll have to first save the file on the remote system's disk, then use your

---

*Of course, the remote (Internet) computer might not have some useful program installed. You'll have to talk that system's manager into finding it and installing it. Installing it on your home PC won't do any good.

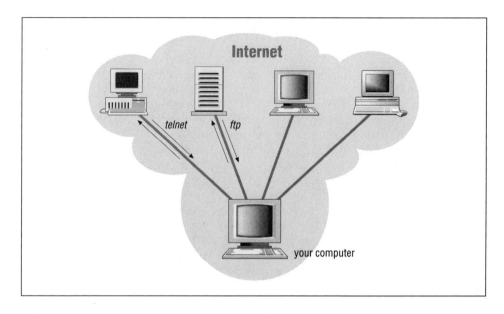

Figure 1-1: A true Internet connection

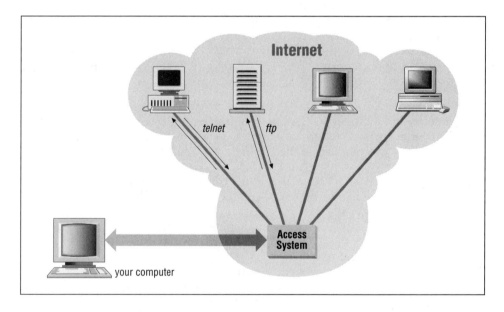

Figure 1-2: A dial-up Internet connection

communications program to move files from the remote system back to your desktop computer. Likewise, you can fetch a file from any of the Internet's public archives; but you still need to go through an extra step of moving that file from the access computer to your personal computer. You also can't use any of the fancier applications that require a graphical display (like Mosaic, discussed in Chapter 13). With this kind of setup, the access computer has no way to get the display information to your local PC.

One step further away, you can get limited access to the Internet. If you're a CompuServe or Bitnet user, you can send mail to the Internet, and (with the right software) read Internet bulletin boards (known as *news*). A UNIX user who uses UUCP* for electronic mail and news is in the same boat. Although it's common for people in this situation to say that they're "connected to the Internet," they aren't in any real sense. With this kind of connection, you can use a few popular Internet services—but you can't use most of them. The fact that I can send a postcard to my friends in Paris doesn't make me a citizen of France.

Some service providers offer software which covers up the limitations of not having a true Internet connection. The software allows you to move files or mail from your home computer to and from Internet sites in one operation. This gives the illusion of being on the Internet even though you may be really accessing it like a dial-up terminal. This is certainly better, but it still leaves you in the hands of the service provider as to what you can or can't do. The real acid test of being on the Internet versus accessing the Internet is, "If I find out about a new or better Internet application program, can I just put the software on my home computer and use it?" I'll be specific: if you can run Mosaic, you can do everything the Internet will let you do.

It doesn't really matter if you are on the Internet, accessing the Internet, or using an alternative network to get to the Internet as long as you can do what you want to do. If all you care about is email, then an account on a timesharing computer with Internet access will suffice and is likely to be cheaper. If you want to use all the latest and greatest features, you probably won't be satisfied without a full connection. You and your pocketbook have to pick. The problem is that Internetting is addictive. You may think today that all you want is email. Through email, you'll find out you are missing something else, so you will need to add that service. With that service you'll find out about another, et cetera, et cetera, et cetera.

Getting Connected?

Here's the big surprise: You may already have an Internet connection and not know it. Most Internet users have a connection through work or school: their corporation or university is connected to the Internet, and they use it for work or for pleasure. If your company has an Internet connection, and you have a computer in your office, getting on the Net should be simple. Ask a system administrator whether or not the company is on the Internet, and (if so) how you can get your office system hooked up. If you're lucky, you may not have to do anything at all—you might be able to sit down, type **telnet**, and go to work. Don't think this is

---

*UUCP is an ancient way of configuring a UNIX computer to automatically dial up another UNIX computer and transfer files. This is the basis for a very popular mail service.

unrealistic: there are *a lot* of people who are this lucky. If you're unlucky and the administrator says that your company or school is not on the Internet, ask the obvious question: "why not?" For a small company, some relatively inexpensive Internet connections can give you the kind of worldwide corporate network that, previously, only companies like EXXON or IBM could afford.

If you're not already connected, there are many ways to get connected. These range from large, fairly expensive solutions that are appropriate for large corporations or universities to relatively low-cost solutions that are appropriate for very small businesses or home use. No matter what level you're at, Internet access always comes via an "access provider": an organization whose job it is to sell Internet access. There are access providers for every level of service from expensive dedicated Internet connections to inexpensive dial up connections for home users. Appendix A, *Getting Connected to the Internet*, lists many (though not all) access providers and the types of service they provide. It also gives you some hints as to how an individual may be able to get connected for little personal cost.*

How This Book Is Organized

This book is organized like a high school woodshop class. First, you talk about the history and theory of carpentry. You then discuss tool use and safety, one tool at a time. On the last day of class, you go on a field trip to the lumber yard to get a feel for what you have to work with.

In Chapters 2 through 4, we'll start with some history and theory. We'll keep the background material to a minimum—just enough so you can understand why the Internet is like it is. We'll discuss a little bit about how the Internet works: not a lot of "this bit moves here," but mostly handwaving and conceptual explanations. This isn't really required reading and can usually be skipped over safely, but it's fairly short, and I think it's important. If you get into a bind and have to guess at what is going on, or what to do next, nothing helps more than a feel for how things work. If you would like to know more about the history of the Internet or its technology, there are other books which go into more detail.†

Most of the book (Chapters 5 to 15) discusses how to use the tools that allow your computer to do things on the Internet. I've tried to focus on what you're likely to do and why: not just which knob to turn and which button to push, but why you need them. A lot of attention is paid to some relatively "fuzzy," but ultimately practical, issues: what's allowed and what isn't? What's polite and what isn't? What's the best way to find the kind of information you want?

---

*The definitive guide to buying an Internet connection is Susan Estrada's book, *Connecting to the Internet*, published by O'Reilly & Associates.

†The best of these is probably Douglas Comer's book, *Internetworking with TCP/IP: Principles, Protocols, and Architectures* (Prentice Hall). Technically, it's quite advanced, but it's the standard work on the topic.

The final large section of this book is a *Resource Catalog*: a list of things we (I had some helpers) found on the Internet. It's organized by subject, so you shouldn't have trouble finding topics that interest you. We found these resources by using the tools explained in this book and just looking around. The list is not complete, but no list is. Pere Marquette didn't throw a dart at a map of the world and decide to look for Indians to convert where the dart landed. He started in a place where he knew there were Indians and began walking from there. This is your place to start. Start at someplace interesting and begin to look and wander. It's amazing what you will find.

If you still think this thing called the Internet is for you, press on, and you can find out what it is.

CHAPTER TWO

WHAT IS THE INTERNET?

What Makes Up the Internet?
Who Governs the Internet?
Who Pays for It?
What Does This Mean for Me?
What Does the Future Hold?

The Internet was born about 20 years ago, out of an effort to connect together a U.S. Defense Department network called the ARPAnet and various other radio and satellite networks. The ARPAnet was an experimental network designed to support military research—in particular, research about how to build networks that could withstand partial outages (like bomb attacks) and still function. (Think about this when I describe how the network works; it may give you some insight into the design of the Internet.) In the ARPAnet model, communication always occurs between a source and a destination computer. The network itself is assumed to be unreliable; any portion of the network could disappear at any moment (pick your favorite catastrophe—these days backhoes cutting cables are more of a threat than bombs). It was designed to require the minimum of information from the computer clients. To send a message on the network, a computer simply had to put its data in an envelope, called an Internet Protocol (IP) packet, and "address" the packets correctly. The communicating computers—not the network itself—were also given the responsibility for ensuring that the communication was accomplished. The philosophy was that every computer on the network could talk, as a peer, with any other computer.

These decisions, like the assumption of an unreliable network, may sound odd, but history has proven that most of them were reasonably correct. With these assumptions, the U.S. was able to develop a working network (the ancestor of the current Internet), and the academic and research users who had access to it were soon addicted. Demand for networking quickly spread. Although the Organization for International Standardization (ISO) was spending years designing the ultimate standard for computer networking, people could not wait. Internet developers in the U.S., U.K., and Scandinavia, responding to market pressures, began to put their IP software on every conceivable type of computer. It became the only practical method for computers from different manufacturers to communicate. This was attractive to the governments and universities, which didn't have policies saying that all computers must be bought from the same vendor. Everyone bought whichever computer they liked and expected the computers to work together over the network.

At about the same time as the Internet was coming into being, Ethernet local area networks (LANs) were developed. LAN technology matured quietly until roughly 1983, when desktop workstations became available and local networking exploded. Most of these workstations came with Berkeley UNIX, which included IP networking software. This created a new demand: rather than connecting to a single large timesharing computer per site, organizations wanted to connect their entire local network to the ARPAnet. This would allow all the computers on that LAN to access ARPAnet facilities. At about the same time, many companies and other organizations started building private networks using the same communications protocols as the ARPAnet: namely, IP and its relatives. It became obvious that if these networks could talk together, users on one network could communicate with those on another; everyone would benefit.

One of the most important of these newer networks was the NSFNET, commissioned by the National Science Foundation (NSF), an agency of the U.S. government. In the late 80's the NSF created five supercomputer centers at major universities. Up to this point, the world's fastest computers had only been available to weapons developers and a few researchers from very large corporations. By creating supercomputer centers, the NSF was making these resources available for any scholarly research. Only five centers were created because they were so expensive—they had to be shared. This created a communications problem: they needed a way to connect their centers together and to allow the clients of these centers to access them. At first, the NSF tried to use the ARPAnet for communications, but this strategy failed because of bureaucratic and staffing problems.

In response, the NSF decided to build its own network, based on the ARPAnet's IP technology. It connected the centers with 56,000 bits per second* telephone lines. It was obvious, however, that if they tried to connect every university directly to a supercomputing center, they would go broke. You pay for these telephone lines by the mile. One line per campus with a supercomputing center at the hub, like spokes on a bike wheel, adds up to many miles of phone lines. Therefore, they decided to create regional networks. In each area of the country, schools would be connected to their nearest neighbor. Each chain was connected to a supercomputer center at one point, and the centers were connected together. With this configuration, any computer could eventually communicate with any other by forwarding the conversation through its neighbors.

This solution was successful—and, like any successful solution, a time came when it no longer worked. Sharing supercomputers also allowed the connected sites to share a lot of other things not related to the centers. Suddenly these schools had a world of data and collaborators at their fingertips. The network's traffic increased until, eventually, the computers controlling the network, and the telephone lines connecting them, were overloaded. In 1987, a contract to manage and upgrade the

---

*This is roughly the ability to transfer two full typewritten pages per second. That's slow by modern standards, but was reasonably fast in the mid 80's.

network was awarded to Merit Network Inc., which ran Michigan's educational network, in partnership with IBM and MCI. The old network was upgraded with faster telephone lines (by a factor of 20) and faster computers.

The process of running out of horsepower and getting bigger engines and better roads continues to this day. Unlike changes to the highway system, however, most of these changes aren't noticed by the people trying to use the Internet to do real work. You won't go to your office, log in to your computer, and find a message saying that the Internet will be inaccessible for the next six months because of improvements. Perhaps even more important is that the process of running out of capacity and improving the network has created a technology that's extremely mature and practical. The ideas have been tested; problems have appeared, and problems have been solved.

For our purposes, the most important aspect of the NSF's networking effort is that it allowed everyone to access the network. Up to that point, Internet access had been available only to researchers in computer science, government employees, and government contractors. The NSF promoted universal educational access by funding campus connections only if the campus had a plan to spread the access around. So everyone attending a four-year college could become an Internet user.

The demand keeps growing. Now that most four-year colleges are connected, people are trying to get secondary and primary schools connected, along with local libraries. People who have graduated from college know what the Internet is good for, and they talk their employers into connecting corporations to the Internet. All this activity points to continued growth, networking problems to solve, evolving technologies, and job security for networkers. Many people are going further: after getting a network connection at work, the next logical step is to get a connection directly to their home.

What Makes Up the Internet?

What comprises the Internet is a difficult question; the answer changes over time. Five years ago the answer would have been easy: All the networks, using the IP protocol, which cooperate to form a seamless network for their collective users. This would include various federal networks, a set of regional networks, campus networks, and some foreign networks.

More recently, some non-IP-based networks saw that the Internet was good. They wanted to provide its services to their clientele. So they developed methods of connecting these "strange" networks (e.g., BITNET, DECnets, etc.) to the Internet. At first these connections, called *gateways*, merely served to transfer electronic mail between the two networks. Some, however, have grown to translate other services between the networks as well. Are they part of the Internet? Maybe yes and maybe no. It depends on whether, in their hearts, they want to be. If this sounds strange, read on—it gets stranger.

Who Governs the Internet?

In many ways the Internet is like a church: it has its council of elders, every member has an opinion about how things should work, and you can either take part or not. It's your choice. The Internet has no president, chief operating officer, or Pope. The constituent networks may have presidents and CEOs, but that's a different issue; there's no single authority figure for the Internet as a whole.

The ultimate authority for where the Internet is going rests with the Internet Society, or ISOC. ISOC is a voluntary membership organization whose purpose is to promote global information exchange through Internet technology.* It appoints a council of elders, which has responsibility for the technical management and direction of the Internet.

The council of elders is a group of invited volunteers called the *Internet Architecture Board*, or the IAB. The IAB meets regularly to "bless" standards and allocate resources, such as addresses. The Internet works because there are standard ways for computers and software applications to talk to each other. This allows computers from different vendors to communicate without problems. It's not an IBM-only or Sun-only or Macintosh-only network. The IAB is responsible for these standards; it decides when a standard is necessary and what it should be. When a standard is required, it considers the problem, adopts a standard, and announces it via the network. (You were expecting stone tablets?) The IAB also keeps track of various numbers (and other things) that must remain unique. For example, each computer on the Internet has a unique 32-bit address; no other computer has the same address. How does this address get assigned? The IAB worries about this kind of problem. It doesn't actually assign the addresses, but it makes the rules about how to assign addresses.

As in a church, everyone has opinions about how things ought to run. Internet users express their opinions through meetings of the Internet Engineering Task Force (IETF). The IETF is another volunteer organization; it meets regularly to discuss operational and near-term technical problems of the Internet. When it considers a problem important enough to merit concern, the IETF sets up a "working group" for further investigation. (In practice, "important enough" usually means that there are enough people to volunteer for the working group.) Anyone can attend IETF meetings and be on working groups; the important thing is that they work. Working groups have many different functions, ranging from producing documentation, to deciding how networks should cooperate when problems occur, to changing the meaning of the bits in some kind of packet. A working group usually produces a report. Depending on the kind of recommendation, it could just be documentation that is made available to anyone wanting it, it could be accepted voluntarily as a good idea which people follow, or it could be sent to the IAB to be declared a standard.

---

*If you'd like more information, or if you would like to join, see "Network Organizations" in the *Resource Catalog.*

If you go to a church and accept its teachings and philosophy, you are accepted by it, and receive the benefits. If you don't like it, you can leave. The church is still there, and you get none of the benefits. Such is the Internet. If a network accepts the teachings of the Internet, is connected to it, and considers itself part of it, then it is part of the Internet. It will find things it doesn't like and can address those concerns through the IETF. Some concerns may be considered valid, and the Internet may change accordingly. Some of the changes may run counter to the religion and be rejected. If the network does something that causes damage to the Internet, it could be excommunicated until it mends its evil ways.

Who Pays for It?

The old rule for when things are confusing is "follow the money." Well, this won't help you to understand the Internet. No one pays for "it"; there is no Internet, Inc. that collects fees from all Internet networks or users. Instead, everyone pays for their part. The NSF pays for NSFNET. NASA pays for the NASA Science Internet. Networks get together and decide how to connect themselves together and fund these interconnections. A college or corporation pays for its connection to a regional network, which in turn pays a national provider for its access.

There is a myth that the Internet is free. It's not; someone pays for every connection to the Internet. Many times these fees aren't passed on to the actual users, which feeds the illusion of "free access." But there are also plenty of users who know very well that the Internet isn't free: many users pay monthly or hourly charges for Internet access from home at speeds up to 56K bits per second (the same as the original network backbones). Right now, the fastest growth areas for the Internet are probably small businesses and individuals, and these users are very aware of the price.

What Does This Mean for Me?

The concept that the Internet is not a network, but a collection of networks, means little to the end user. You want to do something useful: run a program, or access some unique data. You shouldn't have to worry about how it's all stuck together. Consider the telephone system—it's an internet, too. Pacific Bell, AT&T, MCI, British Telecom, Telefonos de Mexico, and so on, are all separate corporations that run pieces of the telephone system. They worry about how to make it all work together; all you have to do is dial. If you ignore cost and commercials, you shouldn't care if you are dealing with MCI, AT&T, or Sprint. Dial the number and it works.

You only care who carries your calls when a problem occurs. If one switch breaks, only the company that owns the switch can fix it. Different phone companies can talk to each other about problems, but each phone carrier is responsible for fixing problems on its own part of the system. The same is true on the Internet. Each network has its own network operations center (NOC). The operations centers talk to each other and know how to resolve problems. Your site has a contract with one of the Internet's constituent networks, and its job is to keep your site happy.

So if something goes wrong, they are the ones to gripe at. If it's not their problem, they'll pass it along.

What Does the Future Hold?

Finally, a question I can answer. It's not that I have a crystal ball (if I did I'd spend my time on Wall Street instead of writing a book). Rather, these are the things that the IAB and the IETF discuss at their meetings. Most people don't care about the long discussions; they only want to know how they'll be affected. So, here are highlights of the networking future.

New Standard Protocols

When I was talking about how the Internet started, I mentioned the Organization for International Standardization and their set of protocol standards. Well, they finally finished designing it. Now it is an international standard, typically referred to as the ISO/OSI (Open Systems Interconnect) protocol suite. Many of the Internet's component networks allow use of OSI today. There isn't much demand, yet. The U.S. government has taken a position that government computers should be able to speak these protocols. Many have the software, but few are using it now.

It's really unclear how much demand there will be for OSI, notwithstanding the government backing. Many people feel that the current approach isn't broke, so why fix it? They are just becoming comfortable with what they have; why should they have to learn a new set of commands and terminology just because it is the standard?

Currently there are no real advantages to moving to OSI. It is more complex and less mature than IP, and hence doesn't work as efficiently. OSI does offer hope of some additional features, but it also suffers from some of the same problems that will plague IP as the network gets much bigger and faster. It's clear that some sites will convert to the OSI protocols over the next few years. The question is, how many?

International Connections

The Internet has been an international network for a long time, but it only extended to the United States' allies and overseas military bases. Now, with the less paranoid world environment, the Internet is spreading everywhere. It's currently in over 60 countries, and the number is rapidly increasing. Eastern European countries longing for Western scientific ties have wanted to participate for a long time, but were excluded by government regulation. Now that the "Iron Curtain" no longer exists, they're well represented. Third world countries that formerly didn't have the means to participate now view the Internet as a way to raise their education and technology levels.

In Europe, the development of the Internet used to be hampered by national policies mandating OSI protocols, regarding IP as a cultural threat akin to EuroDisney. Outside of Scandinavia (where the Internet protocols were embraced long ago), these policies prevented development of large-scale Internet infrastructures. In 1989, RIPE (Reseaux IP Europeens) began coordinating the operation of the Internet in Europe; today, about 25 percent of all hosts connected to the Internet are located in Europe.

At present, the Internet's international expansion is hampered by the lack of a good supporting infrastructure; namely, a decent telephone system. In both Eastern Europe and the third world, a state-of-the-art phone system is nonexistent. Even in major cities, connections are limited to the speeds available to the average home anywhere in the U.S., 9600 bits per second. Typically, even if one of these countries is "on the Internet," only a few sites are accessible. Usually, this is the major technical university for that country. However, as phone systems improve, you can expect this to change too; more and more, you'll see smaller sites (even individual home systems) connecting to the Internet.

Commercialization

Many big corporations have been on the Internet for years. For the most part, their participation has been limited to their research and engineering departments. The same corporations used some other network (usually a private network) for their business communications. After all, this IP stuff was only an academic toy. The IBM mainframes that handled their commercial data processing did the "real" networking using a protocol suite called System Network Architecture (SNA).

Businesses are now discovering that running multiple networks is expensive. Some are beginning to look to the Internet for "one-stop" network shopping. They were scared away in the past by policies which excluded or restricted commercial use. Most of these policies have fallen by the wayside. Now, corporations may use the Internet as a tool to solve any appropriate business problems.

This should be especially good for small businesses. Motorola or Standard Oil can afford to run nationwide networks connecting their sites, but Ace Custom Software can't. If Ace has a San Jose office and a Washington office, all it needs is an Internet connection on each end. For all practical purposes, they have a nationwide corporate network, just like the big boys.

Privatization

Right behind commercialization comes privatization. For years, the networking community has wanted the telephone companies and other for-profit ventures to provide "off the shelf" IP connections. That is, just as you can place an order for a jack in your house for your telephone, you could do this for an Internet connection. You order, the telephone installer leaves, and you plug your computer into the Internet. Except for Bolt, Beranek and Newman, the company that used to run the ARPAnet, there weren't any takers. The telephone companies have historically said, "We'll sell you phone lines, and you can do whatever you like with them." By default, the Federal government stayed in the networking business.

Now that large corporations have become interested in the Internet, the phone companies have started to change their attitude. Now they and other profit-oriented network purveyors complain that the government ought to get out of the network business. After all, who best can provide network services but the phone companies? They've got the ear of a lot of political people, to whom it appears to be reasonable. If you talk to phone company personnel, many of them still don't really understand what the Internet is about. They ain't got religion, but they are studying the Bible furiously.*

Since the talk of the "national information infrastructure" by the current administration, even more players have become involved. The cable TV companies have realized that they also own a lot of wire capable of carrying digital signals; that wire already extends into many homes in the U.S. So they've proposed solving the privatization problem by creating their own network, with no government investment required. Their network would piggy-back on their existing investment in cable TV. It remains to be seen what will come of this initiative; they've obviously got religion (and money to spend), but they may be writing their own bible. It is clear that cable TV companies are interested in applications that haven't been seen on the Internet yet: interactive home shopping, video games, and so on. It's less clear that they understand the traditional uses of data networking and understand that the network can't stop working every time a thunderstorm rolls through.

Although most people in the networking community think that privatization is a good idea, there are some obstacles in the way. Most revolve around funding for the connections that are already in place. Many schools are connected because the government pays part of the bill. If they had to pay their own way, some schools would probably decide to spend their money elsewhere. Major research institutions would certainly stay on the Net; but some smaller colleges might not, and the costs would probably be prohibitive for most secondary schools (let alone grade schools). What if the school could afford either an Internet connection or a science lab? It's unclear which one would get funded. The Internet has not yet become a "necessity" in many people's minds. When it does, expect privatization to come quickly.

We are quickly moving from the era when the network itself was the project, to an era when the network is a tool to be used in "real" projects. This is changing the way that governmental subsidies for networking are being distributed. Rather than funding a network connection to a campus, school, agency, or corporation, subsidy money is moving to project budgets. The people who run the projects can then buy Internet services from a variety of vendors in the open marketplace. This makes a lot of people nervous, because it threatens an existing flow of money (something near and dear to the recipients' hearts). On the other hand, it is probably the only practical way to merge public money and private money into one

---

*Apologies to those telephone company employees who saw the light years ago and have been trying to drag their employers into church.

pool big enough to keep the Internet expanding into the more rural parts of the world.

Well, enough about the history of the information highway system. It's time to walk to the edge of the road, hitch a ride, and be on your way.

CHAPTER THREE

HOW THE INTERNET WORKS

Moving Bits From One Place to Another
Making the Network Friendly

It's nice to know a bit about how things work. It allows you to make sense out of some of the hints you will see in this book, so they don't just seem like capricious rules to be learned by rote. Lest you be scared away, we will explore this with a maximum amount of handwaving. We'll never say "this field is three bits long;" we won't even think about it! If you want to know more, several books on the Internet's implementation are available.*

In this chapter, we will look at packet switched networks and how, by putting TCP/IP on top of such a network, something useful happens. We will talk about the basic protocols that govern Internet communication: TCP and its poor cousin, UDP. These are the network's building blocks. At this point the Internet is fairly boring (frustrating and hard to use). When you put the Domain Name System and a few applications on top of it, it becomes something useful.

If you decide this isn't your cup of tea, feel free to skip the beginning of this chapter. Do read the section on the Domain Name System. It is something that you will be using indirectly for your entire Internet career.

Moving Bits From One Place to Another

Modern networking is built around the concept of "layers of service." You start out trying to move bits from here to there, losing some along the way. This level consists of wires and hardware, and not necessarily very good wires. Then you add a layer of basic software to shield yourself from the problems of hardware. You add another layer of software to give the basic software some desirable features. You continue to add functionality and smarts to the network, one layer at a time, until

---

*Comer, Douglas, *Internetworking with TCP/IP: Principles, Protocols, and Architecture*, Volumes I and II (Prentice Hall).

you have something that's friendly and useful. Well, let's start at the bottom and work our way up.

Packet Switched Networks

When you try to imagine what the Internet is and how it operates, it is natural to think of the telephone system. After all, they are both electronic, they both let you open a connection and transfer information, and the Internet is primarily composed of dedicated telephone lines. Unfortunately, this is the wrong picture, and causes many misunderstandings about how the Internet operates. The telephone network is a *circuit switched* network. When you make a call, you get a piece of the network dedicated to you. Even if you aren't using it (for example, if you are put on hold), your piece of the network is unavailable to others wishing to do real work. This leads to underutilization of a very expensive resource, the network.

A better model for the Internet is the U.S. Postal Service. (Don't get worried . . . .) The Postal Service is a *packet switched* network. You have no dedicated piece of the network. What you want to send is mixed together with everyone else's stuff, put in a pipe, transferred to another Post Office, and sorted out again. Although the technologies are completely different, the Postal Service is a surprisingly accurate analogy; we'll continue to use it throughout this chapter.

The Internet Protocol (IP)

A wire can get data from one place to another. However, you already know that the Internet can get data to many different places, distributed all over the world. How does that happen?

The different pieces of the Internet are connected by a set of computers called *routers*, which connect networks together. These networks are sometimes Ethernets, sometimes token rings, and sometimes telephone lines, as shown in Figure 3-1.

The telephone lines and Ethernets are equivalent to the trucks and planes of the Postal Service. They are the means by which mail is moved from place to place. The routers are postal substations; they make decisions about how to route data ("packets"), just like a postal substation decides how to route envelopes containing mail. Each substation or router does not have a connection to every other one. If you put an envelope in the mail in Dixville Notch, New Hampshire, addressed to Boonville, California, the Post Office doesn't reserve a plane from New Hampshire to California to carry it. The local Post Office sends the envelope to a substation; the substation sends it to another substation; and so on, until it reaches the destination. That is, each substation only needs to know what connections are available, and what is the best "next hop" to get a packet closer to its destination. Similarly with the Internet: a router looks at where your data is going and decides where to send it next. It decides which pipe is best and uses it.

How does the Net know where your data is going? If you want to send a letter, you can't just drop the typed letter into the mailbox and expect delivery. You need to put the paper into an envelope, write an address on the envelope, and stamp it.

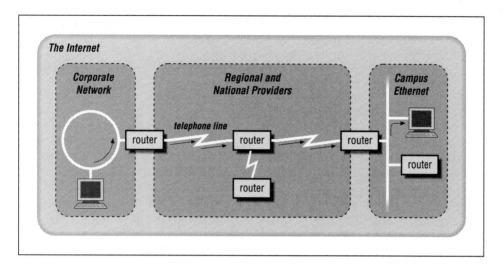

Figure 3-1: Internet hardware

Just as the Post Office has rules that define how its network works, there are rules that govern how the Internet operates. The rules are called *protocols*. The Internet Protocol (IP) takes care of addressing, or making sure that the routers know what to do with your data when it arrives. Sticking with our Post Office analogy, the Internet Protocol works just like an envelope (Figure 3-2).

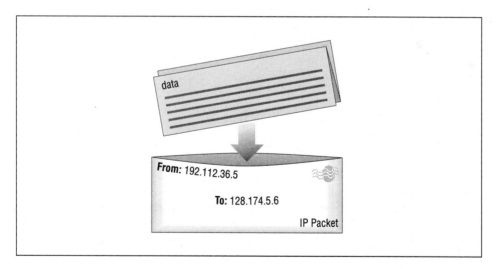

Figure 3-2: IP envelopes

Some addressing information goes at the beginning of your message; this information gives the network enough information to deliver the *packet* of data.

Internet addresses consist of four numbers, each less than 256. When written out, the numbers are separated by periods, like this:

```
192.112.36.5
128.174.5.6
```

(Don't worry; you don't need to remember numbers like these to use the network.) The address is actually made up of multiple parts. Since the Internet is a network of networks, the beginning of the address tells the Internet routers what network you are part of. The right end of the address tells that network which computer or *host* should receive the packet.* Every computer on the Internet has a unique address under this scheme. Again, the Postal Service provides a good analogy. Consider the address "50 Kelly Road, Hamden, CT." The "Hamden, CT" portion is like a network address; it gets the envelope to the right local Post Office, the Post Office that knows about streets in a certain area. "50 Kelly Road" is like the host address; it identifies a particular mailbox within the Post Office's service area. The Postal Service has done its job when it has delivered the mail to the right local office, and when that local office has put it into the right mailbox. Similarly, the Internet has done its job when its routers have gotten data to the right network, and when that local network has given the data to the right computer, or host, on the network.

For a lot of practical reasons (notably hardware limitations), information sent across IP networks is broken up into bite-sized pieces, called *packets.* The information within a packet is usually between one and about 1500 characters long. This prevents any one user of the network from monopolizing the network, allowing everyone to get a fair shot. It also means that when the network is overloaded, its behavior gets slightly worse for all its users: it doesn't stop dead while a few heavy users monopolize it.

One of the amazing things about the Internet is that, on a basic level, IP is all you need to participate. It wouldn't be very friendly, but you could get work done if you were clever enough. As long as your data is put in an IP envelope, the network has all the information it needs to get your packet from your computer to its destination. Now, however, we need to deal with several problems:

- Most information transfers are longer than 1500 characters. You would be disappointed, indeed, if the Post Office would only carry postcards, but refused anything larger.

- Things can go wrong. The Post Office occasionally loses a letter; networks sometimes lose packets, or damage them in transit. Unlike the Post Office, we'll see that the Internet can deal with these problems successfully.

---

*Where the network portion ends and the host portion begins is a bit complicated. It varies from address to address based on an agreement between adjacent routers. Fortunately, as a user you'll never need to worry about this; it only makes a difference when you're setting up a network.

- Packets may arrive out of sequence. If you mail two letters to the same place on successive days, there's no guarantee that they will take the same route or arrive in order. The same is true of the Internet.

So, the next layer of the network will give us a way to transfer bigger chunks of information and will take care of the many distortions that can creep in because of the network.

The Transmission Control Protocol (TCP)

TCP is the protocol, frequently mentioned in the same breath as IP, that is used to get around these problems. What would happen if you wanted to send a book to someone, but the Post Office only accepted letters? What could you do? You could rip each page out of the book, put it in a separate envelope, and dump all the envelopes in a mailbox. The recipient would then have to make sure all the pages arrived and paste them together in the right order. This is what TCP does.

TCP takes the information you want to transmit and breaks it into pieces. It numbers each piece so receipt can be verified and the data can be put back in the proper order. In order to pass this sequence number across the network, it has an envelope of its own which has the information it requires "written on it" (Figure 3-3). A piece of your data is placed in a TCP envelope. The TCP envelope is, in turn, placed inside an IP envelope and given to the network. Once you have something in an IP envelope, the network can carry it.

On the receiving side, a TCP software package collects the envelopes, extracts the data, and puts it in the proper order. If some envelopes are missing, it asks the sender to retransmit them. Once it has all the information in the proper order, it passes the data to whatever application program is using its services.

This is actually a slightly utopian view of TCP. In the real world not only do packets get lost, they can also be changed by glitches on telephone lines in transit. TCP also handles this problem. As it puts your data into an envelope, it calculates something called a *checksum*. A checksum is a number that allows the receiving TCP to detect errors in the packet.* When the packet arrives at its destination, the receiving TCP calculates what the checksum should be and compares it to the one sent by the transmitter. If they don't match, an error has occurred in the transmission. The receiving TCP throws that packet away and requests a retransmission.

---

*Here's a simple example, if you're interested. Let's assume that you're transmitting raw computer data in 8-bit chunks, or bytes. A very simple checksum would be to add all of these bytes together. Then stick an extra byte onto the end of your data that contains the sum. (Or, at least, as much of the sum as fits into 8 bits.) The receiver makes the same calculation. If any byte was changed during transmission, the checksums will disagree, and you'll know there was an error. Of course, if there were two errors, they might cancel each other out. But more complicated computations can handle multiple errors.

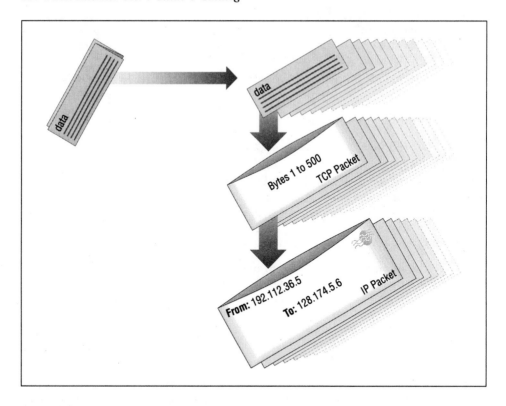

Figure 3-3: TCP packet encapsulation

Other Transmission Protocols

TCP creates the appearance of a dedicated wire between the two applications, guaranteeing that what goes in one side comes out the other. You don't have a dedicated link between the sender and receiver (other people can use the same routers and network wires in the gaps between your packets), but, for all practical purposes, it looks like you do.

Ideal as this may sound, it is not the best approach for every program to use. Setting up a TCP connection requires a fair amount of overhead and delay; if this machinery isn't needed, it's better not to use it. If all the data you want to send will fit in one packet, and you don't particularly care to guarantee delivery, TCP may be overkill.

It turns out that there is another standard protocol that does away with this overhead. This protocol is called the *user datagram protocol* or *UDP*. It is used instead of TCP in some applications; that is, instead of wrapping your data in a TCP envelope and putting that inside an IP envelope, the application puts your data into a UDP envelope, which goes in the IP envelope.

UDP is a lot simpler than TCP because it doesn't worry about missing packets, keeping data in the right order, or any of those niceties. UDP is used for programs that only send short messages, and can just resend the message if a response does not come in a short time. For example, assume that you're writing a program that looks up phone numbers in a database somewhere else on the network. There is no reason to set up a TCP connection to transmit 20 or so characters in each direction. You can just put the name into one UDP packet, stick that into an IP packet, and send it. The other side of the application gets the packet, reads the name, looks up the phone number, puts that into another UDP packet, and sends it back. What happens if the packet gets lost along the way? Your program has to handle that: if it waits too long without getting a response, it justs sends another request.

Making the Network Friendly

Now that we have the ability to transfer information between places on the network, we can start working on making the Internet more friendly. This is done by having software tailored to the task at hand, and using names rather than addresses to refer to computers.

Applications

Most people don't get really excited about having a guaranteed bit stream between machines, no matter how fast the lines or exotic the technology that creates it. They want to use that bit stream to do something useful, whether that is to move a file, access some data, or play a game. Applications are pieces of software that allow this to happen easily. They are yet another "layer" of software, built on top of the TCP or UDP services. Applications give you, the user, a way to do the task at hand.

Applications can range from home-grown programs to proprietary programs supplied by a vendor. There are three "standard" Internet applications (remote login, file transfer, and electronic mail), as well as other commonly used, but not standardized, applications. Chapters 5 through 14 of this book describe how to use most of the common Internet applications.

One problem with talking about applications is that your local system determines how the application appears to you. The commands, messages, prompts, etc., may be slightly different on your screen than in the book or on someone else's screen. So, don't worry if the book says the message is "connection refused" and the error message you receive is "Unable to connect to remote host: refused"; they are the same. Try and distill the essence of the message, rather than matching the exact wording. And don't worry if some of the commands are named slightly differently; most of the applications have reasonable "help" facilities that will let you figure out the right command.

The Domain Name System

Fairly early on, people realized that addresses were fine for machines communicating with machines, but humans preferred names. It is hard to talk using addresses (who would say, "I was connected to 192.112.36.5 yesterday and ... "?) and even harder to remember them. Therefore, computers on the Internet were given names for the convenience of their human users. The preceding conversation becomes "I was connected to the NIC* yesterday and ... ". All of the Internet applications let you use system names, rather than host addresses.

Of course, naming introduces problems of its own. For one thing, you have to make sure that no two computers that are connected to the Internet have the same name. You also have to provide a way to convert names into numeric addresses. After all, names are just fine for people, but computers really prefer numbers, thank you. You can give a program a name, but it needs some way to look that name up and convert it into an address. (You do the same thing whenever you look someone up in the phone book.)

In the beginning, when the Internet was a small folksy place, dealing with names was easy. The NIC (*Network Information Center*) set up a registry. You would send in a form, electronically of course, and the NIC would add it to the list of names and addresses they maintained. This file, called the *hosts* file, was distributed regularly to every machine on the network. The names were simple words, every one chosen to be unique. If you used a name, your computer would look it up in the file and substitute the address. It was good.

Unfortunately, when the Internet went forth and multiplied, so did the size of the file. There were significant delays in getting a name registered, and it became difficult to find names that weren't already used. Also, too much network time was spent distributing this large file to every machine contained in it. It was obvious that a distributed, online system was required to cope with the rate of change. This system is called the *Domain Name System* or *DNS*.

The Domain System Structure

The Domain Name System is a method of administering names by giving different groups responsibility for subsets of the names. Each level in this system is called a *domain*. The domains are separated by periods:

```
ux.cso.uiuc.edu
nic.ddn.mil
yoyodyne.com
```

There can be any number of domains within the name, but you will rarely see more than five. As you proceed left to right through a name, each domain you encounter is larger than the previous one. In the name (**ux.cso.uiuc.edu**), **ux** is the name of a host, a real computer with an IP address (Figure 3-4). The name for that computer is created and maintained by the **cso** group, which happens to be the

---

*A Network Information Center is a repository for information about a network.

department where the computer resides. The department **cso** is a part of the University of Illinois at Urbana Champaign (**uiuc**). **uiuc** is a portion of the national group of educational institutions (**edu**). So the domain **edu** contains all computers in all U.S. educational institutions; the domain **uiuc.edu** contains all computers at the University of Illinois; and so on.

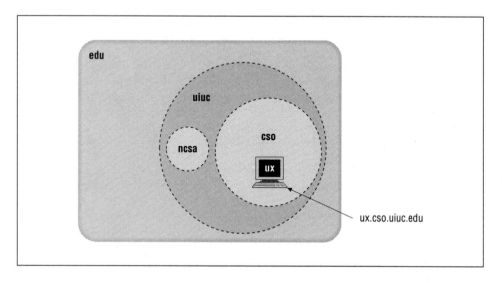

Figure 3-4: Domain authority

Each group can create or change whatever lies within it. If **uiuc** decided to create another group called **ncsa**, it could do so without asking anyone's permission. All it has to do is add the new names to its part of the worldwide database, and sooner or later everyone who needs to know will find out about the new name (**ncsa.uiuc.edu**). Similarly, **cso** can buy a new computer, assign it a name, and add it to the network without asking anyone's permission. If every group from **edu** on down plays by the rules and makes sure that the names it assigns are unique, then no two systems anywhere on the Internet will have the same name. You could have two machines named **fred**, but only if they are in different domains (for example, **fred.cso.uiuc.edu** and **fred.ora.com**).

In practice, being the name administrator for a group requires certain skills and is not fun. Therefore, somewhere around the enterprise level (**uiuc**) or one level below it, there is a person who is responsible for maintaining all lower levels. There is a locally defined procedure for requesting that a name get created or changed.

It's easy to see where domains and names come from within an organization like a university or a business. However, where do the "top-level" domains like **edu** come from? They were created by *fiat* when the domain system was invented. Originally, there were six highest-level domains (see Table 3-1).

Table 3-1: Original High-level Domains

Domain	Usage
com	For Commercial organizations (i.e., businesses)
edu	Educational organizations (universities, secondary schools, etc.)
gov	Governmental organizations, non-military
mil	Military (army, navy, etc.)
org	Other organizations
net	Network resources

As the Internet became an international network, a way was needed to give foreign countries responsibility for their own names. To this end, there are a set of two-letter domains which correspond to the highest-level domains for countries. Since **ca** is the country code for Canada, a Canadian computer might be named:

```
hockey.guelph.ca
```

There are almost 300 country codes; about 150 of those countries have some kind of computer networking. There is a list of the country codes in Appendix B, *International Network Connectivity*, in case you want to see where mail you received came from.

It's worth noting that the U.S. has its own country code, although it hasn't been used much; in the U.S., most network sites use the "organizational" domains (like **edu**), rather than the "geographical" domains (like **va.us**—Virginia). One computer may even have both kinds of names just for completeness. There's no way to "convert" between organizational names and geographical names. For example, even though **uxc.cso.uiuc.edu** happens to be in Urbana, Illinois, U.S.A., there is *not* necessarily a name **uxc.urbana.il.us**. Even if there is, they aren't necessarily the same computer.

Domain Name Lookup

Now that you know how domains relate to each other and how a name gets created, you might just wonder how to use this marvelous system. You use it automatically, whenever you use a name on a computer that knows about it. You never need to look a name up "by hand," or give a special command to find out about some name, although you can if you want. All computers on the Internet can use the domain system, and most do.

When you use a name like **ux.cso.uiuc.edu**, the computer needs to turn it into an address. To do so, it starts asking DNS servers for help, starting at the right end and working left. First, it asks the local DNS servers to look up the address. At this point, there are three possibilities:

- The local server knows the address, because the address is in the local server's part of the worldwide database. For example, if you're in the computer science department of the University of Illinois, your local server probably has information about the computers in your department.

- The local server knows the address because someone else has asked for the same address recently. Whenever you ask for an address, the DNS server keeps it on hand for a while, just in case someone else wants the same address later; this makes the system a lot more efficient.

- The local server doesn't know the address, but it knows how to find out.

How does the local server find out? Its software knows how to contact a *root* server. This is the server that knows the addresses of name servers for the highest level (rightmost) zone (**edu**). It asks the root server for the address of the computer responsible for the **edu** zone. Having that information, it contacts that server and asks that server for the address of the **uiuc** server. Your software then contacts that computer and asks for the address of the server for **cso**. Finally, it contacts that machine and gets the address of **ux**, the host that was the target of the application.

A few computers are still configured to use the old-style *hosts* file. If you find yourself on one of these, you may have to ask its administrator to look up the address you need by hand (or look it up yourself); then the administrator will have to add the machine you want to contact to the local *hosts* file. While you're doing this, you can hint that the administrator *really ought to install* the DNS software so you won't have to do this again.*

Domain Name System Hints

There are a few common misconceptions that you may encounter dealing with names. Here are "truths" to prevent those misconceptions from taking root:

- The pieces of a domain-style name tell you who is responsible for maintaining the name. It may not tell you anything about who maintains the computer corresponding to that IP address, or even (despite the country codes) where that machine is located. It would be perfectly legal for me to have the name **oz.cso.uiuc.edu** (part of the University of Illinois' name space) point to a machine in Australia. It isn't normally done, but it could be.

- The pieces of a domain name don't even necessarily tell you on what network a computer is located. Domain names and networking often overlap, but there's no necessary connection between them; two machines that are in the same domain may not be on the same network. For example, the systems

---

*If you can't get your computer to use the Domain Name System, there are ways you can manually look up a name and find its address. They are listed in the *Resource Catalog* under "Network Information."

uxc.cso.uiuc.edu and **ux1.cso.uiuc.edu** may be on different networks. Once again, domain names only tell you who is responsible for allocating the name.

- A machine can have multiple names. This is especially true of machines that offer services, where the service may be moved to a different computer in the future. My Sun workstation may be known by **ek.cso.uiuc.edu**. It also might be the computer where you can go to get publicly available files at the University of Illinois. So it might also have the name **ftp.uiuc.edu** (ftp being the name of the file-moving program). Sometime in the future, this service might be moved to some other computer. When this happens, the name **ftp.uiuc.edu** would move along with the service (my computer gets to keep its old name **ek.cso.uiuc.edu**). People wanting the particular service use the same name, regardless of which computer is providing the service. Names that symbolically refer to a service are aliases for the unique "canonical name" or *cname* of a computer. You will see symbolic names frequently as you wander about the Internet.

- Names aren't necessary for communication. Unless the error message you receive is "host unknown," the name worked fine. A message like "host unknown" means your system could not translate the name you gave it into an address. Once your system has the address in hand, it never uses the name again.

- It is better to remember names than addresses. Some people feel that the name system is "just one more thing to go wrong." The problem is that an address is tied to a network. If the computer providing a service is moved from one building to another, its network, and hence its address, are likely to change. The name needn't change. The administrator only needs to update the name record so that the name points to the new address. Since the name still works, you don't particularly care if the computer or function has changed locations.

The Domain Name System may sound complicated, but it's one of the things that make the Internet a comfortable place to live. If you don't like the periods wandering around, forget about what they mean: they're just names. However, pretty soon you'll start realizing, "Yes, this resource is at the University of Virginia; this person works for IBM in Germany; this is the address for reporting bugs in Nutshell Handbooks (**nuts@ora.com**)" and so on. The real advantage of the domain system is that it breaks the gigantic worldwide Internet into a bunch of manageable pieces. Although hundreds of thousands of computers are "on the Net," they're all named; and the names are organized in a convenient, perhaps even rational way, making it easier for you to remember the ones you need.

## CHAPTER FOUR

WHAT'S ALLOWED ON THE INTERNET?

Legal Implications
Politics and the Internet
Network Ethics
Ethics and the Private Commercial Internet
Security Consciousness

In earlier chapters, I told you very generally what the Internet is good for, where it came from, and how it works. Now it's time to get to the real nitty-gritty. We will talk about what you are allowed to do on the network; in the next chapter, we will start discussing how to do it.

What you are allowed to do is a very complex issue. It is influenced by law, ethics, and politics. How these interrelate, and which is paramount, vary from place to place. The Internet isn't a network—it's a network of networks—each of which may have its own policies and rules. Lest you give up before starting, the rules are reasonably uniform, and you'll be safe if you keep a few guidelines in mind. Fortunately, these guidelines aren't terribly restrictive; as long as you stay within them, you can do whatever you want. If you feel yourself getting near the edge, contact your network provider to determine exactly what is allowed and what isn't. It may be possible to do what you want, but it's your responsibility to find out. Let's look at the issues so you can see where the borders are.

Legal Implications

Three areas of the law affect the Internet:

- Federal subsidies pay for large sections of the Internet. These subsidies exclude purely commercial use.

- The Internet is not just a nationwide network, but a true global network. When shipping anything across a national boundary, including bits, export laws come into effect and local laws change.

- Whenever you are shipping software (or, for that matter, ideas) from one place to another, you must consider intellectual property and license issues.

First, let's deal with the federal dollars.

Research, Education, and the Federal Dollar

Many of the networks in the Internet are sponsored by federal agencies. Under federal law, an agency may only spend its budget on things that it is charged to do. For example, the Air Force can't secretly increase its budget by ordering rockets through NASA. These same laws apply to the network—if NASA funds a network, it must be used for space science. As a user, you may have no idea which networks your packets are traversing, but they'd better fall within the scope of each network's funding agency. If they don't, it's off to Leavenworth.

Actually, it's not as bad as it sounds. A couple of years ago, the folks in Washington realized that multiple parallel IP networks (NSFNET, NASA Science Internet, etc.—one network per federal agency) was a waste of money (a radical idea). Legislation was passed to create the National Research and Education Network, or *NREN.* This was to be a portion of the Internet dedicated to supporting research and education that was common to all federal agencies. This means that you can use the NREN* to do basic research and education, or in support of research and education.

The importance of the clause "in support of research or education" cannot be over-emphasized. This provision legitimizes important ways to use the network that don't, at first glance, seem appropriate. For example, if a vendor markets software that is used in research or education, it can distribute updates and answer questions through electronic mail. This usage is considered "in support of research or education" (RE). The vendor can't use the NREN for business functions, like marketing, billing, or accounting. For this, it must use a commercial part of the Internet.†

Lately, a lot of attention has been focused on the NII (National Information Infrastructure). The NII is a large and relatively vague proposal for nationwide networking. It could be considered a long-term plan for the NREN's direction; it could be considered a replacement for the NREN; the fact is, right now, no one really knows. There are many players (including the current network providers, phone companies, cable TV companies, and even power companies) trying to make sure the chips fall in their territory. We don't say too much about the NII in this book because we're discussing the network that exists now, not the network that might exist in a few years. It's pretty clear that the NII will have a major impact on networking in the U.S., but until the smoke clears, we won't know what that impact is. Everyone involved is promising easier access, lower prices, and higher data rates, but we'll believe that when we see it.

---

*Actually, the NREN is a real network that hasn't yet been built. The bill also authorizes this traffic on existing federal networks. The correct term for what we have now is the Interim Interagency NREN.

†A copy of the official NSFNET acceptable use policy is included in Appendix C, *Acceptable Use.* It is one of the most restrictive with regard to commercial use. If your usage is acceptable to NSFNET, it is likely acceptable to the other networks as well.

Commercial Use

When your site arranged for its Internet connection, someone needed to tell the network provider whether the connection would be used for research and education, or for commercial purposes. If your site decided it was RE, your network traffic is routed to prefer subsidized NREN routes. If you are a commercial site, your traffic is routed over private routes. As you'd expect, your site's network access fees depend on these decisions; commercial use is generally more expensive than RE because it isn't subsidized. Only someone in your network administration can tell you whether commercial dealings are allowed over your connection. Check before you use it for commercial purposes.

Of course, many corporations join the Internet as research and education sites—and this is appropriate, since the motivation for joining the Internet is often research. For example, a seed company may wish to do joint soybean research with a university. Yet many corporate legal departments decide to declare their connections commercial. This ensures that there will not be a legal liability in the future, when some uninformed employee uses the research connection for commercial work. To many businesses, the added fees are well worth the comfort.

There are a number of commercial Internet providers: Advanced Networks and Services (ANS), Performance Systems International (PSI), and UUNET are a few of them. Each of these companies has its own market niche and its own national network to provide commercial Internet services. In addition, state and regional networks carry commercial traffic for their members. There are connections between each of these and the federally supported networks. Using these connections and some nifty accounting agreements, all of these networks interoperate legally.

Export Laws

Whether you know it or not, exporting bits falls under the auspices of the Department of Commerce export restrictions.* The Internet, being a virtually seamless global network, makes it very easy to export things without your knowledge. Because I'm not a lawyer, I won't get very technical, but I will try to sketch what is required to stay legal. If, after reading this, you think you might run afoul of the law, seek competent legal help.

Export law is based on two points:

1. Exporting anything requires a license.
2. Exporting a service is roughly equivalent to exporting the pieces necessary to provide that service.

The first point is fairly obvious: if you ship, carry, transfer a file, or electronically mail anything out of the country, it needs to be covered by an export license. Luckily, there is a loophole called a *general license* that covers most things. The general license allows you to export anything that is not explicitly restricted and is

---

*This is strictly a U.S.-centric discussion. Other laws apply to servers in other countries.

readily available in public forums in the United States. So anything you can learn from walking into a conference or classroom that does not have security restrictions is probably covered by the general license.

However, the list of restricted items has a lot of surprises and does cover things that you can learn as a student in any university. Networking code and encryption code might be restricted, based upon their capabilities. Many times, one little item is of concern, but by the time the regulations are written, they cover a much wider area. For example, during the Persian Gulf War, it was a lot harder to knock out Iraq's command and control network than anticipated. It turned out they were using commercial IP routers which were very good at finding alternative routes quickly. Suddenly, exporting any router that could find alternate routes was restricted.*

The second point is even simpler. If exporting some hardware, say a supercomputer, is not allowed, then remote access to that hardware within this country is prohibited as well. So, be careful about granting access to "special" resources (like supercomputers) to people in foreign countries. The exact nature of these restrictions depends, of course, on the foreign country and (as you can probably imagine, given the events of the last few years) can change quickly.

When investigating their potential for legal liability, the consortium that runs the Bitnet (CREN) came to the following conclusions:† A network operator is responsible for illegal export only if the operator was aware of the violation and failed to inform proper authorities; the network operator isn't responsible for monitoring your usage and determining whether or not it's within the law. So network personnel nationwide probably aren't snooping through your packets to see what you are shipping overseas (although who knows what the National Security Agency looks at). However, if a network technician sees your packets, and if the packets are obviously in violation of some regulation, then the technician is obliged to inform the government.

Property Rights

Property rights can also become an issue when you ship something to someone else. The problem gets even more confusing when the communication is across national borders. Copyright and patent laws vary greatly from country to country. You might find on the network a curious volume of forgotten lore whose copyright has expired in the U.S. Shipping these files to England might place you in violation of British law. Know who has the rights to anything you give away across the network. If it is not yours, make sure you have permission before giving something away.

---

*This story may actually be a network "urban legend." Everyone on the net talked about this situation, but when I tried to verify it I could not find a definitive source.

†The actual legal opinions are available on the network; see the *Resource Catalog* under Law—Corporation for Research and Educational Networking.

The law surrounding electronic communication has not kept pace with the technology. If you have a book, journal, or personal letter, you can ask almost any lawyer or librarian if you can copy or use it in a particular manner. They can tell you if you can, or whose permission you need to obtain. Ask the same question regarding a network bulletin board posting, an electronic mail message, or a report in a file available on the network, and they will throw up their hands. Even if you knew whose permission to obtain and obtained that permission via electronic mail, it's not clear whether an email message offers any useful protection. Just be aware that this is a murky part of law which is likely to be hammered out in the next decade.

Please note that property rights can be a problem even when using publicly available files. Some software available for public retrieval through the Internet must be licensed from the vendor. For example, a workstation vendor might make updates to its operating system software available via anonymous FTP. So you can easily get the software, but in order to use it legally you must hold a valid software maintenance license. Just because a file is there for the taking doesn't mean that taking it is legal.

Politics and the Internet

Many network users view the political process as both a blessing and a curse. The blessing is money. Subsidies provide many people with a utility they could not afford otherwise. The curse is that their individual actions are under constant scrutiny. Someone in Washington may decide, after the fact, that something you have done can be exploited for political gain. The digitized centerfold you had on your machine can suddenly become the center of an editorial entitled "Tax Dollars Fund Pornography Distribution."* This causes everyone responsible for the Internet's funding no end of grief.

It's important to realize that the Internet has many political supporters, including members of Congress, the Clinton administration, educational leaders, and federal agency heads. They support the Internet because it benefits the country: it increases the U.S.'s ability to compete in international research and trade. Speeding communications allows the research and educational process to speed up; because of the Net, our researchers and their students can develop better solutions to technical problems.

As is typical in the political world, there are also those people who see these benefits as drivel. The millions of dollars spent on the network could be better spent buying pork barrels in their own congressional district.

The bottom line in the politics of networking is that political support for the network is broad, but relatively thin. Any act that can cause political waves might radically change it, probably for the worse.

---

*Something like this actually happened. The files were slightly more explicit than centerfolds, and it did jeopardize the funding of the entire NSFNET.

Network Ethics

For the novice network user, the apparent lack of ethics on the network is fairly disquieting. In actuality, the network is a very ethical place; the ethics are just a bit different than normal. To understand this, consider the term "frontier justice." When the West was young, there was a set of laws for the United States, but they were applied differently west of the Mississippi river. Well, the network is on the frontier of technology, so frontier justice applies here, too. You can delve here safely, provided you know what to expect.

The two overriding premises of network ethics are:

- Individualism is honored and fostered.
- The network is good and must be protected.

Notice these are very close to the frontier ethics of the West, where individualism and preservation of lifestyle were paramount. Let's look a bit more at how these points play off each other on the network.

Individualism

In normal society, everyone may claim to be an individual, but many times their individualism is compromised by the need for a sufficiently large group that shares their concerns. This is called critical mass. You may love medieval French poetry, but try starting a local group to discuss it. It is not convenient. You probably won't be able to find enough people who are interested and willing to meet often enough to support a chain of discussions. In order to at least get some interaction for your love, you join a poetry society with more general interests—perhaps one on medieval poetry in general. Maybe there's only one poetry society in town, and it spends most of its time discussing bad pseudo-religious verse. That's the problem with critical mass. If you can't assemble enough people to form a group, you suffer. You may join a larger group out of necessity, but it may not be what you want.

On the network, critical mass is two. You interact when you want and how you want—it's always convenient, no driving is required. Geography doesn't matter. The other person can be anywhere on the network (virtually anywhere in the world). Therefore, a group, no matter how specific, is possible. Even competing groups are likely to form. Some groups may choose to "meet" by electronic mail, some on bulletin boards, some by making files publicly available, and some by other means. People are free to operate in the manner they like. Since no one needs to join a large group to enjoy critical mass, everyone is part of some minority group. Everyone is equally at risk of being singled out for persecution. Because of this, no one wants to say "this topic should not be discussed on the network." If I said that about French poets, you could attack my favorite group, cross-dressing male adventurers. People understand that others couldn't care less about the information they live and die for. Many Internet users are nervous (justifiably) that support for outside censorship could arise and, eventually, succeed in making the Net less useful.

Of course, individualism is a two-edged sword. It makes the network a nice place for finding diverse information and people, but it may tax your liberality. People have many differing opinions about acceptable behavior. Since a lot of the behavior on the network is between you and a computer somewhere, most people will not be aware of anything you are doing. Those who are, may or may not care. If you put your machine on the network, you should realize that many users feel that any files that they can get to are fair game to retrieve. After all, if you didn't intend to make them available, you shouldn't have put them there. This view, of course, has no basis in law, but a lot of things on the frontier didn't either.

Protecting the Internet

Frequent users find the Internet extremely valuable for both work and play. Since the Internet access frequently comes at no personal expense (or very little), they view this valuable resource as something that must be protected. The threats to the Internet come from two sources:

- Excessive use for unintended purposes
- Political pressures

The NREN is being built with a purpose. A company's commercial connection to the Internet has a purpose. Chances are no one will prosecute a person who uses these connections for unintended purposes, but it is still discouraged by other means. If you use an employer's computer for a bit of personal use, like balancing your checkbook, it will probably be ignored. Likewise, small amounts of network time used for unintended purposes will likely be ignored. (In fact, many seemingly unintended uses, say a high school student playing a game across the network, might actually qualify as intended. She must have learned a lot about computing and networking to get that far.) It is only when someone does something blatant, perhaps organizing a nationwide multi-user dungeon game day on the network, that problems occur.

Unintended use also takes the form of ill-conceived supported usage. The network was not built to be a substitute for inadequate local facilities. For example, using an exported disk system halfway across the world because your employer wouldn't buy a $300 disk for your workstation is unacceptable. You may need the disk to do valuable research, but the cost of providing that storage across the network is outrageous. The network was designed to allow easy access to unique resources, not gratuitous access to common ones.

Heavy network users and network providers are not stodgy. They enjoy a game as well as the next guy. They are also not stupid. They read news. They work on the network regularly. If performance goes bad for no apparent reason, they investigate. If they find that the traffic in a particular area has gone up a hundredfold, they will want to know why. If you are the "why" and the use is unacceptable, you will probably get a polite electronic mail message asking you to stop. After that, you may get some less polite messages; finally, someone will contact your local network provider. You may end up losing your network access entirely, or your employer or campus may have to pay higher access fees (which, I assume, they will not be happy about).

Self-regulation is important because of the politics that surround the network. No reasonable person could expect the network to exist without occasional abuses and problems. However, if these problems aren't resolved within the network community, but are thrown into newspapers and Congress, everyone loses. To summarize, here are some areas that are considered politically damaging to the network and should be avoided:

- Excessive game playing
- Excessive ill-conceived use
- Hateful, harassing, or other antisocial behavior
- Intentional damage or interference with others (e.g., the Internet Worm*)
- Publicly accessible obscene files

It is difficult to justify the NREN's budget to Congress if "Sixty Minutes" is doing a feature on network abuse the Sunday before the budget hearings.

Ethics and the Private Commercial Internet

In the previous few sections, we talked about the political and social climate that got the Internet to where it is today. However, the climate is changing. Every day the percentage of Internet funding which comes from the Federal govenment grows smaller and smaller because of increased commercial usage. It is the government's goal to get out of the networking business and turn over the providing of Internet services to private industry. The obvious question is: if the government is getting out of the Internet business, do I still have to play by its rules? There are two issues to be dealt with: one personal and one commercial.

On the personal side, even though the federal government might be out of the network funding business, most people would rather have someone else pay for their connection than have it come out of their own checkbook. So, if you get your connection through a school, employer, Free-net, or whomever, they may still require you to follow a set of policies. "Freedom's just another word for nothin' left to lose,"† and you may have to give up some freedom to prevent losing your subsidized network connection. It's your responsibility to find out what your network provider considers "acceptable use."

The issue on the commercial side is trying to do business in tune with the Internet's culture. Although the culture is under stress and changing all the time, there is still a lot of sentiment on the Internet against blatant commercialism. Sending an electronic mail message advertising a product to everyone on the Internet is an

---

*The Internet Worm was a program which used the Internet to attack certain types of computers on the network. It would gain unauthorized access to computers and then use those computers to try to break into others. It was a lot like a personal computer "virus," but technically it is called a worm because it did not cause intentional damage to its hosts. For a good description, see *Computer Security Basics* (Russell and Gangemi), O'Reilly & Associates.

†Kris Kristofferson and Fred Foster, *Me and Bobby McGee*, 1969.

affront to most users. It will probably hurt sales by creating a large group of people who would rather not do business with a boorish company.

The Internet culture isn't necessarily opposed to advertising, but it demands that you view advertising as an information service. You can make marketing data available, but you can't force it on people. There would be nothing wrong, in terms of policy or culture, with an auto manufacturer putting up a server with pictures of its cars, technical data sheets, and information about options. If an Internet user wanted to buy a car, he could comparison shop from his terminal, decide what he wanted, and visit one dealer, rather than three, to do a test drive. Most users would be excited by this kind of service, and some resources are beginning to provide it.* In the future, you might even be able to do your test drive over the Internet via a virtual-reality simulation. But we're all trying to avoid a situation where we're deluged with unsolicited email selling everything from vinyl siding to sexy underwear.

Security Consciousness

A computer connected to the Internet is not, in itself, a much different security problem than a machine you can dial in with a modem. The problems are the same; it's the magnitude of the problem that changes. If you have a dial-up modem, anyone can dial the number and try to break in. There are three mitigating factors: the computer's phone number probably isn't widely known; if the intruder is outside your local calling area, he has to pay for the experience (or have stolen something else to get there); and there is only one interface which can be attacked.

If you are on the Internet, the mitigating factors are gone. The general address of your network is easily found, and an intruder would only have to try a few host numbers before stumbling onto an active one. In principle, this is still no worse than computer services that provide dial-in access to their machines through toll-free 800 numbers. The problem is that those services have staff who worry about security, and there is still only one point to break in from: the ASCII terminal port. On the Internet, someone could try to break in through the interactive terminal port, the file transfer port, the email port, etc. It's easy for someone to pull a workstation out of the box and put it on the Internet without thinking about security at all. He or she plugs the machine in, turns it on, and it works. The job is done, until someone breaks in and does something bad. In the long run, it is less time-consuming to put a little thought into security beforehand than to deal with it after the fact.

You can start by having the right attitude towards security. Believe that it is your workstation's responsibility to protect itself, and not the network's job to protect it. A network provider can restrict who may talk over your connection. However, that probably isn't what you want, because it strips away much of the Internet's

---

*O'Reilly & Associate's *Global Network Navigator* (GNN), for example; for information, send email to *info@gnn.com*.

value. Most of this book describes how to reach out to random places and find good things. A network conversation is a two-way pipe. If a remote machine can't talk to you, you can't talk to it either. And if that computer has a resource that you might find useful next month, it's your loss. In order to take advantage of the Internet, you must be a part of it. This puts your computer at risk, so you need to protect it.

Security on the Internet is really a group effort by the whole community. One technique that break-in artists use is to break into a chain of computers (e.g., break into A, use A to break into B, B to break into C, etc.). This allows them to cover their tracks more completely. If you think your lil' ole machine won't be a target because it is so small, dream on. Even if there's nothing of use on your computer, it's a worthwhile intermediate for someone who wants to break into an important system. And some people are out to accumulate notches on their keyboard, counting how many machines they have broken into. Size does not matter.

Discussing security and rumors of security problems is a bit of a problem. Can you imagine the following news story:

> At a news conference today, officials of the ACME Safe and Vault Company announced that their locks will unlock with any combination . . . .

To solve the problem of investigating a purported problem, finding a solution, and informing people without making the problem worse, the government has funded an organization named CERT: the Computer Emergency Response Team. CERT does a number of things. It investigates security problems, works with manufacturers to solve them, and announces the solutions. It also produces a number of aids to allow people to assess the security of their computers. They prefer to work with site security personnel but will, in an emergency, field questions from anyone. If you feel you are out in the woods alone and must talk to someone about security, you can contact them via electronic mail at:

    cert@cert.sei.cmu.edu

There are four ways in which network machines become compromised. In decreasing order of likelihood, these are:*

1. Valid users choosing bad passwords

2. Valid users importing corrupt software

3. Illegal users entering through misconfigured software

4. Illegal users entering through an operating system security flaw

You can draw one very important conclusion from this list. It is well within your ability to protect your system. Let's look at what you can do to stay out of trouble.

---

*A good place to look if you want to learn more about security issues is RFC1244 and the CERT server machine (see the *Resource Catalog* under "Security"). Also, see *Computer Security Basics* (Russell and Gangemi) for a general discussion of security issues, and *Practical UNIX Security* (Garfinkel and Spafford) for UNIX-related system administration issues. Both are published by O'Reilly & Associates.

Passwords

Most people choose passwords for their convenience. Unfortunately, what is convenient for you is also convenient for the hacker. CERT believes that 80 percent of computer break-ins are caused by poor password choice. Remember, when it comes to passwords, computers break in, not people. Some program spends all day trying out passwords; it's not going to get tired when the first three passwords don't work. But you can easily make it very hard to guess the right password. Most password crackers don't pick random letters; they pick common words from the dictionary and simple names. So, pick a good password which:

- Is at least six characters long
- Has a mixture of uppercase, lowercase, and numbers
- Is not a word
- Is not a set of adjacent keyboard keys (e.g., QWERTY)

It is hard for many people to conceive of a password that will meet all the above criteria and will still be easy to remember. One common thing to do is pick the first letters of a favorite phrase, like FmdIdgad (Frankly my dear, I don't give a damn).

When you install a workstation, make sure that you assign passwords to *root, system, maint,* and any other login names that have special powers. Change these passwords regularly. Some machines come out of the box with standard passwords on their system. If you don't change them, everyone who bought the same type of workstation knows your passwords.

Finally, be careful about techniques to bypass password requirements. There are two common ones: the UNIX *rhosts* facility and anonymous FTP. **rhosts** lets you declare "equivalent" login names on multiple machines. You list explicit machine names and logins in a file named *.rhosts.* For example, the *rhosts* entry:

```
uxh.cso.uiuc.edu krol
```

tells the computer on which this file resides to bypass password requirements when it sees someone trying to log in from the login name *krol* on the machine **uxh.cso.uiuc.edu**. When it sees this login name and this host, the computer will assume the login is valid. Obviously, this means that anyone who manages to break into *krol*'s account on **uxh.cso.uiuc.edu** can also break into this machine.

Anonymous FTP (discussed in Chapter 6, *Moving Files: FTP*) is a facility to allow easy retrieval of selected files without requiring a password. It is beyond the scope of this book to tell you how to set up an anonymous FTP server.* However, we will note that it's easy to make more things available through the service than you intended. Make sure you know what you are doing before you turn this facility on.

---

*This is covered in the Nutshell handbook *TCP/IP Network Administration*, by Craig Hunt (O'Reilly & Associates,).

(Note, though: merely using anonymous FTP to retrieve files does not place you at risk.)

Importing Software

The following story illustrates the second most common source of security problems:*

> Two Cornell University undergraduates were arrested for computer tampering. They tampered with a Tetris-style game on a public server at the school. When played, the game would appear to work normally, but would cause damage to the machine running it. It was spread throughout the world by computer networks. The FBI is investigating and expects further charges to be filed . . .

This is a classic "trojan horse" program: something threatening hidden in a gift.

Whenever you put software on your machine you place it at risk. Sharing software can be a great benefit. Only you can decide whether the risk is worth it. Buying commercial software entails minimal risk, especially if you buy from reputable vendors. On the network there are no assurances. You find a computer that has good stuff on it. You want that stuff. You take it and compile it. What can you do to make using it as safe as possible? Here are some rules of thumb:

- Try and use official sources. If you are after a bug fix to Sun Workstation software, it's safer to get the code from a machine whose name ends with **sun.com** than **hacker.hoople.usnd.edu**.

- Get source code if possible. Once you get the source code, read it before you install it. Make sure it isn't doing anything strange. This also applies to **shar** archives, **make** files, etc. I know this may be a daunting task (or impossible for some), but if you want to be safe this is what you need to do. Even common "public domain" or "free" software can be risky.† You have to decide how much risk you are willing to live with.

- Before installing the software on an important, heavily used system, run it for a while on a less critical computer. If you have one machine on which you do your life's work and another which is only used occasionally, put the new software on the second machine. See if anything bad happens.

- Do a complete backup of your files before using the software.

- If you're using a PC or Macintoch, use a virus checker to test the integrity of any software you get from the Net.

---

*This story is a paraphrase of an article in the newsgroup *clari.biz.courts*, February 26, 1992.

†We do not, of course, mean software produced by the Free Software Foundation. That software is trustworthy—at least in its original state. We'll repeat the first point: it's worth making sure you get an official copy of the sources.

Remember: only files that are executed can cause damage. Binary files are the most dangerous; source code is much safer. Data files are never a threat to a computer—though you should be aware that data files may be inaccurate.

Misconfigured Software

This is where it becomes difficult to talk about security. I can't really talk about the problem in concrete terms because it would turn into a hacker's guide to break-in techniques. A more general discussion will have to suffice.

Some system software has debugging options which can be turned on or off at installation or startup time. These options are occasionally left enabled on production systems—either inadvertently, or so the developers can get in at a later time (for example, if you start having problems) and see what's going on. However, any hole that's large enough to let a legitimate software developer in can also let a cracker in. Some break-ins (including the Internet Worm) have occurred through these means. Make sure that, unless needed, debugging options are turned off on system software.

In fact, unless a facility is needed on your system, why turn it on at all? Most vendors configure their operating systems to run everything right out of the box. This makes it easier to install; if all the options are turned on automatically, you don't have to run around figuring out which are needed. Unfortunately, this practice also makes it easier for someone to break in. If you don't plan to let people use a program like **tftp** (trivial file transfer program), why run a server for it?

System Software Flaws

Operating system flaws are either found and fixed, or workaround procedures are developed quickly. A computer manufacturer doesn't want his product to get a reputation as an "easy mark" for break-ins. The bigger problem comes after the manufacturer takes corrective action. You need to get the update and install it before it will protect anything. You can only install software updates if you know that they exist. Therefore, you need to keep up with the current state and release of your operating system. The easiest way to do this is to maintain a dialog with your campus, corporate, or vendor software support staff. For some obvious reasons, vendors don't make public announcements like, "Listen, everyone, Release 7.4.3.2 has this terrible security problem." It's also worth watching newsgroups and mailing lists where your system in discussed. You'll find the relevant newsgroups under *comp.sys*; for example, if you're a Sun user, watch *comp.sys.sun*.

What If My Computer Is Violated?

The first question to ask is really, "How will I know if my computer is violated?" Someone who breaks in tries to be as discreet as possible, covering his tracks as he goes. Once you discover him, you should take corrective action. So, how do you discover a break-in? Most people don't take advantage of security information provided regularly by their computer. Let's say that your machine tells you, "Last login 06:31 26 Jan 1994." Can you remember when you last logged in? Probably not exactly. But you might notice that a login at 6:30 A.M. was strange, given your usual work habits. This is how many break-ins are discovered. The process often starts when someone simply "feels" that something is wrong. For example:

- I don't think I logged in then.
- The machine feels slow today.
- I don't remember deleting or changing that file.

If something like this happens, don't just say, "Oh well" and move on. Investigate further. If you suspect that you have been the target of a break-in, there are a few things you should investigate:

- Examine the password file (on UNIX, */etc/passwd*) and look for unusual entries, typically with lots of permissions.

- List all the tasks (on BSD-based UNIX versions, **ps aux**; on System V versions, **ps -el**) and see if there are any unusual system tasks running.

- Get an extended directory listing (like UNIX **ls -la**) of your normal working directory and any other directory which appears too big or to have changed unusually. Look for unfamiliar files or strange modification dates.

However, before you can investigate, you must know what the password file, the active process list, etc., normally look like. If you don't know what "normal" is, you're certainly in no position to decide whether or not something is abnormal! Therefore, you should check the password files, your working directory, and so on, *now*, and continue to do so regularly. If you perform these checks periodically, you'll make sure that nothing suspicious is going on, and you'll stay familiar with your system.

If you see anything that looks suspicious, get help from either your campus or corporate security department. If you don't have one, ask your vendor. Act quickly to get help; do not try to proceed on your own. Don't destroy anything before you get help. Don't do another disk dump onto a standard tape or diskette backup set; the backup tape you are overwriting may be the last uncorrupted ones around. Don't assume that closing one hole fixes the problem. When a break-in artist gains access, the first thing he will do is cover his tracks. Next, he'll create more holes to maintain access to your system.

All of this may sound frightening, but don't let fear paralyze you. After all the cautions I've given, paralysis might sound like a good option. However, the non-networked world is full of dangers too; if you become overzealous about eliminating danger, you'll spend the rest of your life in a concrete-lined underground shelter (oops, can't do that, radon). Most people structure their lives to keep danger to a manageable level. This is a safe, healthy response: healthy adults don't intentionally subject themselves to dangers that they could easily minimize, and they try to live with the dangers that they can't minimize. They wear seat belts; they don't stop traveling. In the network's world, you need to do the same thing. Make sure your password is good, be careful about installing public domain software, watch your system so that you'll be aware of a break-in if one happens, and get help if you need it.

## CHAPTER FIVE

REMOTE LOGIN

Simple TELNET
What's Really Going On
TELNET Command Mode
Non-standard TELNET Servers
TELNETting to IBM Mainframes

We've been through a lot of background information. We've talked generally about what the Internet can do for you, what you're allowed to do, how the Internet works, how it developed, and so on. We haven't yet said anything concrete about *how* to get anything done; at this point, the Net is still a vague, magical entity. A medieval carpenter might be amazed by a modern woodshop, but it would be useless to him unless he knew what the tools were and how to use them.

Now we're going to get real. In the next few chapters, we'll discuss the basic tools for working on the Internet. We mentioned these tools briefly in the first chapter. In case you've forgotten, though, here's a recap:

telnet   Is used for logging into other computers on the Internet. It's used to access lots of public services, including library card catalogs and other kinds of databases.

ftp   Moves files back and forth. It's most useful for retrieving files from public archives that are scattered around the Internet. This is called anonymous FTP because you don't need an account on the computer you're accessing. Anonymous FTP is covered in Chapter 6, *Moving Files: FTP*.

Electronic mail
                Lets you send messages. You probably know about electronic mail and how useful it can be already. The Internet's slant on email is discussed in Chapter 7, *Electronic Mail*.

USENET News
                Lets you read (and post) messages that have been sent to public "newsgroups." This may sound obscure, but it's really what everyone else calls "bulletin boards" or discussion groups. USENET is the world's largest bulletin board service. We discuss it in Chapter 8, *Network News*.

These are the Internet's basic services. After Chapter 8, we discuss a different kind of service: how to find all the "good stuff" that's available. The problem with the Internet is that it's messy and poorly coordinated. There are incredible resources, but there's no central coordination to help you find what you want. In the last few years, developers have made tremendous progress in sorting out the mess, and providing tools to help you find what's interesting. Chapters 9 through 14 discuss these new tools. If Chapters 5 through 8 discuss the Skil saws and drill presses of the Internet's tool shop, Chapters 9 through 14 discuss the computer-controlled lathes and milling machines.

That's enough introduction. It's time to get started with TELNET. Our goal is to get you familiar with TELNET and its use. We will look at a simple TELNET session, talk a bit about what is happening behind the scenes, and then look at some more esoteric uses.

Simple TELNET

As we've said, **telnet** is the Internet's remote login protocol. It lets you sit at a keyboard connected to one computer and log on to a remote computer across the network. The connection can be to a machine in the same room, on the same campus, or in a distant corner of the world. When you are connected, it is as if your keyboard were connected directly to that remote computer. You can access whatever services the remote machine provides to its local terminals. You can run a normal interactive session (logging in, executing commands), or you can access many special services: you can look at library catalogs, find out what's playing in Peoria, access the text of *USA Today*, and take advantage of the many other services that are provided by different hosts on the network.

The simplest way to use **telnet** is to type:

```
% telnet remote-computer-name
```

at command level. We're using a UNIX system's C shell, so the command prompt is the percent sign (%). If you're using some other computer system (like DOS, VAX/VMS, or a Macintosh), the command will be fundamentally the same, though the details might be slightly different. Here's a very basic example:

```
% telnet sonne.uiuc.edu
Trying...
Connected to sonne.uiuc.edu.
Escape character is '^]'.

SunOS UNIX (sonne)

login: krol                          logging in to remote system
Password:                            password not echoed by the system
Last login: Sat Sep  7 17:16:35 from ux1.uiuc.edu
SunOS Release 4.1(GENERIC) #1:Tue Mar 6 17:27:17 PST 1990
sonne% ls                            command executed by remote system
Mail         News         development         project1
sonne% pwd                           command executed by remote system
```

```
/home/sonne/krol
sonne% logout                           logout from re
%                                        back to local
```

We told TELNET to find a remote computer ca'
the computer, it started a terminal session. O
appears to be the same as if you were at a *r*
particular, you must log in and log out just a
computer. After you have logged in, you c/
priate for the remote system; because **sonne.u.**
tem, all of the standard UNIX commands (like **ls** ana ,
log out from the remote system, **telnet** quits. Any furthe.
cuted by your local system.

That's really all that TELNET is: it's a tool that lets you log in to remote cc
In the course of this chapter, we'll discuss a number of fancy **telnet** commanas .
options, and we'll see that you can use it to access some special-purpose "servers"
with their own behavior. But the simple **telnet** command above (plus an account
on the remote computer) is all you need to get started.

What's Really Going On

Let's take a deeper look at what happens when you start a TELNET session. An
application consists of two pieces of software that cooperate: the *client*, which
runs on the computer that is requesting the service, and the *server*, which runs on
the computer providing the service. The network, using either TCP or UDP services, is the medium by which the two communicate.

The client, which is the program that began running on your system when you
typed in the **telnet** command, must:

- Create a TCP network connection with a server
- Accept input from you in a convenient manner
- Reformat the input to a standard format and send it to a server
- Accept output from the server in a standard format
- Reformat that output for display to you

---

*TELNET may not communicate your exact terminal specification to the remote host. This is especially
true if you start from some strange-sized terminal like an X terminal (more on these later). You might
have to do something to set the terminal specifications after you log in. On BSD UNIX, you would do
this with **setenv TERM** and **stty** (to specify the number of rows and columns on your screen). For example, if you're using the **xterm** terminal emulation program that has 46 lines and 82 columns, you'd
give the following commands:

```
% setenv TERM xterm
% stty rows 46
% stty columns 82
```

oftware runs on the machine delivering the service; if the server isn't
e service isn't available. On UNIX systems, servers are often called *dae-*
stem jobs which run in the background all the time. These "silent
wait for their services to be required and when they are, spring into
. When a typical server is ready to accept requests it:

nforms the networking software that it is ready to accept connections

Waits for a request in a standard format

- Services the request

- Sends the results back to the client in a standard format

- Waits again

A server must be able to handle a variety of clients, some running on the same kind of computer, and some running on IBM/PCs, Macintoshes, Amigas—whatever happens to be out there. To make this possible, there is a set of rules for communicating with the server. This set of rules is generally called a *protocol*. In this case, since it is a protocol used between pieces of an application, it is called an *application protocol*. Anyone can write a client on any type of computer. As long as that client can communicate across the network to the server and can speak the protocol properly, it can access the service. In practice, this means that your Macintosh (or IBM PC, etc.) can use TELNET and the other Internet tools to do work on an incredible number of different systems, ranging from UNIX workstations to IBM mainframes.

An application protocol usually allows the client and server to differentiate between data destined for the user, and messages the client and server use to communicate with each other. This is frequently done by adding a few characters of text onto the beginning of each line. For example, if the server sends the client a line which begins with the characters "TXT", then the rest of the line is data to be passed on to the screen. If the line begins with "CMD", it is a message from the server software to the client software. Of course, you never see any of this; by the time the message gets to you, the control information is stripped off. So let's get back to looking at how all this relates to TELNET.

TELNET Command Mode

TELNET has more features than our first example would lead you to believe. The clue to this was the "Escape character is ‘ ^] ’ " message. TELNET sends any character you type to the remote host, with one exception: the *escape character*. If you type the escape character, your **telnet** client enters a special command mode. By default, the escape character is usually **CTRL-]**. Don't confuse this with the ESC key on the keyboard! The TELNET escape character can be any character that you will never want to send to the remote system. The ESC key on the keyboard is a special nonprintable character which you frequently need to send to remote systems to flag commands. Also, remember that there are exceptions: the escape character isn't always **CTRL-]**. **telnet** clients that run on machines with slick interfaces generally use menus or function keys instead of an obscure escape character.

You can also enter the command mode by typing **telnet** alone, with no machine name following it. When you're in command mode (no matter how you got there), you will see the prompt `telnet>`; this means that TELNET is waiting for you to type a command. Typing a question mark (?) will get you a list of the commands available:

```
telnet> ?
Commands may be abbreviated.  Commands are:

close         close current connection
display       display operating parameters
mode          try to enter line-by-line or character-at-a-time mode
open          connect to a site
quit          exit telnet
send          transmit special characters ('send ?' for more)
set           set operating parameters ('set ?' for more)
status        print status information
toggle        toggle operating parameters ('toggle ?' for more)
z             suspend telnet
?             print help information
```

Although there are a number of commands, and even more subcommands (try a **set ?** sometime), only a few are generally used:

close   Terminates the connection which currently exists or is being created. It automatically disconnects you from the remote system; it may also quit from TELNET if you specified a hostname with the **telnet** command. This command is useful if you get into a bind across the network and want to get out.

open *name* Attempts to create a connection to the named machine. The name or address of the target machine is required. Most TELNETs will prompt for a machine name if it is not specified. Note that you must **close** any existing connection before opening a new one.

set echo   Turns local echoing on or off. *Echoing* is the process by which the characters you type appear on your screen. Usually, the remote computer is responsible for sending the character back to your terminal after it receives it. This is called "remote echoing," and is generally considered more reliable, because you know that the remote system is receiving your keystrokes correctly. "Local echoing" means that the local computer (in this case, the **telnet** client) sends the characters you type back to the display screen. Because remote echoing is more reliable, TELNET usually starts with echoing turned off. To turn it on, enter command mode and type the **set echo** command. To turn it off again, just type **set echo** again. (This command is like a light switch: giving the command repeatedly turns echoing on or off.) It has the same effect as the half/full duplex switch on modems and computer terminals, if you have any experience with them.

How do you know whether local echoing should be on or off? If local echoing is turned off and it should be on, any characters you type won't be echoed; you won't see the commands you send to the remote system, but you will see the output from these commands. If local echoing is turned on and it should be off, you'll see every character you type twice. In either case, the solution is the same: enter command mode and type **set echo**.

set escape *char*

Sets the escape character to the specified character. You will usually want to use some kind of control character, which you can either type "as is" (for example, if you want to use **CTRL-b**, just type **b** while holding down the CTRL key), or by typing a caret (^) followed by the letter (for example, ^**b**). It is important that your escape character be a character that you'll never need to type while doing your normal work. This can be a problem—many programs (the *emacs* editor in particular) assign meanings to virtually every key on the keyboard.

The ability to change the escape character is really useful if you are running daisy-chained applications. For example, you **telnet** from system A to system B, log in and then **telnet** to system C. If what you are doing on system C goes bad, and if the escape characters are the same, there is no way to break the B-to-C connection; typing the escape character will always put you into command mode on system A. If you use a different escape character for each TELNET session, then you can choose which one to put into command mode by typing the appropriate character. This applies not only to **telnet**, but also to other applications with escape characters, like terminal emulators (for example, the popular **kermit** program).

quit

Gets you out of the **telnet** program gracefully.

z

Temporarily suspends the TELNET session to allow other commands to be executed on the local system. Connections and other options remain set when the session is resumed. The session is resumed by normal operating system means, which on BSD UNIX is usually an **fg** command. System V UNIX places you in a subshell to do other commands. To return to your TELNET session you exit the shell. (This facility depends on operating system support, so it may not be available on all systems.)

Carriage Return   Without issuing a command (a blank line in command mode) returns you to your session on the remote machine from command mode. In addition, many of the other commands implicitly take you out of command mode.

Here's a sample session, in which we log in to **sonne.uiuc.edu**, go into command mode for a few commands, and then return to **sonne**:

```
% telnet sonne.uiuc.edu
Trying...
Connected to sonne.uiuc.edu.
Escape character is '^]'.

SunOS UNIX (sonne)

login: krol                                    logging in to remote system
Password:
Last login: Sat Sep  7 17:16:35 from ux1.uiuc.edu
SunOS Release 4.1(GENERIC) #1:Tue Mar 6 17:27:17 PST 1990
sonne% ls
Mail         News         development         project1
sonne% pwd
/home/sonne/krol
sonne% CTRL-]                                  enter telnet command mode
telnet> ?                                      print help message
Commands may be abbreviated.  Commands are:

close          close current connection
display        display operating parameters
...                                            several commands omitted
z              suspend telnet
?              print help information
telnet> set escape ^b                          change escape character
escape character is '^B'
sonne% pwd                                      back to sonne; give a command
/home/sonne/krol
sonne% logout                                  and quit
%                                              back to local system
```

Note that the **set** command implicitly takes you out of command mode. If it didn't, of course, you could just enter a blank line to get back to **sonne**.

Non-standard TELNET Servers

I may have given you the impression that TELNET is only useful for logging on to other computers. This is not strictly the case. If I were writing an application and would be happy with the VT-100 style connection that the TELNET protocol supports, why not use **telnet** as the client and write a special server that does what I want it to do? All I have to do is make the server talk the TELNET protocol. On the positive side, it saves me the trouble of distributing a special client program to everyone who is going to use my application. It also gives the users an interface with which they are already familiar: anything that works with TELNET will work with the new application. On the negative side, it means that the server machine is virtually dedicated to the single application: anyone who **telnet**s to it will, by default, end up in my application.

To you, it also means that when you connect to a computer using TELNET, you won't get the normal login prompt, which I hope you are familiar with by now.* You get whatever the writer of the service wanted to give you. So, you need to approach these services with a bit more caution. Here are a few notes which you might keep in mind when dealing with one of these beasties:

- Almost every special-purpose server is different. Some have good user inter-faces; some have horrible user interfaces. What you get is what you get. Most have help facilities (some useful, some not so useful).

- Most servers will ask for a terminal type of some sort when you enter. "VT100" is probably the most common choice—many terminal emulators, and most window systems, deal with it. If you don't know what kind of terminal to ask for, if your terminal isn't represented, or VT100 does strange things, then fall back to "hardcopy" or "dumb."

- On their first screen, most servers will tell you how to log out, or terminate your session. Look for this information when you start a session; that will keep you from getting stuck. Of course, you can always use TELNET's escape char-acter to get out of a session. (Make sure you know what it is.)

TELNET to Non-standard Ports

Requiring that you dedicate a computer to a non-standard service limits non-stan-dard servers to applications where user friendliness is .paramount. However, there's another solution to this problem which strikes a compromise between friendliness and capital investment. What you really want to do is use the user's existing **telnet** client program, but write a special application server without pre-venting the serving machine from offering normal TELNET services. This can be done, but to understand how you need to know a bit more about how the Internet works. Since most computers provide many different servers (for **telnet** and other applications), there needs to be a way for the software communicating with the network to decide which server is to handle a request. This is accomplished by assigning each server a specific *port* number as identification. When the server starts running, it tells the network software which port it is responsible for servic-ing.† When a client program wants to connect to some service, it must specify both the address (to get to a particular machine) and a port number (to get to a

---

*There's one variation of a "non-standard" server that's worth knowing about. Sometimes you get a standard login prompt; then you use a special login name (like "library") to start a special application program. You're still using the standard TELNET server.

†These are "virtual" ports that are used by software to differentiate between various communications streams. Don't confuse them with terminal ports, SCSI ports, etc., which are actual hardware plugs.

particular service on that machine). Frequently-used applications have standard port numbers assigned to them; TELNET is assigned to port 23, for example.*

Now we can see how to use a standard client for another application—all we need is some way to make use of another port number. Private applications have to use an unassigned port that the client and server agree upon. If we write our non-standard server and tell it to listen to some other port (say, for example, port 10001), and if we can tell users to "connect" their **telnet** client to port 10001 on our machine, we're home free.

In fact, there are many such applications scattered around the Internet. When applications are provided over non-standard ports, the documentation about the service (or the person telling you to use it) must tell you which port to use. For example, let's try to use the Weather Underground, which provides access to weather information for cities across the United States. Its entry in the *Resource Catalog* looks like:

    Access: *telnet madlab.sprl.umich.edu 3000*

This tells you to "connect to **madlab.sprl.umich.edu** using **telnet**, but don't use the default port (23); use port 3000 instead." The non-standard port number is just added to the end of the **telnet** command. Here is the actual session accessing that service:

```
% telnet madlab.sprl.umich.edu 3000
Trying 141.212.196.79...
Connected to madlab.sprl.umich.edu.
Escape character is '^]'.
-------------------------------------------------------
*                University of Michigan
*                WEATHER UNDERGROUND
-------------------------------------------------------
*
*        College of Engineering, University of Michigan
*        Department of Atmospheric, Oceanic,
*              and Space Sciences
*        Ann Arbor, Michigan  48109-2143
*        comments: sdm@madlab.sprl.umich.edu
*
* With Help from:
*        The UNIDATA Project,
*        University Corporation for Atmospheric Research
*        Boulder, Colorado  80307-3000
*
```

---

*On BSD UNIX systems, the standard port numbers can be found in the file */etc/services*. Standard port number assignments are documented in an RFC titled "Assigned Numbers." At the time of this printing, this number is RFC1340, but it gets updated periodically; newer versions will have a different number.

```
----------------------------------------------------------
* NOTE:> New users, select option "H" on the main menu:
*        H) Help and information for new users
*
----------------------------------------------------------
```

```
Press Return for menu, or enter 3 letter city code:
```

There are two things worth noting about this session. First, rather than receiving the usual login prompt, you ended up right in the middle of an application. Every non-standard server has its own set of commands. You need to read the screens carefully to learn how to use them. Most servers tell you fairly early in the session how to log out and how to access its help facility. In this case, you enter a carriage return to get to the main menu and then an **H** to get to help information.

Second, because you never saw a login prompt, you never had to log in—you didn't even need an account on **madlab.sprl.umich.edu** to use the service. Of course, the non-standard server can have its own login procedure; you may need to register with some authority to use the service, and that authority may want to bill you for your usage. But many services are free and open to the public.

In this example, we used TELNET to connect to a non-standard port and thus accessed a special service. In practice, you will see both solutions: non-standard TELNET servers that use the standard port (port 23), and are therefore dedicated to a particular task, and non-standard servers that use a non-standard port. Our *Resource Catalog*, and other databases of network resources, tell you when a non-standard port is necessary.

Mimicking Alternate Clients

Another use for **telnet**ting to a different port is to masquerade as a different client. This technique is used primarily to debug the client-server relationship when developing applications. If I were having trouble with my network news-reading program (more on net news later) and didn't know whether the problem lay with the client or with the server, I could bypass the client on my machine by using the command:

```
% telnet sonne.uiuc.edu 119
```

This command connects me directly to the news server on **sonne** rather than the TELNET server; 119 happens to be the port that the news server uses. At this point, I could type in NNTP (the news distribution protocol) commands to exercise the server and see if it is acting as expected.

TELNETting to IBM Mainframes

If you've used computers for very long, you've probably come to expect IBM mainframes to exhibit their own behaviors, just to confuse the rest of the world. TELNET is no exception. As far as TELNET is concerned, we can divide IBM applications into two classes: "line-mode" applications and "3270" (or "full-screen") applications. We'll consider each of them separately.

First, line-mode applications. These are more or less what you're used to. Line mode means that the terminal sends characters to the computer a line at a time. This is the way most common terminals behave, and it's the way TELNET normally behaves. So line-mode applications don't present a problem. You might have to issue the **set echo** command to **telnet**, since line-mode applications sometimes don't echo the characters you type. But with this warning, you're all set. You can **telnet** to an IBM system, start your application (giving the **set echo** command if the characters you type don't appear on your screen), and everything will work normally.

Now for 3270 applications, which are (unfortunately) nowhere near as simple. First, what does "3270" mean? For a long time, IBM computers have used a proprietary full-screen terminal known as a 3270.* The 3270 was designed to make data entry (filling in forms, etc.) easier for the user and less of a load on the system. Therefore, it has many features that you won't find on garden-variety terminals: protected fields, numeric fields, alphabetic fields, etc. There are also several special-purpose keys, notably *programmed function* (PF keys), which may have special commands tied to them. The terminal operates on block transfers, which means that it doesn't send anything to the host until you press the ENTER key or a PF key; when you do, it sends a compressed image of the screen changes since the last transmission. Obviously, then, a 3270 application is going to require some special handling. It is usually possible to use a 3270 application in line mode, but it will be pretty unpleasant.

To use a 3270 application on its own terms, you really need a "terminal emulator" that can make your system act like a 3270 terminal. In many cases, the IBM mainframe that you're connected to will provide the terminal emulation itself. In this case, you can use the usual TELNET to connect to the computer. When TELNET connects, the mainframe will ask you what kind of terminal you are using. After you tell the system your terminal type, you're ready to go. You don't need to do anything special, but you do need to know what the special keys are on your terminal, so read on.

If the host you contact does not provide some kind of 3270 emulation, you need to use a special version of TELNET that has an emulator built in. This version is called **tn3270**. First, how do you know when you need **tn3270**? If you **telnet** to a system and see a message like this:

```
% telnet vmd.cso.uiuc.edu
Trying 128.174.5.98...
Connected to vmd.cso.uiuc.edu.
```

---

*Actually, there are a whole series of 3270-class terminals with a variety of characteristics (screen width, etc.). The original terminal was called a 3270; later, improved versions were known by model numbers like 3278 or 3279. So if some documentation talks about "emulating a 3278," it's refering to a particular flavor of the 3270 emulation that we're discussing here.

```
Escape character is '^]'.
VM/XA SP ONLINE-PRESS ENTER KEY TO BEGIN SESSION .
```

you know you're talking to an IBM mainframe. Two flags should give you a clue to this. One is the string "VM" in the message (or it might say "MVS"); these are the names of IBM operating systems. The other clue is that the message is entirely in capital letters, which is common in IBM-land. (Of course, there are other operating systems that do all their work with uppercase letters.) In this case, you should be able to use the computer system with regular TELNET, but it will be cumbersome; **tn3270** will probably work better.

You should also try **tn3270** if something funny happens to your session:

```
% telnet lib.cc.purdue.edu
Trying 128.210.9.8...
Connected to lib.cc.purdue.edu.
Escape character is '^]'.
 Connection closed by foreign host.
```

TELNET managed to connect to the remote system, but something went wrong, and the remote system gave up. In this example, the remote system is so entrenched in the 3270's features that it quit and closed the connection when it found you were not using them. (Note: many things can cause a connection to close immediately; this is only one of them.)

In this case, using **tn3270** gives you completely different results. Here's how you start:

```
% tn3270 lib.cc.purdue.edu
Trying...
Connected to lib.cc.purdue.edu.
```

Then the screen clears and you see:

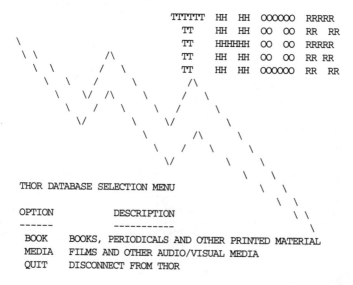

```
            TTTTTT  HH  HH  OOOOOO  RRRRR
              TT    HH  HH  OO  OO  RR RR
              TT    HHHHHH  OO  OO  RRRRR
              TT    HH  HH  OO  OO  RR RR
              TT    HH  HH  OOOOOO  RR RR



THOR DATABASE SELECTION MENU

OPTION          DESCRIPTION
------          -----------
 BOOK    BOOKS, PERIODICALS AND OTHER PRINTED MATERIAL
 MEDIA   FILMS AND OTHER AUDIO/VISUAL MEDIA
 QUIT    DISCONNECT FROM THOR
```

```
TYPE OPTION AND PRESS ENTER ==> ▮
THOR RECORDS ARE CURRENT AS OF 11/15/91
```

This is more like what the designer of the THOR system wanted.

Using a system in 3270 mode usually involves "filling in the blanks" and hitting PF keys or ENTER to get work done. You get to the blanks you want to fill in by moving the cursor to them and typing. When you want to send the completed form to the computer, you hit ENTER. Optional commands can be executed by hitting PF keys rather than ENTER. The bottom of the screen frequently lists the functions that are available through the PF keys; they often vary, depending on what you are doing. If the screen gets too full, or if the system prints an "important" message, the keyboard will lock until the screen is cleared using the CLEAR key. Obviously, this is not your run-of-the-mill terminal.

tn3270 is the only practical way to use some machines on the network, but it is confusing. The first problem is finding the program. Sometimes it is a funny mode of TELNET; if your **telnet** client detects that it is talking to an IBM system, it may start talking **tn3270** automatically. With some versions of TELNET, you may find a **tn3270** option in the command menu, or, you may be able to specify it in the command line. For example, in a popular IBM PC version of the client, the normal line-mode **telnet** command is **tn**. It looks like this:

```
C:\> tn vmd.cso.uiuc.edu
```

If you want to do full-screen (3270-style) **telnet**, you use a slightly different command: we need the **-t 3278** option. (As we said before, 3278 is one of IBM's variations on the 3270 theme—it's the same, as far as we're concerned):

```
C:\>  tn -t 3278 vmd.cso.uiuc.edu
```

On most systems, **tn3270** is a stand-alone program. If you need it, try typing **tn3270** and see if it starts. **tn3270** is currently part of the normal distribution of BSD 4.3 UNIX, but some older systems may not have it. It comes with most TCP/IP products for microcomputers. You can use Archie to locate a free copy of the software (for UNIX or any other system). See Chapter 9, *Finding Software*, for information about how to use the Archie service.

Once you've found **tn3270**—or even if the mainframe is taking care of 3270 emulation for you—you need to figure out how the 3270's special keys have been mapped onto your keyboard. There is no agreement on how to do this; it differs from system to system. That is, some implementations map the PF keys to the numeric keypad that's to the right of the keyboard (PF1 being 1, PF2 being 2, and so on); other emulators map the key sequence PF1 to ESC 1; some use the special function keys that are often placed above the keyboard; etc. In this book, we can't describe the different variations that you might encounter, because it is determined by the person who installed the emulator or **tn3270** you are using. However, we can tell you what you need to know and how to "feel" your way around. You need to know what keys move the cursor, clear the screen, and transmit the PF key and "reset" key codes.* In addition, make sure you know how to escape to command mode, so you can close the connection if things go wrong. This should be similar to the regular **telnet** program's escape command.

If you are lucky, the program's documentation, or the person who installed the program, might be able to provide a key map. If not, here are some hints to help you:

- Make sure that you identify your terminal correctly. (If you are using an ADM 3A terminal and the computer thinks you are using a VT100, things will be really confused.)

- To position the cursor, first try the arrow keys, if they exist on your keyboard. If there are no arrow keys, or if you try the arrow keys and the cursor doesn't move, try the h, j, k, l keys (just like the UNIX text editor *vi*, if you are familiar with that). Failing that, the TAB key almost always works. It takes you to the next field you can type into. By using TAB repeatedly, you can move the cursor around, albeit inconveniently.

- ENTER is usually the carriage return or the ENTER key near the numeric keypad.

- To find the function keys: first try any keys marked F1, F2, etc., or PF1, PF2, etc. You are looking for the screen to change, or for a message like "PF4 Undefined" to appear. (This message means that you have successfully sent a PF key, but no command has been assigned to it.) If that doesn't work, try the numeric keypad, or the sequence ESC *number*; e.g., try typing **ESC 1** to send PF1. If you still have no luck, you need to search for the key map (as described below).

- To clear the screen, try **CTRL-z**, **CTRL-l** (lowercase L, not the digit one), or **CTRL-home**. One of these should work.

- Implementations running on menu-driven workstations sometimes use menu items to send special keys.

If these hints didn't help, and you are using regular TELNET to contact the host (i.e., if the terminal emulator is running on the remote system, not your local system), you're out of luck. Try to contact the help desk for the remote computer and ask for a copy of their key mappings. If you are using **tn3270**, there is one more thing you can try: look around for a file named *map3270* (or something similar), either in same directory as the program, the system area or folder, or the */etc* directory. It should contain a list of terminal types and, for each terminal type, the key sequences which do good things. Unfortunately, its form is fairly unreadable. This

---

*Reset unlocks the terminal after you have typed something illegal. Some implementations don't support reset.

is a portion of the entry for VT100-type terminals from the standard BSD UNIX distribution:

```
vt100 | vt100nam | pt100 | vt125 | vt102 |          the list of terminals
    direct831 | tek4125 | pcplot | microvax{          this map describes
enter = '^m';
clear = '^z' | '\EOM';                               the clear key is
...                                                   control-z or ESC O M
# pf keys
pfk1 = '\EOq' | '\E1'; pfk2 = '\EOr' | ...           PF1 is either ESC O q
...                                                   or ESC 1; PF2 is ...
# local control keys

escape = '^c';  # escape to telnet command mode
master_reset = '^g';
...
}     # end of vt100, etc.
```

This particular key mapping is the basis for many **tn3270** implementations. There may be a guide for reading it at the beginning of the file to help you along, but the two major notational hints you need are: a \E stands for the ESC key on the keyboard, and the ^ stands for the control version of the following letter. That is, ^c stands for hitting the c key while holding down the CTRL key.

A final word of caution. There are many **tn3270** programs that don't work well in more specialized IBM applications. You may find that your version of **tn3270** works just fine doing mundane things on an IBM system (e.g., electronic mail, editing files, etc.), but as soon as you start the big software package you really wanted to use, it dies with a message:

```
Unexpected command sequence - program terminated
```

This is because the original **tn3270** program, which is the basis for a lot of implementations, could not handle certain correct, but infrequent, 3270 control codes. Therefore, **tn3270** will work correctly until you try to run a program that uses one of the codes that it can't handle. There is only one solution to this problem: try to get a better, usually newer, version of **tn3270**.

## CHAPTER SIX

MOVING FILES: FTP

Getting Started With FTP
Anonymous FTP
Handling Large Files and Groups of Files
Special Notes on Various Systems
Last Words: Some Practical Advice

O ften, you will find information on the Internet that you don't want to examine on a remote system: you want to have a copy for yourself. You've found, for example, the text of a recent Supreme Court opinion, and you want to include pieces of it in a brief you are writing. Or you found a recipe that looks good, and you want to print a copy to take to the kitchen. Or you found some free software that just might solve all your problems, and you want to try it. In each case, you need to move a copy of the file to your local system so you can manipulate it there. The tool for doing this is **ftp**.

ftp is named after the application protocol it uses: the "File Transfer Protocol" (FTP). As the name implies, the protocol's job is to move files from one computer to another. It doesn't matter where the two computers are located, how they are connected, or even whether or not they use the same operating system. Provided that both computers can "talk" the FTP protocol and have access to the Internet, you can use the **ftp** command to transfer files. Some of the nuances of its use do change with each operating system, but the basic command structure is the same from machine to machine.

Like **telnet**, **ftp** has spawned a broad range of databases and services. You can, indeed, find anything from legal opinions to recipes to free software in any number of publicly available online databases, or archives, that can be accessed through **ftp**. For a sampling of the archives that you can access with **ftp**, look at the *Resource Catalog*. If you're a serious researcher, you will find **ftp** invaluable; it is the common "language" for sharing data.

ftp is a complex program because there are many different ways to manipulate files and file structures. Different ways of storing files (binary or ASCII, compressed or uncompressed, etc.) introduce complications and may require additional thought to get things right. First, we will look at how to transfer files between two computers on which you have an account (a login name and, if needed, a password). Next, we'll discuss anonymous FTP, which is a special service that lets you access public databases without obtaining an account. Most public archives provided anonymous FTP access, which means that you can get files from the archive without arranging for a login name and an account in advance. Finally, we'll discuss some common cases (accessing VMS, VM, DOS, or Macintosh systems) which require some special handling. Unfortunately, there are a number of partial implementations of **ftp**, so all facilities may not be available on your system.

Getting Started With FTP

First, we'll consider how to move files between two computers on which you already have accounts. Like **telnet**, **ftp** requires you to specify the machine with which you would like to exchange files. This can be done with the command:

```
% ftp remote-machine-name
```

This starts the **ftp** program and connects to the named machine.

When **ftp** makes the connection with the remote computer, you will be asked to identify yourself with a login name and password:

```
% ftp sonne.uiuc.edu
Connected to sonne.uiuc.edu.
220 sonne FTP server (SunOS 4.1) ready.
Name (ux.uiuc.edu:krol): krol        send login name krol
331 Password required for krol.
Password:                            type the password; it isn't echoed
230 User krol logged in.
```

With some operating systems, like DOS and the Macintosh system, **ftp** may not ask for a password; it may only demand a login name, since there is no password security on the system. On these machines, protection from unwanted access is usually handled by disabling the FTP server software.

If you respond to the "name" prompt with a carriage return, many versions of **ftp** will send the login name that you are using on the local system. In the above example, the name of the local system and the default login name are shown in parentheses (**ux.uiuc.edu:krol**). Therefore, as a shortcut we could have typed a carriage return instead of the full login name. The login name you use will determine which remote files you can access, just as if you were logging into it locally. However, remember that you have to use a login name and password that are appropriate for the remote system.

After the remote system has accepted your login name and password, you are ready to start transferring files. **ftp** prints `ftp>` to prompt you for further commands. **ftp** can transfer files in two directions. It can take a file on the local machine (the one initiating the transfer) and **put** it on the remote machine; or it can **get** a file from the remote machine and place it on the local machine. The **get** and **put** commands have the syntax:

```
ftp> get source-file destination-file
ftp> put source-file destination-file
```

The *source-file* is the name of the existing file (the file that you want to copy); *destination-file* is the name of the newly created copy. The *destination-file* name is optional; if it is omitted, the copy is given the same name as the source file. In the following example, we start by logging into machine **ux.uiuc.edu** under the name **edk**. We transfer the file *comments* from the machine **sonne.uiuc.edu** under login name **krol**'s default directory to the originating machine. Then we transfer the file *newversion* to **sonne.uiuc.edu**, renaming the new copy to *readthis*:

```
ux login:    edk                          send login name edk to ux
password:                                 type the password; it isn't echoed


     Welcome to ux.uiuc.edu


ux% ftp sonne.uiuc.edu
Connected to sonne.uiuc.edu.
220 sonne FTP server (SunOS 4.1) ready.
Name (ux.uiuc.edu:edk): krol             send login name krol
331 Password required for krol.
Password:                                 type the password; it isn't echoed
230 User krol logged in.
ftp> get comments                         request copy of file comments
200 PORT command successful.              be moved from sonne to ux
150 ASCII data connection for comments (128.174.5.55,3516) (1588 bytes).
226 ASCII Transfer complete.
1634 bytes received in 0.052 seconds (30 Kbytes/s)
ftp> put newversion readthis              copy newversion to sonne
200 PORT command successful.              from ux; rename it as readthis
150 ASCII data connection for readthis (128.174.5.55,3518)
226 ASCII Transfer complete.
62757 bytes sent in 0.22 seconds (2.8e+02 Kbytes/s)
ftp> quit                                 end this session
221 Goodbye.
ux%
```

There are a few things worth mentioning about the example. First, knowing how to quit from any program is as important as knowing how to start it. When we finished transferring the files, we gave the **quit** command to terminate the **ftp** program. The command **bye** does the same thing; depending on your background, you may find **bye** easier to remember.

Notice that we did not show you how to look around and figure out which files you actually wanted; we just "knew" that there would be a file named *comments* in our home directory on **sonne**. Don't be afraid; omniscience isn't required. **ftp** has commands to list and change directories; we'll explain them a little later in this chapter. But if you already know what you're looking for, **put** and **get** are all you need.

ftp is fairly verbose; it gives you a lot of information about what it's doing. Unfortunately, the messages are rather arcane and inconsistent; **ftp** was designed before "user-friendliness" was invented. All of the messages begin with a "message number," which is eminently ignorable. However, the message texts (arcane though they may be) are worth scanning.

Finally, after each transfer, the program tells you what it transferred, how big it was, and the average transfer rate. The transfer rate will vary, depending on the load on the sending and receiving machines and what network route the packets are taking. You might find this information interesting but, if not, you can ignore it.

Common Problems

In the previous example, we typed the password and login name correctly. However, you won't always be so lucky. If you make a mistake, you'll get a "Login incorrect" message. There are two ways to handle this. You can exit **ftp** and try again; or you can give the **user** command, followed by your login name, to restart the login process. You'll be prompted again for your password and can continue from there:

```
ux% ftp sonne.uiuc.edu
Connected to sonne.uiuc.edu.
220 sonne FTP server (SunOS 4.1) ready.
Name (ux.uiuc.edu:edk): krol          login name krol
331 Password required for krol.
Password:                             type the password incorrectly
530 Login incorrect.
Login failed.
ftp> user krol                        start again with the login name
331 Password required for krol
Password:                             this time, get the password right
230 User krol logged in.
ftp>
```

It's a bit confusing, because if your first attempt to log in fails, you get an `ftp>` prompt, but you can't do anything with it. You have to complete the login process before proceeding.

There are, of course, other things that can go wrong. You can misspell the name of the computer you're trying to reach; this will probably earn you the message "unknown host" (or something of that sort). Check the spelling of the hostname. If the host you're trying to access has crashed, or is unreachable for some other reason, you'll see the message "host not responding," "host unreachable," "connection timed out," or something along those lines. In this case, your only solution is to wait and try again later. If the situation persists for a long time, try contacting whoever is responsible for the remote system. (You'll find more troubleshooting help in Chapter 15, *Dealing with Problems*).

If you misspell the name of the file you're trying to transfer, you'll see a message saying "no such file or directory," or the equivalent. Make sure you typed the name correctly, and make sure that the file you want to copy actually exists; we'll show you how to do that in the next section. If you try to get a file that you aren't allowed to take, you'll get a message saying "access denied," or something like that.

Finally, remember that some files you may find on the Net are huge (all right, pretty big—over a million characters). Some systems place file size limits on their customers, or your disk may not have room for large files. Make sure you have room for the file before you start to transfer it. In the next section, we'll see how to find out just how big a file is.

Browsing on a Remote Machine

When you are using **ftp**, you frequently don't know exactly what files you want and where they are located; you usually need to browse around to figure out what you want to transfer. There are a few useful commands and techniques to allow this. The basic commands to list directory information on the remote machine are **dir** and **ls**. The two commands have the same format:

```
ftp> dir directory-name local-file-name
ftp> ls directory-name local-file-name
```

Both commands list the files in directory *directory name* on the remote machine, putting their output into a local file. Both arguments are optional. The second argument (the *local-file-name*) tells **ftp** to put the listing into the given filename on the local system. If you want the listing to appear on your terminal rather than saving it in a file, just omit this argument. Since that is what you usually want, the *local-file-name* argument is rarely used.

The first argument, *directory-name*, gives the name of the directories or files that you want listed. If it is omitted, **ftp** lists all the files in the current remote directory. The first argument may contain "wildcard" characters, which are useful if you want to list something like "all files ending in the extension *.txt.*" However, there are no easy rules for wildcards; the wildcards are interpreted by the remote system. Therefore, their meaning will differ somewhat depending on what kind of computer you are trying to browse. Luckily, on *most* computer systems, the asterisk (*) is a wildcard that matches any group of characters. For example, on many machines the command:

```
ftp> dir test*
```

lists only files whose names begin with *test*. The biggest difference between systems is whether or not a wildcard can match a period.* On computers running the UNIX operating system, it can; so *test** would match filenames like *test.c* and *test.sh*, in addition to filenames like *test1* and *test*. On computers running the VAX/VMS or MS-DOS operating system, the filename and extension are considered different entities, so we would expect *test** to only match files with no extension (like *test1* and *testout*). However, that's not the whole story. Many servers on these machines interpret a wildcard without an explicit extension to have the extension .*. That is, the name *test** is interpreted as *test**.* (match any name starting with *test*, with any extension). Note that you can use a wildcard in either the name, the extension, or both. So you can use names like *test**. to match files beginning with *test* with no extension, or **.txt* to match any file with the extension *txt*.

Now, back to the basic listing commands, **ls** and **dir**. Their output should be quite different. The **ls** command, by default, gives you a simplified listing of filenames with no additional information. It is designed primarily for making a list of files that can be easily used as input to another program. It should look something like this:

```
ftp> ls
150 Opening ASCII mode data connection for file list.
nsfnet
CIC
campus
scott
```

The **dir** command produces more complete information:

```
ftp> dir
150 Opening ASCII mode data connection for /bin/ls.
total 2529
-rw-------  1 krol    cso    110 Oct 31 08:18 .Xauthority
-rw-r--r--  1 krol    cso    821 Nov 21 15:11 .cshrc
-rw-------  1 krol    cso     68 Mar  4 1989  .exrc
```

The output of this command looks like a full directory listing on the remote system. So, if you are connected to a computer running the VMS operating system, it will look like the output from a VMS **direct** command. If you are connected to a UNIX machine, it will look like the output from a Berkeley UNIX **ls –lga** command. This is because the client tells the server to send the directory information; the server executes an appropriate command, and then sends the listing back to the

---

*This is, admittedly, a UNIX user's way of looking at the world. To do justice to VMS and DOS, we'll say it more precisely. On these systems, filenames have two fields, a "name" and an "extension," separated by a period. A wildcard can appear in either field (or both). But, since the name and extension are different entities, a wildcard in the name can't match any characters in the extension, and vice-versa. Under UNIX, there is no formal difference between a "name" and the "extension." Many (probably most) filenames have extensions, but there's nothing special about the extension; it's just part of the name.

client untouched. There are some sloppy **ftp** implementations for which the **dir** and **ls** commands are synonyms.

The ultimate in directory commands, which only works if the remote system is running UNIX, is **ls –lR**. This is a "recursive" listing; it lists all files in the current directory and, if there are subdirectories, lists the files in those subdirectories too. It continues until it has exhausted the subdirectories of the subdirectories, listing just about every file which you can get to with **ftp**. Output from this command looks like:

```
ftp> ls -lR
200 PORT command successful.
150 Opening ASCII mode data connection for /bin/ls.
total 2529
-rw-------  1 krol    cso     110 Oct 31 08:18 .Xauthority
-rw-r--r--  1 krol    cso     821 Nov 21 15:11 .cshrc
drwx------  3 krol    cso     512 Oct  3  1989 iab
-rw-r--r--  1 krol    cso    2289 Jan  5 12:34 index

iab:                      contents of iab directory above
total 51
-rw-r--r--  1 krol    cso   25164 Sep  1  1989 crucible
-rw-r--r--  1 krol    cso   14045 Oct  3  1989 iab
drwx------  3 krol    cso    1024 Jan  3  1990 ietf
-rw-------  1 krol    cso   10565 May 15  1989 inarc

iab/ietf:                 contents of subdirectory ietf of iab
total 416
-rw-r--r--  1 krol    cso   24663 Jan 17  1990 agenda
drwxr-xr-x  2 krol    cso     512 Jul 13  1989 reports

iab/ietf/reports:
total 329
-rw-r--r--  1 krol    cso   46652 Jul 13  1989 jun89
-rw-r--r--  1 krol    cso   53905 May 11  1989 mar89
-rw-r--r--  1 krol    cso   53769 Jun 15  1989 may89
-rw-------  1 krol    cso   47429 Dec 15  1988 nov88

226 Transfer complete.
```

Be careful: it may produce large amounts of output. It is often a good idea to save the results of **ls –lR** in a file with the command:

```
ftp> ls -lR filename
```

So you do a few **dir** commands and see some files which are likely candidates to **get**, but you're still not sure exactly which file you want. You could **get** the file, **quit** or suspend the FTP program, list the file, restart **ftp** if you find out that the file isn't what you want, and so on, but it would be a pain. What you would really like to do is list the file on your terminal to see if it is the right one. Many **ftp** implementations provide this facility; to invoke it, use a minus sign (–) instead of a destination filename:

```
ftp> get source-file -
```

For example:

```
ftp> get index -
200 PORT command successful.
150 Opening ASCII mode connection for index (2289 bytes).
The following archives are available at this site:

activism    Files related to activism in general, NOT to any
            particular "cause."

...lines deleted ...

226 Transfer complete.
2289 bytes received in 0.41 seconds (5.5 Kbytes/s)
```

The problem with this technique is that the entire file is transferred to your terminal; this can be more than you want to see. One solution in this situation is to try to suspend the output with CTRL-S; typing **CTRL-S** stops your computer from sending characters to the screen. To see more, type **CTRL-Q**, which lets your computer continue. CTRL-S and CTRL-Q are fairly standard "suspend" characters; they'll probably work on your computer.

A more drastic approach is to send an interrupt to the server, telling it to stop sending. (On UNIX, this is a CTRL-C character). This cancels the current transfer. Unfortunately, this will not stop the output immediately. The CTRL-C has to traverse the network to the sender and tell it to stop. While this is occurring, the server continues merrily pumping the file towards your terminal, so your system is still queuing data for your terminal, which is slower than the network. All of this means that you've got a lot more to look at before the interrupt takes effect.

On some systems, **ftp** allows you to pass the output of the listing into another program, which may treat it more rationally. Two obvious candidates in a UNIX environment are **more** and **grep**.* For example:

```
ftp> get source-file "|more"
```

lists a screen worth of data and waits for you to tell it to send more. And:

```
ftp> get source-file "|grep RFC"
```

---

* **more** prints a file a screen at a time. **grep** prints only lines which contain a specified character or string.

scans the file as it is sent and only prints the lines which have the characters "RFC" in them.*

Neither command diminishes the network load very much. The sender doesn't know that the receiver is handling the output in a special way, so it still tries to send the file as quickly as possible. In the first case, congestion at the receiving end forces your system to tell the sender to stop sending temporarily. In the second case, the entire file is sent, even though only pieces of it are typed. If you are likely to scan the file repeatedly for different strings, it is more efficient to get it once and process it locally on your system than to send it repeatedly across the network.

You can also use the "|more" trick to handle long directory listings. However, there's a catch: the command **ls** "|more" doesn't work. **ftp** will think you're trying to list a file named |*more*—and you won't get anything back, unless the server happens to have a file with that rather odd name. Instead, use:

```
ftp > ls * "|more"
```

Actually, you don't need a *; you could have a directory name, the **-lR** option, or anything else reasonable, provided that "|more" is the third item on the command line.

Directories in FTP

There are a number of commands in **ftp** to deal with filesystem directories—probably more commands than you'd ever need to use. There are so many commands because two sets of directories are involved during an **ftp** session: the working directory on your local machine and the directory on the remote machine. Moving around the local directory is easy:

```
ftp> lcd directory
```

The usage rules for **lcd** are the same as for the UNIX **cd** command. These can be summarized as:

- If no directory is given, **lcd** sets your position back to the default directory for your account.

- If the directory starts with a slash (/), **lcd** moves you to the specified directory regardless of your current position (absolute positioning).

- If the directory is . ., **lcd** moves you up one level from the directory at which you are currently positioned.

- If the directory starts with an alphanumeric character, **lcd** looks for the directory as a subdirectory of the current one.

---

*We won't describe the intricacies of **more**, **grep**, and pipes. If you're a UNIX user, you should know about them. If you don't, we strongly recommend that you look them up—but until you've figured them out, you can treat the "|**more**" and "|**grep** *string*" notations as "magic cookies": type them as is, and they'll work. If you're not using UNIX, your system may provide some other way to handle this problem; check your documentation.

Manipulating the remote directory is a bit more restrictive,* and is done using the **cd** command:

```
ftp> cd directory
```

When you create a connection to a remote computer using **ftp**, you are initially placed in the same directory you would have been in if you had logged into that machine directly. You are also governed by the file and directory access permissions of the login name you are using on that computer. That is, you can't do anything you couldn't do if you were using a terminal connected directly to it.

The format of the directory specification is the same as for the **lcd** command, except that there is often no easy way to return to your default directory. If you were logged in directly, a UNIX **cd** command with no argument would return you to your default directory. **ftp** requires an argument to its **cd** command, and most implementations will prompt you for it if you omit it.

One way to get around this problem is to know the full directory path you are using on the remote computer. If you know it, whenever you get lost you can just specify the whole thing to **ftp** and be back on familiar turf. If you get lost, you can use the **pwd** command to find out where you are. **pwd** returns the path of the current working directory:

```
ftp> pwd
/mnt/staff/krol
```

ASCII and Binary Transfers

Now that you can move around and find files, let's think a bit more about how to transfer data. **ftp** has two commonly used ways ("modes") of transferring data, called "binary" and "ASCII." In a binary transfer, the bit sequence of the file is preserved, so that the original and the copy are bit-by-bit identical, even if a file containing that bit sequence is meaningless on the destination machine. For example, if a Macintosh transferred an executable file to an IBM VM system in binary, the file could not be executed on the VM system. (It could, however, be copied in binary mode from that VM system to another Macintosh and be executed there.)

ASCII mode is really a misnomer: it should be called "text" mode. In ASCII mode, transfers are treated as sets of characters; the client and server try to ensure that the characters they transfer have the same meaning on the target computer as they did on the source computer. Again, think of a Macintosh file being transferred to an IBM VM system. If the file contains textual data, the file would be meaningless on the IBM VM machine, because the codes used to represent characters on the Macintosh are different than those used on the IBM. That is, the bit pattern used to represent an "A" on the Mac is not the same bit pattern as that used on the VM

---

*This is especially true if you are using the guest account, *anonymous*. We'll discuss "anonymous FTP" extensively later in this chapter.

system. In ASCII mode, **ftp** automatically translates the file from a Mac text file to an IBM VM text file: hence the file would be readable on the IBM machine.

If you are confused by this, think of giving someone a journal article published in German. Binary mode would be equivalent to photocopying the article, in which case it is useless unless the recipient understands German. (But if the recipient photocopies the article again and gives it to someone who reads German, it is useful even if the original recipient didn't understand it.) ASCII mode is equivalent to translating the article before giving it to the other person. In this case, it becomes useful to the person who doesn't understand German, but probably loses some detail in the translation process.

In the previous example, some of the messages made a big point of saying that this was an ASCII transfer. This is appropriate, because the two files we were transferring were both text files. We don't know what kind of machine we're taking them from, and we don't care; we just want to make sure that we can read the files on our machine. To make sure that **ftp** is in ASCII mode, enter the command **ascii**. To put **ftp** into binary mode, enter the command **binary**. The command **image** is a synonym for **binary**; you'll find that a lot of **ftp** messages use the phrase "image mode," or "I mode" when they mean binary. For example:

```
ftp> binary          now we're ready to transfer a binary file
200 Type set to I.   I stands for "image," or "binary"
ftp> put a.out       transfer a UNIX executable (binary)
ftp> ascii           now we're ready to transfer a text file
200 Type set to A.   A stands for "ASCII," or "text"
ftp> get help.txt    retrieve a text (ASCII) file
```

Even if you are transferring files between identical machines, you need to be aware of the proper mode for the type of file you are transferring. The **ftp** software doesn't know the machines are identical. So, if you transfer a binary file in ASCII mode, the translation will still take place, even though it isn't needed. This may slow the transfer down slightly, which probably isn't a big deal, but it may also damage the data, perhaps making the file unusable. (On most computers, ASCII mode usually assumes that the most significant bit of each character is meaningless, since the ASCII character set doesn't use it. If you're transferring a binary file, all the bits are important.) If you know that both machines are identical, binary mode will work for both text files and data files.

This means that it is important to know what kind of data you want to transfer. Table 6-1 gives you hints for some common file types.

Many database and spreadsheet programs use a binary format to store their data, even if the data is inherently textual. Therefore, unless you know what your software does, we recommend trying binary mode first for database or spreadsheet files. Then see whether or not the file you have transferred work s correctly. If not, try ASCII mode. For word processing programs, you can get a few additional clues. The so-called "WYSIWYG" word processors (word processors that have an elaborate display that matches the actual output very closely) usually store documents in a binary format. Some of these programs have a special command for writing text (i.e., ASCII) files that can be transferred in ASCII mode, but you may lose some formatting information. The simpler (and older) word processors that don't have fancy WYSIWYG display capabilities typically store data in an ASCII format.

Table 6-1: Common File Types and Modes

File	Mode
Text file	ASCII, by definition
Spreadsheet	Probably binary
Database file	Probably binary, possibly ASCII
Word processor file	Probably binary, possibly ASCII
Program source code	ASCII
Electronic mail messages	ASCII
UNIX shell archive	ASCII
UNIX tar file	Binary
Backup file	Binary
Compressed file	Binary
Uuencoded or binhexed* file	ASCII
Executable file	Binary, but see below
PostScript (laser printer) file	ASCII
Hypertext (HTML) document	ASCII
Picture files (GIF, JPEG, MPEG)	Binary

* **uuencode** is a UNIX utility that we will mention in Chapter 7, *Electronic Mail*. The UNIX UUCP utilities use it to encode binary files in an all-ASCII representation, which makes them easier to transfer correctly. **BinHex** is a similar utility used on DOS and Windows systems.

Executable files are generally binary files; however, there are exceptions. Programs that are compiled and executed directly by the processor are always binary. However, most operating systems provide at least one "scripting" language that allows you to write sequences of commands that are then interpreted by another program. UNIX provides several scripting languages, including the "shell" itself; it is very common to write programs from basic UNIX commands. With some operating systems, scripts are called "command files." Scripts are always text files.

On the Internet, many hypertext files are stored in a format called HTML, which stands for "hypertext markup language." This is an ASCII format that's used by the World-Wide Web (described in Chapter 13). There are many places on the Net where various types of video images (weather maps, satellite images, etc.) are available. The most important file formats for video images are called GIF and JPEG, both of which can encode elaborate multicolor images; and MPEG, which is used for "movies." These are all binary formats, and should therefore be transferred in binary mode. You probably need extra software to view these files; that's also available through the Internet.

On UNIX, you can use the **file** command to figure out the type of most files. This utility wasn't written with **ftp** in mind, so it gives you a lot more information than you really need. Here are some examples, taken from a SunOS system:

```
% file /bin/spell /bin/ls outline.txt telnet.ms grosbeak.gif
/bin/spell:     executable shell script
/bin/ls:        sparc pure dynamically linked executable
outline.txt:    ascii text
telnet.ms:      [nt]roff, tbl, or eqn input text
grosbeak.gif:   data
```

These commands tell you that the file */bin/spell* is an executable shell script, which you'd transfer using ASCII mode. This might surprise you; most people assume that any file in the UNIX */bin* directory is a binary executable. That's not true. The file */bin/ls* is a true binary executable, so you would transfer it in binary mode. *outline.txt* and *telnet.ms* are text files that you'd transfer in ASCII mode. *telnet.ms* happens to be input for the **troff** typesetting program. **file** can't figure out what *grosbeak.gif* is, but it does tell you that the file contains "data"—which means that it's binary, and should be transferred in binary mode. (It happens to be a GIF image.) If you don't know what mode to use, binary is probably the best bet. Non-ASCII computers are becoming less common, so the translation step often isn't needed.

Many FTP implementations provide several additional modes (e.g., **tenex**, an obsolete operating system format; **jis78kj**, a *kanji* character set for Japanese), but they are not commonly used.

Transferring Multiple Files

The **get** and **put** commands that we discussed earlier can only transfer one file at a time. On occasion, you want to transfer groups of files. To do so, you can use the **mput** and **mget** commands. They have the syntax:

```
ftp> mput list of files
ftp> mget list of files
```

The **mput** command takes the files in the list and moves them to the remote system. The **mget** command moves files from the remote system to the local system. In both cases, the filenames will be the same on both the local and remote systems. The list of files can be arbitrarily long and can include wildcards.

The actual rules for how wildcards are expanded are more complicated than the **ftp** documentation lets on. You can usually use an asterisk (*) to match zero or more characters and forget about the complexities. On UNIX systems, you can use a question mark (?) to match any single character. On other systems, you'll have to do some experimentation or some careful reading of the documentation to see what's legitimate.* Here's a typical session using **mget** and **mput**:

---

*The actual rules go something like this: When you're using **mput**, you're moving files from your local system to the remote system. The wildcards are expanded by your local system, and use the local system's wildcard rules. When you're using **mget**, you need to locate files on the remote system. In this case, **ftp** uses the remote system to see what, if anything, matches the wildcards. Therefore, the wildcard rules that **mput** and **mget** obey may differ, and **mget**'s rules depend on the remote system.

```
ftp> cd work                          change the remote directory
250 CWD command successful.
ftp> ls b*                            see what files are there
200 PORT command successful.
150 ASCII data connection for /bin/ls (127.0.0.1,1129) (0 bytes).
b.tst
bash.help
bsdman.sh
226 ASCII Transfer complete.
remote: b*
29 bytes received in 0.03 seconds (0.94 Kbytes/s)
ftp> mget b*                          try to transfer the files
mget b.tst? yes                       first file: do I really want it?
200 PORT command successful.
150 ASCII data connection for b.tst (127.0.0.1,1133) (68112 bytes).
226 ASCII Transfer complete.
local: b.tst remote: b.tst
81927 bytes received in 0.41 seconds (2e+02 Kbytes/s)
mget bash.help? no                    second file; do I really want it?
mget bsdman.sh? no                    third file; do I really want it?
```

Now let's try to "put" a group of files. This time, we'll explicitly put two filenames on the command, just to show you that it can be done.

```
ftp> mput login tblsz.c               now try to put some files
mput login? yes                       first file: do I really want it?
200 PORT command successful.
150 ASCII data connection for login (127.0.0.1,1139).
226 Transfer complete.
local: login remote: login
2785 bytes sent in 0.03 seconds (91 Kbytes/s)
mput tblsz.c? y                       second file: do I really want it?
200 PORT command successful.
150 ASCII data connection for tblsz.c (127.0.0.1,1141).
226 Transfer complete.
local: tblsz.c remote: tblsz.c
975 bytes sent in 0.04 seconds (24 Kbytes/s)
ftp>
```

Note that the command we just gave, **mput login tblsz.c**, does *not* mean "put *login* on the remote system with the filename *tblsz.c*," as it would if it were a simple *put* command. It means "copy all the files on the command line to the remote system, in the current remote directory, without changing their names."

ftp normally asks you whether or not you want to transfer each file; you have to type y (or **yes**, or RETURN) to transfer the file.

Typing **n** (or **no**)* cancels the transfer. Being prompted for each file is annoying (particularly if you're transferring a large group of files), but it helps prevent mistakes. If you really dislike being prompted, or you need to transfer a huge group

---

*Actually, anything that begins with the letter **n** will do. In some implementations, anything that does *not* begin with the letter **n** is taken as a "yes," so be careful!

of files, give the command **prompt**; that disables prompting. The whole group of files will be transferred without further intervention. Giving the **prompt** command again re-enables prompting.

There are a few things to watch out for:

- Remember that you don't get to specify a name for the destination file. All the names on the command line are interpreted as source files. It's particularly tempting to try to copy a group of files into a directory; watch out for this! You cannot use a command like the following:

  ```
  ftp> mput ch*.txt book
  ```

  where *book* is the name of a remote directory. Instead, you must first use **cd** to change the remote directory.

  ```
  ftp> cd book
  ...
  ftp> mput ch*.txt
  ```

  The same goes for **mget** commands.

- You cannot use **mput** or **mget** (or, for that matter, the regular **get** and **put**) commands to copy a directory. You can only use them to copy groups of plain files. Copying a directory yields unpredictable results. If you need to transfer a directory, create an archive of some sort and transfer the archive. We'll discuss how to do this later in the chapter.

- You may find that the **mget**, with wildcards, doesn't always work properly; it appears to depend on whether or not the **ls** command is implemented correctly by the remote FTP server. *Caveat emptor.*

FTP Command Summary

The following table summarizes **ftp**'s most useful commands. It includes all of the commands that we have discussed so far. These commands are available on most, if not all, **ftp** clients. **ftp** will show you the commands that are available on your particular client if you type **help**.

account *info*	Supplies additional accounting or security information which must sometimes be given within a session. Later, we'll see a situation in which the **account** command is needed for accessing IBM mainframes.
ascii	Enters ASCII mode, for transferring text files.
binary	Enters binary mode, for transferring binary files.
cd *remote-directory*	Changes the working directory on the remote machine.
close	Ends the **ftp** session with a particular machine and returns to **ftp** command mode. After a **close**, you can **open** a connection to a new system or **quit** from **ftp**.

delete *filename*   Deletes the named file on the remote system.

dir *file destination*   Gives a full directory listing on the remote machine. *file* and *destination* are both optional. *file* can either be a single file or a wildcard construction. The listing shows all filenames that match the specification. If *file* is omitted, the listing shows all files in the current remote directory. The *destination* is where the output should be put. It can either be a file on the local machine or a command through which to filter the file. If *destination* is omitted, the listing appears on the terminal.

hash   Tells **ftp** to print a pound sign (#) every time a block of data is transferred by a **get** or **put** command. Useful if you are not certain the network is working; it gives you a visual signal that data is actually moving. It is also lets you know that something's happening when you're transferring a very long file. If **ftp** is already printing hashes, the **hash** command tells it to stop.

help *command*   Prints a short bit of documentation about the command.

lcd *directory*   Changes the default directory on your local machine to the named directory.

ls *file destination*   Gives a short directory listing on the remote machine. The arguments are the same as for **dir**.

mget *file-list*   Gets multiple files from the remote machine. The file list can be either a list of filenames separated by spaces or a wildcard construction.

mput *file-list*   Puts multiple files onto the remote machine. The file list can be either a list of filenames separated by spaces or a wildcard construction.

open *machine-name*   Connects to the named machine. This is useful if you want to **connect** to a new system after transferring files from another system. You must **close** your old connection first.

prompt   With **mget** or **mput**, the **prompt** command tells **ftp** to prompt you for confirmation before transferring each file. This is useful if you want to make sure you're not needlessly transferring files or (worse) overwriting files that already exist. If prompting is already enabled when you give the **prompt** command, **ftp** turns it off and transfers all the files without asking any questions.

pwd   Prints the name of the current remote directory.

quit   Closes the connection, if one exists, and exits **ftp**.

user *username*   Sends the username to the remote machine to log in. This
                                is useful if you typed your username or password incor-
                                rectly. Rather than closing the connection and opening a
                                new one, you can try again by issuing a **user** command.

Most **ftp** implementations actually have 70 or 80 commands, so this is obviously a
shortened list. However, most of the commands are only needed for esoteric purposes; unless you have very special needs, the commands we listed above will
suffice.

Anonymous FTP

So far, the facilities we've discussed make it difficult to make a file available for
everyone to use. For example, if I wanted to distribute a software package, I'd
have to put it on the system and then pass out login/password combinations to
everyone who wanted to get the software. This would be a burden, particularly for
the administrator, but also for the user.

Anonymous FTP bypasses this limitation. It allows users who don't have a login
name or a password to access certain files on a machine. Of course, there are
strong restrictions: anonymous users can normally only **get** files (i.e., copy them);
they can't install new files or modify files that already exist.* And there are strict
limits on which files that they can copy.

When anonymous FTP is enabled, a special login name is created called *anonymous*. If you start **ftp**, connect to a remote computer, and give *anonymous* as your
login name, **ftp** will accept any string as your password. It is generally considered
good form to use your electronic mail address as the password, so the managers of
the server have some idea of who is using it and can easily contact you if necessary. (In fact, some systems are starting to demand you use a valid email address
before they will let you in.) After signing in as *anonymous*, you are allowed to **get**
those files which are expressly permitted to the anonymous FTPers.

These additional restrictions on which files you can access with anonymous FTP
are enforced by changing the **cd** command. When you enter a system anony-
mously, you are placed at a particular place in the file directory system. That initial
directory is the starting point for all anonymous FTP access. From there, you can
only move to subdirectories by giving the name of the subdirectory, or move back
from a subdirectory to its "parent" by using the .. argument. Positioning yourself
absolutely, by specifying a directory beginning with a slash (/), is usually not
allowed. Technically, it is legal; but **cd /pub** has been redefined to mean "move to
the *pub* subdirectory of the initial anonymous FTP directory." You can use **cd /** if
you get lost in an anonymous FTP session and need to get back to your starting

---

*An archive manager can create directories that can be written by anonymous FTP users. Such direc-
tories are often used to let users submit articles or software for inclusion in an archive. If the archive
manager has set up an incoming anonymous FTP directory, you can use use ftp's normal **put** and
mput commands to place files there.

point. Your other option is to use **cd ..** repeatedly to move up to where you started. The command **cdup** is a synonym for **cd ...**

Remember, when you are using anonymous FTP, you are a guest on someone else's system. Sometimes there will be usage restrictions posted:

```
230-Available for anonymous ftp only between 5 pm EST
230-and 8 am EST.
```

These are displayed when you first log in. Please observe them—if you don't the server might become disabled for us all.

Well, I guess it's time for an example. You were browsing through the *Resource Catalog*, and ran across a document called *Not Just Cows*, a directory of useful agriculture-oriented Internet resources. The entry for this document gave the following access information:

```
ftp ftp.sura.net login anonymous; cd pub/nic;
get agriculture.list
```

This tells you to get a copy of the document via anonymous FTP from **ftp.sura.net**. Your dialog with **ftp** to get this resource would look like this:

```
% ftp ftp.sura.net                        start up ftp to the server
Connected to nic.sura.net.
220 nic.sura.net FTP server (Version 6.9 Sep 30 1991) ready.
Name (ftp.sura.net:krol): anonymous     anonymous login
331 Guest login ok, send email address as password.
Password: krol@ux1.cso.uiuc.edu          password doesn't really echo
230 Guest login ok, access restrictions apply.
ftp> cd pub/nic                           move to the directory
250-######WELCOME TO THE SURANET NETWORK INFORMATION CENTER##########
250-SURAnet                                   info@sura.net
250-8400 Baltimore Blvd.                      301-982-4600(voice)
250-College Park, Maryland  USA 20740-2498    FAX 301-982-4605
250-    Many of the documents available in this ftp archive are geared
250-towards the new user of the Internet. SURAnet has provided several
250-"How To" guides for network navigation tools such as, telnet, ftp,
250-and email. These "How To" guides are available in the directory
250 CWD command successful.
ftp> dir                                  list files
200 PORT command successful.
150 Opening ASCII mode data connection for /bin/ls.
total 4096
-rw-rw-r--   1 mtaranto 120        1226 Jun  4 17:39 .message
-rw-rw-r--   1 mtaranto 120        7545 Jul 15 18:30 00-README.FIRST
-rw-rw-r--   1 mtaranto 120       47592 Mar  5 17:04 BIG-LAN-FAQ
-rw-rw-r--   1 root     120      216594 Jan  3  1992 Internet-Tour.txt
drwxr-sr-x   2 mtaranto 120         512 Jul 22 13:37 NREN
-rw-r--r--   1 mtaranto 120        1657 Jul 10 20:17 NSFNET.policy.statement
drwxr-sr-x   2 mtaranto 120         512 Jun 29 13:17 ZEN
-rw-rw-r--   2 root     120        2555 Jan  3  1992 acceptable.use.policy
-rw-rw-r--   1 mtaranto 120       85677 May 11 17:29 agricultural.list
-rw-rw-r--   1 mtaranto 120       27840 Apr 17 14:10 archie.manual
        <remainder of list deleted for space>
```

```
226 Transfer complete.
1752 bytes received in 1.2 seconds (1.4 Kbytes/s)
ftp> get agricultural.list NJC          move the file
200 PORT command successful.
150 Opening ASCII mode data connection for agricultural.list (85677 bytes).
226 Transfer complete.
local: NJC remote: agricultural.list
88383 bytes received in 2.8 seconds (31 Kbytes/s)
ftp> quit
221 Goodbye.
%
```

Let's examine the preceding example and see what happened. Once you were connected to **ftp.sura.net**, which was specified on the **ftp** command, you used *anonymous* as the login name. As a password, you sent your email address—it didn't print when you typed it. Next you issued the **cd pub/nic** to move to the directory specified in the *Resource Catalog* entry. The server responded with a message (all the lines beginning 250). Some newer FTP servers automatically display a file on your terminal whenever you enter a directory.* This feature is becoming increasingly common; it's very helpful, because you don't have to hunt down a *README* or *INDEX* file to find out what's in the directory. After reading the introductory message, you list the files in the directory to see whether there's anything else you might want; finally, you get around to copying the file named *agricultural.list* on the remote computer to *NJC* on your home computer.

That's all there is to it. Anonymous FTP is just like regular FTP, except that you don't need a password. The *Resource Catalog* in this book lists many FTP archives that you can access; the Archie service can give you more information about what is available, and where to find it.

Handling Large Files and Groups of Files

Network users often need to transfer extremely large files, or large batches of files, across the network. You may need a large database, an archive of a discussion group, a set of reports, or the complete source code to BSD UNIX. All of these tend to be large. In this section, we'll discuss techniques for handling large files (compression) and ways to accumulate large groups of files into a single archive to make them easier to transfer. Because most anonymous FTP sites already store files as compressed archives, we'll also discuss how to "unpack" such a file once you've transferred it to your system.

Compressed Files

To reduce the cost of storage and transmission across the network, large files are frequently stored in *compressed format*. There are many techniques for data compression, and consequently a number of different compression programs that can

---

*The initial message is stored in the file *.message*; you'll see it in the directory listing.

be used. Text files run through a good data compression program can be reduced anywhere from 30 percent to 70 percent in size.

Moving compressed files across the network really isn't a problem. They should always be treated as *binary* files. The problem is that getting the file to the target system is only half the battle. After it is there, you must uncompress it before it is usable. This may or may not be easy, since there is no one standard for compression utilities.

Compressed files are usually flagged by an unusual suffix or extension on the filename. The most common compression utilities are:

Table 6-2: Common Compression Programs

Compression Program	Decompression Program	File Suffix	Typical Filename
compress	uncompress	.Z	*rfc1118.txt.Z*
gzip	gunzip	.z or .gz	*textfile.gz*
pack	unpack	.z	*textfile.z*
Stuffit	unsit	.Sit	*program.Sit*
PackIt	unpit	.pit	*report.pit*
PKZIP	unzip41	.ZIP	*package.ZIP*
zoo210	zoo210	.zoo	*picture.zoo*

If you are looking at the files available on a remote system and see these suffixes, that's a hint that the files are probably compressed. The suffix gives you a hint about what utility should be used to uncompress it. The program you need to uncompress the file will vary depending on what kind of computer you are using and what kind of compression was used. This is only the tip of the iceberg; there are about as many compression programs as there are types of computers. A very useful chart is available via **ftp** (see, I told you **ftp** was useful); after you finish the chapter, you can get it yourself. See the *Resource Catalog* for "Computing: Compression and Archival Software Summary."

On UNIX, compression and decompression are usually done using the **compress** and **uncompress** utilities. Let's take the file we just retrieved, *NJC*, check its size, and compress it:

```
% ls -l NJC*                     list all files starting with NJC
-rw-r--r--  1 krol      61411 Dec 20 14:46 NJC
% compress -v NJC                -v says tell me how much compression
NJC: Compression: 57% - replaced with NJC.Z
% ls -l NJC*                     now I have a .Z file only
-rw-r--r--  1 krol      26230 Dec 20 14:46 NJC.Z
```

Now we have a file called *NJC.Z*. The original file was 61411 characters long; the compressed file is only 26230 characters long, for a savings of roughly 57%. This means that the compressed file will take less than half as much storage and half as much time to transfer from one computer to another. For a relatively small file (and 60 KB is not terribly large), the savings may not be important; but if you're storing many megabytes of data, and have a slow communications line, a 57 percent savings is very significant.

Let's decompress *NJC.Z*, to make the original file again:

```
% uncompress NJC.Z
% ls -l NJC*
-rw-r--r--  1 krol        61411 Dec 20 14:46 NJC.txt
```

We have the same useful file back. Note that its size hasn't changed; the uncompressed file is still 61411 bytes, just like the original. This is a quick, unreliable, and (frankly) unnecessary check that the file was decoded correctly.

Moving a Whole Directory

When you're using **ftp**, you often want to receive a whole file structure: a directory or collection of directories, not just a single file. **ftp** really isn't designed to do this effectively; it's not convenient to move 50 or 100 files at a time, and there are no standard commands for moving entire directories.

While this situation comes up all the time, it is particularly common when you want to get a set of files from a remote FTP archive. For example, someone who distributes a free software package by putting it in an FTP archive usually needs to make dozens (maybe even hundreds) of files available. Rather than telling users to "ftp these 50 files," he or she usually uses a backup utility to aggregate all of these files into a single file (shown in Figure 6-1).

On the source computer containing the files to be distributed, the person responsible must copy all the files into one package. When someone gets the package, he or she must open it up to get the group of files that are contained. On a UNIX system, this single file is typically created using **tar**, as follows:

```
% cd book                          let's see what's in the directory
% ls                               we plan to dump
README        ftp.2      news           tmac.Seffnuts
applications  ftp.bak    nut.guide      tmac.Sioc
% cd ..                            move to parent directory
% tar -cf book.tar book            dump directory book into book.tar
% ls -l book.tar                   how big is book.tar
-rw-r--r--  1 krol     802816 Dec 21 06:35 book.tar
```

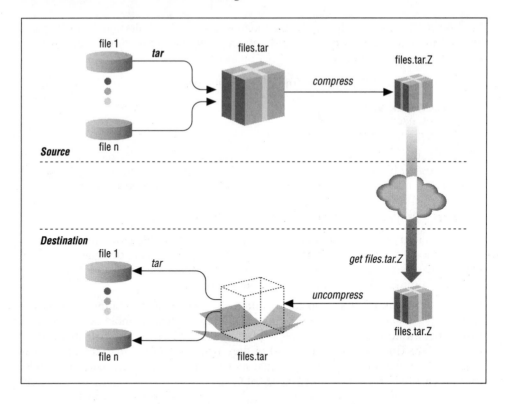

Figure 6-1: Moving many files

The directory to be packaged is called *book* and can be seen to contain a number of files. From the parent directory of *book*, the **tar** command is used to create a file named *book.tar*, which contains all the data to be distributed. The file is quite large and is of no benefit to the owner anymore (he has the directory already). So, it makes sense to compress it as follows:

```
% compress -v book.tar
book.tar: Compression: 60.13% -- replaced with book.tar.Z
% ls -l book.tar*
-rw-r--r--  1 krol       321717 Dec 21 06:35 book.tar.Z
```

That's better, only 40 percent as much disk space. The friendly system administrator now puts this file into the anonymous FTP directory, where it can be fetched by anyone in the world.

Some time later, you decide you want to pick up the "book" package and install it on your computer. You begin by using anonymous FTP to contact the server and retrieve *book.tar.Z*:

```
% ftp ux1.cso.uiuc.edu               start an ftp to the server
Connected to ux1.cso.uiuc.edu.
220 ux1.cso.uiuc.edu FTP server (Version 5.60) awaits your command
Name (ux1.cso.uiuc.edu:): anonymous   log in as appropriate
```

```
331 Guest login ok, send ident as password.
Password:
230 Guest login ok, access restrictions apply.
Remote system type is UNIX.
Using binary mode to transfer files.   note binary mode
ftp> get book.tar.Z                     get the aggregate dump file
200 PORT command successful.
150 Opening BINARY mode data connection for book.tar.Z (321717 bytes).
226 Transfer complete.
321717 bytes received in 2.4 seconds (1.3e+02 Kbytes/s)
ftp> quit                               quit ftp
221 Goodbye.
```

You now have the compressed **tar** file; you only need to undo all the operations done to it to make it usable. Sometimes people are confused by the order of doing these multiple operations. You must undo them in exactly the opposite order they were performed to create the file. The rule of thumb is to do whatever it takes to handle the filename extensions right to left. So, with a file like *book.tar.Z*, you must first get rid of the *Z*:

```
% uncompress book.tar.Z              file is unusable until uncompressed
% ls -l book*                        now one file book.tar
-rw-r--r--  1 krol        802816 Dec 21 07:00 book.tar
```

Now you have an uncompressed **tar** file, *book.tar*. Get rid of the **tar** and you are done:

```
% tar -xf book.tar                   extract all files in book.tar
% ls -l book*                        same file as before
-rw-r--r--  1 krol        802816 Dec 21 07:00 book.tar

book:                                and a whole new directory
total 792
-rw-r--r--  1 krol          4630 Sep  3 10:43 README
-rw-r--r--  1 krol         14461 Nov 11 15:18 applications
     <remainder deleted for space considerations>
```

You will find the command **tar -tf** *filename* useful, too. This lists the files that are present in the **tar** file; by looking at the list, you can figure out whether or not you got the right file.

From time to time, you will see other complications. At some sites, extremely large archives are cut into many smaller pieces (usually 100 KB or so). Each piece is typically assigned a two-digit decimal number, which is the last part of the filename. For example, you might see files named *book.tar.Z.01*, *book.tar.Z.02*, etc. Transfer all of these files to your system. (Yes, this is a pain; yes, we did tell you that archive managers use **tar** to avoid large collections of files. If it's any consolation, remember that something large enough to require this treatment probably includes several hundred files. This is why **mget** exists.) Then assemble them in order; usually, a command like the following will work correctly:

```
% cat book.tar.Z.* > book.tar.Z
```

This command assumes that the administrator has named each chunk of the archive so that **cat book.tar.Z.*** will produce the files in the right order. That's usually the case.* Then proceed as normal; use **uncompress** to get a tar file, and **tar** to extract the source files from the archive:

```
% uncompress book.tar.Z
% tar xf book.tar
```

Some hints:

- Before you unpack a **tar** file, it's a good idea to give the command **tar -tf book.tar** to find out what files are contained. Make sure that unpacking the archive won't overwrite any files that you want. One drawback of **tar** is that it can't rename files as it unpacks them; the names you see are the names you'll get.

- You can combine the uncompress and unpack steps into one command with **zcat book.tar.Z | tar -xf -**. This way, you don't leave an extra temporary file lying around.

- An increasing number of archives are using the **gzip** program (GNU-zip) for compression, which uses the extension **.z** or **.gz**. The corresponding un-compress tool is called **gunzip**; and **gzip -d** corresponds to **zcat**. GNU-zip is free software that's distributed by the Free Software Foundation; their FTP archive is listed in the *Resource Catalog*, in the "Computing" section. It may come with your system, but it probably doesn't; you'll have to get your own copy.

Shell archives

If you're using a UNIX system, you will also see *shell archives* from time to time. A shell archive is simply a composite file that is a Bourne shell script, or command file. Executing this shell script extracts the files. For example, say that you retrieve a file called *goodies.shar* from your favorite anonymous FTP site. To unpack this, just give the command:

```
% sh goodies.shar
```

It is very common to see shell archives that have been compressed, cut into chunks, or both. You should already know how to handle these special cases: reassemble the chunks, do whatever's necessary to decompress the file, and then use **sh** to unpack the archive.

---

*Here's how to tell. If the archive administrator used leading zeros (i.e., 00, 01, 02, ... 09, 10, 11) in the number part of the name, the filenames will sort correctly. If the administrator omitted the leading zero (and there are ten or more files), they won't. Another way to tell is to give a command like **ls -l book.tar.Z.***; if it lists the files in the right order, you're in good shape.

When you're unpacking a shell archive, you're executing a program that someone else gave you. As we all know by now, it's unwise to place much trust in programs someone else wrote. There have been reports of malicious shell archives that delete all your files and take other hostile actions. Therefore, two warnings:

- *Always* look at the archive's contents before unpacking it. Make sure it doesn't do anything unreasonable. You'll have to learn a little shell programming (though not much) to do this.

- *Never* unpack a shell archive when you are logged in as "root." Should the archive do something hostile, you won't have any protection.

While there are many programs for creating a shell archive, and therefore many slightly different formats, don't worry: any properly constructed shell archive can be unpacked by any UNIX Bourne or Korn shell. If you want to create a shell archive, any number of **shar** programs are available from the Internet.

Other archival utilities

In my experience, **tar** archives are by far the most important, with shell archives a close second. There are a few other archive types you may see from time to time. You will occasionally see archives created by the UNIX **cpio** utility. You may see archives created by various programs on DOS systems (FASTBACK, ZIP, PCBACKUP, etc.) or the BACKUP utility on VMS operating systems. Unfortunately, most archival tools are specific to one operating system—if you're using a Macintosh, you probably don't have a **tar** command, let alone a VMS BACKUP command. Likewise, if you're using a UNIX system, you probably don't have a DOS FAST-BACK program lying around. As a rule, therefore, an archive is only useful if you're unpacking it on the same kind of computer that created it. (The archive might be stored on another kind of computer, which is not important—as long as it is treated as a binary file.)

However, all is not lost. If the Internet presents some problems, it also gives you a way to resolve these problems. If you have the time and energy to poke through the acres of free software that are available on the Net, you *may* be able to find a program that will unpack a strange archive format on your system. There are definitely UNIX implementations of VMS BACKUP floating around; if you look hard enough, you might be able to find equivalent utilities for other operating systems. (The chapter on Archie tells you how to locate software.) There is even some commercial software available for unpacking different backup formats; it costs money, but you don't have to debug it yourself.

Special Notes on Various Systems

ftp's biggest virtue is that it lets you move files between computers regardless of their type. In many cases, you don't need to know anything about the remote systems. However, this isn't completely true; in practice, whenever you have two systems, you usually end up needing to know something (certainly not much, but something) about the remote system.

The problems are relatively minor, and typically have to do with the way the remote system specifies filenames. As much as possible, **ftp** uses a uniform, UNIX-like notation for filenames and addresses. However, this can be confusing, since **ftp** doesn't try to interpret **dir** listings and other output generated by the remote system: it just sends the command's output back to you verbatim. Deciphering the output from **ls**, **dir**, or any other command usually isn't too difficult. It's fairly easy to find the filename, the file's size, and the last modification date, and that's usually all the information you care about. But you do need to know how to convert remote filenames into a form that **ftp** understands.

Here are a number of examples using **ftp** to access various kinds of systems that you will find as servers on the Internet. Remember that these are examples. There are many vendors of TCP/IP software for the Macintosh, Digital Equipment, and IBM computers. The server you are contacting might look a bit different from the examples we show here. Also, in most of the examples, the remote system tells you what kind of computer it is. This is not always the case. If you don't know what kind of system you're using, your best bet is to look for *README* files; there's often one that explains what archive you're looking at, what kind of a system you're using, and so on. If this doesn't work, do a **dir** and try matching the format to the examples.

Target: Digital Equipment VMS Systems

VMS systems have a fairly feature-rich file structure. Logging into one presents no particular problems:

```
% ftp vaxb.cs.usnd.edu
Connected to vaxb.cs.usnd.edu.
220 FTP Service Ready
Name (vaxb.cs.unsd.edu:krol): anonymous       anonymous ftp
331 ANONYMOUS user ok, send real identity as password.
Password:
230 ANONYMOUS logged in, directory HSC1$DUA1:[ANON], restrictions apply.
Remote system type is VMS.
```

ftp was nice enough to tell you that it's talking to a VMS system, so you know what to expect. This is not always the case. The software necessary to take part in the Internet does not come automatically on VMS. A site wanting Internet access must buy a software package from one of several companies; the competing implementations are all a bit different. Another clue that you're communicating with a VMS server might be the word Multinet:

```
220 ftp.unsd.edu MultiNet FTP Server Process 3.3(14)...
```

Multinet is the name of a popular software product for VMS systems; if you see it, you're probably dealing with a VMS server.

The complexity surrounding VMS lies in its file structure. We have been placed in a directory containing files accessible via anonymous FTP; the complete name of this directory is *HSC1$DUA1:[ANON]*. This name consists of two parts: *HSC1$DUA1* is the name of a disk; and *[ANON]* is a directory on that disk.*

Now that we have logged in, let's try a **dir** command to see what's available:

```
ftp> dir
200 PORT Command OK.
125 File transfer started correctly
Directory HSC1$DUA1:[ANON]

AAAREADME.TXT;9    2-MAY-1991 15:45:51    730/2    (RWED,RE,,R)
ARTICLES.DIR;1    28-MAY-1990 10:20:14   1536/3    (RWE,RE,RE,R)
LIBRARY.DIR;1     30-APR-1991 11:13:06   1536/3    (RWE,RE,RE,RE)
WAIS.DIR;1         1-OCT-1991 10:21:16    512/1    (RWE,RE,RE,RE)

Total of 4 files, 1448 blocks.

226 File transfer completed ok
```

Each file consists of a name (e.g., *AAAREADME*), an extension (e.g., *TXT*), and a version number (e.g., *9*). Ignore the version number;† you will almost always want the most recent version of a file, which is what you'll get if you pretend the version number doesn't exist. The extension tells you something about the file. *TXT* is the extension for text files, so these files may be read directly. Files with the extension *DIR* are directories. There are a number of other standard extensions, like *FOR* for FORTRAN files, *EXE* for executable files, *COM* for command files. The filenames will be listed in uppercase, but VMS doesn't care whether you use upper- or lowercase letters.

We see that the default directory for anonymous FTP has three subdirectories. Let's use **cd** to look at the subdirectory *wais.dir*. When you use **cd** to change directories, you use the directory name without the extension:

```
ftp> cd wais
200 Working directory changed to "HSC1$DUA1:[ANON.WAIS]"
```

Now our working directory is *HSC1$DUA1:[ANON.WAIS]*. Notice that VMS specifies a subdirectory by listing each subdirectory after a period within the brackets. So this subdirectory is roughly equivalent to the UNIX path *HSC1$DUA1/ANON/WAIS*. Likewise, it's equivalent to the DOS path \ANON\WAIS, on a disk named *HSC1$DUA1:*.

---

*If we had been using regular **ftp**, rather than anonymous FTP, we probably would have been placed in a "default directory," which is similar to the UNIX "home directory." The home directory name would probably be *HSC$1DUA1:[KROL]*.

†All right, we'll explain it. VMS has the peculiarity that it keeps old versions of your files, until you explicitly tell it to delete them. This can waste tremendous amounts of disk space, but it does make it easy to undo your mistakes.

Unfortunately, the people who sell TCP/IP software for VAX/VMS systems don't agree about how the **cd** command should work, particularly when you want to move through multiple levels of directories. With some VMS FTP servers, you have to use a VMS-style directory specification, like this:

```
ftp> cd [x.y.z]
```

If the FTP server you're using expects this syntax, then to move up a level, you must use the command **cdup**; the UNIX-style **cd** .. will not work.

Other implementations expect you to specify multiple directories using the UNIX "slash" notation:

```
ftp> cd x/y/z
```

Which do you use? As I said, it depends on the software the FTP server is running. The easiest way to find out which syntax to use is to try one approach; if it doesn't work, try the other. No harm will be done if it doesn't work. If you want to be safe, you can move through one directory level at a time:

```
ftp> cd x
ftp> cd y
ftp> cd z
```

This strategy works in either case. And, once again, you must omit the *.dir* extension from the directory's name whenever you use it in a **cd** command.

get and **put** work in the usual way. You must specify the extension as part of the filename. You can include the version number, but it's easier to omit it (unless you want an old version for some special reason).* In this example, we will move two levels down the directory tree and retrieve the file *waissearch.hlp* from there:

```
ftp> cd wais/doc          change to directory anon/wais/doc
200 Working directory changed to "HSC1$DUA1:[ANON.WAIS.DOC]"
ftp> get waissearch.hlp   get the file waissearch.hlp
200 PORT Command OK.
125 ASCII transfer started for
    HSC1$DUA1:[ANON.WAIS.DOC]WAISSEARCH.HLP; (1076 bytes)
226 File transfer completed ok
1076 bytes received in 0.35 seconds (3 Kbytes/s)
ftp>
```

As long as you aren't confused by the VMS-style file specifications, you should have no problems dealing with VAX/VMS systems.

---

*If you specify an old file version be sure to specify a local filename. If you don't, you will probably end up with a filename that has a semicolon in it. The semicolon will really confuse UNIX, and probably isn't too healthy for DOS or Windows systems.

Target: MS-DOS Systems

MSDOS systems look very much like other network servers. You log in using the normal procedure:

```
% ftp server.uiuc.edu
Connected to server.uiuc.edu.
220-server.uiuc.edu PC/TCP 2.0 FTP Server by FTP Software ready
220 Connection is automatically closed if idle for 5 minutes
Name (server.uiuc.edu:): krol
331 User OK, send password
Password:
230 krol logged in
Remote system type is MSDOS.
```

Note that the remote system tells you that you are connected to a system running DOS.

It's also fairly obvious how to interpret the output of the **dir** command:

```
ftp> dir
200 Port OK
150 Opening data connection
        336          FS.BAT    Tue Dec 17 21:36:56 1991
          0          MBOX      Thu Nov 07 14:46:30 1991
        123          NS.BAT    Tue Jan 08 22:34:44 1991
<dir>                NETWIRE   Tue Jun 11 02:37:34 1991
<dir>                INCOMING.FTP  Tue Dec 17 21:42:24 1991
226 Transfer successful. Closing data connection
```

Filenames on a DOS computer consist of a filename (e.g., *FS*) and a three character extension (e.g., *BAT*). Subdirectories are flagged with the character string **<dir>** at the beginning of their line.

When you're dealing with a DOS server, you may be confused by the way that it handles directories. First, directories are disk-specific; you sometimes need to specify the disk on which the directory resides. Disks are identified by a single letter followed by a colon (:). The following **cd** command changed the "working disk" to the **h** disk:

```
ftp> cd h:
200 OK
```

If you now do another directory command, you will see a different set of files:

```
ftp> dir
200 Port OK
150 Opening data connection
<dir>                SYSTEM    Wed Dec 31 00:00:00 1980
<dir>                PUBLIC    Wed Dec 31 00:00:00 1980
226 Transfer successful. Closing data connection
```

Changing directories within a disk is done with a normal **cd** command, like the following:

```
ftp> cd public
200 OK
```

This command changes to the subdirectory *public*. You can also move down multiple directory levels at once with a command:

```
ftp> cd h:public/ibm_pc/msdos
200 OK
```

The trick is that DOS uses backslashes (\) to separate directory levels. However, when you access a DOS server with **ftp**, the server will try to be Internet-compatible and accept the slash rather than the backslash. If you use a backslash (as an experienced DOS user would expect), you'll get an error message:

```
ftp> cd h:public\ibm_pc\msdos
550 can't CWD: Error 2: No such file or directory
```

To add to the confusion, when you check the current directory, **ftp** prints the name using backslashes:

```
ftp> pwd
250 Current working directory is H:\PUBLIC\IBM_PC\MSDOS
```

Once you are positioned in the directory where the file you want lives, moving the file works as expected:

```
ftp> get config.bak
200 Port OK
150 Opening data connection
226 Transfer successful. Closing data connection
99 bytes received in 0.12 seconds (0.82 Kbytes/s)
```

The moral of the story is very simple. When you're accessing an MS-DOS system using **ftp**, use slashes instead of backslashes. With this in mind, you won't be confused.

Target: IBM VM Systems

IBM VM systems require a little more special handling. Most of the special handling is needed because VM doesn't have a hierarchical filesystem. On VM, you have disks; each disk can have multiple passwords (one for read-only access and one for read/write access); and filenames are short but have two parts. When you **ftp** to a VM system and log in, it looks like this:

```
% ftp vmd.cso.uiuc.edu
Connected to vmd.cso.uiuc.edu.
220-FTPSERVE at vmd.cso.uiuc.edu, 14:46:14 CST MONDAY 12/16/91
220 Connection will close if idle for more than 5 minutes.
Name (vmd.cso.uiuc.edu:krol):          took the default name: krol
```

```
331 Send password please.
Password:
230 KROL logged in; no working directory defined. Remote system type is VM.
```

Once again, **ftp** was nice enough to inform you that the remote system is VM. It also tells you that, even though you are logged in, you can't get at the files you want. The message "no working directory defined," which you see when **ftp** confirms that you are logged in, tells you that you aren't ready to transfer files yet.

When you do a **cd** command on a VM system, you are really asking to get at another disk. Disks are functions of a login name and an address. So, to cram this into a **cd** command you need to say:

```
ftp> cd login-name.disk-address
```

For example, the command:

```
ftp> cd krol.191
```

starts the connection to the disk addressed 191 of user krol. (You can find the names and addresses of the disks you normally use when logged in to a VM system by doing a **q disk** command while you are logged in.) A disk password is usually required; to supply the password, use the **account** command immediately *after* the **cd** command. Continuing the previous example:

```
ftp> cd krol.191
550 Permission denied to LINK to KROL 191; still no working directory
ftp> account j9876hoh
230 Working directory is KROL 191
```

Note that message 550 implies your **cd** command failed, even though it looked correct at the time. The **account** command, which you must give next, "fixes" the original **cd** command, so you can access files. Also, since your local system does not really know what the **account** command does on the remote computer, it makes no attempt to hide your password. Take precautions to make sure that others don't find out your password.

Now you have established a directory to work in. The output from a **dir** command looks like this:

```
ftp> dir
200 Port request OK.
125 List started OK
ACCNT   LEDGER   V   80    59     5 12/20/90  9:04:24 LEN
AGENDA  MEETING  V   73    34     2  9/24/91 10:23:01 LEN
ALL     NOTEBOOK V   80  5174   233 12/10/91 15:17:11 LEN
```

Each filename on an IBM VM system consists of two character strings. Each string has at most eight characters. The first string is called the "filename" and the second is call the "filetype." Above, the filenames are in the first column (e.g., *ALL*), while the second column shows the filetype (e.g., *NOTEBOOK*).

If **dir** doesn't show you all the files you expect to see, it's because there is also a file mode (1 or 0) associated with a file. A file with the mode 0 is considered "private" and cannot be seen with the read password. If you give the write password, you can see all the files. Again, the read and write passwords are set by the owner of the disk.

The filename and filetype both must be specified if you try to move a file. Since both are variable length, you use a period (.) to separate the two. So:

```
ftp> get all.notebook mbox
```

transfers the file *all* of type *notebook* to the file *mbox* on the local machine.

If you're doing anonymous FTP and the remote host is a VM system, you still have to give a **cd** command before you can access any files. You don't have to give a second password with the **account** command. When you actually **get** files, you must (as you'd expect) give a complete, two-part filename.

Target: Macintosh

Using **ftp** to access a Macintosh server is fairly straightforward, once you get connected. Getting connected might be a problem if the Mac is on a network that dynamically assigns addresses. Many Macs are connected to *Localtalk* networks, which in turn are connected to the Internet through a gateway. Some Localtalk gateways assign Internet addresses to computers as they are turned on, taking addresses from a pool reserved for the Localtalk net. This means that the address or name of a machine might change from day to day; the address that works today might not work tomorrow. This isn't usually a problem with public archives; anyone who configures their Macintosh as a public server usually makes sure that its address is assigned permanently. (Otherwise, complaining users would make his life miserable.) You are most likely to run into addressing problems when someone tells you to "grab this file from my Macintosh" on the spur of the moment. The system's owner gives you a numeric IP address, letting you grab the file—as long as he doesn't turn the system off first. Newer Macintoshes usually don't have this problem, because they can handle Ethernet cards and be connected directly to the Internet.

When you get connected to a Macintosh, **ftp** may ask you for a name; even if it does, it will not require a password. The name is used for logging purposes only.

```
% ftp 128.174.33.56               used an IP address this time
Connected to 128.174.33.56.       rather than a name
220 Macintosh Resident FTP server, ready
Name (128.174.33.56:krol):        send default name
230 User logged in
```

Doing a **dir** command will get a listing which looks like this:

```
ftp> dir
Accelerator
```

```
Administration/
Applications Combined
Article T3 connections
```

There are two things to note about this listing. One is that subdirectories, which in the Mac world are called *folders*, are flagged by the trailing slash (/). The second is that filenames can have spaces in them, which requires special handling. If a filename contains spaces, you must put the entire name within quotes. For example:

```
ftp> get "Applications Combined" applications
```

This gets the file *Applications Combined*, putting it into the file *applications* on the local machine. Aside from the Macintosh, most systems cannot handle names with spaces properly. Therefore, in this example, we made a point of specifying a local filename without a space.

Changing directories is handled in the usual way. The command:

```
ftp> cd Administration
```

changes the current directory to *Administration*. If we wanted to move through multiple folders and subfolders, we would list the whole path separated with slashes:

```
ftp> cd Administration/Personnel
```

Last Words: Some Practical Advice

Because using **ftp** is fairly straightforward, it is easy to get enthralled with the power it puts at your fingers and lose sight of its limitations. Here are a couple of hints that you may find useful:

- **ftp** allows you to create, delete, and rename files and directories on a remote system. Treat this ability as a convenience to use occasionally, rather than a technique to use all the time. If you are making a lot of changes on a remote system, instead of moving files, it is probably easier to use **telnet** and do your changes as a timesharing session.

- Directions about anonymous FTP are frequently sketchy. Someone will tell you "anonymous FTP to **server.public.com** and get the Whizbang editor, it's really neat." Servers set up for distributing free software (or other large public archives) frequently have many, many files stashed in various directories. If you can't find what you are after, try looking for files in the default directory named *README*, *index*, *ls-lR*, or something similar. If you're lucky, you'll find information about how the server is organized.

- On UNIX, **ftp** allows you to make some convenient things happen by putting instructions in the *.netrc* file of your home directory. The *.netrc* file is usually used to give instructions for logging into remote computers. You shouldn't set up automatic logins for computers needing a private login name and password, because you should never put your password in a file. But if you use one anonymous FTP server frequently, say **ftp.sura.net**, you could bypass the login step by putting something like this in *.netrc*:

```
machine ftp.sura.net
login anonymous
password krol@ux1.cso.uiuc.edu
```

More information about this facility can be found in your FTP documentation.

- When you copy a file with FTP, the file gets created with the standard access permissions that are used for any new file you create. If the file has special permissions on its originating system, they will not be preserved. In particular, if you transfer a file that requires execute permission (like *.plan* or *.Xsession*), you'll have to give a **chmod +x** command before you'll be able to use it.

- Some **ftp** servers allow you to put extensions on filenames that are really file reformatting commands to the server. The two most common ones are .**tar** and .**Z**. For example, if a file named *program* exists, and you issue the command **get program.Z**, the server automatically compresses the file before the transfer. With the .**tar** ending (e.g., **get pub.tar**), the file or directory is converted to a UNIX **tar** archive before transmittal. This makes it possible to transfer an entire directory tree with a single command. As you might expect, the server does nothing special if a file with the suffix already exists. For example, if *program.Z* already exists, the server will give it to you as is, without trying to compress it.

  These are extensions to the normal FTP service which will probably become more widespread in the future. Right now, they may work and may not. If you use a server regularly, you might give them a try to see if they work.

- Some clients get confused by the extensive messages new FTP servers send after **cd** commands. If nothing comes out after a **cd** command, but you start seeing long messages after other commands, your **ftp** client may be getting confused. Here's what you might see:

```
% ftp ftp.sura.net                              start up ftp to the server
Connected to nic.sura.net.
220 nic.sura.net FTP server (Version 6.9 Sep 30 1991) ready.
Name (ftp.sura.net:krol): anonymous         anonymous login
331 Guest login ok, send email address as password.
Password: krol@ux1.cso.uiuc.edu             password doesn't really echo
230 Guest login ok, access restrictions apply.
ftp> cd pub/nic                              move to the directory
250-######WELCOME TO THE SURANET NETWORK INFORMATION CENTER###########
ftp> get NJC                                 the following messages should
                                             have been displayed before this line
250-SURAnet                                  info@sura.net
250-8400 Baltimore Blvd.                     301-982-4600(voice)
250-College Park, Maryland  USA 20740-2498   FAX 301-982-4605
250-    Many of the documents available in this ftp archive are geared
250-towards the new user of the Internet. SURAnet has provided several
250-"How To" guides for network navigation tools such as, telnet, ftp,
250-and email. These "How To" guides are available in the directory
250 CWD command successful.
```

Try disconnecting and logging in again, but this time prefix your password with a minus sign, −. The minus sign tells the new **ftp** server not to send the additional messages.

CHAPTER SEVEN

ELECTRONIC MAIL

When Is Electronic Mail Useful?
Hints for Writing Electronic Mail
Acquiring Electronic Mail Addresses
Choosing an Email Package
The UNIX Mail Program
MIME: Multi-purpose Internet Mail Extensions
When Electronic Mail Gets Returned
Mail Lists and Reflectors
File Retrieval Using Electronic Mail

Most network users get their start by using electronic mail (*email* for short). After sending a few hesitant messages (frequently followed up by a telephone call to ask if the mail arrived), most email users quickly become comfortable with the system. Your confidence, too, will grow after you've gotten past the first few awkward messages; you'll be using mail frequently and with authority, customizing the system to meet your own needs and establishing your own mailing lists. Soon you will find that email means much more than faster letters and memos. You can take part in electronic conversations about mystery writers, the stock market, or just about anything else you'd like. You might even decide that your telephone is superfluous.

How quickly you become comfortable with electronic mail has a lot to do with your knowledge of the medium and some basic technical decisions you make in choosing and using your email system. There are any number of electronic mail programs for each kind of computer. To get enough background to describe good email software, we will start out discussing general facilities of electronic mail, mail addressing, and how electronic mail works. After that, using UNIX **mail** as an example, we will look at what features exist in email packages. Finally, we will talk about how to use those features in concert to move files, take part in discussions, and deal with problems that you might run across.

When Is Electronic Mail Useful?

Like any other tool, electronic mail has its strengths and weaknesses. On the surface, it appears to be just a faster way of delivering letters, or their equivalent. To know when electronic mail is appropriate, think about how it differs from other communications media. In some ways, email is very similar to the telephone; in other ways, it's similar to traditional postal mail. Table 7-1 makes a quick comparison.

Table 7-1: Comparison of Communication Techniques

	Telephone	Email	Post
Speed	High	Moderate	Low
Synchronized	Yes	No	No
Formality	Varies	Moderate	Varies
Accountability	Low	Moderate	High
Conferencing	Small group	Any to all	One-way only
Security	Moderate	Low	High

First, let's think about how quickly each medium gets a message from one point to another. The telephone offers immediate delivery and works at a fairly high communication speed (although it is still far less than the speed at which email travels). The time it takes to deliver electronic mail ranges from seconds to a day; and, as I'm sure you know, postal delivery can be overnight in the best case, but often takes several days. The price you pay for the quick communication of telephony is that the caller and the sender must be synchronized; that is, they must both be on the phone at the same time. Email and postal mail are both asynchronous; the sender sends when the time is ripe, and you read it at your leisure. This comes in handy if you are trying to communicate a long distance (e.g., over many time zones) when daily schedules are quite different.

The delivery time for email consists of two parts: the time it takes the network to deliver the message to your mail computer and the delay in your reading it once it is there. The first part is a function of how your mail machine is connected to the network; it can only be changed with an outflow of money. The second part is under your control. If you don't check your email regularly, then quick delivery is meaningless. Your messages just sit there waiting for you to come look at them. Electronic mail becomes more useful as the delay in machine-to-human delivery is reduced. Try and keep it under a few hours. When electronic mail is delivered (and read) quickly, it can become almost as convenient and fluent as a personal conversation.

Formality and accountability are closely related. On the telephone, formality varies: with some people you are very formal; with others, very casual. The same is true of postal mail. You have a lot of time to construct messages and multiple formats to choose from (handwritten notes, typed business letters, etc.). These formats and other cues (e.g., a perfumed envelope) give signals, both to yourself and your reader, regarding the purpose of the note. Email is always typed, and there is no chapter in any high school typing book on the format of an email letter. Also, individuals are somewhat hidden in email (i.e., the big boss's email address looks just like everyone else's). Since email often flies between parties at a rate approaching a conversation, and since most people are more comfortable being friendly than combative, many people tend to drift into informality in their electronic messaging. This can be a problem when it comes to accountability: the necessity of writers to take responsibility for their messages.

Written media tend to hold writers more accountable for their actions than spoken media. If you are having a telephone conversation and make some comments you wish you hadn't, you can later claim that you didn't say them or that the hearer misunderstood (or take comfort knowing that only one person heard them). If you try and do this with email, someone will have saved a copy of the message in a file and will trot it out to be rehashed. The only factor that reduces email accountability is that the sender's identity can be spoofed. I could send you an email with the return address **president@whitehouse.gov**, offering you a seat on the Supreme Court. It is also possible to forge paper mail, but it is a lot more difficult: I would have to mimic stationery, postmarks, signatures, etc.

Next, we need to examine group communications. The telephone is a fine medium, but only for small groups. Conference calls allow groups to talk with each other, but as the group gets larger, scheduling and setup get prohibitively difficult. On the other end of the spectrum, bulk mail is easy to use and can reach millions with little difficulty. The problem with junk mail (aside from being a nuisance) is that all messages originate from one point and go to the whole group. Communications from any point (i.e., any member of the group) cannot easily be sent to the whole group. Electronic mail allows you to set up arbitrarily large groups, and any member of the group can communicate with the whole at any time. This makes it very useful both for disseminating information and for querying a group.

Finally, the security of electronic mail is usually low compared to the other media. If I am careful with the post, a letter could remain within locked boxes or the Postal Service until it gets into the recipient's hands. If it is opened along the way, damage to the envelope normally makes the intrusion obvious. Telephone tapping by normal folks requires access to the facilities at one end or the other to intercept a conversation. Once a conversation makes it outside your building and into the telephone network, it is technically difficult for anyone to intrude without the phone company's help. Email, however, takes a fairly predictable route through computers, some of whose security may be questionable. Also, there are error modes where a message might be undeliverable and a computer, not knowing what else to do, delivers it to a mail administrator. Administrators will not normally snoop or spread your message around, but still, if security is an issue, having your mail fall into the hands of someone else—even a responsible administrator—is unsuitable. "Privacy-enhanced mailers" try to encrypt the message to combat these security deficiencies, but they are not in general use. As a general rule, you can't trust email's security, and therefore you shouldn't use it when security is an issue.

Hints for Writing Electronic Mail

If you read much email, you'll see a lot of messages that should never have been sent—and that the sender probably wishes he or she hadn't sent. To prevent making such mistakes yourself, you should develop some electronic mail "etiquette." Creating good habits while you're beginning can prevent big embarrassments later on. Here is some advice:

- Never commit anything to email that you wouldn't want to become public knowledge. As was discussed previously, you never really know who may end up reading your email message. This may be on purpose (e.g., if a co-worker covers someone's email while he's on vacation), or by mistake, either yours or a misbehaving computer's. The threat does not end when the mail is deleted from the mail system. Email messages are frequently caught in system backups and sit on tapes in machine rooms for years. With enough effort, an old message might be found and resurrected. (This was how much of Oliver North's connection to the Iran-Contra affair was documented.)

- Don't send abusive, harassing, threatening, or bigoted messages. While abuse, harassment, and even bigotry are hard to define, there's one good rule of thumb: if a message's recipient complains, stop. Email can usually be traced to its originating machine, and systems on the Internet are liable for the misdeeds of their users. You don't want your system administrator (or the system administrator of your electronic mail link) to receive complaints about your activity. It could come back to haunt you.

- Writers frequently approach electronic mail as a friendly conversation, but recipients frequently view email as a cast-in-stone business letter. You might have had a wry smile on your face when you wrote the note, but that wry smile doesn't cross the network. You also can't control when the message will be read, so it might be received at the worst possible moment. Consider sitting around after work having a drink with a co-worker and saying "You really blew that sale." You could judge his frame of mind before speaking so you're sure he will take it jokingly. That same thing in email, which he reads after just being chewed out by the boss, comes off as "YOU REALLY BLEW THAT SALE!!!"

- Be very careful with sarcasm. Consider this exchange with the big boss (a real hands-on manager):

  You worked with Sam a while ago. What would you think of promoting him to regional sales manager?

To which you respond:

  He's a real winner!

Does he get the promotion? The answer could either mean that he won the last three "salesperson of the year" awards, or that he hasn't sold anything for the past three years. There is no body language, nor perhaps any personal knowledge on the recipient's side (e.g., she may not know that you are quite the wisecracker). Some help is available for these situations. For example, inserting a "smiley" face into a message denotes "said with a cynical smile." So:

He's a real winner! :-)

means he couldn't sell his way out of a paper bag. Another symbol is the wink meaning "it's better left unsaid, but catch my drift." Like:

Sam and Bertha spent a long time in her room last night working on the presentation. ;-)

A sentence whose meaning is left to the reader. ;-)

There are many others which are used less frequently. In general, their meanings are pretty discernible, so you'll have to figure them out for yourself. :-(

Aside from basic mail etiquette, there are a couple of style guidelines that, if followed, make email easier to read and understand:

- Keep the line length reasonable (less than 60 characters). You want it to display on just about any terminal. If the note gets forwarded, it might be indented by a tab character (usually 8 columns). Messages that consist of a single extremely long line are particularly obnoxious. You have a RETURN key; use it! This may be especially hard if your mail package automatically goes to a new line when one gets too full. Frequently these new lines are not inserted in the text; they only show up on your screen. When the message gets to its destination, it appears as one long line.

- Use mixed case. Even though some operating systems don't understand lowercase letters, virtually all modern terminals can generate them. All uppercase sounds harsh, like shouting. UPPERCASE CAN BE USED FOR EMPHASIS!

- Don't use exotic features of your terminal (bold, italics, etc.). These frequently send a string of control characters, which wreak havoc on some types of terminals.

- Read your message before you send it and decide if you'll regret it in the morning. On most systems, once you send it, you are committed to it.

How Electronic Mail Works

Electronic mail differs from the other applications we are looking at because it is not an "end to end" service: the sending and receiving machine need not be able to communicate directly with each other to make it work. It is known as a "store and forward" service. Mail is passed from one machine to another until it finally arrives at its destination. This is completely analogous to the way the U.S. Postal Service delivers mail; if we examine that, we can draw some interesting conclusions.

The U.S. Postal Service operates a store and forward network. You address a message and put it into a post box. The message is picked up by a truck and sent to another place and stored there. It is sorted and forwarded to another place. This step is repeated until it arrives at the recipient's mailbox. If the recipient's mailbox happens to be in a place where the U.S. Postal Service cannot deliver directly (e.g., another country), you can still send the message; the U.S. Postal Service will pass the message to the Postal Service of that country for delivery.

We can infer a couple of things about the Internet from this analogy. First, if you correctly address a message, the network will take it from there. You needn't know much about what's going on. We can also infer that messages can be moved between the Internet and other mail networks. This is true, but the address required may be more complex in order to get to and through the foreign network.

Just as in the Postal Service, if the destination and source are not on the same network, there needs to be a place where the email from one network is handed to the email service of another. Points of connection between email networks are computers called "application gateways." They are called "gateways" because they can be viewed as magic doors between worlds; they are "application gateways" because they know enough about the email applications on both sides to reformat messages so they are legal on the new network. To send mail through a gateway, you frequently have to give an address which contains both information about how to get to the gateway, and information about how to deliver the mail on the other side. We'll discuss addressing further below.

Finally, before you can put a postal letter into a mailbox, you put it in an envelope. The same happens to email, except that the "envelope" is called a *mail header*. The header is the **To:**, **From:**, **Subject:** stuff on the front of the message. Just as an envelope may get changed *en route* (e.g., a hand-scribbled "not at this address" here, a yellow sticker with a forwarding address there, etc.), the mail header gets stuff stuck into it while the message is traveling to help you figure out what route it took, just in case it doesn't get through.

It's All in the Address

Whether or not your email gets to its destination depends almost solely on whether or not the address is constructed correctly. (Email sometimes fails because machines or pieces of the network are unavailable, but usually the network tries to send mail for days before giving up.) Unfortunately, email addresses are a bit more complex than the simple host addresses we've seen so far.* They are more complex for several reasons:

- The world of email is bigger than the Internet.
- Email needs to be addressed to a person, not just a machine.
- Personal names are sometimes included as comments in email addresses.

Let's start with the Internet's addressing rules. On the Internet, the basis for all mail is the domain name of the machine which is acting as a mail agent (the machine that's handling the addressee's mail—say **ux1.cso.uiuc.edu**). In fact, this is all that the network, per se, worries about. Once it has delivered a message to

---

*An authoritative work on email addressing is, *@#!%, The Directory of Electronic Mail Addressing & Networks*, O'Reilly & Associates.

the named machine, the network's task is over. It's up to that computer to deliver it the rest of the way, but the machine requires more information about further routing: at the minimum, the name of a user, but possibly extended information for routing the mail to another kind of network. So, how do you send mail to other networks? For most networks, it's easy—like it is for Delphi. You just tack something on to the user's user ID on his net. We'll tackle these easy cases first; then we'll look at the more difficult ones.

Table 7-2: Addressing Users of Other Networks

Network	Send Mail To	Notes
Alternex	*user*@ax.apc.org	
ALAnet	*user*%ALANET@intermail.isi.edu	American Library Assn.
America Online	*user*@aol.com	User name lower case, spaces removed
Applelink	*user*@applelink.apple.com	
ATTmail	*user*@attmail.com	
BIX	*user*@bix.com	
CGNet	*user*%CGNET@intermail.isi.edu	
Chasque	*user*@chasque.apc.org	
Comlink	*user*@oln.comlink.apc.org	
Delphi	*user*@delphi.com	
Econet	*user*@igc.apc.org	
Ecuanex	*user*@ecuanex.apc.org	
eWorld	*user*@online.apple.com	
Genie	*user*@genie.geis.com	
GeoNet	*user*@geo1.geonet.de	For recipients in Europe
	user@geo2.geonet.de	For recipients in the United Kingdom
	user@geo4.geonet.de	For recipients in North America
Glasnet	*user*@glas.apc.org	
Greenet	*user*@gn.apc.org	
Nasamail	*user*@nasamail.nasa.gov	
Nicarao	*user*@nicarao.apc.org	
NIFTY-Serve	*user*@niftyserve.or.jp	
Nordnet	*user*@pns.apc.org	
Peacenet	*user*@igc.apc.org	
Pegasus	*user*@peg.apc.org	
Prodigy	*user*@prodigy.com	(alphanumeric ID rather than name)

Table 7.2: Addressing Users of Other Networks (continued)

Network	Send Mail To	Notes
Pronet	*user*@**tanus.oz.au**	
Web	*user*@**web.apc.org**	

It would be nice if all the email gateways in the world were that simple. Unfortunately, they're not. Here are the more difficult addressing problems:

Bitnet
: Bitnet addresses normally have the form *name@host. bitnet*. Change this address to something like *name%host*, and use that for the login name part of the address. Use the address of a Bitnet-Internet gateway for the machine name side (for example, **cunyvm.cuny.edu**). Separate the two with an "at" (@) sign. For example, rewrite the address **krol@uiucvmd.bitnet** as **krol%uiucvmd@cunyvm.cuny.edu**.* If you are going to do this regularly, find out the best gateway for you to use from someone local.

Compuserve
: Compuserve addresses consist of two numbers separated by a comma. Change the comma to a period and use that on the left-hand side of the address. To the right of the @ use **compuserve.com**. So, a Compuserve address of 76543,123 would be addressed **76543.123@compuserve.com**.

Fidonet
: Fidonet addresses consist of a first and last name, and a set of numbers of the form a:b/c.d. Separate the first and last names with a period (.) and send to p*d*.f*c*.n*b*.z*a*.**fidonet.org**. For example, send mail to Willie Martin at 1:5/2.3 by using the address **willie. martin@p3.f2.n5.z1.fidonet.org**. Some machines still may have trouble with an address like this. If yours does, try sending the above add ress to the gateway machine: **willie. martin%p3.f2.n5.z1.fidonet.org@zeus.ieee.org**.

Sprintmail
: Complete Sprintmail addresses look like "John Bigboote" /YOYODYNE/TELEMAIL/US. If the address is used within Sprintmail, it can be abbreviated to John Bigboote/ YOYODYNE. These first two parameters are the person and an organization. When someone gives you a Sprintmail address, this

---

*This is a non-standard format for an address, known as the "BBN hack", but it is in common use, is easy for people to understand, and it works. The standard way of doing this would be @cunyvm.cuny.edu:krol@uiucvmd.

is all they will provide. The positional parameters need to be plugged into a command like the following*:

/PN=*John.Bigboote*/O=*YOYODYNE*/ADMD=TELEMAIL/C=US/@sprint.co m.

Even if the person only gives you the first two parts of the address, the complete address should be used when sending it to **sprint.com**.

MCImail

There are multiple ways of addressing MCImail. MCI mailboxes have both an address and a person's name associated with them. The address looks a lot like a phone number. If that's what you have, then use that number on the left side of the @, and use the gateway name **mcimail.com** on the right side. For example: **1234567@mcimail.com**. If you are given the name of a person on MCImail, you can send mail by addressing it to **firstname_lastname@mcimail.com**, like: **John_Bigboote@mcimail.com**.

UUCP

Change the UUCP address, which looks like **name@host.uucp**, to *name%host*. Use that for the login name portion of the address. Use the address of a UUNET-Internet gateway as the machine name. Internet service providers provide these gateways for these constituents. Of course, separate the two with an "at" sign. For example, a user receiving mail via uucp from PSI, Inc. should be sent mail through **uu.psi.com**, like **john_w%yoyodyne@uu.psi.com**. You can ask your e-mail or system administrator for a good gateway for you to use.

Many people also give UUCP addresses in the form: . . .**!uunet!host!name**. This is a UUCP "path"; it means "you figure out how to get the mail to the system named **uunet**, and then **uunet** will send it to **host**, which will deliver it." Convert this to: *name%host@gatewaymachine*. You pick the proper gateway by examining the UUCP path address. If it has **uunet** as part of the address you could use **uunet.uu.net**, if it has **uupsi** as part of the address you could use **uu.psi.com**, etc. On very rare occasions, you may see gateway names other than **uunet** or **uupsi** in the path; you will have to figure out the Internet address of the gateway. Giving addresses as "paths" is, fortunately, becoming less common. If you are forced to use a UUCP path address, be careful. When you're using the UNIX C shell, you must "quote" the exclamation points with a backslash (\), like **mail \!uunet\!host\!name**. If you give the address inside the **mail** program, you don't need the backslashes.

---

*This is called an X.500-style address. X.500 is a ISO standard form of addressing that no one really likes; but it will probably be around for a long time.

Acquiring Electronic Mail Addresses

Once you decide to jump into the email world, you have to start collecting email addresses. There is no national registry of email addresses. There are a few specialized servers that one can peruse to try and find someone's address. These servers are known as *white pages* servers because they provide the electronic equivalent to the white pages telephone book. (Chapter 10, *Finding Someone*, tells you how to use the common ones.) But the easiest and best way of acquiring these addresses is via information sent directly to you, be it a business card, a phone call, a postal letter, an email message, or a newsgroup posting.

This method of acquiring email addresses has two advantages over all others:

- You are fairly sure it is an email address which is current and checked regularly. An address found in an index might be an old email address used at a previous employer, or an address on a machine which no longer exists.

- If there are typically problems getting to the person's email address, the address he gives out will probably reflect the best way to get to his machine. For example, if Joe's business card gives his email address as **joe%bizarrenet@bizarregate.com**, that's the address you should try first.

Sometimes when you try to glean email addresses from mail you receive, you will see an address which looks like:

```
John Bigboote<johnb@yoyodyne.com>
```

This address is in a slightly more elaborate format than anything we've seen so far:

```
comments<email-address>
```

Adding comments to the email address is a really nice thing to do. As in the example above, the comment is usually the addressee's name. Putting the name in a comment makes it a little more obvious to other recipients who also got the message. This is especially true if the person's email address is computer generated, like **ajzxmvk@uicvmc.bitnet**. Wouldn't you like to know who reads that mail! If you get a message as part of a mail distribution list, and if the list's manager has included comments, you can look at the **To:** field and easily see who else got the message—even if the email addresses themselves are not recognizable. (You might want to squirrel away some of those addresses in case you want to send one of them a message later.)

Choosing an Email Package

Electronic mail systems evolved in two separate environments: on wide area networks (WANs), where the goal was to provide a "least common denominator" service to everyone in the world, and on local area networks (*LANs*) where feature-rich service to a work group in a small area was the target. As a result, people on wide area nets were frustrated because email was hard to use, but they could send email to anyone. People on LANs were frustrated because they could easily send email to virtually no one. As email evolved, the wide area network mailers added nicer user interfaces and features, while the LAN products added the ability to send over wide area networks. We have reached the point where most email systems can exchange basic email with any other email system. This means that if you have a choice between email packages, the decision will be made on the basis of how you plan to use email and the extended features and comfort of the packages, not on connectivity.*

When you decide how to approach email, a number of questions will affect the decision:

- With whom are you going to be exchanging mail?
- How closely are you "tied" to them?
- What do you like in a user interface?
- How much do you travel?
- Are you happy sending text, or do you want to send other data?

Many facilities are common to all mailers. Other features (like digitized pictures and voice) can only be used when the sender and recipient both use similar mail software and operating system utilities. If your goal is to transfer all kinds of files between a small circle of friends with as little trouble as possible, then you and your friends should agree on a single mail system and use it. If that is not a big concern, then you should pick the email software that you find the easiest to use and with which you can feel at home. That is, if you like Macintoshes, you should pick something that works, looks, and feels like a Macintosh. Don't pick something else just because all your friends are using it.

If you are a frequent traveler, you should investigate systems that allow you to connect a portable computer to the network (even by dial-up) and download mail. You can then read your mail and queue new messages while disconnected from the network. The next time you connect to the Net, the queued mail gets sent. So you could dial up in Chicago, download 20 messages, read and respond to them at 30,000 feet over Cleveland, queue your responses and, finally, send the queued mail and pick up a new batch when you arrive in Washington D.C. These systems are based on the Post Office protocol or *POP*, which allows remote interaction between a workstation and a mail repository.

So, pick your mail system to suit your needs. If your needs are not that great and you are mainly concerned with basic messaging, then pick something that is free and that other people are using.

The UNIX Mail Program

The UNIX **mail** program is the Chevy Impala of electronic mail packages. It doesn't make anyone ecstatic about using it, but it gets the job done. That's why I chose it. With a few commands, you can use all of its basic features. While you may

---

*That is not to say that some decisions will not cost more than others. Connecting a LAN-based mail system to the Internet may require a dedicated PC and some fairly expensive software.

never use the **mail** program, it provides a good basis for discussing how to use a mail system.*

To start the **mail** program, give the command:†

```
% mail address-string
```

The *address-string* is optional. If it is there, the command sends a message to those people listed in the address string. You can usually use either spaces or commas to separate different addressees in the list. If the address string is absent, **mail** enters command mode. One of the things you do in command mode is read your incoming messages.

Reading Your Mail

To read your mail, enter command mode. If you don't have any mail to read, the program tells you:

```
% mail
No mail for krol
```

If you have messages waiting, **mail** lists the first 20 new message headers:

```
% mail
"/usr/spool/mail/krol": 5 messages 1 new
     1 LISTSERV@bitni Fri Nov  8 16:02 128/6172 "File: "LISTSERV FILELI"
     2 LISTSERV@bitni Fri Nov  8 16:08 164/9834 "File: "BITNODE FILELIS"
  U  3 daemon@pit-man Sat Nov  9 09:26  72/2817 "Reply from mserv re: s"
  U  4 akida          Sat Dec 28 05:53  12/298  "Overthruster found"
 >N  5 buckaroo       Thu Jan  2 19:15  11/305  "Aliens in Grovers Mill"
 &
```

Each message has a status and a number. The status is flagged by the letter (or the lack of a letter) at the beginning of each line. These letters might be:

N   New message received since the last time you entered mail in command mode to read messages.

P   Signifies a preserved message, which you have read and decided to put back in your "in-basket" within this invocation of the *mail* program.

U   Unread message. New messages turn into unread messages if you exit mail without reading them.

no letter   The message was read and preserved in a previous mail session.

---

*If you think I have an oversimplified view of email, look into **mh** and the whole book dedicated to its use (*MH and xmb: Email for Users and Programmers*, O'Reilly & Associates). For yet another approach to UNIX mail, consider Z-Mail, which was known as **mush** in an earlier incarnation (discussed in *The Z-Mail Handbook*, O'Reilly & Associates).

†Unfortunately, some UNIX systems have two different mail programs with almost the same name. The proper command may be **mailx**.

The message number is used in various commands to refer to that particular message (more on this when we talk about commands). Finally, notice that one message has a greater-than sign (>) pointing to it. This is the current message. If you give any commands without specifying a message number, the command applies to the current message.

The & that follows the message list is **mail**'s command prompt, telling you that it's waiting for you to type a command. You only need to know about four commands to read email for fun and profit. Commands are usually single letters, but there are a couple which are longer to avoid ambiguity. To read messages, use the print command, which has the general format:

    & **p** *messages*

The *messages* parameter is optional. If you leave it off, the current message is displayed on the screen. The parameter can take one of the following forms:

    & **p** 3   *display message #3*
    & **p** 3-5   *display message #3 through #5*
    & **p** $ *display the last message*
    & **p** 3-$ *display message #3 through the last message*

All commands that allow a message number as a parameter operate in this same fashion. Remember that you can use $ to indicate the last message.

The print command is also the default command. So the following commands are the same:

    & 3
    & **p** 3

Therefore, a carriage return with no command just prints the current message.

The fast print command gives you an in-basket "table of contents," just like the menu you receive when you start up **mail**. The initial list tries to give you 20 new messages, starting with the oldest. Should you have more, you can move around in the menu by issuing successive **f** commands:

    & **f** 1-20   *display sender & subject 1 to 20*
    & **f** 21-$ *display sender & subject 21 to the end*

You can also use the **z** command to list messages. **z** prints message descriptions for the next screenful of messages. If you want to move backwards in the list, use the command **z-**.

Unless you do something special, any messages you read while you are in a mail session get moved from your in-basket into the file *mbox* when you quit. The usual commands to change this action are:

d *messages*   Delete the messages specified (or the current one if not specified). This deletes those message numbers from the menu and deletes the messages themselves at the end of the mail session.

pre *messages*   Preserve the specified messages (or the current one if none are specified). That is, keep them in your in-basket, where they may be viewed in future sessions.

q   Exit the mail program.

Sending Messages

In this section, we'll tell you how to originate a new email message. You can also respond to a message that someone sent you; we'll cover that later.

To send a message, either enter the UNIX **mail** command, followed by a list of addresses, or enter the **mail** command from within the **mail** program (i.e., after the & prompt). Both forms of the commands have the same syntax:

```
% mail address-list     --or--
& mail address-list
```

The address list can be one or more addresses separated by commas. If the addresses are not full domain names, like **krol@ux1.cso.uiuc.edu**, then the mail program usually completes the address by adding the domain of the machine it is running on. So, if **krol** has a mailbox on **ux1.cso.uiuc.edu**, then **mail krol** works fine on the computer **ux1.cso.uiuc.edu**. If you execute it on the computer **yoyo-dyne.com**, it will fail, because on that computer, **mail krol** means **mail krol@yoyo-dyne.com**.

Next, **mail** prompts you for a subject:

```
% mail johnb@yoyodyne.com
Subject: Do you have the Overthruster
```

Enter a meaningful synopsis of the message as a subject. That and your name will be all the recipient has to decide on the priority to give this message.* After you type the subject, start typing the text of your message. You won't get another prompt. Here's how we completed the message we started above:

```
% mail johnb@yoyodyne.com
Subject: Do you have the Overthruster
John Warfin was wondering if you had acquired the
overthruster yet?  He is pretty excitable.
.
```

Notice the period in column one. A period on a line by itself signifies the end of the message to the UNIX **mail** program. When the message is completed, it is sent and you return to whatever you were doing before issuing the command. That is, you return to the UNIX prompt if you sent your message from the UNIX command

---

*Not all **mail** programs prompt for the subject by default. Sometimes, you have to put a line reading `set ask` (or, for some versions, `set asksub`) into the file *.mailrc* in your home directory. We strongly recommend that you *always* put a subject on your message. That makes it much easier for the recipient (who may get hundreds of messages a day) to handle.

line; you return to **mail**'s command mode if you sent your message from command mode.

Typing the message like can be very inconvenient, particularly if the message is long. It's hard to correct mistakes, particularly if you don't notice them until you're already typing the next line. You can use the **vi** editor to compose your message by giving the command ~**v**, putting the ~ in the first column on the screen. The ~**v** command starts the **vi** editor; if you've already typed part of the message, you should see it within **vi**. Use **vi** commands to edit your message; then, when you're ready, save the message and quit. You'll be back within **mail**; type a period in the first column to end the message and send it.

If you don't like **vi**, quit **mail** and give the UNIX command:

```
% setenv EDITOR my-favorite-editor
```

where *my-favorite-editor* is the name of an editor you'd rather use. For example, if you like the **emacs** editor, give the command **setenv EDITOR emacs**; then, use the ~**e** command while composing a message. **mail** will start **emacs** for you. These two commands do very similar things. ~**v** starts the "visual" editor **vi**. ~**e** starts the editor specified by the environment variable; if you haven't set one, it starts the **ex** editor. (You don't want to use **ex**!)

The ~**e** command belongs to a large set of commands called *tilde escapes*. Tilde escapes are commands issued while typing in the message body. They are flagged by a tilde in column one of a line. You'll see several more tilde escape commands as we work through common **mail** features. (If you want to see which ones are available try ~**?**.)

A Shopping List of Features

I wish I could give you the definitive list of email packages and tell you which one to get, but there are at least five for UNIX systems, three for IBM VM systems, five for PCs, and three for Apple machines. They all have some common features which can be used when sending mail to any other mailer, some features which look similar but are implemented differently and therefore can't be used with other kinds of mailers (they don't *interoperate* in the vernacular), and some features which are unique. So here are some common features of mail systems, what they do, and how much interoperability you can expect.

Universally Supported Features

Aside from the basic ability to send mail, almost any email facility gives you the following features, which can work with other mail systems.

Aliasing

Aliasing is the ability to define nicknames for people. If you don't like typing complete Internet addresses (and who does?), you can decide that **edk** is shorthand for **krol@ux1.cso.uiuc.edu**; if you then use **edk** as the recipient of a message, your system will substitute the complete address for you. Don't decide on aliases arbitrarily: pick some convention and stick to it. Having an alias doesn't do you any good if you can't remember or guess it. You may need to remember an alias even though you haven't used it for a long time. It is common to use a first name, followed by the last initial, as an alias. It is also common to have nicknames that are tied to "functions," rather than a specific person (e.g., secretary or boss); over time, the person may change, but the function will remain the same.

With UNIX **mail**, you can put alias definitions in the file *.mailrc*, which stores your personal mail configuration commands. To define aliases, add lines to the file in the form:

```
alias nickname actual-address
```

So, the following line would define the **edk** alias that we discussed above:

```
alias edk "Ed Krol<krol@ux1.cso.uiuc.edu>"
```

This example includes a comment in the address, a practice we recommended earlier. After you have defined an alias, you can use it anywhere you would normally use an address. With the alias I defined above, the following two commands are synonymous:

```
% mail krol@ux1.cso.uiuc.edu
% mail edk
```

Caution: if you happen to assign a nickname that's the same as a login name on your local computer, your mailer will use the nickname rather than the login name. That is, if I have an alias defined as:

```
alias krol "Karen Rolex<karen@blitzos.com>"
```

then the command:

```
% mail krol
```

sends a message to Karen Rolex (whose address is **karen@blitzos.com**), not the local user **krol**.

Folders

Folders let you save messages in an organized way. For example, you could have a folder for each project you're involved with, and one called "personal." As mail arrives, you can file it in the appropriate folder for future reference. These can usually be examined from within the **mail**-reading program, using the same facilities you would normally use to read incoming mail. You merely tell **mail** to read the mail in a folder instead of the incoming mail.

In UNIX, a folder is a file that contains messages stored in a format the **mail** program can understand. The file *mbox*, where **mail** stores the message that you don't delete, preserve, or file elsewhere, is really just the default folder. To create another folder or append to an existing one, use the **s** command. It has the format:

```
& s folder-name
```

This command saves the current message in the named folder. The following command stores the current message in a folder named **ietf**:

```
& s ietf
```

Switching to a different folder is accomplished with the **folder** command, with one of the following forms:

```
& folder name          switch to the named folder
& folder #             switch back to the previous folder
& folder %             switch to your in-basket
```

When you switch folders, **mail** lists the contents of the new folder. This list looks just like the list that **mail** gives when you start the **mail** program. For example:

```
% mail "/usr/spool/mail/krol": 1 message 1 new
>N 1 johnb@yoyodyne.cso   Fri Jan  3 13:27  11/307  "junk"
& folder mbox
Held 1 message in /usr/spool/mail/krol
"mbox": 2 messages
   1 quayle@lawyersRus. Fri Nov 15 19:48  46/1852 "More stupid remarks"
>  2 Kennedy@senate.gov Thu Nov 21 10:09  52/2352 "Candidate wanted"
&
```

Once you are in a folder, you can use all of the normal commands (**print**, **delete**, etc.) to manipulate or read your archived messages.

Forwarding

Within UNIX **mail**, "forwarding" has two slightly different meanings. First, forwarding means automatically sending all mail received by a particular login on one computer to another. This is particularly useful if you have accounts on several different computers. So that you don't have to check mail on different computers constantly, you may want any mail sent to any of your accounts to be forwarded to the one where you normally read mail.

UNIX uses the file *.forward* to accomplish this. You create this in your home directory on each system from which you want mail forwarded. In the file, you place the mail address to which you want the mail to be sent. For example, the following *.forward* file is taken from **johnb**'s home directory at **yoyodyne.com**; it contains a single line:

```
krol@ux1.cso.uiuc.edu
```

This file causes any mail sent to **johnb@yoyodyne.com** to be forwarded to **krol@ux1.cso.uiuc.edu**.

Forwarding also means taking a message you have received and sending it on to someone else who might be interested. This can usually be done either in its entirety, or as a part of a message which you compose. (This is another big boss tool: she forwards you the original message, adding something like, "Take care of this, Sam." Suddenly, it's your problem.)

With UNIX **mail**, this is not as convenient as it should be. In **mail**, you must start a new message to the person to whom you want to forward the message. Then you insert the old message into the new message with the ~m or ~f commands. The ~m and ~f both take an optional parameter, which is the message number to be inserted. If it is not given, the current message is inserted. The difference between ~m and ~f is that ~m adds a tab character at the beginning of each line of the old message. This is useful when you want to insert text into the old message—for example, to respond to a previous message point by point. The lines that are indented by tabs belong to the original message; the lines that aren't indented are your additions. On the other hand, ~f inserts the old message exactly as received. This is useful either when the message contains something to be processed by a computer (in which case, the format is critical), or when you expect the new recipient to respond point by point. Let's peek at the big boss' **mail** session while she forwards a complaint to Sam:

```
% mail
"/usr/spool/mail/krol": 2 messages 2 new
>N  1 pking@ux1.cso.uiuc.e  Fri Jan  3 13:48   16/621   "ctp-100 price"
 N  2 whiner@bigaccount.com Fri Jan  3 14:00   13/559   "Bad service"
& mail sam
 Subject: complaint from Mr. Whiner
See if you can make him happy:
~m 2
Interpolating: 2
(continue)
.
```

When Sam checks his mail, he receives a message like this:

```
/cso/staff/sam-6>mail
"/usr/spool/mail/sam": 1 message 1 new
>N  1 Bertha the Boss Fri Jan  3 14:12   23/718   "complaint from Mr. Whi"
& 1
From bertha Fri Jan  3 14:12:56 1992
Date: Fri, 3 Jan 1992 14:12:55 -0600
From: Bertha the Boss<bertha@fledgling.com>
To: sam@fledgling.com
Subject: complaint from Mr. Whiner

See if you can make him happy

        From whiner Fri Jan  3 14:12:06 1992
        Received: by fledgling.com id AA09908
           (5.65d/IDA-1.4.4 for bertha); Fri, 3 Jan 1992 14:12:05 -0600
           Date: Fri, 3 Jan 1992 14:12:05 -0600
        From: whiner@bigaccount.com
        Message-Id: <199201032012.AA09908@fledgling.com>
```

```
To: bertha@fledgling.com
Subject: Bad Service

I got bad service from your office...
```

Inclusion of Text Files

You often want to send someone a text file via electronic mail. You would like to keep the file intact and insert a copy of it into the message being sent. That way, the file will be immediately useful to the recipient, who doesn't have to use **ftp** to get it. You can also insert an explanation into the message, telling the recipient what to do with the file.

An example may make this clearer:

```
% mail johnb                    start a normal message
Subject: Check this out
Here is the draft proposal.  Make changes and get
back to me ASAP.
~r draft                        include file draft
"draft" 300/13427               300 lines 13427 chars long
.
```

In this example, you built a mail message by typing some introductory text, and then inserting a copy of your file called *draft*. To insert the file, you used the ~r command. The general format of this command is:

```
~r filename
```

You can give this command at any place in the text of the message, provided that the ~ is in column one, and provided that you're not using an editor to construct the message.* The named file is unchanged by the command.

Mailing Lists

With electronic mail, it is just as easy to send a message to a group of people as it is to send a message to a single person. The facility that makes this possible is called a "mailing list." It allows an alias or nickname to stand for a group of recipients; for example, the alias **staff** can be defined as "all employees." When you send mail to the name **staff**, the mail is actually delivered to everyone in the group.

With many mailers, including UNIX **mail**, this is a simple extension of the **alias** command we discussed earlier. Instead of listing one recipient after the alias name, you can list many. If all the names won't fit on one line, you can put multiple alias lines in succession:

```
alias staff tommy@banzai.edu, pecos@banzai.edu
alias staff akida@banzai.edu, newjersey@banzai.edu
alias staff buckaroo@banzai.edu, rawhide@banzai.edu
```

---

*That is, you can't type ~r while you're using **vi** or some other editor. Any reasonable text editor has its own commands for inserting files—use them instead.

With these entries in your *.mailrc* file, you can send mail to them all by typing:

```
% mail staff
Subject: Staff Meeting at 9am
To discuss the 8th dimension
.
```

Your mailer expands the mailing-list name to a set of normal email addresses. This means that the recipients' email addresses will be listed in the **To:** part of the header.

Reply

Replying is a shorthand for telling your mailer that you want to send a response back to the person who sent you a particular message. It saves you the trouble of typing in the email address. Your mailer typically copies the **From:** (or **Reply-To:**) field from the original message to create the **To:** line of a new message; to create the new **Subject:** line, your mailer just copies the original and adds "Re:" at the beginning to show that this is a response to an earlier message.

Replies can be tricky. Your mailer may not be able to convert the original **From:** field into something reasonable. Whether or not a reply will work correctly depends on whether the sender's return address is complete and acceptable to your mailer. If it doesn't work, you might need to look at the **From:** address and modify it, based on your experience (see the section "Acquiring Email Addresses" earlier in this chapter).

Like most mailers, UNIX **mail** has two commands to support this feature:

```
& r message#
& R message#
```

The **r** command sends a message back to the original sender and all of the original recipients. **R** only sends the reply back to the original sender.* The *message#* is optional. If it is not given, the current message is used. Which form of the reply command you choose obviously depends on the nature of your message. If you're taking part in a discussion, you probably want all of the recipients to receive your response (**r**). If you're just providing some information (like "Yes, I can make it to the company picnic"), you can assume that the other recipients probably don't need to get your reply (so you would use **R**).

Let's let Sam respond to the complaint from Mr. Whiner he was sent earlier:

```
& 1
>From bertha Fri Jan  3 14:12:56 1992
Date: Fri, 3 Jan 1992 14:12:55 -0600
From: Bertha the Boss<bertha@fledgling.com>
To: sam@fledgling.com
Subject: complaint from Mr. Whiner
```

---

*A few UNIX **mail** programs have these functions reversed. Just watch carefully the first time you use it.

```
See if you can make him happy

    From whiner Fri Jan  3 14:12:06 1992
    Received: by fledgling.com id AA09908
      (5.65d/IDA-1.4.4 for bertha); Fri, 3 Jan 1992 14:12:05 -0600
      Date: Fri, 3 Jan 1992 14:12:05 -0600
    From: whiner@bigaccount.com
    Message-Id: <199201032012.AA09908@fledgling.com>
    To: bertha@fledgling.com
    Subject: Bad Service

    I got bad service from your office...
& R
To: bertha@fledgling.com
Subject: complaint from Mr. Whiner
I took care of it.
.
```

mail doesn't automatically insert the message that you're replying to into the body of the reply (many mailers do). If you want it, you must insert it with the ˜m or ˜f command, just as you would with any other message.

Commonly Supported Features

There are several common features that are supported by most mail programs. If your mailer supports any of these features, then you can use them when sending messages to any other mailer—regardless of its type.

Carbon copies

All mailers let you put several addresses in the **To:** field of the header. It is frequently useful to differentiate between those to whom the message is primarily directed, and those who receive it for their information. To do so, the mail-forwarding software recognizes that a line beginning with **Cc:** contains a list of addresses; anyone listed on the **Cc:** line will also receive a copy, just as if he or she were listed on the **To:** line. Thus, the **Cc:** field has the same meaning as the old cc: line on a business letter. Many mailers have a facility for creating a **Cc:** line automatically. If the mailer allows you to edit the header, you can create a **Cc:** line manually.

UNIX **mail** gives you two ways to generate a **Cc:** line. First, you can use the tilde escape ˜c anywhere in the text of the message:

```
~c johnb@yoyodyne.com            ˜must be in column 1
```

You can also add the line **set askcc** to your *.mailrc* file. This tells the mailer that whenever you end a message, it should ask you who should get "carbon copies." When **askcc** is set, a typical **mail** session might look like this:

```
& mail johnb
Subject: Can you make the meeting
remember the meeting at 0900.  Can you make it?
.
```

```
Cc: secretary
&
```

Some UNIX systems have this facility turned on as an installation option; if yours does, your mail package will ask for a carbon copy list, even if you don't set the **askcc** variable.

Blind carbon copies

Blind carbon copies are copies sent to a list of readers, just like carbon copies. However, the header line that lists the recipients is automatically deleted from the outgoing mail. Therefore, none of the other recipients will know who (if anyone) received "blind carbon copies." Since there is no record in the received message that these copies were ever sent, later actions which use data in the header (for example, replies to the message) will not include these recipients in their action.

Blind cc's in UNIX **mail** are available through the tilde escape ~b. The facility works just like the ~c. There is no switch to prompt for blind carbons. If the mailer allows you to edit the header, you can create a **BCC:** line manually.

Signature files

Signature files are a way to append additional information to outgoing mail messages. They are often used to include information about who you are and how you can be contacted. So, if you don't think:

```
From: johnb@yoyodyne.com
```

conveys a lot of information about yourself, you could set up a file which gives your name, postal address, phone number, FAX number, other email addresses, etc. For example, such a file might look like:

```
----------------------------------------
John Bigboote       | Yoyodyne Industries
johnb@yoyodyne.com  |
(212)333-4444       | "The Future Begins Tomorrow"
----------------------------------------------------
```

Remember, if the recipient cannot get email back to you, the information in your signature file might be the only means at his disposal to get in touch with you. Keep it short and useful, however. It is really pushing it (and irritating) when your signature includes your dog's and kid's names, pictures of your favorite cult icons, and takes up 15 to 20 lines.

There is no signature file facility in UNIX **mail**. The best you can do is make a file and then do a ~r at the end of each message to include it.

Unusual and Non-standard Features

The following features are found in some electronic mail packages, but can't be assumed to be available to everyone. Some of them, like attaching documents, are becoming more common because there are standard ways of doing them. Others, like notification of reading, will probably never become standard. As a result, you can't assume these will work unless you know the recipient's mailer has the feature you need, and is compatible with your mailer. None of these features are available in standard UNIX **mail**.

Attaching documents

Some electronic mail systems allow you to mail files as separate entities along with a message. That is, when you send a message to someone you can say: "send this file, too." When the message is read, the receiving mailer asks the person reading the message where the file should be stored. These files can be either binary or ASCII, and system information about the file is preserved in the move. For example, you could send a message saying "Take a look at the spreadsheet I've enclosed and get back to me," and attach an Excel spreadsheet from a Macintosh. When the recipient reads the message and accepts the attachment, his Mac automatically creates an Excel spreadsheet file on his machine.

A facility called "multimedia mail" is related to attached documents. This extension allows you to send digitized voice and pictures as part of a message—together with other attachments (like binary data). The new standard Internet way of doing this is called MIME; we'll discuss it more fully later in this chapter. Remember, digitized sound and video take a lot of time to transmit and a lot of disk space to store.

Notification of receipt

Notification of receipt automatically sends you a message when the mail you've sent is placed in the recipient's electronic in-basket. This prevents someone from saying "Well, I never got the message"; just as with the Post Office, a "return receipt" proves that the mail was delivered.

Notification of reading

This feature automatically sends you a message when the mail you've sent is displayed by the recipient. It doesn't mean that he actually read or understood it. It does mean that he is not being truthful when the excuse is: "I just read it this morning." You know it was displayed two days ago!

Message cancel

Message cancel allows you to take back a message after you have sent it. This can be handy if you often write cantankerous messages and then wish (later) that you hadn't sent them. Obviously, there's a limited window during which you can cancel a message. The length of this window varies with the message's destination (where the mail is going) and how the mailers are connected. If the message is sent to another user within the same mail system, it can usually be cancelled until it is read. If it is addressed to an in-basket on another mail system, it usually cannot be retrieved after it has passed out of the sender's system.

Sending Binary Data as ASCII

At times, you want to send a binary file (for example, files from WordPerfect, disk dumps, etc.) through electronic mail. **ftp**, which is designed for transferring files, may not be possible or practical. Email can reach many places that **ftp** can't: it can traverse networks which are not directly connected to the Internet, or networks which provide only mail service. In addition, **ftp** can't send a file to many recipients; you may want to post an executable of your new NEWS reader to a large mailing list, in which case **ftp** will be impractical.

So electronic mail looks like what you need. Unfortunately, it is a text-only medium. That is, it only deals with messages that are constructed from characters. As we said a few pages ago, any mailer will let you insert a text file into a message. However, relatively few mailers allow you to send binary (i.e., non-text) files directly, and those that do probably aren't compatible with each other—though MIME is establishing standards in this area.

But with a little additional work, it's possible for any mailer to transmit a binary file, provided that both the sending and receiving computers have a utility to convert binary files into some ASCII representation. All UNIX systems have such utilities; one is called **uuencode**, and we'll use it as an example below. Many other systems have an equivalent utility; if you're a programmer, it's not difficult to write your own, and give it to your friends.

Of course, the ability to transfer a binary file doesn't mean that the binary file will be *useful* at the destination. You may be able to mail a **tar** dump of a directory to someone; but that **tar** dump is only useful if the recipient has a utility capable of reading **tar** files. If those files are executable files, they will only work if the sender and recipient have the same kind of computer. However, whether or not the binary data you send is *useful* is a different problem that has nothing to do with electronic mail.

At any rate, if we have the same utilities available on the systems at each end, we are home free. You need to find a program that converts a binary file into a printable character representation of the binary data. You could do this yourself, if you wanted, by taking each byte, turning it into a number between 0 and 255, and storing this sequence of three-digit numbers in another file. You would have to write the inverse program at the other end to convert this representation back into binary. But why bother? As we said, most systems have this kind of utility available. **uuencode** comes with UNIX; **btoa** is available on many UNIX systems; and both are available in the public domain for PCs. **BinHex** performs a similar function in the Macintosh world. With these utilities, you can encode the file, turning the binary file into a textual representation. Once you have a textual representation, you can send it through electronic mail. The recipient takes the message, edits off the headers (sometimes this is not necessary), decodes it, and has the original binary file.

Maybe an example is in order:

```
% uuencode overthruster < overthruster > temp
% mail john@yoyodyne.com
Subject: Program
Here is the program you wanted (you need to uudecode it):
~r temp
"temp" 7216/447224
.
Cc:
%
```

The first line (**uuencode**) takes the file *overthruster* and encodes it as printable text. It puts the output into the file *temp* (making it about a third bigger as well). In the process, it flags the file internally with the name *overthruster* (more on this later). Next, we begin an email message to **john@yoyodyne.com**, and give him a little hint about what to do with it (always a good idea). The ˜r line is this mailer's command for copying a file into a message; here, we copy the *temp* file that we created earlier. The next line informs us that the file *temp* was inserted and that it is 7216 lines and 447224 characters long.* Typing a period (.) in column one says "end of message"; a return in response to the **Cc:** prompt says, "no carbon copies to anyone."

Some time later, John logs in to check his mail. He'll see:

```
% mail
"/usr/spool/mail/john": 1 message 1 unread
>N 1 krol            Sat Nov 2 19:57 7245/448458 "Program"
& 1
Received: from uxh.cso.uiuc.edu by uxc.cso.uiuc.edu with...
   (5.65c/IDA-1.4.4 for <john@yoyodyne.com>);
   Sat, 2 Nov 1991 19:56:31 -0600
Received: by uxh.cso.uiuc.edu id AA22546
   (5.65c/IDA-1.4.4 for john@yoyodyne.com);
   Sat, 2 Nov 1991 19:56:16 -0600
Date: Sat, 2 Nov 1991 19:56:16 -0600
From: Ed Krol <krol@uxh.cso.uiuc.edu>
Message-Id: <199111030156.AA22546@uxh.cso.uiuc.edu>
To: john@yoyodyne.com
Subject: Program

Here is the program you wanted (you need to uudecode it):
begin 755 overthruster
M```!@0D```!I`I$U;Q```10```````!<`````````!,`J<```````````*4H`
M``````````````````````!*`````#C``````"#`!`A```";`!`!`P@``````
```

---

*Some email systems have limits on the size of any one message, like 1000 lines or 50,000 characters. If you run into one of these limits you can use the UNIX **split** utility to break up a file into multiple pieces and mail them separately.

```
CTRL-C  Interrupt
& s encodedprog
"encodedprog" [New file] 7244/448458
& q
% uudecode encodedprog
```

He sees one message from "krol," and it's huge (7244 lines). In response to the & prompt, he enters a **1**, meaning "read message 1." It starts like a normal, everyday message until the line starting with **begin**; this is the start of an encoded binary file. After seeing a few lines, he interrupts the listing (in this case by pressing CTRL-C) and issues the command **s encodedprog**. This command saves the current message in a new file named *encodedprog*. He then runs **uudecode** on the new file. It ignores any text before the **begin** line, and decodes the ASCII garbage that follows. In doing so, it creates a new binary file that matches the original. It gives the binary file the name you called it on the **uuencode** command (**overthruster**), which was recorded on the "begin" line. In the end, John has the **overthruster** program.

MIME: Multi-purpose Internet Mail Extensions

MIME is a specification for automatically sending objects other than text in email messages. It allows you to avoid all that **uuencode** and **uudecode** stuff we just showed. Even if you and the recipient of a message are using different mail packages, if both packages are MIME-compliant, you should be able to transfer any kind of object you desire—within reason.

Although MIME is primarily a specification for attaching files to email messages, for most people MIME is associated with multimedia, and their expectations go a little farther. MIME mailers usually know how to process several kinds of file attachments themselves; in particular, images, audio recordings, and movies. (The ability to display any of these depends on your computer having the appropriate hardware and, most likely, some additional software.) So you could send a message describing the new remote-control toy you're trying to market, attached to a video of the toy chasing the dog around the living room. The recipient could read the message and—without doing anything extra—watch the video. (Of course, he might curse you for sending a gigantic file to him, especially if he pays for connection time.)

At their most exotic, some MIME messages can even contain software that executes on your system. For example, you might receive a message about the condition of homeless shelters in New York. After you read the message, it automatically creates a new screen that displays a model "letter to your congressman" and says "If you would like to send this letter via electronic mail, check here." The letter is composed, signed, and sent automatically.* Although letting someone else execute software on your system sounds dangerous, there's a very clever bit of engineering here: this software is written in a special language that your MIME

---

*Whether or not this feature constitutes a great leap forward in cultural progress is up to the reader.

mailer understands, and it isn't allowed to do anything that could possibly be harmful.

All these features are both a blessing and a curse, wrapped up into one package. The blessing is that it allows people with less technical know-how than you now have to send all kinds of files as part of their email. The curse is that they don't realize that they are using features that aren't universal, and that some recipients may not be able to decipher their messages.

What MIME Does

Let's look at a slightly less esoteric example that will give us some insight into what MIME really does. If you want to send someone an Excel spreadsheet, you can attach the spreadsheet file to your message as a document. If the recipient's email package is not MIME-compliant, she will see something like this:

```
From e-krol@uiuc.edu Mon Jan  3 11:19:49 1994
Date: Mon, 3 Jan 1994 11:19:39 -0600
Message-Id: <199401031719.AA25021@ux1.cso.uiuc.edu>
X-Sender: krol@ux1.cso.uiuc.edu
Mime-Version: 1.0
Content-Type: multipart/mixed; boundary="=====_3514124==_"
To: ajzxmvk@ux1.cso.uiuc.edu
From: e-krol@uiuc.edu (Ed Krol)
Subject: Here is the spreadsheet
Status: RO

--=====_3514124==_        this is the normal text part
Content-Type: text/plain; charset="us-ascii"

Hi, Martha. Here's the spreadsheet you wanted.

--=====_3514124==_        this is the included file
Content-Type: application/mac-binhex40; name="Projected_Costs_List"
Content-Disposition: attachment; filename="Projected_Costs_List"

(This file must be converted with BinHex 4.0)

:&&"bEfTPBh4PC#"$Eh0dFb"-DA0d!&K-8c0B3d9-!3!!!%!&!!!!!2`H#3)'!!!
!%!$f"9`!)!!+8QpcFb"@C@&MD#!J)#!J)#!J)#!J)#!J)#!J)!X#'!"@!`!
```

When MIME sent the message, it added some additional lines that are, essentially, directions to the recipient's mail package. Whether you're sending or receiving the message, you don't have to understand these directives; they're processed automatically. However, you hope that the recipients' mail software understands them! There's no way to tell, in advance, whether or not it does.

Here's how the directives work. They divide the messages into a number of *parts* separated by *boundary* markers. A boundary marker is just a string of characters that's guaranteed not to occur anywhere in the message. The message header defines the boundary marker; it's not the same in every message.

Following the first boundary marker, you will see one or more lines that look like more mail headers. These lines describe the *type* of the part: that is, they tell the recipient's mailer how to unpack the message. The first part in the preceding message is *text/plain*: this means that it's plain old text, using the U.S. ASCII character set. There's a very short message in here that the recipient will see as a regular, textual email message. The second part of the message is a file named *Projected_Costs_List*, of the type *application/mac-binhex40*. The recipient's mailer is supposed to understand this file type and decode the file automatically (possibly asking the user for permission first).

So: MIME mailers are supposed to understand how to decode different kinds of files. If things work correctly—and they often do—MIME will leave the decoded *Projected_Costs_List* file on the recipient's computer, with no additional work of coding or decoding necessary on the user's part. However, there's still a compatibility problem here. There are many MIME types. A MIME-compliant mail package must be able to handle messages in the MIME format, but isn't required to handle all possible message types. In general, the sender's and recipient's mail packages each define a set of MIME types that they know about; some of them will overlap and some will not. If your mailer is MIME-compatible, but it encounters an unfamiliar message type, you might see something like this:

```
This message contains data in an unrecognized format,
application/mac-binhex40, which can either be viewed
as text or written to a file.

What do you want to do with application/mac-binhex40 data?
1 -- See it as text
2 -- Write it to a file
3 -- Just skip it
```

In this case, you can salvage the message by saving the message (or just the offending part) in a file, and decoding it by hand—just as you would with an old-fashioned mailer. The MIME message will usually tell you what you need to do. In this example, you need to find a utility that can decode BinHex 4.0 files and use it to make the file readable.* Remember: just because you or your email package managed to decode the message, it may not be usable on your computer. If you received the spreadsheet we sent in the example, you'd need to have Microsoft Excel on your computer to read it.

One other feature of MIME is that it can avoid sending a file unless the recipient wants it. Instead of putting the file into the mail message as an encoded insertion, it adds a directive telling the recipient's mailer how to FTP the file automatically. (Of course, the sender has to make sure that the file is available in an FTP archive somewhere). This feature lets you choose whether or not you want to receive a file; if you don't want the file, you save storage on your computer and reduce network traffic. For example, you could "mail" the draft of a new user's manual to everyone in your company. The user's manual wouldn't actually be sent, though; it

---

*See Computing/Compression and Archival Software Summary in the *Resource Catalog*.

would sit in an FTP archive until individual readers decided that they needed it. Those who wanted the user's manual could receive it without even knowing how to use FTP—their MIME mailer will handle the FTP transfer for them. Those who don't want the manual can easily ignore it.

Here is one such inclusion:

```
--OtherAccess--          This is the boundry flag
Content-Type:   Message/External-body;
        name="draft-ietf-atommib-sonet-03.txt";
        site="ds.internic.net";
        access-type="anon-ftp";
        directory="internet-drafts"

Content-Type: text/plain
Content-ID: <19931228115236.I-D@CNRI.Reston.VA.US>

--OtherAccess--
```

It instructs a MIME-compliant mail package to **ftp** the file *draft-ietf-atommib-sonet-03.txt* from the host **ds.internic.net**. Now, there's an obvious problem. It's easy for the recipient to get the file if he or she is connected directly to the Internet. But if the recipient is on another network with an Internet email gateway, **ftp** won't work. If you find youself in this state, you may be able to salvage the message by using the **ftpmail** facility (explained later in this chapter) by hand.

Pine: A MIME Example

So far, I've spent a fair amount of time talking about how MIME can make your life difficult, and I may have given you the impression that it's more likely to cause you grief than it is to be really helpful. That's not true. Most of the time, MIME mailers do what you want: they're incredibly helpful for transferring all sorts of files that otherwise get you into trouble. And the things MIME *doesn't* get right are things normal email doesn't dare try.

So let's look briefly at how MIME simplifies email life. Several packages are capable of handling MIME messages: **metamail** is one (free extensions to the standard BSD mailer we've been discussing); Z-Mail is another (a popular commercial mailer that runs on many different systems); and **pine** is another free software product that's gaining popularity. We'll look at **pine** briefly. We won't try an exhaustive overview of its features; it has a reasonable help facility. Its simplicity and its menu orientation allow many people to use it really quickly.

pine was designed at the University of Washington to be used by students.* Its functionality is pretty basic, but it's easy to use. It runs in full-screen mode on standard ASCII terminals. Therefore, it will work over dial-up lines with VT100

---

*You can get **pine** via anonymous FTP from **ftp.cac.washington.edu**, in the directory **/mail**. There are executable binaries for many UNIX systems in the **unix-bin** directory, in addition to binaries for other platforms; see the *README* file.

emulation and on old-fashioned terminals; it doesn't require a fancy graphical display.

You start **pine** with the command:

```
% pine
```

You are greeted with a screen that summarizes the most common commands:

```
PINE 3.05        MAIN MENU        Folder:inbox  1 Message

   ?   HELP         - Get help using Pine
   C   COMPOSE      - Compose and send a message
   I   MAIL INDEX   - Read mail in current folder
   F   FOLDERS      - Open a different mail folder
   A   ADDRESSES    - Update your address book
   O   OTHER        - Use other functions
   Q   QUIT         - Exit the Pine mail program


 ? Help       Q Quit       F Folders .   O Other
 C Compose    I Mail Index A Addresses
```

All the commands are single keystrokes; there aren't any weird "tilde" commands, like we had in UNIX **mail**. Let's repeat our earlier example: we'll send the **overthruster** program to johnb@yoyodyne.com This time, we don't need to worry about uuencode; we'll send the program as a MIME attachment, which uses its own coding. To send a message, press **C** (the compose command). Now MIME displays a mail entry template:

```
PINE 3.05    COMPOSE MESSAGE    Folder:inbox  1 Message

To      : johnb@yoyodyne.com
Cc      :
Attchmnt: 1. /cso/staff/krol/overthruster (185 KB) ""
Subject : Program
----- Message Text -----
Here is the program you wanted.




 ^G Get Help ^C Cancel   ^R Read File^Y Prev Pg  ^K Del Line ^O Postpone
 ^X Send      ^J Justify  ^W Where is ^V Next Pg  ^U UnDel Lin^T To Spell
```

The cursor is initially in the `To:` field. We type the destination address, and then use **TAB** to move to other fields. When we get to the `Attachmnt:` field, we type the name of the file to send; in this case, *overthruster*. We only typed *overthruster*; when **pine** noticed that we had typed a complete filename, it added the rest of the path, the file size, and the other information. That's all we have to do to send the program; MIME does the rest. We then type in a subject and the message text. When that's done, we type **CTRL-X** to send the message.

Now let's peek over John B's shoulder at Yoyodyne and watch what happens when he receives the message. He again starts with **pine**'s main menu, which gives him a command summary and tells him that there's one message waiting in his "inbox":

```
PINE 3.05      MAIN MENU      Folder:inbox  1 Message

  ?  HELP         - Get help using Pine
  C  COMPOSE      - Compose and send a message
  I  MAIL INDEX   - Read mail in current folder
  F  FOLDERS      - Open a different mail folder
  A  ADDRESSES    - Update your address book
  O  OTHER        - Use other functions
  Q  QUIT         - Exit the Pine mail program

              [Folder "inbox" opened with 1 message]
  ? Help      Q Quit      F Folders    O Other
  C Compose   I Mail Index A Addresses
```

He chooses **I** to see mail in the current folder *inbox*.

```
PINE 3.05      MAIL INDEX      Folder:inbox  Message 1 of 1

  N 1   Jan  5 Ed Krol            (256K) Program




  ? Help       M Main Menu  P Prev Msg    - Prev Page  F Forward     D Delete
  O OTHER CMDS V View Mail  N Next Msg SPACE Next Page  R Reply       S Save
```

By positioning the cursor on the message he wants to read and pressing **V**, he displays the message we sent him:

```
PINE 3.05      VIEW MAIL    Folder:inbox  Message 1 of 1 100%

Date: Wed, 5 Jan 1994 13:18:59 -0600 (CST)
From: Ed Krol <krol@ux1.cso.uiuc.edu>
To: johnb@yoyodyne.com
Subject: Program
Parts/attachments:
 1 Shown  2 lines Text
 2     251 Kb   File "overthruster", ""   What we are interested in
----------------------------------------

Here is the program you wanted


   [Part 2, ""  Attached file "overthruster"  251Kb]
   [Can not display this part. Use the "A" command to save in a file]

  ? Help       M Main Menu  P Prev Msg    - Prev Page  F Forward     D Delete
  O OTHER CMDS I Mail Index N Next Msg SPACE Next Page  R Reply       S Save
```

As we would expect, **pine** displays the printable part of the message, and says that the file *overthruster* is attached—but that it doesn't make sense to display it on the screen. **pine** also gives John B a hint about how to save the message: press **A**. When he does this, **pine** responds:

```
Enter attachment number to view or save (1 - 2) :2
^G Help          ^C Abort           RETURN Enter
```

John B tells it he wants to save the second part of the message by pressing a **2**. Remember, MIME messages can have many parts; in this message, part 1 was our explanatory text ("Here is the program you wanted"), and part 2 is the file itself. **pine** then asks:

```
Save or View attachment? (s/v) [s]
```

This shows one the limitations of **pine**. It knows how to deal with two kinds of objects, binary files and GIF files.* If the attachment were a graphics file, we could view it (assuming that our terminal supports graphics) by pressing **v**. In John B's case, he really wants to save the attachment in a file, which he does by pressing **s**. The [**s**] indicates that **s** is the default, so typing RETURN would be just as good. **pine** then asks for a filename, suggesting *overthruster* (the same one the sender used):

```
File (in home directory) to save attachment in: overthruster
```

If John doesn't like that, he can backspace over it and type another name. Since he is happy with *overthruster*, he enters a **RETURN** and is done. There's no encoding or decoding, no weird file formats to understand.

That's all we're going to say about **pine**. It's worth exploring if it's available to you. If you try it, remember that each screen has a help command that describes the commands you can enter at that point.

When Electronic Mail Gets Returned

When electronic mail cannot be delivered, you normally get a message telling you why. This takes the format of a really ugly, strange message in your in-basket:

```
% mail
"/usr/spool/mail/krol": 1 message 1 unread
>N 1 MAILER-DAEMON@uxc.cs Sun Nov 3 09:03 29/1233 "Returned mail: Host un"
&
```

At this point, all you know is that your mail didn't go through; you have no idea why. To find out, you have to wade through the cryptic message that got returned.

---

*GIF (Graphics Interchange Format) is a common format for storing color graphic images. Many of the images you find around the network are stored as GIF files (pronounced "jif").

There are three common reasons for electronic mail to fail:

- The mail system can't find the recipient's machine.
- The recipient is unknown at that machine.
- The mail can find the machine but still can't deliver the message.

Let's investigate these causes one at a time.

Unknown Hosts

When you send a message to someone, the network tries to make some sense out of the stuff to the right of the @. If it can't make sense of it, or if it can't look up the address of the named machine, the mailer that gives up sends you a message saying that the host is unknown. Look at the previous example, in which we encoded a binary program and sent it to **johnb@yoyodyne.com**. Assume that the Net was unable to recognize the system **yoyodyne.com**. Eventually, you'll get a returned message like this:

```
& 1
From MAILER-DAEMON@uxc.cso.uiuc.edu Sun Nov  3 09:03:18 1991
Date: Sun, 3 Nov 1991 09:02:57 -0600
From: Mail Delivery Subsystem <MAILER-DAEMON@uxc.cso.uiuc.edu>
To: krol@ux1.cso.uiuc.edu
Subject: Returned mail: Host unknown

     ----- Transcript of session follows -----
550 yoyodyne.com (TCP)... 550 Host unknown

     ----- Unsent message follows -----
Received: from ux1.cso.uiuc.edu by uxc.cso.uiuc.edu with SMTP id AA17283
    (5.65c/IDA-1.4.4 for <johnb@yoyodyne.com>); Sun, 3 Nov 1991 09:02:57 -0600
Received: by ux1.cso.uiuc.edu id AA17906
    (5.65c/IDA-1.4.4 for johnb@yoyodyne.com); Sun, 3 Nov 1991 06:22:30 -0600
Date: Sun, 3 Nov 1991 06:22:30 -0600
From: Ed Krol <krol@ux1.cso.uiuc.edu>
Message-Id: <199111031222.AA17906@uxh.cso.uiuc.edu>
To: johnb@yoyodyne.com
Subject: The program you wanted.
```

In response to the & prompt, you entered the message number that you wanted to read (just like any other message). You see a message from the MAILER-DAEMON on a machine named **uxc.cso.uiuc.edu**. **uxc.cso.uiuc.edu** is an intermediate mail handler. Your mail was sent to this system *en route* to **yoyodyne.com**; this is where it ran into trouble. Past the header of the returned mail message, in a section marked "Transcript of session," you find a message that the host **yoyodyne.com** is unknown to the network. After this,, you will usually find the unsent message itself. This saves you the trouble of re-entering it. However, you have to delete the junk from the front before resending the message.

What should you do when something like this happens? First, check the address: is the name **yoyodyne.com** spelled correctly? Second, check whether the address is complete. When presented with an incomplete name like **yoyodyne**, many machines add a domain suffix automatically; they assume that the suffix should be the same as their own. So, on a machine named **ux1.cso.uiuc.edu**, the address **yoyodyne** will be expanded to **yoyodyne.cso.uiuc.edu**. This is a nice shorthand, because most mail is directed within the same organization. However, you must be careful to provide the proper domain when sending mail to someone outside your organization.

A variant of this problem occurs when people give out partial addresses, assuming that you'll be able to figure out the rest. For example, someone might give you an address like **joe@turing.cs**. He is assuming that you know he's in the CS department of the University of Illinois (Urbana-Champaign), which is the domain **uiuc.edu**, and that his complete address is therefore **joe@turing.cs.uiuc.edu**. If you don't realize this and simply use the address **joe@turing.cs**, the mail-forwarding software will get confused—in this case, really confused. To a computer, **turing.cs** looks exactly like the complete name of **turing** in Czechoslovakia (**.cs** is Czechoslovakia's country code). If you're lucky, **turing.cs** doesn't exist, and you'll get an "unknown host" message. If you're unlucky, **turing.cs** does exist, and you'll be even more confused. (If you're really unlucky, **joe@turing.cs** will even exist, and he'll get your mail.) The moral of the story is twofold. First, you may need to finish the address yourself from your own knowledge of where the person really resides. Second, when you give your address to someone, always give a complete address; don't assume that your correspondents will be smart enough to figure out the rest.

One last warning. You might find a returned message where the unknown host has multiple highest-level domains:

```
yoyodyne.com.cso.uiuc.edu
```

If you run across something like this, you have run into a misconfigured mailer. **yoyodyne.com** was a perfectly fine address. Some mailer along the way decided it wasn't and tried to complete it by tacking on its own domain, **.cso.uiuc.edu**, really screwing things up. In this case, there is nothing you can do. Find someone who knows about mailers and ask for help.

What was wrong with the particular message we have been discussing? Let's assume that John gave you the address **yoyodyne.com** and that you spelled it correctly. Since the domain **.com** is a valid highest-level domain, name completion shouldn't be a problem. So, it looks like nothing is wrong from the network's standpoint. At this point, I would assume that the computer **yoyodyne.com** does not exist. Either John gave it to you in error, or it passed out of existence over the course of time.

It's also possible that your computer just doesn't know about the system you're trying to send to. Some mailers have lists of valid hostnames which are not updated continuously. The target machine may just not be in the list. If you think this may be the problem, talk to whoever manages the mail system you are using.

Similar errors may occur when you reply to someone's message. Some mailers fail to fill out their full name in the **From:** section of the header. Let's assume that johnb@yoyodyne.com uses one of these mailers; he sends you a message, in which the **From:** field simply says johnb@yoyodyne. Since the **From:** field has nothing to do with delivering the message, you receive the message just fine. The **From:** field gets copied to the **To:** field when you do a reply. You then have exactly the same situation as above. Your mail is addressed to johnb@yoyodyne. Your computer will complete the name, but probably not correctly. In this situation, if your mailer allows you to edit the header, you can compose a reply and then fix the address. If you aren't allowed to do this, you will have to skip **reply** and start a new message.

If none of these hints apply, you have no recourse other than calling the person to see if some other address might work better.

Unknown Recipients

Now, let's assume that your mail made its way to the correct host. Eventually, a machine forwarding your mail makes contact with the destination machine and tells it the recipient's name. What happens if the destination machine hasn't heard of the message's addressee? In this case, the returned mail header looks something like:

```
>From daemon Mon Nov  4 14:44:31 1991
Received: by uxh.cso.uiuc.edu id AA08280
   (5.65c/IDA-1.4.4 for krol); Mon, 4 Nov 1991 14:44:26
Date: Mon, 4 Nov 1991 14:44:26 -0600
From: Mail Delivery Subsystem <MAILER-DAEMON>
Message-Id: <199111042044.AA08280@uxh.cso.uiuc.edu>
To: krol
Subject: Returned mail: User unknown Status: RO

     ----- Transcript of session follows -----
While talking to yoyodyne.com:
>>> RCPT To:<johm@yoyodyne.com>
<<< 550 <johm@yoyodyne.com>... User unknown
550 johm@yoyodyne.com... User unknown
```

This failure is frequently caused by mistyping the username in the address. (That's what happened above, I mistyped john.) It is also possible that the username is correct, and the hostname is incorrect, but legal. For example, if you address a message to **johnb@ux2** rather than **johnb@ux1**, you may get a "User unknown" message. The machine **ux2** exists, but there is no user **johnb** on it. (In the worst case, the wrong person may receive your mail: some "johnb" that you've never met, but who happens to have an account on **ux2**.)

Mail Can't Be Delivered

The previous examples show the most frequent ways of failing, but if you're clever you may find others. You may see the message:

```
----- Transcript of session follows -----
554 <johnb@yoyodyne.com>... Service unavailable
```

This message tells us that, although the machine was located and in communication, it wasn't accepting electronic mail at this time. In this case, your best bet is to wait a while and try again, perhaps during normal working hours. (Or, if you tried during working hours, try again during off-hours.) Some machines are set up so that they won't accept mail on weekends or some other arbitrary time.

In the previous cases, you would receive notification of the problem almost immediately. For example, if the destination host is unknown to the network, you will receive notification as soon as a system that's handling the mail tries to look up the destination and fails. This should happen in minutes or, at most, a few hours. There is an additional common failure mode in which the problem might not be known for days: the machine is known to the network, but unreachable. In these cases, the sending machine may try to send the mail for two or three days (or more) before it gives up and tells you about it. This looks like:

```
From: Mail Delivery Subsystem <MAILER-DAEMON@ux1.cso.uiuc.edu>
Message-Id: <199111091804.AA27807@ux1.cso.uiuc.edu>
To: e-krol@uiuc.edu
Subject: Returned mail: Cannot send message for 2 days
Status: RO

    ----- Transcript of session follows -----
421 deadhost.cso.uiuc.edu (TCP)... Deferred:
    Connection timed out during user open
    with deadhost.cso.uiuc.edu

    ----- Unsent message follows -----
```

This message can mean several different things:

- The network may be faulty, making it impossible to contact the remote system.
- The remote system may be dead; for example, it may be having severe hardware problems.
- The remote system may be misconfigured; it isn't uncommon for someone to change the configuration of their system and forget to "tell" the network.

Note that the message does not imply that the host was completely unreachable for the entire two days. After a few failures, the sending machine might only try to send the message every few hours or so. If the machine is having hardware problems, the network's chances of contacting it when it's working may be very small.

Failures Involving Multiple Recipients

So far, all of the examples of failures have been for mail destined for one person. It's easy to become confused when something goes wrong with mail sent to several recipients. The returned mail might look like this:

```
Subject: Returned mail: User unknown
Status: RO


     ----- Transcript of session follows -----
While talking to ux1.cso.uiuc.edu:
>>> RCPT To:<willie_martin@ux1.cso.uiuc.edu>
<<< 550 <willie_martin@ux1.cso.uiuc.edu>... User unknown
550 willie_martin@ux1.cso.uiuc.edu... User unknown


     ----- Unsent message follows -----
Date: Thu, 7 Nov 1991 10:43:40 -0600
From: Ed Krol <krol>
To: krol@ux1.cso.uiuc.edu, willie_martin@ux1.cso.uiuc.edu
Subject: Willie do you exist?
```

Who got the mail, and who didn't? You can figure out the answer by looking at the "unsent message" section. The message was destined for both krol@ux1.cso.uiuc.edu and willie_martin@ux1.cso.uiuc.edu. The "Transcript of session" tells us it is complaining about **willie_martin**, not about **krol**. You can conclude that **krol** received the message safely, and that there's something wrong with **willie_martin**'s address. You only need to resend the message to **willie** when you correct his address.

Last Ditch Help

By convention, every computer that exchanges mail should have a mailbox named **postmaster** defined. Mail addressed to **postmaster** should be read by the email administrator for the host computer. If you need any help with a particular machine, you can send a request to:

postmaster@*hostname*

Some things you might consider sending a message to **postmaster** about are:

- Help finding the email address for someone you know to be using that host
- Help finding the proper gateway for sending email to external networks
- Complaints about the actions of someone on that host (e.g., harassing messages)

Mail Lists and Reflectors

In an earlier section, we discussed aliases and learned how to define an alias with multiple recipients. For example, I can define a group alias for a few suspicious people:

```
alias aliens johnb@yoyodyne.com, johnw@yoyodyne.com
```

After I have created this alias, I can send a message to **aliens**, and it will be delivered to both **johnb** and **johnw**. This is a natural way to implement group discussions through electronic mail. It works fine for small groups, or for personal groups that only you use. As the group grows and other people want to use the same group definition, it turns into a maintenance nightmare. Whenever anyone is added to or deleted from the group, everyone who wants to use the alias must change his or her own personal definition. "Everyone" never does, so someone gets left out and doesn't receive a message, and there is hell to pay.

You really want a centrally maintained mailing list, so that you can make a single change that is effective for everyone. As long as you (or some other responsible person) maintains the **aliens** mailing list, everyone—senders and recipients—will be happy. This is typically implemented by a *mail reflector*. A mail reflector is a special email address set up so that any message sent to it will automatically be resent to everyone on a list. For example, let's assume that we've set up a mail reflector for **aliens**, rather than a simple alias. Now I can send a message to **aliens@yoyodyne.com**. The mailer on **yoyodyne.com** will take my message and resend it to **johnb** and **johnw**. It doesn't take much of a machine to act as a mail reflector, but it does take someone with system administrator privileges to set one up.* In this section, we'll tell you how to use lists that other people have set up; we won't discuss how to create your own.

In the tradition of computing, we need to make things even more complex. The mail reflector we discussed above works well for a private (though large) group. What if, rather than a private list of people, it were a list available to anyone who wanted to take part in a discussion? Suppose we want to allow anyone in the world who is interested in discussing pencil collecting to access the address **pencils@hoople.usnd.edu**. From there the mail will be forwarded to all the other participating collectors. You will receive everyone else's messages automatically; likewise anything you send to this address will be "broadcast" to pencil lovers worldwide.

For this to work there must be a method for saying "Please add me to the list." Sending that message to **pencils@hoople.usnd.edu** is not a reasonable solution. It sends the message to everyone on the list. Doing this may work, but it is considered bad form (making you appear to be a geek among pencil collectors everywhere). Worse, the person who manages the list may not get your message at all.

---

*One of the reasons for this is that if you create multiple mail reflectors, which have each other as members, they could send messages to each other forever.

The list maintainer may be an email administrator who doesn't care at all about pencil collecting.

Unfortunately, the correct way to subscribe to a list depends on how the list is maintained. Historically, the Internet uses special addresses for administrative requests. Whenever you create a public mail reflector, you create a second mailbox on the same machine. This mailbox has the same name as the mailing list, with the suffix **-request** added. This special mailbox is "private"; anything it receives isn't broadcast, but instead is sent to the mailing list's maintainer. So the correct way of subscribing is to send a message to:

```
pencils-request@hoople.usnd.edu
```

This is still a bit of a chore for the list maintainer, who must read the requests and edit the list manually. A nice utility named **listserv** for maintaining lists (and more) without human intervention grew up in the BITNET community on IBM/VM machines.* Since BITNET **listserv**s were accessible to both the BITNET and the Internet communities, they grew quite popular. So popular, in fact, that there has been a proliferation of **listserve**-like software running on all sorts of computers. Luckily, these packages, like **mailserv**, **majordomo**, and **almanac**,† accept a similar command set, so signing up for mailing lists isn't quite as confusing as it might have been.

To subscribe to a mailing list that's managed by one of these automatic packages, you send a specially formatted message to a special address on the computer that runs the mailing list. The "addressee" is often—but not always—the name of the program that's managing the list. For example, to subscribe to a pencil collector's list, you might send a message to **listserv@hoople.usnd.edu**. The messages would consist of one line, with no subject:

```
subscribe pencils your name
```

where **subscribe** is a keyword and **pencils** is the name of the group. Your name in the above example is strictly for documentation and the format doesn't really matter—though many groups won't let you sign up without giving your name. Be sure you send the subscription request from the account where you want to receive the mailings! The list processor gets your email address directly from the message headers, so if you use the wrong account, the mail will go to the wrong place. Once you have subscribed, whenever anyone sends a message to **pencils@hoople.usnd.edu**, you will get a copy.‡

---

*BITNET is a message and file retrieval network which has been around for a long time within the educational community. It used to be a real network, with phone lines of its own. While BITNET probably still has a few phone lines, it now uses the Internet to handle a lot of its traffic.

†**almanac** appears to be most heavily used by Agricultural Extension services. It looks like a good program, though, so expect it to spread.

‡A few mailing lists add an additional step: they require "subscription confirmation." This means that they will send you a standard message, requesting that you forward it back to them—possibly with some additional information. In any case, the message you receive should contain precise instructions about what to do.

If the mailing list were managed by **majordomo**, the address might be **major-domo@hoople.usnd.edu**; the message you'd send to subscribe would be identical. Similarly, if the mailing list is managed by **almanac**, you would send your subscription request to an address like **almanac@hoople.usnd.edu**. You'd send the same message, except that **almanac** doesn't require your personal name: the message would be simply **subscribe pencils**. (**almanac** has another good feature: you can send the message **send mail-catalog** to a server to get a list of all mailing lists the server manages.)

No matter who manages the list, the following rules hold:

- The address you send your request to probably serves many different lists: **list-serv@hoople.usnd.edu** could maintain mailing lists for pencil collectors, cat lovers, and fans of obscure Baroque composers.

- The address to which you send the subscription request and the address to which you send actual list postings are different.

- Many lists do not repost mail to the submitter, so you may not get the warm fuzzy feeling of seeing your message sent back to you. If you really want a copy, send a carbon copy to yourself.

Dropping Your Subscription

Now that you can get on a list, how do you get off it, or *unsubscribe*? Mailing lists can be as annoying as any other form of junk mail. Unsubscribing is known in the **listserv** parlance as **signoff**, and is done by sending the following command to the list server:

```
signoff pencils
```

This subscribe/signoff pairing was viewed as a bit obscure by the developers of **majordomo** and **almanac**, who chose the obvious:

```
unsubscribe listname
```

for their lists. Of course, if you want to unsubscribe to an Internet-style mailing list, just send a message to the administrative (**list-request**) address.

If you want more information about what any of these automated mailing list packages can do, send the message:

```
help
```

to any list server you can find—no matter what type of server it is. It will mail a help guide back to you.

This has been a lot of information. Let's summarize with a table. In the table below, *hostname* is the computer that manages the list, and *list* is the name of the list.

Table 7-3: Subscribing to Mailing Lists

List type	Subscription Address	Subscription Message	Termination Message	Posting Address
Listserv	listserv@*hostname*	Subscribe *list* yourname	Signoff *list*	*list*@hostname
majordomo	majordomo@*hostname*	Subscribe *list* yourname	Unsubscribe *list*	*list*@hostname
Internet	*list*-request@hostname	Anything	Anything	*list*@hostname
almanac	almanac@*hostname*	Subscribe *list*	Unsubscribe *list*	*list*@hostname

If this seems complicated, remember that there are exceptions! (Not what you wanted to hear.) When you subscribe to a mailing list, the first message you receive will probably be a "form letter" describing the list in detail and telling you how to sign off. If you're likely to forget, save this message in a file!

If you think about what happens when a mail reflector is in operation, you will realize that it isn't terribly efficient. If five people from the Yoyodyne corporation all subscribe to the **aliens** mail reflector at **hoople.usnd.edu**, five messages will be sent from **hoople.usnd.edu** to **yoyodyne.com** for every original message sent to **aliens@hoople.usnd.edu**. This sends unneeded, extra traffic across the Internet. There is a way to get around this suboptimal behavior and, also, make the list more responsive to local personnel changes. The system administrator for **yoyodyne.com** can create a local mail reflector that only resends messages to its employees (Figure 7-1).

Then he subscribes the **Yoyodyne** reflector's address to the national reflector at **hoople**. So, when a message gets sent to **aliens@hoople.usnd.edu**, one message is sent to **aliens@yoyodyne.com**, which resends it to the five subscribing employees.

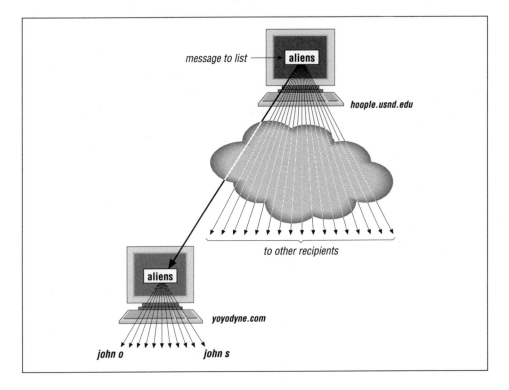

Figure 7-1: Local mail reflectors

Moderators and List Etiquette

A couple of final pieces of trivia about using mailing lists. First, some lists are *moderated*. With a moderated list, the messages are not automatically transmitted. Instead, a moderator first screens the messages to determine whether or not they are appropriate. This is usually not a big deal, but may lead to some delays in reposting. It also means that inappropriate or grossly impolite postings will be screened out—though the meaning of "inappropriate" depends on the tastes of the moderator and the expectations of the particular list.

Many mailing lists have their own etiquette rules. Some are free-for-alls, some have very strict standards about the behavior of their members. The form letter you get when subscribing will tell you what expectations the list has, if any. Be sure to obey these rules; don't make inappropriate postings.

Finally, be careful when responding to list messages. Some messages require personal responses to the original sender; for others, it's more appropriate to send your response to the list. For example, consider a meeting announcement requesting an RSVP. Your RSVP should be sent to the person requesting the information—don't expect that everyone on the list cares that you're coming. On the other hand, replies to requests for information of general interest (e.g., "Anyone know how to make a million dollars legally?") should probably be sent to the list. Be careful about using your mailer's **reply** command. Sometimes, your reply will go to the entire list by default; other times, replies are sent to the originator by default. Exactly what happens depends on how the mail reflector was set up. A mail reflector should set the message's **From:** line to the address of the reflector, and should insert a **Reply-To:** line containing the address of the original sender. If this is done, and if your mailer works correctly, the reply should go to the original sender. However, not all mail reflectors are set up correctly, and not all mailers handle **Reply-To:** lines properly. Only experience will tell you for sure. One thing about email lists: you'll hear about it, via email, if you do something obnoxious.

File Retrieval Using Electronic Mail

Earlier, we discussed how you can use email to send a file to someone else as a substitute for FTP. The reverse is also true in some special cases: you can, on occasion, use email to request and receive files from FTP archives. This requires a special kind of server at the FTP archive site. You send this server a special message, telling it which file you want it to send. Upon receiving this message, the server gets the file and sends it back to you through the mail. The reason for this service is, again, so that you can retrieve files even if the server is on another network (like BITNET) or over a UUCP connection. Archie, Gopher, and Veronica services are also available via email; I'll discuss these when I discuss Archie and Gopher.

There are three ways of requesting files via electronic mail:

- Specialized "Internet-style" servers that give access to a specific set of files at one location.

- Mailing list servers, like **listserv**, **majordomo**, and **almanac**, that give access to a specific set of files at one location. These are functionally equivalent to the Internet-style servers, but for historical reasons, they work differently. **listserv** is especially prevalent, since BITNET has no equivalent to FTP. Many **almanac** servers have cropped up recently.

- General FTP-mail gateways (**ftpmail** and **bitftp**). These servers allow you to send a message describing what you want to get. The server then performs anonymous FTP for you, and mails the results back. This differs from the previous two in that **ftpmail** can get any publicly available file anywhere on the Internet.

If you have access to FTP, you won't need to use these facilities; it's easier to use FTP directly.

Internet-style Servers

The first method of retrieval is used by Internet information repositories that have to be widely accessible. To get a file from one of these Internet-style servers, send a mail message to the server in which the message body containing the command **send**, followed by the name of the file you want. For example:

```
% mail mail-server@rtfm.mit.edu
Subject:
send usenet/comp.mail.misc/Inter-Network_Mail_Guide
.
Cc:
```

This message asks the machine named **rtfm** at MIT to send a copy of the file **usenet/comp.mail.misc/Inter-Network_Mail_Guide** back to the original sender (i.e., the **From:** line of the requesting message). If you don't have enough information, or if your request fails, a message with the command **help** as the body requests information about what facilities are available through that server. One common pitfall: filenames on Internet servers are usually case-sensitive, so be careful to use capital and lowercase letters appropriately; you must match the filename exactly.

Listserv-style Requests

Here you will need to be cognizant of the kind of server you are using, since there are some differences both in syntax and interpretation of the commands you give to retrieve files.

Listserv file retrieval commands

The **listserv** commands for requesting files are similar to the commands used for mailing-list maintenance. Send your request to the name **listserv**, on the machine providing the service. The message body should have lines of the form:

```
get filename filetype
```

where *filename* and *filetype* are the two components that make up an IBM/VM filename.* For example, assume you want to get a list of files that are available about BITNET network nodes. This list is in the file *bitnode filelist* and is available from the server **bitnic.bitnet**. To get the file, send the message:

```
get bitnode filelist
```

to the address **listserv@bitnic.bitnet**. There are a couple of funny things that you'll notice the first time you try to fetch something from a **listserv** server. You will receive at least two messages back: a message acknowledging the request and telling you it will be sent, and a message that contains the requested data. The data may arrive in multiple messages, because BITNET has a limit on the size of an individual message. If the file you want is too long, it will be divided into smaller chunks. Finally, with a **listserv** request, you don't have to worry about upper- and lowercase letters. **listserv** servers are not case-sensitive. All requests are converted into uppercase before being serviced.

---

*There is more about this in Chapter 6, *Moving Files: FTP*, in the section "Target: IBM/VM Systems."

Majordomo file retrieval

The commands to do file retrieval using **majordomo** are the same as those for **listserv**, with two differences.

- The files available are list-dependent.
- The filenames are case-sensitive.

On **listserv** servers, all the files available to be fetched are sitting there on the server in one big pool, so they must all have unique names. The authors of **majordomo** thought this was a problem, so **majordomo** software maintains a separate pool of files for each mailing list it maintains. This implies that the server needs two pieces of information: the name of the file and the list that it came from.

The second difference is merely a result of **Majordomo**'s UNIX background. On UNIX systems, upper- and lowercase characters are different. Therefore the file *REPORT* is a different file from *report.* You must type the filename you want exactly.

Now that the background is out of the way, we can look at the command you need:

```
get listname filename
```

Listname is the name of the mailing list, and *filename* is the file that you want sent to you. You put this in the body of the mail message and send it off, just as you would with **listserv**.

Almanac file retrieval

almanac servers work a little differently than the others. **almanac** servers are organized in terms of topic-oriented "folders." To get a list of the folders available at an **almanac** server, send the following message to the server:

```
send catalog
```

Folders can have many files (and other folders) within them. Once you know what folders are available, you need to look inside the folders that interest you. To do so, send a command like:

```
send foldername catalog
```

Finally, when you have a catalog that contains a file you want, send a request like this to get the file:

```
send foldername filename
```

For example, to receive the document named *0001* from the folder *ers-reports*, send the command:

```
send ers-reports 0001
```

Many folders and files have aliases, or shortened names that make requests more convenient. The catalog will show any aliases that are available. Aliases can be used instead of the file or folder name. You can also use wildcards to request multiple files or groups of files: for example,

```
send ers-reports "*"
```

retrieves all the files in the folder *ers-reports*. Beware—commands like this may retrieve many, many files. If you are paying for connection time, you may have a big bill!

For more information about what **almanac** does, send it a "help" message.

The FTPmail Application Gateway

You can also request a file through email by using an FTP application gateway called **ftpmail**. **ftpmail** may be used to retrieve files from any **ftp** server on the Internet. Requests to use the **ftpmail** service are made by sending messages to an **ftpmail** server. The original server was **ftpmail@decwrl.dec.com**, but several more have appeared; we'll give you a list of known servers later. The server includes your subject text in the mail it returns to you, but otherwise ignores it—so you can use the subject line for your own reference. For example, let's assume that you are really into juggling and want to get a copy of the Juggling FAQ, available in the directory */pub/juggling* on the computer **cogsci.indiana.edu**. You might do the following:

```
% mail ftpmail@decwrl.dec.com
Subject: juggling FAQ
connect cogsci.indiana.edu      ftp from this computer
chdir pub/juggling              move to target directory
get FAQ                         request the file
quit
.
Cc:
```

You can get complete information about how to use **ftpmail** by sending it a message with the single word "help" in the body, but some of the more useful commands are listed here:

connect *hostname login password*

Specifies the host to contact. Each request must have one **connect** statement in it. If you don't list a *hostname* with the command, **ftpmail** assumes that the file is located on the host **gatekeeper.dec.com** (which isn't a very good assumption). *login* and *password* are optional. If they are not given, they default to "anonymous" and your email address.

binary Specifies that the files are binary and should be encoded into ASCII before being transmitted. By default, the files are encoded with the **btoa** utility.

uuencode Specifies that binary files should be encoded with **uuencode** rather than **btoa**.

compress   Specifies that binary files should be compressed with the UNIX **compress** utility.

chdir *directory*

Change to the specified *directory* when the **ftp** connection is made to the server computer.

dir *directory*

Return a directory listing of the specified *directory*. If none is specified, return a listing of the current directory.

get *file*   Specifies the *file* to be sent to you from the **ftp** server via electronic mail.

chunksize *number*

Specifies the maximum number of characters which will be sent in any one message. If a message is larger than the number specified (the default is 64000), the file is split into as many messages as required for transmission. When you receive all the pieces, you have to reassemble them in order.

quit   Tells the server to terminate the request.

The **ftpmail** utility will be quite happy to mail you any file. It's up to you to tell it if it should treat it as a binary file or not. If it is binary and you don't tell it so, what you get will be useless.

Other FTPmail Servers

The original FTPmail server at **decwrl.dec.com** is very heavily loaded—obviously because it fulfills a need. However, it may take days for it to respond. Their help file says that it may take a week or more. Therefore, some other servers have appeared that you might want to try. Table 7-4 lists some FTP-email gateways we know about. It's a good idea to use a server that's close to you. In particular, avoid the European servers if you're not in Europe. It's a good idea to use a server that's located near you.

Now, how do you use these servers? Before doing anything else, get the help file. All of the servers respond to the single word "help" sent as the body of a mail message. That's the easy part.

Describing more than the help command is difficult. The problem is that the five servers we've mentioned have three different command sets! However, we can give you a couple of examples. That, plus the help file of the server you want to use, should get you started.

FTPmail to IEUnet

Here's how to get the file we retrieved earlier from the IEUnet server. Send the following message to **ftpmail@ieunet.ie**:

```
begin
send cogsci.indiana.edu:/pub/juggling/FAQ
end
```

By default, the file will come back **uuencode**d, unless you specify some other encoding with the ENCODE command. You can include several **send** comands if you want. Note that the command includes the hostname, the directory, and the filename as a single string.

BITFTP

The three BITNET servers, fortunately, have the same user interface. Here's how to get a file from them. Send the following message to **bitftp@pucc.princeton.edu**, **bitftp@vm.gmd.de**, or **bitftp@plearn.edu.pl**:

```
FTP cogsci.indiana.edu
USER anonymous
cd /pub/juggling
get FAQ
QUIT
```

You can include more **get** commands if you wish.

Table 7-4: FTPmail and BITFTP servers

Server	Location
ftpmail@decwrl.dec.com	United States
ftpmail@ieunet.ie	Ireland
bitftp@vm.gmd.de	Germany
bitftp@pucc.princeton.edu	New Jersey
bitftp@plearn.edu.pl	Poland

Taking a Break

You are well on your way to Internet competency now. Maybe you ought to consider a vacation. After all, lots of other net-citizens are obviously taking vacations—you've probably received a few messages like this already:

```
>From krol@uxh.cso.uiuc.edu Thu Jan  6 11:54:12 1994
Date: Thu, 6 Jan 1994 11:54:23 -0600
From: krol@ux1.cso.uiuc.edu
Subject: Out of town
X-Sender: vacation program
Precedence: bulk
Apparently-To: johnb@yoyodyne.com
```

```
I will be out of town for the next week.
In case of emergency contact my secretary
at secretary@maced.cso.uiuc.edu
```

These messages are the result of a UNIX program called **vacation**. **vacation**'s job is simple; it replies to incoming mail automatically when you're away. If you're a UNIX user and your system administrator allows it, you can also use **vacation** to generate automatic responses.

To set **vacation** up, you have to do three things. All of these things need to be done in the home directory of the account where you read your mail. First, you run a database initialization program:

```
% vacation -i
```

vacation keeps a list of who sends you messages and only sends one automatic reply per person per week. This command just sets up the recordkeeping structure and reinitializes it between trips.

Second, type the message you want sent into the file *.vacation.msg* in your home directory, using the editor of your choice. The message should look something like this:

```
From: krol@ux1.cso.uiuc.edu
Subject: Out of town
X-Sender: vacation program
Precedence: bulk
I will be out of town for the next week.
In case of emergency contact my secretary
at secretary@maced.cso.uiuc.edu
```

It's a normal email message, except that it doesn't have a **To**: field. You, of course, will need to substitute your email address in the **From**: line, above. Notice the two lines **X-Sender**: and **Precedence**:. It is considered good form to insert these lines. **X-Sender**: is a comment telling the recipient that the message was automatically generated. The **Precedence**: **bulk** line tells the mail-forwarding software in the network to give this message low priority. (It's third-class mail, not express mail.)

Finally, just before you catch the plane, you need to modify your *.forward* file to look something like this:

```
\krol, "|/usr/ucb/vacation krol"
```

You need to substitute your UNIX login name for **krol** in the above example in both places. **vacation** starts processing your incoming mail as soon as you make this change.

The "vacation cookbook" I just gave only works for messages that contain **krol** in the **To**: field. If you have other email addresses, **vacation** ignores them. There are a number of options to make **vacation** respond to other messages, but that's not normally needed.

Now that you've set up **vacation**, you can relax in the sun, knowing that all the people who are making electronic demands on you will be informed that you are unavailable. When you get home, you will find all the messages you received in your mailbox, as usual, but you need to shut off **vacation** forwarding. You can do that with either of these commads:

```
% rm .forward              remove it
% mv .forward forward      rename it to forward
```

If you are going to use **vacation** rarely, you might just delete the file. If you travel a lot and anticipate switching **vacation** on and off, you might want to just change the name. Then, to turn **vacation** back on, you only need to give these commands:

```
% vacation -i              restart the database
% mv forward .forward      rename the forwarding file
```

CHAPTER EIGHT

NETWORK NEWS

Newsgroups and News System Organization
Getting Started
Reading News
Posting Articles
Summary of nn Commands and Features
A Philosophically Different Newsreader: tin

L et's say you have a question like: Where should I stay on my first trip to Disney World? or: Why won't my Western Digital Ethernet card work in my 286 machine with NCSA Telnet? or: What is wrong with my laser? It won't lase.

Wouldn't it be nice to ask the world to solve your problem? Wouldn't you like to carry on a discussion about your favorite obscure hobby with obscure hobbyists worldwide? On the surface, email discussion groups seem to provide all you could possibly want for worldwide discussions. As you get into it, however, you find that there is a problem with the volume of messages. There are discussions you take part in for work, and those you participate in for recreation and enjoyment. Having these messages mixed in with the messages from the big boss, to which you need to react immediately, is an information disaster waiting to happen. Network news is a way to take part in even more discussions, yet keep them organized and separate from your mail.

News has another advantage: it's ideal for browsing and doesn't require a lot of commitment. If you're marginally interested in an obscure hobby, you can "drop in" and read up on the latest discussions once a month, or once a year. You don't have to subscribe to a mailing list, and you won't receive lots of mail that's only vaguely interesting—which, at best, you'll have to delete. Of course, something about network news turns lots of these "marginal interests" into all-consuming passions. If electronic mail is the application that forces people to use the Internet the first time, net news is the application that keeps them coming back.

Network news is the Internet equivalent of a discussion group or a "bulletin board system" (BBS) like those on CompuServe or private dial-up facilities. To the user, network news organizes discussions under a set of broad headings called *newsgroups*. A newsreading program presents those discussions in an orderly way: a menu of classical music discussions, followed by a menu of pencil collecting discussions, followed by a menu of chemical engineering items, etc. Inside each newsgroup, there are usually multiple discussions going on under specific subjects. In the classical music newsgroup, you might see discussions of Beethoven's Ninth

Symphony, breaking in reeds for an oboe, and Bach's children. All of these discussions will be going on simultaneously. The newsreader helps you keep everything in order. It keeps track of the items you have already seen and only displays new items that have arrived since your last session. Once the newsreader has shown you what articles are available for any topic, you can select and read the items that interest you. If you forget where you have seen something, you can search for an article based on its author, subject, or an author-given synopsis. You can also set up your newsreader to view or discard certain items automatically, based on the author's name or the article's subject.

As with most Internet applications, there are many newsreading programs from which you can choose. On UNIX systems, the most common newsreaders are probably **rn**, **trn**, **nn**, and **tin**:

- **rn** is one of the oldest readers that's still in widespread use. I've chosen not to discuss it; it lacks a few important features, so you might find it frustrating. **rn** was written before there was much news flowing around. It assumes that you want to read most items that come along in the groups to which you are subscribed. Now, there is so much news flowing that it is easy to get inundated with stuff you don't care about.

- **trn** is a descendant of **rn** that supports *threads*; i.e., it lets you read news items in order within a topic. A more thorough discussion of threads comes later. We won't discuss **trn** either, though it's a good, modern newsreader.

- I will use **nn** to illustrate the features of the news system. It has a good set of features and was designed to be used in a busy news environment. It has become very popular among UNIX users.

- **tin** is the "new kid on the block"—that is, the newest of the four readers I've listed. It seems to be particularly popular among new users; many people feel that it's easy to use, but it doesn't sacrifice any of the functionality you get with **nn**. Because it's become quite popular in a short time, I've ended this chapter with an introduction to **tin**.

There tend to be a lot of similarities between different newsreaders, so looking at the commands and features of **nn** will give you a start on whatever newsreader you finally decide to use.* Despite these similarities, nowhere on the Internet are religious wars so evident as when discussing which newsreader is best. Ignore these arguments. The important thing is not whether or not you use **nn**, **trn**, **tin**, or some other program, but rather that you use a reader that supports threads. This feature separates the cream from the milk. **nn**, **trn**, and **tin** all support threads, as do other readers.

Newsreaders differ in how they organize and present the news. Which is best for you is a personal matter. Some people like to read magazines cover-to-cover, and some people pick and choose articles. The same is true of the news. **nn** is a "cover

---

*****nn** is a very complicated program; its entry in the UNIX reference manual is over 50 pages long, significantly longer than this chapter. Therefore, we won't pretend to discuss all of **nn**'s features; we are only introducing you to the "important" ones.

to cover" kind of a reader. If that's not your style, you might be interested in the **tin** program, which gives you a bit more freedom to jump around according to your whims.

Newsgroups and News System Organization

Newsgroups are organized hierarchically, with the broadest grouping first in the name, followed by an arbitrary number of subgroupings. The name of each group is separated from its *parent* and its *subgroups* by a period (.), a notation you're probably familiar with by now. So:

rec.music.folk

is a *recreational* discussion, one which most people take part in for fun, in the general category of *music*. Specifically, it's a discussion of *folk* music.

Now the big question: "Just what newsgroups are available to me?" The answer is, of course, "It depends." It depends mostly on what computer your newsreader uses for its news server. To understand this, we need to look a little at how news works. Figure 8-1 shows what the news system looks like to users. There is a *newsreader*, which interrogates a news server to receive menus of articles, and calls for the articles themselves as required. The server collects news from a number of places: USENET, local news sources, mail reflectors, and Clarinet. It holds these articles for a certain pre-set period (controlled by the server's administrator) and eventually discards them.

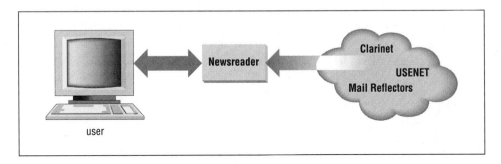

Figure 8-1: User's view of the news system

Most of the server's newsgroups come as part of *USENET*, a set of newsgroups generally considered to be of interest globally, and free. USENET is one of the most misunderstood concepts around. It is not a computer network. It does not require the Internet. It is not software. It is a set of voluntary rules for passing and maintaining newsgroups. Also, it is a set of volunteers who use and respect those rules. (If you want the whole story, get the article "What Is USENET" that's listed under "USENET News" in the *Resource Catalog*.) USENET is made up of seven well-managed newsgroup categories. The rules for how to use, create, and delete groups have been around since before the Internet. (Yes, USENET predates the Internet; in those days, news was passed via regular dial-up connections. There are still many sites that participate in USENET in this fashion.) The seven major news categories are:

comp   Computer science and related topics. This includes computer science proper, software sources, information on hardware and software systems, and topics of general interest.

news   Groups concerned with the news network and news software. This includes the important groups *news.newusers.questions* (questions from new users) and *news.announce.newusers* (important information for new users). If you are new to USENET, you should read these for a while.

rec   Groups discussing hobbies, recreational activities, and the arts.

sci   Groups discussing scientific research and applications (other than computer science). This includes newsgroups for many of the established scientific and engineering disciplines, including some social sciences.

soc   Groups that address social issues, where social can mean politically relevant or socializing, or anything in between.

talk   The *talk* groups are a forum for debate on controversial topics. The discussions tend to be long-winded and unresolved. This is where to go if you want to argue about religion.

misc   Anything that doesn't fit into the above categories, or that fits into several categories. It's worth knowing about *misc.jobs* (jobs wanted and offered) and *misc.forsale* (just what it says).

Servers may also have newsgroups they create locally. Any server administrator can create whatever groups he or she likes, corresponding to the interests of the server's users. These might include discussions of campus events, local network outages, and employee announcements. Although these are local groups, they can still be passed to other servers that want to carry them. In a large corporation, each department might have its own news server; the servers would be able to pass the employee-announcements group between themselves. Of course, the servers wouldn't pass groups like this to the outside world. Local newsgroups are named by the local server's administrator, who must choose names that don't conflict with other newsgroups.

Now we start getting to the confusing part. To a user, the news system looks like Figure 8-1. In actuality, it is implemented as shown in Figure 8-2. A server's administrator makes bilateral agreements with other administrators to transfer certain newsgroups, usually over the Internet, between each other. A site that provides your server with one or more newsgroups is known as a *news feed*. Certain servers will provide feeds for some groups, other servers for other groups. A server administrator may make any arrangements for news feeds from any servers that are necessary to provide the set of groups to be offered. Over the years, this has caused some useful local groups to be distributed almost as widely as the core USENET groups.

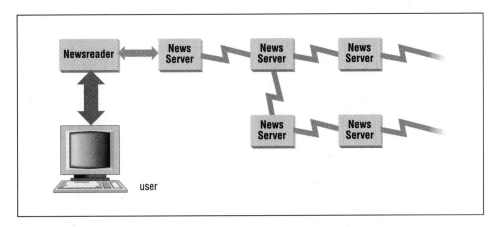

Figure 8-2: Implementation of the news system

These widespread local groups are known as "alternative newsgroup hierarchies."* Since they look like the USENET newsgroups (except that they have different names), the term USENET is frequently expanded to include these groups as well. The most common alternative newsgroups are:

alt   Groups that discuss "alternative ways of looking at things." There are a lot of truly bizarre newsgroups here (including one that tracks the wanderings of an itinerant West-coast evangelist). In a few groups, the postings lack any coherence at all, and make you wonder what, er, stimulants were influencing the authors. However, there is also a lot of useful information. Some important groups (like *alt.gopher*) were created here rather than going through the voting process required to create an "official" newsgroup. (These groups sometimes migrate to official newsgroups as their topics gain acceptance.) On the whole, though, discussions tend to be out of the mainstream.

bionet   Groups of interest to biologists

bit   The most popular BITNET *listserv* discussion groups

biz   Discussions related to business. This newsgroup hierarchy allows postings of advertisements or other marketing materials; such activity is not allowed in other groups.

de   Technical, recreational, and social discussions in German

*If you are interested in a complete list of all official and alternative newsgroup hierarchies, you might check out the newsgroup *news.groups*. These lists are posted regularly there. If you use **nn**, give the command **nn -x -X -n/"David C Law" news.groups** to get these lists, plus a bit more.

fj	Technical, recreational, and social discussions in Japanese (some require software to display the Kanji character set)
hepnet	Discussions primarily of interest to the High Energy Physics community
ieee	Discussions related to the IEEE (Institute of Electronic and Electrical Engineers)
info	A group of mailing lists on a wide variety of topics, which are transformed into newsgroups
gnu	Discussions related to the Free Software Foundation (FSF) and its GNU project. This includes announcements of new FSF software, new developments to old software, bug reports, and questions and discussion by users of the Foundation's tools.
k12	A group dedicated to teachers and students, kindergarten through high school
relcom	Various groups originating in the former USSR (some require special software to display the Cyrillic alphabet)
u3b	Discussions related to the AT&T 3B computer series
vmsnet	Discussions of Digital Equipment's VAX/VMS operating system and DECnet

Several of these groups are *gatewayed*: in particular, the *bit*, *info*, and *gnu* groups. This is another way of creating newsgroups. The output of a mail reflector or a list server can be converted into a newsgroup. This allows people who would rather use the organizational facilities of news to take part in a mail reflector-style discussion without subscribing to the mailing list themselves. A few computers subscribe to a mailing list, reformat the mail so it's appropriate for the news system, and then distribute it to anyone who wants a news feed.

Finally, several commercial information services are distributed via network news. One example of this is *Clarinet*, which is a news hierarchy that broadcasts articles from the traditional wire services, plus syndicated columns. For a server to offer this service, the organization that owns it must contract with Clarinet for the service; this contract places limits on where the server can distribute the Clarinet newsgroups. The distribution is usually limited to a particular corporation, campus, or work group. These newsgroups are prefixed by the header *clari*.

All of these groups generate an amazing amount of network traffic; a typical server subscribes to over 2500 newsgroups and receives about 50 Megabytes/day. This leads to other limitations on which newsgroups are available from any particular server. A server administrator may choose not to accept a certain group because it is very active and eats up too much disk space. This also limits the amount of time old news items will reside on a server. It's possible to go back and read news items you passed by earlier, provided that the server hasn't yet deleted (or *expired*) the article. The amount of time that any article remains on the system depends entirely on how long the administrator feels those items can be stored. It varies from a few days to months and may be different for each group. This also means that if you go away on vacation, some items may come and go before you get a chance to read them. Luckily, many important work-related newsgroups have their conversations archived at various places. The locations of these archives are usually announced via the group.

Last, we must deal with (how can I write this delicately?) censorship. Some administrators decide that some groups (especially in the *alt* category) are not for consumption by the server's clientele. So they choose not to carry them. If you are offended, you have two choices: find another server or beat up on your administrator.

This point is very fuzzy and leads to much animated discussion about basic freedoms. There are many reasons that an administrator might decide not to offer a group; strictly speaking, censorship usually isn't among them. A server administrator is the steward of a machine. That computer is owned by someone, and it has a purpose, aside from being a news server. The administrator walks a fine line between accepting as many newsgroups as possible and not diverting too many machine resources to news. If you look at this logically, on most servers (other than perhaps at the Kinsey Institute) the group *sci.engr.chem* has a lot more to do with the machine's intended purpose than *alt.sex*. Hence, if disk space runs low, the group to be cut is *alt.sex*. If you use that machine as a news server, you are using someone else's property. There is no basic freedom to use other people's property. You can suggest that *alt.sex* (or any other group) be carried, but not demand it.

Getting Started

This is probably the hardest part. The biggest problem with starting to read the newsgroups is that your client software has no idea where your interests lie. Typical network news servers offer 2500 newsgroups or so, and the first time you use a client, you are most likely subscribed to all of them. Most of them you will find uninteresting. The straightforward approach is to *unsubscribe* to the groups one by one. Obviously, this process is slow and boring: the client displays a page, you say unsubscribe, it says, "do you really want to," you say, "yes," repeat 2450 times. Clearly, there must be an easier way to start.

Some people never even bother to start—they just use standard UNIX commands to read news. They rely on the fact that on a computer running a news server, news items live in the directory */usr/spool/news*, and they just **grep** for keywords. This is OK, but from an information organization standpoint, this is even worse than using an old reader like **rn**. The biggest problem is that it can't be guaranteed to work! If you look back to Figure 8-1, the computer running the newsreader has no news files on it. Whenever you read news, it asks the computer running the server for articles. So, this approach only works if the server is running on the same system on which you are trying to read news. In the past, that was common, but it's less and less frequent these days.

Assuming you are not the type who rolls his own cigarettes and doesn't believe in power tools, you will want to use a reader. So, let's get back to a shortcut for getting started with **nn**. We're going to discuss this shortcut even before telling you how to read news; you won't *want* to read news if you don't have some control over what you read. The shortcut is very specific to the **nn** newsreader, but it may give you some insight into configuring other newsreaders correctly. Other newsreaders have different files and utilities for handling this problem; you may have to use your ingenuity to find out what works. Whatever you do, your first step will be the same: you must tell your computer which groups you want to view.

Setting Up nn

Two files govern **nn**'s action when dealing with groups: *.nn/init* and *.newsrc.* *.nn/init* is used to set configuration variables and to tell **nn** what groups you want to read (and what groups you want to ignore). Use this file to specify which groups you never want to read. The other file, *.newsrc,* keeps track of what groups you are subscribed to and what articles in each group you have read.* Use it to unsubscribe to particular groups that have not been excluded in the *init* file. Let's just start doing it step by step, explaining what is happening along the way.

1. If your home directory does not contain a subdirectory named *.nn* (you can check with **ls -a .nn**) create one with **mkdir .nn** while you are in your home directory (you can get there with a **cd** command with no arguments).

2. Using the editor of your choice, create a file in the *.nn* directory named *init* (using the **vi** editor, give the command **vi .nn/init**). The contents of the file should look like:

   ```
   sequence
   !bionet
   !gnu
   (List as many groups as required)
   ```

   The first line must be the word "sequence." Subsequent lines specify the groups that you never want to subscribe to. In this case, you are excluding any groups starting with *bionet* or *gnu.* You can add any amount of detail to get the job done. For example, if you don't care about any groups about TV that might pop up, you could add the lines:

   ```
   !alt.tv
   !rec.arts.tv
   ```

---

*On UNIX systems, just about all newsreaders use the file *.newsrc* to maintain your newsreading history.

These would exclude only those portions of the *alt* and *rec* groupings. When you have listed all the groups you don't care about, exit the editor.*

3. Issue the **nn** command. When **nn** starts, immediately type **Q**. This quits **nn**, but not before it creates the file *.newsrc*. This file lists all the groups offered by the server you are using.

4. Edit *.newsrc*. (If you are using **vi**, use the command **vi .newsrc**.) Your display should begin something like:

        alt.activism:
        alt.aquaria:
        alt.atheism:
        alt.bbs:
        alt.callahans:
        alt.co-ops:
        alt.cobol:
        alt.config:
        alt.conspiracy:
        alt.cosuard:

5. Issue a "global replace" command that turns all colons (:) into exclamation points (!). This unsubscribes you to everything by changing all colons to exclamation points. (A : after the newsgroup name flags the group as subscribed, an ! as unsubscribed.) If you're using **vi**, give a **:%s/:/!/** command.

6. Find the groups you want to participate in, either by using a search command if you know the group's name (*/name* for **vi** users), or by scrolling through the file (use CTRL-f to move down a screen at a time in **vi**). When you find a group you want to subscribe to, change the exclamation point (!) following the name back to a colon (:). By changing the ! to a :, you are flagging that group as subscribed. Repeat as necessary. For **vi** users, position the cursor over the ! and type **r:**.

7. Save the file and exit the editing session (in **vi**, the command **ZZ** does both).

You are now subscribed to those groups whose names are followed by a colon (:) and that aren't listed in the *.nn/init* file as "don't care" groups.

These instructions are a bit more extensive than is absolutely necessary to do a minimal job. You can easily do steps 1 and 2, cutting the number of groups to around 200; then use **nn** to unsubscribe to the rest, one at a time. Or you can do steps 3 through 7 to set up your current subscriptions correctly; in this case, you'll automatically be subscribed to any new groups that are created, and you'll have to get rid of them by hand. Steps 1 and 2 prevent you from subscribing automatically

---

*How do you know what groups you're not interested in? This is a chicken-and-egg problem; you don't have a newsreader running, so you can use it to tell you what's available. You can make some very broad cuts on the basis of the top-level summaries we've already given, but you might want better control. One way to find out for sure is to ask your news server. Find out the name of the news server your system uses and **telnet** to its **nntp** port with the command: **telnet your.servers.name nntp**. This command connects you to the server. You should then type the command **list newsgroups**, which will do just that. After you see all the groups fly by, exit by typing **quit**.

to newly created groups in any of the categories listed in *.nn/init.* In the long run, the complete seven-step procedure does just what you want.

Reading News

Now we're through with preliminaries: selecting the newsgroups that you're interested in. Once you're through with this somewhat messy process, you can start the fun part: reading news and creating your own news items.

What Is a News Item?

A news item is very similar to an electronic mail message. It has the same general parts as an email message: a header and a body. The body of a news item is the message's text, just as you'd expect. The header tells the news software how to distribute the item throughout the Internet and also tells you something about the item's contents. The header information is used to build an index on news servers; this index allows the clients to build menus and search for items of interest without having to pass around the complete set of articles. Thus, the header has information about the submitter, the subject, a synopsis, and some indexing keywords. The header is built when you create a new item. You needn't worry about its format, but you do need to provide the information. (The program you use to post the news will ask you for the information it needs.) You will see a header if you save an item in a file for later use, since the header is saved as well.

Each news item is considered part of a discussion *thread*. The act of creating (*posting*) a new article on a completely new topic creates a new thread. News readers who want to add their "two cents" to the discussion then make *follow-on* postings. A follow-on posting creates another article, but tells the news software that it is part of the thread created by the original posting. This allows it to be logically tied together in the presentation.

Using a Newsreader

As we said earlier, we will describe the **nn** newsreader, one of the more popular newsreaders available for UNIX. You can expect other newsreaders to have features that are more or less similar; and, no matter what the commands are, the basic tasks you want to perform (select newsgroups and individual news items, search for different topics) will be identical. Once you understand what you should be able to do, figuring out how to make your personal newsreader do it should be simple.

The **nn** newsreader has two distinct phases (or modes) of operation: the *selection* phase and the *reading* phase. In the selection phase, you are presented with a menu of news postings in a group you subscribe to, and you select the ones you really want to read. Assume I went through the laborious newsgroup selection process that we outlined, and ended up subscribing to the single group *rec.music.folk*. When I next give the command **nn**, I will get a menu like this:

```
% nn
Newsgroup: rec.music.folk          Articles: 6 of 6/1
a Mr. Chicago      19  World Cafe
b John Storm        8  >
c Willie Martin     4  >>
d John Bigboote    34  lyric request: HARD TIMES
e Jimmy Gretzky     ?  Jimmy Driftwood
f Jimmy Gretzky     ?  Guitar Strings
  -- 13:16 -- SELECT -- help:? -----All-----
```

The format of the listing is pretty simple. There is a title line at the top, telling you what newsgroup you're currently looking at. The rightmost part of the line, beginning **Articles:**, tells you there are six articles you haven't seen in this group. The **6/1** says there are six articles you haven't seen in all the groups you are subscribed to; there is only one group with unread articles. (Of course, so far you have only subscribed to one group.) At the bottom of the screen, you see a status line. This line tells you the current time; it says that you are now in selection mode; it tells you how to get help (by typing **?**); and it states that you're currently looking at the headings for all the unread articles in the newsgroup.

The middle of the listing shows entries for the selectable articles, or news items. Each line has the following format:

ID author   size   subject

The items in each line mean:

ID   A letter used to select (or unselect) a particular article for reading. For example, to select the sixth item on the screen, type **f**. If you change your mind, another **f** unselects it. On many terminals, **nn** uses reverse video or more intense lettering to highlight the items which have been selected.

author   The name of the person who posted the article. Most news senders include their login name as the name in this field. Some newsreaders allow you to post news with a *nom de plume* (e.g., Mr. Chicago above). These pseudonyms are frequently used in discussions where anonymity promotes a more complete expression of opinion (as in *alt.sex*).

size   The number of lines of text in the article. Some newsreaders fail to provide this information when posting, so you will sometimes see a **?** in the size field.

subject The subject of the article, as typed by the submitter. Notice that some subject entries have text, and some only have one or more **>** characters in that field. The lines which have textual subjects are the original postings for their thread. Lines which have a **>** are reactions or follow-on postings to the original. Multiple **>**'s flag these as follow-ons to the follow-ons. In the preceding example, item **b** is a follow-on to the original "World Cafe" posting. Item **c** is a comment on what John Storm said in item **b**.

Typing a SPACE takes you to the next step in the process. If the status line looks like this:

```
-- 09:37 -- SELECT -- help:? -----Top 6%-----
```

it is telling you that there are more articles to be scanned in selection mode; so far, you have only seen six percent of the selectable articles in this group. In this case, a SPACE gets you the next menu (the next "page") of unread articles. If you have seen all of the selection menus, typing a SPACE displays the first article that you have selected. If you haven't selected anything, typing a SPACE moves you to the next newsgroup to which you are subscribed. If you haven't subscribed to any more newsgroups, typing SPACE exits **nn**. Of course, a **?** displays a help menu; there are many more options.

Often, there will be more than a screenful of news articles to scan—particularly when you've just subscribed to a new newsgroup. To move between screens of articles, use **>** to move forward a page and **<** to move backwards.

Now, let's assume that you selected Jimmy Gretzky's second posting on Guitar Strings by typing the letter **f**. When you reached the last menu, you typed a SPACE. **nn** displays the first item you have selected, one page at a time. Here's Jimmy Gretzky's posting:

```
Jimmy Gretzky: Guitar Strings     Thu, 21 Nov 1991 16:24
I've been following this newsgroup for a long time, to
my knowledge there's never been a discussion of guitar
strings.  I have two primary questions:
 1. What's the brand that the good people buy?
 2. How long before a gig should you change
    your strings?
Thanks for any opinions.
-- Jimmy Gretzky   "The old axe man"

-- 13:30 --rec.music.folk-- LAST --help:?--Bot--
```

Now you're in the reading mode. Once again, there are a number of different options available; if you type a question mark to get help, you'll see the list of options available in this mode. You can read the articles you have selected by pressing the space bar until you have waded through them all. In reading mode, typing a SPACE takes you to the next page of the article you're reading, or to the next article that you have selected. If you want to move to the previous page of your current article, type BACKSPACE.

If you select multiple items to read, **nn** presents them to you in the order in which they were displayed in the menu, oldest to youngest for each thread. So, if you select an original posting with some follow-up messages, you'll see the original first, then the follow-ups. If you get bored with a long item and want to skip to the next one, use the **n** command. Sometimes, after selecting a large number of articles in a thread, you may decide that the whole thread is going nowhere and want to skip the remainder of it. To do so, use the reading mode's **k** command. It skips to the first article you have selected in a different thread.

When you have finished reading all the articles, typing SPACE takes you back to selection mode for your next subscribed newsgroup (if there are more groups waiting to be read). If you've finished all the groups, **nn** terminates normally. (Later, we will discuss a few other options.)

If you come back later and start **nn** again, you will work through a similar dialog—except that **nn** will display only news items that have arrived since your last news-reading session. This time, you might see a subject line with both a **>** and a subject heading. These are follow-on items for a thread whose original message is not displayed because you saw it in a previous session.

When you're in selection mode, you don't have to wade through an entire newsgroup menu before you start to read. The commands **X** and **Z** take you to reading mode immediately and display the first article that you selected. The only difference between the commands is that **X** says you are done selecting; when you're finished reading, you will move on to the next group. **Z** returns to the selection menu for the same group after you have read the articles.

In either reading or selection mode, if you need to quit reading before you've gone through all the groups, type the command **Q**. This command exits **nn** normally, updating the list of news items that have been displayed. When you next start **nn** after issuing a **Q**, you are given the option of starting at the beginning of your group list, or continuing where you left off. You do this in response to a question like:

```
Enter clari.biz.market.ny (1 unread)?
```

In this example, *clari.biz.market.ny* is the name of the group you were reading when you quit. Answer **y** to the question, and you are placed back in this group. Answer **n**, and you start at the beginning of the groups you normally read.

Steering a Newsreader

The last section took you through a typical reading session and showed you some of the turns you might take in the process. Now that you have been introduced to newsreading, let's talk about navigating. As you come back to news time and time again, your biggest problem will be the amount of information that's there for the taking. There's so much information that it's difficult to know where to step without getting caught in the tar pits. How can you move back and forth to read the material that interests you, ignoring material that looks interesting but really isn't?

When you're in **nn**'s selection mode, you can:

- Go forward and back between groups
- Go forward and back within the selection menus of a single group

- Go to reading mode

- Quit

When trying to move around in **nn**, or in any newsreader, it's important to think about what mode and group are you in, and where you want to go next. Groups are presented in the same order each time you enter **nn**. You will get a feel for when a group will be presented in the normal course of events. If you want to leave the current group and skip forward to the next, type **N**. Type **P** to return to a group that you've previously read or skipped over.

If you want to stay in the same group, you can page back and forth in selection menus with **<** and **>**. Once you have selected a few things, you needn't page all the way through the menu before reading. We've already mentioned the **Z** and **X** commands, which allow you to jump to reading mode directly. Use **Z** if you want to return to the same group after reading what you have already selected. **X** allows you to read, but will finish the group normally and after reading move on to the next group.

Similar options are available in reading mode as well. You can move back and forth between articles with the **n** and **p** commands. You can page forward and back within an article with SPACE and BACKSPACE. And, even if you have said you never want to return to selection mode for this group again (with an **X**), you can get back there with an equal sign (**=**).

If you want to jump immediately to a particular group (perhaps a group you're not subscribed to), use the **G** (go to) command. After you type **G**, you'll see the prompt:

```
Group or Folder (+./~ %-sneN) █
```

Forget about the complicated sequence of letters. Type the name of a newsgroup, followed by RETURN. Alternately, type the name of a file of news articles that you've saved. (The next section describes how to save articles.) In our case, we'll jump to the group *rec.music.folk*. Next, we're asked how many articles we want:

```
Number of Articles (uasne)  (a) █
```

u means all unread articles, and **a** means all articles, whether or not you've read them. You can also type a number, saying how many articles you want to select from; **nn** will pick the most recent. If you just press RETURN without doing anything, you'll get the default (in this case, all articles—though it may be different on your system). After you type RETURN, **nn** puts you into the article-selection menu to pick the articles you want to read.

All of the commands described here (and more) are listed following our discussion of **nn**.

Saving News Articles

After reading a news article, you will often want to print it, mail it to someone, or just save it for later. You can save a file while you're in reading mode by entering the **s** command, which appends the current item to the end of a file. In response to an **s**, **nn** suggests a filename, which it forms by taking the full name of the newsgroup you're reading; turning the dots into slashes; and interpreting the whole mess as a filename, within your *News* directory. This sounds confusing, but in practice it's not bad. If you want to save an article while reading *rec.music.folk*, **nn** generates the path *~/News/rec/music/folk*—or, equivalently, *+/rec/music/folk*. (~ is a UNIX abbreviation for your home directory; + is the newsreader's abbreviation for *~/News*.) This is a great filename for archiving, because it keeps saved entries from the various newsgroups separate in an orderly set of files.

```
Save on (+~|) +rec/music/folk █
```

To accept this filename and store the article, type RETURN. If there's already an article in *News/rec/music/folk*, **nn** adds the new article after whatever's already there; you won't lose any old articles.

If you'd rather use a different name for the file, backspace until you erase the portion of the string you want to replace. Since the + represents your *News* directory, it's a good place to save news articles, so we'll keep it. But we want a simpler filename: just *guitar*. So we delete *rec/music/folk* and then type our new name after the +:

```
Save on (+~|) +guitar
```

When you are satisfied with the name, hit a carriage return. In this case, the news item is appended to the file *guitar* in your *News* directory. If the file does not exist, **nn** asks you to confirm that you really want to create it:

```
Create /home/krol/News/"guitar" ?
```

You can respond with a **y** or **n** as appropriate. **nn** creates any directories it needs to in order to create the file as requested.

You can use **nn** to read the articles you've saved by using the **G** (goto) command. If you've used **nn**'s default filenames, this is particularly easy. Type **G**; when **nn** asks you for a newsgroup or a folder, respond with the pathname of the saved articles you want to open. You can use the + shorthand for "the News directory of your home directory." For example, let's revisit the file we just saved. When you type **G**, you'll see the prompt:

```
Group or Folder (+./~ %=sneN) █
```

When you type +, **nn** realizes you want a folder; you'll see this:

```
Folder +█
```

Then type **guitar**, followed by RETURN, and you're done. You can also use abbreviations like ~ (your home directory) and . (the current directory). You *can't* type a filename (i.e., something starting with a letter) by itself. If **nn** sees a character first, it assumes you're typing a newsgroup name. If these rules seem unnecessarily complicated, perhaps they are. Keep all your articles in a *News* directory, use + all the time, and you won't need to remember them.

It's possible for an administrator to set up **nn** to use different default file-naming schemes. The first time you save an article with **nn**, watch carefully to make sure the filename it picks is what you expect. If it isn't, you can change the filename to something you like better—but it's better to figure out the administrator's naming conventions. Fighting system-wide defaults is always a pain.

Controlling What You Read

There are few needles in the haystack. For every news item that's truly worth reading, there are many that are a waste of time: either they're on a topic that's completely uninteresting, or an initially-intelligent discussion has degenerated into name-calling, or it's clear the participants didn't know what they were talking about in the first place. So you shouldn't be surprised to learn that all newsreaders support some commands to limit the number of articles that are inflicted on you.

Subscribing and unsubscribing

At the beginning of this chapter, we took you through a relatively laborious procedure for limiting the number of newsgroups that you read. We said that you subscribed to a limited number of groups (out of the many that are available). Just as with a magazine, you can change your subscription status at any time: you can subscribe to new groups and unsubscribe to groups you're currently receiving.

Subscribing and unsubscribing are done with the U command while viewing the group's selection menu. If you are subscribed to the group *alt.callahans*, issuing a U will unsubscribe you with the following dialog:

```
Unsubscribe to alt.callahans ?
```

If you answer **y**, **nn** unsubscribes you.

Subscribing presents an obvious problem: if you haven't yet subscribed, how do you view the selection menu in the first place? The easiest way to do this is to start a separate **nn** session with some command-line options.* You can tell **nn** to read a group, even though you aren't subscribed to it, by starting it with the command-line option **-X**. Start **nn** with the command:

```
% nn -X group-list
```

If you do this, you will read the specified groups in the normal fashion. For example, to subscribe to the group *alt.callahans*, type the command:

```
% nn -X alt.callahans
```

---

*There are other ways. You can also move to unsubscribed groups using the G command. This isn't an **nn** manual, and using G has more side effects.

You will see the selection menu for this group's unread articles. If you now enter the U command, the response will be:

```
Already unsubscribed. Resubscribe to alt.callahans ?
```

Answering with a **y** resubscribes you. If you list groups on the command line, **nn** reads only those groups in this session; you won't see the other groups that you've subscribed to. So you see only *alt.callahans* this time, but the next time you enter normally with **nn**, the newly subscribed group appears in its normal place.

By the way, **-X** is useful if you want to "look in" on a group periodically, without subscribing to it. For example, you might want to read *rec.arts.poems* once a year, but you don't want to read it regularly, and you don't want it cluttering up your selection menus. Don't bother to subscribe to it; just invoke **nn -X rec.arts.poems** when the urge strikes.

Killing and auto-selecting items

Killing means automatically ignoring some postings within a group. You specify certain criteria. If an article meets the criteria, the newsreader ignores it when building the selection menu; you never see it. Auto-selection is the opposite of killing. You set some criteria. If an article meets the criteria, the newsreader automatically selects the article for you when it presents the selection menu. Killing is far more frequently used. This is because judicious use of kill criteria saves you time. There are fewer items to scan, and it takes less time to transmit menus. In this section, we will concentrate on killing. The process for auto-selection is almost identical.

In **nn**, setting kill criteria is done in either mode. You give the newsreader a word or a phrase to search for,* and tell the newsreader whether you want to kill based on the message's contents (as given in the subject field), or the author. **nn** saves this search string in one of your startup files. In the future, whenever **nn** creates its lists of interesting articles, it will check each article to see whether or not it matches one of the kill criteria. If it does, the newsreader will ignore the article. (Likewise, if you have specified auto-select criteria, **nn** will automatically select those articles for you.)

How does this work? Let's say you are reading *rec.humor*, and you see this selection menu:

```
Newsgroup: rec.humor          Articles: 671 of 671/1

  a willie martin     9  >>>racial
  b aaly055           ?  >>>>
  c Peter Johnson    39  >
  d M K T            30  >>>
  e M K T            13  >>>
```

---

*In practice, this can be any string; indeed, it can be a full UNIX "regular expression." If you're not a heavy-duty UNIX user and don't want to learn about regular expressions, just search for words or phrases.

```
 f Earl Butz         18  >>>
 ...
 -- 10:07 -- SELECT -- help:? -----11%-----
```

You decide you don't like racial jokes, so you want to suppress their display. Type the command **K**, which is used for *both* killing and auto-selecting. **nn** returns with:

```
AUTO (k)ill or (s)elect (CR => Kill subject 30 days) █
```

At this point, you have three choices. Type **k** to enter a slightly longer dialog about killing the topic; type **s** to enter a similar dialog about auto-selecting the topic; and type RETURN for a "shorthand kill." The shorthand kill uses the subject of a displayed item and remains in effect for 30 days. If you enter a carriage return, **nn** asks:

```
AUTO (k)ill or (s)elect (CR => Kill subject 30 days)
from article: a
```

to which you respond with an **a**, saying "don't let me see any articles with the same subject as article **a**." Now, for the next 30 days, any items which are part of that thread are ignored.

In this case, you decide the default criteria are not strong enough. If someone posts a new joke with the subject "Racial Joke", you will still see it, because it doesn't match your kill criterion exactly. You really want to suppress permanently any item with the word "racial" in its subject. To do this, start out with the command **K**, but don't type a RETURN; instead, enter a **k**, and the dialog continues:

```
AUTO (k)ill or (s)elect (CR => Kill subject 30 days)k
AUTO KILL on (s)ubject or (n)ame (s) s
KILL Subject: (/)racial
KILL in (g)roup 'rec.humor' or in (a)ll groups (g)g
Lifetime of entry in days (p)ermanent   (30)p
CONFIRM KILL Subject perm: racial y
```

The dialog is fairly self-explanatory, but a few points should be explained. Note that **nn** gives you the option of killing the subject either in this group only, or in all groups. Since you may want to read about racial bias in *soc.politics*, you choose to restrict the suppression to the group *rec.humor.*

The newsreader also lets you set the lifetime of the kill: it can be permanent (i.e., forever), or for a fixed period (by default, 30 days). You may wonder why anyone would want a non-permanent kill—with racial jokes, you probably do want to banish them permanently. However, there are other reasons for killing articles where the same considerations don't apply. You may be generally interested in the subject, but you're not interested in the current discussion. For example, you, being quite the rocket scientist, enjoy reading *rec.models.rocketry*. An article with the subject "Designing rocket motors" appears, and you think "great." However, when you start to read the thread, you find out that it is really basic stuff, and you're just not interested. You don't want to ignore articles on rocket motor design forever; you just want to wait for the current thread to die. Although it's anybody's guess how long a particular discussion will last, a 30-day kill is appropriate.

Aside from the racial example, there is another situation in which a permanent kill may be preferable to a temporary kill. Some groups have an internal structure. Although the group isn't divided into subgroups, the readers of the group have agreed to put certain codes into their subject lines to allow their messages to be categorized easily. For example, the *rec.arts.tv.soaps* group uses codes to indicate what soap opera is being discussed. On the selection menu, it looks like this:

```
Newsgroup: rec.arts.tv.soaps        Articles: 630 of 630/1

a Sherri Lewis       42   >OLTL: Blair-ramblings
b John R. Anderson   ?    >>>>OLTL: Gabrielle's son
c M. T. Czonka       24   >>>
d S. A. Winslow      143  >>>DOOL: Friday 10th of January
e Lisa J. Huff       38   AMC: Terrence Was: The Wedding
f S. A. Winslow      18   >>>DOOL: One Stormy Night Update
g Willie Martin      50   >GH--Faison,etc.
h Willie Martin      126  >GH: More Ramblings
i Liz Wolf           ?    >DOOL : please clear some things up
j Liz Wolf           ?    >>
k Jason Castillo     15   >>
l Liz Wolf           ?    >OLD KL: Question

-- 13:33 -- SELECT -- help:? -----8%-----
```

In this example, if the only soap you are interested in discussing is "Days of Our Lives," you could auto-kill all articles that do not contain the string "DOOL" in their subject.

If a newsgroup has established conventions like this, someone regularly posts a key showing which flag strings to use.

Catching Up

Some time, when you are reading twenty or thirty groups regularly, you will go on vacation. You will come back to find thousands of articles in those groups waiting for you to scan. When confronted with this daunting task, you may decide that you really *do* need to read all the messages in some of those groups; but for most of them, you'd just as soon flush all of the old articles. Most newsreaders provide you with a facility to do this; it is generally called *catching up*. **nn** provides this through the command-line option **-a0**. To begin catching up, give the command:

```
% nn -a0
```

nn then responds:

```
Release 6.4.16,  Kim F. Storm, 1991

Catch-up on 2031 unread articles ?
(auto)matically (i)nteractive i

  y - mark all articles as read in current group
  n - do not update group
  r - read the group now
```

```
        U - unsubscribe to current group
        ? - this message
        q - quit

    Update bit.listserv.cdromlan (2)? (ynrU?q) y
    Update comp.dcom.lans (3)? (ynrU?q) U
    Update rec.arts.disney (12)? (ynrU?q) n
    Update rec.music.folk (1)? (ynrU?q) n
        ...
```

The first question asks whether you want to catch up automatically or interactively. An *automatic* catchup tells **nn** that you want to mark all of the unseen articles, in all groups, as read, so you won't be bothered with them again. It doesn't do anything to change your subscription status; if you were subscribed to the group before, you're still subscribed, and you'll see any future articles that arrive. To do an automatic catchup, type **auto**.

Your other alternative is an *interactive* catchup, for which you type **i**. **nn** starts by telling you the possible responses, and then proceeds through the groups you're subscribed to, one at a time. In this case, you choose to update *bit.listserv.cdrom-lan* (**y**), meaning that it marks all the messages in that group as read, but you remain subscribed to the group. You decided to unsubscribe to the group *comp.dcom.lans* (**U**), so you'll never see any messages from it again. You decided not to update the last two groups, meaning that you still want to read the articles that arrived during your vacation (**n**).

The next time we invoke **nn**, you won't see *comp.dcom.lans* at all; you unsubscribed to the group, so **nn** will skip it. You will see the newsgroup *bit.list-serv.cdromlan*, but only the new articles that have appeared since the catchup. You will also see *rec.arts.disney* and *rec.music.folk* in full, including the articles that arrived while you were away.

rot13

In an attempt to keep political pressures at bay, there is a voluntary rule that potentially offensive postings to widely-read newsgroups should be encrypted with a code called **rot13**. The intent of **rot13** isn't to keep any information confidential; it is just to prevent readers from accidentally seeing something they would rather have avoided. If you go to the trouble of decoding the message, you deserve what you get.

You are most likely to see encrypted messages in groups like *rec.humor*. Such groups are read by a wide range of people, with many different tastes. In groups in the *alt* area, where some of these same topics are commonplace, it is not needed. The easily offended should not be wandering through the *alt* groups anyway.

A posting which is in **rot13** will usually be flagged on the selection menu line:

```
 e Ed Krol          38 Joke offensive to some (rot13)
```

If you decide to live dangerously and read it, you will see a posting like this:

```
Ed Krol: Joke offensive to some  Thu, 21 Nov 1991 16:24

Lbh qvqa'g rkcrpg or gb trg
bssrafvir va cevag, qvq lbh?
------
Ed Krol    Speaking for myself not my employer
```

Now you're curious and want to see what this is all about. To read the text, you must decrypt it using the **D** command; this causes the screen to be repainted with:

```
Ed Krol: Joke offensive to some  Thu, 21 Nov 1991 16:24

You didn't expect me to get
offensive in print, did you?
------
Rq Xeby    Fcrnxvat sbe zlfrys abg zl rzcyblre
```

Notice that the entire text of the message is changed, even the signature (which was not encrypted to start with).

If you need to read some **rot13** text, and you can't figure out how to make your newsreader deal with it, you'll have to create your own decoding command. The code could be implemented with one of the coding rings found in cereal boxes. It's merely the alphabet rotated 13 letters: "a" mapped to "n", "b" to "o", "A" to "N", etc. All non-letters remain the same. (As we said, this code isn't designed to keep anything secret; it's just to allow readers to ignore offensive material.) In UNIX, this can be translated to:

```
% tr "[a-m][n-z][A-M][N-Z]" "[n-z][a-m][N-Z][A-M]"
```

So, if you're curious, save a message and use **tr** to translate it. If you're not using UNIX, you'll have to cook up your own translation command.

Posting Articles

After reading news for a while, you might get your courage up enough to take part in a discussion. There are two basic ways of taking part: adding to an existing discussion thread or starting a new discussion.

Adding to an Existing Discussion

Let's start by adding a follow-up item to an existing discussion thread. This is a bit easier, because all the work of describing the thread (i.e., building the header) is done for you. It is like replying to an electronic mail message. Remember Jimmy Gretzky's question:

```
Jimmy Gretzky: Guitar Strings    Thu, 21 Nov 1991 16:24
I've been following this newsgroup for a long time, to
my knowledge there's never been a discussion of guitar
strings.  I have two primary questions:

1. What's the brand that the good people buy?

2. How long before a gig should you change
   your strings?

Thanks for any opinions.
--
Jimmy Gretzky    "The old axe man"
```

You, being a folk guitarist from way back, see this request for comments on guitar strings and wish to respond. So, while viewing this article, you enter **f**, meaning "make a follow-on posting." Note that the **f** has a different meaning now that you are in reading mode. **nn** asks you:

```
Include original article? n
```

To which you responded "no," because nothing would be gained by including the questions. You then get popped into the **vi** editor* and can enter your reply by using normal editor commands. After you are done, you have something like this:

```
Newsgroups: rec.music.folk
Subject: Re: Guitar Strings
References: <1991Nov21.162445.17611@yoyodyne.com>

I've been playing acoustic guitar for a long time and
I've found one brand of strings that I think is the
best.  I use GHS Bright Bronze, which are the
mellowest-sounding I've ever found.
```

Save the file and exit your editing session normally (for **vi**, the command **ZZ** does both). At this point, **nn** asks you what you want to do next with the line:

```
a)bort c)c e)dit h)old m)ail r)eedit s)end v)iew w)rite
Action: (post article)
```

which gives you the option of revising your posting (**e**), chickening out (**a**), or posting what you just did (with RETURN or **s**). You hit RETURN, and your posting is on its way to the world. It will take a while for it to get there, so be patient. (There are other options, obviously, but you can go pretty far without ever using them.)

---

*If you don't like **vi**, you can give the command **setenv EDITOR emacs** (or whatever editor you like) before you start **nn** and use that editor instead.

Some newsgroups are *moderated*; that is, all items in the group are reviewed by a moderator, who relays the postings that are of genuine interest to the rest of the group. A moderated group is thus more like a magazine or journal than a free-for-all discussion. As you might expect, moderated groups have much higher "quality," albeit at the cost of spontaneity. Posting to a moderated group is no different than posting to any other group. The news servers know which groups are moderated and who moderates them; your news item will be forwarded to the appropriate moderator automatically.

Starting a New Discussion

The only difference between a follow-on posting and creating a new thread is that for a new thread, you must supply the information to fill out the header. To begin a new discussion, use the command:

```
:post
```

at any time during an **nn** session. **nn** will ask you what newsgroup you want to post to:

```
POST to group rec.music.folk
```

In this case, you typed the name of the folk music group, *rec.music.folk.* You don't have to be looking at the group, or even subscribed to it. After you type the group's name, **nn** asks you for the subject, keywords, and a summary of the article. These are the items which go in the header to allow searches. Finally, you need to tell the newsreader how far you want your posting disseminated. This exchange looks like this:

```
Subject: Is Mike Seeger Still Touring?
Keywords: traditional
Summary: Wondering if Mike Seeger is still alive
Distribution: (default 'world')
```

The first three lines (Subject, Keywords, and Summary) will be passed from news servers to the newsreaders, allowing them to build selection menus and kill or auto-select your article. Therefore, make it good. It is all the reader has to judge whether your posting is interesting or not. (The actual text of an article is only sent from a news server to a newsreader when someone selects the article for reading. Readers pick which articles they want to read on the basis of the subject, so misleading subject lines can be really annoying.)

The distribution line gives the news system some idea about how far you would like the posting passed. You should treat this as a statement of the minimum coverage required for the article. There is no guarantee that it will not be propagated farther than you think. Once you pick a distribution that goes beyond your local server, you are depending on remote servers' configurations to be correct. This is probably too optimistic.

There is no way to find out exactly what distribution lists are available for a server. There is a set of standard distributions which is available on most servers, but they describe only wide areas. They are shown in Table 8-1.

Table 8-1: Common Distribution Keywords

Keyword	Distribution area
world	Worldwide distribution (default)
att	AT&T
can	Canada
eunet	European sites
na	North America
usa	United States
IL,NY,FL . . .	The specified state

The problem comes with smaller, local distributions whose names are made up by the local server's administrator. So only your administrator can tell you for sure.

This is not quite as hopeless as it sounds. Most of the time, the default for the group is what you want. This is OK, even if it sounds too large. Newsgroup propagation is voluntarily arranged between sites, and most of the time a group of local interest is not sent too far even if you specify "world" as the distribution. The person who runs a neighboring server for the Megabucks Corporation certainly doesn't want his disk filled up with discussions about the problems with dorm rooms on a remote campus. That server will be set up to ignore the group *hoople.campuslife*.

However, you should restrict distribution if you are trying to contact local people through a worldwide group. What if you wanted to find lunch-hour running partners in your area? One way to approach the problem would be to assume that avid runners would read *rec.running* and post to this group. But *rec.running* is a worldwide group. If you posted a request for jogging partners to this group, you would probably get snide replies like "Sure, meet on the steps of Paddington Station at noon." Quite a jog. What you want to do is post to that group, but use a limited distribution: "campus," "local," "hoople," or whatever your local distribution identifiers are. Similarly, if you're offering an old car for sale, you might want to restrict distribution to your state (unless you're willing to deliver the car): for example, IL, NY, or CA.

One final word of warning about the distribution. You cannot specify a distribution that does not contain your server. For example, you can't specify a distribution of Florida while sitting on a machine in New York. This is because news is distributed by flooding: it is "poured" into the system by your server to its neighbors, and flows outward. If you specify Florida in a message that's distributed from New York, about the time it gets to New Jersey, machines start saying "Why did you give this to me?" and throw it away.

After you've specified the distribution, you've completed the header. You then begin an editing session and proceed just as you did when writing a follow-on posting. Write your message, exit your editor, and tell **nn** whether you want to abort, send, or revise your message.

Replying via Email

You sometimes want to reply to the submitter of an item privately, through electronic mail. This is useful when the comments you want to make are not of general interest, or should not be widely distributed. To make this easy, **nn** has a mail facility built into it. To invoke it, use the **r** command while reading an item. The mail interface then proceeds much like a follow-on posting. For example, if you were reading the same Jimmy Gretzky item you have been reading throughout this chapter, and you typed an **r**, you would see something like this:

```
Include original article? n
```

You are then given an editing session (using **vi** or your favorite editor) with a mail header already built:

```
To: gretzky@ux.uiuc.edu
Orig-To: gretzky@ux.uiuc.edu
Subject: Guitar Strings
Newsgroups: rec.music.folk
References: <1991Nov21.233330.1466@ux.uiuc.edu>

Are you the same Jimmy Gretzky who was in the class
of '80 at PS12 in Sheboygan?
```

Again, when you are done, exit from the editor normally. You'll return to **nn**, which will ask you:

```
a)bort e)dit h)old m)ail r)eedit s)end v)iew w)rite
Action: (send letter)
```

Of the possible responses, the most useful are to abort sending the message, send the message (a carriage return will do this, too), or edit the message again.

Other Hints and Conventions

Here are some other gems which are known to most experienced news users:

- Read before you post. Take some time getting to know both the system and the group. If you see any postings marked **FAQ** (Frequently Asked Questions), read them. These postings may be in the group itself, or they may be in the special group *news.answers*. Your question may have already been discussed *ad nauseam*, and you will look like a novice just asking it again.

- Format your postings nicely. Use a subject which is descriptive. People will choose to read your postings based on the subject. Busy people tend to have less time to read news than they would like, so they choose items which don't appear to be a waste of time. A subject like "Question" will probably be ignored because I would have to be an expert on everything to know I could answer it. Try "Guitar String Question." Never use "gotcha" subjects (e.g., "Subject: Sex", but in the body, "Now that I have your attention, I have a question about insects"). On the other end of the posting, signatures are fine but keep them short.

- Be polite. You asked a question of the network. Someone took their time to answer; a thank-you message back is appreciated. Disagreements are fine, but attacking someone personally for their postings is not good form (although common). This is known in the trade as *flaming*.

- Post and reply appropriately. Post to the smallest distribution that will get the job done. Read the whole thread before responding. If someone asks, "What's the answer?" and someone already said "The answer is 42", you don't add anything by repeating it. Some of this is inevitable because of the delays in news propagation, but avoid contributing to the problem intentionally. If the answer is not of general interest, reply by email.

- Don't automatically include the article to which you are responding. Too many times, articles get longer and longer with each response, because people include all previous discussion. The people who are reading the group chose to read your posting based on the subject. If it is a follow-on posting, they probably have read the initial postings, too (they had the same subject). Please don't make them read it again. If you want to respond point by point, edit the discussion down so only the relevant sentences are included.

- Controversy is fine, but keep it in its place. There are groups designed for pro/con discussions, and there are groups where people of a like mind meet to commiserate. Don't post anti-gun sentiments on *rec.hunting*; it won't do anything but get you tons of hate email. In any group, flag controversial opinions with IMHO (In My Humble Opinion) like "IMHO, Mossberg makes the best firearms."

- Be patient; news takes a while to be distributed. When you post something, it goes into a queue on your server; it then needs to be indexed and passed on to the rest of the world. All of this is done by background tasks on the server. So your posting won't appear on your system immediately, and may take a day to get to the rest of the world. Also, don't expect responses immediately, even by email. Some people feel guilty reading *rec.arts.disney* on company time. Therefore, a lot of people read recreational groups only on the weekend.

- The biggest problem with reading news is that there is so much, and it is all so interesting. It is easy to be enamored with it. Be selective about which groups you read. It could mean your job, your family, or your college career.

Summary of nn Commands and Features

In the following sections, we're going to summarize the **nn** commands that we have discussed. If you're not using **nn**, these lists may not be of too much value, but take heart; they do provide a "checklist" of worthwhile features.

Command-line Options

In most of the previous examples, we have assumed that you invoked **nn** with no options. In reality, the general format for invoking **nn** is:

```
% nn options group-list
```

If you specify a group-list, **nn** examines only those groups listed in this session. The groups you listed are examined only if you are subscribed to them, unless you specify the -X option. If you specify the initial part of a group name in the list, all groups in that hierarchy are examined. For example:

```
% nn -X rec.arts.
```

will show you any groups beginning with *rec.arts*. If you don't specify a group list, then all groups you are subscribed to are examined. Options control various aspects of the particular invocation. Some of the more useful ones are:

-a0   Used to catch up on all groups to which you subscribe. (Explained more fully in the "Catching Up" section of this chapter.)

-i   Makes searches of the **n** or **s** command case-sensitive, which means that uppercase letters and lowercase letters are considered different. Normally, case is ignored in matching.

-m   Displays all articles meeting other criteria (specified with other control-line options like a group list, -s, etc.) on one selection menu, rather than one menu per group. This is useful if you are searching for a particular article and don't know what group it is in. Using -m prevents **nn** from marking new items in this session as "seen."

-n*string*   Searches the groups specified in this invocation and selects items whose author name matches the string. (Think of "n" as an abbreviation for "name.") The string may either be a single word, like -nkrol, a complete name like "**ed krol**", or a search expression like -n/"ed.*" to search for all authors beginning with "ed". The search is case-insensitive, but otherwise the name has to match exactly; that is, -n"ed krol" won't match "Edward Krol".

-s*string*   Searches the groups used in this invocation and selects items whose subject matches the string. The string may either be a single word like -sgolf, a phrase like -s"u.s. **open golf scores**", or a search expression like -s/"go.*"; the latter searches for articles whose subject contains a word beginning with "go".

-x   Tells **nn** to consider all articles for display, subject to other criteria (e.g., search strings), regardless of whether you have viewed the article previously. Useful when you read an article once and later want to go back and read it again. (Use of -x prevents **nn** from marking new items in this session as seen.)

-X   Tells **nn** to consider groups even if you are not subscribed to them. Useful when you are looking for an article in groups to which you are not subscribed.

Here's an example. You remember having seen an interesting posting by John Wadsworth. However, you don't remember the newsgroup it was in. But you do know it was in a newsgroup that you regularly subscribe to. To find it, you can give the command:

```
% nn -x -n"john wadsworth"
```

We used **-x** to search all articles in all newsgroups that we have subscribed to, including articles we have already read. To make an even wider search that includes all articles in all groups, we could have done:

```
% nn -X -n"john wadsworth"
```

Given our example, this wider search isn't necessary; in fact, it's a waste of resources. We remember reading the article, so it must be in a newsgroup to which we subscribe. Therefore, **-x** is appropriate.

When would you use **-X**? Let's say someone else told you about an interesting article, but she didn't remember where it appeared. In this case, **-X** is appropriate. However, you should be judicious in the use of the **-x** and **-X** options. **-x** relaxes the limits on items within groups which are searched. **-X** suppresses limits on what groups are searched. If you use both parameters, the search looks at every news item on the server, which could take a long time. It is better if you can say, "well, I'm sure that article would have appeared in one of the 'talk' groups." Then you can give the command:

```
% nn -X -x -n"john wadsworth" talk.
```

Some Selection Mode Commands

The following list shows the most important commands available to you while in selection mode. It includes all of the commands that we have covered, and a few that we haven't. There are many additional commands that we won't mention; the commands we've listed below are certainly all you need to get going and may be all that you ever need.

lowercase letters
Select news items; type the ID letter that appears on the left side of the menu. If the news item is already selected, typing its ID letter unselects it.

space bar
Moves to the next logical step in the process of selecting or reading. If you're reading the selection menu, typing the space bar moves you forward to the next menu page, if one exists. If none exists, you move to the first selected item. When you are reading an item, pressing the space bar moves you to the next page of that item. When there are no more pages, you go to

the next item. When there are no more items, you move to the next news-group. If there are no more groups, the program terminates.

<   Moves you back a page in the menu.

>   Moves you forward a page in the menu.

G   Jump to (go to) another group or a folder of saved news messages.

K   Starts the kill dialog to suppress listing of some items (see the section "Kill-ing and Auto-selecting Items" earlier in this chapter).

N   Moves forward to the next group. Any items selected in the group you are leaving remain selected, in case you return to that group.

P   Moves backward to the previous group. Any items selected in the group you are leaving remain selected, in case you return to that group.

Q   Quits the **nn** session normally. This updates the list of items shown so you won't see articles a second time.

S   Saves the articles you have selected in a file.

U   Toggles the subscription status of the current newsgroup. If you are cur-rently subscribed, U unsubscribes you. If you are currently not a subscriber, it subscribes you.

X   Moves to reading mode if anything is selected, or to the next group if not. Marks all items on the menu as having been seen, so you won't see them again. After reading the articles, you won't return to the selection menu.

Z   Same as X, except that after reading, you **will** return to this group's selection menu.

Some Reading Mode Commands

Here are the most useful commands for reading mode. Again, we've listed all of the commands covered in the text, plus a few more; and again, there are many more commands available, but you may never need them.

space bar

    Moves down one page in the article or if on the last page of an article to the next article or menu. Note that this is different from the command used to page forward in selection mode.

backspace

    Moves up one page in the article. Note that this is different from the com-mand used to page backward in selection mode.

=   Switches back from reading mode to selection mode for the current group.

C   Cancels this article. It is a way you can retract an article you posted. People will probably see it before you retract it, so you may still catch some grief about it. This can only be used on items you submitted.

D   Decrypts an article posted in **rot13**, making it readable.

f   Starts a follow-on posting to the current article (see the section, "Adding to an Existing Discussion" earlier in this chapter).

k   Kills the remainder of the current thread. If you select an article and five follow-on articles, then decide you don't care to read them, a **k** skips those articles and any other ones in the menu for that session.

K   Enters the kill dialog to automatically ignore or select articles (see the section "Killing and Auto-selecting Items"). Remember the difference between **k** and **K**. Uppercase **K** lets you permanently kill (or auto-select) a group of articles; **k** is used to ignore follow-on articles in the current session that you don't want to bother reading.

n   Stops reading the current article and moves to reading the next selected article.

p   Stops reading the current article and moves to the previously selected article.

r   Replies to the selected item via email (see "Replying via Email" earlier in this chapter).

s   Saves the selected item in a file (see "Saving News Articles" earlier in this chapter).

U   Toggles the subscription status of the current newsgroup. If you are currently subscribed, U unsubscribes you. If you are not currently a subscriber, it subscribes you (see "Controlling What You Read" in this chapter).

Q   Quits the **nn** session normally. This updates the list of items shown so you won't see the same articles a second time.

A Philosophically Different Newsreader: tin

Although we've only discussed one newsreader, there are probably dozens out there, each doing more-or-less the same job. One reason why so many newsreaders exist is that no one reader suits everyone's habits. For example, you've seen that **nn** maintains a subscription list of groups in which you are really interested. It wants you to scan each subscribed group in a set order. You may quit before you've looked at each group, but when you return you have two options: start at the beginning or start where you left off. What if you have two distinct sets of newsgroups, those to which you must be really responsive (perhaps for work), and those which you read when you have the time (perhaps for recreation)? There are a number of ways you could do this with **nn**, but it would be like pulling teeth. It's not the way the program was meant to be used, so whatever you do, you'll be fighting against it.

tin is another popular newsreader. It does all the things **nn** does, but has a different philosophy about how to present newsgroups. We are going to introduce you to **tin**, without providing as much detail as we did for **nn**. Since you now know how to use one newsreader, you know what they all can do. If you prefer **tin**'s presentation style, our discussion will get you started. **tin** has a good built-in help facility; to get at it, type **h** at any time.

nn divides reading news into two parts, selection and reading. **tin** groups the process into three parts: group selection, thread selection, and reading. When you enter **tin**, you first see a list of all the groups to which you are subscribed:

```
          Group Selection (2585)              h=help

   1    596  alt.1d                     ?
   2    199  alt.3d                     Discussions of 3 dimensi
   3    162  alt.abortion.inequity      Paternal obligations of
   4         alt.abuse-recovery
   5   1384  alt.activism               Activities for activists
   6    291  alt.activism.d             A place to discuss issue
   7    183  alt.adoption               Adopting people.
   8     12  alt.aeffle.und.pferdle     German TV cartoon charac
   9      7  alt.alien.vampire.flonk.flonk.flonk
  10    588  alt.alien.visitors         Space Aliens on Earth!
  11     47  alt.amateur-comp           Discussion and input for
  12         alt.anarchism
  13    490  alt.angst                  Anxiety in the modern wo
  14         alt.angst.xibo.sex         Tightening the screws of
  15     36  alt.appalachian            Appalachian region aware
  16    317  alt.aquaria                The aquarium & related a

<n>=set current to n, TAB=next unread, /=search pattern, c)atchup,
g)oto, j=line down, k=line up, h)elp, m)ove, q)uit, r=toggle all/unread,
s)ubscribe, S)ub pattern, u)nsubscribe, U)nsub pattern, y)ank in/out
```

This is the group selection menu, asking which groups you want to read. Before doing anything else, notice that **tin** lists the most useful commands you can give from this screen at the bottom.

As with **nn**, since we just started reading news, we are subscribed to 2585 groups. This is too many for comfort. But, unlike other readers, **tin** gives you an easy way way to prune your subscriptions to a reasonable number. You can unsubscribe to large sets of groups at one time with the U (unsubscribe pattern) command. This command allows you to specify a "regular expression" search string; it unsubscribes you to any groups which match the string. For example, after you enter U, **tin** responds:

```
Enter regex unsubscribe pattern>
```

You then type the regular expression **alt\.***, followed by a RETURN to unsubscribe to all the *alt* newsgroups; i.e., all groups containing the string *alt.* in their name.* This single command whittles your subscription list down by a bit more than 700 groups. By repeating the process, you can get the list down to a manageable size quite easily.†

There's one trick that's worth knowing. Let's say that you've unsubscribed all the *alt* groups, but later decide you want to read *alt.aquaria*. It's hard to subscribe to a group (or even to visit it briefly) if it's not on the group selection menu—so how do you get it there? The easiest way is to type y, which "yanks" all groups that you have access to onto your menu, whether you've subscribed to them or not. You'll see a few thousand groups reappear. Subscribe to the group or groups you want, using the S command: type S, followed by the group's name (**alt.aquaria**). You can select some of these unsubscribed groups and read a few articles, just to make sure the group is something you really want. When you've finished updating your subscriptions, type y again. The second time you type y, all the unsubscribed groups will disappear. Now that you've unsubscribed to groups you never want to see, you can select the newsgroups you want to read in this **tin** session.

The group selection menu has several useful features. For each group, an index number on the left allows you to see that group's article list immediately by entering the index number, followed by a carriage return. Next to the index is the number of unread articles in that group. The numbers here are quite large, because we have not read news before. Most groups only get a few postings a day. The group name is shown next. On the right is a short, sometimes meaningful, description of the group.

Now let's read some articles. Basic use of **tin** is deceptively easy. One line on the screen is shown in reverse video; if your terminal doesn't support reverse video, **tin** uses an arrow instead:

```
        Group Selection (11)                    h=help

   1   439  misc.books.technical  Discussion of books about technical top
   2        rec.arts.sf.movies    Discussing SF motion pictures.
   3    90  rec.folk-dancing      Folk dances, dancers, and dancing.
   4    73  sci.anthropology      All aspects of studying humankind.
   5   196  sci.classics          Studying classical history, languages,
   6    62  soc.couples           Discussions for couples (cf. soc.single
   7   227  soc.culture.nordic    Discussion about culture up north.
   8    35  misc.kids.computer    The use of computers by children.
   9        fedreg.commerce
  10        sci.bio.ecology       Ecological research.
```

---

*In actuality, you said "Match the characters 'alt', followed by a period, followed by anything." In a regular expression, a period means match any one character. In this case, we need to match the period at the end of alt. So we need a way to say "I want to match a period; I don't want a period to have a special meaning." That's what the backslash does: It says "I really mean this character '.' and not some special meaning." The * on the end says to match anything from there on out. Regular expressions are fairly complex—but if you remember this little incantation, you'll be able to get by.

†If you want to, you can use the same trick we tried with **nn**: enter **tin** once to let it create your *.newsrc* file and quit immediately. Then edit the *.newsrc* file.

```
11    1  sci.anthropology.paleo

<n>=set current to n, TAB=next unread, /=search pattern, c)atchup,
g)oto, j=line down, k=line up, h)elp, m)ove, q)uit, r=toggle all/unread,
s)ubscribe, S)ub pattern, u)nsubscribe, U)nsub pattern, y)ank in/out
                    *** End of Groups ***
```

On this menu, you move between newsgroups by using the arrow keys on the keyboard. As you'd expect, the up arrow moves you to the previous newsgroup; the down arrow moves you to the next. So, if you are positioned on *misc.books.technical*, a down arrow moves you to *rec.arts.sf.movies*. A right arrow key accesses whatever is in the current position. If you are on *misc.books.technical*, you can press the right arrow to see the threads of the articles in that group:

```
      misc.books.technical (128T 154A 0K 0H R)          h=help

   1  +     4 Sale: *Cheap* Unix/dBase/Beginner's/Prog Duc Cheng
   2  + 2   numerical analysis recommendations sought   Craig Levine
   3  +     standard IGES file format                   Oren H. Hershel
   4  +     Bookstores info.                            Antonio Cleopatra
   5  + 3   Anyone know of companies that locate out o  S. Slade
   6  +     "The Unicode Standard"                      Rob Warren
   7  +     books in ascii via ftp sought               Wilbur Wright
   8  + 2   >>> Technical Books for sale (X/UNIX/C/C++  S. Slade
   9  + 3   Books on Internet needed                    Andrew Jones
  10  + 2   RAID literature                             Betty Brelin
  11  +     looking for books on FoxPro ver.2.5 (for D  Adrian Hall
  12  +     "Scientific C++" wanted, by Guido Buzzi-Fe  Calvin Hobbs
  13  + 2   books forsale                               Dilbert
  14  +     PASCAL BOOKS!!!!   DISCOUNT SALE!!!!         Jian Ng
  15  +     books for sale                              Peter Rzewski
  16  +     Books forsale                               Willie Martin

<n>=set current to n, TAB=next unread, /=search pattern, ^K)ill/select,
a)uthor search, c)atchup, j=line down, k=line up, K=mark read, l)ist
thread, |=pipe, m)ail, o=print, q)uit, r=toggle all/unread, s)ave, t)ag, w=post
```

This looks a lot like the previous screen, with a reference number on the left. The + tells you that you have not yet read this thread. Some of the threads have a number before the title, showing how many articles are in the thread. Finally, the display shows the thread's subject and the author of the first article. Like **nn**, **tin** uses the > flag to show that you've missed beginning of the thread and some responses—for an example, look at article 8.

As on the group selection menu, you navigate with the arrow keys. Pressing the right arrow key reads a thread. So if you press the right arrow key while article 1 is highlighted, you'll see something like this:

```
Fri, 22 Oct 1993 19:43:44  misc.books.technical   Thread 1 of 128
Lines 39 4 Sale: *Cheap* Unix/dBase/Beginner's/Program No responses
dcheng@poi.uhcc.Hawaii.Edu        Duc Cheng at University of Hawaii
```

SCO Xenix OS Ref. Manual $15

```
SCO Xenix Develpment Sys. Programmer's Ref. $15
Microsoft Fortran Compiler User Manual $10
Using Norton Backup Manual $6
Using Norton Desktop for Windows Manual $7
Microsoft Win386 Manual Set $5
The Whole Internet, Users Guide and Catalog $10
Quattro Pro Manual Set $18
Lotus Agenda Manual Set $18


A/UX Handbook(422 pages) was $29.95
Excel Macro for the IBM (276pages) was $21.95
Using Clarion Professional Developer (761pg) was $26.95


<n>=set current to n, TAB=next unread, /=search pattern, ^K)ill/select,
a)uthor search, B)ody search, c)atchup, f)ollowup, K=mark read,
|=pipe, m)ail, o=print, q)uit, r)eply mail, s)ave, t)ag, w=post
```

Pressing the SPACE bar pages you through the article; when you get to the last page (screen) of the article, pressing the SPACE bar displays the next article in the thread. (The down arrow does the same thing.) When you're finished with the thread, pressing the SPACE bar automatically returns you to the group's thread selection menu. If you get tired of reading this thread, you can return to thread selection by pressing the left arrow key. To jump forward to the next article in a thread, press the TAB key.

Following Up and Posting

To post a follow-up message to an existing article, press either **f** or **F** while reading the article to which you want to reply. The only difference between these commands is that **f** copies the text of the original article into the your response; **F** does not. In either case, **tin** pops you into the editor of your choice; as with **nn**, it's determined by the EDITOR environment variable. When you exit the editor, **tin** asks:

```
q)uit e)dit p)ost: p
```

If you hit a carriage return at this point, your article is sent on its way. If you decide to change the article, type **e**; **tin** starts your editor again, letting you modify your article. If you decide that silence is true wisdom, typing **q** gets you out of the mess you created.

Starting a new thread is done with the **w** command. It's similar to **nn**'s **:post** command, but there's one important difference. **:post** asks you where you want your article posted. **tin**'s **w** command posts your new thread to the currently selected group. So, if you type a **w** while reading an article in *misc.books.technical*, your new posting will be sent to the group *misc.books.technical*.

The only difference between a follow-up article and a new posting is that you'll be asked for a subject when you're making a new posting:

```
post Subject[]>
```

After all, you're starting a new thread of discussion. Enter the subject for your new thread. After providing the subject, you'll see the same dialog as before.

One thing to note: **tin** remembers the subject of your most recent post during a session. If you post another note later in the day, you may see something like:

```
post Subject[Unix Book For Sale]>
```

"Unix Book For Sale" was the subject of the last posting you made. If you want to re-use this same subject line, you only have to press RETURN.

Quitting tin

All of **tin**'s command menus have a **quit** option: just type **q** to quit. Unfortunately, this is a bit misleading. "Quit" doesn't mean "exit **tin**"; it means "exit the current operation, and go to the next higher level." For example, if you're reading an article, you need to type **q** to quit reading and return to the thread menu; then you have to type **q** again to go to the newsgroup selection menu; and **q** a third time to get out of **tin**.

So—what if you want to get out of **tin** easily? There must be an easier way. There is—type **Q**. Whatever you are doing, the **Q** command takes you all the way out.

CHAPTER NINE

FINDING FILES

How Archie Works
Contacting Archie
Using Archie With Telnet
Using Archie by Electronic Mail
Archie Using a Client
Post-processing Archie Output
Archie Under the X Window System

Historically, one of the biggest problems on the Internet has been finding what you know exists. Anonymous FTP servers sprang up early on, giving you the ability to fetch files from repositories on the network, but the existence of those files was largely communicated by interpersonal networking. Part of the apprenticeship for a network guru was knowing enough other people and attending enough conferences to find out where things were hidden. This worked just fine while the Internet was a small network used by computer professionals. Now that the Internet provides resources to the masses, the "good ole boys" network no longer works. Plenty of new users don't have access to an experienced administrator with the right contacts. And there are now so many resources online that not even the best administrator could keep track of them all. You may know that such-and-such a database or public domain program exists, but finding it is like finding the proverbial needle in the haystack.

This sounds like a job for a computer. Enter Archie, a system which allows you to search indexes to locate files that are available on public servers. It's the place you should start if you are searching for programs, data, or text files. Currently, Archie indexes about 1200 servers and 2.5 million files. You ask it either to find filenames which contain a certain search string or to suggest files whose description contains a certain word. It returns the actual filenames that meet the search criteria and the name of the servers containing those files. Once you decide which of the files is most likely to meet your needs, you can easily move the file to your computer with anonymous FTP.

First, we'll look at how Archie works. It's so amazingly simple that it took years for someone to think of it. From there, we will move to how to use Archie. Like a lot of services on the Internet, Archie can be accessed in multiple ways. It's simplest to use Archie through TELNET, using a public-access client, because you don't need any additional software. From TELNET access, we'll go to the other extreme: sending queries to Archie servers through email. Email access is useful if you're connected to some other network that only provides electronic mail access to the Internet.

Then we'll discuss using an Archie client program on your own computer. We'll focus on the simple line-oriented client program (**archie**), because you can run it on virtually any kind of computer and any kind of display. The really lucky folk have the **xarchie** client installed on their computer; it's the best Archie client around, and includes a built-in FTP client. It requires a UNIX system with a graphic display. (There are also Archie clients for PC and Macintosh systems; we won't discuss them.) Finally, you can access Archie through a service we haven't talked about yet, named Gopher. We'll discuss Gopher access to Archie in Chapter 11.

How Archie Works

If this were a murder mystery, this would be the time to unveil the killer. In the preceding chapters, I have given you all the clues necessary to build an Archie service. The answer to "whodunit?" is "some people at McGill University."*

The answer to "howdunit?" is "to ask, via the network, for people who were running servers to register them." The perpetrators run a program once a month which contacts those servers via **ftp** (Figure 9-1). When it contacts each server, it builds a directory listing of all the files on that server, using standard **ftp** commands (**ls -lR**, to be exact). When you come along some time later and say, "find me a file which contains the string 'eudora' in its filename," Archie just scans all the merged directories and sends you the filenames that match your search string, together with the names of the servers where each file is available.

This is the basic service that was created. It became obvious that some people choose strange, non-intuitive names for their files, like a filename of *MacPOPclient* for the Macintosh electronic mail program named Eudora. The Archie developers then asked for people to send information on the major packages they provide They used this information to create a service called **whatis**, a set of alternative indexing keywords for files on the network that can be used to locate software or data files even if the filename bears no resemblance to its contents. Since this service requires human intervention, it is a lot spottier, but nonetheless useful.

---

*Archie development continues, but no longer at McGill; development work now takes place at a company named Bunyip.

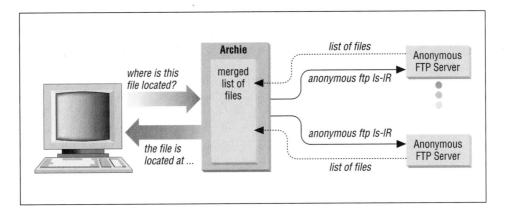

Figure 9-1: How Archie works

As Archie's usage grew, the service changed to meet the increased demand. Currently, there are many Archie servers scattered across the Internet. Each server builds an index of the FTP archives close to itself, then the servers share the information. This allows the updates to be more timely, without severely loading the network. For the most part, however, you don't care about how the system works. The mechanics are hidden from you; all you need to do is contact any Archie server (they all have the same data) and look up the data you want.

Contacting Archie

To use Archie, you must choose an Archie server. There are a number of servers, all of which are equivalent; that is, each has the same information.* You only care about picking the server that will answer your queries fastest.

Start the search for a good archie server with your service provider. If your provider recomends a particular server, try it first. Some providers set up private servers available only to their clientele. (As competition increases, service providers are offering more special services like this). If so, you're lucky: the private server will almost certainly give you excellent response. If your service provider has such an offering, it's probably mentioned in their documentation. If not, ask your system administrator, or your service provider's support staff, if there's a preferred Archie to use.

If you can't find the best archie server from documentation (and I wouldn't look too long) or word of mouth, pick one of the systems listed in the following table. The "nice" way to pick a server is to choose one that is close to you on the

---

*At least in theory. From time to time, differences between Archie servers creep in. They're usually resolved eventually; the Archie developers at Bunyip are working on ways to solve these problems. In the meantime, if you don't find what you're looking for, you can try another server—but only *after* you've made sure that everything else is correct (you're doing the right kind of search, you typed the search string correctly, etc.). The differences between servers are very minor.

network. This is not easy to do, since you probably don't know exactly where the wires providing your Internet connection go after leaving your campus or company. The best approximation you have is to pick one that is geographically close. Using a server in Australia from the U.S. might be cool, but it is a poor use of slow transoceanic network links. Table 9-1 shows a list of public Archie servers and their general locations.

Table 9-1: Available Archie Servers

Name	Suggested Usage Area
archie.au	Australia
archie.edvz.uni-linz.ac.at	Austria
archie.univie.ac.at	Austria
archie.uqam.ca	Canada
archie.funet.fi	Finland
archie.th-darmstadt.de	Germany
archie.ac.il	Israel
archie.unipi.it	Italy
archie.wide.ad.jp	Japan
archie.kr	Korea
archie.sogang.ac.kr	Korea
archie.rediris.es	Spain
archie.luth.se	Sweden
archie.switch.ch	Switzerland
archie.ncu.edu.tw	Taiwan
archie.doc.ic.ac.uk	United Kingdom
archie.unl.edu	USA
archie.internic.net	USA
archie.rutgers.edu	USA
archie.ans.net	USA (for ANS* customers)
archie.sura.net	USA

Archie is a very popular service. It is not unusual for a server to be handling over 40 requests simultaneously. In order to protect the responsiveness of the service, some servers have limits on the number of concurrent requests that can be handled. If you try to use a server and hit one of these limits, you will get a message like:

```
Due to serious overloading on the archie server,
we have been forced to restrict the number of concurrent
interactive (telnet) sessions to 10.

Connection closed by foreign host.
```

---

*ANS is one of the Internet service providers.

The actual text of the message will vary from server to server, but the intent should be clear. If everyone uses a server close to them, it naturally spreads the load around and minimizes this irritation.

Using Archie With Telnet

After you decide what server is the best one for you to use, the common way to use it is to **telnet** to that hostname. It will come back with a standard UNIX login prompt, to which you respond with the login name **archie**:

```
% telnet archie.au
Trying 139.130.4.6...
Connected to archie.au.
Escape character is '^]'.


        Welcome to Archie.AU (aka plaza.AARNet.EDU.AU)


login: archie
Last login: Tue Jan 25 21:55:05 from 143.108.1.4
SunOS Release 4.1.3: Wed Oct 20 18:12:43 EST 1993

# Message of the day from the localhost Prospero server:

NOTE: By default this version of archie returns 'au' sites only.

As usual, contact owner-archie@archie.au if you have any problems.

# Bunyip Information Systems, 1993

# Terminal type set to `vt100 24 80'.
# `erase' character is `^?'.
# `search' (type string) has the value `sub'.
Archie.au>
```

At this point, we are talking to Australia's Archie and can set parameters and make searches. This initial screen gives you a lot of information that will help with your searches. Don't ignore it. According to this screen, Archie thinks you're using a VT100-style terminal, with 24 lines that are 80 characters long; you are doing substring searches, meaning that the characters you search for can occur anywhere in the filename, ignoring case; and you will only find files on Australian computers. You can change any of these parameters, and we'll tell you how in a bit. If these conditions are all OK, you can begin searching.

When you're finished searching, you leave Archie with:

```
archie> quit
```

This terminates the TELNET session and returns you to your local computer.

Searching by Filename

The most common and reliable way to look things up in Archie is to search for likely filenames. It is reliable because you know that the information you find was correct within the past thirty days. If you find a file in the index, you will almost certainly find the same file when you go to fetch it with anonymous FTP. To begin this search, pick a minimal search string that will probably occur in a filename you are looking for. Use the command:

```
archie> prog searchstring
```

to start the search. The search string is interpreted as specified by the "set search" command.

For example, let's say someone suggested you check out the Eudora package to do electronic mail from your Apple Macintosh. You might try:

```
Archie.au> prog eudora
# Search type: sub, Domain: au.
# Your queue position: 1
# Estimated time for completion: 00:01
```

When you enter a search command, the Archie server puts you in a queue with the rest of the people trying to do searches. It tells you where you are in the queue and estimates how long will be before it can work on your request. In this case, you are first in the queue, and can expect to wait 00:01 (no minutes and one second) to get service. Don't be surprised if it takes a long time to get an answer. Most Archie servers are very heavily loaded.

After the search is complete, the server returns a list of FTP archives and filenames that fit the criteria. Eudora, being a very popular package, is offered by nine servers in Australia alone. An abbreviated listing of this search looks like:

```
Host sunb.ocs.mq.edu.au     (137.111.1.11)
Last updated 11:44 23 Jan 1994

  Location: /Mac/networking
    FILE -r-xr-xr-x 960108 bytes 06:34 28 Oct 1993 eudora-14-manual.hqx
    FILE -r-xr-xr-x 510354 bytes 06:20 28 Oct 1993 eudora-14.hqx
    FILE -r--r--r-- 263976 bytes 01:00 11 Jun 1992 eudora1.3b34.sit.hqx

Host csuvax1.murdoch.edu.au     (134.115.4.1)
Last updated 20:02 24 Jan 1994

  Location: /pub/pc/windows
    DIRECTORY drwxr-xr-x     512 bytes  14:05 11 Nov 1993  eudora

Host ftp.connect.com.au    (192.189.54.17)
Last updated 20:02 24 Jan 1994

  Location: /pub/mac
    DIRECTORY drwxr-xr-x     512 bytes  10:50 22 Nov 1993  eudora

Host ftp.utas.edu.au    (131.217.1.20)
```

```
Last updated 19:39 24 Jan 1994

  Location: /pc/win31/mail
    DIRECTORY  drwxrwxr-x      512 bytes  22:49  1 Nov 1993   eudora

  Host uniwa.uwa.edu.au    (130.95.128.1)
  Last updated 11:27 23 Jan 1994

  Location: /pub/mac/freeware
    DIRECTORY  drwxrwxr-x      512 bytes  10:22 17 Jan 1994   eudora
```

For each match it finds, Archie tells you the name of the host that offers one or more files that matched the search string. The first host in the example is **sunb.ocs.mq.edu.au**. Next Archie tells you the directory where the file resides (*/Mac/networking*), and finally, it lists the filenames within that directory (*eudora-14-manual.hqx*).

Sometimes a search will match a word in a directory path, but no filename in that directory. In that case, the location line give you the path to the directory that matched the search criterion. Instead of a line beginning with FILE, you will see a line beginning with DIRECTORY, like:

```
  Host uniwa.uwa.edu.au    (130.95.128.1)
  Last updated 11:27 23 Jan 1994

  Location: /pub/mac/freeware
    DIRECTORY  drwxrwxr-x   512 bytes  10:22 17 Jan 1994   eudora
```

This shows that what was found is a directory that might contain something useful. If you decide that this entry is promising, you'll have to use anonymous FTP to find out exactly what it contains.

Since many anonymous FTP servers have the file you want, you now face a new problem: which one to use. This is a significant problem: you find out lots about the files "out there," but you get little or no information to help you decide which file is best to use. Here are a few suggestions:

1. If the program runs on several kinds of computers, you have to decide which file contains the version you want. It turns out there are both PC/Windows and Macintosh versions of Eudora. The only help Archie gives you is in the directories and filenames. There are no standards for these names, but most server administrators try to name directories in an intuitive, descriptive way. In this example, you'll find that many copies of *eudora* reside in some sub-directory called *mac*, which probably stands for Macintosh. File that reside in directories like *pc*, *windows*, or *win31* are probably the Windows version of the package. Filename suffixes provide another clue. Certain kinds of compression and file encoding techniques are common on certain kinds of computers. In particular, *.sit* and *.hqx* are frequently used on Macintoshes. (There is a nice table of these in Chapter 6, *Moving Files: FTP.*) So *eudora-14.hqx* is probably a Macintosh file.

2. Multiple versions of the same software may be available. If you're lucky, a version number will be encoded in the filename, as in these examples:

   ```
   eudora-14.hqx
   eudora1.3b34.sit.hqx
   ```

   If some friends told you about the software, you might ask which version they are running. Otherwise, you might pick the latest version possible. Again, there are no standards for how version numbers are encoded into the filename. You could guess that 14 is a later version than 1.3, and you would almost certainly be right.* Sometimes, the directory name will be a clue. If you found directories named */mac/eudora/old* and */mac/eudora*, you might presume that the newer software is in the latter directory.

   Also, remember that the terms *alpha* and *beta* are used to denote test versions of software. Unless you are adventurous, stay clear of these.

3. Pick an official-looking server. (Remember the security discussion from Chapter 4, *What's Allowed on the Internet*.) Try to pick a server that is run by someone who should be in the business of delivering software, like a computer center, network provider, etc.

4. Finally, pick a server that is close. Earlier, we said that you should pick an Archie server that's relatively close to you, to minimize the total network traffic and spread the workload among the different servers. The same logic applies here. To encourage you to use an FTP site that's nearby, some Archie servers (like the one we're using here) only tell you about files within a certain domain—in our example, Australia. It's always possible (and sometimes necessary) to make worldwide searches, but on many servers that's not the default.

   There's one other important reason to pick an FTP server that's local. If you pick up a file from a server that's not in your native land, the file might not be in your native language. If you speak English and grab Eudora from a server in Finland, you might get a surprise: you might find that all the menus and prompts have been translated into Finnish.

If I were an Australian trying to decide from which of the sites shown in the example to get Eudora, I would probably look in the */pub/mac/eudora* on the **ftp.connect.com.au** server. First, the server is run by connect.com, a network service provider in Australia. They have an interest in distributing reliable software to their clients. I don't really know exactly what they have, since the search found only a directory, but it is the first place I would look.

I passed up the obvious choice of **sunb.ocs.mq.edu.au**, because I can't tell enough about its pedigree. It is probably a Sun workstation in "ocs", maybe in the "office of computer science" at some university, but I can't tell. If I had some knowledge

---

*In fact, *eudora-14.hqx* is version 1.4. Files aren't always named exactly as you'd expect them to be; you may need some creativity to figure out what the names mean.

of the site, I might know it was okay to get software there. Lacking that, I would steer clear of it.

Controlling Filename Matching

The discussion of Archie reflects servers running the latest version (3.1) of the Archie software. Some variables like (**match_path** and **match_domain**) may not exist in earlier versions. The basic search commands and controls will work on any version.

There are other ways to search besides the "substring ignoring case" search we did in the last section. At any time in a session you can check how the matching is done with the command:

```
archie> show search
# 'search' (type string) has the value 'exact'.
```

Different servers default to different types of searches. Some are case-sensitive, some insensitive. Some allow full UNIX regular expression searches. The above server is set to an "exact" match. This means you must match the filename exactly, including case. If you are browsing for software, this probably isn't what you want. If you are looking for the package Eudora, you usually want the search to match Eudora, eudora, or EUDORA.

You can change the way your search is conducted with the command:

```
archie> set search type
```

type indicates how Archie should conduct your search. It must be one of the following:

exact   The search string given must exactly match a filename.

regex   The search string is treated as a UNIX regular expression to match filenames.

sub   The search string matches any filename that contains it as a substring. The case is ignored when doing the matching. This is probably the most useful search type for general-purpose use.

subcase   The search string matches any filename which contains it as a substring. The case of the matching substrings must match as well.

There is no way to specify part of a directory name in the **prog** command that you use to start the search. That is, if you say, **prog eudora**, Archie will find directories and files named *eudora*. You may not say **prog pub/eudora** (*eudora* in the directory *pub*). In most cases, this is reasonable: the directory structure depends entirely on the FTP server that has the file you want. If you know the directory in which a file resides, it's a good bet that you know the server, too, and don't need Archie.

If you really want to look for a file in a specific directory, you can, but it takes two commands. First, you must specify which directories to search. You do this by setting the **match_path** variable with the command:

```
archie> set match_path path-list
```

The *path-list* is a list of strings separated by colons. One of these strings must be found in the directory path. This is always a substring match, ignoring case, regardless of the search type you have chosen. For example, let's say that you're interested in finding a PC version of the Eudora package; software for the Macintosh won't do you any good. Therefore, you'd like to restrict your search to directories named *pc* or *win31*. To make this search, give these two commands:

```
archie> set match_path pc:win31
archie> prog eudora
# Search type: sub, Domain: au, Path: win.
# Your queue position: 8
# Estimated time for completion: 01:14
working... -

Host ftp.utas.edu.au    (131.217.1.20)
Last updated 13:56  2 Feb 1994

    Location: /pc/win31/mail
       DIRECTORY    drwxrwxr-x     512 bytes  22:49  1 Nov 1993  eudora
```

   ...   *(additional matches deleted)*

The first command says that either *pc* or *win31* must occur in the complete directory name; the second command runs the search. Of course, these aren't the only directories in which you might find the software; they're only good guesses. If you don't find anything, try a broader search. Remember to give the command **unset match_path** first; the **set match_path** stays in effect until it is changed to something else, or **unset**.

Controlling a Search Geographically

The newer Archie servers allow you to restrict a search to a particular geographic area—more formally, a particular set of domains. There are a few reasons why you'd want to do this:

- In our Australian example, we noted that the server only returned information about files on servers within Australia. We won't consider the possibility that a reader in the U.S. wants to use this server; as we've said, that's impolite. However, an Australian who's looking for something obscure might need to search FTP sites world-wide.

- If you're looking for a popular piece of software, Archie may present you with a huge list of FTP archives, world-wide, where you might find it. Rather than wading through such a huge list, you might want to restrict the search to servers within your area.

- If you're looking for specialty software, you might have ideas about where to find it. For example, if you're looking for a version of Eudora that's been translated into Japanese, you're most likely to find good, up-to-date software by searching the .**jp** domain.

To restrict (or broaden) an Archie search, you use the **set match_domain** command:

```
archie>set match_domain domain-list
```

The *domain-list* is a list of all the domain suffixes you want included in the search. They are listed without a preceeding period, and separated by colons. For example, to search for files located in the United States, issue the command the following command prior to your search:

```
archie> set match_domain us:com:mil:edu:gov
```

Typing this string each time you want to do a search in a particular area could get tedious, but luckily there is a short cut. Each Archie server may have defined a list of mnemonics for groupings of commonly used domains. You can find out what mnemonics are defined on your particular server using the command **domains**, like:

```
archie> domains
Domains supported by this server:

africa          Africa          za
anzac           OZ & New Zealand au:nz
asia            Asia            kr:hk:sg:jp:cn:my:tw:in
centralamerica  Central America sv:gt:hn
easteurope      Eastern Europe  bg:hu:pl:cs:ro:si:hr
europe          Europe          westeurope:easteurope
mideast         Middle East     eg:.il:kw:sa
northamerica    North America   usa:ca:mx
scandinavia     Scandinavia     no:dk:se:fi:ee:is
southamerica    South American  ar:bo:br:cl:co:cr:cu:ec:pe:ve
usa             United States   edu:com:mil:gov:us
westeurope      Western Europe  westeurope1:westeurope2
westeurope1                     de:ie:pt:es:uk:at:fr:it:be:nl
westeurope2                     ch:cy:gr:li:lu:tr
world           The World       world1:world2
world1                          europe:scandinavia:northamerica
world2                          southamerica:mideast:africa:anzac:as
```

So, instead of typing **set match_domain us:com:mil:edu:gov**, we could have typed:

```
archie>set match_domain usa
```

Remember, the names you may use are only guaranteed to work on one particular server. Don't use the previous list as a reference; give the **domains** command to see what will work on the server you are using.

Searching the Descriptive Index

Archie also lets you search a descriptive index; this is called a **whatis** search. It searches the so-called "software descriptions database." When administrators place a file in their FTP archives, they may contribute to an index entry for the file to help people find it. The index entry creates a relationship between a filename and a set of keywords. When you do a **whatis** search, your search string is used to examine the keyword list. The search is done with the command:

```
archie> whatis searchstring
```

If the search string matches any of the keywords in the descriptive database, Archie prints the name of the files associated with the keywords. (Searches of the desriptive database are always case-insensitive substring searches, regardless of your search type). Once you have a filename that sounds appropriate, you must do a filename search to find out where it is located.

Let's say you were looking for a gene sequence map for E.Coli bacteria.* If you do a **prog coli**, Archie would return over 100 filenames. Most of the matches are obviously not what you want: the broccoli recipes, the horse colic database, etc. There are a few like *colidb* which might be good, but that's all you know. So you decide to try a **whatis** search to get more information:

```
archie> whatis coli

ECD        Escherichia coli db (M. Kroeger, Giessen)
NGDD       Normalized gene maps for E.coli, S.typh., etc.
                    (Y. Abel, Montreal)
```

The file *NGDD* looks like just what the doctor ordered. To find out where it lives you do a **prog** search, just like you did before:

```
archie> prog NGDD
# Search type: sub, Domain: edu:com:mil:gov:us.
# Your queue position: 2
# Estimated time for completion: 02:40

Host ncbi.nlm.nih.gov   (130.14.20.1)
Last updated 02:23  4 Mar 1992
  Location: /repository
    DIRECTORY rwxrwxr-x     512  Jun 25  1990    NGDD
```

This looks even more promising now. It even comes from a reliable source, the National Institute of Health (**nih.gov**). Notice, however, that what Archie found is not a file called NGDD, but a directory by that name. So you don't quite know what you really have. You need to anonymous FTP to **ncbi.nlm.nih.gov** and go to the */repository/NGDD* (**cd repository/NGDD**) directory. Once there do a **dir** command to see what files are there.

---

*As this example shows, Archie isn't just good for looking up software; it's good for finding all kinds of resources.

Remember the one caveat. The **prog** index is up to date to within 30 days. The **whatis** index is not. Someone can create an entry, and sometime later delete the file. So you may occasionally find something with **whatis**, but not be able to locate it with the **prog** command.

As time goes on, the problem with updating the descriptive database has gotten worse. The "whatis" index is depends too much on centralized human processing. So much so, that the Archie maintainers have stopped making changes to it. They have designed a new system that allows FTP system administrators to maintain their own information. Unfortunately, this new system isn't widely used yet. For now, Archie users are stuck with an index of pretty old information.*

Other Archie Commands

We talked about the **archie** commands which are used regularly. There are a number of other commands which can be useful on occasion. Here is a selection of the other commands you might need:

bugs
Displays a list of the current known bugs in the Archie system.

find
Synonym for the **prog** command.

help
Displays a list much like this one.

list *regexp*
Displays a list of anonymous FTP servers that are indexed in the Archie system. If a regular expression is specified, only servers which match the expression are displayed.

mail *destination*
Sends the result of the last search to an email address. The *destination* is optional. If given, it is taken to be an email address to which the search results should be mailed. If no destination is specified, the value of the variable **mailto** is used as the destination.

manpage
Displays the complete reference manual description of the Archie system.

set *variable value*
Used to set parameters for controlling your Archie session. The variable name is required (there is a list of variables in the next section). The value is required only if the variable is not a Boolean (on or off) variable. For Boolean variables, **set** *variable* turns the variable on. For other variables, the value is remembered and used appropriately.

---

*This new system is part of the IAFA templates work being done in the IETF. The templates are forms to be filled out by the administrator of each archive and left on the system in a specially named file. They are gathered during the archie data acquisition visit to each server, so they would be more up to date, and maintained by people much closer to the data. It is moving towards standardization, but is not there yet.

show *variable*

Displays the value of the specified variable. *variable* is optional. If it is not specified, **archie** displays the value of all variables. **show**, with no variable name, is a good way to get a list of valid variable names or to find out your server's default settings.

servers

Gets a current list of all the known **archie** servers.

unset *variable*

Turns off a Boolean variable or clears the value of a string variable.

version

Returns the version number of the Archie server you are using.

Archie Configuration Variables

Here is a partial list of the variables that can be manipulated with the **set**, **unset**, and **show** commands that are not discussed elsewhere in the text:

mailto *address*

Sets a default email address; this address is used whenever the **mail** command is given without a parameter.

match_domain

Specifies a list of top-level domains; the FTP server on which any file resides must belong to one of these domains for a match to occur. Explained more fully in the "Controlling Filename Matching" section.

match_path

Specifies a list of directory components that must be in the pathname for a match to occur. Explained more fully in the "Controlling Filename Matching" section.

maxhits *number*

Limits the amount of output to *number* entries. (*Number* must be between 1 and 1000.)

pager

XX "pager command:Archie" Determines whether the output should stop whenever the screen is full. If **pager** is set, output will be held until you enter a carriage return when the screen is full. This is a Boolean variable. Use **set pager** to turn it on, **unset pager** to turn it off).

sortby *keyword*

Declares the sort order of the output. For a list of the kinds of sorting available, try **help set sort**.

search *keyword*

Sets the search type. This was explained more fully in the "Controlling Filename Matching" section of this chapter.

term *type row col*

Declares that you are using a *type* terminal (e.g., **VT100**) which has *row* rows on the screen and *col* columns. The type can be any one of the typical terminal abbreviations available in UNIX. *row* and *col* are optional. If they are omitted, the standard size for the declared terminal type is used.

Using Archie by Electronic Mail

In addition to logging into an Archie server directly, you can use Archie via electronic mail. While it's less convenient than an interactive session, there are two reasons why you might want to use mail. First, you may be forced to: your network might not allow you to contact Archie via TELNET. This would be the case, for example, if your only connections to the outside world are through UUCP or Bitnet. Many of the servers that **archie** indexes provide access through **ftpmail** (Chapter 7, *Electronic Mail*) for those networks which can't do **ftp**. Second, you may not care to wait around for Archie to do the lookup. If you hear about something great at 4:59 and have to run for the train, send an email query—the answer will be there when you get to work the next morning. The same logic applies if Archie tells you that it's busy, or if it's unavailable for some reason.

The commands for using Archie by mail are a subset of those available using **telnet**. You build a message with search commands in it and send it to:

```
archie@server
```

where *server* is one of the servers mentioned earlier. Commands must begin in column one of a line. You can have as many commands as you like in a message. Any command which cannot be understood is interpreted as **help**. So if you do anything wrong, you get help whether you need it or not. Since interactive responsiveness is not an issue, the arguments all use more powerful search types like **regex**. You can set all of the variables (like **match_path** and **match_domain**) just as you would with the TELNET interface. You can also use any other commands that make sense in the mail environment. Here's a summary of the most common commands for the email interface:

path *email-address*	Tells **archie** to send the responses to *email-address* rather than the address given in the **From:** field of the requesting message. It is useful if you are traversing email gateways and not enough information is conveyed to Archie in the **From:** field for the return trip. If you send requests and never receive an answer, try specifying a very explicit route back to your computer and see if it helps.
compress	Causes the output sent to you to be compressed and **uuencoded** before being sent. It is suggested you use this option whenever you expect the output to exceed 45K bytes.
prog *regexp*	Looks for filenames that match the regular expression.
help	Returns a help file for mail **archie**.
list *regexp*	Returns a list of all the servers whose names match *regexp*.

servers   Returns a list of all the known Archie servers.

whatis *keyword*   Returns a list of files that match the keyword argument in
                       the **whatis** database. This can then be used in a subsequent
                       mail message with the **prog** command to look up the loca-
                       tion of these files.

quit   Causes processing to be terminated and any lines following
                       this command to be ignored. This is useful if you have a
                       signature file, which Archie might try to interpret as com-
                       mands.

For example, let's say you wanted to find an archive for the *sci.geo.meteorology*
newsgroup. Of course, since you are interested in meteorology in general, you
might also want to go fishing and see if there are any other good meteorology files
available. To do this, use your favorite mail program to construct a message like
this:

```
% mail archie@archie.rutgers.edu   use any server you like
Subject:                           no subject necessary
prog meteorology
      .
```

Some time later, you will receive a message back from the server, containing the
results:

```
>From archie-error@dorm.rutgers.edu Sat Apr 11 06:33:30 1992
Received: from dorm.rutgers.edu by ux1.cso.uiuc.edu with SMTP
Date: Sat, 11 Apr 92 07:32:35 EDT
Message-Id: <9204111132.AA04307@dorm.rutgers.edu>
From: archie@dorm.rutgers.edu
To: Ed Krol <krol@ux1.cso.uiuc.edu>
Subject: archie reply: prog meteorology
Status: R

Sorting by hostname
Search request for 'meteorology'

Host cnam.cnam.fr    (192.33.159.6)
Last updated 02:06  8 Apr 1992
 Location: /pub/Archives/comp.archives/auto
   DIRECTORY rwxr-xr-x  512  Feb  5 21:20   sci.geo.meteorology

Host earth.rs.itd.umich.edu    (141.211.164.153)
Last updated 06:48 10 Apr 1992
 Location: /mac.bin/development/libraries/MacVogl :c4/fonts
   FILE       rw------- 3034  Oct 17 06:55   meteorology

Host rtfm.mit.edu   (18.172.1.27)
Last updated 06:27 26 Mar 1992
 Location: /pub/usenet
   DIRECTORY rwxrwxr-x  512  Feb 19 01:56   sci.geo.meteorology
 ...
```

Well, you found what you were looking for at **cnam.cnam.fr** in France, and at **rtfm.mit.edu** in Massachusetts. You also seem to have come across some Macintosh fonts that might be useful in meteorology at the University of Michigan (**earth.rs.itd.umich.edu**). They could be worth playing around with!

Archie Using a Client

The most convenient way to do Archie lookups is with the **archie** command installed on your system. If you have this command available to you, you can do searches with:

```
% archie -modifiers string
```

string is the search string, as in all the other **prog** lookups we have discussed previously. The modifiers control the type of search. Some of the modifiers available to you are:

-c   Tells **archie** to return files whose names contain the search string. Uppercase and lowercase letters must match exactly.

-e   Tells **archie** to return files whose names match the search string exactly. This is the default.

-r   Tells **archie** the search string is a UNIX regular expression.

-s   Tells **archie** to return files whose names contain the search string; the case of the letters is ignored.

-l   Tells **archie** to reformat the output so it is suitable for input into another program.

-h*name*   Tells the **archie** client to use the server specified by *name* for the request. With many clients, you can set an environment variable to default this to whatever server you like to use. On UNIX, the variable to set is **ARCHIE_HOST**.

-m*number*   Tells **archie** to return no more than *number* files. If you don't specify this parameter, Archie returns at most 95 matches.

Any given request can only include one of the **-c**, **-r**, or **-s** modifiers. If **-e** is used with any of the other search switches, an exact match is tried before doing the more time-consuming search types.

Let's see if we can find the source for the **archie** command for a UNIX workstation, just in case you might want to install it yourself:

```
% archie -s -m5 archie
Host ab20.larc.nasa.gov
 Location: /usenet/comp.sources.amiga/volume89/util
   FILE -rw-rw-r--   5015  Mar 15 1989  archie.1.Z

Host nic.funet.fi
```

```
Location: /pub/archive/comp.sources.amiga/volume89/util
  FILE -rw-rw-r--   4991  Aug  1 1989  archie18.1.Z

Host wolfen.cc.uow.edu.au
  Location: /ab20/usenet/comp.sources.amiga/volume89/util
    FILE -rw-rw-r--   5015  Aug 16 1991  archie.1.Z
    FILE -rw-rw-r--   4979  Aug 16 1991  archie18.1.Z

Host wuarchive.wustl.edu
  Location: /usenet/comp.sources.amiga/volume89/util
    FILE -rw-rw-r--   5054  Mar 16 1989  archie.1.Z
```

This search says: "Search for filenames that contain 'archie', ignoring case (**-s**); return the first five files you find (**-m5**)." We found five **archie** clients but they all appear to be for Amiga computers. Since that's not what we're looking for, we'll have to issue the search again, making **-m** bigger. I'm sure you get the idea.

Post-processing Archie Output

Archie's output normally looks like the examples in this chapter. This is fine for human consumption, but occasionally you might want to take Archie's output and use it as input to another program. In this situation, it would be more convenient if all the information about each file were printed on one line, rather than on multiple lines.

Two options give you "one line per file" output formats. They are controlled by the variable **output_format**. Normally, this variable is set to **verbose**, which produces the familiar format. By setting it to **terse**, you get a one line per file output like this:

```
Archie.au> set output_format terse
Archie.au> prog eudora
# Search type: sub, Domain: au, Path: win31:pc.
# Your queue position: 1
# Estimated time for completion: 02:29
working...

tasman.cc.utas.edu.au  22:49  1 Nov 1993 512 bytes /pc/win31/mail/eudora
csuvax1.murdoch.edu.au  14:05 11 Nov 1993 512 bytes /pub/pc/windows/eudora
ftp.utas.edu.au  22:49  1 Nov 1993 512 bytes /pc/win31/mail/eudora
```

This is our same old search for Eudora for PCs and Windows in Australia. Same files, different format. The output is still fairly readable, particularly the date.

The command **set output_format machine** generates output that can be read easily by a computer, but isn't quite so convenient for humans. It gives additional information about file access modes, and displays the file's date in a numeric format. Otherwise, the output is fairly similar to what we saw above:

```
19931101224900Z tasman.cc.utas.edu.au 512 bytes drwxrwxr-x /pc/win31/mail/eudora
19931111140500Z csuvax1.murdoch.edu.au 512 bytes drwxr-xr-/pub/pc/windows/eudora
19931101224900Z ftp.utas.edu.au 512 bytes drwxrwxr-x /pc/win31/mail/eudora
```

If you are using a local **archie** client, use the –l option to get machine-readable output.

Archie Under the X Window System

The Cadillac (or, if you prefer, the Lamborghini) of Archie clients is **xarchie**.* It provides a nice graphical interface to the Archie service. In addition, it includes a built-in FTP client, so you can use **xarchie** to explore directories at FTP sites (a deficiency we've noted with the other clients we've discussed)—and even to retrieve files for you. If you're using the X Window System, this is the client to try!

We won't discuss it thoroughly, but we will show you how it's done. Starting **xarchie** is easy—just type:

```
% xarchie &
```

xarchie starts by displaying a screen like this:

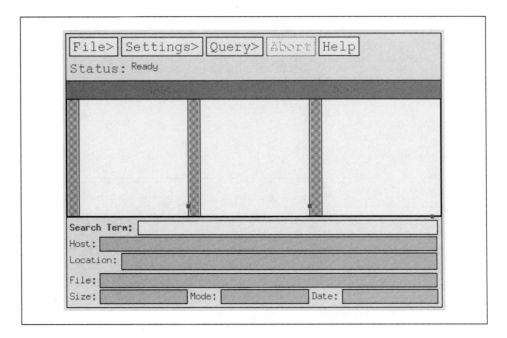

Figure 9-2: Initial xarchie screen

Doing a search is easy. Use the **Setting** pull-down menu to change any options (search type, Archie server) as appropriate. Then, put the cursor in the **Search Term** box, type the filename you want to search for, and press RETURN. Archie then fills the left column of the central display with a list of FTP sites that have

---

*Available via anonymous FTP from **ftp.cs.rochester.edu**.

matches. If Archie found more FTP sites than fit on the display, you can use the scroll bar to the left of the column to move up and down in the list. (The left mouse button scrolls down the list; the right scrolls up.) To find out specifics about the files available at any FTP site, click on that site's name. **xarchie** then displays the directories at that site that have matches in the central column. **xarchie** displays the actual match (directory or file) in the right column. If more than one directory contains matches, the right column is left blank; click on a directory in the center column to see the matches it contains.

Here's how a typical search looks. We'll find the PDIAL list, which is a list of Internet service providers. We used the **Settings>** pull-down menu to select a case-sensitive substring search (again, probably the most useful kind of search when you're looking for a file). We then typed the name *pdial* in the **Search Term** field, followed by a RETURN. After waiting for **xarchie** to do the lookup, we see:

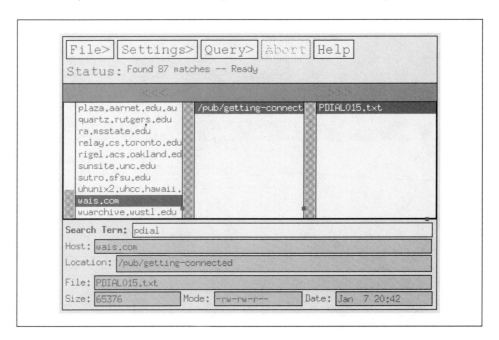

Figure 9-3: xarchie search results

The leftmost column shows where versions of this file are found. The FTP archive **wais.com** contains a version of our file; the filename (*PDIAL015.txt*) is in the right column, and the directory (*/pub/getting-connected*) is in the center. If the name in any column is too long, you can "stretch" it by dragging the "handle" at the bottom.*

---

*Looking up the *pdial* list is a good exercise in what to watch out for when searching the Net. There are many versions out on the net. Most of them are out of date to one extent or another; some are more than a year out of date. Some are tagged with version numbers; some aren't.

If several directories at the FTP archive contain matches, **xarchie** lists the directories in the center column and leaves the right column empty; to find the filenames, click on one of the directories.

Here's where having FTP built-in comes in handy. Earlier, we said that Archie searches often match a directory, rather than a file. In that case, you're stuck—you have to FTP to the site and look up the directory to find what's in it. However, with **xarchie**, you'll see a directory name (rather than a filename) in the right column. Double-click on the directory name; **xarchie** then gets a list of files in the directory and displays the files in the rightmost column.

Whether or not you need to list a directory, you can use **xarchie**'s built-in FTP client to transfer files. Click on the name of the file you want; you can select multiple files by holding down the SHIFT key while you're clicking. Then go to the pull-down menu under **File>**. You'll see several options. **Open** transfers a text file to your system and displays it in a window. (The window has its own option for saving the file). **Get** FTPs the file to your system, without displaying it, and can be used for any kind of file.

The **Settings>** pull-down menu is used to select the search type, the Archie server you want to use, and other features. If you've read the previous discussion, using it should be simple easy. One note—the **Other** item at the bottom doesn't really mean "other settings"; it's a "form-style" interface to setting Archie options that lets you set several options at once.

One final trick. The central **xarchie** display only has three columns—and sometimes Archie needs more, particularly if it matches a directory name, and you ask it to fill in the files within the directory. In this case, you can "scroll" the main display to the left or right by clicking on the arrows (<<< and >>>) just above the screen.

CHAPTER TEN

FINDING SOMEONE

Why Isn't There a Single Internet Directory?
CSO Directories
Finding a User on a Specific System
Whois
The USENET User List
X.500 Directory Services
Knowbot Information Service
Netfind

I t seems only natural that if the phone company can provide a "white pages" telephone directory of its customers, then the Internet should have one, too. Well, it does. The problem is that, just like the phone company, there are multiple phone books for various parts of the Internet. It is easy to find out Willie Martin's phone number if you know he lives in Chicago. If you don't know where he lives, it is nearly impossible. The same is true of the Internet. You can probably find someone, but the more you know, the easier it will be.

Making a rare attempt not to be confusing, the technical community calls this service service the *white pages*, named after the phone book. On the surface, it looks like building a global white pages service should be easy; after all, we have computers. But it's not as easy as it looks. There are a couple of reasons why there is no single service for the entire Internet. We'll discuss this first, then we'll discuss how to look people up.

Discussing how to use the white pages isn't as easy as it should be. There are many different kinds of white pages directories. On top of that, there are usually several different ways to interrogate each kind of directory. For example, one kind of white pages directory is named *whois*. There is a **whois** command for accessing these directories; you can also make **whois** queries through TELNET, Gopher, WAIS, and the World Wide Web. In this chapter, we'll focus on the "native" software interfaces to directories; for example, the **whois** command. We'll cover the alternative interfaces (like Gopher) in the chapters on those other services. Most of the time, these services present white pages directories as simple index lookups.

Why Isn't There a Single Internet Directory?

There are three reasons why a single, unified Internet user's directory doesn't exist:

- The ease with which users change location and work habits
- Lack of standards for directories
- Worries about security and privacy

These factors delayed the creation of such a directory. Progress is being made now that some of the fundamental problems have been solved, but it is still slow. Let's examine these issues more closely.

Mobile Users

Let's consider the first point by comparing an Internet directory to the telephone directory. You want a phone. You call the company, pay them some money, give them some information, get a phone, and they put you in the directory. If you move, you cancel your service, and the company takes you out of the directory. If you stop paying your bill, the company discontinues your service and takes you out of the directory. You are forced to play the phone company's game: each time you get a new phone, you have to give them information and pay their fees. Under these circumstances, creating and maintaining a directory is easy: the phone company always has all the information it needs.

On the Internet, there is no one group to deal with, no one has to collect information, and in many cases no money changes hands. If my workstation is on the network and you want to be on, I can set up an account for you in five minutes. I'll set up an account for you and boom! you're an Internet user with all the capabilities of the other hundreds of thousands of users. Since there is no monthly charge for the account, there is no reason to turn your account off if you stop using it. It just sits there looking like the active accounts.

This illustrates how difficult it is to keep data accurate, but it's really only the tip of the iceberg. First, many people on the network have multiple accounts. Sometimes they are on co-located computers: everyone in the office has accounts on each other's workstations. Sometimes, they are widely separated: I may have an account at the San Francisco office so I can work while I am there. In either case, having an account on an Internet-connected machine makes me an Internet user. It doesn't mean I will ever use that account again. If you send an urgent email message to my account at the San Francisco office, I probably won't read it until next year, when I'm there for the annual sales meeting.

In order to maintain a good directory, someone needs to maintain it; in turn, the maintainer needs the cooperation, even if it's forced, of the user. On the Internet, the first part is easy. The second is almost impossible. Many campuses and corporations maintain internal staff directories. Some of these include electronic access information and some are online. That doesn't mean the information is up-to-date.

Most of the information is gathered when a person is hired and deleted when he retires or quits. Updating the information is optional and frequently not done.

Standards

If everyone creates his own version of a service to serve a particular community (say a university campus), it's difficult for those outside the community to use it. Even if outsiders can get access to the software, you still need one program to access Joe's Directory of Fishermen Online, another to access Mary's Directory of Physics Grad Students at the University of Omaha, and so on. After an awkward period of confusion, a standard technique emerges and is agreed upon. Anyone who knows the standard can then use the service regardless of where it is located.

A long time ago (by computing standards anyway) the Organization for International Standardization started trying to develop a standard for directory services called *X.500*. There were some non-standard servers already, built for special groups. As the X.500 standard took longer and longer to complete, more special directory services with their own facilities got built out of need. Now X.500 is a reality, but a lot of the other services are still there working just fine. Almost every campus or corporation has its own local service. The people who use them are reluctant to change for the sake of changing. If it ain't broke, why fix it?

Security and Privacy

Remember when we discussed security and said that a common way to break into a system was to find a valid username and try common passwords? Since an email address usually contains the recipient's login name, some people think making this information public is a breach of security. It makes it slightly easier for a cracker to break in. Therefore, as a matter of policy, some systems refuse to provide any information about users.

The other side of the coin is personal privacy. Some people believe that they should be able to control whether or not their email address and user name are publicly accessible. Some countries have very strict personal privacy laws that forbid any personal information to be released without express permission. This is not a problem for voluntary systems, where you ask to be included. But it arises when you try to include people in directories automatically, without their consent. Most corporations and campuses have email information gathered, but administrative procedures may not be in place to protect the users' privacy. Rather than deal with the administrative problem directly, these organizations solve the problem by refusing to give out any information.

Now that you understand some of the issues, let's look at what directories are available and how to use them. The facilities are not presented in any order of preference; rather, each one has its own place. You have to decide which one will most likely produce results based on whatever information you already know. Again remember, even the best online directory is out of date and gives only approximate information. If you really want to know for sure, gather the information yourself; that's much more accurate. If you need to know Jane Doe's email address, give her a call, or look up her business card.

CSO Directories

CSO-style directories are one of the most prevalent on the Internet. A large number of colleges and universities use them to put their student and staff information online. To use these directories directly, you need a client called **ph**. This client isn't easy to get. It's primarily available at sites running CSO directories and is occasionally included as part of another package (for example, the mail package Eudora). Most people access CSO directories through Gopher, which does a lot more than white pages queries. Because they're usually accessed through Gopher, we'll defer a detailed discussion of CSO directories until Chapter 11, *Tunneling through the Internet: Gopher.*

Finding a User on a Specific System

finger is an old and widely-used facility that examines the user login file (*/etc/passwd*) on a UNIX system. It lets you find out someone's login name (hence the email address) plus his or her personal name, given that you know what computer your correspondent uses. **finger** also tells you whether or not the user you're asking about is currently logged in to the target machine. Although **finger** is closely tied to UNIX, there are clients that allow you to make finger-style queries from other types of systems as well.

The general format of the **finger** command is:

```
% finger name@host
```

The *name* is optional and specifies the name you want to look up. The **finger** command goes to the specified *host*, and returns information on all users whose first or last name matches *name*, or who have chosen *name* as their login ID. *Host* is the name of the computer where you want the inquiry to be made. It is also optional. If you are asking about someone on your local system, you can omit **@host**; that is, if you don't specify a host, **finger** searches the computer on which you gave the command.

The mechanics of how the search is done are confusing. The *name* you give must be one of the following:

- An exact match, case-sensitive, for a user's login name. It may help you to remember that UNIX login names are almost always all lowercase.
- An exact match, case-insensitive, for a user's first name, as listed in the system's accounts file (for UNIX users, the so-called GECOS field of */etc/passwd*).
- An exact match, case-insensitive, for a user's last name, as listed in the accounts file.

In practice, it's not that bad. If you use lowercase letters for everything, you'll be fairly safe: you won't inadvertently exclude login names, and you'll still find any first and last names that match.

For example, you know that Ed Krol uses the computer **ux1.cso.uiuc.edu**. To find his email address, you might try:

```
% finger krol@ux1.cso.uiuc.edu
[ux1.cso.uiuc.edu]

Login name: ajzxmvk          In real life: Marge Krol
Directory: /mnt/other/ajzxmvk   Shell: /bin/csh
Last login Mon Dec  3, 1990 on ttyq5 from dc-mac49
No Plan.

Login name: krol             In real life: Ed Krol
Directory: /cso/staff/krol    Shell: /bin/csh
Last login Sun Mar  8 20:01 on ttyr3 from beretta
No Plan.
```

This query found two Krols on the machine **ux1.cso.uiuc.edu**: the first is Marge Krol, with the login name *ajzxmvk*; the second, Ed Krol with the login of *krol*. There is other information of interest here. If you were looking for a place to send email you might gather that sending mail to **ajzxmvk@ux1.cso.uiuc.edu** is futile. That account was last used in 1990; obviously, it's not regularly used. Ed Krol, on the other hand, used his account last Sunday, March 8, at 20:01. Using this one for email probably would be successful.

On the surface, both of these logins appear to be owned by shiftless people with no plans. "No Plan" actually refers to the file *.plan*. If the file *.plan* exists in the user's home directory, **finger** displays its contents. The file *.project* is treated similarly; if it exists, its contents are displayed at the end of *finger*'s report.* Let's look at what happens when I create those two files:

```
% finger krol@uxh.cso.uiuc.edu
[uxh.cso.uiuc.edu]

Login name: krol             In real life: Ed Krol
Office: 3337886
Directory: /cso/staff/krol    Shell: /bin/csh
On since Mar  9 19:23:37 on ttyp3 from mossberg.cso.uiu
Project: Write this damn book.
Plan:
Keep plugging away working early mornings and
weekends until it is done.
```

Notice that the contents of the *.plan* and *.project* files were displayed.

---

*For this to work, the files must have world read permission, and your home directory must have world read and execute permissions.

finger is often used to get a list of the people who are currently using a system. To do this, just omit the login name from your command (remember to put the @ sign before the hostname). The following command uses **finger** to find out who's logged in to the system **uxc.cso.uiuc.edu**:

```
% finger @uxc.cso.uiuc.edu
[uxc.cso.uiuc.edu]

Login Name            Tty Idle Login         Office Phone
joh   John Debgrat p0       Mar 9 19:33 1705 UCB 443-7584
opr   Operator       co 3:12 Mar 6 15:01
halph Hal Philland p2    55 Mar 9 17:52 114 DCL  542-4664
madd  Maddox Ross  p3 5:26 Mar 9 12:15 169 DCL  542-8765
```

Notice that the output looks quite different and gives information about the current login, as well as some personal information.

Finger as a general information server

finger's ability to display a plan file provides a simple and effective way to distribute small amounts of information. It's often used for this purpose, playing a role as a very simple database server. For example, in the account for **quake@ geophys.washington.edu**, someone maintains a listing of recent earthquake information in the *.plan* file. So, if you use **finger** to inquire about that login, you get something like this:

```
% finger quake@geophys.washington.edu
Login name: quake                      In real life: Earthquake Information
Directory: /u0/quake                   Shell: /u0/quake/run_quake
Last login Mon Feb 28 06:23 on ttyp0 from 192.102.245.2
New mail received Sun Feb 27 21:27:46 1994;
  unread since Sun Feb 27 00:57:52 1994
Plan:

Recent events reported by the USGS National Earthquake Information Center
  DATE-(UTC)-TIME  LAT(N) LON(W)   DEP  MAG     COMMENTS
  yy/mm/dd hh:mm:ss  deg.   deg.    km
  94/02/20 01:54:36   2.00N 126.60E 33.0 5.6Ms    NORTHERN MOLUCCA SEA
  94/02/23 08:02:08  30.90N  60.60E 33.0 6.1Ms    NORTHERN IRAN
  94/02/23 23:39:52  18.60N 146.80E 33.0 5.5Ms    MARIANA ISLANDS
  94/02/24 00:11:14  31.10N  60.50E 10.0 6.2Ms    NORTHERN IRAN
  94/02/26 02:31:12  31.10N  60.60E 10.0 5.9Ms    NORTHERN IRAN

Recent earthquakes in the Northwest located by Univ. of Wash. (Mag > 2.0)
  DATE-(UTC)-TIME  LAT(N) LON(W)   DEP  MAG QUAL COMMENTS
  yy/mm/dd hh:mm:ss  deg.   deg.    km   Ml
  94/02/04 22:22:32  42.40N 122.05W  5.8 2.0  B    30.0 km  NW of Klamath Falls,
  94/02/05 15:25:52  42.25N 121.90W  6.9 2.0  B    11.6 km WNW of Klamath Falls,
  94/02/06 14:54:09  47.71N 120.33W  3.6 2.5  C FELT 11.2 km  NW of Entiat
  94/02/07 13:22:36  42.26N 121.98W  7.7 2.0  A    18.4 km WNW of Klamath Falls,
  <the list continues - remainder deleted to conserve space>
```

If you look through the *Resource Catalog*, you'll find a couple of organizations that provide similar information through **finger**.

When finger fails

finger requires that a server be running on the target computer to service the request. If you try to use **finger** on an uncooperative host, you will get a message like this:

```
% finger krol@sonne.cso.uiuc.edu
[sonne.cso.uiuc.edu]
connect: Connection refused
```

In this case, there is nothing you can do. **finger** is simply unavailable on the remote computer. You might complain to the administrator—but, likely as not, the administrator has decided that running **finger** is a security risk (a point that's been hotly debated on the Net). You must try other means to find the information you require.

Whois

whois is the name of a particular white pages directory, a general kind of directory, and an application to access it. The confusion arises because **whois** was the original way of doing Internet directory lookups (on what was at the time the ARPAnet). When you are the only game in town, people aren't too accurate with names. You would say, "Gotta run, email me, I'm in **whois**," and everyone would know how to look you up.

The original directory was maintained by the Defense Data Network (DDN) Network Information Center (NIC) and at its peak contained about 70,000 entries. In its prime you were automatically listed in the directory if you had any authority over an IP network or a domain name; in addition, anyone who wanted to be listed could get in the directory by filling out a form. Life was good, and simple.

With the ARPAnet's decommissioning, the DDN NIC stopped supporting a global white pages directory for the Internet. The DDN NIC still exists, but it only supports a directory of people in a restricted part of the Internet call MILNET (used by the U.S. Department of Defense and its contractors). Currently, the Registration Services portion of the InterNIC, the new Internet information provider,* maintains the **whois** directory for non-military network and domain contacts.

This new **whois** directory is a little different from its predecessor. It doesn't accept random listings from people who want to be included; it is restricted to people with authority over some bit or piece of the Internet. It is restricted because the **whois** technology was never designed to support really huge directories (it doesn't "scale well"). You can still use these two **whois** directories to find someone, but they only really help if you're looking for someone connected with the networking infrastructure.

---

*There is a longer explanation of what the InterNIC is and how it works in the introduction to the Resouce Catalog.

That's still not the entire story. When the initial database was split up, the DDN NIC wanted only DDN people, and Registration Services of the InterNIC wanted only network and domain contacts. No one wanted the network hangers-on, who requested to be listed for no particular administrative reason. These fell to yet another party, the Database Services section of the InterNIC, whose task is to begin building the big global white pages directory. They started their task by putting up these old records in yet a third directory. This directory is really a WAIS database, but it is searchable through the **whois** interface.

There are many ways to access these directories. We'll discuss the **whois** command and **telnet** access in detail here. You can also get to these directories through the InterNIC's Gopher, WAIS, and World Wide Web servers, but we won't be discussing these tools for a couple of chapters. To use the **whois** command, just type **whois**, followed by the last name of the person you are looking for:

```
% whois krol
Krol, Ed (EK10)          Krol@UXC.CSO.UIUC.EDU
    University of Illinois
    Computing and Communications Service Office
    195 DCL
    1304 West Springfield Avenue
    Urbana, IL  61801-4399
    (217) 333-7886

    Record last updated on 27-Nov-91.

    Please note that all INTERNET Domain, IP Network Number, and ASN
    records are now kept in the new Internet Registry, RS.INTERNIC.NET.
    This whois server only contains DOD Information.
```

What actually can you search for? Individual names are stored as:

```
last name, first name, titles
```

Matches always begin at the beginning of this text, so it is easiest to look up people by last name. If you are hazy about spelling, you can search on a portion of the last name by ending the search string with a period. For example, the search string *kro.* matches all names beginning with the three characters *kro*:

```
% whois kro.
Krokeide, Per-Arne (PK117)                        +47-2-800200
Krokoski, Chester (CK124)  OOSCT1G@GW3.ARMY.MIL   (817) 287-3270
Krol, Ed (EK10)            Krol@UXC.CSO.UIUC.EDU  (217) 333-7886
Krolikoski, Stan (SK139)   KROLIKOS@WPAFB.AF.MIL  (507) 253-7200
Kroll, Carol (CK43)        carol@CS.UTEXAS.EDU    (512) 835-6732
<only a portion of the matches>
```

If you match more than one item, **whois** gives you a shortened output format, shown above. The funny string in parentheses, like (EK10) for "Krol, Ed", is a unique identifier known as a *handle*. If you have someone's handle, you can get his or her complete record with another **whois** command:

```
% whois \!ek10
```

The exclamation point tells **whois** that you want to look up a person by handle rather than name. If you're on a UNIX system, and using the C shell, you have to put a backslash (\) prior to the exclamation point to ensure that the string is not processed as a history reference. You can omit the backslash if you're using another UNIX shell (like the Korn shell), or if you're not using UNIX.

When we first looked up Ed Krol, the last line of the **whois** output said something about this directory containing "only DOD information." The **whois** command has the domain name of a server to query built into it. And, because the DDN NIC has been around forever (in the Internet's time scale), that's the server **whois** will look up. This was a good idea back when the DDN was the only game in town. Unfortunately, it's not such a good idea now that there are many servers around. When the **whois** database was divided, many **whois** clients pointed to the wrong database. All of a sudden, it wasn't possible to find people anymore.

To get around this problem, the two major **whois** players, **nic.ddn.mil** and **rs.internic.net**, forward requests to each other. This comment is a gentle reminder that says "Hey stupid, I found the guy you were looking for in the **rs.internic.net** database. Why don't you go there directly next time and save me the trouble?" Most **whois** commands let you specify an alternate server by using the –h option, followed by the server's address. For example, the command below says "look up the handle *ek10* at the InterNIC":

```
% whois -h rs.internic.net \!ek10
```

Be forewarned: some **whois** clients support the –h option, and some don't. This is really too bad, because there are other **whois**-style services around. Some sites who got into the game early standardized on **whois** for their online phone books. You can access any of these special servers by issuing the **whois** command with a special hostname, as in the previous example.*

So far, we've only mentioned searching two of the three major **whois** directories. How do you get at the third? This time, we'll point **whois** at **ds.internic.net**:

```
% whois -h ds.internic.net krol
```

The server at **ds.internic.net** automatically searches all three directories in sequences. Because this server accesses all three databases, it's the best one to use for most requests—unless you know you're looking for someone involved with network management.

---

*There are lists of **whois** servers available. See the *Resource Catalog* under "White Pages."

You can also access the Registration Services **whois** using **telnet**. Start by **telnet**ting to the **ds.internic.net** address.* When you get there, give **whois** as a login name, and start making queries. For example:

```
% telnet internic.net
Trying 198.41.0.5...
Connected to internic.net.
Escape character is '^]'.

SunOS UNIX (rs) (ttyp8)

******************************************************************
* -- InterNIC Registration Services Center  --
*
* For gopher, type:                 GOPHER <return>
* For wais, type:                   WAIS <search string> <return>
* For the *original* whois type:    WHOIS [search string] <return>
* For registration status:          STATUS <ticket number> <return>
*
* For user assistance call (800) 444-4345 | (619) 455-4600 or (703) 742-4777
* Please report system problems to ACTION@internic.net
******************************************************************
Please be advised that the InterNIC Registration host contains INTERNET
Domains, IP Network Numbers, ASNs, and Points of Contacts ONLY. Please
refer to rfc1400.txt for details (available via anonymous ftp at
either nic.ddn.mil [/rfc/rfc1400.txt]  or ftp.rs.internic.net
[/policy/rfc1400.txt]).

Cmdinter Ver 1.3 Sun Feb 27 14:33:08 1994 EST
[vt100] InterNIC > whois
Connecting to the rs Database . . . . . .
Connected to the rs Database
InterNIC WHOIS Version: 1.0 Sun, 27 Feb 94 14:33:23

Whois: krol
Krol, Ed (EK10)          Krol@UXC.CSO.UIUC.EDU
    University of Illinois
    Computing and Communications Service Office
    195 DCL
    1304 West Springfield Avenue
    Urbana, IL 61801-4399
    (217) 333-7886

    Record last updated on 27-Nov-91.
Whois: ^D
[vt100] InterNIC > ^D
%
```

When you are done, you need to send two **CTRL-D** characters: one to end the **whois** session and one to close the connection to the InterNIC.

---

*Not every **whois** server allows TELNET access.

The **whois** database contains more than just people. There are several other kinds of entries. Do you care? Yes, for two reasons. First, if you make broad searches, you will probably see some odd stuff returned. Second, you may occasionally need other kinds of information. After the information about users, the most useful data in the **whois** database concerns network and domain ownership. Let's try to find some information about the networks at the University of Illinois. This time, let's do it by email. First, construct a message like the one below, and send it to **mailserv@internic.net**, using your favorite email program:

```
% mail mailserv@internic.net
Subject:
whois University of Illinois
.
```

In about a day, you will get a response containing an answer to the request. It will look something like this:

```
>From mailserv@internic.net Tue Mar  1 07:34:59 1994
Date: Tue, 1 Mar 94 06:17:58 EST
From: mailserv@internic.net (Mail Server)
To: krol@uxh.cso.uiuc.edu
Subject: Re: whois university of illinois

University of Illinois (ILLINOIS-DOM)                    ILLINOIS.NET
University of Illinois (NET-NCSA-K12-NET) NCSA-K12-NET       192.17.6.0
University of Illinois (NET-UI-ISDN-NET) UI-ISDN-NET         192.17.7.0
University of Illinois (NET-UIUC-CAMPUS-B) UIUC-CAMPUS-B    128.174.0.0
University of Illinois (NET-UIUC-NCSA) UIUC-NCSA            130.126.0.0
University of Illinois (ASN-UIUC) UIUC                               38
University of Illinois (GARCON) VIXEN.CSO.UIUC.EDU        128.174.5.58
University of Illinois (UIUC)   A.CS.UIUC.EDU            128.174.252.1

<output truncated for space considerations>
```

Our query was about the University of Illinois. But you can use the same technique to inquire about people, domains, and other networks.

The USENET User List

MIT maintains a list of the names and email addresses of everyone who posts USENET news. This list is generated by automatically extracting names and addresses from all the news postings that pass through MIT—which includes just about all of the official and alternative newsgroups described in Chapter 8, *Network News*. The extraction itself is fairly simple. Most news messages contain a line like the following:

```
From: krol@ux1.cso.uiuc.edu (Ed Krol)
```

A newsreader like **nn** or **tin** uses this information to tell you that someone named Ed Krol posted the message. MIT's address service uses this line to infer that the email address **krol@ux1.cso.uiuc.edu** will probably work if you want to contact Ed Krol.

To use this service, send an email message to **mail-server@rtfm.mit.edu**. The body of the message should look like:

```
send usenet-addresses/search-string
```

Search-string is the name that you are interested in finding. The *search-string* can only be one word without spaces. Matches will not occur on a partial word. So you can't use "kro" to find "krol." For example, to look up "Ed Krol" using the USENET address database, send a message like this:

```
% mail mail-server@rtfm.mit.edu
Subject:
send usenet-addresses/krol
.
```

Some time later, you will receive a response:

```
From daemon@bloom-picayune.MIT.EDU Mon Feb 28 09:52:54 1994
Date: Mon, 28 Feb 1994 10:41:09 -0500
From: mail-server@BLOOM-PICAYUNE.MIT.EDU
To: Ed Krol <krol@uxh.cso.uiuc.edu>
Subject: mail-server: "send usenet-addresses/krol"
Reply-To: mail-server@BLOOM-PICAYUNE.MIT.EDU
Precedence: junk
X-Problems-To: owner-mail-server@rtfm.mit.edu

-----cut here-----
        krol <krol@TISLINK.TIS.ANL.GOV> (Apr 21 93)
Ed Krol <krol@UX1.CSO.UIUC.EDU> (Aug 3 93)
Melanie.Krol@f152.n321.z1.fidonet.org (Melanie Krol)    (Aug 26 93)
Ed Krol <e-krol@UIUC.EDU>        (Dec 5 93)
e-krol@uiuc.edu (Ed Krol)        (Jan 8 94)
krol@ux1.cso.uiuc.edu (Ed Krol) (Jan 8 94)
Ed Krol <krol@ux1.cso.uiuc.edu> (Oct 15 93)
meajjk@ercx44.Skferc.Nl (Jan Jitze Krol)        (Apr 21 93)
        Rosemary Krol <B42603BC@ANLCV1.BITNET>  (Apr 11 93)
Andrzej Krol <genda@LILY.ICS.AGH.EDU.PL>        (Aug 3 93)
genda@galaxy.uci.agh.edu.pl (Andrzej Krol)      (Feb 11 93)
krol@Mari.Unit.NO (Kristian Olsen)      (Mar 11 93)
```

Notice that the search found multiple Krols, and a few possible email addresses for Ed Krol. You have to figure out, or guess, which address is most likely to reach the person you are looking for.

If your search request fails to locate anyone, the response will look like this:

```
From daemon@bloom-picayune.MIT.EDU Mon Feb 28 09:49:36 1994
Date: Mon, 28 Feb 1994 10:24:25 -0500
From: mail-server@BLOOM-PICAYUNE.MIT.EDU
To: Ed Krol <krol@uxh.cso.uiuc.edu>
Subject: mail-server: "send usenet-addresses/ekrol"
Reply-To: mail-server@BLOOM-PICAYUNE.MIT.EDU
Precedence: junk
X-Problems-To: owner-mail-server@rtfm.mit.edu
```

```
-----cut here-----
No matches for "ekrol".
-----cut here-----
```

This service has a few minor limitations. First, it doesn't know about people who don't post news at all, or who only post to local newsgroups, or who post with restricted distribution that doesn't include the MIT campus.

Somewhat more important, this service depends on information in the **From:** field of news postings. Many users use pseudonyms when they are posting messages. So, if Ed Krol has his newsreader configured to post with an alias like "Mr. Hockey" you won't find "Ed Krol" in this directory. If you happen to know that Ed's alias is "Hockey," you could look this up, instead.

X.500 Directory Services

None of the services we have mentioned so far "scale well." That is, **whois**-style directories work just fine for 70,000 entries, but would fail horribly if asked to list millions of users. As is often the case, the Internet is the victim of its own success; when **whois** was planned, no one thought that the database would ever have 70,000 entries, to say nothing of the millions of Internet users who aren't listed.

At the beginning of this chapter, we mentioned the X.500 directory service, adopted by the Organization for International Standardization (ISO). Unlike **whois**, X.500 does scale well. In fact, it is the only currently available technology which does, so it has been chosen for the global online Internet directory that the InterNIC is building. Unfortunately, although it solves the scaling problem, it creates another: the standard offering is very cumbersome to use directly. We'll start by talking a bit about the philosophy of X.500, then move on to looking at how to do a search with a public client.

Native X.500

Let's go back to our first analogy: the phone company. If you were looking up Willie Martin in Chicago, you could start at one end of a shelf of phone books and look at each one sequentially, but it would take all day. Instead, you would find the U.S. section of the shelf, within that find the Illinois section, then find the Chicago directory, and finally look up Willie. This is known as a tree structure. Figure 10-1 shows how to model a collection of phone books as a tree.

If you want to find a person, you start at the top and pick the most likely path. When you finally get to the node at the bottom, which has the directory information, you can look up Willie. The path from the top of the tree to the bottom should identify a particular Willie:

```
World, US, IL, Chicago, Willie Martin
```

This points to your Willie, not the one in Grovers Mills.

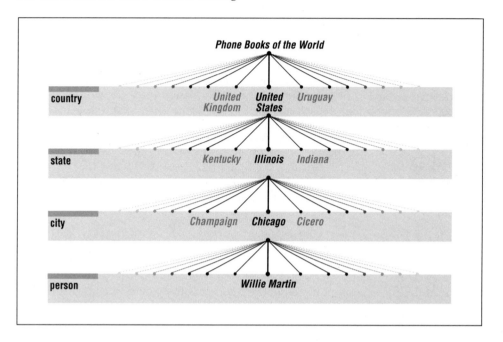

Figure 10-1: Phone book structure

X.500 views "the white pages problem" as a library of telephone books. Each participating group is responsible for its own directory, just as Ameritech is responsible for the Chicago phone book. Figure 10-2 shows the tree structure for the X.500 directory service. The structure is very similar to our phone book model, though the labels for each level are different. The levels shown are fairly static. At the organization level, each organization has responsibility for its own lower structure. This is analogous to the set of phone books for Illinois, where any changes to the books, or to their structure, are made by Ameritech.

Therefore, with the X.500 service, once you know the right organization you can probably find the name you want without trouble. If you like, you can poke around and find out about the organization's internal structure, but you don't need to. Limiting your search to the organization will suffice for doing queries.

How does this work? If I were searching for my buddy Bill Schrader, who works for Performance Systems International, I would type something like:

```
c=US@o=PerformanceSystemsInternational@cn=Schrader
```

As you can see, direct X.500 has a fairly complex syntax. You might not have considered **whois** terribly "friendly," but X.500 is worse! To be fair, X.500 was designed to be used by computers, rather than people. And, as we know, computers aren't bothered by complexity.

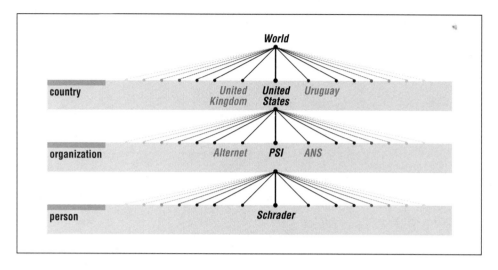

Figure 10-2: X.500 tree structure

X.500 access

The ISO usually decides that standard terminology isn't good enough to describe what they do, so they always develop their own language. X.500 clients are known as Directory User Agents (DUA). To do a white pages search, you need to get the DUA you are using to contact a Directory Server Agent (DSA), which actually does the search for you. If you are lucky enough to have a DUA on your local computer, you can use it to do queries. If you don't, you need to get at a public DUA somehow.

There are several ways to contact public DUAs: Gopher, WWW, and TELNET all work. We'll concentrate on TELNET access using the client at **ds.internic.net**.* The InterNIC's DUA breaks down the X.500 directory structure into four levels:

1. Person
2. Department
3. Organization
4. Country

How does this work in practice? **telnet** to **ds.internic.net** and log in with the password **x500**. It looks like this:

```
%telnet ds.internic.net
Trying 198.49.45.10...
Connected to ds.internic.net.
Escape character is '^]'.
```

---

*Older books on the Internet, including the first edition of this book, recommended the public client called, **fred**, run by PSI, Inc. on the computer **wp.psi.com**. Fred appears dead. The computer is still there, but as soon as you give the password "fred" it cuts the connection. Use the InterNIC; it is more reliable.

```
          InterNIC Directory and Database Services

<introductory text deleted to conserve space>

SunOS UNIX (ds)

login: x500
Last login: Mon Feb 28 03:20:14 from slip-2-3.ots.ute
SunOS Release 4.1.3 (DS) #3: Tue Feb 8 10:52:45 EST 1994

******************************************************************

      Welcome to the InterNIC Directory and Database Server.

******************************************************************


          Welcome to the InterNIC X.500 Directory Service

Connecting to the Directory - wait just a moment please ...
You can use this directory service to look up telephone numbers and
electronic mail addresses of people and organizations participating
in the Directory Service. You will be prompted to type in:

:- the NAME of the person for whom you are seeking information
:- their DEPARTMENT (optional),
:- the ORGANIZATION they work for, and
:- the COUNTRY in which the organization is based.

On-line HELP is available to explain in more detail how to use the
Directory Service.  Please type ?INTRO (or ?intro) if you are not familiar
with the Directory Service.

?         for HELP with the current question you are being asked
??        for HELP on HELP
q         to quit the Directory Service (confirmation asked unless at the
          request for a person's name)
Control-C abandon current query or entry of current query
```

Once you give the login name "x500," you are logged in without a password, and
the search software is available to you.

Let's say you want to look up your old friend Bill Schrader again. You remember
he changed jobs and now works for the firm "Performance something or other."
How do you find him? First, you need to find the organization's exact name. Let's
look at all the organizations that start with the letter "p". This can be done by
responding to the first two questions (person's name and department name) with
a RETURN, and typing "p*" when you're asked for the organization:

```
Person's name, q to quit, * to list people, ? for help
:-                type RETURN
Department name, * to list depts, ? for help
:-                type RETURN
Organisation name, * to list orgs, ? for help
```

```
:- p*
Country name, <CR> to search `United States of America', * to list countries, ?
for help
:-                  type RETURN
United States of America
```

The **p*** says: "find all the entries starting with p of type *organization*." Note the use of the * as a wildcard to match any string of zero or more characters. The results of this search is:

```
Got the following approximate matches.  Please select one from the list
by typing the number corresponding to the entry you want.

United States of America
     1 Pacific Northwest Laboratory
     2 Performance Systems International
     3 Portland State University
     4 Princeton University
     5 Princeton University Plasma Physics Laboratory
     6 United States Postal Service
     7 Pace University

It was not possible to search all the parts of the Directory necessary
to complete this search - part of the database is currently inaccessible.
There may thus be more results than those displayed.
```

Number two looks like a good candidate for Bill's employer. Let's display it by responding to the following query with a **2**:

```
Organisation name, * to list orgs, ? for help
:- 2
United States of America
  Performance Systems International
     postalAddress          PSI Inc.
                            Reston International Center
                            11800 Sunrise Valley Drive
                            Suite 1100
                            Reston, VA 22091
                            US
                            PSI Inc.
                            5201 Great American Parkway
                            Suite 3106
                            Santa Clara, CA 95054
                            US
                            PSI Inc.
                            165 Jordan Road
                            Troy, NY 12180
                            US
     telephoneNumber        1-703-620-6651 (Corporate Offices)
                            +1 800-836-0400 (Operations)
                            +1 800-82PSI82 (Sales)
                            +1 518-283-8860 (Troy Office)
                            +1 408-562-6222 (Santa Clara Office)
```

```
     fax                  +1 703-620-4586
                          +1 518-283-8904
                          +1 408-562-6223
```

Yes, that's it. Now let's try to look up Bill:

```
    Person's name, q to quit, * to list people, ? for help
    :- schrader
    Department name, * to list depts, <CR> to search all depts, ? for help
    :-              type RETURN
    Organisation name, <CR> to search `Performance Systems International',
             * to list orgs, ? for help
    :-              type RETURN
    Country name, <CR> to search `United States of America', * to list countries, ?
    for help
    :-              type RETURN
```

Notice that Performance Systems International became the "default organization" for this search because we displayed it in the previous search. So here we just had to press RETURN at the Organization prompt, rather than retyping the name. Here is the successful result:

```
    United States of America
      Performance Systems International
        Reston
          William Schrader
            postalAddress        PSI Inc.
                                 Reston International Center
                                 11800 Sunrise Valley Drive
                                 Suite 1100
                                 Reston, VA 22091
                                 USA
            telephoneNumber      +1 703-620-6651 x310
            fax                  +1 703-620-4586
            electronic mail      wls@psi.com

    Person's name, q to quit, <CR> for `schrader', * to list people, ? for help
    :- q
    If you have any comments, or have had any difficulties while using this
    service, or if you would like further information, please contact:

      InterNIC Directory Services Help
      email:          admin@ds.internic.net

    Connection closed by foreign host.
```

The quit command, **q**, tells the client that you're finished. This ends the session and logs you out, returning you to the system you started from.

Remember that X.500 is a decentralized database. Every participating organization is responsible for its own server. Sometime a server may be unavailable. If this occurs you will get the message:

```
The search for 'schrader' has failed, probably because a Directory
server is unavailable. In the meantime, displaying organisation details.
For information on people, try again a little later.
```

This means that the server that's responsible for the organization "Performance Systems International" was unavailable; you had better try other means to find your name. You might try the same query a few hours later, on the chance that PSI's server is only temporarily out of commission.

Knowbot Information Service

The Knowbot Information Service (KIS) is an experimental white pages meta-server. That is, it does not itself hold any white pages data. Instead, it knows about other servers, and allows you to query them all through one set of commands. You say "find krol" and it contacts **whois** servers, X.500 servers, **finger** servers, and so on. You don't have to think about what tool to use; Knowbot does that for you.

On the surface, this sounds so nice that you're probably wondering why I bothered talking about the other servers. For two reasons: First, Knowbots are actually an area of research that far exceeds just white pages services. (They are discussed more generally in Chapter 14, *Other Applications.*) KIS is one of the first Knowbot applications. Since the area is so new, any part of it may change or become unavailable for a time. I didn't want you to be left high and dry should this occur.

The second is that the Knowbot "ease of use" philosophy currently is somewhat constrained by practicality. KIS could easily be made to access every host on the Internet when looking for a person, but the search would take days. Therefore, you don't really escape the basic phone book problem: you need to know something about how to search before you can search effectively. A Knowbot can use **finger**, but only if you tell it what host to inquire on. It can use X.500, but only if you tell it an organization. In short, you have to know enough about these services to use them through KIS, but why bother? It is far easier to inquire with **finger** directly than to have a Knowbot do the search for you.

Nevertheless, Knowbots are useful, because they know how to access some unusual directories. One such service is the MCImail directory, which contains information about users of MCI mailboxes. Another unusual directory is the RIPE directory, which contains the names and addresses of Internet networking people in Europe. Let's see how it works.

KIS can be used with **telnet**. You **telnet** to port 185 of **info.cnri.reston.va.us**. On UNIX, you'd use the command:

```
% telnet info.cnri.reston.va.us 185
```

You'll be asked to add your email address to the KIS "guestbook"; if you want to be private, you can ignore this. The easiest way to use KIS is to type the name you want to find at the prompt. For example, let's look up "krol" again, this time using KIS:

```
% telnet info.cnri.reston.va.us
Trying 132.151.1.15...
Connected to info.cnri.reston.va.us.
Escape character is '^]'.

                Knowbot Information Service
KIS Client (V2.0).    Copyright CNRI 1990.    All Rights Reserved.


The KIS system is undergoing some changes.
Type 'news' at the prompt for more information
Type 'help' for a quick reference to commands.

Backspace characters are '^H' or DEL

Please enter your email address in our guest book...
(Your email address?) > krol@ux1.cso.uiuc.edu

> krol
Connected to KIS server (V1.0). Copyright CNRI 1990. All Rights Reserved.

Trying whois at ds.internic.net...

The ds.internic.net whois server is being queried:

No match for "KROL"

The rs.internic.net whois server is being queried:

Krol, Ed (EK10)          Krol@UXC.CSO.UIUC.EDU
    University of Illinois
    Computing and Communications Service Office
    195 DCL
    1304 West Springfield Avenue
    Urbana, IL 61801-4399
    (217) 333-7886

<This goes on to match a number of other krols in various directories>

> quit
```

You can make as many requests as you like in this fashion. When you are done, type **quit** to exit.

If your request had not been serviced at the NIC, the Knowbot would have gone ahead and tried a number of other places. Unless you tell it otherwise, it will try, by default, the following directories:

1. DDN NIC and InterNIC **whois** servers

2. MCImail

3. RIPE

KIS knows how to search in many more places, including most of the places we have visited in this chapter and some we haven't. You can get a list of all the directories it knows about with the command **services**:

```
> services
nic
mcimail
ripe
latin-america-nic
x500
finger
nwhois
quipu-country
quipu-org
>
```

If you want one of these listed directories, like the combined Latin-American directories, used in the search, add it with the **service** command:

```
> service latin-america-nic
```

When you are done, you can exit by typing **quit**.

Netfind

Netfind is a useful but intrusive way to find people. It isn't really a white pages directory; it's more like a private investigator. You tell Netfind to find someone, give it some idea about where to look, and it searches that general geographical area for you. On the surface this sounds really great, but it should be employed only in the most desperate cases. It's not extremely efficient—either of your time, or of the computer resources on the Net. And, like a private investigator, it *is* intrusive.

Netfind does its work in two phases. In the first phase, it takes the list of "hints" you gave and locates every domain in that geographical area. If the list is small enough, it then uses a variety of means, like **finger**, to interrogate each machine in the area. If there are too many domains, Netfind shows you the list and asks you to pick a likely few, then does its **finger**ing within your selected domains. Already you might see the problem. If you don't know where someone is, you might not know enough to pick likely domains.

The most common way to do a Netfind search is to **telnet** to a Netfind server; alternatively, you can use Netfind through an integrated package like Gopher. As before, we will concentrate on TELNET access here. To start, pick a server from Table 10-1 and **telnet** to it.

Table 10-1: Public Netfind Access Sites

Computer Name	Location
archie.au	Melbourne, Australia
bruno.cs.colorado.edu	Boulder, Colorado
dino.conicit.ve	Venezuela
ds.internic.net	Herndon, Virginia (InterNIC Directory Services)
lincoln.technet.sg	Singapore
malloco.ing.puc.cl	Santiago, Chile
monolith.cc.ic.ac.uk	London, England
mudhoney.micro.umn.edu	Minneapolis, Minnesota
netfind.oc.com	Dallas, Texas
nic.nm.kr	Taejon, Korea
nic.uakom.cs	Slovakia (former USSR)

Once there, you enter a search string something like this:

```
name hint hint hint....
```

Name is usually the person's last name, and the hints are keywords used to constrain the search to an area. In all of the search strings you give, case is ignored. The hints can be city and state names (if you know them) or domain names (separated by spaces rather than periods. For example let's look for "krol" at a university in Illinois:

```
krol university illinois    look at universities in Illinois
```

Netfind says the search is too broad, and it returns a list of hundreds of domains where it would be happy to look, some of which are:

```
cs.uiuc.edu (computer science department, university of illinois, urbana-champaign)
csl.uiuc.edu (university of illinois, urbana-champaign)
cso.uiuc.edu (computing services office, university of illinois, urbana-champaign)
cso.niu.edu (northern illinois university, dekalb, illinois)
csrd.uiuc.edu (university of illinois, urbana-champaign)
```

The search is too broad because it will look at the University of Illinois, Urbana; the University of Illinois, Chicago; Illinois State University; and so on. If you really wanted to narrow the search, you could do Urbana, but there are still hundreds of domains at the University of Illinois, Urbana. The search only becomes productive if you know that this guy works for the Computing Services Office (cso):

```
Please form a more specific query.
Enter person and keys (blank to exit) --> krol illinois university cso
( 0) check_name: checking domain cso.uiuc.edu.  Level = 0
( 1) check_name: checking domain cso.niu.edu.  Level = 0
MAIL FOR Ed Krol IS FORWARDED TO krol@ux1.cso.uiuc.edu
```

```
NOTE:     this is a domain mail forwarding arrangement - so mail intended
          for "krol" should be addressed to "krol@cso.uiuc.edu"
          rather than "krol@ux1.cso.uiuc.edu".

( 0) check_name: checking host ux1.cso.uiuc.edu.  Level = 0
The domain 'cso.niu.edu' does not run its own name servers,
          and there is no aliased domain IP address/CNAME/MX record for
          this domain -> Skipping domain search phase for this domain.
SYSTEM: ux1.cso.uiuc.edu
          Login name: ajzxmvk                    In real life: Marge Krol
          Directory: /mnt/courtesy/ajzxmvk        Shell: /bin/csh
          Last login Thu Jan 20 17:06 on ttysk from goofy.aiss.uiuc.
          No Plan.

          Login name: krol                       In real life: Ed Krol
          Directory: /cso/staff/krol              Shell: /bin/csh
          On since Feb 28 08:15:46 on ttyph from maced
```

But if you know that much about "krol", you can look directly in the University of Illinois' online white pages server and be sure, rather than **finger**ing every machine at the campus.

The bottom line is that if you have any clue about someone's whereabouts, it's probably better to use a few of the online white pages servers than Netfind. If, when you last heard of your buddy Willie Martin, he was a computer programmer at an Illinois university, it would probably be faster to try every online phone book in Illinois looking for "martin, wil*" than to use Netfind. If you look in a White Pages directory for "martin, wil*", and it doesn't find someone, you can be reasonably sure he is not there and move on to another directory. With Netfind, you never know. You might look for Martin in an Illinois university, and it would return hundreds of departmental domain names, most of which hire programmers. You can waste a long time searching and come up empty.

Even if you know someone's whereabouts, there's no guarantee that Netfind will work. Let's say that you know Willie is a chemist at the University of Illinois. But there's no reason to believe that you'll find him by searching the Chemistry department. There's a good chance you will—but he may pick up his mail at a computer with a domain of **cso**. Netfind works best when you can make good educated guesses about where people are located; and those guesses are often really hard to make.

CHAPTER ELEVEN

TUNNELING THROUGH THE INTERNET: GOPHER

The Internet Gopher
Finding Internet Resources
Remembering Where You Are With Bookmarks
Gopher Development

In the past few chapters, we've talked about tools that allow you to do particular tasks: find people, software, or data. The next three chapters introduce you to some tools that can do a lot more. They try to be "friendly" and help you to search a variety of online resources. To understand what each of these tools does, think of your local public library. It's convenient, and it has a fairly good collection on its shelves. It also belongs (most likely) to a system of cooperating libraries. The library in the next town belongs to the same system, and it has a lot of the same material as yours. But it also has some different materials. If your library doesn't have something, the neighboring library will honor your library privileges. You don't even need to visit the other library in person. You talk to your local librarian, arrange an inter-library loan, and the materials you need are shipped from the next town to you.

This chapter discusses **gopher**, a lookup tool that lets you prowl through the Internet by selecting resources from menus. If you want to use one of the resources that Gopher presents, it helps you access it. This is like helping you browse the remote library's card catalog and automatically sending the material you want. It doesn't really matter where the library is located, as long as it is part of the Gopher system.

In the next chapter, we'll look at Wide Area Information Service (WAIS). This service helps you search indexed material. You can search for particular words or phrases; it gives you a list of online files that contain those words. WAIS is like walking into a library with a quote ("these are the times that try men's souls"), and having the library automatically check out everything that contains it.

In Chapter 13, *The World Wide Web*, we'll discuss the newest arrival from the Internet's toolshop: the World Wide Web. On the surface, the Web looks like a variation on Gopher: it's another menu-based service that helps you access different resources. However, the Web is based on a much more flexible "hypertext"

233

model that allows cross-references, or links, between related resources. Some of these related resources may also be different media. It allows pictures, text, and audio to all appear as one image. And, unlike the Gopher, the Web is a "read/write" resource (at least potentially). It really offers a different paradigm for working: if you have a Web server and a hypertext editor, it will support all kinds of collaboration and joint authorship. The number of Web servers on the Internet is growing by leaps and bounds. It's still a chore to create hypertext because hypertext editors are scarce; but the potential here makes the World Wide Web one of the most interesting new tools on the Internet.

The Internet Gopher

Gopher, or more accurately, "the Internet Gopher," allows you to browse for resources using menus. When you find something you like, you can read or access it through Gopher without having to worry about domain names, IP addresses, changing programs, etc. For example, if you want to access the online library catalog at the University of California, rather than looking up the address and **telnet**ting to it, you find an entry in a Gopher menu and select it. Gopher then "goes fer" it.

The big advantage of Gopher isn't so much that you don't have to look up the address or name of the resources, or that you don't have to use several commands to get what you want. The real cleverness is that it lets you browse through the Internet's resources, regardless of their type, just as you might browse through your local library, with books, filmstrips, and phonograph records on the same subject grouped together. Let's say you're interested in information about the American West: history, climatological data, minerology, and so on. You can use Gopher to wander around the Internet, looking for data. By looking through a menu of "online catalogs" or "libraries" (the exact menu item will vary, depending on your server), you see that the University of California library catalog is available, and you know that its collection of Western Americana is very strong; so you access the catalog and try to look up relevant books. (You may even be able to use Gopher to arrange inter-library loans through the online catalog, if the library permits it.) A search of FTP archives finds some data about the relationship between drought cycles and snow pack, which is interesting; looking further, you could probably find some meteorological statistics from the time of the Gold Rush.* Yes, you still need to know what you're looking for, and a little bit about where the resource might be located, but Gopher makes the search less painful.

To think about how to use Gopher, it's best to return to our well-worn library image. Think of the pre-Gopher Internet as a set of public libraries without card catalogs and librarians. To find something, you have to wander aimlessly until you stumble on something interesting. This kind of library isn't very useful, unless you already know in great detail what you want to find, and where you're likely to find it. A Gopher server is like hiring a librarian, who creates a card-catalog subject

---

*I don't know if such a database exists—but you could certainly use Gopher to check. A little experience will teach you a lot more than this book.

index. You can find something by thumbing through the subject list, then showing the card to the librarian and asking "Could you help me get this, please?" If you don't find it in one library, you can electronically walk to the next and check there.

Unfortunately, Gopher services usually did not hire highly trained librarians. There's no standard subject list, like the Library of Congress Subject Headings, used on most Gophers to organize things. The people who maintain each server took their best shot at organizing the world, or at least their piece of it. It's the same state we would be in if one library had things filed under a subject called "Folklore, American" and another had the same works under "Funny Old Stories." Each server is a bit different—you have to approach each one with an open mind.

Gopher does not allow you to access anything that wouldn't be available by other means. There are no specially formatted "Gopher resources" out there for you to access, in the sense that there are FTP archives or white-pages directories.* But, once you find something you want to "check out," Gopher will also help you with that. Gopher knows which application (**telnet**, **ftp**, white pages, etc.) to use to get a particular item you are interested in and does it for you. Each type of resource is handled a bit differently. However, they are all handled in an intuitive manner, consistent with the feel of the Gopher client you are using.

If you've followed the discussion so far, you should realize that it doesn't really matter what Gopher server you contact first. Your home server only determines the first menu you see. The other menus all come from whichever server is appropriate at that point. Each server, like each library, has a unique collection.† Popular files, like collections of frequently asked questions, may be in several places. Obscure collections of data might only be found through a single server. If you don't find what you want at your initial library, you can search elsewhere. When you find what you like, get it by inter-library loan. With libraries, this can take a while; with Gopher, getting material from somewhere else is instantaneous.

Finally, the system is smart enough to enforce licensing restrictions. Some software or resources (e.g., online newspapers) may only be licensed for use within a particular city or campus. You may access a remote Gopher server, but it may prevent you from accessing a particular resource because you are not local. This is annoying, but inability to enforce licensing has been a major stumbling block in the delivery of online information. Gopher seems to have taken a step in the right direction.

Gopher is a lot harder to talk about than to use. So, if you are mildly confused, just press on. Find a **gopher** client and play with it! The information is there for the taking. It's there to be used. No one is watching you and laughing at your mistakes. So make some!

---

*Some files might only be available through Gopher, but that is strictly a security issue. If you access those files through Gopher, they come to you via **ftp**.

†In reality, the collection might be housed elsewhere, but you don't care—it will be fetched automatically should you request it.

Where Gopher Was Born

The name "Gopher" is an interesting pun. It started out as a distributed campus information service at the University of Minnesota, home of the "Golden Gophers." Since its primary function is to "go fer" things, the name **gopher** was coined.

The service was designed so that each piece of a bureaucracy could have control over its own server and data. That is, the school administration could have a computer in the administration building which could deliver information on administrivia. The athletic department could have a sports-schedule server in its offices. Each academic department could provide a server with a class schedule; and so on. There could be as many servers as there were groups who wanted to provide them.

Gopher's developers then created a special application that could guide students to the information, with no training required. To do this, they organized the system by topic, so that it looks like one large database, rather than hundreds of smaller databases. It can access files in FTP archives, phone numbers from white-pages servers, library catalogs and other databases with special-purpose (TELNET-based) servers, whatever. Only Gopher knows where the data really is, how to access it, and that there are multiple servers providing it.

It didn't take much effort to see that if this could work for a bunch of servers in various departments, it could work for servers all over the world. All it took was the Internet to connect them all together. In the space of about four years, the Gopher system has gone from one site to over 1300 sites.

Finding a Gopher Client

To access the Gopher system, you need a **gopher** client program. The special client software must be installed on a computer that is on the Internet. There are free **gopher** clients for just about any computer you might have: UNIX, Macintosh, IBM/PC, X Windows, VAX/VMS, VM/CMS, and probably more by now.

Each client has the "look and feel" of the system it runs on. If you are an IBM/PC user, the PC version will work just like other PC applications. The Macintosh version will look like a hypercard stack with buttons to push. The X Windows version also has a *point-and-click* interface. Almost anything that you can do with one **gopher** client you can do with another. It may be easier if you have a mouse, but it works just fine without one. Ultimately, the choice of a client isn't important; find one that suits your taste. You can get the software you need from the anonymous FTP site **boombox.micro.umn.edu**, in the directory *pub/gopher.* You can also use Archie to find other sources for the client software—in fact, that's a good way to practice.

Whichever client you decide to install, it will be pre-configured with the Internet address of a home server. Since all servers are public, it doesn't really matter where it points initially. You can start the client, get a menu, and use **gopher**. When you have some experience, you can decide which Gopher server you want to be your home and change the configuration accordingly.*

As in the other chapters, to illustrate **gopher** I had to pick a client. I chose to use the UNIX non-graphical version (sometimes called the *curses* version because it uses UNIX's standard terminal interface package of that name). I chose this version for two reasons. First, all it requires is a terminal emulator. You don't need a mouse or a super graphics monitor. Second, when you're starting off with **gopher**, you're more likely to access the client on a "public" client computer somewhere, rather than setting up a new client on your own system. If you use **telnet** (or a dial-up modem) to access a Gopher server on a remote system, you're most likely to see the UNIX curses client.

If you want to try **gopher** at one of the public gopher sites, pick one from Table 11-1 that is geographically close to you. **telnet** to the computer name shown and login using the corresponding login name. It will automatically start **gopher** for you when you login.

Table 11-1: Public Gopher Access Sites

Computer	Login	Location
consultant.micro.umn.edu	gopher	North America
ux1.cso.uiuc.edu	gopher	North America
panda.uiowa.edu	*none required*	North America*
gopher.msu.edu	gopher	North America
gopher.ebone.net	gopher	Europe
info.anu.edu.au	info	Australia
gopher.chalmers.se	gopher	Sweden
tolten.puc.cl	gopher	South America
ecnet.ec	gopher	Ecuador
gan.ncc.go.jp	gopher	Japan

* **panda.uiowa.edu** uses a different line-oriented gopher client (called **panda**) than the one we discuss. It works just fine, but you may need to check out the help facility to use it.

NOTE

Public-access gophers are fine for getting the flavor of the Gopher system, but you will be severely hampered in certain areas. Any use which either leaves the Gopher system, such as accessing TELNET resources; requires disk space, such as saving files you find; or emailing the results will be

---

*How you change the configuration varies from client to client. Check the documentation that comes with the client you have installed.

prohibited. If you want to do these things, you must access a client on a computer on which you have your own account.

How Gopher Works

When you first start up a **gopher** client, it contacts its home server and asks for its main menu. The server sends the menu and some hidden information to your client. The hidden information tells your client what each item on the menu represents (e.g., a text file, a directory, a host, a white-pages server, etc.), the IP address of a server for that item, a port number to use, and a directory path to a file. The IP address could be the home server itself, if that's where the resource resides; it could just as easily be another server somewhere else. It doesn't matter; when you pick a menu item, the client does the same thing. Your client saves its current position (in case you want to return) and contacts the new server. Then the process repeats itself.

Eventually, you will choose a resource rather than a menu. Your **gopher** client will choose an appropriate utility for dealing with the resource you select, whatever it is. If it is a file, the client **ftps** it for you. If the resource is a "login" resource (i.e., a system you can log in to), it creates a TELNET session. If it's a collection indexed by Archie or WAIS, Gopher uses Archie or WAIS to find out what's relevant. The **gopher** client you are using allows you to speak to it in a screen-oriented, menu-driven fashion. It takes what you say and turns it into real commands for the appropriate application. So, if you are in Gopher, you never have to type an **ftp get** command.

Finding Internet Resources

Getting started is easy. To start a **gopher** client on UNIX, give the command:

```
% gopher
```

Or **telnet** to one of the public-access clients. Whatever client you use, and whatever Gopher server it connects to, your first menu will look something like this:

```
                Internet Gopher Information Client v1.12S

                            Root Directory

        --> 1.   Welcome to the U of Illinois Gopher.
            2.   CCSO Documentation/
            3.   Computer Reference Manuals/
            4.   Frequently Asked Questions/
            5.   GUIDE to U of Illinois/
            6.   Libraries/
            7.   National Weather Service/
            8.   Other Gopher and Information Servers/
```

```
 9.   Peruse FTP Sites/
10.   Phone Books/


Press ? for Help, q to Quit, u to go up a menu     Page: 1/1
```

If your initial server resides at the University of Minnesota, you may find items in the menu about Minnesota campus events. If you use the University of Illinois, you will find items of interest to its students. In addition to these "local interest" categories, though, you will always find a few topics of general interest (for example, items 6, online library catalogs; 7, current weather and forecasts; and 9, software and data sources), and a way to reach other servers (item 8). You're also likely to find some introductory information (item 1). Usually it will be pretty obvious what an item is from the menu entry. If it isn't, try accessing it and see if it looks interesting.

gopher keeps track of several different types of entities. The most important are directories and text files; we'll see the others later. All clients use some kind of flag to show you what kind of entity any menu item represents. The client we're using puts a slash at the end of a line to denote a directory.* A directory is really equivalent to another menu. That is, if you select a directory and access it, you'll see another menu—this time, one that's more specific to your topic. (Selecting item 8 gives you a menu of other Gopher servers.)

With this Gopher implementation, you move between menu items by typing the line number you want, or by using your terminal's arrow keys to move up and down the screen. (On a version with a graphical interface, you'd point at the item you want and click a mouse button, or something along those lines.) As you move around the menu, the arrow on the left will show you which item is selected. If you are interested in "Frequently Asked Questions," you would move the cursor (i.e., the arrow) to number 4.† Notice that the line has a slash (/) on the end of it, meaning that it's a directory; expect another menu when you access it. When you want to access this directory, or any other resource you have selected, type a carriage return or right arrow. In this case, your screen changes to:

```
Internet Gopher Information Client v1.12S


       Frequently Asked Questions


--> 1.   About Frequently Asked Questions.
    2.   New Users/
    3.   AIX and IBM RS6000/
    4.   Binaries Sent via News or E-mail.
    5.   Bulletin Board Systems.
    6.   C Language/
    7.   Consumer Information/
```

---

*Fancier clients (like Macintosh or X clients) will most likely use an icon.

†"Frequently Asked Questions" (or FAQs) are, in net-speak, lists of common questions organized by topic. There are thousands of such lists scattered in various archives; many are "published" periodically through the USENET News. These lists exist so that users can resolve the most common problems themselves, rather than asking an expert (who probably answers the same question 100 times a day).

```
     8.  Credit/
     9.  E-mail Questions/
    10.  Experienced Internet User Questions.
    11.  FAQs from Finland/
    12.  File Compression Questions/
    13.  GNU EMACS/
    14.  Glossary of Networking Terms.
    15.  Home Owner/
    16.  How to find sources.
    17.  Internet Naming Conventions/
    18.  LISP/


Press ? for Help, q to Quit, u to go up        Page: 1/2
```

You can do several other things besides selecting a menu item. Sometimes a menu won't fit onto a single screen. The **Page** item in the lower right-hand corner shows you how much material there is and where you are. (This example happens to be page 1 of 2.) To move between pages, press the < key to move backward and > to move forward. Sometimes you may find yourself in a menu with many pages, perhaps more than 20. An easy way to search for things with a menu is with the / command. In response to this command, **gopher** asks:

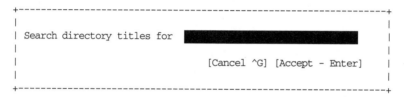

You enter the string you are searching for and then enter a RETURN. Gopher positions the cursor at the next menu item which contains that string. If Gopher can't find the string you're looking for, you'll get a message saying "Search failed."

If you find yourself somewhere you didn't want to be, or if you decide that you're done with a topic, you can move "up" to where you came from by pressing the **u** key. If you did this now, you would move back up to the main menu. If you really get lost, you can get back to your main menu any time by pressing **m**. Finally, when you are done with **gopher**, press the **q** (quit) key to exit. That, in a nutshell, is what it takes to use **gopher**.

Looking at Text Files

The first menu we looked at only showed us directories. But this second menu (Frequently Asked Questions) has some entries that end in periods rather than slashes. These are text files. To read a text file, access it just like you accessed a directory: select it and press the RETURN or right arrow key. For example, let's say you want to peek at the "Glossary of Networking Terms." Type **14**, which is the line number. When the **gopher** client detects a numeric key, it changes the bottom line from `Press ? for Help . . .` to:

```
Move To Line: 14
```

It stays in this mode until a RETURN is typed. The carriage return moves the selection arrow to line 14 and accesses the document; you'll see something like this on your screen:

```
Network Working Group                    O. Jacobsen
Request for Comments: 1208               D. Lynch
                        Interop, Inc.
                        March 1991


                A Glossary of Networking Terms

Status of this Memo

      This RFC is a glossary adapted from "The INTEROP
      Pocket Glossary of Networking Terms" distributed
      at Interop '90.  This memo provides information
      for the Internet community.  It does not specify
      an Internet standard.  Distribution of this memo
      is unlimited.


Introduction
--More--(1%)[Press space to continue, 'q' to quit.]
```

The UNIX **gopher** client honors the PAGER environment variable. This is the UNIX facility to determine how a program should act when it displays text that's longer than your screen. If you have this variable set, **gopher** uses the pager you have specified (e.g., **more** or **pg**). For example, to use the utility **more** as your pager, give the following command before starting **gopher**:

```
% setenv PAGER more
```

If PAGER isn't set, this **gopher** client uses the internal pager seen here; typing a SPACE advances you to the next screen of text. Clients that are more window-oriented use a scrollbar to page back and forth.

When you get to the end of the article (by pressing the space bar) or quit (by pressing **q**), **gopher** asks what you want to do next:

```
Press <RETURN> to continue, <m> to mail, <s> to save: █
```

Type a carriage return if you want to return to the menu from which you selected this item. If you want a copy of the document you are looking at, you can get one either by email or as a file*. You can email a copy of the file to yourself (or anyone else) by pressing **m**. You'll see a prompt like this:

```
Mail document to: ▐
```

Then type your email address,

```
Mail document to:krol@ux1.cso.uiuc.edu
```

followed by a RETURN. Eventually, you'll receive the document as an email message; you can use your favorite email program to read it and save it, just like any other message.

Alternately, you can save a copy of the item in your file space on the computer running the **gopher** client. This might not be of much use if you are using a public client, since you won't have any file space on the client's computer. If you ran the client on a computer that allows you to create files, you can wander the world, collecting souvenirs as you go. When you get home, you can admire your collection. To save a file, press **s**. **gopher** asks:

```
Enter save filename: ▐
```

Type the filename you want for the saved article. **gopher** saves the article in the *current directory* (the one that was in effect when the **gopher** client started). You may use any legal filename; the name may contain directory components (for example, *rfc/1208*). If you use a pathname like this, the directories must already exist.† It doesn't matter what Gopher server you happen to be using or where the data resides: **gopher** knows how to move the file to the computer that's running your client.

In the next few sections, we'll visit a few other menus. These should give you a feeling for how to navigate through Gopher, and what kinds of information you're likely to find.

Moving to Other Servers

By poking around with **gopher** on your home server, you might find 80 percent of everything you ever wanted to find. Now you need to find the other 20 percent. You can do this by poking around on other servers. **gopher**'s main menu will usually have an entry that looks something like:

```
--> 8.  Other Gopher and Information Servers/
```

The wording may change from server to server. Sometimes it may be one level down in menus, underneath "Other Services" or something like that. It may be hidden, but it's always there.

---

*Mail and save are disabled if you are using a public access gopher.

†Many **gopher** implementations don't know how to create directories.

Moving from one server to another isn't different from any other search: you look through menus and pick a resource. So, after picking the "Other Gophers" entry, you may have to go through a few screens to find one you want. Some servers break them up alphabetically, according to the server's name:

```
1.  Gopher Servers (A-G)/
2.  Gopher Servers (G-T)/
3.  Gopher Servers (U-Z)/
```

Some break them up by geographical area, usually by continent. Move around until you find an entry you want to try:

```
--> 1.  CICNET gopher server/
    2.  CONCERT Network -- Research Triangle Park, NC, USA/
    3.  Cornell Information Technologies Gopher/
    4.  Cornell Law School/
```

Notice that other servers are flagged as directories: their menu entries end in a slash. If you think about it, this makes sense—if you access any of these servers, you get a menu of services. It's not important that the services are provided by another server.

From the list above, you might be able to gather that some servers are general, like the one we have been using. Some, like the server at the Cornell Law School (number 4), have a particular focus. On a focused server, you might not find any of the specific items we've seen so far, like the glossary of network terms, or a general directory of white pages services. But you will always find a way to move to other Gophers. If your interests lie in the area of one of these special servers, you might consider making it your home base; the Cornell Law School server would be an obvious choice if you're specifically interested in legal questions. It can place much of the information you need for day-to-day existence at your fingertips—and someone else maintains it for you!

If you already have a particular server in mind, there's an easier way to get to it than going through a chain of gopher menus. You can point your gopher client at a particular server by putting the server's Internet name on the command line. Let's say you want to access the Cornell Law School gopher, **fatty.law.cornell.edu**. To do so, just add the Internet address to your **gopher** command:

```
% gopher fatty.law.cornell.edu
```

You'll start with Cornell Law School's main menu; you don't have to track the server down. Given the rate at which gophers multiply, this is a more effective way to get started; it's how we list Gopher resources in the *Resource Catalog*. If you're using a public Gopher client, you don't have this luxury; you'll have to hunt down your Gopher servers through a chain of menus. That's one good reason for getting your own client.

Index Searches

Let's say that you're a biologist, and are looking for strains of Drosophila (fruit flies) for a particular experiment. You go to the Indiana University Biology Archive (**gopher ftp.bio.indiana.edu**), and see an item called "Flybase." After selecting that item and poking around a little more, you get to a menu called "Stocks." That menu is cluttered with "questionable" items:

```
          Internet Gopher Information Client v1.12S


                           Stocks

     --> 1.  Search stocks at Bloomington, USA  <?>
         2.  Search stocks at Bowling Green, USA  <?>
         3.  Search stocks at Umea, Sweden  <?>
```

What does this mean? Gopher isn't sure what these items are?

Not at all. The symbol <?> refers to a type of entry that we haven't seen yet. These are *indexed directory* resources. In a normal Gopher directory (/), you select the directory and see a menu of everything in it. An index is similar. When you select an item that ends with <?>, you get an opportunity to do a keyword search through a database. First, you'll be asked for a search string; Gopher then searches for items that match your string and presents you with a special menu containing only the items it found—rather than a complete list of the directory's contents. For your experiment, you need a strain of Drosophila with purple eyes. So, after finding the "Stocks" menu, you select resource 1, "Search stocks at Bloomington, USA." Then you see this display on the screen:

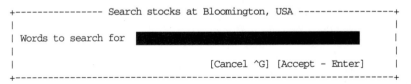

```
+---------------- Search stocks at Bloomington, USA ----------------+
|                                                                   |
| Words to search for  [                                        ]   |
|                                                                   |
|                              [Cancel ^G] [Accept - Enter]         |
+-------------------------------------------------------------------+
```

Now you can type keywords. If you've previously performed a search, Gopher will remember the keywords you used last time and show them on the screen. This makes it easier to repeat your search if you don't get what you want the first time. If you want entirely different keywords, just backspace over your old keywords and start again. (If you're using a UNIX client, typing CTRL-u will probably do the trick.)

In our case, we want to find out about Drosophila with purple eyes, so we type the keyword "purple", followed by RETURN.

```
Words to search for: purple
```

When you type RETURN, **gopher** searches the index and builds a "custom" directory menu that only contains items matching your search criterion. In this case, then, you'll see a new menu that only contains items that match the keyword "purple":

```
            Internet Gopher Information Client v1.12S

            Drosophila Stocks (genotype,breakpt,...): purple

      --> 1.   Genotype: D. mauritiana  pr-3.
           2.   Genotype: D. simulans  pur osp-3.
           3.   Genotype: D. simulans  pur e.
```

This menu isn't any different from the other menus. You're looking at a list of files (the entries end in periods). Therefore, selecting item 1 just displays the file:

```
      >>>
      Genotype: D. mauritiana  pr-3
      Comments: Coyne stocks, 1990; purple eye
      Stock #:  2520  Stock Center: Bloomington

      Press <RETURN> to continue, <m> to mail, <s> to save: █
```

(If you're a biologist, you presumably know how to use this information!)

Indexed searches are a great feature, but there are some tricks. The Gopher interface is very general and, as with anything very general, there are several causes for confusion. First, you have no idea what kind of computer or software is really doing the search. Gopher can do searches through Archie servers, WAIS servers, and others. Each of these servers has its own search rules, and interprets keywords differently. Some, like Archie, only let you search for a single word. Some servers accept strings of keywords, but the meanings of these keywords may change as you move from index to index. For example, consider the string:

```
      clinton and gore
```

Does this mean that for the search to match, the item must contain the words "clinton", "and", and "gore"? Or is the "and" a directive telling the server to find entries that contain the word "clinton" and the word "gore"? You don't know, and you can't tell beforehand. You don't want a list of every item containing the word "and"!

Another problem is that Gopher tends to reduce the search capabilities of different servers to the intersection of their features. You get to use the features they all have in common, not the best of any one. For example, you can access WAIS servers through Gopher. WAIS searches are extremely powerful, much more sophisticated than anything you've seen so far. (You should be drooling by now!) However, if you use a WAIS server through Gopher, much of its power is lost, because you can't use all its facilities with Gopher's simple line-oriented keyword interface.

You may also find that the resources which are most useful to index also tend to have licensing restrictions. Most of the time, you're allowed to search the database, but you're not allowed to see the information that you find. For example, the

University of Minnesota's Gopher server has the UPI press feed (derived from the Clarinet newsgroup) as an indexed resource. You can access it:

```
Internet Gopher Information Client v1.12S

                     UPI News

       1.  About UPI News.
   --> 2.  Search Today's News <?>
       3.  Search entire news archive <?>
       4.  Search last month's news archive <?>
       5.  Search this month's news archive <?>
       6.  Stories/
```

And search it for "clinton":

```
+-------------------- Search Today's News -------------------------+
|                                                                  |
| Words to search for  clinton                                     |
|                                                                  |
|                               [Cancel ^G] [Accept - Enter]       |
+------------------------------------------------------------------+
```

It gives you a menu of articles that match the search key:

```
Internet Gopher Information Client v1.12S

             Search Today's News: clinton

   --> 1.  Today/biz/Israeli report: Pan Am security was lax before bombing.
       2.  Today/feature/PEROT CAN CASH IN BY IGNORING ISSUES.
       3.  Today/news/What Newspapers Are Saying.
       4.  ..news/Israeli report: Pan Am security was lax before bombing.
       5.  Today/news/UPI NEWS AT A GLANCE.
       6.  Today/news/Voters still unhappy with their choices.
       7.  ..news/Florida Perot supporters say they've got enough signatures.
       8.  ..Bush, Clinton get big wins but Perot could be a factor in th.
       9.  Today/news/Clinton takes campaign to Congress.
```

But, when you try to read an article, you get:

```
We cannot off campus allow connections to this server.
Sorry

Bummer.....

Press <RETURN> to continue, <m> to mail, <s> to save: █
```

This is because the license that allows the University of Minnesota to have the UPI news feed online forbids them from distributing it off-campus. Gopher knows where you are coming from and enforces this restriction. A few restrictions are a minor price to pay. Keep in mind that the alternative to licensing restrictions is not unlimited access to data; in reality, the alternative would be no data at all.

With a little experience, you will hardly notice the differences in how searches work. Here are a couple of hints to help you through:

- Gopher searches are always case-insensitive; uppercase and lowercase letters are considered the same.

- When you approach a new index, keep the search simple. If you want articles containing "clinton" and "gore," just look for "gore." He is likely to appear in fewer articles, hence the resulting menu will be shorter. If your search is too broad, no harm done, the menu will just be longer.

- If you use a particular resource regularly, take five minutes to experiment. Find an article and read it. Jot down a few terms from the article. Try a few searches with multiple keywords, including some with "and", "or," and "not" in between them. See what happens; are words like "and" considered part of the search string, or are they keywords? Remember that the rules change from resource to resource; that is, two different resources that you access from the same Gopher server may behave differently.

- If you move from Gopher server to Gopher server, the way a search is conducted for a similarly named resource may vary. If you always use a resource from the same Gopher server, the search semantics will remain the same.

- There is no obvious way to cancel a search once you have started. If you react instinctively with a CTRL-C, you will cancel the **gopher** client. The best you can do is let it complete and give you a bizarre collection of menu items.

Searching for Things in Menus

We see that it is fairly easy to move around in one gopher server and to move from gopher server to gopher server. This points to a problem: how do you find the item you want among the tens of thousands of gopher menus available? Until two people at the University of Nevada at Reno built the Gopher equivalent to Archie, there was no way to know. With a typical hacker's sense of humor, they named their Archie-like facility Veronica, after the comic-book character.

Basic Veronica

Veronica acquires its data exactly like Archie: it visits Gopher servers worldwide and traverses their menus, remembers what is there, and builds a combined index of Gopher menus. The most amazing thing about Veronica is that you know how to use it already! It appears to be just another index search. You select it just like any other search menu item. It asks you for words to search for and builds you a custom menu. The menu items are items from all the Gophers worldwide which contain the words you are looking for.

To access Veronica, look around on any Gopher server for a menu item like this:

```
19. Search titles in Gopherspace using Veronica <?>
```

Select this item; your next menu will look something like this:

```
              Internet Gopher Information Client v1.12S

              Search titles in Gopherspace using Veronica

      1. Search gopherspace by veronica at PSINet <?>
 --> 2. Search gopherspace by veronica at SUNET <?>
      3. Search gopherspace by veronica at University of Cologne <?>
      4. Search Gopher Directory Titles using PSINet <?>
      5. Search Gopher Directory Titles using SUNET <?>
      6. Search Gopher Directory Titles using University of Cologne <?>
      7. FAQ:  Frequently-Asked Questions about veronica  (1993/08/23).
      8. How to compose  veronica queries (NEW June 24) READ ME!!.



 Press ? for Help, q to Quit, u to go up a menu          Page: 1/1
```

The first thing to notice is that there several menu entries, associated with several different Veronica servers. The number of servers varies from place to place and from time to time. Some Gopher servers are smart enough to know when a Veronica server is unusable, and delete unusable servers from their menus dynamically. Others leave them all there and let you try and fail.

There are many servers, because they are heavily used; one server could not handle the searches for the whole Internet. How do you know which one to use? Well, there is no way to know beforehand which is the best. They all contain the same data, but you can't tell which are busy and which aren't. As with Archie, start by trying a server that's close to you; if that doesn't work, try one slightly farther away, until you reach one that responds. When you select a Veronica server, Gopher asks you for your search words. Healthcare is a big political topic, and you'd like to follow the debate. So you are interested in finding a place where you can drop in occasionally and find out what's new. So you start by typing your search term:

```
+-------------Search gopherspace by veronica at SUNET-------------+
|                                                                 |
| Words to search for  healthcare                                 |
|                                                                 |
|                             [Cancel ^G] [Accept - Enter]        |
|                                                                 |
+-----------------------------------------------------------------+
```

At this point, you can cancel the search by typing CTRL-g; you'll return to the previous menu. To proceed with the search, press RETURN. If all goes well, you will be rewarded with a menu of items related to health care:

```
              Internet Gopher Information Client v1.12S

          Search gopherspace by veronica at SUNET: healthcare

 --> 1. PubH 5753    Strategic Management in the Healthcare Industry.
      2. healthcare-reform-group.
```

```
     3. Healthcare Professionals to Review Healthcare Reform Options .
     4. womancare - healthcare for women, by women.
     5. Conference on Healthcare for the Poor and Uninsured:...
     6. 06/21/93 - Orange County Healthcare Agency/Cal EPA Inspection.
     7. PREFERRED FAMILY HEALTHCARE, INC. - 1.
     8. PREFERRED FAMILY HEALTHCARE, INC. - 3.
     9. PREFERRED FAMILY HEALTHCARE INC. - 2.
    10. PREFERRED FAMILY HEALTHCARE INC. - 4.
    11. PREFERRED FAMILY HEALTHCARE INC. - 5.
    12. PREFERRED FAMILY HEALTHCARE INC. - 6.
    13. CFP: Neural Networks in Medicine and Healthcare.
    14. Bloodborne Pathogens      Healthcare Workers with AIDS.
    15. Bloodborne Pathogens      B.Review of the Epidemiology of ...
    16. Bloodborne Pathogens      (4)Information Provided to the...
    17. Bloodborne Pathogens      (5)Healthcare Professional's Written...
    18. President's Remarks on NAFTA, Healthcare, and the Canadian...


   Press ? for Help, q to Quit, u to go up a menu          Page: 1/9
```

This search gave you more than you bargained for: nine pages worth!

Nine pages might be acceptable if you're only going to do the search once: your kid comes home and says, "I need a periodic table for chemistry quick!" You find it, you pick it up, look at it, and are done. But that's not the only way to use search information. If you occasionally want to find out what's new on a particular topic, you'd rather find a few collections of information than a long list of scattered resources. This means searching for a directory, rather than for individual resources. That's why the Veronica menu contained items like the following:

```
   5. Search Gopher Directory Titles using SUNET <?>
```

The first search we did found any item that matched our keywords; this item only searches for directories (which are, by definitions, collections of things). The actual mechanics of the search are exactly the same in either case: Veronica asks you what to search for; you enter a string followed by a return. If we did our healthcare search, looking only for directory titles, we would get a more reasonable number in response:

```
              Internet Gopher Information Client v1.12S

       Search Gopher Directory Titles using SUNET: healthcare

    -->  1.   HealthCare/
         2.   HealthCare/
         3.   HEALTHCARE/


   Press ? for Help, q to Quit, u to go up a menu          Page: 1/1
```

That's more to your liking. You don't need a complete list of healthcare resources; you just want a few places where you can poke around from time to time.

These examples show basic Veronica usage at its best. Frequently, you will select a Veronica server and get a message like:

```
Internet Gopher Information Client v1.12S

Search gopherspace at University of Cologne: healthcare

--> 1. *** Too many connections - Try again soon. ***.
```

If this happens, try another server or try the server later. **Gopher** remembers your search string, so you won't have to enter it time and time again.

Advanced Veronica

When we talked about index searches earlier, I said you don't know what kind of software is actually doing the search for you. You couldn't try really sophisticated search strings unless you had inside knowledge of the index server. Well, Veronica servers are smarter than the average server. They all do limited boolean and substring searches.

Boolean searches allow you to use the words "and", "or", and "not", together with parentheses, to allow you better control of the search. For example, if you were interested in healthcare as it relates to women or families, you could have used the search string:

```
healthcare and (women or family)
```

This string is interpreted as a mathematical expression; "healthcare and" applies to all the items within the parentheses. So the meaning of this expression is: return any items that contain both of the words "healthcare" and "women" or both of the words "healthcare" and "family". The result would be:

```
Internet Gopher Information Client v1.12S

Search gopherspace by veronica at SUNET: healthcare and (women or
family)

--> 1. PREFERRED FAMILY HEALTHCARE INC. - 4.
    2. PREFERRED FAMILY HEALTHCARE, INC. - 3.
    3. womancare - healthcare for women, by women.
    4. PREFERRED FAMILY HEALTHCARE INC. - 5.
    5. PREFERRED FAMILY HEALTHCARE INC. - 2.
    6. PREFERRED FAMILY HEALTHCARE INC. - 6.
    7. PREFERRED FAMILY HEALTHCARE, INC. - 1.
```

As a shorthand, the "and" is assumed between any two adjacent words, unless there is another directive present. That is, searching for "healthcare and women" is the same as "healthcare women". Why type it if you don't need it?

If you think carefully about the search we just did, you'll realize that it might exclude some entries we would like see because they contain "woman" (or even "womyn") rather than "women". To handle situations like this, use the partial-word character *. In our current search, **wom*** takes care of most possibilities—in

addition to finding articles about the care of wombats. (Nothing's perfect.) The *
may only be used at the end of a word.

Finally, our fishing expedition also landed a lot of information about "Preferred
Family Healthcare, Inc." If I had to guess, this would be information about a particular insurance plan available to employees on a campus somewhere. Not too interesting to us, and we could have excluded it with the Boolean "not". So, we can
further refine our search to:

```
healthcare (wom* or family) not inc
```

We want "healthcare and some word starting with 'wom' or healthcare and family,
but if the menu item has 'inc' anywhere in it, ignore it."

Jughead—the searcher you never see

We have explored two kinds of searches in Gopher, an index search of a particular database and an index search of the whole Gopher community. What about
something in the middle? Remember the section "Where Gopher Was Born"? The
idea was that each department of a University could have its own Gopher server:
one for administration, one for athletics, etc. All of these servers were part of one
community. Using Veronica, there's no way to say, "Search only at the University
of Minnesota's Gophers"; that's what Jughead is for.

Jughead is an indexing facility that indexes a particular set of Gopher servers.
You'll rarely see the name Jughead. Rather, you will see another kind of index
search in a Gopher menu (usually a site's main menu), like this:

```
5. Search Gopher Menus at the University of Minnesota <?>
```

For you, it's just another index search. The underlying technology is Jughead, but
you use it just like you would use any other index item.

White-pages Servers

In Chapter 10, *Finding Someone*, we discussed white-pages services, which are
essentially electronic phone books. However, we omitted one important group of
over 300 phone book servers: those available through Gopher. White-pages services are offered through **gopher** in two ways: as normal index searches, and as
"CSO name servers."* If you find a menu item on a Gopher server called something like "Phone books" and follow it down through a bunch of geographic areas,
you will eventually get to lists of white-pages servers for different groups of
people. On that list, you might see the following entries:

```
    142. Penn State University <CSO>
--> 143. Performance Systems International <?>
```

---

*So named because they were developed from the CSnet name server code at the Computing Services
Office of the University of Illinois, Urbana.

The items flagged <CSO> are CSO-style servers, and the ones labelled <?> are Gopher index servers.

Gopher index white-pages searches

White-pages directories offered through the Gopher index facility work just like you would expect them to. You select the directory you want to use, it gives you a familiar dialog box, you fill in your search term, and Gopher looks up the name. For example, let's pick the Performance Systems International server and look up Bill Schrader, as we did in Chapter 10:

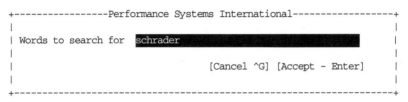

```
+-----------------Performance Systems International------------------+
|                                                                    |
| Words to search for  schrader                                      |
|                                                                    |
|                          [Cancel ^G] [Accept - Enter]              |
|                                                                    |
+--------------------------------------------------------------------+
```

You type in the name and press RETURN. Gopher looks up the name and returns some information about it in a menu item named **Raw Search Results**. If you select that menu item (often it's the only one), you will see:

```
William Schrader (1)                           wls@psi.com

President

Chief Executive Officer
PSI Inc.
   Reston International Center
   11800 Sunrise Valley Drive
   Suite 1100
   Reston, VA 22091
   USA

Telephone: +1 703-620-6651 x310
FAX:       +1 703-620-4586

Locality:    Reston, Virginia
...
```

In principle, these searches are easy. The catch is that you can never be too sure of what you're allowed to search for. Some of these places have indexed the whole text of their internal directory; some have only indexed names; and some are somewhere in between. Keep it simple and search only for first and last names.

CSO directory searches

When CSO directories were first developed, you needed a special client program to look up names. The software for this client isn't widely available; if you're not at a site that has a CSO name server, you probably don't have access to it. (That's why we didn't cover it in Chapter 10, *Finding Someone*.) However, Gopher knows how to perform CSO name-server lookups; so, once you're comfortable with Gopher, you can access these online directories too.

Let's go back to the main menu of my local Gopher server at the University of Illinois. Item 10 on this menu was labeled **Phone Books**. If you select this item, you will see something like "Phone books at other institutions". If you select this, you'll see another menu, dividing all possible phone books into geographical menus. Eventually, you'll wind your way down to something like this:

```
          Internet Gopher Information Client v1.12S


                North America

       175. University of Houston <?>
       176. University of Idaho Faculty/Staff <CSO>
   --> 177. University of Illinois Urbana-Champaign <CSO>
       178. University of Iowa <CSO>
       179. University of Kansas School of Engineering <CSO>
       180. University of Kentucky <CSO>
       ...
```

The **<CSO>** suffix at the end of a line tells you it represents CSO-style white-pages servers. The entries are mostly large universities, where CSO servers are most popular. If you access one of these items, just like you accessed the file we used in the previous example, you can look things up in the selected directory.

For example, let's say that you accessed the server for the University of Illinois by entering a carriage return. Now you get a new menu for entering search criteria:

```
          Internet Gopher Information Client v1.12S

  +-------------University of Illinois Urbana-Champaign-------------+
  |                                                                |
  | name                                                           |
  | alias                                                          |
  | email                                                          |
  | curriculum                                                     |
  | phone                                                          |
  | office_phone                                                   |
  | home_phone                                                     |
  | fax                                                            |
  | permanent_phone                                                |
  | address                                                        |
  | office_address                                                 |
  | office_location                                                |
  | home_address                                                   |
  | permanent_address                                              |
  |                                                                |
  |   [Switch Fields - TAB]        [Cancel ^G] [Accept - Enter]    |
  |                                                                |
  +----------------------------------------------------------------+
```

The cursor is originally positioned on the **name** field. You can type the words you want to search for there. If you want to constrain the search with any of the other fields, you can press TAB to move down the screen to the relevant field and add what is necessary. Don't press RETURN until you have filled in everything you want; RETURN starts the search.

CSO's search rules make sense, but they're a little different from what you might be used to. Each word in the name is taken as an item, with wildcard characters allowed.* The words in the search string must all be found in the target for the target to match. Substrings don't automatically match. If you met Ed Krol over a beer, and tried to look up "Ed Krol" when you got thirsty, you would likely be drinking alone. "Ed" would not match "Edward" or "Edwin", and his first name is not Ed. Therefore, it is usually safer to search for wildcarded first names like "Ed*". Order and case are not important. That is:

> name   `Ed* Krol`

would match "Edward M Krol", because both "Ed" followed by any characters and "Krol" were in that name. Similarly,

> name   `Krol Ed*`

would also work. You needn't match every word in an entry, like the middle initial M. After entering either of these strings, type RETURN to start the search. When it's finished, you'll see:

```
        -------------------------------------------------------
                alias: e-krol
                 name: krol edward m
               e-mail: krol@ux1.cso.uiuc.edu
                phone: (217) 333-7886
              address: 1121 dcl, MC 256
                     : 1304 w springfield : urbana, il 61801
           department: computing and communications services office
                title: asst director

        Press <RETURN> to continue, <m> to mail, <s> to save:
```

As with the text file that we retrieved earlier, you can either continue (i.e., look up another address), save this output in a file, or mail it to yourself.

One quirk of CSO-style servers is that they only index entries based on some fields in an item. You might think that you could find the person whose address is 1121 DCL by filling in line 4 and doing the search. You can't, because there is no index for the data based on the address. Your search must be based on the person's name, phone number, or email address. You can use any fields, however, to further constrain a search. For example, let's say you got a note from your secretary saying "L Ward at 244-0681 called." You don't recognize the name; after

---

*For review: * matches any sequence of characters. [*list*] matches any single character between the brackets (e.g., [abc] matches a, b, or c). CSO name servers do not honor UNIX regular expressions or the ? wildcard character.

playing telephone tag for a while, you decide to try email. So you do a lookup on "L* Ward":

```
name       L* Ward
```

The result is:

```
query name=L* Ward

Too many entries to print.
```

The search was too broad, and the server is refusing to print all the matching entries (you are usually limited to about 20). You can further constrain the search by adding the telephone number:

```
+-------------University of Illinois Urbana-Champaign--------------+
|                                                                  |
| name                                                             |
| alias                                                            |
| email                                                            |
| curriculum                                                       |
| phone                   244-0681                                 |
| office_phone                                                     |
| home_phone                                                       |
| fax                                                              |
| permanent_phone                                                  |
| address                                                          |
| office_address                                                   |
| office_location                                                  |
| home_address                                                     |
| permanent_address                                                |
|                                                                  |
|   [Switch Fields - TAB]        [Cancel ^G] [Accept - Enter]      |
|                                                                  |
+------------------------------------------------------------------+
```

Now you'll be rewarded with a single matching entry:

```
--------------------------------------------------------
           alias: l-ward1
            name: ward lynn e halpern
          e-mail: ux1.cso.uiuc.edu
           phone: (217) 244-0681
         address: 1541 dcl, MC 256
               : 1304 w springfield
               : urbana, il 61801
      department: computing services office
           title: res programmer
           hours: 7:30am - 6pm"ish" (Mon-Fri)

Press <RETURN> to continue, <m> to mail, <s> to save:
```

FTP Through Gopher

Now that you know about Gopher and indexes, you can use Gopher as an alternative interface for FTP. Gopher's FTP features currently allow you to move files from anonymous FTP servers to the computer running your **gopher** client. (I'd say "your own computer" but at first, it's more likely that you'll be using a **gopher** client on another system. This is one big motivation for running the client on your computer or workstation—you can move files directly to it.)

If you look back to Gopher's main menu, you'll see an item labeled "Peruse FTP Sites." On our **gopher**, it's item 9. The name may change from server to server, but you should be able to recognize which item we mean. Once you've selected this item, you'll see one of two types of menus; which menu you'll see depends on how your Gopher server works with FTP sites. Some servers use FTP directly, in which case you'll see an alphabetic list of sites, annotated with their holdings:

```
           Internet Gopher Information Client v1.12S

                      Peruse FTP Sites

    --> 1.  About Peruse FTP Sites.
        2.  About Anonymous FTP.
        3.  a FTP sites/              sites starting with "a"
        4.  b FTP sites/              sites starting with "b"
        5.  c FTP sites/              sites starting with "c"
        ...
```

If you see a menu like this, you'll have to search through a series of menus to find the server and file you want. In this case, let's say that you're looking for information about the effect of snowpack on drought, and that you vaguely remember that the files you want are on a server whose name starts with "c". So you select the menu for the "c" servers:

```
           Internet Gopher Information Client v1.12S

                        c FTP sites

        1.  c.scs.uiuc.edu 128.174.90.3     adventure, dungeon, world,/
        2.  cadillac.siemens.com 129.73.2.39     unknown/
        3.  caf.mit.edu 18.62.0.232     giraphe3/
        4.  calpe.psc.edu 128.182.62.148  GPLOT, GTEX/
        5.  calvin.nmsu.edu 128.123.35.150  unknown/
        6.  casbah.acns.nwu.edu 129.105.113.52  unknown/
        7.  casper.na.cs.yale.edu 128.36.12.1     multigrid repository/
    --> 8.  ..Drought info for/
        9.  cayuga.cs.rochester.edu 192.5.53.209    JOVE, NL-KR mail list/
        10. cc.curtin.edu.au 134.7.70.1     internet access sw, chemical/
        ...
```

You're lucky: **gopher** has suppressed the hostname because it's too long, but the annotation shows that item 8 is a likely source. It doesn't matter that the name is truncated; internally **gopher** knows how to access the source. So select item 8, and type a RETURN:

```
Internet Gopher Information Client v1.12S

   caticsuf.cati.csufresno.edu 129.8.100.15
             Weather/Drought info for

     1.  bin/
     2.  dev/
     3.  etc/
--> 4.  pub/
     5.  usr/
```

Now you have contacted the FTP server **caticsuf.cati.csufresno.edu**, which you believe contains the data you want. You need to find out more precisely what information it has that's useful. To search through this server's files, you use a series of **gopher** menus—not FTP-style **ls** or **dir** commands. Start by looking for a *README* file, if one exists. Unfortunately, it doesn't. So, knowing a little about FTP, you guess that the *pub* directory (item 4) is a good place to start. When you select item 4, you see lots of subdirectories, including these:

```
     4.  beer/
--> 5.  drought/
     6.  ethics/
```

The *drought* entry looks appropriate, so you select it. You get another directory; this time, you find an entry on *snowpack*, which is just what you're looking for. If you select that item, Gopher will display it on the screen and ask whether or not you want to save it or mail it elsewhere. What's interesting about this process is that the machine you're receiving the file from doesn't belong to the Gopher system at all; it's just an anonymous FTP server somewhere.

Of course, the process we just described really isn't all that convenient. Gopher makes the search a little more convenient, but you still have to know (or at least, have an idea) which server has the data you want. That's where the other kind of FTP menu comes in. Some Gopher servers use Archie to look up FTP resources. This builds an indexed resource, accessible by menu, of the entire world's supply of anonymous FTP servers! If the Gopher server you are using is using one of these, you will see a menu like this:

```
                FTP Sites

--> 1.  Read Me First.
     2.  Exact Word FTP Search <?>
     3.  Partial Word FTP Search <?>
     4.  University of Minnesota - Gopher, POPMail/
     ...
```

We're no longer looking at "raw" directories, as in the previous example; we're looking at indexed directories, accessed via Archie. That is, rather than traversing a series of menus to find a server, you can use a Gopher-style indexed-directory search to find the file you want. You're actually using Archie—but, as you'd expect, Gopher hides the details of Archie from you. You can perform two kinds of searches, corresponding to two of Archie's search types: you can perform exact string matches (item 2) or Archie substring searches (item 3). If we pick 3, Gopher responds:

```
+--------------Search of Most FTP sites (archie)-----------------+
|                                                                |
| Words to search for                                            |
|                                                                |
|                         [Cancel ^G] [Accept - Enter]           |
|                                                                |
+----------------------------------------------------------------+
```

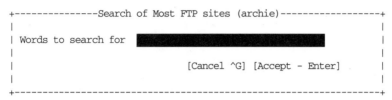

To which we respond by typing **snowpack**. After the search is completed, we get a menu:

```
            Internet Gopher Information Client v1.12S

            Partial Word FTP Search: snowpack

 --> 1.  caticsuf.cati.csufresno.edu:/pub/drought/snowpack  General Info.
     2.  caticsuf.cati.csufresno.edu:/pub/drought/snowpack.
```

This menu shows us two items, both of which match the search criterion we specified. If we select item 2, we get the same item we found previously:

```
            DEPARTMENT OF WATER RESOURCES
            Hydrology and Flood Operations

                WATER SUPPLY CONDITIONS
                  as of March 15, 1991

   Precipitation,  Northern Sierra 8-station index:
        Mar 1 - Mar 15:  12.1" (est.)
        March average:    7.0"
        Pct of Mar avg:   172%
   ...
```

Don't be surprised if you see both interfaces: an Archie-like indexed directory, plus an alphabetical list of FTP servers. Archie's resource list is probably more reliable, but both are useful in their own way. The indexed list is obviously appropriate if you're looking for information about a particular topic and don't know where to find it. The alphabetical list may be easier if you already know where the data is (you don't have to try constructing an appropriate search), or if you've heard that the FTP server at **hoople.usnd.edu** has some great stuff, and you'd like to check it out.

Gopher works just fine for text (ASCII) files, but binary files are more troublesome. To handle a binary file appropriately, **gopher** must be able to guess the file's type, based on extensions to the name (e.g., *.tar.Z*, *.hqx*, etc.). If it finds a file it recognizes as binary, **gopher** flags it for you with the **<BIN>** suffix. There is a lot of development in this area; the way **gopher** handles these files may vary from client to client. For example, the Macintosh client may work perfectly with binary files and unpack them if they end with the extension *.hqx*. The UNIX version may transfer the files in binary but leave them intact. The X version may be able to transfer picture files of various types and display them for you automatically. Another version might throw up its hands and say "I'm sorry; no can do binary." All of this is changing (hopefully for the better), so just try it and see what happens.

Even if your **gopher** client refuses to handle binary files (or if it tries, but does something unreasonable), it still isn't useless. The equal sign (=) command shows, technically, what **gopher** is doing. If you select a resource like item 2 and press =, you'll see something like this:

```
Name=snowpack
Type=0
Port=7997
Path=caticsuf.cati.csufresno.edu@/pub/drought/snowpack
Host=gopher.uiuc.edu

Press <RETURN> to continue, <m> to mail, <s> to save: █
```

The important thing here is **Path**. It tells you exactly where the resource is located. Even if **gopher** can't transfer the file for you, you still know that the hostname is **caticsuf.cati.csufresno.edu**. You can use anonymous FTP to access this host, **cd** to *pub/drought*, and retrieve any files you want with your FTP client. Once you have the file, you would do whatever decoding is necessary to make it usable.

The = command gives you Gopher's internal information on any kind of resource; what you do with that information varies by resource type. If it is a **telnet** resource, you'll have to use **telnet** to access it; if it's a file, you'll need to use FTP; etc. If it is a **gopher** resource, you can only be guaranteed access with **gopher**. In a pinch you might try anonymous **ftp** to the same machine name, but it might not work.

Using Telnet Through Gopher

Gopher can connect you to resources using **telnet** as an interface. You do this in the same fashion as every other resource: walking through the menus, and then selecting a resource that interests you. For example, while browsing through a menu under the title **Libraries**, you notice the resource below:

```
--> 23. University of California MELVYL <TEL>
```

This is an online, TELNET-style interface to the University of California's card catalog. The marker <TEL> at the end of the entry tells you that this is a **telnet** resource. When you select a **telnet** resource, **gopher** gives you a warning and a help screen:*

```
       Warning!!!!!, you are about to leave the Internet
          Gopher program and connect to another host.
       If you get stuck press the control key and the ] key,
                    and then type quit


            Now connecting to melvyl.ucop.edu

               Press return to connect:
```

Gopher gives you this warning because it loses control of your session once **telnet** starts; it regains control when **telnet** finishes. If you get hung up somewhere in TELNET, you're on your own. Control-right bracket (CTRL-]) is the common way to get to **telnet**'s command mode.†

Depending on the resource, the warning screen may have some hints about how to use it. For example:

```
       Use login "Guest"
```

or:

```
       When you get connected do a "DIAL VTAM"
```

In other cases, you are on your own. You may need to contact the site to arrange an account. Just because you are getting there through **gopher** doesn't mean you bypass security.

Now that you have read the warnings, type RETURN to get connected to the resource:

```
       Trying 31.1.0.1...
       Connected to melvyl.ucop.edu.
       Escape character is '^]'.

       DLA LINE 145 (TELNET) 06:56:54 05/06/92    (MELVYL.UCOP.EDU)

       Please Enter Your Terminal Type Code or Type ? for a List of Codes.

       TERMINAL?
```

When you are done and log out, you will return to **gopher** and to the menu where you selected the resource.

---

*This facility is very different in the Macintosh Hypercard Gopher.

†If you are using **telnet** to access a public Gopher client, remember the cautions about escape characters when running multiple TELNET sessions! Also, note that public Gopher servers usually won't allow you to access a TELNET resource. To get to TELNET resources, you need to run a client either from your own computer or from an account of your own. Chapter 5, *Remote Login*, describes TELNET in detail.

Remembering Where You Are With Bookmarks

By now you should have gotten good enough at moving around in **gopher** to have experienced one of its frustrations: getting to somewhere through a long series of menus can be tedious. You start at your main menu, pick other Gophers, pick USA, North Carolina, NCSU Library Gopher, Library without Walls. You did all of this just so you can look at the resource you really wanted to use. This isn't so bad when you're just prowling around to find out what's interesting; but what if you find a resource you want to use every Friday? It gets mighty old mighty fast.

The solution to this problem is called a *bookmark*. Bookmarks are available in almost all clients; they let you "mark" a particular place, so that Gopher can return to it later—possibly in another session.

What if you find yourself doing Veronica searches regularly? Rather than searching through menus to find the Veronica items, you might to place a bookmark on the directory where Veronica searches live. Creating a bookmark is a two-step process. First, position yourself at the menu item you want to remember:

```
--> 19. Search titles in Gopherspace using Veronica/
```

That accomplished, create the bookmark with the **a** command. Pressing **a** yields a dialog box:

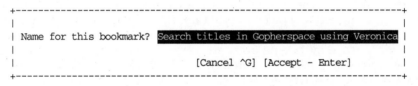

```
+--------------------------------------------------------------------+
|                                                                    |
| Name for this bookmark? Search titles in Gopherspace using Veronica |
|                                                                    |
|                        [Cancel ^G] [Accept - Enter]                |
+--------------------------------------------------------------------+
```

It's asking you to give the bookmark a name so you can recognize it later. It suggests using the item's menu string as a name. If that's OK with you, press RETURN and you're done. If you want to give the bookmark some other name, backspace over the suggested name and type whatever you like. Press RETURN when you're finished.

You now have a bookmark. You can do a search now, move somewhere else, or quit. It doesn't matter what you do since you can always jump back to this directory. You do this with the **v** command, which brings up a menu of all the bookmarks you have set:

```
               Internet Gopher Information Client v1.1

                            Bookmarks

   --> 1. Search titles in Gopherspace using Veronica/

   Press ? for Help, q to Quit, u to go up a menu          Page: 1/1
```

To jump straight to the Veronica directory, just select it like any other menu item.

Some time in the future, you might want to get rid of a bookmark. You may not need the resource any more, or the resource may have disappeared or moved. (The Internet in general, and Gopherspace in particular, is constantly in flux.) To delete a bookmark, go to the Bookmarks menu (with a **v**), select the bookmark you want to delete, and press **d**.

Bookmarks are especially useful after Veronica searches. You might get back a bunch of articles you really think are great. You haven't a clue where they live. You might figure it out with an **=**, but why bother? Just set a bookmark on the articles you want to remember and you're done.

A variation of the bookmark command remembers how you got to a particular menu, rather than an item within the menu itself. This is the **A** command. On the surface, this appears to be a two-keystroke shortcut: I can use **A** to mark the previous (or parent) menu, rather than using **u** to move to the previous menu, and **a** to set a bookmark. Why would you do this? Well, there's one obvious reason. Often you get to a directory that looks interesting; but you don't know that it really contains what you want until you look at some of the items within it. Now, when you're looking at those items, you can say "yes, this entire directory is something worth remembering" and type an **A**.

The real beauty of **A** isn't as a shortcut. It allows you to remember searches. That is, if you type **A** after performing a search, **gopher** remembers the search menu and the search string you used. Let's say you want to save our previous Veronica search for articles related to women's healthcare. By the time we finished refining the search, it was pretty complicated—**healthcare (wom* or family) not inc**—and not something you'd want to type every week when you check for new articles. To save the search itself, make the Veronica search; check to see that it found the resources you want; and type **A**. That saves the search as a bookmark. In the future, when you select the bookmark, **gopher** will re-run your search, rather than just delivering the articles you already know about. It's an easy way to check periodically for new resources.

Bookmarks can only be used to remember your position in the Gopher system. If you leave **gopher** to access something through **telnet**, you can place a bookmark on the actual <TEL> resource, but you can't place one within the resource. For example, you can place a bookmark to get you to:

```
23. University of California MELVYL <TEL>
```

When you enter this resource you will get the message "Warning!!!!!, you are about to leave the Internet Gopher program" ... remember? Among other things, this message means that Gopher can no longer keep track of where you are. If it can't do that, it can't set a bookmark. For example, you can't remember a particular menu or resource within MELVYL.

Pointing to Another Server

Earlier, we said that every Gopher client is configured with a "default server" that it contacts when it starts, and that you can specify an alternate server on the command line as follows:

```
% gopher server-name
```

There are two reasons you might want to go directly to a server. The first is to get someplace quick. If you know that the information you want is offered by one particular server, you can go there directly, rather than hunting through a bunch of menus. With thousands of servers out there, finding the one you want on a menu can be tedious. (The *Resource Catalog* in this book assumes that you'll be using Gopher this way.)

Second, there will be times when your main menu server is unavailable. Your boss comes in and says, "I need a copy of Clinton's budget proposal by ten today." You say "no problem" and fire up Gopher, but it responds:

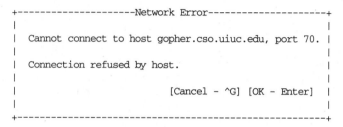

```
+--------------------Network Error--------------------+
|                                                     |
|  Cannot connect to host gopher.cso.uiuc.edu, port 70. |
|                                                     |
|  Connection refused by host.                        |
|                                                     |
|                      [Cancel - ^G] [OK - Enter]  |
|                                                     |
+-----------------------------------------------------+
```

What do you do? It's easy: just pull the name of another Gopher server out of your back pocket and add it to the command:

```
% gopher gopher.internic.net
```

How do you get server names like **gopher.internic.net**? The easiest way is to prowl around through the **Other Gopher and Information Servers** menu. When you find a particularly well-stocked server, use the = command and scribble down its name.

Gopher Development

Since the Gopher service is still under development, the features that are available are changing—hopefully for the better. Client programs for other types of computers are being developed by volunteers. Also, as they are developed, some may have different features. Some clients may omit certain features; other clients may have strange implementations of some features. So be forewarned; if you expect some surprises, you'll be able to deal with them without too much trouble.

Every day, people are learning more and more about how to put various kinds of resources up on the network. In some respects, that's making a big mess even bigger. However, it's also driving the development of new servers and indexing tools to make the Net more usable and friendly. It also means that your favorite Gopher server will be somewhat different every time you visit it. You'll just have to learn how to relish life in a changing world.

Other Gopher Clients

In this chapter, we've discussed a simple line-oriented **gopher** client for UNIX. That was an obvious choice, since it's what you'll see if you stick your toe in the water by **telnet**ing to a public Gopher client. However, there are many other clients available: **xgopher** for the X Window System, TurboGopher for the Macintosh (quite highly regarded), and several clients for Windows. But the best Gopher client is—ironically—not a Gopher client at all. It's Mosaic (available in UNIX, Windows, and Macintosh versions), a browser for the World Wide Web. We'll see it in Chapter 13; stay tuned!

A Last Word

I hope I've given you some idea of what's available through Gopher—that is, almost everything. One thing that I can't give you is a better sense of how Gopher is organized: for example, where to look if you're an archaeologist, or a financial analyst, or a software developer, or a Dante scholar. Gopher may help to guide you to the resources, but you still have to know your resources fairly well. In a traditional library, there's no substitute for browsing through the stacks and seeing what looks interesting. The same is true for Gopher: there's no substitute for exploring. Not only will you become familiar with the various commands, you'll also find out where the "good stuff" is. And you'll probably find some useful services that you didn't know existed.

## CHAPTER TWELVE

SEARCHING INDEXED DATABASES: WAIS

How WAIS Works
Getting Access
Public WAIS Clients
Adding Sources

Wide Area Information Service (WAIS, pronounced "wayz") is another of the Internet's services. It's great for searching through indexed material and finding articles based on what they contain. That is: WAIS lets you search through Internet archives looking for articles containing groups of words.

WAIS is really a tool for working with collections of data, or databases. To many people, databases connote a file full of numbers—or, once you've seen a little of what WAIS can do, a set of articles about some topic. That's too narrow a view. WAIS can deal with much more; the format of the information presented doesn't matter much. It doesn't really look at the data in the process of a search, it looks at an index. If you or someone else takes the trouble to build an index, WAIS can select information and present it to you regardless of its format. It's most common to see indexes for various kinds of text (articles and so on), but you can build an index for anything. For example, someone could build an index from descriptions of great works of art; the data tied to the index could be the works of art themselves, stored in some standard graphical format (e.g., GIF). You could then search for "gothic", and up would pop Grant Wood's painting "American Gothic." There are many such indexes built from data that is available elsewhere (such as **whois** and **archie** indexes). Some of them are useful and some are not, but you can search them and frequently come up with what you want.

I confess that I dislike the "official" terminology used to discuss WAIS. The database language is overly abstract and prevents you from seeing what WAIS can do. I like to think of WAIS databases as private libraries devoted to a particular topic: for example, a library of architectural building standards and codes. Since I find this an easier way to view things, that's how we'll talk about them for the rest of the chapter.

Like Gopher, WAIS allows you to find and access resources on the network without regard for where they really reside. In Gopher, you find resources by looking through a sequence of menus until you find something appropriate. WAIS does the same thing, but it does the searching for you. You tell it what you want; it tries to find the material you need. A WAIS command is essentially: "find me items about this in that library." WAIS then looks at all the documents in the library (or libraries) you gave it and tells you which documents are most likely to contain what you want. If you like, WAIS then displays the documents for you.

There are more than 500 free WAIS libraries on the network now. Since they are maintained by volunteer effort and donated computer time, coverage tends to be spotty. For topics where there are a lot of willing volunteers, coverage is good: as you'd expect, there are many libraries for computer science, networking, and molecular biology. Some literature libraries exist, such as Project Gutenberg's collection and various religious texts. Coverage in the social sciences is pretty thin at this time; however, libraries are always being added. There is a way to ask: "Is there a library for this topic?" So, you can easily check whether or not WAIS has any resources that are relevant to you.

Some commercial information products, like the Dow Jones Information Service, provide their product through a WAIS interface. You have to pay a fee to use services like this. Once you've arranged for payment, these services are no different than the free network WAIS services.

We'll introduce you to WAIS by discussing how it works. There are some good and bad points about how WAIS does its job. It takes a little practice to get WAIS to do what you want; you have to ask it the right questions. It's a bit easier to understand how to construct these questions if you know what WAIS does with them. Once that is behind us, we can do some searches. Finally, you can use WAIS to build and search private libraries; we'll touch on that briefly.

How WAIS Works

WAIS is a distributed text-searching system. It is based on a standard (named Z39.50*) that describes a way for one computer to ask another to do searches for it. WAIS is one of the first systems based upon this draft standard. At this point, it's also the most common.

To make a document available through a WAIS server, someone must create an index for that server to use in the search. For textual information, every word in the document is usually indexed. When you request a search from a WAIS client, it contacts the servers that handle the libraries you suggested. It asks each server, in turn, to search its index for a set of words. The server then sends you a list of documents that may be appropriate, and a "score" telling how appropriate it thinks each one is. The scores are normalized, so that the document that best matches

---

*Z39.50 is a draft ANSI standard for requesting bibliographic information. It has been under development for a long time within the library and computing communities.

your search criterion is given a score of 1000; others get proportionally less. So, if you say, "Find me documents that contain 'clinton and gore,'" WAIS looks in the index and counts how many times each document contains the word "clinton," the word "and," and the word "gore." The sum of these counts, weighted slightly by what the word is, is converted to a score for a document. After all the libraries have been searched, WAIS gives you the titles of the documents that received the highest scores. There's a limit to the number of documents it reports—usually between 15 and 50, depending on which client you use. You can then pick which documents to view, and WAIS will display them for you.

You should see a problem already. How many times can you conceive of selecting a document because it contained the word "and"? You might have thought that "and" meant the logical *and* operation in WAIS. In fact, there are no special words in WAIS; every word counts in the ranking. A document that contains 1000 matches for "and," but no matches for "clinton" or "gore" might just have the best score; or, more likely, a score high enough to place it in the top 10. Remember that WAIS is a relatively new facility, and all the kinks haven't been worked out. As the software matures, some of these problems will be resolved.

A second problem that may not be as obvious is that WAIS lacks "contextual sensitivity." You could ask WAIS to find articles containing the words "problem children," but it would also be just as happy with an item containing the sentence, "The children had a problem; they'd lost their lunch money." You can't tell WAIS that the words must occur in a certain order, and you can't provide any information about the context in which they occur.

Finally, once a search has taken you astray, you can't tell WAIS to exclude any "wrong turns" or portions of a source. That is, you can't give a command like, "find articles with the words 'problem children,' but throw out articles that contain references to lunch." There is also no way to ask, "What's been added to this source since last year?" This makes it hard to do searches repeatedly in a changing source. If your source is an index of papers from a journal, there is no way to say, "Look for the articles that have been published since the last time I checked."

So much for the bad aspects. Even with these flaws, you'll find that WAIS is one of the most useful lookup tools on the Internet. And it's possible that future versions of WAIS will solve these problems. WAIS has one really unique feature going for it: *relevance feedback*. Some clients allow you to find articles that are similar to the articles you've already found. Let's say your search for "problem children" turned up an article titled "Educational Problems In Gifted Children," in addition to the spurious "lunch money" article. "Educational Problems..." happens to be exactly what you're looking for. Relevance feedback allows you to take some text from that article and have WAIS extract good words from it to use in future searches. These searches can be done either within the same source or in a different source.

Getting Access

Accessing WAIS is a lot like accessing Gopher. In order to use it, you need a computer running a WAIS client program. You can install the client program on your own workstation, or you can access a computer that already has the client installed and run it there. Again, as with Gopher, there are WAIS clients for most standard operating systems and computers: Macintosh, DOS, X Windows, NeXT, UNIX, and so on. In all the other sections of the book, I have always said, "I'll illustrate with the UNIX version so nothing special is required to run it." Well, I could do that with WAIS, too. There is a UNIX line-oriented interface called **swais**. The problem is that explaining how to do WAIS searches using **swais** is pretty confusing. You have to give a lot of commands and use a lot of keystrokes just to set up the search, and it's not at all obvious what is happening. It is a lot easier to visualize what's happening with a graphical client, like **xwais**, which runs under the X Window System. So, in the next section, I'll first do a few examples with the X client. When you know what's happening, I'll show you how to use the line-oriented client (**swais**), too.

The line-oriented client is important because it is available at a number of public-access sites around the Internet. As with Gopher, you can **telnet** to a particular computer and login with a special ID, like "wais", and do some simple searches. You can also do WAIS searches through Gopher and the World Wide Web (which we'll discuss in the next chapter). Most Gopher servers have a line like this on the main menu:

```
9.  Other Gopher and Information Servers/
```

If you select this item, the next menu will have an entry:

```
6.  WAIS Based Information/
```

This item lets you use the Gopher index interface to search any WAIS source for which there is no charge. The only thing you can't do with this facility is search multiple sources at one time.

You might want to use one of these public servers the first time to try things out. If you decide you want to use it regularly, get yourself a better client (like Gopher, WAIS clients are getting better all the time). They are all available for free from various places. You can use **archie** to find them. Look for something called *freeWAIS*.* Two FTP archives where you can find this software are **ftp.cnidr.org** in the U.S. and **nic.funet.fi** in Europe. As with the other software we've discussed in this book, the choice of a WAIS client is primarily a matter of taste.

---

*Although the development of WAIS was done by Thinking Machines, Apple, Dow Jones, and KPMG Pete Marwick, most of the current work on the free software (*freeWAIS*) is coordinated by the Clearinghouse for Networked Information Discovery and Retrieval (CNIDR).

Formulating a WAIS Search

Now that we're through the preliminaries, let's get started. In order to get properly started, though, you need to make a leap of faith and forget how you would normally deal with computer databases. When many users try WAIS for the first time, they ask the question "What libraries of documents are out there, anyway?" This is the wrong approach. People are used to relying on the computer for some tasks and their brain for the others. The brain is usually responsible for scanning lists to look for interesting items. In order to use WAIS most effectively, you must trust WAIS and let it do the scanning for you.

When you start the WAIS client for X Windows, **xwais**, the first thing you'll see is the main window, which appears in Figure 12-1. WAIS clients maintain two libraries: a library of questions and a library of sources.* This window shows both. The **Questions** section at the top contains identifiers for queries you may want to make again. If you want to see what is new in a particular field every month, you can re-execute the search in its original form, or modify it and issue it again. Here we see one saved question, named *child-sources.*

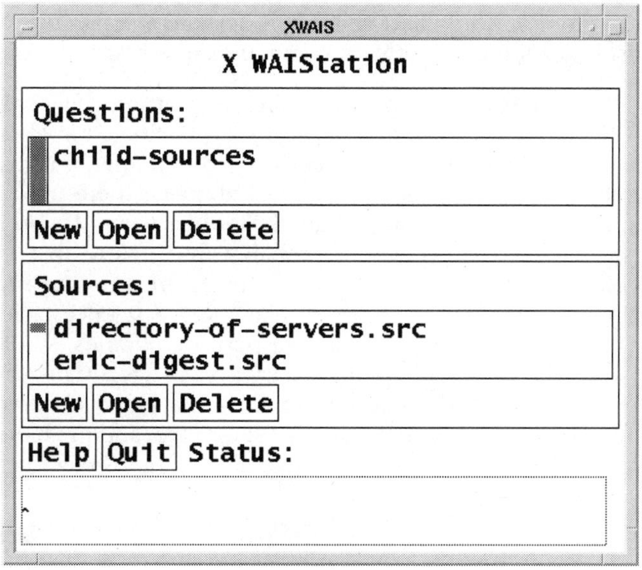

Figure 12-1: Main window

---

*These libraries are stored in directories named *wais-questions* and *wais-sources* in your home directory for the account you use to run this client.

The **Sources** section, just below the **Questions** section, is for source library mainte-nance. It shows a scrollable list of libraries that your client knows how to locate and search.

The **Questions** and **Sources** sections each have three buttons:

New   Creates a new question or source window

Open   Displays an existing question or a source that you have selected by clicking on it. The **Open** button is used to change and re-execute a question, or to change source entries.

Delete   Deletes an existing question or a source that you have selected

Towards the bottom of the window, there are two buttons. The **Help** button gets you help if you click on it. **Quit** terminates **xwais**.

Finding a library

There is a list of public WAIS libraries, but that list is a WAIS library itself. If you know about one library, the *directory-of-servers*, you've got it all. But instead of reading the list of libraries yourself, you should start your search by asking WAIS: "What library do I look in for 'gifted children'?" To start the process, click the **New** button. This displays another window, with a template for asking a question.

So, now it's time to compose a question. Before starting, I'll give you a clue. "Gifted children" is much too narrow a term; if you look for libraries that are appropriate for "gifted children," you're not likely to find any. This makes sense, if you think about traditional (books and paper) libraries: there are probably very few libraries in the world with "gifted children" in their name. If you had an index of important special collections, you'd probably find a few that contained the words "gifted children," but not too many. If you restricted your search to these libraries, you'd miss many libraries with excellent social science collections, some of which may be more useful than the special-purpose libraries. WAIS is no differ-ent. The right way to find an appropriate library is to use really broad terms. Think about what kind of people would be concerned about gifted children. You might think of social workers, educators, parents, etc. Since adding more terms to a search in WAIS makes it easier to match, try to search the *directory-of-servers* with your relevant terms:

```
social work
education
parenting
```

Type your keywords into the **Tell me about**: window, as shown in Figure 12-2.

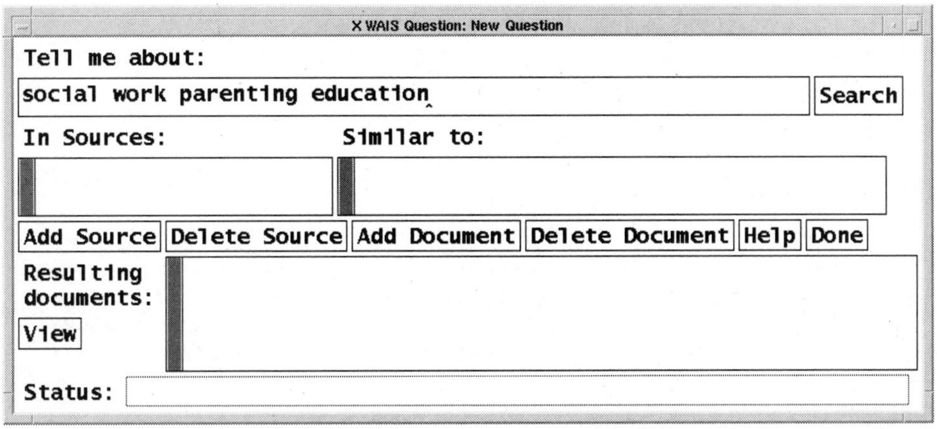

Figure 12-2: Directory-of-servers query

After you've filled in the relevant terms, click on the **Add Source** button. This displays a pull-down menu of all the libraries listed in your client's library of sources, shown in Figure 12-3.

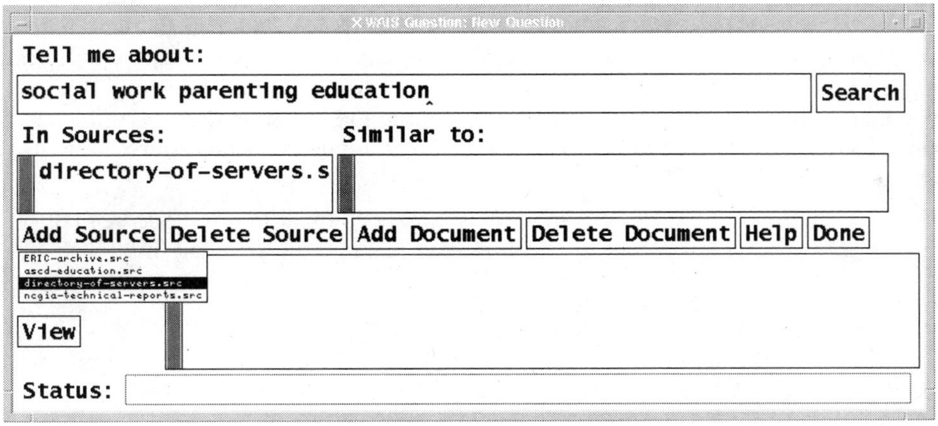

Figure 12-3: Selecting a source

Move the arrow to the *directory-of-servers*, which appears in reverse video, and let the button go; the *directory-of-servers* will appear in the **In Sources:** box. Now you're ready to run your query. So, with bated breath, push the **Search** button.

If you did things correctly, WAIS will fill in the **Resulting documents:** section of the window, as shown in Figure 12-4.

```
┌──────────────────────────────────────────────────────────────────────┐
│ ⌐                          X WAIS Question: New Question            ◻ ⌐│
│ ┌──────────────────────────────────────────────────────────────────┐ │
│  Tell me about:                                                       │
│ ┌────────────────────────────────────────────────────┐ ┌──────────┐  │
│  social work parenting education̯                        │ │ Search │  │
│ └────────────────────────────────────────────────────┘ └──────────┘  │
│  In Sources:                    Similar to:                           │
│ ┌───────────────────────────────┐ ┌────────────────────────────────┐ │
│ │▌ directory-of-servers.s        │▌                                  │ │
│ └───────────────────────────────┘ └────────────────────────────────┘ │
│ ┌───────────┐┌─────────────┐┌─────────────┐┌───────────────┐┌────┐┌────┐│
│ │Add Source ││Delete Source││Add Document ││Delete Document││Help││Done││
│ └───────────┘└─────────────┘└─────────────┘└───────────────┘└────┘└────┘│
│  Resulting      │▌ 1000   986 ascd-education.src    /proj/wais/wais-sources│
│  documents:     │   625   518 ncgia-technical-reports.src   /proj/wais/wai│
│ ┌──────┐        │   375  1020 ERIC-archive.src    /proj/wais/wais-sources/ │
│ │ View │        │   375  1 2K eric-digest.src    /proj/wais/wais-sources/ │
│ └──────┘                                                               │
│ ┐ Status: ┌─────────────────────────────────────────────────────────┐ │
│          └─────────────────────────────────────────────────────────┘ │
└──────────────────────────────────────────────────────────────────────┘
```

Figure 12-4: Results of directory search

Look at the first result:

```
1000  986 ascd-education.src /proj/wais/wais-sources
```

The 1000 is its score; this score indicates that it fit your search criteria better than any other source, not that it was a perfect match—but you're more likely to find interesting articles here than anywhere else. The size is listed next: 986 characters.* The name of the index, *ascd-education.src*, sounds promising. When you make your next search, looking for actual articles (rather than promising libraries), you'll select *ascd-education.src* in the **Add Source** menu, and add it to your search list, **In Sources**. At the end of the line, you see the filename of this source. You can ignore this for now.

If you scroll down the list of prospective sources, you will find their scores fall off significantly after the top four. So, you decide to draw the pass-fail line there and use the top four for the real search:

```
ascd-education.src
ncgia-technical-reports.src
ERIC-archives.src
eric-digest.src
```

Now that you've successfully searched for something, it's really tempting to click the **Done** button and get rid of the search window. Don't be so hasty. You'll need this information again in a bit. The *directory-of-servers* is like the Yellow Pages telephone directory. It tells you what telephone numbers to call for different services, but it doesn't call them for you. The *directory-of-servers* likewise tells you where to look to find what you want. You'll need to take the sources you just found, and use them in the next search. Leave the window on the screen, and you won't have to write the names of those four libraries on a piece of paper to use them.

---

*This is the size of the item you found. In this case it is the size of the server descriptor. The 986 characters has nothing to do with the size or completeness of the ascd-education library itself.

It's time to think about what we just accomplished. There are a couple of obvious questions which WAIS users ask at this point. First: "How do the *directory-of-servers*, the library of sources, and the **In Sources:** area of the screen relate?" To make sense of this, you need to keep in mind what you know and what your client knows. In the beginning, you know what you want to ask, but you don't know where to tell your client to look. Your client knows how to look in all the servers listed in its library of sources, but you have to tell it which ones. The *directory-of-servers* solves this quandary by suggesting where you should send your client looking. Once you've found out which libraries are useful, you can fill in the **In Sources** part of a question and send WAIS off.* On occasion, you may find that a search through the *directory-of-servers* suggests libraries that your client doesn't know about. Perhaps they are new and your client's source library doesn't have their entries yet (remember, your client can only search libraries found in its Sources library). For now, let's assume that any source suggested to you by the *directory-of-servers* is in your client's library of sources.

The second question is simply "Why do we bother?" Why don't we just tell WAIS to "look everywhere"? There are several reasons. First, selecting sources is one way to narrow the search. If you ask WAIS to look up items about "cars," you could get articles on toys, automobiles, and Computer Aided Registration Systems (CARS). Selecting some suitable libraries, like "automobile-repair-records," focuses your search.† Wading through hundreds of articles to decide which are relevant is a waste of your time—that's what WAIS is supposed to do. Second, searching everywhere could take a long time. You don't go to the library and start at one end of the shelves looking at every title to find something of interest. You know automobile repair starts at 629.28, so you find that section and browse only that section.

Asking your question

Now that we've got these questions out of the way, let's get back to behavior problems: how do we compose an appropriate question? The real search is similar to the directory search with which we started. Go to the main menu and click the **New** button in the question area. Now you have a new question menu; fill in some relevant keywords:

```
behavior problems in gifted children
```

Then you fill in the sources section. That is, you fill in the "phone numbers" you found above from the "yellow pages." You do this as before, with the pull-down menu under **Add Source**, but you need to do it four times, once for each source. Now you are ready. You click the **Search** button, and off you go. In a bit, the results return, as shown in Figure 12-5.

---

*You may also find that searching the *directory-of-servers* leads you to another directory of servers: for example, *JANUS-dir-of-servers* (which happens to be a good place to look for legal and U.N.-related resources). That's OK; just add this new directory to your source list and ask a general question again.

†I used this for illustration; I don't think this library exists—yet.

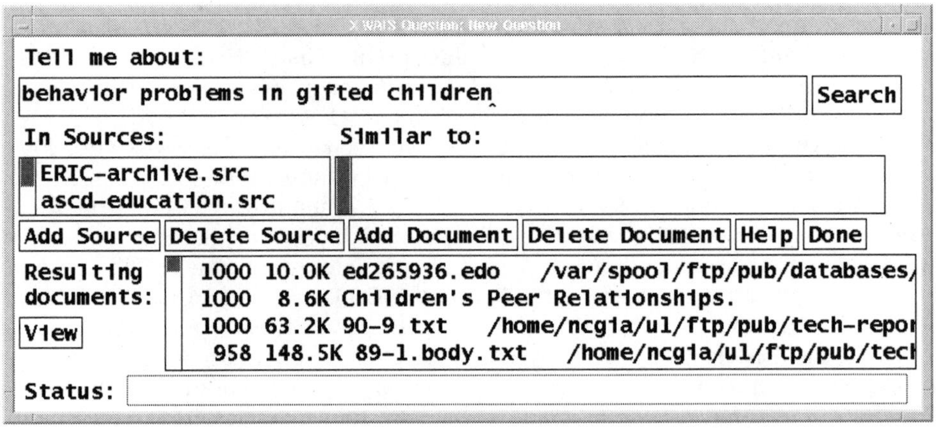

```
┌─────────────────────────────────────────────────────────────────────────┐
│                      X WAIS Question: New Question                        │
├─────────────────────────────────────────────────────────────────────────┤
│  Tell me about:                                                           │
│  ┌──────────────────────────────────────────────────────┐  ┌──────────┐  │
│  │behavior problems in gifted children                  │  │ Search   │  │
│  └──────────────────────────────────────────────────────┘  └──────────┘  │
│  In Sources:                   Similar to:                                │
│  ┌────────────────────────┐    ┌────────────────────────────────────┐    │
│  │ ERIC-archive.src        │    │                                    │    │
│  │ ascd-education.src      │    │                                    │    │
│  └────────────────────────┘    └────────────────────────────────────┘    │
│  ┌──────────┐┌─────────────┐┌──────────────┐┌─────────────────┐┌────┐┌────┐│
│  │Add Source││Delete Source││Add Document  ││Delete Document  ││Help││Done││
│  └──────────┘└─────────────┘└──────────────┘└─────────────────┘└────┘└────┘│
│  Resulting      1000 10.0K ed265936.edo    /var/spool/ftp/pub/databases/  │
│  documents:     1000  8.6K Children's Peer Relationships.                 │
│  ┌──────┐       1000 63.2K 90-9.txt     /home/ncg1a/u1/ftp/pub/tech-repor  │
│  │ View │        958 148.5K 89-1.body.txt   /home/ncg1a/u1/ftp/pub/tech    │
│  └──────┘                                                                  │
│  Status: ┌───────────────────────────────────────────────────────────┐   │
│          └───────────────────────────────────────────────────────────┘   │
└─────────────────────────────────────────────────────────────────────────┘
```

Figure 12-5: Result of behavior problems search

Now that's what you wanted: a set of articles which sound interesting. (If you
want to see more of the titles, you can expand the window horizontally.) The
item's size field tells you the size (in bytes) of what will be fetched. If you click on
Children's Peer Relationships and push **View**, WAIS will fetch the article (8.6K
characters worth) for you and will display it in another window. This is shown in
Figure 12-6.

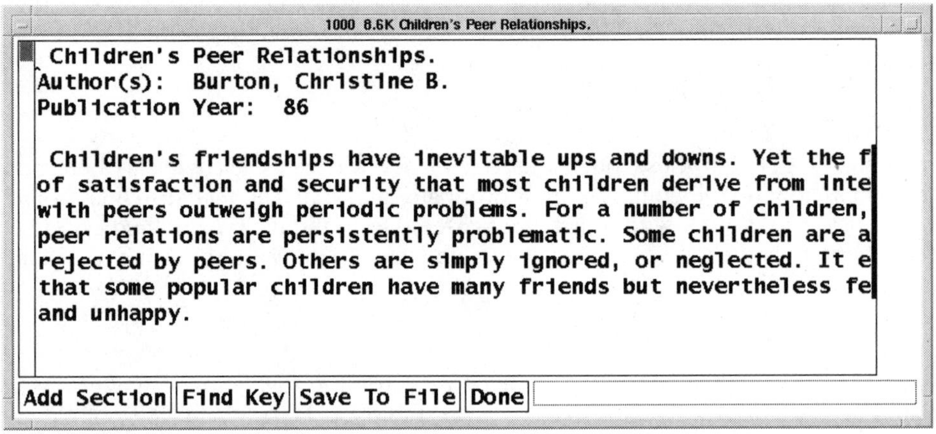

```
┌─────────────────────────────────────────────────────────────────────────┐
│                1000 8.6K Children's Peer Relationships.                   │
├─────────────────────────────────────────────────────────────────────────┤
│  Children's Peer Relationships.                                           │
│  Author(s):  Burton, Christine B.                                         │
│  Publication Year:  86                                                    │
│                                                                           │
│  Children's friendships have inevitable ups and downs. Yet the f          │
│  of satisfaction and security that most children derive from inte         │
│  with peers outweigh periodic problems. For a number of children,         │
│  peer relations are persistently problematic. Some children are a         │
│  rejected by peers. Others are simply ignored, or neglected. It e         │
│  that some popular children have many friends but nevertheless fe         │
│  and unhappy.                                                             │
│                                                                           │
│  ┌─────────────┐┌──────────┐┌──────────────┐┌──────┐                      │
│  │ Add Section ││ Find Key ││ Save To File ││ Done │                      │
│  └─────────────┘└──────────┘└──────────────┘└──────┘                      │
└─────────────────────────────────────────────────────────────────────────┘
```

Figure 12-6: Article you retrieved

This screen lets you do four things, in addition to reading the article:

Add Section   Adds a previously selected section of the article to the relevance feedback section of the question window. (This is the **Similar to:** field, shown in Figure 12-5.)

Find Key   Skips forward in the text to the next occurrence of a word that was one of the search terms and highlights it.

Save to File   Saves the article in a file on the computer running the client. The client asks you for a filename. WAIS then stores the article by that name in a directory, *wais-documents*, under your home directory.

Done   Gets rid of the article and the window.

Finally, with your problem solved, you can push the **Done** button on the question window. WAIS will ask you if you want to save the question. If you do, you need to provide a filename. After saving a question, it will appear in your "question library." Next time you want to ask the same question, just select it from the **Questions** section of the main window and click on the **Open** button.

Refining a Search

Relevance feedback lets you use the results of a search to further refine the search. You do this by selecting items, either in whole or in part, that you have already found and moving them to the **Similar to:** area of the question window. If you want to use the whole article, you select the article on the question screen and click on **Add Document**. The result of this action is shown in Figure 12-7.

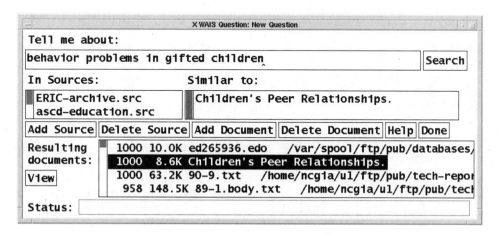

Figure 12-7: Feedback search setup

In this example, you selected "Children's Peer Relationships" as the most appropriate article to use.

To use a portion of an article as feedback, you must be viewing the document. Select the text you want with the mouse and click on the **Add Section** button in the view window. When you move back to the question window, the feedback section will refer to the selected portions of the document. You can select multiple pieces of the same article, or of different articles, in the same manner. When you are done selecting, click **Search** to try the search again, this time with the added selection criteria.

NOTE

Relevance feedback is the section of clients undergoing the most development. If a client is going to die on you, this is where it will happen. If your client runs into trouble, check whether a newer one is available.

From start to finish, there are a lot of steps. A summary of how to go about searching is in order:

1. Select the *directory-of-servers*.

2. Ask a general question of the *directory-of-servers* to find any libraries that are relevant to your topic. Do this as often as you need, to find good libraries.

3. Select the libraries that look interesting.

4. Ask a specific question to find the articles (or other items) that you're searching for.

5. If you're not satisfied with the results, refine your search (possibly using relevance feedback) to get a new set of articles.

As I've said, formulating good WAIS searches can be tricky. With some practice, though, you'll get the hang of it.

When Searches Don't Go as Planned

Sometimes your searches won't retrieve what you want; you may get articles that are unrelated, or you might find nothing at all. There are two possible problems: you either used inappropriate keywords or the wrong sources. That's one reason why most WAIS clients let you save your questions. Some questions are hard to construct. Once you have one that works, you may not want to let it go. Even if you don't want to ask the same question next time, you may find it easier to modify an old search than to start from scratch. It is not unusual to do a search many times, modifying it slightly each time until you get what you want.

Of course, saving your searches doesn't solve the problem at hand: searches that aren't effective in the first place. The only real solution is to keep trying until you find something that works. However, we can give you some hints about how to proceed:

*   If the search results are reasonable, but not what you really want, refine the search, either by adding keywords yourself or using relevance feedback.

*   View an article even if it isn't what you really want. It may give you some ideas about terms appropriate to the field you're searching. You won't find

many matches for "God" in the Koran, but you will find "Allah". WAIS does not automatically try synonyms. This technique might also turn up some variant spellings ("behavior" versus "behaviour") or relevant synonyms (like "Llah").

- If WAIS doesn't find anything, and if you're confident of the sources, try a simple search first, for which you're sure there will be some articles. Look at the results; this may give you some clues about the best words to search for.

- If you keep getting irrelevant articles, try to limit the number of sources you use. The problem is that a highly rated source can, on occasion, provide a lot of irrelevant articles. So you've got to find out which source is providing the irrelevancies, and eliminate it from your search. Unfortunately, not all WAIS clients tell you which source a particular document came from. You might be able to guess by checking whether the article's filename corresponds to the source's name. (This won't always help, but it's worth trying.) It you need to, you can delete a source and try the search again. If it's better, leave it out. If it's worse, put it back and delete another.

Public WAIS Clients

Using the line-oriented, public client **swais** is not particularly hard. (Remember, **swais** is not really different. It is just a particular WAIS client, which is used when you are using a line-mode terminal.) Just like Gopher, it may be available on the computer you normally use. If it is, you should be able to access it just by entering **swais**. For the sake of the discussion, I will assume that you are using a public client. So, the first thing you must do is pick a likely prospect out of the Public WAIS Servers table and **telnet** to it.

Table 12-1: Public WAIS Servers

Name	Login	Location
info.funet.fi	wais	Europe
swais.cwis.uci.edu	swais	Western US*
cnidr.org	demo	Eastern US
sunsite.unc.edu	swais	Eastern US
quake.think.com	wais	Eastern US

* This server has a limited number of databases, mostly of interest only to University of California, Irvine students and staff. It can still be used to practice and investigate **swais**.

When you are connected, use the login shown, and you will automatically be placed in **swais**. For example:

```
% telnet quake.think.com
Trying 192.31.181.1...
Connected to quake.think.com.
Escape character is '^]'.
```

```
SunOS UNIX (quake)

login: wais
Welcome to swais.
Please type user identifier (i.e user@host): krol@ux1.cso.uiuc.edu
TERM = (unknown) vt100
Starting swais (this may take a little while)...
```

What happens next will vary significantly from place to place. When the number of WAIS databases was small, each of these public clients would have all known databases in their available-source list. Now that there are over 500 WAIS libraries, if they were all in the source list, it would be around 25 pages of sources to wade through.

Since you have no storage to build a personal set of interesting sources, and working with all the databases at once is unwieldy, many of these public clients start with a single source: the *directory-of-servers*. Even if you know exactly which source you want to use, you must still search the *directory-of-servers* to find it. This search retrieves the database's descriptor records. You then add the descriptors to the list of sources available in your current session, and select them to do your real search. If the client you use gives you the whole list of sources at this point, you may skip the first search of the *directory-of-servers*—provided that you already know which sources you want. Just find them (in the 25-page listing) and select them. (It still might be easier to go through the *directory-of-servers*.)

Let's say that you'd like to find an interesting fish dish to make for dinner tonight. After connecting to **quake.think.com** and logging in, you are greeted with this basic **swais** screen:

```
SWAIS                          Source Selection
Sources:  1
    #           Server                  Source                Cost
001:    [     quake.think.com]  directory-of-servers          Free




Keywords:

<space> selects, w for keywords, arrows move, <return> searches, q quits, or ?
```

You have at your disposal one source, the *directory-of-servers*. First select that source, as the one you want to use. (You don't have much choice; it's either this or nothing.) To select a source, move down to the line on which it's listed, either by using your arrow keys or typing the source's number, followed by RETURN. Once you have yourself positioned, press SPACE to select the source. Since there is only one source available to you, you should only need to press SPACE. An asterisk appears in the display to flag the *directory-of-servers* as a selected source:

```
001: * [     quake.think.com]  directory-of-servers          Free
```

Once you have chosen a source, you need to enter the keywords you want to search for. Pressing **w** signals that you want to enter keywords; the client positions the cursor near the bottom left of the screen, and prompts you:

```
Keywords: ethnic cooking
```

You type in the words you are interested in, separated by spaces. We're looking for some interesting fish recipes, so we'll start with "ethnic cooking." Why not just start with "fish"? At this point, we're still looking for cookbooks in our electronic card catalog; we aren't yet looking for recipes. Once we find some cookbooks, we'll do a more specific search.

After typing the search string, press RETURN; that starts the actual search. When the search is completed, it will return a screen similar to this, showing the results:

```
SWAIS                            Search Results
Items:  8
  #     Score    Source                Title                     Lines
001:   [1000] (directory-of-se)  ANU-Aboriginal-Studies            73
002:   [1000] (directory-of-se)  ANU-CanbAnthropology-Index        86
003:   [1000] (directory-of-se)  ANU-SSDA-Australian-Census       106
004:   [1000] (directory-of-se)  ANU-SSDA-Australian-Opinion      114
005:   [1000] (directory-of-se)  ANU-SSDA-Australian-Studies      126
006:   [1000] (directory-of-se)  ANU-Thai-Yunnan                   83
007:   [1000] (directory-of-se)  recipes                           15
008:   [1000] (directory-of-se)  usenet-cookbook                   21


  <space> selects, arrows move, w for keywords, s for sources, ? for help
```

This is really interesting. You found eight sources; they all get a score of 1000. Some of them are mighty odd. This is a good illustration of how WAIS works. You were looking for the words "ethnic" and "cooking." The ANU resources are a bunch of sociological sources which matched the single word "ethnic." Sources 7 and 8 matched the single word "cooking." Since each source matched one word, they were all given the same score.

Now that you know what sources to use, you need to add them to the list of sources available to you. Select each source that looks interesting, either by using the arrow buttons or typing its number and a RETURN. When you have positioned the cursor, type the **u** command (use this source). This will cause the left bottom line to say things like "Initializing connection..." followed by "Adding source...", but won't change the display you are looking at. In this example, you would do two **u** commands, one while positioned at line 7 and one at line 8 (type 7 RETURN u 8 RETURN u).

To see the effect of what you have done, give the **s** command to view sources. Its output will now look something like this:

```
SWAIS                        Source Selection
Sources:  3
    #           Server               Source                  Cost
001: *  [     quake.think.com]   directory-of-servers         Free
002:    [     wais.oit.unc.edu]  recipes                      Free
003:    [ cmns-moon.think.com]   usenet-cookbook              Free

Keywords: ethnic cooking

   <space> selects, w for keywords, arrows move, <return> searches, q quits, or ?
```

Notice that you now have three possible sources to search, but you still have the *directory-of-servers* selected (remember the asterisk). If you were to search for a recipe now, you would only search the *directory-of-servers*: not what you had in mind. You must do two things: first get rid of the current selected sources, then select the sources you want. This is pretty easy. Press = to de-select all current sources. It will get rid of all the asterisks in the display. Next, select the sources you want just as you selected *directory-of-servers* initially: move to lines 2 and 3 and press the SPACE bar.

You've finally set up the environment for doing the search you originally wanted. You need to change keywords, so you enter a **w** again. Surprise: it positioned you after the keywords, "ethnic cooking," that you entered earlier. You need to clear these out by typing **CTRL-U**. After clearing the keyword list, list the ingredients you are looking for in the recipe:

Keywords: **garlic fish rice onion**

Pressing RETURN signals the end of keyword entry and starts the search. Let's see what you caught:

```
SWAIS                      Search Results                  Items: 40
    #   Score    Source             Title                   Lines
001:   [1000] (cmns-moon.think)  SARDINE-FRY(M)    USENET Cookbook   47
002:   [1000] (      recipes)    gidh@buckn Re: COLLECTION  LONG I  936
003:   [ 946] (      recipes)    arielle@ta Re: Appetizers (Long)  1591
004:   [ 946] (      recipes)    arielle@ta Re: Appetizers          1590
005:   [ 931] (cmns-moon.think)  RICE-BEAN-BAKE     USENET Cookbook  61
006:   [ 931] (cmns-moon.think)  CURRIED-RICE       USENET Cookbook  67
007:   [ 924] (cmns-moon.think)  CABBAGE-SALAD(SL)  USENET Cookbook  45
008:   [ 917] (cmns-moon.think)  TARAMOSALATA-1(A)  USENET Cookbook  61
009:   [ 917] (cmns-moon.think)  HOT-FANNY-1(S)     USENET Cookbook  64
010:   [ 910] (cmns-moon.think)  TORTILLA-SOUP(SPV) USENET Cookbook  74
011:   [ 910] (cmns-moon.think)  STROGANOFF-1(M)    USENET Cookbook  56
012:   [ 889] (cmns-moon.think)  PONCIT(M)          USENET Cookbook  54
013:   [ 889] (cmns-moon.think)  PEANUT-SAUCE-1(M)  USENET Cookbook  62
014:   [ 889] (cmns-moon.think)  CUBAN-BEANS(MV)    USENET Cookbook  67
015:   [ 882] (cmns-moon.think)  BLACK-EYE-RICE(B)  USENET Cookbook  57
016:   [ 882] (cmns-moon.think)  AFRICAN-STEW(MV)   USENET Cookbook  56
017:   [ 869] (cmns-moon.think)  PICADILLO(M)       USENET Cookbook  92
018:   [ 862] (cmns-moon.think)  CHICKEN-WINE(M)    USENET Cookbook  52

   <space> selects, arrows move, w for keywords, s for sources, ? for help
```

You can view any one of these items by selecting it, as before, and pressing SPACE. Notice that a lot of these items don't have much to do with fish—next time, you might be better off with a more restrictive search. The first item, SAR-DINE-FRY, looks appetizing. It's highlighted, so it's already selected; just press SPACE to see the recipe:

Recipe From The Net

SARDINE-FRY(M)   USENET Cookbook   SARDINE-FRY(M)

SLOPPY SARDINES

    SARDINE-FRY - Sardines with garlic and tomato. A quick and easy meal for two people. This is a recipe conjured up by my friend, Carole Senior.

INGREDIENTS (serves 2)
2	cans of sardines
1	small onion chopped
1/2	green pepper, chopped
6 oz	tomatoes (1 small can)
1/2	garlic clove, crushed
pinch	salt and pepper
2 Tbsp	cooking oil
1 cup	uncooked white rice
2 cups	water

PROCEDURE
    (1) Heat the oil in a small frying pan.
    (2) At the same time place the water, rice and a pinch of salt
        into a small saucepan and simmer for 15 minutes.
    (3) Place the chopped onion and pepper in the frying pan and
        cook until the onion becomes soft.
    (4) Add the tomatoes, garlic, sardines, salt and pepper to the
        frying pan and cook for 10 to 15 minutes, stirring occasionally.
    (5) Serve over the rice.

RATING
    Difficulty: easy. Time: 5 minutes preparation, 15 minutes cooking.
    Precision: measure the rice.

CONTRIBUTOR
    Andy Cheese, Department of Computer Science, University of Nottingham, UK
    abc@uk.ac.nott.cs   mcvax!ukc!nott.cs!abc

The USENET Cookbook. Copyright 1991 USENET Community Trust. Permission to copy without fee all or part of this material is granted provided that the copies are not made or distributed for direct commercial advantage, the USENET copyright notice, title, and publication date appear, and notice is given that copying is by permission of the USENET Community Trust.

You're done! If you want to get your own copy of the message, type **q** to get back to the list of recipes; then type **m** to mail the recipe to yourself. You'll be prompted for your email address. When you are done with **swais**, type **q** to exit from the program.

We've now demonstrated all the commands you need to use the **swais** client, but there are a few more which might make your life a bit easier:

/*string* Search for a particular string in the results.

S   Save an article in a file. (This doesn't work on public WAIS clients.)

r   Use an article for "relevance feedback."

Adding Sources

When we composed the question before about "behavior problems in gifted children," we first looked up some interesting source libraries in the *directory-of-servers*. We then used the **Add Source** pop-up menu to add these to the source list for our "real" question. Now it's time to ask: how does a source get onto the **Add Source** menu?

In our example, we assumed that the WAIS client already knows about all the sources—at least, all that were interesting to you. This is normally a good assumption. However, you'll occasionally find sources that your WAIS client doesn't already know about. These sources may show up in the *directory-of-servers*, and therefore may appear in searches through the directory, but you won't find them on the **Add Source** menu. (It's also possible to discover sources that aren't even listed in the *directory-of-servers*; we'll describe that situation later.) Remember that the *directory-of-servers* is like the phone book's Yellow Pages; likewise, the **Add Source** menu is like a set of "speed dial" buttons on your telephone. If you look up your favorite pizzeria in the Yellow Pages, you'll find it listed there; but you could just press the speed dial button on your phone (you probably programmed it last year). However, if you want to try a new pizzeria, you'll have to look it up in the Yellow Pages *and* program it into your phone.

To see why this analogy is relevant, think about what the *directory-of-servers* is. It's just another library (or database). The actual information isn't on your client—it's on a server in some remote part of the world (probably Cambridge MA, where Thinking Machines, one of the WAIS developers, is located). You can make WAIS searches on that server, and dig up any information that it knows about. And, from time to time (fairly often, in fact) people create new WAIS libraries, tell the folks at Thinking Machines who maintain the *directory-of-servers*, and these new sources appear there. Your client doesn't know anything about these new sources, any more than your phone automatically knows about every number in the Yellow Pages. How could it? You find a new library in the library of servers, and you'd like to use it; but your local client doesn't even know the name of the

system on which to find it. This information is available, but it's all in Cambridge.*
How do you tell your WAIS client about the new library?

This is called "saving," or "adding," a source. It's really quite easy. Most WAIS clients let you copy a source entry directly. In fact, if you have used the public **swais** client, you've already done this. When you used the **u** command to "use" a source, you actually were telling **swais** to add the source you selected to the sources library. With the public client, you get a source library scratch space when you start; it is destroyed when you leave.

It's just as easy to do this in **xwais**, if not easier. Let's say your question to the *directory-of-servers* about "social work" accidentally turned up a strange source called *beer.src*, with a fairly low score. This probably isn't relevant, but you think it's interesting; it might contain recipes for home-brew, or something else you'd like. You ignored it when you were looking up articles about "behavior problems in gifted children," but now you want to see if you can find a new recipe for lager. So you pop up a new question window and start searching the **Add Source** menu. Surprise! *beer.src* doesn't show up. With the X client, go to the menu where you searched the *directory-of-servers* for relevant libraries—i.e., the question in which you discovered this new library. Click on *beer.src*, and then "view" the library. You'll see a new window with a description of the library. This window will have a button labeled **Save**. If you click on that button, your client will save the source automatically; you don't need to type anything.

Now you can go back to your new question. This time, when you search through the **Add Source** menu, you'll see *beer.src*. Your client now knows about it; you've added it to the "speed dialing" library. Add it to your search list, just like any other source.

New Sources That Aren't in the Directory-of-Servers

Most of the time, you'll discover new sources through the *directory-of-servers*. However, on occasion you'll find one through other means. You might be prowling through a newsgroup and see a message like this:

```
I just created a new and most wonderful source:

(:source
     :version  3
     :ip-name "nic.sura.net"
     :tcp-port 210
     :database-name "/export/software/nic/wais/databases/ERIC-archive"
     :cost 0.00
     :cost-unit :free
```

---

*It's actually a credit to WAIS that this is so confusing. If we had to think in detail about what information was where, and who knew what, everything would be clear. After all, if someone told you "There's a great new FTP archive about gerontology," you'd know that you don't have enough information to use the archive; you'd immediately ask "where?" But WAIS really gives you the illusion that all the data is available locally. You still have to ask "where" (or get WAIS to ask "where") but it almost seems like you shouldn't have to.

```
         :maintainer "info@sura.net"
         :description "ERIC (Educational Resources Information Center)
Digests

Information provided by EDUCOM

ERIC Digests are:

- short reports (1,000 - 1,500 words) on one or two pages, on topics
  of prime current interest in education.
- targeted specifically for teachers and administrators, and other
  practitioners, but generally useful to the broad educational
community.
- designed to provide an overview of information on a given topic,
  plus references to items providing more detailed information.
- produced by the 16 subject-specialized ERIC Clearinghouses, and
reviewed
  by experts and content specialists in the field.
- funded by the Office of Educational Research and Improvement (OERI),
  of the U.S. Department of Education (ED).

Created with WAIS Release 8 b4 on Apr 10 13:02:45 1992 by
lidl@nic.sura.net
")
```

Most of this message (everything following the first line) is a standard WAIS descriptor for the source. To tell your client about this source, go to the **Sources** section of the main menu. Click the **New** button. After you push that button, **xwais** puts up a blank template for you to fill in the information necessary to add a source.* If you were to fill in the template given for the "ERIC-archive" source shown in the previous example, it would look like Figure 12-8. Retyping the source by hand may be painful, but if you're using a window system, you should have a copy/paste mechanism to move large chunks of text automatically.

When you are done adding or changing an entry for a source, you can either save your changes, or throw them away by using the **Accept Changes** or **Discard Changes** button, at the bottom of the window.

---

*Before copying the source descriptor by hand, though, it might save you some work to search the *directory-of-servers* to see whether or not it's been added "officially" to the list. Anyone who creates a new library is supposed to tell Thinking Machines. This doesn't always happen, but it's worth checking.

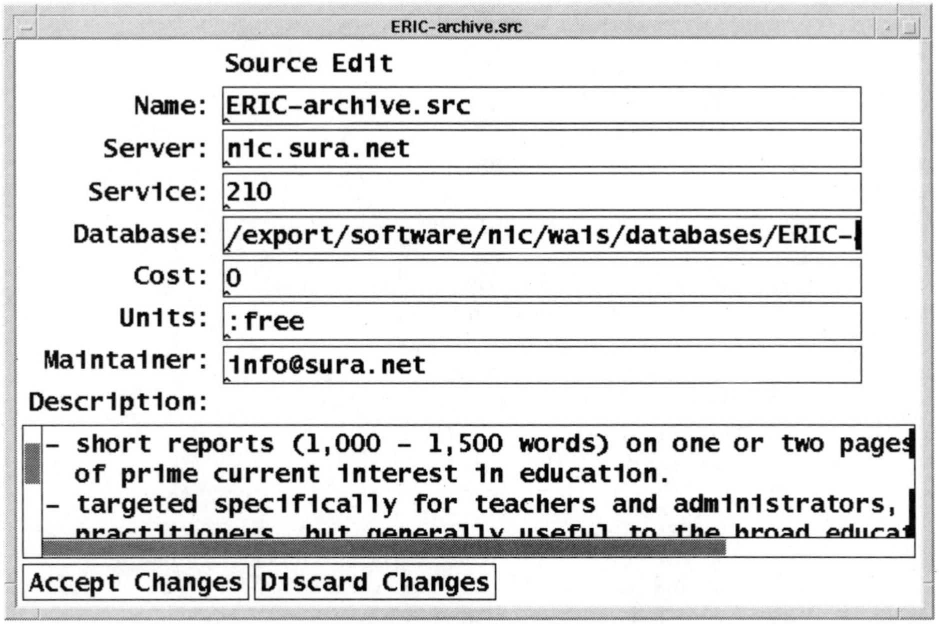

Figure 12-8: Source maintenance window

Building Your Own Sources

The software archives that provide WAIS clients also provide programs and documentation for creating your own sources and offering your own servers. One of these, **waisindex**, takes a set of files and builds an index from them. It knows about various forms of data: normal text, various text formatters (e.g., LaTeX), mail folder format, etc. These formats are shown in Table 12-2.

Table 12-2: Waisindex Input Formats

Name	Description
text	Simple text files
bibtex	BibTeX/LaTeX format
bio	Biology abstract format
cmapp	CM applications from Hypercard
dash	Entries separated by a row of dashes
dvi	*dvi* format
emacsinfo	GNU documentation system
first_line	First line of file is headline.
gif	*gif* files, only indexes the filename
irg	Internet *Resource Catalog*
mail_digest	Standard Internet mail digest format
mail_or_rmail	mail or rmail or both

Table 12.2: Waisindex Input Formats (continued)

Name	Description
medline	MEDLINE format
mh_bboard	MH bulletin board format
netnews	Net news format
nhyp	Hypertext format, Polytechnic of Central London
one_line	Each line is a document.
para	Paragraphs separated by blank lines
pict	*pict* files, only indexes the filename
ps	PostScript format
refer	**refer** format
rn	Net news saved by the **rn** newsreader
server	Server structures for the *directory-of-servers*
tiff	*tiff* files, only indexes the filename

So if you want to build a WAIS index for the email you receive, you can. It's really beyond the scope of this book to tell you how to do this. Many people find that once they learn WAIS, it is a valuable tool for searching many other things. If you'd like to experiment, look for **waisindex** via Archie. It is also part of the distribution package for UNIX WAIS servers, available by anonymous FTP to **think.com** in the directory *wais*.

CHAPTER THIRTEEN

THE WORLD WIDE WEB

Getting Started
The Web and Gopher
Navigating the Web With www
Navigating the Web With xmosaic
Working With Other Services
Setting Up Your Own Home Page
Hints for Mosaic Users
Where the Web is Going

The World Wide Web, or WWW, is the newest information service to arrive on the Internet. The Web is based on a technology called *hypertext*. Most of the development has taken place at CERN, the European Particle Physics Laboratory; but it would be a mistake to see the Web as a tool designed by and for physicists. While physicists may have paid for its initial development, it's one of the most flexible tools—probably the most flexible tool—for prowling around the Internet. The Web and its tools are still under development, so don't be surprised if they don't work as you expect. They're certainly worth playing with, and will probably become the predominant method for accessing the Internet in the next few years.

To try the Web, **telnet** to **info.cern.ch**. This will automatically drop you into a public-access client program (or *browser*, to use the Web's terminology).* This is a line-oriented browser that will work with a traditional terminal. Several other browsers are available; if you decide to install your own (and that's highly recommended if you want to use the Web frequently), you can choose between the line-oriented browser, and several browsers for the X Window System, the NeXT workstations, the Macintosh, and PCs.† As of this writing, the most advanced browser available is called Mosaic. It works on UNIX under the X Windows system (where it's called **xmosaic**), the Macintosh, and Microsoft Windows.

---

*More precisely, a *browser* is any program for reading hypertext. Web clients are basically hypertext readers, so they're called browsers.

†One good software source is the anonymous FTP site **info.cern.ch**. Look in the directory *pub/www/bin*; you'll see directories for several different machines. In any of these directories, the file *www* is the line-oriented browser; *erwise* is an X-based browser. **cello** is a browser for Windows. Mosaic browsers are also available at CERN, but the best place to look is at NCSA's FTP archive: **ftp.ncsa.uiuc.edu**.

What Is Hypertext?

Hypertext is a method of presenting information where selected words in the text can be "expanded" at any time to provide other information about the word. That is, these words are *links* to other documents, which may be text, files, pictures, anything. For the sake of illustration, let's assume that your library has a hypertext card catalog. If you pull up the card for a particular book, it might look like:

```
TITLE:    The river and the prairie : a history
          of the Quad-Cities, 1812-1960
AUTHOR:   Roba, William Henry.
PUBL.:    (Davenport, Iowa) : Hesperian Press,
DATE:     1986

SUBJECT:  Quad Cities (Iowa-Ill.)--History.
          Davenport (Iowa)--History.

FORMAT:   157 p. : ill., map ; 24 cm.
CONTENTS: Includes bibliographical references and notes.
```

If the italicized words are links, you can expand the author's name and get a biographical sketch. If you expand "prairie," you might end up in a hypertext Oxford English Dictionary and see:

```
prairie ('pre&schwa.rI). Also 8, 9 parara, pararie, praira, 9 praire,
prairia.   a A tract of level or undulating grass-land, without trees,
and usually of great extent; applied chiefly to the grassy plains of
North America; a savannah, a steppe.
```

Since this is another hypertext document, there are links in it as well. You can plunge deeper by expanding *savannah*, ending up in a hypertext encyclopedia positioned at a whole article on savannahs—complete with pictures and possibly even movies. You can repeat the process as long as you like, getting deeper and deeper into a topic.

The amount of hypertext on the Net has exploded in the past few years. Many musem exhibitions, magazines, and other hypertext presentations are available, including O'Reilly & Associates' *Global Network Navigator* (GNN). The big problem is a scarcity of tools to build the linked structure. Most of the hypertext documents available now were painstakingly built by hand. Hypertext editors are just being written; as time goes on, you will begin to see more hypertexts, and better tools for creating them.

In this chapter, we'll start by discussing a simple line-oriented browser, **www**. It isn't fancy, but it's very usable, particularly if you access the Internet via an account on another system. After introducing the Web and **www**, we'll discuss Mosaic, a "high-octane" browser. Then we'll go on to discuss techniques that are common to all browsers, and close with some additional hints for Mosaic users, and some thoughts about where the Web is going.

Another browser worth knowing about is **lynx**. It's a line-oriented browser, like **www**, but has some additional features. A public-access **lynx** client is available by **telnet**ing to **ukanaix.cc.ukans.edu**. You may also find that some Internet service providers offer **lynx** browsers to their clients.*

Getting Started

What is WWW about? It's an attempt to organize all the information on the Internet, plus whatever local information you want, as a set of hypertext documents. You traverse the network by moving from one document to another via *links*. For example, using the line-mode browser at CERN, you might see something like this:

```
                              Welcome to the
                              World Wide Web
                THE WORLD WIDE WEB

   This is just one of many access points to the web, the universe of
   information available over networks. To follow references, just type the
   number then hit the return (enter) key.

   The features you have by connecting to this telnet server are very
   primitive compared to the features you have when you run a W3
   "client" program on your own computer. If you possibly can, please
   pick up a client for your platform to reduce the load on this
   service and experience the web in its full splendor.

   For more information, select by number:

A list of available W3 client programs[1]
Everything about the W3 project[2]
Places to start exploring[3]
The First International WWW Conference[4]

   This telnet service is provided by the WWW team at the European Particle
   Physics Laboratory known as CERN[5]
     [End]
   1-5, Up, Quit, or Help:
```

This is CERN's current *home page*. Your home page is the hypertext document you see when you first enter the Web. The bracketed numbers are links. To follow any link, just type the number, followed by a RETURN. On a graphic browser, the links would be highlighted (maybe in a different font, underlined, or in color); to follow a link, you'd click on the word with your mouse. Let's return to the **www** browser

---

*The software is available via anonymous FTP from **ftp2.cc.ukans.edu**, in the directory *pub/lynx*.

and see what happens when we select one of the links. If you type 3 RETURN, you'll see:

```
                                                     Overview
                                                     of the Web
                    GENERAL OVERVIEW OF THE WEB

     There is no "top" to the World Wide Web. You can look at it from
     many points of view.  Here are some places to start.

       by Subject[1]          The Virtual Library organises information by subject
                              matter.

       List of servers[2]     All registered HTTP servers by country

       by Service Type[3]     The Web includes data accessible by many other
                              protocols. The lists by access protocol may help if
                              you know what kind of service you are looking for.

     If you find a useful starting point for you personally, you can configure
     your WWW browser to start there by default.

     See also: About the W3 project[4]  .
       [End]


     1-4, Up, Quit, or Help:
```

Have you guessed? Typing **1** gets you to a subject index of resources available on the Internet. You can go from there to aeronautics, astronomy, music, literature, or any other subject area. That's about all you need to know to navigate successfully. By the way, CERN's subject index (also called the "Virtual Library") is a great service in itself. It's a useful way to see what kinds of resources are available at a glance.

For comparison, Figure 13-1 shows the home page that you'll see when you start the **xmosaic** browser. It's a different home page, but the same idea: you navigate from one page to another by selecting links. The only difference is that you don't have to type numbers any more: instead, you navigate by clicking with the mouse on the underlined words.

Any of these hypertext pages can be changed, hopefully for the better, at any time. It's important to realize that the home page, the index of Virtual Library, and everything else that's available is not built in to your browser. They are just hypertext documents that can be modified at will. Some screens aren't even documents in the traditional sense (i.e., files that exist on some system's disk); they are generated "on the fly" by gateways between the Web and other services. Therefore, don't be surprised if you see text that doesn't match our sample screens. The Web is constantly changing; that's part of its beauty.

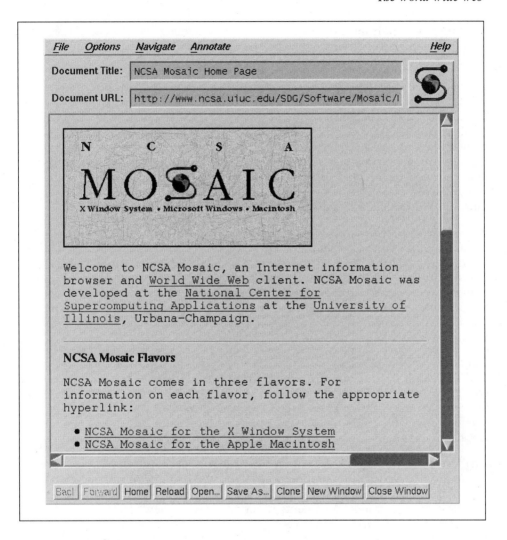

Figure 13-1: NCSA Mosaic home page

The Web and Gopher

You may be asking what's so great about this. After all, what we've done so far isn't that different from what you can do with Gopher.

That's really not true, though. While there are a lot of similarities, the Web and Gopher differ in several ways. First, the Web is based on hypertext documents, and is structured by links between pages of hypertext. There are no rules about which documents can point where—a link can point to anything that the creator finds interesting. So a text about chemistry might point to a periodic table entry for Lithium, which might in turn point to some other articles discussing the properties of Lithium, which might point to an FTP server containing spectral data for various Lithium compounds. Newer browsers like Mosaic add another dimension: documents can contain illustrations and sound.

Gopher just isn't as flexible. Its presentation is based on individual resources and servers. When you're looking at an FTP resource, this may not make much of a difference; in either case, you'll see a list of files. But Gopher doesn't know anything about what's inside of files; it doesn't have any concept of a link between something interesting on one server and something related somewhere else. By nature, Gopher menus only allow short descriptions; the Web's hypertext model can provide as much (or as little) description as required for each item. And, though some Gopher clients can understand pictures and sound, they can't integrate pictures or sound with other kinds of data.

Second, the Web does a much better job of providing a uniform interface to different kinds of services. Providing a uniform interface is also one of Gopher's goals; but the hypertext model allows the Web to go much further. What does this mean in practice? For one thing, there are really only two Web commands: follow a link (which we've already demonstrated) and perform a search (which we'll discuss momentarily). No matter what kind of resource you're using, these two commands are all you need. With Gopher, the interface tends to change, according to the resource you're using.

Simple as the Web is, it's still flexible. For example, the Web allows you to read USENET news. If you read any news, you've probably noticed that each posting contains references to other messages. A client restructures news postings as hypertext, turning these cross-references into links: so you can easily move between original postings, follow-ups, and cross-references, just by selecting links. Gopher doesn't have any way of organizing news articles; they're just there.

Finally, the Web eliminates the barrier between your data and "public data." If you set up a WWW server and an appropriate hypertext editor, you can integrate your own personal notes into the Web. (Your notes, of course, remain private; but they can have links to public documents.) Ten years ago, a few dozen boxes full of index cards was *de rigeur* for anyone writing a dissertation or an academic book. With the Web, a few hypertext documents make all that obsolete. Rather than copying a quote and sticking it into an index box, you can just create a link from a notes file to the document you're quoting. Editing your own hypertext files is beyond the bounds of this book, but it's an important topic, and something that should become easier in the future. (Today, browsers are pretty much read-only tools; in the future, though, browsers and editors will be integrated.)

The best way to see the difference between Gopher and the Web is to look at some real hypertext documents. If you're using the simple **www** browser, probably the easiest way to familiarize yourself with hypertext is to spend some time reading the World Wide Web documentation. To get to the online documentation, start the **www** browser and give the command **manual**. I highly recommend this exercise, even if you don't care about the documentation itself; it's a good way to see what's possible. If you're using Mosaic, you can go a lot further. Try looking at "Dinos Under Glass" (a dinosaur display), the Vatican Library exhibit, or GNN. All of these resources are listed in the Resource Catalog.

Navigating the Web With www

To start the line-oriented browser, use one of these commands:

```
% telnet info.cern.ch    --to use the public browser at CERN
% www                    --to use a local client
```

The CERN browser is fine for experimentation, but if you're going to use the Web heavily, you should get your own. Whichever you do, you'll see a home page; at the bottom of the home page (and every other page you read), you'll see a line like this:

```
1-7, Back, Up, <RETURN> for more, Quit, or Help:
```

These lines summarize some of the commands that are available for moving from one document to another. They're the most useful. Most simply, typing a number selects a document; **Back** returns you to the previous document; **Up** moves to the previous page of the current document; **RETURN** takes you to the next page of the current document; **Quit** exits the Web; and **Help** shows you a help screen.

However, these simple commands aren't really enough; if you reach a dead end, you may not want to type **back** 30 times before returning to some recognizable point. Therefore, there are a number of navigational short-cuts:

Home   Moves you to the home page, which is the page you saw upon entering the Web. If you use an off-the-shelf browser, it will probably be the introductory page from CERN.

Recall   The **recall** command is the equivalent of the **gopher** bookmark. It lets you return to any of the documents you have already visited. This is a much more convenient way of navigating than simply crawling back and forth. By itself, **recall** lists the documents you have already visited, with numbers:

```
Back, Up, Quit, or Help: recall

Documents you have visited:-

R  1)    in Welcome to CERN
R  2)    in User Guide for the WWW Line Mode Browser
R  3)    Commands -- /LineMode
R  4)    in Welcome to CERN
R  5)    in Academic information
R  6)    in Commercial data available through WWW-WAIS
R  7)    abstracts index
R  8)    in batch (in abstracts)
R  9)    Document
```

To return to any of these documents, give the command **recall**, followed by the document's number. In this example, **recall** 7 takes you back to the abstracts index. To save typing, you can abbreviate the command to **R** 7.

Next Goes to the next article in a list of articles. Or, more precisely, follow the next link. Let's say that I'm looking at a hypertext article about shale. I see something interesting, so I follow a link to another article—say, the seventh. The **next** command takes me to the next link from my previous article (in this case, the eighth link from the original article about shale). This command comes in handy if you want to read the responses to a posted news message in order.

Previous Goes to the previous article in a list of articles; similar to **next**.

Top Moves to the beginning (first screen) of the current document.

Bottom Moves to the end (last screen) of the current document.

There's more to life than moving around; you may want to print a document, or save your own copy of it. So there are a few more commands:

Print Prints the current document. (Your administrator may need to fiddle with things to make it work properly.) This command is only meaningful if you're running your own browser. Obviously, if you're using a public browser, like the one at CERN, printing a document somewhere in Switzerland isn't going to help much.

> *filename* Saves the current document in the local file *filename*. Only available on UNIX systems. Again, it's only meaningful if you're running your own browser.

>> *filename*
Appends the current document to the local file *filename*. Only available on UNIX systems.

| *unix-command*
"Pipes" the document into the given UNIX command. For example, you might pipe a large document (like the cross-reference index to the CIA world fact-book) into a UNIX **grep** command to eliminate the entries you don't care about. Only available on UNIX systems.

Commands like **next**, **up**, and so on can be abbreviated; you only need to type enough letters to distinguish the commands from others. In most cases, the first letter is sufficient.

Navigating the Web With xmosaic

Mosaic was designed as a World Wide Web browser—probably the nicest one there is. It presents a multimedia interface to the Internet. It does more than present hypertext, with links into other documents; it's a *hypermedia* tool, which means that it can handle audio, pictures, and even video (moving pictures). And it simplifies the interface to different services. It's the Internet's "Swiss Army knife:" just about all the tools you need, wrapped into one package. There are times when specialized tools do a better job—but if you could only install one piece of network navigating software on your system, Mosaic would be the one to choose. Remember, though, that Mosaic requires a direct connection to the Internet; you can't run it if you're only dialing into a timesharing account. Also, Mosaic will be painfully slow if you don't have a 9600-baud (or better) modem.

In this chapter, we'll discuss **xmosaic**, the X Window (UNIX) version of the Mosaic browser. There are also versions for Microsoft Windows and the Macintosh. All the versions are available via anonymous FTP from **ftp.ncsa.uiuc.edu**. For most purposes, the UNIX, Windows, and Mac versions of Mosaic are identical. Some details (like customization) differ from one version to another; the Windows and Macintosh versions are typically about six months behind the UNIX version for new features;* but the point-and-click user interface, and even the menus, are largely the same from one version to another.

Getting Started

Starting Mosaic is very simple; just type:

```
% xmosaic
```

When Mosaic starts up, you'll see the home page that we showed earlier in this chapter, shown again in Figure 13-2.

Let's start with a tour of the screen. The line across the top contains a series of *pull-down menus.* When you move the mouse to one of these menus and hold the left button down, you'll get a list of choices. Move the mouse down to the choice you want and release the button. If you've used computers much in the past decade, I shouldn't have to say much more about menus. For your information, the Exit command (to get out of mosaic) is located at the bottom of the File menu. On the right side, you'll see a Help menu. You can view all of Mosaic's documentation through the online help system.

Underneath the menu bar, you see a Document Title, which is a brief explanation of what you're looking at. The Document URL is the "Uniform Resource Locator" for the document you're viewing. It's a technical explanation of exactly where the document was found, and what kind of document it is. (URLs are discussed later in this chapter).

---

*This isn't strictly true; the Macintosh version has a few features that X doesn't yet support, or supports on some platforms, but not others (for example, QuickTime movies).

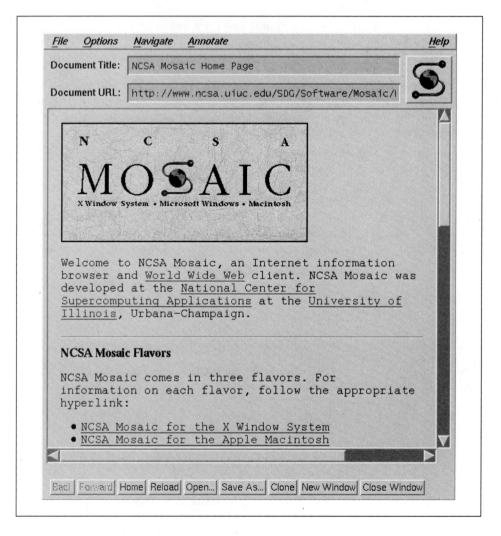

Figure 13-2: NCSA Mosaic home page

At the bottom of the screen, there is a group of buttons. These are one-step commands, without menus; they're shortcuts for commonly used operations. For example, the **Back** button takes you to the item that you previously viewed.

At the right side of the screen, you see a *scroll bar* that you can use for looking at documents that are longer than one page. Click at the bottom of the scroll bar to move further down (i.e., towards the end); click at the top to move up. If the document is too wide, Mosaic also puts a scroll bar at the bottom of the screen. However, scrolling left and right is terribly inconvenient; it's easier to resize the screen so it's wide enough to display the whole document.

Like all Web browsers, Mosaic starts by finding a home page somewhere on the Internet. Unless your browser has been specially configured, you'll see Mosaic's default home page, which comes from the National Center for Supercomputing Applications at the University of Illinois (where Mosaic was born). You can create your own, or collect any of several home pages scattered around the net. The home page consists of illustrations and text. Underlined text is a link to another document; if you click on that text with the left mouse button, Mosaic downloads and displays a new document, including any graphics that are part of it. For example, if you click on the phrase "World Wide Web," Mosaic displays a document about the Web: a brief explanation, plus additional links to more detailed explanations.

Now, let's say you follow a link, then decide that it wasn't what you wanted. To return to the previous page, click on the Back button at the bottom left of the screen. When you see the old page again, you'll notice that the link you selected looks different: it may be a different color and it may be underlined with dashes instead of a solid line. This is a notice that you've already followed the link. It doesn't mean that you can't look at the same link again; you certainly can. It's just notification that you've been there before. After you've played with Mosaic for a while, you'll starting seeing "already visited" links on pages you can swear you've never visited. You're not going crazy, and Mosaic isn't making a mistake; it means you've visited this link before, but you took another route.

In addition to providing a nice user interface and multimedia support, Mosaic presents you with several online catalogs, plus other demonstrations. Several good choices are listed on the home page; right now, The NCSA Mosaic Demo Document and Suggested Starting Points for Internet Exploration are worth trying. The demo document includes several audio links; these are icons that look like loudspeakers. Selecting the link downloads an audio file and plays it on your system.*

Another source for navigation suggestions is the Navigate menu at the top of the screen. If you select the Internet Resources Meta-Index option, you'll see a large list of different resources, sorted by type: World Wide Web, WAIS, Gopher, and TELNET. Near the top of this list, you'll find something familiar: the "Whole Internet Catalog," a part of the *Global Network Navigator*. GNN is ORA's online magazine; it's updated frequently with news and articles of interest to the networking community. The "Whole Internet Catalog" is an online version of the Resource Index in this book, with an additional twist: once you've found a resource, you can click on a link and access it.

---

*Most of the more esoteric multimedia functions require "helper" programs, along with Mosaic. So, if you click on an audio link and nothing happens, you might need an audio player installed. Common ones are available from **ftp.ncsa.uiuc.edu**.

If you click on the link to GNN, you'll see its home page, as shown in Figure 13-3.

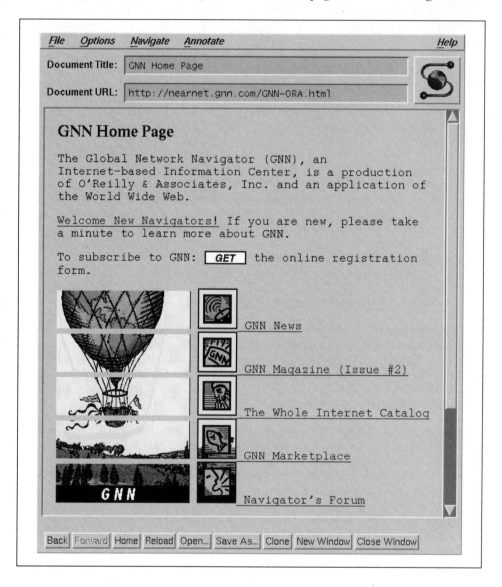

Figure 13-3: Global Network Navigator home page

You can download a copy of GNN's home page and use it as your own home page; see "Setting Up Your Own Home Page" later in this section. If you go directly to the catalog (either from the meta-index or from the GNN Home Page), you'll see a subject index (see Figure 13-4).

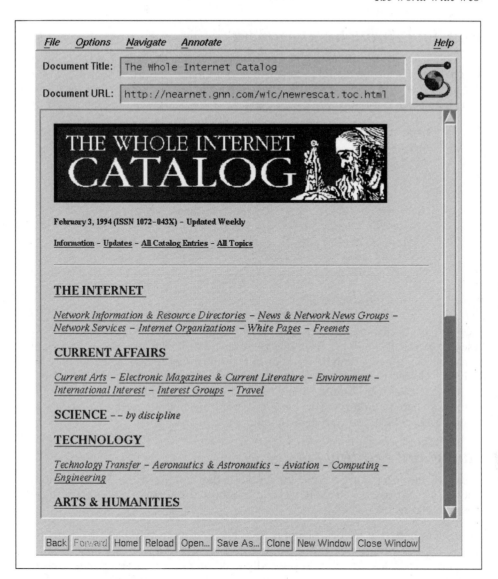

Figure 13-4: The Whole Internet Catalog subject index

If you poke around, you can also find other well-known Internet resource lists, like Yanoff's list of Internet services. Most of these lists have been converted into hypertext documents, with links to the resources themselves. One great way to explore is to look at NCSA's "What's New" list in the "Internet Resources Meta-Index" under World Wide Web. The resource lists, which are updated regularly, are an easy way to find out about the newest and most interesting resources.

Searching Through a Document

So, you've found an interesting document, and Mosaic has displayed it on your screen. But it's ten pages long, and you're only interested in part of it. How do you find what you want? Go to the **File** menu, and select the **Search in Current** item. You'll see a pop-up window like this:

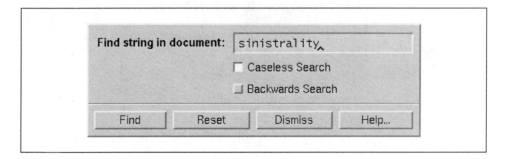

Figure 13-5: Search through current document window

Click on the **Backwards Search** item if you want to search backwards; click on **Caseless Search** if you want to toggle between case-sensitive and case-insensitive searching. Type your search word (or phrase) into the editing window, and click on **Find**. Mosaic then finds your string, highlights it, and puts it in the center of the display. Click on **Dismiss** to get rid of the search window. The **Reset** button erases the search string that's in the window (if any), and moves you back to the position from which you started searching.

Saving and Printing Files

To save a file, click on the **Save As** button at the bottom of the Mosaic window. (There's also a **Save As** item in the **File** menu at the top.) You'll get the menu shown in Figure 13-6.

There's lots here that you can ignore. Don't worry about the filter; that's for processing the file with another program before saving it. And don't worry about the **Directories** and **Files** lists; they supposedly make it easier to select where your file is saved, but that's debatable. You only care about the name and format of the saved document. The **Format** item is another pull-down menu that gives you four choices:

Plain Text   Save the document as a text file, but without any special attempt to format it nicely. Graphics and anything fancy are omitted.

Formatted Text
            Save the document as a text file, but include some rudimentary formatting. No graphics.

PostScript Save the document as a PostScript file which can be sent to a Post-Script printer. Graphics are included in the PostScript file.

HTML Save the document as an HTML file, which can then be read as a hypertext document by Mosaic or another World Wide Web browser.

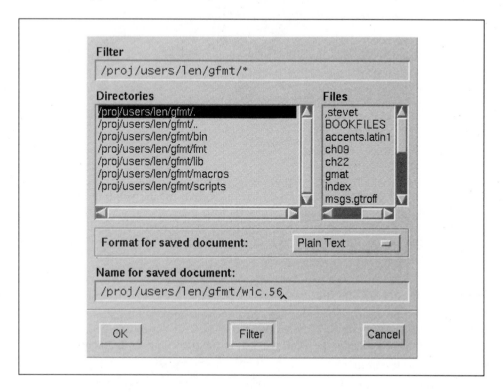

Figure 13-6: Save document window

You also have to specify a filename. The input window under **Name for saved document** shows the directory in which you started Mosaic. Move the mouse into this window, and edit the path shown: if the directory that's shown is OK, just add a filename; otherwise edit the directory and add a filename to the end. Don't forget to specify a filename! If you forget, Mosaic will pick a filename for you—and it won't pick something reasonable.

When you're ready, click on the **OK** button to save the file. If you change your mind, click on the **Cancel** button.

Printing a document is similar—but even simpler. When you select the **Print** option in the **File** menu, you'll see this:

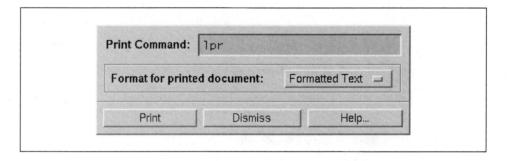

Figure 13-7: Print document window

The **Print Command** should be whatever command you use on your system to print a file. For a UNIX system, **lpr** will work. **Format for the printed document** is the same pull-down menu we just discussed, with the same four choices: you can print plain text, formatted text, HTML (also plain text, but including all the special commands that make the Web work), or PostScript, which will print just as it is displayed on the screen.

Advanced Navigation

Once you can move around, save files, and know where to find some interesting things, you're most of the way there. But Mosaic does a lot to make Internet navigation easier for you. In this section, we'll describe three special features:

- How to use the hotlist
- How to work with multiple windows
- How to use the window history

Using the hotlist

When you start using Mosaic, you'll spend a lot of time clicking on items and following links. You'll soon find out that some documents are particularly interesting to you—whether it's the GNN home page (which really deserves to be seen) or the Library of Congress Gopher server. And you won't want to be constantly mousing around searching for something, when you already know exactly what you want.

To solve this problem, Mosaic provides a concept of a *hotlist*. A hotlist is similar to a Gopher bookmark. It is a permanent list of documents that you find interesting and can access with a single menu selection. Once you've found an interesting document, adding it to your hotlist is easy. Just go to the **Navigate** menu at the top of the screen; then select **Add Current to Hotlist**, as shown in Figure 13-8.

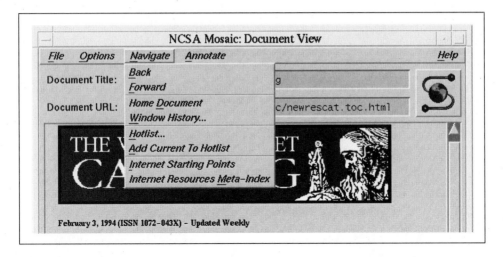

Figure 13-8: Mosaic Navigate menu

Later, when you want to select an item, choose the **Hotlist** item from the **Navigate** menu. You'll see a menu of the hotlist items you've selected in the past:

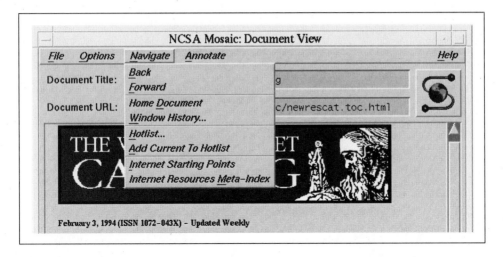

Figure 13-9: Mosaic Hotlist window

Double-click on one of these items to view it. Then click on the **Dismiss** button to make the hotlist menu go away. What's particularly handy about the hotlist is that it lasts between sessions; once you add something to the hotlist, it stays until you delete it.

There are a few other buttons you can push:

Add Current   Add the current document to the hotlist (same as using the Navigate menu).

Remove   Delete the selected document from the hotlist.

Edit Title   Provide your own title, without changing the hotlist entry pointer. You'll get a new screen, in which you can type a more memorable or convenient title.

Mail To   Send the hotlist to someone through email; you'll be asked to provide an email address and (optionally) a subject. The hotlist is sent as an HTML file, which means that the recipient can read it with his or her Web browser.

Window history

Like the simple **www** browser, Mosaic keeps track of the documents you have seen and lets you move back to your previous selections. At the simplest level, you can use the **Back** button on the bottom of the screen to move to the previous document. Once you've moved back, you can also move forward again by using the **Forward** button. (Moving forward doesn't make sense until you've moved back at least once; Mosaic won't let you try it).

You can also get a **Window History** from the **Navigate** menu. When you select this item, you'll see a menu that lists every document you've looked at with this window. (As you'll see below, you can have several windows; each window has its own history.) The document you're currently looking at will be highlighted. To view any document in the list, double-click on it with the mouse. Use the **Dismiss** button to get rid of the window when you're done with it.

Working with multiple windows

The three buttons at the bottom-right of the screen let you create multiple Mosaic windows on your screen, so you can look at several documents at a time. Their functions are:

Clone   Create a new window that's a copy of the current window.

New Window   Create a new window, looking at your home page.

Close Window   Get rid of a window. Getting rid of your last remaining window is the same as quitting Mosaic, except that you won't be asked for confirmation.

Cloning can be particularly useful when you're exploring a "tree" of items: that is, following lots of search paths from a common point. Clone the window that you're searching from; then, when your search reaches a dead-end, just jump back to your original window rather than retracing your steps. It's sort of an instant book-mark. Cloning is also useful if you want to follow several different search paths, or if you want to read several windows at a time.

The **Help** button also starts a new Mosaic window. This may seem odd—after all, why not display the help files in the main Mosaic window? In practice, it's nice to have one window for exploration and another for reading the documentation. You don't have to disturb your main search whenever you run into a problem.

Making Annotations

One of Mosaic's ground-breaking features is that it lets you add your own private comments to any Web document. This is the first computer interface I've seen that allows you to write notes in the margin! Annotations are stored on your system; when you read an annotated document, Mosaic adds your annotations to the end as a hypertext link. To read an annotation, click on the link; Mosaic then displays your comment.

To create an annotation, select the **Annotate** item within the **Annotate** menu at the top of the main Mosaic window.* Figure 13-10 shows the pop-up window you'll use for creating your annotation.

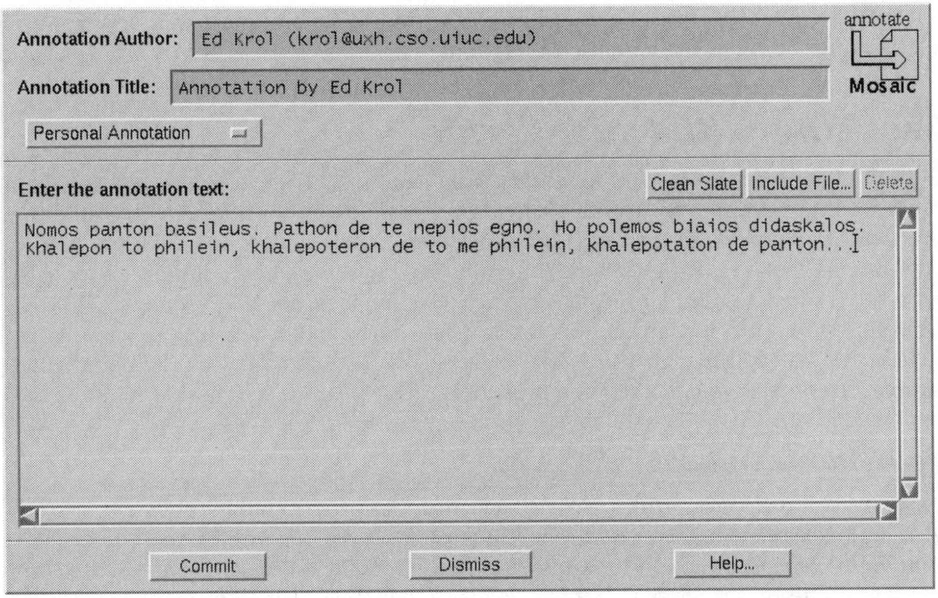

Annotation Author:	Ed Krol (krol@uxh.cso.uiuc.edu)
Annotation Title:	Annotation by Ed Krol

annotate

Mosaic

Personal Annotation

Enter the annotation text: Clean Slate Include File... Delete

```
Nomos panton basileus. Pathon de te nepios egno. Ho polemos biaios didaskalos.
Khalepon to philein, khalepoteron de to me philein, khalepotaton de panton...
```

Commit   Dismiss   Help...

Figure 13-10: Creating an annotation

*****Audio Annotate** is even fancier; it lets you record your voice as an annotation. Audio annotations re-quire special software to be installed on your computer.

Type your comment where Mosaic says "Enter the annotation text." The **Clean Slate** button deletes everything you have written. The **Include File** button lets you insert the contents of a file within your annotation. However, the most important buttons are:

Commit   Save the annotation, making it permanent.

Dismiss   Discard the annotation.

Once you have written an annotation, you can edit it or delete it. First, select the annotation so that it's visible on your screen. Then go to the **Annotate** menu at the top of the screen. You will see two additional items that you weren't allowed to select before: **Edit This Annotation** and **Delete This Annotation**. The Edit option takes you back to the editing window we just discussed. You can modify or rewrite your annotation; then click on the **Commit** button when you're done.

If you select the **Delete** option, Mosaic asks you for confirmation; then it deletes your annotation.

Making annotations to text and hypertext files should come naturally enough. However, you can go further. When you start playing with other kinds of resources (a topic we'll take up momentarily), try adding annotations to FTP menus, Gopher menus, etc. This may be where annotations are most useful: you can make your own notes about what you've found on any particular server, supplementing the often inadequate *README* files.

Working With Other Services

If Web clients like **www** and **xmosaic** could only read hypertext documents, they would be interesting and useful—but not that interesting or that useful. While the amount of hypertext on the net is growing, there still isn't that much. Many hypertext documents—and the "Whole Internet Catalog" is a prime example—consist largely of links to more prosaic services: Gopher servers, FTP servers, TELNET servers, and so on. In this section, we'll discuss how other services behave when you access them through the Web using **www** and **mosaic**. It's actually quite simple; for most services, the Web presents a very clean, nicely usable interface.

Searchable Indexes

As you go travel through the web, you'll find lots of searchable indexes. Searchable indexes present many different kinds of resources: Veronica searches, WAIS searches, CSO phone book lookups, and so on. What's nice is that the same user interface is used for all searches, no matter what their type. In many cases, you don't even need to know what kind of search you're making.

If you're using the **www** browser, the **Find** command (abbreviated F) is used to search. You'll see **FIND <keywords>** in the command list at the bottom of the screen whenever a search is possible. Here's an example:

```
                   LANGLEY TECHNICAL REPORTS SERVER
    This LTRS gateway searches citations at
        NASA Langley Research Center[1]
        ICASE - Institute for Computer Applications in Science and
    Engineering[2]
    Please enter search words...
        original code for gateway by: d.j.bianco@larc.nasa.gov

    [End]
FIND <keywords>, 1-2, Back, Up, Quit, or Help:
```

To make a search, type the **Find** command, followed by one or keywords, then RETURN. Here's the same screen, viewed through **xmosaic**:

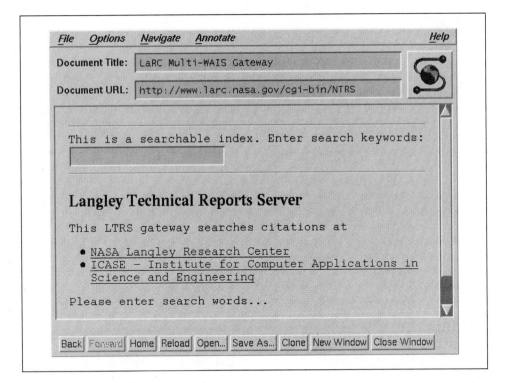

Figure 13-11: Searchable indexes

The item labelled "This is a searchable index. Enter search keywords:" tells you that you're looking at something you can search. Move the cursor into the small editing window and type the keywords you want to search for, followed by RETURN. If you search for the keyword "mars", you'll find three relevant items.

(Go ahead and try it.) The location of the search item varies from page to page, depending on the author's design; you won't always find it in the same place.

Gopher and FTP Servers

The World Wide Web is a great way to access FTP and Gopher servers; you'll find these poking up frequently in various resource lists and indexes. For the most part, using them should be fairly self-explanatory, but there are a few niceties that you don't get elsewhere.

Web browsers use the same interface for both Gopher and FTP services. For example, the line-oriented browser presents an FTP or Gopher directory the same way it presents other menus. You get a list of items; each item (whether it's a file or a directory) has a number next to it. To select any item, type its number; if it's a text file, **www** displays the file for you to read it. (If it's a binary file, you'll get an error). If you select a directory, **www** displays the directory.

xmosaic is substantially more sophisticated. Again, you get a list of files that you can select. Each filename has an icon next to it, telling you something about the file's contents. Here's a typical screen.

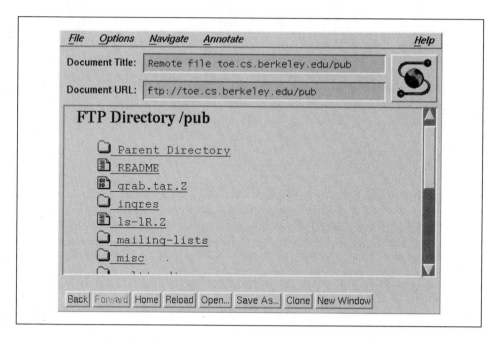

Figure 13-12: Mosaic viewing an FTP archive

Table 13-1 shows the icons you'll see (some of these are shown in the previous figure).

Table 13-1: Common Mosaic Icons

File type	Icon
Directory	File folder
Text file	Sheet of paper with writing
Compressed text file	Sheet of paper with writing
Binary file	Sheet of paper with zeros and ones
Picture	Sheet of paper with a pencil
Movie	"Film strip"
Audio	Loudspeaker
Phone books	Question mark
Veronica searches	Question mark
Searchable indexes	Question mark
TELNET services	Box with "TEL" inside

If you select a directory, Mosaic displays the items in the directory as if it were a Gopher client. If you select a file, Mosaic does what it can to display the file. Unlike the line-oriented browser, Mosaic knows about file types. In particular:

- If it's a text file, it displays the file on the screen. Use the **Save As** button to save it.

- If it's a compressed text file, Mosaic uncompresses the file and displays it. Currently, **xmosaic** understands the UNIX **compress** and the Free Software Foundation's **gzip** commands; it doesn't understand other kinds of compression. Again, use the **Save As** button to save the file.

- If it's a picture, a movie, or an audio file, Mosaic downloads the file and plays it, if possible.

- If it's a binary file, Mosaic automatically pops up the **Save As** menu; trying to display it would be meaningless. In practice, "binary" is a catch-all for files Mosaic doesn't otherwise recognize.

Mosaic's knowledge isn't flawless; it can be confused (particularly by files with two or more extensions, like *foo.tar.gz*), and there are things it doesn't understand. But it makes a good—and usually useful—attempt to do something intelligent with binary files.

If you've followed this discussion, you're probably already asking: how do I save pictures, audio, and video? Good question. By default, Mosaic doesn't; it plays the file, and then it's gone. If you've just downloaded a five-megabyte audio file and would like to listen to it more than once, you might find this frustrating. To save files that Mosaic normally plays, go to the **Options** menu, and select the **Load To Local Disk** option. When this option is in effect, Mosaic will *not* display pictures, movies, or sounds. Instead, it immediately pops up the **Save As** menu, allowing you to save the file.

When you access an FTP server, Web clients automatically insert a **Parent Directory** link at the head of the directory list. This makes it easier to navigate around the server's file system; clicking on this icon is equivalent to **cd ..** or **cdup**. One particularly nice feature for FTP users: Mosaic handles the mechanics of anonymous FTP for you; it logs in automatically. However, there are a few limitations worth noting:

- Web clients don't handle groups of files: it's strictly one file at a time. There's no equivalent to **mget**. If you habitually collect lots of stuff, **ftp** might work better.

- There's no equivalent to the **put** command; the Web is strictly for downloading files.

- It's not possible to find out how large a file is before downloading it. So you can suddenly find that you have transferred two megabytes, and you have no idea how much more is to come.

Now, a few notes about Gopher servers. An inherent limitation of Gopher, no matter whether you're using a Gopher client or a Web client, is that there's no concept of a parent menu; hence, there's no equivalent to the **Parent Directory** icon. To move back "up" a tree, you have to use the **Back** button or **Window History**. If you're using **xmosaic**, you could also use the Hotlist to record particularly interesting menus.

Gopher's Veronica searches are presented as searchable indexes; they are identical to other searches that you find.

Using TELNET Servers

Accessing a TELNET server is more-or-less what you'd expect; on UNIX, Mosaic creates a new window with a TELNET session running in it. On a Macintosh or Windows system, it will do something equivalent.

If you select a **telnet** resource while using the line-oriented browser, you will temporarily "drop out" of the Web and start a **telnet** session. When you end the **telnet** session, you'll return to the Web. For security reasons, you can't access TELNET resources from a public browser (like the one at **info.cern.ch**). If you try, you'll see a message telling you that TELNET access is not allowed. Get your own browser and try again.

Using WAIS Servers

There are many WAIS resources available through the World Wide Web. As you might expect, WAIS resources appear as searchable indexes. I find that Web browsers make perfectly adequate WAIS clients. They don't let you do fancy things, like relevance feedback, but they get the job done.* We've already seen

---

*That is, when the WAIS-WWW gateways are working—which, lately, hasn't been very often. However, there are many "private" gateways to particular WAIS resources—like the NASA Langley cover page we looked at a few pages back—so you should know how to work with WAIS sources.

what WAIS is, so perhaps the best approach would be to search for something concrete. Imagine that you're an economist and need some accurate data about France. There are several places to look. But, while scanning the index of academic information, your eye falls on the CIA World Fact Book:

```
Geography                    CIA World Fact Book[14], India: Miscellaneous
                             information[15] , Thai-Yunnan: Davis collection[16],
```

It certainly looks like you might find something useful there! So, after selecting item 14, you see the factbook's cover page:

```
                    CIA

Connection Machine WAIS server.  Operated between 9AM and
9PM East coast time.  The 1990 World Factbook by the CIA which
contains a
good description of every country.  The entry for WORLD is also
particularly good.

Descriptions of 249 nations, dependent areas, and other entities with
information on population, economic condition, imports/exports, conflicts
and wars, and politics.  Produced annually by the
CIA.  Search 'World Factbook' for table of contents.

FIND <keywords>, 1, Back, Quit, or Help:
```

To search a database (in this case, a WAIS database), just type **find** followed by a keyword. You can use **f** as an abbreviation for **find**; you can even omit the command entirely, if your keywords don't overlap with any commands. If you're using Mosaic, type your keyword into the **searchable index** box on your screen.

Here's the frustrating part. After searching for the keyword **france**, you get a list of 40 documents: various obscure French territories, former colonies, countries with territorial disputes involving France, and so on. There are so many listings that WAIS hits its built-in limit (40 items) without finding what you want. This is a WAIS problem, rather than a limitation of the Web. It's hard to construct an appropriately narrow question. Relevance feedback would really help here, but it's not yet possible to use that feature within the Web.

So we need a better question. Adding the keyword **economy** to the search doesn't help—virtually every article in the database will have something about the economy. An inspired guess: how many articles would refer both to France and to Paris? Let's see:

```
FIND <keywords>, 1-40, Back, <RETURN> for more, Quit, or Help: find france paris
                                                       france paris (in CIA)
                    FRANCE PARIS

Index CIA contains the following 40 items relevant to 'france paris'.

France  Geography Total area: 547,030 km2; land area: 545,630 km2; includes
                  Corsica[1]
                  Score: 1000, lines: 415
```

```
France  Geography Total area: 547,030 km2; land area: 545,630 km2; includes
                  Corsica[2]
                  Score: 1000, lines: 415
French Guiana (overseas department of France)[3]
                  Score: 1000, lines: 299
  ...
```

By constructing a somewhat contrived question, we've managed to get the article we wanted—the factbook's main entry about France—at the top of the list. Let's see what we've managed to dig up:

```
FIND <keywords>, 1-40, Back, Up, <RETURN> for more, or Help: 1
                                                 Document
0000073CIA
920120
CIA World Factbook 1991
France

Geography
Total area: 547,030 km2; land area: 545,630 km2; includes Corsica
and the rest of metropolitan France, but excludes the overseas
administrative divisions

Comparative area: slightly more than twice the size of Colorado

Land boundaries: 2,892.4 km total; Andorra 60 km, Belgium 620 km,
Germany 451 km, Italy 488 km, Luxembourg 73 km, Monaco 4.4 km,
Spain 623 km, Switzerland 573 km

Coastline: 3,427 km (includes Corsica, 644 km)
  ...
```

If you read through enough of this, you'll eventually find statistics about the French economy. You'll also find estimates of the number of Communists around, the size of the armed forces, and other statistics of understandable interest to the CIA.

I intentionally picked a slightly difficult problem so you could see how WAIS searches are refined. Ironically, looking for a "first-world" country with a long history is likely to be more difficult than looking for an obscure third-world country: searches for obscure entities are, by nature, more tightly focused. Experience will help you with the inspired guesses; further development will improve the quality of the servers and clients.

Despite these kinds of problems, the World Wide Web and WAIS really are a natural pair. With some improvements to the browsers (for example, incorporating relevance feedback) and perhaps some improvement to WAIS, WWW could easily become the ideal WAIS client.

The WAIS Directory of Servers

It's possible to search the WAIS directory of servers directly. You can either look up WAIS servers explicitly (there's an item for WAIS servers on many home pages) or you can look for any WAIS resource. Once you've found a WAIS resource, you'll see (on its cover page) a link to the directory of servers. If you select this link, you'll see a description of the directory of servers; you can then search the servers for whatever topic interests you. In the example below, we search for WAIS libraries relevant to classical literature:

```
FIND <keywords>, 1, Back, Quit, or Help: find classical literature

                       CLASSICAL LITERATURE

Index directory of servers contains the following 9 items relevant to
'classical literature'.

indian-classical-music.src[1]
                       Score: 1000, lines:  30
bryn-mawr-classical-review.src[2]
                       Score:  400, lines: 107
bionic-algorithms.src[3]
                       Score:  333, lines:  18
...
```

We're interested in looking up articles about Plato, so the Bryn Mawr Classical Review looks like what we want. Selecting item 2 gets us to strange nowhere-land:

```
FIND <keywords>, 1-9, Back, Up, <RETURN> for more, or Help: 2
The index cover page has been retrieved. Please see the index itself[1]
[End]
```

This is an intermediate step that will soon be eliminated. Logically, it's the same as copying a list of interesting WAIS libraries into your next WAIS query. For the time being, just select 1; this gets you to the review's cover page:

```
                              BMCR

The _Bryn Mawr Classical Review_ is a review journal of books in Greek and
Latin classics.

   In its new format the BMCR will distribute reviews as they become
available:  that is, as soon as they have been submitted and gone through
the minimal editorial massaging (inserting missing commas, removing
libelous assertions) that we do.
FIND <keywords>, 1, Back, Up, <RETURN> for more, Quit, or Help:
```

Now you can type **find plato**, and get a list of relevant articles. We're back in familiar territory.

Don't hesitate to use the directory of servers if the Web drops you into some strange place that you weren't expecting.

Reading Network News

There are a few documents with links to newsgroups—not a lot, though. If you find one of these, you can use your Web browser as a newsreader. To save the suspense and trouble of looking, you can find an entry into the newsgroup world by looking at "Data Sources By Service," which is in the "Starting Points for Internet Exploration" document. If you don't even want to search that much, here's a URL for a list of newsgroups:

```
http://info.cern.ch/hypertext/Datasources/News/Groups/Overview.html
```

(The next section, "Going Outside the Web," tells you how to go directly to this document rather than finding it through links).

Once you've gotten to this page, you'll see a list of "top-level" newsgroups: *rec*, *comp*, *alt*, and so on. Select the top-level group you want; when you see the next page, select an interesting newsgroup within that category. If all goes well, you'll see a list of articles that are available in the group.

That's if all goes well. What might go wrong? Really only one thing. To read news, you must either have a news server (an NNTP server) running on your local system, or you must access one somewhere else on the network. If you don't know what that means, ask your system administrator—if you can read news, you have access to an NNTP server somewhere. If the server isn't on your own machine, and you're using UNIX, set the environment variable NNTPSERVER to the name of your server before starting your browser.

Frankly, reading news isn't one of the Web's strong points. It has a few good features that you won't find elsewhere: for example, cross references to other articles are rendered as links to those articles. Therefore, it's easy to go from any article to its predecessors. However, many basic newsreader features are missing. You can't reply or post articles, the browsers don't have a concept of "subscribing" or "unsubscribing," they don't keep track of articles you have read, and so on. Unless you're the type who insists on using a Swiss Army Knife for everything, you're better off using **nn** or **tin** for a newsreader.

Going Outside the Web

Although the World Wide Web spreads further every day, it doesn't encompass the entire Internet. There are many resources that you can't reach by following links. And there are also many resources for which you would rather *not* follow links. After all, if you know you want anonymous FTP to **ftp.uu.net**, why should you have to go through three or four menus to find it? It's easier to go directly to the FTP server you want than to look around until you find some page with a link.

Before we can go to an arbitrary resource on the Net using a World Wide Web browser, we have to answer two questions:

1. How do you do it? (What's the command?)

2. How do you name the resource you want?

The first question is mechanical and fairly simple. Both **www** and Mosaic have commands for finding resources directly. The second is more involved; we'll need to introduce the concept of a URL, or Uniform Resource Locator. Fortunately, URLs are standardized, so they're the same for all Web browsers, and other tools.

Opening other resources

If you're using the WWW line-oriented browser, just type the **go** command, followed by the URL of the resource you're interested in. For example, to jump directly to O'Reilly & Associates' Gopher server, type the following command **go gopher://gopher.ora.com**. The ugly thing after the **go** command is the URL. We'll explain it a little later.

With XMosaic, click on the **Open** button at the bottom of the screen. (There is also an **Open** item under the **File** menu—it does the same thing.) When you click on **Open**, you'll get a menu like this:

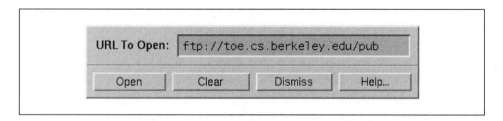

Figure 13-13: Opening a resource

Type the URL of the resource you want into the editing window. Clicking on the **Clear** button erases the window; clicking on the **Open** button tells Mosaic to access the resource and display it appropriately.

Uniform Resource Locators

Now you only need to know how to construct a URL. Here's a brief and simplified synopsis:

For FTP resources, a URL has the format:

```
file://internet-name/remote-path
```

where the *internet-name* is the name of the server you want to access, and the *remote-path* is the file you want. If you don't specify the *remote-path*, the browser shows you the FTP server's root menu—that is, the directory you'd see when you log in. If you specify a directory, the browser shows you that directory; you can then use point-and-click navigation to find the file you want. And if you specify a file, the browser gets the file for you, without any further navigation. (Line-oriented browsers like **www** may have trouble if you specify a binary file). For example, to get the file *ls-lR.Z* from **ftp.uu.net**, use the URL **file://ftp.uu.net/ls-lR.Z**. To get UUNET's root directory, use the URL **file://ftp.uu.net**.

Mosaic assumes that FTP servers are "well-behaved"—that is, that they behave like UNIX FTP servers, which are a *de facto* standard. In particular, they need to accept an *anonymous* login. That's usually the case, but you may run into trouble with servers that require **ftp** or something else as the anonymous login name. Using a more general form of the URL can help:

```
file://username@internet-name/remote-path
```

For example, to access the server **foo.bar.edu** that requires the login name **ftp**, use the URL **file://ftp@foo.bar.edu**. You may still have trouble with servers that break the rules in other ways; IBM mainframes are most likely to be tricky. If you can't make things work, get out the old-fashioned FTP client we discussed in Chapter 6.

This syntax also allows you to specify a password following the username; use a colon to separate the two. As you might guess, you can use this feature to **ftp** to a private account. However, your password will be visible as you type it; furthermore, Mosaic has the additional disadvantage of showing your password in the URL field at the top of its display. For this reason, we do not recommend using a Web browser for private FTP.

For TELNET resources, a URL has the format:

```
telnet://internet-name:port
```

The *internet-name* is the name of the host you want to access. The *port* is optional; you only need it if the TELNET server you want uses a non-standard port.

For Gopher resources, a URL has the format:

```
gopher://internet-name:port
```

Again, the *internet-name* is the name of the host you want to access. The *port* is only needed if the gopher server uses a non-standard port. For example, to TEL-NET to the MTV gopher server, use the URL **gopher://mtv.com**.

It's worth noting that Gopher URLs are really much more complicated; what I've shown above is about all that's useful to a human. There is no good way to specify a particular directory on a Gopher server, unless you're a computer.

For network news, a URL for a newsgroup has the format:

```
news:newsgroup-name
```

For example, to read the newsgroup *alt.3d*, use the URL **news:alt.3d**. There is currently no way to specify a news server, though this may be possible in the future. On UNIX systems, the environment variable NNTPSERVER specifies your news server.

For Hypertext resources, a URL for a hypertext page has the format:

```
http://internet-name/remote-path
```

The *internet-name* is the name of the server, and the *remote-path* is the pathname for the file you want to read. It's assumed to be an HTML file and can contain links to embedded pictures and other documents.

By the way, do you find the process of constructing a URL laborious and confusing? There's a solution. Once you've constructed the URL and visited the item you want, just add it to your hotlist!

Setting Up Your Own Home Page

When your browser starts, it presents you with a default home page. However, you're not stuck with the home page it gives you; you can select other home pages around the net. There are many reasons to select a different home page:

- You may find another home page that's more to your liking; for example, you might like starting with ORA's "Whole Internet Catalog" or CERN's "virtual library." Or you might prefer some specialized subject index that's appropriate for your own interests.

- The server that provides the default home page for your browser may be over-loaded—and therefore inconvenient, or even impossible, to use. You can find another home page, or (when the server isn't badly loaded) make your own copy of its home page.

- If you want to learn HTML, the markup language in which World Wide Web documents are written, you can download a home page from somewhere else, and customize it—i.e., add your own favorite resources.

There are many ways to pick your own home page; the online documentation for Mosaic says there are 37, but I think that's an exaggeration. No matter how many ways there really are, there are two *important* ways: via the command line and via the WWW_HOME environment variable.

To specify an alternate home page on the command line, use one of these commands:

```
% www alternate-home-page
% xmosaic alternate-home-page
```

Formally, the *alternate-home-page* is the URL of the home page you've selected. It can be located anywhere on the net. However, if the home page is on your own system, you can dispense with the complicated URL mechanism and just give a filename. For example, if you've saved the GNN home page as the file *gnn-home.html*, you can look at GNN by giving the command:

```
% xmosaic gnn-home.html
```

You can also use the WWW_HOME environment variable to specify a home page. It should be set to the URL for your home page—again, a local filename will suffice:

```
% setenv WWW_HOME gnn-home.html
% xmosaic                          --or--
% www
```

Now all you have to do is find a suitable home page from somewhere on the net and save it. Remember to save it in HTML format, otherwise it won't be useful as a home page.

Hints for Mosaic Users

We've covered most of what you need to use **xmosaic** and **www** effectively. However, since Mosaic is the ultimate power tool, a few formal hints are in order. You would probably figure out most of these yourself, but we can get you pointed in the right direction.

Cancelling

If you get tired of waiting, or if you decide you've made a mistake, you can cancel most operations by clicking on the spinning-world icon in the upper-right corner of the screen.

Minimizing Delays While Loading Images

If you're using Mosaic over a medium-speed link (e.g., between 9600 and 19,600 baud), you'll find it takes a fair amount of time to load graphics. For many documents, that isn't a problem; for example, GNN includes many graphics, but it's organized in relatively short chunks, so that waiting for them to "come down the line" isn't burdensome. However, there are documents that contain so many graphics that you can easily spend 10 minutes or more waiting. The worst offenders in this regard tend to be the Exhibitions and Museums.

To eliminate the time it takes to load the pictures, go to the **Options** item in the title bar at the top—then select the **Delay Image Loading** item (see Figure 13-14).

Now, when you load a document that contains embedded graphics, you'll see icons instead of pictures. To download a picture, click on the icon. You can read the text, figure out which illustrations should be interesting, and get those as desired. If you want all the illustrations in the current document, go back to the **Options** menu and select the **Load Images in Current** option. You'll get all the images for the current document, but you won't load images in the future.

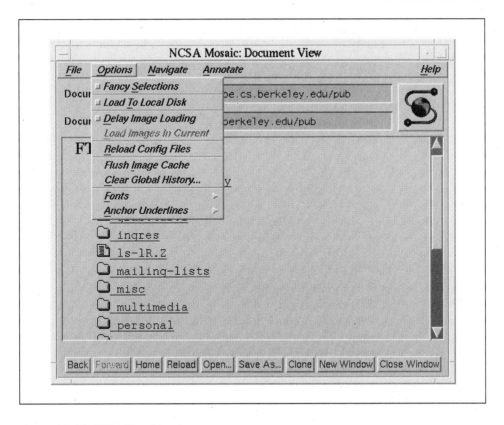

Figure 13-14: NCSA Mosaic options menu

To return to normal image loading, go back to the **Options** menu and select **Delay Image Loading** again.

Getting the Big Picture — or the Big Sound

Often, pictures are miniatures of a larger image. In these cases, the picture itself is a link, and probably has some kind of noticeable outline. When you click on a picture, Mosaic transfers the full-size image and displays it on your system. (Remember, though: a full-size figure can be as large as a megabyte and may take a long time to transfer, unless you have a high-speed network connection).

The same is true with sound and video icons. When you click on a sound or video icon, Mosaic transfers the file and renders it appropriately: by sending it to software that can "play" sound files or motion pictures. Be aware, though, that sound and video require even bigger files than pictures! Even the "What is NCSA Mosaic" audio file, from the Demo Document, which only lasts about 30 seconds, is about 1/4 megabyte. At moderate speeds, it takes much longer to transfer the file to your system than to play it.

You may need some external software to view large pictures, listen to sound files, or watch movies. For UNIX X Windows systems, here's a quick summary of the programs Mosaic expects to find:

Purpose	Program	Comment
Display large pictures	xv	**xloadimage** and other programs that display GIF and JPEG files will work, but the program must be named **xv**.
Display PostScript	ghostscript	
Display movies	mpeg_play	
Play audio files	showaudio	Any player of Sun-style .au files will work, but the program must be named **showaudio**.
Record audio		Depends on your system

If you want to use audio or various image types, make sure that you have these programs and that they're named properly.*

Keyboard Shortcuts

Most of Mosaic's commands are bound to *hot keys* and can be executed from the keyboard. This is useful if you dislike endless mousing around. Here's a table:

Key		Function
a	A	Annotate; pop up the Annotate screen.
b	B	Back; go to the previous document.
c	C	Clone
d	D	Document source
f	F	Move forward in window history.
h		History; pop up the history screen.
H		Hotlist; pop up the hotlist screen.
l	L	Local; open a local file.
m	M	Mail the current document to someone.
n	N	New; create a new window.
o	O	Open; visit a new document (specified by URL).
p	P	Print the document on the screen.
R		Refresh the screen.
s	S	Search; find text in the document.
ESC		Close the window.

You can also use your computer's up arrow and down arrow keys to scroll up and down. The left and right arrows scroll the display to the left or right, if you're displaying something that's wider than your screen. You still have to use the mouse

---

*You can use the *.mailcap* file to customize these names. Mosaic's online documentation describes how to create the *.mailcap* file. However, if you're using UNIX, it's easier to create symbolic links from the name Mosaic expects to the program you have.

to select items, but if you get used to these shortcuts, you can avoid using it for basic commands.

When Things Go Wrong

If Mosaic tells you that the information server you want could not be accessed, you can use the **Reload** button to tell it to try again. Obviously, if a server isn't responding, trying again won't help; your best bet is to try later. But it can help if the problem is on your end: if your connection to the Internet is congested, or momentarily flaky, a retry might be all you need to set things right.

There's one other trouble spot that I can imagine, though I haven't actually experienced it. Maybe you wondered how Mosaic knows how to display links you've already visited differently from links you haven't? Mosaic keeps track of your global history in a file called *.mosaic-global-history* in your home directory. Obviously, the global history will grow over time and could eventually become extremely large—possibly filling up your filesystem, or at least causing your system administrator some grief. It doesn't grow as quickly as you might think, since this file only tracks URLs you've visited, rather than the files themselves. But it could become a problem, particularly if you're short of disk space. You should periodically truncate this file; to do so, select the **Clear Global History** item in the **Options** menu.

Where the Web is Going

In the first edition, we ended with a discussion of where the Web is going. Here's a recap, taking into account events of the past year and a half. At this point, the World Wide Web is becoming one of the most important information delivery systems on the Internet. It has been immensely successful, and continues to be so, in large part because of Mosaic, which has encouraged people of all kinds—not just physicists—to build hypertext documents.

Other Kinds of Documents

When we first wrote about the Web, we said that it consisted mostly of textual documents, and that there was a significant need for browsers that could make intelligent decisions about processing different kinds of files. We've seen tremendous progress in this area. Mosaic could go further in terms of processing different file types correctly, but we're 90 percent of the way there.

Making Your Own Links

Mosaic's annotation facility allows you to link public documents (and even FTP directories) to your own notes; your notes can also contain links to other documents.

Creating Hypertext Documents

You can create your own WWW documents by editing them with a traditional editor like **vi** or **emacs**. This how most of the original documents on the Web were created. But look at all the stuff you need to enter just to get the beginning of the GNN homepage to look as it appears on page 298:

```
<HEAD>
<TITLE> GNN Home Page </TITLE>
<ISINDEX>
<BODY>
<H1>GNN Home Page
</H1>
<P>
The Global Network Navigator (GNN), an Internet-based
Information Center, is a production of O'Reilly & Associates, Inc.
and an application of the World Wide Web.
<P>
```

You would really like a tool that helps you to add all the extra stuff without memorizing and typing all the commands.

There are two ways of doing this: with a special editor or with a conversion package. HTML editors are few and far between, but they are becoming more available every day. Currently, the best HTML editor exists on NeXT workstations; it's the only one that can display what you enter exactly as it will appear. For UNIX, there are extensions to **emacs** that allow you to enter the special commands by typing a few keystrokes. For the Macintosh, there is a Hypercard stack that does about the same with pull-down menus.

The most dynamic area of HTML generation is in creating programs to convert other, more common, *rich text* formats into HTML. For example, you can convert Wordperfect or Microsoft Word documents with different fonts and styles into HTML easily. The documents will look the same, but they still won't have links to other documents. You will have to add these by hand if you want them.

In the future (i.e., after simple hypertext editors are available), special-purpose editors designed for collaborative work may be developed. This is clearly an exciting research topic; although there are some ideas, no one yet knows exactly what such an editor would be like.

How Can I Help?

Obviously, software developers (particularly in the area of hypertext editors) are still needed. But there are many more mundane needs. Creating texts (even "plain" texts) and making them available via FTP servers is a help in its own right. People are also needed to maintain information in a particular subject area. The online documentation for the Web contains information about what kinds of help are needed, and who to contact.

In short, the Web is much more than a lookup service. It's really a way to structure information. It's one of the newest and most exciting developments on the Net. Check it out.

## CHAPTER FOURTEEN

OTHER APPLICATIONS

The R Commands
X Windows
Disk and File Sharing
Time Services
FAX Over the Internet
Conversations With Others
Games
The Uncategorizable: MUDs
Audio and Video
Robotic Librarians

We have covered all of the standard, system-independent, and useful software that an average Internet user needs to make the network useful. There are many other Internet facilities that don't fit these categories. Some of them are useful, but system-specific (e.g., they can only be used between UNIX systems). Some are useful to system administrators and software developers, but not to a "general purpose" user. Some are new and haven't made it to the Internet's mainstream. And some never will. Notwithstanding these problems, no book on the Internet could be complete without introducing a few such applications.

This chapter is a brief introduction to the clutter of "miscellaneous" applications that you'll find. The facilities discussed are treated unevenly. Some facilities are really useful to normal network users and are discussed in detail. Some of the other facilities may be useful, but require a third-order guru with "root" or "system" privileges to implement. In these cases, I've only given a brief, conceptual explanation—enough so that you'll know what exists and what to ask for.

The R Commands

The *R* commands are a time-honored part of the BSD (Berkeley) UNIX system. These commands are networking versions of other standard commands. Most of them are based on common UNIX commands, like **cp**, which copies files. The command **rcp** is just the obvious network-based extension of **cp**: whereas **cp** copies files within one computer's filesystem, **rcp** copies files from one system to another via the network—similar to **ftp**. Likewise, the **rlogin** command is a network-based version of **login**—which makes it similar to **telnet**.

You're probably asking the obvious questions. Why would you ever need these UNIX-specific commands? What's wrong with **ftp** and **telnet**? Strictly speaking, you don't need the **R** commands; you can get by with the "standard" Internet utilities just fine. However, the **R** commands are more convenient. They have a simple command-line interface, and if set up appropriately, they eliminate the need to log in to the remote system. As we talked about in Chapter 4, *What's Allowed on the Internet*, this feature can also be a big security risk.

Because of their origins in BSD UNIX, the **R** commands aren't available on every system. You can only assume that they'll work if *both* computers (the local system and the remote system) are running some variant of BSD UNIX. The **R** commands are included with most (but not all) networking packages for System V UNIX. They are also included with some (but not most) networking packages for non-UNIX systems. As you might expect, details of the commands (and, in some cases, which commands are implemented) vary from one version to another.

Security and Validation

All of the **R** comands involve multiple computer systems: the system on which the command is issued (the local system), and one or more remote systems, accessed through the network. I mentioned above that they can be a security problem because they can short-circuit the normal login procedure. Security on the local system isn't a problem; if you're giving commands at all, you must have logged in first. The local system knows who you are and what you're allowed to do. The security problem is on the remote system, which isn't normally in the habit of giving people access without prior screening. Security on the remote system is governed by two files, */etc/hosts.equiv* and *.rhosts*.

There may be one */etc/hosts.equiv* file for any computer. Keeping this file up-to-date is the system administrator's job. If your local computer's name is listed in the *hosts.equiv* file on a remote computer, then anyone on your local system can execute **R** commands on the remote system without having to give a password, provided that he has an account with a matching login name on the remote system. You'll be put into the matching account on the remote system. You'll then be able to access any file that you could access when you're logged in directly. More colloquially, we say that the computer "hosts" are "equivalent."

If this sounds confusing, perhaps an example will clarify things. **system1.usnd.edu** is a computer with two accounts, Ren and Stimpy. Another computer, **system2.usnd.edu** has two accounts with the same names. Its */etc/hosts.equiv* file contains the line:

```
system1.usnd.edu
```

In this case, Ren on **system1.usnd.edu** can use **R** commands to execute commands under the Ren account on **system2.usnd.edu** without having to give a password. The same is true for Stimpy: when he's logged into **system1**, he can use the Stimpy account on **system2** without providing a password.

However, the reverse isn't true. **System1** doesn't have a *hosts.equiv* file, so neither Ren nor Stimpy can execute **R** commands on **system1** from **system2**. These facilities need not be symmetrical—and, in practice, they rarely are. Note, too, that I haven't said that Ren and Stimpy can't use the **R** commands. I've only said that they won't have password-free access. If an **R** command doesn't give you password-free access, it will ask for the password when it is necessary.*

The file *.rhosts* offers similar functionality, but is maintained by any user for his or her own account. It allows the owner of an account to grant access to any other user without requiring a password. The account names no longer have to match. Let's say the owner of the account Ren creates a file named *.rhosts* in his home directory on **system1**.**usnd.edu**. This file contains the following line:

```
system2.usnd.edu Stimpy
```

Now Stimpy, on **system2.usnd.edu**, can access Ren's account on **system1** without a password. You may have as many entries in your *.rhosts* file as you like, one per line.

As we've said, this is a security hole. If someone breaches security on one computer, he can also bypass security and gain access to another computer as well. For this reason, */etc/hosts.equiv* is rarely used; *.rhosts* files are used regularly, but caution should be maintained. You should regularly examine your *.rhosts* file to make sure you want to continue granting access to the accounts listed. Also, be aware that anyone who breaks into your account can modify your *.rhosts* file to guarantee continued access to your account.

Finally, you should be aware that some system administrators forbid users to create *.rhosts* files, and may have "search and destroy" programs to delete them. I won't debate the wisdom of this policy. But I will suggest that, if such a policy is in effect, you obey it.

Remote Login

The **R** equivalent to the **telnet** command is called **rlogin**. Like **telnet**, it lets you start a terminal (login) session on a remote computer. The most common form of the command is simply:

```
% rlogin hostname
```

The **hostname** is the name of the computer you wish to contact—for example, **system2.usnd.edu**.† If you have password-free access, the next thing you'll see is a prompt from the remote system, after it executes the user defined auto-login

---

*Unfortunately, because **rcp** doesn't know how to ask for a password, you can use it only when the remote system is configured to allow you password-free access.

†If the remote computer is in the same "domain" as yours—i.e., if everything after the "local" name matches—you should be able to abbreviate the full name to something like **system1** or **system2**.

procedures defined in the files *.cshrc* and *.login*. Here, Ren on **system1** logs onto **system2**:

```
system1% rlogin system2.usnd.edu
system2% whoami
Ren
```

You've bypassed the login step entirely. The **whoami** command tells you your login name (Ren), which should normally be the same login name that you are using on **system1**. It's instructive to compare this to **telnet**: after the command **telnet system2.usnd.edu**, you'd still have to give a login name and a password. With **rlogin**, you don't have to worry about that: you're ready to start typing commands immediately.

What if you don't meet the criteria for password-free access? In that case, you'll see a password prompt:

```
system1% rlogin system2
Password:                                type the password here
Last login: Thu Jun  4 03:32:30 from MacEd
system2%
```

Notice: this time I didn't specify **usnd.edu**, because it was the same on the local and remote systems.

If you want, you can log into a different account on the remote system. If Ren wanted to log into Stimpy's account, he would add the account name after the system name, using the -l option:

```
% rlogin system2 -l Stimpy
```

Again, whether or not **rlogin** will ask for a password depends on the *.rhosts* file in Stimpy's home directory on **system2**. If it had an entry like this:

```
system1.usnd.edu Ren
```

system2 would grant access to Stimpy's account without a password.

When you are done, you log out in the normal manner, which returns you to the system where you issued the **rlogin** command.

One advantage of **rlogin** over **telnet** is that it automatically forwards your terminal environment to the remote computer. So, if you have an odd terminal like a Whizbang 23 with 132 columns and 60 rows and you've told the local system about it, when you **rlogin** to a remote system, the remote system will automatically know about your terminal.*

---

*Not quite true. The remote system will know what your terminal *is*—but it may not know how to handle it. An appropriate terminal description must exist on the remote system. It doesn't do the remote computer any good to know that you're sitting in front of a Whizbang 23 if it doesn't know what that terminal's properties are. Most UNIX systems come with a broad database of terminal descriptions, though, so you should be in good shape most of the time.

Escape sequences

When we were discussing TELNET, we told you how to "escape" and return to **tel-net**'s command mode. This lets you run commands on your local system without terminating your session on the remote system. **rlogin** has the same kind of feature: you can temporarily suspend a session or terminate it abruptly by using a tilde-escape sequence (a beast we met in the chapter on electronic mail). These are command sequences beginning with the character tilde (~), often pronounced "squiggle."

The tilde escape sequences are:

~CTRL-z   Suspend the remote login session. You'll instantly return to your local system. However, the remote session isn't terminated; you can return to the remote system with the **fg** command.*

~.   Abort the remote login session. This is similar to a **logout**, except more brutal. If possible, use the regular **logout** command; only use **~.** if you're stuck.

The tilde must be the first character on the line—otherwise, **rlogin** will think you're typing normal text. If it doesn't hurt what you are doing, it's a good idea to type a RETURN before issuing one of these commands.

One warning: if you're new at this, it's easy to get excited and create a dozen or so **rlogin** sessions to the same host. You start one; suspend it; forget it's there; start another one; and so on. While this isn't particularly harmful, it's not good style. If you don't think about what you're doing, it's also easy to **rlogin** to a system; **rlogin** back to the first system; then **rlogin** to the second again; *ad infinitum.* This is also a bad practice, and it wastes network resources: every character you type has to go back and forth between the two systems like a ping-pong ball. If you find yourself doing this often, you need to learn about **~CTRL-Z**.

Moving Files

As I said earlier, you can move files between systems using the **rcp** command. Access to remote filesystems is governed by the *.rhost* and */etc/host.equiv* files, just as with **rlogin**. The syntax of the **rcp** command is:

```
% rcp source-file destination-file
```

Source-file describes the file to be moved; *destination-file* tells **rcp** where to put the new copy. Both arguments contain two kinds of information: the name of a file

---

*Two notes. First: This requires a feature known as "job control," which isn't supported on most System V UNIX implementations prior to System V Release 4 (SVR4). SVR4, which is now the basis for most commercial UNIX implementations, supports job control. Second: by **CTRL-Z** we mean "the suspend character," which is almost always set to **CTRL-Z**. However, it can be set to other values—so beware.

(or a directory) and the name of a computer. This requires a new syntax, in which the file specification has two distinct parts:

```
hostname:filename
```

If you just give a *filename*, **rcp** will assume that you mean a file on your local system. Neither the *source* nor the *destination* needs to be local—often, they're not. You can copy a file from your local system to a remote system, or from a remote system to a local system, or from one remote system to another remote system.

This can most easily be understood through a couple of examples. All of the following commands were issued from Ren's account on **system1.usnd.edu.**:

```
% rcp program  system2:program         #1
% rcp system2:thesis/data  data.old     #2
% rcp system2:data  ux1.cso.uiuc.edu:data.old  #3
```

Example 1 copies the file *program* to a file with the same name on **system2**. The file is put in Ren's home directory. (This is the equivalent of an **ftp put** command.) Because you didn't specify the whole domain name for **system2**, it is assumed to be in the same domain as **system1**—i.e., the full name of the remote system is **system2.usnd.edu**.

Example 2 copies the file named *data* in the *thesis* directory on **system2** to the file *data.old* on **system1** in Ren's directory. In this case, the file is moving from the remote system to a local system.

Finally, in 3 you copy a file named *data* on **system2** to the file *data.old* on the computer **ux1.cso.uiuc.edu**. The copy does not need to involve files on the system issuing the commands.

When you use **rcp**, you can copy any files to which you have read access on the remote system. This is determined by the account you're using on the remote system.* So, in example 2, Ren must have permission on **system2** to read the file *thesis/data*; otherwise, the **rcp** command will fail.

Only being able to access files through a single account sounds like a real pain. In real life, it's not as bad as it sounds—that's all you can do on the local computer, anyway. If the file permissions are set up carefully (which may require some cooperation from several different system administrators), you should be able to access what you need. It's obviously helpful to have the same login name on every system you use. It's also a good idea to have groups structured reasonably.† For

---

*Similar, though somewhat more complicated rules, determine whether or not you're allowed to copy the file to the destination. In any case, though, there's nothing especially "network-ish" to this. If the destination computer would allow you to copy the file with **cp**, you should be able to copy it with **rcp**.

†UNIX has three sets of file permissions. One set determines what the owner of the file can do to it (read, write, or execute it). Another set determines what the public can do to it (world permission). Finally, there's something known as "group permission." The idea is that if you are part of a project team, you might give all members of the team, but not the general public, access to a file.

example, if Ren and Stimpy tend to work on the same files, they should be put into the same group; that will make it easier for them to move files back and forth. (If you don't understand UNIX groups, look at any book on Unix system adminis- tration. The Nutshell Handbook, *Essential System Administration*, is a good choice.)

So far, we've only shown **rcp** with "relative" pathnames which (implicitly) start at your home directory on the remote machine. There's no reason you can't use an "absolute" pathname, as in the following command:

```
system1% rcp prog system2:/staff/Stimpy/prog
```

This command will work correctly if you're allowed to write the file *prog* in the directory */staff/Stimpy*.

The most interesting feature of **rcp** is its ability to copy a directory, including all the files contained in it. You do this by adding the **-r** switch to the command. In the following example, you can see that there is a directory on **system1** named *resources* containing quite a number of files:

```
% ls resources                                   check files locally
README        foo.ms         prompt        text
data          geography.us   split.output
data.add      macros         splitter
% rcp -r resources system2:book/resources        copy the directory
% rlogin system2                                  login to system2
Last login: Tue Jun  9 05:35:15 from uxh

% ls book/resources                              Yes! there they are
README        foo.ms         prompt        text
data          geography.us   split.output
data.add      macros         splitter
```

This directory is copied to **system2** with the single **rcp** command. If there are any subdirectories within *resources*, they'll be copied, too.

Distributing Files

Copying files from here to there is nice as far as it goes, but there are times when it would be nice if it were more automated. A common problem that falls into this category is maintaining a set of files on various computers. This problem doesn't ring a bell for you, huh? Well, consider Archie again. How can all the Archie servers in the world get copies of the information they provide? They could all go out and gather it themselves, but that would be wasteful of the Archie servers, the FTP servers, and the network. It would be better for one server to gather the infor- mation and give the necessary files to all the other servers periodically.* So, once a week you need to pass five or six files to ten or twelve computers. It sounds like a

---

*This is not how the Archie system really works. I am only using it as an example to illustrate the problem.

boring job, doesn't it? The sort of thing you're likely to forget if you're the slightest bit busy? That's why **rdist** was created.*

rdist is a sophisticated (and complicated) program. If the *.rhosts* file on each computer is set up correctly, **rdist** allows you to move groups of files to any number of computers on the network. The movement is controlled by a command file. From the command file, you can direct **rdist** to rename files as they are moved, conditionally move files based on modification dates, and notify people of the updating. I'm not going to show you how to use **rdist** in all its glory. Most people will never need it. I'm only going to give a quick and fairly simple example that should be sufficient for most problems you will ever face. If you need more, check the **rdist** documentation.

For an **rdist** example, let's think about designing a simple "Archie." Let's assume that data is gathered in two files, *archie.dat* and *whatis.dat*, on the computer **archie.mcgill.ca**. Once a week, you need to give these files to the secondary systems **archie.unl.edu** and **archie.sura.net**. Implementing this with **rdist** is very simple:

- First, you need to make sure the *.rhosts* files on the destination computers allow the access. So use **telnet** or **rlogin** to access these hosts and make sure that they're set up correctly.

- You need to create an **rdist** control file, which we'll call *moveit*. The control file basically tells **rdist** what files you want to distribute, and where you want to distribute them. Here's the listing; everything after a pound sign (#) is a comment:

```
(whatis.dat archie.dat) ->          # files to move
      (archie.unl.edu archie.sura.net) # destination hosts
      notify archiemgr;              # send email to archiemgr
```

Notice the **notify** statement. It directs **rdist** to send a message to the account **archiemgr** whenever **rdist** updates the files. Since there is no hostname appended to the login name, **rdist** sends the message to **archiemgr** on each of the computers it touches.

- Now that you've set up the control file, you just need to give the **rdist** command whenever you want to transfer the files:

```
% rdist -f moveit
updating host archie.unl.edu
updating: whatis.dat
updating: archie.dat
notify @archie.unl.edu ( archiemgr )
updating host archie.sura.net
updating: whatis.dat
updating: archie.dat
notify @archie.sura.net ( archiemgr )
```

---

*By the way, **rdist** is one of the few **R** commands that doesn't have a "non-network" analogy. There's no such thing as *dist*—it really isn't needed.

- In real life, typing **rdist** every week is almost as bad a burden as distributing the files by hand. So you'd probably run **rdist** through the UNIX **cron** facility, which allows you to schedule a program to run at a given time or at regular intervals (like every Sunday at 3 A.M.). We won't discuss **cron** here—it has nothing to do with networking. See the documentation, or any book on Unix system administration, for more information.

X Windows

The X Window System is not a network application in itself. It is a special way of delivering network applications. It is an industry-standard way of displaying graphical information and reading information from graphics and keyboard devices.

To understand what the X Window System does, you need to understand the problem it solves. One long-standing problem with computer graphics was that every graphic display is different. To drive a Tektronix graphics terminal, for example, you need completely different commands than to drive a Hewlett-Packard display. A third graphics display would be different again.* So, if you bought a fancy program to display car crash simulations, you might have to buy a special graphics display to run it; this would probably be a different display than the one you used to do stress analysis; and so on. Each program might only know about a few of the many output devices available.

Some developers at MIT did some thinking about this problem and suggested the following approach. What if:

- we designed, not as hardware but as a set of software facilities, a mythical graphics device with all the bells and whistles you might want.
- programs wrote software to drive this mythical device, not particular hardware.
- software was written for each workstation to translate mythical terminal commands into actual commands to drive their particular display.

Then, any software that could drive the mythical terminal could be used on any computer that simulated the mythical terminal. The mythical terminal was dubbed an X-terminal.

It turns out that describing, programming, and setting up a computer for the X Windows environment, as the system is called, is not easy. But, luckily for you, using it is a snap. Each application you use under X has the same look, feel, and features. So once you learn the X Window System, you can easily figure out how to use any application that runs under it. You have a standard set of buttons and menus available to you, regardless of what you are doing.

---

*The same actually is true of normal terminals, like a VT100. However, normal terminals are "more or less" the same; they differ mostly in their advanced features. Certainly all character-based terminals take the same approach: you send them characters, they display them on the screen. With graphics terminals, there's really no common ground. Each manufacturer's terminal is completely different from everyone else's. As a result, software to support all the different types would be unmaintainable.

To use X, you need a suitable display, mouse, and software for your workstation. All the necessary pieces are available to make almost any computer work in the X environment. As I said before, you may need some help getting set up to use X,* but once you start, you should feel comfortable pretty quickly. Most of the time, you use the same commands you always did, except that some of them are preceded with an "x", like **xgopher** or **xwais**.

To get a feel for the X Window System, think of a typical personal computer. It has a monitor, a mouse, a keyboard, and a main computational unit. What if rather than wiring them all directly together, you connected the monitor, mouse, and keyboard as a group to the computer by the Internet—then they would no longer have to be colocated. We'll call the monitor-mouse-keyboard package an *X terminal*. There are products called X terminals that are exactly like this—but keep in mind that the X terminal can be an independent computer in its own right.

So far so good, but now let's make the model a bit more complex. What if you sat at your X terminal and ran **telnet** on your computer, now in another location. You might log onto a computer somewhere else on the Internet, say **yoyodyne.com**, and once there, run another program. With traditional terminals, data would be sent from **yoyodyne.com** to your computer and then forwarded to your terminal. With X, the data can be sent directly to your X terminal, with no forwarding.

Since **yoyodyne.com** communicates with your computer by knowing its IP address (or domain name), and your computer communicates with your X terminal group by knowing its IP address, there is no reason why the X application on **yoyodyne.com** cannot send data directly to your X terminal. To do this, the X application needs to know the IP address and some other information about the display you want it to use. With UNIX, this is normally conveyed to the application through the environment variable DISPLAY, which is set by the X system software when you begin your X session. The problem is that some TELNET clients don't pass this variable to the remote system when you log in.† To get around this problem, make sure you set the DISPLAY variable appropriately on the computer running the application.

For example, assume you normally use **ux1.cso.uiuc.edu** for all your computing with X. You decide to try **xwais**, but find it doesn't have the client installed. So you **telnet** to **wais.uiuc.edu**. When you fire up **xwais**, you get the message:

```
Error: Can't Open Display
```

---

*O'Reilly & Associates publishes the definitive set of X manuals, should you really get into it.

†Since TELNET predates the X system, the ability to do this was added later, as a standardized extension. Not all vendors have embraced this standard.

To solve this problem, you only need to set your DISPLAY variable. The problem is: what to set it to? The easy way to find out is to print it on your original system before you do the **telnet**:

```
% printenv DISPLAY
ibmxtrm1.cso.uiuc.edu:0.0
% telnet yoyodyne.com
```

Once TELNET has established a connection, and you've logged in to the remote system, you need to give a **setenv** command to set DISPLAY properly. Just set it to the same value you got above:

```
% setenv DISPLAY ibmxtrm1.cso.uiuc.edu:0.0
```

One more "gotcha" you may need to deal with is authorization. An oddity of X is that an application may put a window on any terminal it has the address for, regardless of who owns that terminal. This could lead to a lot of obnoxious behavior, so most system administrators prevent their system from receiving X displays from strange places. Most of the time this is fine; there is rarely a good reason for commandeering a display somewhere else on the network. However, occasionally you want to use a service, but happen to find yourself at a strange X terminal or workstation, and you get an authorization failure. For example, let's say you are at the workstation **theotormon.beulah.com**, and you can't get an application to work right. You're sure that it works back on your own system, **rintrah.blake.com**—so you'd like to log into your own system, run the application there, but display it across the Internet on **theotormon**. Using a remote display across the Internet is often very slow, but X lets you do it—and there are times (like this) when it's necessary.

The problem is convincing **theotormon** to let **rintrah.blake.com** use its display. This is done with the **xhost** command, followed by the name of the computer that will be running the application. Log in to **theotormon** and give the command:

```
% xhost +rintrah.blake.com
```

Then **telnet** (or whatever) to **rintrah.blake.com**, set the DISPLAY variable, and start the application. If you worry about such things, you can give the command **xhost -rintrah.blake.com** when you're finished; that will prevent an unauthorized user on **rintrah** from grabbing **theotormon**'s display without permission.

Disk and File Sharing

Up to this point we have talked about copying a file from a remote system in order to use it—or putting that file back onto the remote system to make it available to someone else. But it's possible to do better. The next logical step is to use the file where it is. That is, why can't you just use the network to make a disk somewhere else on the network appear to be part of your computer's hardware? Then you could access it just like any other disk, without needing special commands. You might not even know, or care, where the file was physically located.

If it's on your local system, that's fine; if not, it still "looks like" it's on the local system.

As you might expect, there are a few ways of doing this. Just as with email, there are two basic approaches: those that grew up in the Internet community and those that grew up in the LAN/microcomputer community. The basic functionality of these approaches is identical. Depending on what type of computer you're using, your computer sees a disk file structure like */remote/* . . . (UNIX), a D: disk (DOS), or an icon (Macintosh) for another disk. The differences lie in the software required.

The Internet approach is the network filesystem, *NFS*. It was championed by Sun Microsystems and is a UNIX-oriented approach. If you're using a UNIX workstation, you probably have the necessary software already. For most other systems, NFS implementations are available for an extra cost. It requires careful cooperation between the managers of all the systems sharing disks. As a result, NFS can be hard to set up when the systems can't be tailored easily to fit the NFS environment. The biggest advantage of NFS is that it was based on the Internet protocols from the beginning. As a result, you can use it to access disks anywhere that the Internet reaches (provided, of course, that the necessary arrangements have been made in advance). The drawback is that performance can be very slow: it's limited by the rate at which you can move data across the Net.*

Approaches that have grown out of the LAN/microcomputer community are based on so-called "LAN Operating Systems" like Novell Netware or Microsoft LAN-manager. These products were designed for file sharing within a local area network. The competitive pressures of the marketplace made the manufacturers design for access speed. The speed issue forced them to use proprietary network protocols optimized for a particular hardware and software platform. They were not designed for generality: they were stripped bare to work fast. Since LAN operating systems were designed for the small business market, the designers did not consider UNIX worthy of support. And they didn't use the Internet's TCP/IP protocols, so they were inherently limited to a local network.

Over time, these two camps have grown together. Some third-party vendors now provide NFS support for non-UNIX computers and gateways to support NFS in other environments, like Appletalk. Coming from the other direction, many LAN operating system suppliers have enhanced their products to use TCP/IP, hence the Internet, as a transport medium. Some have also begun to offer NFS support.

In either case, it is nice to know these facilities exist as a tool to solve certain problems. However, before you can use any of them, a system administrator will have to make the necessary arrangements. So, if you think you need these facilities, give your local administrator a call. It is beyond the scope of this book to tell you which approach is best and how to install it.

---

*A newer alternative to NFS—namely the "Andrew Filesystem," also called AFS and sometimes called DFS—will solve some of these problems. AFS has been in use in some research environments for a while, but solid commercial products are now on the market.

Time Services

Computers have had built-in clocks since the early days of computing, mainly to help figure out what happened when something went wrong: did event A happen before event B, or after it? What if you start two jobs: one to create a file and one to use it, in that order. The second job fails because the file was not found. To see what happened, you check the log to see whether the second job ran faster than the first, and tried to use the file before it was created.

Before networking, time synchronization didn't matter much. Whenever you needed to compare two times, the times that you were comparing were all taken from the same clock. It didn't really matter if that clock was inaccurate; it would still tell you that event A took place before event B. With the advent of networks, the same problems existed, but you needed to compare events that happened on different computers. Each computer's clock was set by a half-asleep myopic operator, who typed in the time from the wall clock when the system booted. Needless to say, there was a lot of error entering this data. So, the times on various computers were never quite the same. Did event A occur before B? You never really knew, particularly if the times were close.

In order to get around this problem, a program called **timed** was developed for UNIX. **timed** just runs in the background and watches clocks. It contacts other **timed** programs running on other computers on the same local network, and compares their clocks. Each computer adjusts its clock slowly until the whole network reaches some average network time. From then on, **timed** continues monitoring to make sure the clocks stay synchronized, making slight modifications if needed.

This was good as far as it went. The next problem was: how do you synchronize clocks on computers that are widely separated? How do you keep a computer in California synchronized with a computer in Massachusetts? This problem is much harder: you have to account for the time the synchronizing messages take to reach their destination, including (if you really need accuracy) the time it takes for an electrical signal to travel down a wire at the speed of light. To handle this case, a more advanced service was developed: the network time protocol, or NTP. NTP uses time servers at various points on the Internet. These time servers are all synchronized to something called Coordinated Universal Time, which they get through a variety of means like listening to time synchronization broadcasts from the U.S. Naval Observatory, and make the time available to computers that need it. This is a really hard problem, considering that the network distributing the information has variable delays. So a lot of fancy computations are done to derive some statistically reasonable time to the requesting computer.

These are neat things, but in reality, using them may be beyond your control. In order to set up either **timed** or NTP, you need to be a system administrator. For NTP, you also need to find a willing time server. If you feel you are in need of these services, you might ask your network service provider for the best time sources on their portion of the Internet. (It's possible to buy the necessary hardware and software to become your own time server, but this costs thousands of dollars.)

FAX Over the Internet

These days everyone seems to have access to a FAX machine. To use one, you need a communications medium. Since the Internet is a communications medium, you would assume the technologies should merge: it should be easy to send FAX transmissions over the Internet. Well, the technologies are indeed merging, but certainly not as smoothly nor as quickly as you would anticipate. The reason for this is, I think, primarily a "not invented here" phenomenon. The people who developed FAX are making money hand over fist, because it works fine over phone lines. They aren't primarily computer networking people, and they're perfectly happy sending FAX transmissions over the phone. On the other hand, computer people have viewed FAX as a lesser service, because the documents are not machine-readable, merely machine-transferable and -displayable. That is, you can't FAX a document to a computer and then edit it with a text editor. What's there is not text, but a picture of the page. It's only those of us who might find the facility useful who are tugging at the coat tails of the manufacturers saying, "pardon me, but can you make FAX work over the Internet?"

As I said, the technologies have merged to a limited extent. You can take a file (either a text file, or a file in any number of standard display formats) and send it via a modem to a FAX machine. Likewise, you can receive a FAX and have it placed in a file, where you can examine it with a display program. All the software you need is available commercially. If you poke around, you should be able to find the necessary software on the Net for free. (Try getting the file *pub/systems/fax-3.2.1.tar.Z* from the anonymous FTP server **transit.ai.mit.edu**.) There are a number of sites (often college campuses) that have local email-to-FAX gateways; these gateways are often restricted to the site's local users.

In 1993, a group of people got together and tried an experiment to provide Internet FAX services on a wider basis. They recognized that the ability to send FAXes over the Internet means that you could transfer the "FAX" file by whatever means to another system across the Internet. Then you could view it or re-FAX to its destination by placing a local phone call, saving long-distance charges. If sites were already paying for Internet services, why not make it more useful?

This group has solicited sites in various geographical areas to act as FAX gateways. If you volunteer, you allow a system on your site to receive FAXes from anywhere in the world via the Internet, and then you relay these FAX transmissions by phone to FAX machines in your local calling area.

To send a FAX via this service, you have to create a really strange email address that contains the destination FAX machine's phone number. For example, say you

wanted to send a FAX to Ed Krol, whose FAX phone number is 1-217-555-1234.*
You would send an email to the following address:

```
remote.printer.Ed_Krol/1120_DCL@12175551234.iddd.tpc.int
```

The mailbox (the part to the left of the @) always starts with **remote.printer**. After
remote.printer, you can put some text that will be printed on the FAX's cover
sheet. To get things through the email system, where spaces in names are forbid-
den, use an underscore (_) in place of a space, and a slash (/) to signal a new
line. So the address above puts the following text on the cover:

```
Ed Krol
1120 DCL
```

This address format is relatively new; if you have trouble getting it to work, try
using an address like this one:

```
remote.printer.Ed_Krol/1120_DCL@4.3.2.1.5.5.5.7.1.2.1.tpc.int
```

Note that the phone number is listed in the host part of the domain name in
reverse order.

No matter what the address looks like, the body of the mail message is just a normal email message. The text of this message is printed on the recipient's FAX
machine. If you're using a MIME-compliant mailer (discussed in Chapter 7, *Electronic Mail*), you can also include images in various standard formats.

International FAXes are no different, except that the phone numbers are longer. If
you send an international FAX through the Internet, omit the international access
code, but leave the country code on the phone number.

If this all sounds too good to be true, it sort of is. The area covered by volunteer
gateways is constantly growing, but there is no guarantee that the area you want
to reach is covered. And, like any volunteer service, it can be unreliable. If one
of the relaying systems crashes while its owner is at work or on vacation, there's
no staff to rush out and get it fixed. The best way stay on top of Internet FAXing
is to send email to **tpc-faq@town.hall.org** to receive the documention. (The message itself can be null; all they care about is your email address.) You can also
send email to **tpc-coverage@town.hall.org** to receive a list of the areas currently
covered. If you would like to volunteer to serve as a gateway in your local area,
the document will tell you how.

Conversations With Others

Several facilities allow you to "connect" to someone at another Internet site and
type messages back and forth. These facilities are generically called **talk** (for two-
way conversations) or **chat** (for group discussions). Of course, communications are
what you make of them. **talks** and **chats** can be business-oriented, helping you win

---

*Don't send FAXes here; I just made this number up!

the Nobel prize. Or someone may be giving you grief because your team lost the big playoff game. They can be used either way, so it is hard to condemn or restrict their use.

Talking

The UNIX **talk** program is probably the most common application used for direct communication with others. To use **talk**, two people must agree to communicate with each other. The process starts when one person calls the other, using **talk** to set up the communications link. Let's say that Stimpy on **cat.nick.org** wants to talk to Ren on **chihuahua.edu**. He starts by issuing the command:

```
% talk Ren@chihuahua.edu
```

If Ren is logged in, a message like this will appear on his screen:

```
Message from Talk_Daemon@chihuahua.edu at 13:15 ...
talk: connection requested by Stimpy@cat.nick.org.
talk: respond with:  talk Stimpy@cat.nick.org
```

Just in case Ren doesn't notice, the terminal's "bell" will beep a few times. If Ren wants to talk back, he must issue the command **talk Stimpy@cat.nick.org**. When he does this, a connection is made and the screen clears. The screen is then divided vertically into two halves. Anything Stimpy types to Ren is displayed on the top half of his screen, and the bottom half of Ren's screen, and vice versa. In this example, Stimpy's screen would look like this:

```
[Connection established]
Happy, Happy, Joy, Joy




------------------------------------------------------------
What is it, man!



```

Stimpy typed everything that appears above the line; Ren's replies appear below the line. It's a little hard to describe how this works, but you'll get used to it fairly quickly once you try.

talk displays everything you type, one key at a time, as you type it in. You can't edit something before you send it off, as you can with email. **talk** doesn't even wait until you finish typing the line. So if you are a bad typist, the other person can see how slowly you type, and every mistake you backspace over. This can be dangerous. Ill-advised comments still appear for an instant, even though they are erased. So, if you type "get off my case" while you're talking to the big boss, you're in trouble. Even if you change your mind and backspace over it, you've already dug your grave. It was displayed long enough for her to read it.

talk pages (the message and the bell) can be irritating: for example, you may not want one appearing suddenly on your screen when you're proofreading the final copy of a report. This is easily prevented. The command:

```
% mesg n
```

disables incoming **talk** conversations. You can still call other people, and they can connect to a call you make. The only thing that is affected is your ability to receive **talk** messages initiated by someone else. This remains in effect until you log off or give the command:

```
% mesg y
```

If you are not participating, the requesting person will get the message:

```
[Your party is refusing messages]
```

Some programs, like text formatters, may put your session into **mesg n** mode for you. They do this so their output won't be messed up by random **talk** messages. When they finish, they return you to the state you were in before you invoked them.

There is no way for a caller to know if your refusal is temporary or permanent. If you try to contact someone and see that he's refusing messages, you can only try again later, send electronic mail, or make a phone call.

NOTE

> Some **talk** programs are incompatible. You may get a "connection requested" message, but when you try to connect, your talk program never realizes you were trying to connect to that person. The problem is that older versions of **talk** tend to send characters out in a manner that is specific to a particular vendor's hardware. The only thing you can do is look for a program called **ntalk**, which works exactly like **talk**, or **ytalk** (explained under "Chats" in the next section).

Chats

chats are generalizations of **talk** where multiple people converse at once. Some of them are extensions of the talk program we just discussed, and some are like an electronic cocktail party, except without drinks. Groups gather to **chat** about various subjects. You can feel free to wander from group to group and take part as you like. Sometimes you might feel the need for a private conversation with someone in the discussion—i.e., drop out of the "chat" and revert temporarily to a two-person "talk." All this is possible within the framework of **chat** facilities.

Ytalk

Ytalk is a newer talk client.* It allows you to have conversations with people using **talk**, **ntalk**, or **ytalk**. It gets around all of the incompatibility problems of the previous two and also allows you to have multiple conversations going at one time. **ytalk** works just like **talk**: to strike up a conversation, give a command like this:

```
% ytalk person@machine
```

and the screen separates into "to" and "from" halves, just like before.

You can also accept other conversations, or list multiple names on the ytalk command line. As you get connected, the screen subdivides again and again until there is no room left. If everyone in a conversation is using **ytalk**, everything you type appears on everyone's terminal, and vice versa. If you are talking to someone who is using a more traditional talk program, he or she will only see a private conversation with you, even if you have other connections open.

Ytalk is very new and still under development. It was available for normal character-oriented terminals, with the developers promising an X version. The only documentation right now is a *README* file which comes with the software.

Internet Relay Chat

The Internet is sometimes described as "an anarchy that works." If that's true, then Internet Relay Chat, or *IRC*, is a microcosm of it. The model for a Chat has always been a cocktail party, where people gather into groups and talk about whatever interests them; IRC is a really big party. There are usually many simultaneous users worldwide, and over 15,000 connections a day.

Granted that this is an anarchy, still—what allows you to accomplish anything at all? With many simultaneous users, what's the difference between an IRC chat and shouting at a friend at the other side of a basketball stadium? Chats work because you aren't on line chatting away simultaneously with everyone in the world. Chats are divided into small groups called "channels." There can be any number of channels in IRC, and any number of people within a channel. Some channels exist all the time, like #hottub (a channel modeled after a hot tub at a ski resort) where anyone can talk to anyone else about anything at any time. And some channels come and go as the need arises.

Each channel has at least one operator, and possibly more, who is responsible for managing the channel. The first person in a channel is the first operator. He or she can then give away operator privileges to others, who can then give it away to others, etc. That's about all there is for law and order on the IRC.

---

*Ytalk is not very readily available, but it is being talked about more and more on the net. You might want to bring it up with your system administrator, or find it using Archie and install it on your personal system. Right now it only exists for UNIX.

Like most of the applications we've discussed in this book, you can get at the IRC in two ways. You can use **telnet** to contact a public client running on some other system; or you can have your own client on your local computer. In the case of IRC, using a public client isn't a very good option. They exist, but they are very dynamic: they come and go all the time, and are very hard to keep track of. Therefore, it's really better to have your own client. The best way to find out where to get client software and public-access clients is to read the newsgroup *alt.irc*. That will also provide an introduction to the IRC culture, if you don't already belong to it.

The hardest part about using IRC is getting started. IRCs do have a culture all their own. Let's throw caution to the wind, flash our ID to the bouncer at the door, and walk in:

```
% irc TWI
```

Getting in is pretty easy; it's like a campus bar. You type the name of your client (usually called **irc**), and a nickname (in this example "TWI"). From now on you are known in the IRC world by that nickname, or like the campus bar, your fake id. Your client then contacts an IRC server somewhere in the world, and you're in:

```
*** Welcome to the Internet Relay Network TWI
*** If you have not already done so, please read the new user information with
+/HELP NEWUSER
*** Your host is irc.uiuc.edu, running version 2.8.16
*** This server was created Tue Mar 1 1994 at 15: 39:50 CST
*** umodes available oiws, channel modes available biklmnopstv
*** There are 1605 users and 763 invisible on 100 servers
*** There are 80 operators online
*** 819 channels have been formed
*** This server has 139 clients and 14 servers connected
*** Message of the Day:
***
*** The University of Illinois at Urbana IRC Server.
***
*** The NO BOTs server.
***
*** Fetch a list of IRC Servers by anon ftp from h.ece.uiuc.edu
***
*** End of Message-of-the-Day
*** Mode change "+i" for user TWI by TWI
-service.de- * This Nickname is already used frequently by another
person.
+Please try to avoid confusion and choose another one.
[1] 05:05 TWI (+i) * type /help for help
```

As you can see there is a bit of a jargon problem here, but I'll try and translate some of the highlights of this introductory screen.

- First, this screen suggests that you issue the command **/help newuser** if you're just starting out. All IRC commands start with a slash; that's what differentiates them from the stuff you are typing to others on your channel.

- There are 1605 people currently using IRC worldwide, with 80 operators controlling 819 channels.

- You are connected to a server running at the University of Illinois, Urbana. It doesn't matter which server you connect to; IRC is a distributed system, so messages you type are relayed to other servers, and from there to the users connected to those other servers.

- This particular server does not allow "BOTS" (IRC slang for software robots) to take part in conversations on channels. Bots have been known to take over a channel by continual jabbering. This is often done maliciously. (I told you this was an anarchy.)

- Finally, the server says that someone has already chosen my nickname, and I should pick another. There is a central registry where people may register their nicknames, but you really should be involved with IRC for a while before you go that far, so I'll leave you on your own for this fine point.

To pick another name I give the command:

```
/nick newname
```

To request the nickname "maddog," I give the command:

```
/nick maddog
```

At this point, it's a good time to give the commands:

```
/help newuser
/help intro
/help etiquette
```

They will tell you about all the commands you need to know, and how to fit into the IRC culture. Just to give you a feel for what an IRC session is like, we'll continue with maddog's exploits.

First, since you are new to the game, you might give the **/list** command to list the channels that are active. That might be a bad idea; you'd get a list of 800 channels, which wouldn't really be manageable. To get a more reasonable number, give a command like this:

```
/list -min 10
<a bunch of lines deleted here>
*** #malaysia  18     Steal Someone's Nick And Get Excited!
*** #warung    37     Hari Raya Menjelang..Hehehe
*** #Talk      21     *** Topic for #talk: *** Topic for #talk:
+#talk
*** #Unix      21     I await the wisdom of the Internet.
*** #Twilight_ 35     How do you go from 170 clients to 114 in 2
+minutes? (a lot of K: lines)
*** #amiga     39     we all wonder _why_ cyclone lives anyway
*** #hkfans    10     Welcome to the arena.
*** #indo      22     #medan is under our control...
*** #thailand  16     }=- Welcome to land of smiles -={
```

```
*** #chat     22     The Pseudo-Friendly Channel (tm)
[1] 08:12 maddog (+i) * type /help for help
```

The names of the channels are listed, followed by the number of people currently active, followed by an optional (and sometimes useless) description of the channel. The lines with a + in column 1 are continuations of the previous line; many IRC clients use this convention.

Well, let's join the **#talk** channel, and see what is happening:

`/join #talk`

A message is sent to everyone else on the channel telling them that maddog has joined the channel, and your screen lights up with the following. (Remember you have just walked in on multiple ongoing conversations; unless you frequent the channel, listen for a while before blurting in.)

```
*** Topic for #talk: *** Topic for #talk: *** Topic for #talk: *** Topic for
+#talk
*** Users on #Talk: maddog Molok Jordan @KEWL_KAT @Tango ILikeFish alpha-S
+claudio @JABBAH @DasBot @SnuffBot panda ella Lw Styng OverNet jevans @YaZoO
+o662 @Ekim dHitMan Keimaster @PikerBot
<KEWL_KAT> can you see why it didn't work? MOLOK!!!!
<panda> molok...
<claudio> all: i must bid you, adieu.
<KEWL_KAT> oops
<alpha-S> claudio exits???
<KEWL_KAT> I needed an enter in there =]
<Lw> heheh Yaz: good way to test the new Feature.. :)
*** Cybrarian (bubtb@alf.uib.no) has joined channel #talk
<YaZoO> lw :d
* panda jumps in front of alpha's car.. *crunch*
<claudio> au revoir mes amis
*** Molok has left channel #talk
<Cybrarian> Hi ppl
*** cob (sin_aarr@ask.gih.no) has joined channel #talk
<ILikeFish> panda : Well, let me know!  I need to go to to offy later, so I'll
+have a look too.
[1] 08:17 maddog (+i) on #talk (+nt) * type /help for help
```

At this point, anything you type will be sent to everyone in the channel, unless it is preceded by a slash (in which case, it's interpreted as a command). Anything you type is preceded by your nickname. So if Maddog types "hi all", everyone sees:

`<maddog>hi all.`

As you can see, the normal chatting channels are free-for-alls, demanding a lot of attention. They're really pretty useless. Most people who are really into IRCs don't frequent these; most of the time, they "channel shop" until they find a place where they feel at home. Then they come back repeatedly, developing a set of friends who know their nickname.

When you are done with one channel and want to leave, you can do so with:

```
/leave #talk
*** maddog has left channel #talk
```

When you get enough of IRC, you may leave it with **/quit**.

IRC is not just a place for college undergraduates to waste time until they flunk out. There are channels used by kids, and channels used by professionals. It's not all that different from getting together with coworkers for a beer after work to gossip about the job. People do the same thing through IRC. If they wanted to, a group of microbiologists could create a channel called #bacteria, and chat about the day's happenings and discoveries.

Finally, I feel I need to give you some warnings. First, IRC can be addicting. Some people get so into their electronic community that they ignore all their real-life responsibilities. Many people who get enamored with IRC know little else about computers, and think they know a lot about their IRC friends. Well, they may not know all that much. All they really know is their friends' nickname and a signon, which might be fraudulent. There have been many cases in which people have gotten into trouble by following the advice of some IRC buddy. In one case I know of, someone was complaining about how slow IRC was and someone else said, "I have a file that can make it go faster; do you want it?" The file was a *.rhosts* file that allowed the second user access to the first user's account without knowing his password. (*.rhosts* files were explained earlier in this chapter.)

All this is not to say that you should avoid IRCs. If that's what interests you, go ahead and try. Just be careful; don't do anything that might get you in trouble, or cause trouble for someone else.

Games

The Internet gives you many ways to waste time, both yours and the network's. Some people read recreational newsgroups. Others talk to other people or play games. There is fairly wide disagreement by system administrators about the validity of these uses. For this reason, I don't want to encourage you. But if I didn't tell you about them, you'd find out they exist on your own.

Computer games have been around for ages. In fact, the UNIX operating system was invented in order to play a game called "Space Travel."* However, the past few years have spawned a number of person-to-person games played via the computer. These range from traditional games, like Chess and Go,† to real-time simulation games. The traditional games are not really a problem on the network, since they consume few resources. The others, however, have the ability to consume both computers and networks.

---

*Maurice J. Bach, *The Design of the UNIX Operating System* (Prentice Hall: 1986), page 2.

†Check out "Recreation" in the *Resource Catalog*.

In real-time simulation games, each player is the commander of something (like the starship Enterprise, a tank, or an F16 fighter). The players all take part in a simulated battle, complete with cockpit displays and visual effects. These games were really designed to be played over LANs, because of their high-speed communication requirements. They require more speed than most inter-campus Internet connections provide. As a result, if you play these games over the Internet, two things will happen:

- You will get other network users (and maybe some administrators) mad at you, because you're dragging the network's performance down.

- You will lose. You are at a competitive disadvantage, because the speed with which you can react to threats is limited by your link to the Internet's speed.

Play if you must, but be discreet and considerate. There is no inalienable right to play games on the Internet.

The Uncategorizable: MUDs

Multi-User Dungeons (MUDs) were created in around 1980 as a network accessible version of the *Dungeons and Dragons* adventure game. In the beginning that's exactly what it was. You could create a character, wander through the dungeon, meeting other characters, fight various foes, and accumulate treasures and experience. They've changed a lot since then: there are still the original adventure-style games, but there are also MUDs that are more oriented towards conversation, towards teaching, and even some oriented towards various kinds of experimentation. The thread that holds MUDs together is that they are all games in which people interact with their surroundings.

Note that I said "Games"—plural. Unlike most of the other software discussed in this book, MUDs are very hard to categorize. There are perhaps a half dozen basic categories (MUD, MUSH, tinyMUD, MUSE, MOO, etc.) and many variations within each category. Each kind of MUD has its own client and server software, but they all support the same general type of game. A MUD and a MUSH might both describe a Star Trek–sort of world, but what you can do will be different. Have I muddied this up enough? Basically, there are two things that determine what any MUD will look like: the software it is running on, and the database which describes the world. A MUSH looks a lot like another MUSH in basic characteristics, but the world defined might be drastically different.

By now, it's probably completely unclear what exactly MUDs are. Certainly, the majority of them are still dungeon or combat games of some form. However, consider what it takes to build one of these dungeon games, and you'll realize that there are other possibilities, too. You build a world complete with a variety of objects, and manipulate those objects with commands like "take axe", "look book", etc. It takes very little to turn a fantasy world into a poor person's virtual reality. What if there were a MUD designed for teaching Chemistry? If you give the commands "pour water into beaker" and "pour acid into beaker" in that order it's OK; if you give the commands in the other order, you get a message like:

```
The mixture foams and gets very hot, cracking the beaker.
Concentrated sulphuric acid splashes in your face!
```

It's arguably better to learn this way than by playing around with real chemicals. So, in addition to their role as diversions, some MUDs have found a home in education. There isn't a chemistry lab MUD that I know of, yet. I used it as an example, because it shows fairly well what you might do with a MUD's facilities. Currently, most of the educational MUDs I know about are in the social sciences, computer science, or humanities. One such MUD is a model of a society: it has its own newspaper, a bar, a town hall, etc. There are some MOO-style MUDs used as conferencing tools in molecular biology and genetics. If interest and discussion is any measure, many more MUDs for research and education will be springing up in the near future.

Some of the games even let players of sufficient experience modify the game. In the Dungeon games, you might be allowed to "dig" a new section of tunnel. In the chemistry MUD, you might be able to define a new experiment. Changing things usually means you need to learn a bit of programming in some language; it might be the C programming language, or some language specific to your MUD. Don't even think about modifying a game until you have a *lot* of experience!

There are two basic problems with MUDs. First, you need to find one that matches your interests. Then you need to figure out how to use the MUD once you find it. So, how do you get started in MUDing? Start with the FAQ posted to the newsgroup *rec.games.mud.announce*. The first part give you a general introduction to MUDs. The second part also tells you, in general, which software is used for what kind of MUD. For example, if you are into combat, you might look for DIKU sites (DIKU is a particular class of MUD, which tends to be used for the traditional slaughter-and-pillage games). If not, you might look at tinyMUSHs. There is not always an exact correlation between the type of software that's used and the type of game that's played, but it's a start.

Once you have read the FAQ, you can look at the MUD newsgroups:

```
rec.games.mud.announce
rec.games.mud.diku
rec.games.mud.misc
rec.games.mud.tiny
```

This is where you'll see announcements about MUD software, ongoing games, and so on. Even if the first MUD you learn is not destined to be your eventual home, it will be fairly painless to make the transition to other MUDs of the same class (i.e., other MUDs using the same software). And—even if you're not enamored of the first MUD you play—you will find out about others from the adventurers you meet while playing.

Now, how do you do all of this? Well, it's possible to play a MUD with nothing but **telnet**; all you need to do is **telnet** to a special port on the MUD server. However, that's a pretty painful way to play; you are much better off with a client on your local system. Again, there are many clients, and they're all slightly different; the best way to find out about them is to read the FAQ on MUDs, which is posted to the above groups. Good luck!

Audio and Video

It is either trivial or very hard to send audio or video over the Internet, depending on how you look at it. If you only want to send a snippet of voice, a song, or a short video, it's easy. All these things are just files: rather large files, but nonetheless just files. For example, Carl Malamud produces an Internet radio show called *Internet Talk Radio.* He tapes interviews with well-known people within the networking community. He then places the digitally encoded interviews on a number of anonymous FTP servers. If you want to hear what the "Geek of the Week" said, you can download one of these files with FTP (or a higher-level tool like Mosaic) and play it through your workstation. These are large files (15 MB), but they're still just files: you download them and play them at your leisure.

Most recent workstations and PCs either have the equipment and software needed to create your own audio or video files, or make it available as an option. Once you've captured the audio or video, you can mail it to your friends using a MIME-compliant mailer, or put it in an FTP archive. The files are large, but that's just an inconvenient detail.

The hard thing about audio and video is doing it in "real time".* That is, it's very difficult to have a phone or video conference over the Internet. The problem is that the Internet was not really designed to do this. To understand, think about the telephone. When you dial a phone number, you are essentially renting a phone line all the way from your house to whomever you are calling. It is yours and you are paying for it whether you are talking or not. No one else can use it as long as you have it reserved.† The Internet gets its cost advantage over traditional telephone service by sharing telephone lines. If data networking required placing a long-distance phone call every time a computer wanted to use a resource elsewhere, it would be prohibitively expensive—much more expensive than the network of high-speed leased lines that is currently in place. The problem with sharing resources is that things can get busy. When a network like the Internet gets busy, data just moves slower. There's no such thing as a busy signal. If you're FTPing a file or using a TELNET server somewhere, that's exactly what you want. But real-time applications can't deal with slowdowns. A video playback application needs some number of frames per second, regardless of what else is happening in the world. You would be very annoyed if your networked

---

*Technically, these are known as isochronous applications. They require a steady stream of equally spaced information.

†That's no longer quite true. However, if you're a stickler for accuracy, you don't have to think back too far to get to a time when it was true.

video conference suddenly went into slow motion (to say nothing of the technical problems this would cause).

Today, real-time video and audio work on the Internet only because the paths they take are not busy. It's generally accepted that if many people tried to do live audio or video, the Internet would get real slow, real fast. There is, however, a lot of research on two topics, resource reservation and multicasting, to try and expand the usability of the Internet to these areas.

Resource reservation is just what it sounds like: allowing someone to pay for a dedicated piece of the Internet for a while. You might be doing a video conference with someone and would like to tell your service provider "I'd be willing to pay five dollars per minute for a guaranteed television channel between here and Stanford."

Multicasting involves using the lines you have wisely. Imagine doing a three-way video conference with sites in London, Washington DC, and New York. The obvious way to set up the conference would be to open three channels, one between each site. There are two problems with this. One is that as the number of sites goes up, the number of channels goes up faster. The second is that some channels are more expensive than others. It would be much more cost-effective for London to open one channel to the US, and have the channel duplicated once it crossed the ocean. One of the copies would be sent to Washington and one to New York, thereby saving a transoceanic channel.

The work to support audio and video is being done in Internet Engineering Task Force meetings. It's currently a significant topic of research and discussion; by the time the third edition of this book appears, it may be a reality.

Robotic Librarians

We talked about Knowbots in Chapter 10, *Finding Someone*, as a white pages server. This is only a minor use of the Knowbot concept. The model for Knowbots is a reference librarian. You don't go into a library and ask, "I need to know this. Could you look it up in that book?" If you knew where to look it up, you could do it yourself. (Besides, this is what WAIS does.) You ask only, "I need to know this." The reference librarian is trained to know how to find it. Robotify this model and you have a Knowbot.

Knowbots are generally thought of as software worms that crawl from source to source looking for answers to your question. As a Knowbot looks, it may discover more sources. If it does, it checks the new sources, too. When it has exhausted all sources, it comes crawling home with whatever it found.

Clearly, this is a very futuristic view of the information retrieval problem. It is probably an idea whose time has not quite come. There are pilot projects and research in the area, but the fields of networking, computing, and information science are not quite ready to support them. Perhaps they will be by the fourth edition of this book.

## CHAPTER FIFTEEN

DEALING WITH PROBLEMS

The Ground Rules
Gather Baseline Information
The Battleplan
Talking to Operations Personnel
Dealing With Coaxial Ethernets
Token Ring Notes

The network is not infallible. You will eventually walk up to your workstation and type:

```
% telnet ux1.cso.uiuc.edu
Trying 128.174.5.59...
```

You wait and wait until finally after a few minutes it prints:

```
telnet: Unable to connect to remote host: Connection timed out
```

Now what?

You don't have to be an ace network technician to deal with this situation, but you do need some guidance about managing in the face of adversity. First, we'll talk about what usually breaks, then what you need to know to attack a problem. After that, I'll give you a reasonable approach to deal with common network problems. It's not an exhaustive guide. I could easily construct scenarios that would lead you astray with this approach, but they would not be common in real life. Finally, I'll give you some hints about how to deal with some common LANs.

If you are easily offended, you may be upset by some of the suggestions in this chapter. Don't be. When the pressure is on, people lose common sense. If you read this chapter when there is nothing wrong (and you should) you might think

"I'm not stupid. Of course I'd check the power cord." I don't think you are dumb. When you are in the swamp up over your knees, it's very easy to forget the most common-sense trouble spots.*

The Ground Rules

When you're thinking about what's wrong with the network, there are two rules to keep in mind:

1. The cheaper the component, the more likely it will fail and the less likely it will be noticed by someone who is able to fix it.

2. You need to know what's right before you can figure out what's wrong.

What do these rules mean? The Internet is frequently described as an amorphous cloud, as in Figure 15-1.

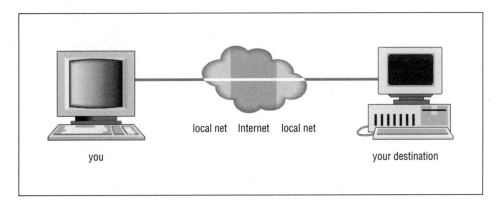

local net   Internet   local net

you   your destination

Figure 15-1: The Internet cloud

Think about this cloud in the context of rule 1. As you move away from your workstation, you know less and less about what happens to your packets; you enter the cloud. As you get closer to the cloud, components get more expensive. Inside the cloud are a bunch of expensive computers and telephone lines. If one of them fails, a lot of people could be affected: a campus or even an entire country could be disconnected. So the cloud is monitored continuously and built as redundantly as possible. If something goes wrong, technicians notice and take corrective action immediately.

On the other extreme, you are probably sitting at a $5000 workstation talking to a network over a $150 Ethernet interface connected to a $5 piece of cable running across the floor. If something happens to these, no one except you will notice.

---

*You might also be offended if you're an experienced administrator; a lot of the solutions here are, admittedly, simplistic. Remember that this chapter isn't for you; you'll get to do your job if the techniques in here don't work. If I can cut down your work load significantly, I feel I've succeeded.

In between, an area of reduced visibility, there will be a campus or corporate network connecting you to the Internet cloud. It is medium-priced, fairly well protected, and frequently monitored during business hours.

Most unexpected network outages occur fairly close to the ends: either around your computer or the one you are trying to reach. It may be in your computer or between your computer and the wall, but the closer you get to the cloud, the less likely the problem is to occur. This doesn't mean that problems are "always your fault." There is a destination computer sitting just as far from the cloud as you are, somewhere else in the world. The problem is just as likely to be on the other end. And, on rare occasions, there are problems in the cloud itself. But that should be your last assumption, not your first.

When something goes wrong, your major goal is not fixing the problem. If you can, great, but more often than not, the problem will be something you can't control. Although you are close to the point of failure, much of the time fixing it will be beyond your means. This isn't necessarily because you're not a skilled technician; it's a function of failure probabilities, how things are built, and who has spare parts. Even if the problem occurs in your building, it could be in a locked network closet. This is where the cloud starts: wherever the network gets beyond your control. Your goal is finding out when you can expect it to be fixed. Do you sit in your office at midnight banging on the return key, or do you go home and watch David Letterman? If it's 10 P.M. and you deduce that the problem's a bad cable, you can go home; the guy who has the key to the supply cabinet won't be back until morning. If you learn that you're accessing a service that's temporarily off-line until 11 P.M., you might stick around and play some network Go.

Even if you can't fix the problem, you can help by narrowing down the area to be searched by others. When a technician is handed a stack of trouble tickets with equal priorities, it's natural to work on the most specific problem first. What would you do if someone handed you some assignments, and one said "It don't work," while the other said "Bad Ethernet cable—needs new one"? You could go to the second and fix the problem in five minutes, making someone happy. The other might be just as easy, or it might take hours—you don't know. If you attack them in the opposite order, both users could be unhappy for a long time. The problem gets even worse if there are multiple technicians responsible for different pieces of your connection (e.g., one does PC Ethernet cards, another does cables)—you have to call the right one. The moral is simple: even if you can't fix the problem, the more you know, the better the service you'll get.

Now we start getting into rule 2. You need to learn a little about your network and your network neighbors while the network is running correctly. When things go wrong, a few simple tests will show you what's changed. You don't need anything special for these tests. You already have the tools you need: a **telnet** program and your eyes.

Gather Baseline Information

To do any reasonable amount of network troubleshooting, you need to push the cloud back a bit. You need some information on your local connection to the network and the router that connects you to the rest of the Internet. If you push back the cloud, every network in the world looks something like Figure 15-2.

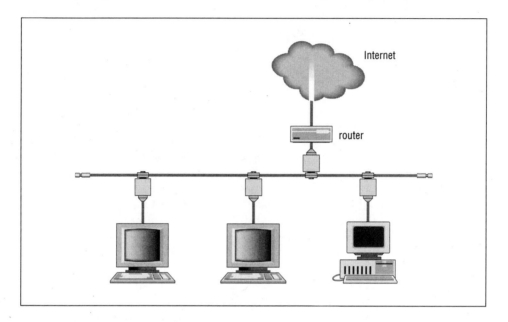

Figure 15-2: Network schematic

The technology may change from place to place. The wiring might be thin coax Ethernet, phone wire Ethernet, token ring, or something else. In any case, a wire connects your computer to something else. You need to find out a little about the "something elses": who is responsible for them and how fast they respond. So right now, go shopping for the following items:

1. The IP address of your computer and another computer on the same LAN. (There may not be any others.)

2. The IP address of the router closest to your computer that is responsible for connecting you to something larger (the router in Figure 15-2).

3. A list of who to call, by hour of the day and day of the week, when something goes wrong with your LAN (item 1) and your closest gateway (item 2). These aren't necessarily the same person.

4. The state of the status lights on any networking equipment you have access to.

These points are just guidelines. What is appropriate varies from connection to connection. For small sites or dial-up users, there may not be any other IP addresses, and there might not be anyone local to call: just you and your service provider. For really large sites, the network infrastructure may be complicated, but so is the support structure. The heartening thing is that the more complex your network is, the more local help you are likely to find. In a really large network, "who to call" is probably a single phone number, answered 24 hours per day, seven days a week. In almost every case, the information required is quite manageable, but you need to modify the shopping list based on how your connection is made.

Don't underestimate the importance of items 1 and 2: the numeric Internet address of your system, a neighbor's, and the closest router. Elsewhere, we've always used computer names to contact things, rather than IP addresses. Troubleshooting is the exception to this rule. In order to use a name to make contact, your computer may automatically seek out a Domain Name Server to convert the name to an address. This requires a healthy network. If your net is in sad shape it won't be able to do this; the tests you run using a name will be meaningless. An IP address is immediately usable, so it eliminates one source of error.

The Battleplan

Let's get back to the task at hand. You walked into your office to work on the big project at 10 P.M. and you can't connect to the "Federal Information Exchange." Your first question should be "do I have time to fiddle with the problem?" If the project is really important, you might not want to waste an hour worrying about a network problem. It might be better to try using your buddy's computer in the next office (he's not using it—he has a life). If his connection works, then you can get your work done. You also have a clue to the problem: something's wrong with your computer or its connection to the network.

Well, your buddy's office is locked and you have to get the report out tomorrow. So let's look at the problem. Throughout this discussion, we need to assume that your connection has been working and just quit. It's beyond the scope of this book to tell you how to configure your system for the first time. Your service provider or corporate/campus network group should help you with this.

Know the Hours of Operation

The computers that provide network resources range from personal computers to gigantic mainframes. Most of these, along with the network control computers, require some kind of periodic maintenance. Most sites schedule maintenance during odd hours, like 2 A.M. Saturday morning, when the network load is usually light. However, scheduled "down time" varies from resource to resource. If you use a resource regularly, you should try to find out what its hours are supposed to be. You may save yourself a midnight attempt to access a resource that isn't available, anyway. Also, remember that the Internet is worldwide. Friday during business hours in the United States is 2 A.M. Saturday morning in Japan.

If you are trying sources randomly, you won't be aware of the site's schedule. If you try in the middle of the night, you run a greater risk of finding a computer out of service. The computer may be down for scheduled maintenance, or it may have crashed, and no one is around to bring it back up. Remember, many resources are volunteer efforts. If the last volunteer locks up the office and goes home at five, it could be the next morning before someone can restart a crashed application.

Read the Error Message

When some people get an error message, they become so flustered that they only see:

```
ERROR - glitzfrick framus gobbledegook
```

Relax, read the error closely, and write it down. You need to write it down so that if you have to report it to someone, you have the exact text of the message. Nothing is more frustrating, for the network technician and the network victim, than a message like "It said 'error something something something'." Before you start calling out the troops, you might be able to fix your own problem. Even if you don't understand the whole message, you should be able to pick out a couple of words to help you along. Several words and phrases crop up regularly: "unknown," "unreachable," "refused," "not responding," and "timed out." Let's try and deal with each of these, mapping them into some telephone-call scenarios.

unknown   You called directory assistance and asked for Willie Martin's phone number. The operator responded "I'm sorry; there is no listing for Willie Martin." This problem usually shows up when your computer tries to convert a name into an IP address. You told the computer to call **ux1.cso.uiuc.edu**. It tried to find the address, but was told that the computer didn't exist. Either you misspecified the name (e.g., spelled it wrong) or the computer couldn't convert it. This might be because your computer doesn't use the Domain Name System, but rather the old system in which all names are looked up in a file (under UNIX, */etc/hosts*).* There could also be a problem with the Domain Name System. This is almost certainly something you can't handle; get on the phone. In a pinch, if someone can tell you the IP address you need, you can use it and bypass this problem.

unreachable   You dialed the number and get the message "I'm sorry; the number you have reached is out of service." This is a real network

---

*UNIX systems will probably have an */etc/hosts*, with one or two entries in it, even if they are using the Domain Name System. So, if you find */etc/hosts* but there are only two entries, don't conclude that you're not using DNS. You're almost certainly wrong. For that matter, even if you find a huge host table, you still can't conclude that you're not using DNS—that table might be left over from the "olden days."

problem. A portion of the network is down. The network is telling you, "I know where you want to go, but you can't get there from here." If this happens, there is nothing you can do: call for help.

refused You tried to make a person-to-person call and got the correct number, but the person you want is not there. The computer at the far end needs to accept connections for a particular service (e.g., TELNET). Your computer successfully contacted the destination computer and asked to make the connection to a service, but the destination said "no." There are several possible reasons for this. The computer may be running, but not available for user access. This is frequently the case during maintenance periods or while doing filesystem dumps. It's also possible that the service has been cancelled: i.e., the system's manager has decided not to provide it. For example, you might hear that a great game is available if you **telnet** to **game.edu** at port 5000. When you try this, you get a "connection refused" message. This probably means that the computer's owner decided not to allow game playing anymore.

timed out This may mean that you called and no one answered, or that you were put on hold indefinitely. When TCP sends messages to a remote computer, through whichever application you are using, the local TCP process expects responses in a reasonable length of time. This is usually a few minutes. If it doesn't get one, it gives up and sends you this message. It usually means that the destination computer or a piece of the network is dead. This can happen in the middle of an ongoing conversation. Try again in about ten minutes. This is long enough for most systems to recover from a crash automatically, if they are going to. If it still doesn't work, investigate further. (You would get this message if the network cable suddenly fell off your computer.)

not responding This is very similar to a "timed out" message, but the conversation is happening with UDP rather than TCP. (Different applications use different protocols. From your point of view, it shouldn't matter.) It does mean that packets were sent to the remote site and nothing came back. As with the "timed out" message, try again in about ten minutes. If it still doesn't work, investigate further. (Again, you'd get this message if the network cable suddenly fell off your computer.)

Did You Change Anything?

If you've ever used a computer, or helped others use computers, the following dialog should come as no surprise:

> "It stopped working."
> "Did you change anything?"
> "No, it was working yesterday and then it just stopped."
> "You're sure?"
> "Well, I did change the screen color in my configuration file,
>   but that wouldn't affect it."

If it worked yesterday and doesn't work today, something has changed. It may be your computer, it may be the network, it may be the destination. Changes you've made are the easiest to undo, but the hardest to acknowledge as a problem. People change things on their computers because they're trying to accomplish something. If I tell you that your changes caused some problem, you'll probably think that I'm trying to impede progress. But in many cases, your recent changes probably *did* cause the problem. If you have changed anything, a file or some hardware thingy, and your network connection hasn't worked right since, don't consider it unrelated, even if the relationship appears remote. Before looking anywhere else, try to undo the change. You only have to go back to your old version of *config.sys* (or whatever the file might be). You did copy *config.sys* to *config.bak* before you made the change, didn't you?

A good rule of thumb is to assume that the problem is at your end of the connection before you suspect problems at the other end. Make sure your end is working correctly before looking elsewhere. "Why?" you ask. "Didn't you say that the problem is equally likely to be at the far end?" Yes, that's true. But think about this: the far end is as likely to be in Japan as in Chicago, and almost certainly isn't close to you. Before making a long distance phone call to Japan, make sure that the problem's not on your end.

Try a Different Destination

Since you didn't change anything, you need to find out what has changed. First, try accessing a different destination. You don't even have to leave your seat. Look in the *Resource Catalog* and pick any destination that allows TELNET access; then **telnet** to it. If you get through, the problem is probably at the first destination you tried to reach. A successful **telnet** to any remote destination tells you that your system is working, and the network as a whole is working. If you are desperate to use that resource, you can call them up and ask them what the story is. Or you could just call it a night. In any case, your network connection is working just fine. Once the "remote end" gets its act together, you should be able to reach it.

Just to be comprehensive, I'll repeat a tip I gave earlier. If you get a message with a phrase like "host unknown" in it, your computer is having trouble looking up the Internet address of the remote system you want. Make sure you spelled the name correctly. Then see if you can find the (numeric) Internet address of the remote system. Using the numeric address should solve your problem.

Try Your Neighbor's System

Since you are still reading, I assume that didn't fix it. Earlier, I suggested that you go to your buddy's office, and try again. If you can get to whatever resource you want, you know two things:

- You can work until the office's owner shows up in the morning.

- The problem is most likely with your workstation—it certainly isn't with the resource you want to access, or the network.

If you can't reach the resource you want, your local network or (in rare circumstances) the Internet itself is in trouble. Eventually, you'll need to call someone and ask for help. But there are still a few things to check.

Try to Reach a Local System

On the shopping list, we told you to get the IP address of another computer on the same local network. Here's where you use that information. Try to **telnet** to that machine. You should see its login prompt:

```
% telnet 192.33.44.56
Trying 192.33.44.56
Connected to 192.33.44.56
Escape character is '^]'.

login:
```

If you get this far, you've proven that your system is probably working. If you can reach local systems but not remote systems, the problem is most likely somewhere on your local net—very likely a router, or some other piece of hardware that connects your network to the rest of the Internet. If you know a lot about how your local net is structured, you can make lots of experiments and maybe even pinpoint the trouble spot. However, that's not really your job. It's time to start making phone calls.

Look Around Your Office

Now, assume that the finger of Murphy's law is pointing directly at you—or your computer. It's time to start looking around your office. In World War II, the problem was gremlins. They caused bombs not to explode, engines to stop, etc., all for unknown causes. For the network, the problem is usually people: janitors, office-mates, you. It's amazing how many network problems are caused by damage to that $5 piece of wire between your computer and the wall. Janitors knock it out with a broom, or you roll over it a hundred times with a chair wheel and cut it. If you find something obviously wrong (for example, thick Ethernet transceiver cables* on the back of a computer have a tendency to fall off), fix it (or get someone to fix it).

---

*A 15-pin connector, explained more fully later in "Dealing With Coaxial Ethernets."

CAUTION

If you are on a coaxial cable Ethernet (a round cable running to your computer, not a flat one) don't do anything until you read the section on dealing with Ethernets later in this chapter.

If you have access to any networking equipment, look at it. Do the lights look normal? Are they on at all? If none of the lights are on, check the power to the unit. If they are on, but abnormal, there is probably nothing you can do except note the colors of the lights and call someone for help.

There is one situation where you might be able to help yourself out. Are you on a *10baseT* Ethernet* or a token ring LAN? These are probably the most common types of local area networks in the Internet these days, so the odds are pretty good that you fit into this category. For both kinds of network, each computer plugs into a separate port (plug) in a box called a "multiport repeater" (if you're on an Ethernet) or "media access unit" (MAU, for a token ring). Each port usually has a status light next to a plug. Locate the plug next to your computer's connection.† Is the light next to the cable from your computer red or off, and are the lights next to the other cables green? If so, try moving your plug to a vacant port. Did the new port's light turn green when you plugged your cable in, or did it remain red or dark? If it is now green, leave it there and try your computer again. You may have been plugged into a bad port and have bypassed the problem. If the new light turns red or remains unlit, it means that there is something wrong with the wire to your computer, or the interface card in it. Unless there is something obviously wrong, like a loose cable, it's hopeless to proceed without some other test equipment. (If you are on a token ring LAN, there is a section on token ring hints later in the chapter.)

Check Your Local Connection

If you can't get through to any remote destination, but you can connect to computers in your local "group," the problem is somewhere between your computer and the router that connects your group of computers to the Internet. "Group" is a pretty fuzzy term. You may be in a group by yourself, particularly if you connect using a dial-up, SLIP, or PPP connection. Your "group" may be a large number of computers sharing a local network and connected to an on-site router; at the extreme, your "group" may be a whole campus or corporate network.

---

*This is an Ethernet that uses normal telephone wiring and modular phone jacks, like the ones your home telephone uses to plug into the wall. They are also referred to as Ethernet on *UTP*, unshielded twisted pair.

†If you can't find your computer's connection, call it a day (or a night). Wiring closets are often messy places. If the cables aren't clearly labelled, or if there isn't an up-to-date map telling you what each cable is, don't touch anything. I'm also assuming that you properly have access to the network equipment. In many cases it's locked away to prevent random people (i.e., you) from moving wires. If you do take it upon yourself to move some wires, be sure to tell the person responsible for the network what you did, so he can get the port fixed and update any documentation necessary.

Now, you have to figure out whether the problem is within your area (your LAN or computer), or somewhere further away and out of your control. In this case, what you should do depends on how you're connected to the Net. Dial-up connections, in which you get network services by logging in to some "directly connected" computer over a modem, are significantly different from "direct connections." With SLIP or PPP, you have the worst of both worlds: you have to use the dial-up debugging techniques until the connection gets made and then deal with problems as if you had a dedicated connection. This is because these protocols set up temporary IP protocol connections between your computer and the service providers, just as if you had a dedicated connection.

Dial-up connections

Once again, by "dial-up connections" we mean that you dial into another computer over a phone line, log into it as a regular user, and use that computer's network services. What happens if you can't log into the remote computer? The problem is clearly not with the Internet, since you haven't gotten anywhere close to it.

Again, most problems fall into a few common categories. Although the symptoms and remedies listed below aren't exhaustive, they should take care of most situations:

Phone doesn't dial

> There is a problem in either your terminal emulator software, or between your computer and the modem. Your terminal emulator and modem are speaking different speeds or using different data formats. Check that out. It could also be that the location of the modem is not what your software thinks it is. (PCs have two communications ports, called COM1 and COM2; you have to pick the one your modem is plugged into. A similar thing happens on Macintoshes with the "phone" or "printer" plug. For that matter, most UNIX systems have two or more terminal connectors on the back.) Other possibilities are that your telephone line is dead, or the phone cable isn't plugged into the modem or the wall, or the modem isn't plugged into the computer. Even if you *know* that everything is wired correctly, checking never hurts. Also: find the phone jack where your modem plugs into the wall. Try plugging a regular telephone into the jack. Do you get a dial tone? If not, call your phone company.

Ring, no answer

> Check the number you dialed. Was it correct? If you dialed correctly and the remote system doesn't answer, the remote system may be down, or its modem may be bad. Check the published hours of operation to make sure it should be up. If it should be working, try the same phone number a few times. Better yet, if you have any alternate numbers, try them. If you have two phone lines available, try dialing the number with a phone on the line that doesn't have the modem. While it is ringing, dial with your modem phone and see if it gets through. (Sometimes if there are multiple phone lines through one number, one bad line will always answer the call. If you keep it busy with another

phone, your modem call might get to a good one.) Even if you get through eventually, call your service provider and report the problem so it can be fixed.

Answer, then nothing

Here's one common scenario: the modem dials correctly, the remote system answers, the modems whistle a few tones at each other, and you get the message "Connected" (or its equivalent) on your screen. Then nothing happens; everything goes dead. This usually points to a problem with your service provider's gear. Either the provider's modem is bad, or the port on the computer it is connected to is bad. Either way, the only thing you can do is call in and report it. You might try again a few times. If you have an alternate number, try it. Getting a different modem to answer might bypass the problem.

There's one other possibility. There are certain modems that "don't like to talk to each other," particularly if they're made by different manufacturers. However, we're assuming that you're trouble-shooting a connection that has worked for you in the past. Unless you've just bought a new modem, incompatible modems probably aren't the problem.

LAN, PPP, or SLIP connections

If you're directly on some kind of local network, or if you connect to a service provider using PPP or SLIP, your situation is somewhat different. Try and **telnet** to the closest router that services you. You should know this address—it was on the shopping list at the beginning of the chapter! If the router responds at all, then your computer and connection are OK. The problem is in the "cloud"; it must be solved by whoever worries about the router and the network that it's connected to. This could be your service provider, the networking staff for your campus or corporation, or (if you have a large in-building network) someone in your department.

Note that we said, "If the router responds at all." You might see a login prompt, or just the message "connection refused." Both of these are equally good responses. You don't know how to log in to the router, or the router may not be interested in letting anyone log in—who cares? To get either of these messages, you had to traverse your local network connection and get to something bigger. It isn't your problem. Call the appropriate person and report it.

Some Consolation

It may sound like there's not much you can do. In some senses, that's true. Think of your washer, dryer, or VCR. If they break, you can make sure all the plugs and hoses are tight, or maybe pull out a jammed cassette. There are a few things you can fix. But, much of the time, there is nothing you can do but call up the lonesome Maytag repairman and talk about the problem knowledgeably. As we said earlier, even if you can't solve the problem yourself, the more information you can gather, the better service you'll get.

Talking to Operations Personnel

Whenever pilots talk on the radio to air traffic controllers, they are taught that every message should say:

- Who you are
- Where you are
- What you want to do

These same guidelines apply to calling network operators. First, they need to know who you are—otherwise, they can't ask you for more information, or tell you that they've solved the problem. "Where you are" (the name of your computer and possibly its IP address) and "what you want to do" (the name of the remote computer and the service you want to get) allow operators to figure out the path your communications should take. This is the essential data necessary to diagnose and solve a problem. However, it is the minimum required. In addition, keep in mind why you've called the network operators. If you've followed our short procedure above, remember what you've done, why you did it, and what the results were. Why are you convinced that the problem isn't on your desktop? The answer to this question contains very important clues about the nature of the problem.

The operator you call should be the one operating the network closest to you. Your local network operators are the only ones who monitor connections to your campus or building. It isn't like calling up the President of GM to get some action on your car. In the network world, a national operator only knows about his network's connection to regional networks. Once he or she determines that the NSFnet, or NREN, or whatever isn't at fault, he will call the regional network responsible for your connection. In turn, the regional network will call your campus or corporate networking center. Very likely, they will then call you. Save yourself some time: start at the bottom.

Dealing With Coaxial Ethernets

Traditional coaxial cable Ethernets are special because, in many cases, fiddling with the wiring can break the network for other working computers. An Ethernet that uses coaxial cable has two parts: the *bus* and a number of *taps* (shown in Figure 15-3). The bus is the cable which snakes from computer to computer. There are two kinds of cable: "thick" and "thin." In thick Ethernets, the cable is about 3/8 inch in diameter, and yellow or orange with black marks every two meters. Thin Ethernets usually use grey, white, or black cable 1/5 inch in diameter. Each end of the bus must have a special "cap" called a *terminator*. Between the two terminators may be a number of taps. A tap is where one computer connects to the network. For thick Ethernets a tap is built in the *transceiver*, a little box a bit bigger than a pack of cigarettes hanging off the cable. This box allows your computer to connect to the Ethernet. A *transceiver* or *AUI* cable runs between it and your computer. For thin Ethernets, a tap looks like a "T" made of metal tubing, shown in Figure 15-4. It's usually located on the back of your computer. In this case, there is still a transceiver, but it is built into your computer.

If your computer only has a transceiver cable port, it might have an external transceiver next to the cable, just like a thick Ethernet would have.

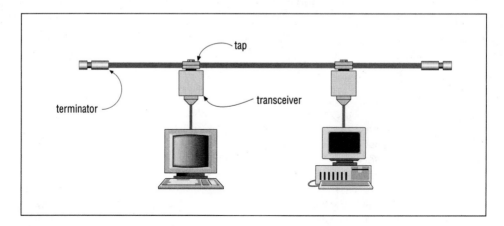

Figure 15-3: Typical thick Ethernet

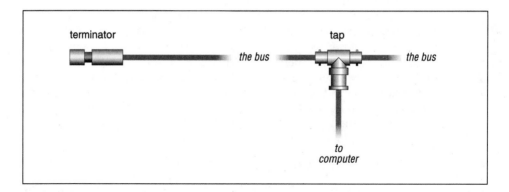

Figure 15-4: Thin Ethernet—tap and terminator

Why do you care so much about the parts of an Ethernet? Whatever you do, the bus must always remain "electrically intact." This means that there must be an unbroken connection from one end (one terminator) to the other. If the bus is broken for any reason, it stops working for *everyone* connected to it.* So, by improperly disconnecting the Ethernet cable in your office, you can easily make enemies out of friends. Two rules for dealing with Ethernets will get you through most situations:

---

*You might think that the network would still work, although in pieces: two computers should still be able to communicate if they're both on the same side of the break. Sorry. Life isn't so simple.

1. You can do anything to the connection from your Ethernet tap to your computer without affecting other people.

2. If you need to break the bus for repairs, warn others and make it quick.

Rule 1 is pretty straightforward. If you need to disconnect your computer from the network, leave the "T" in the cable, and disconnect the vertical part of the "T" from the computer (shown as "to computer" in Figure 15-4). On thick Ethernets, leave the tap and transceiver in the cable, but disconnect the transceiver cable.

The second rule is a bit harder. You must recognize that there are times when it's necessary to do things to the bus. If it's damaged or cut and everyone is down, it is not an issue. It's down and you're doing everyone a service by fixing it. If it's working for everyone but you, you have a problem. This is quite common if a thick Ethernet transceiver dies. Fixing your connection could take everyone off the air. In this case you have two choices: do it when they're not around or do it so fast they hardly notice.

Since most protocols, like TCP, are designed to deal with communication glitches of short duration, you can break an Ethernet for ten seconds or so without permanently impacting people's work. Whatever they're doing will stop momentarily, but that's it. If you break their connection for too long, first they will notice the lack of response, then later (usually over a minute) TCP will time out.

NOTE

Whether or not you should touch the cable at all depends on your environment. On some networks, the policy might be "no one but a cable technician or network administrator touches the wiring." Abide by your local rules.

Token Ring Notes

If you are on a token ring net, here are a few pointers. First: some MAUs don't have status lights. On these, you have no help figuring out if your port is bad or not. If you're desperate, you might just try plugging your computer into a vacant port.

Second: If you move the plug on a MAU, you may need to reboot your computer before you try again. (On some systems, you may only need to restart the Internet software.) The software has to perform a special "ring insertion" to become active on the network. A ring insertion only happens once, when the software first starts running. Your system won't automatically notice that it's back on the network and try to insert itself again. So if you change the cabling, you need to force a ring insertion before you can be active on the network. This may be possible within your TCP/IP software package. If you can't figure out how to do it gracefully, a reboot always works.

In any case, try and leave the network in the same configuration that you found it (with perhaps some bad cables replaced and now in working order).

THE WHOLE
INTERNET

CATALOG

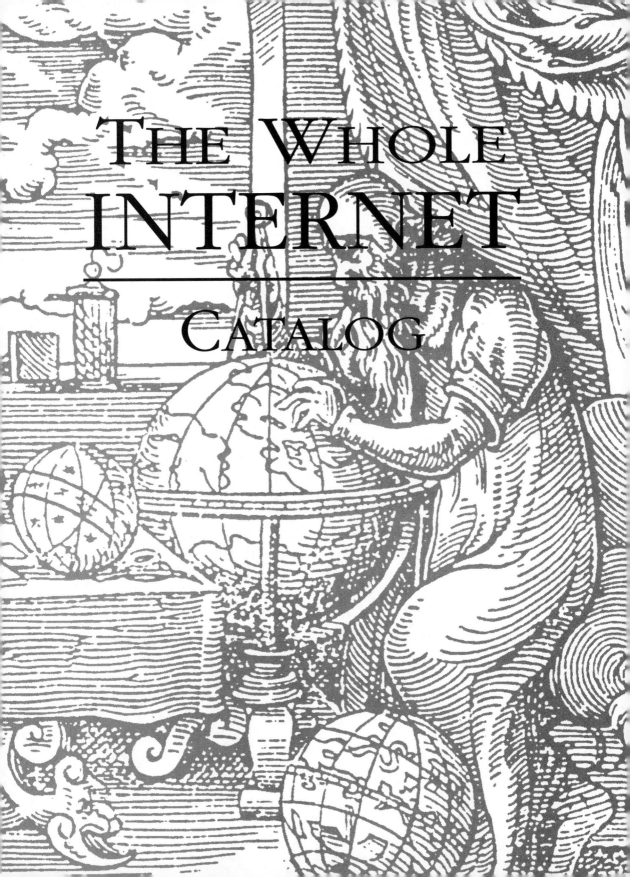

RESOURCES ON THE INTERNET

Stalking the Wild Resource
A Few Special Resources
How We Did It
Using the Catalog

Up to this point, I've given you a lot of "how to" advice. Now it's time to discuss "to what?" There are lots of resources out there—but there's no official list. Anyone who has an Internet connection can put a new resource online at any moment without telling anyone—and they do. So the trick is finding out what's available. First, we'll discuss how to use the tools we've covered to find resources. Next, we'll talk about a few resources we know about which we think are pretty special. One of these, the Global Network Navigator (GNN), is the basis for the *Resource Catalog* in this book. We'll talk about how the *Resource Catalog* in GNN was created and how it eventually ends up in this book. Finally, we'll introduce the format and use of the catalog. In the J.C. Penny catalog, this section would be called "how to order." Then you'll be ready to start shopping in the catalog itself.

Remember, the Internet is dynamic. The half-life of an Internet resource is about four years.* Translated into practical terms, this means that given any index of network resources, in the next year about a quarter of them will change in such a way that the index's information about them is unusable. That's as true of the *Resource Catalog* in this book as it is for any (and every) other resource list out there. The moral of the story is that resource lists are nice, but they aren't the final word. They are always partly out of date; and they're always missing the latest and greatest things on the Net.

Another problem is that quality of network resources varies greatly. While resource lists try to focus on the "best" resources they can find, it's certainly true that beauty is in the eye of the beholder. To become truly fluent in using the Net, you must learn how to find your own truffles amid the muck.

---

*It's probably not a coincidence that this is also the average time a student, whether undergraduate or graduate, remains at the same institution.

Stalking the Wild Resource

In the chapter on Gopher and WAIS, I drew some analogies between the Internet and a library without a card catalog. It's time to start thinking about that again. You may be without an official card catalog, but you are not without tools. The major tools at your disposal are your friends, network news, and mailing lists, and the Archie, Gopher, WAIS, and World Wide Web services. Let's look at how each of these may be used to find the resource of your dreams.

Friends

Your friends are your friends because you have interests in common with them. In addition to your regular friends, you will make a set of network friends through email. These friends may be looking for the same things you are; or even if their interests differ, they may be aware of resources that you want. In the real world, a friend who knows you are into female mystery writers might tell you "Sara Paretsky has a new book out": he knows you are interested and will appreciate the tip. In the network world, a friend who knows you are interested in agriculture resources might send you a message saying "Have you seen *Not Just Cows*, the Internet ag resources guide?" He, being a pencil collector, would love to hear from you if you found a complete pencil-pricing database. Life on the network is not all that different from "real life."

Network News and Mailing Lists

Network news and mailing lists are resources themselves. Newsgroups are shown in the catalog by topic. Lists of mailing lists are compiled and are listed under Network Information. These resources are also gateways to other resources. If you are interested in pencil collecting and follow the rec.pencil-collecting group (or a mailing list—same facilities, but different technology) for a while, one of three things will happen. First, someone might post a news item announcing a great find, like "Pencil Collecting Database Found." Second, these great finds will probably be collected into a group of frequently asked questions (FAQ). FAQs are posted to the newsgroup or to *news.answers* periodically (usually monthly).* By reading the FAQs, you can instantly be brought up-to-date on whatever the newsgroup is discussing.

If you don't find what you want in a FAQ, you can "go fishing" for an answer. Write a posting to the pencil-collecting newsgroup (or mailing list) asking "Does anyone have a database of current pencil prices?" It is easy to cast out and see what you can catch.

---

*FAQs have been archived, so they are available when you want them via ftp. See the "USENET Periodic Posting Archives" (under *Network News*) in the catalog for their location.

Archie

Archie (discussed in Chapter 9) is primarily a service for locating files by name. It makes a slight attempt to allow searches by topic, but this facility is limited and dated. However, in reality Archie is more general-purpose than this description implies. People who maintain anonymous FTP servers try to name things logically. Frequently, they use the structure of a filesystem to help organize: related files are stored in the same directory, which will probably have a useful name. In these cases, Archie doesn't tell you exactly what you want to know, but gives you an idea where you might look. For example, to locate pencil-collecting information, you might try the following command:

```
% archie -s pencil

Host blandsworth.usnd.edu
    Location: /pub
        DIRECTORY drwxr-xr-x   512  May 17 05:19  pencils
```

You didn't search for a particular topic, you searched for a file starting with "pencil." What Archie found was not a file, but a directory named */pub/pencils*, on the computer **blandsworth.usnd.edu**.

At this point, you don't know if there is anything useful to you on that computer or not. But—let's face it—how many people would create a directory named *pencils* for numerical analysis software? Not many. There's a good chance that this directory will contain something to do with pencils—maybe not exactly what you're looking for, but probably something interesting. All you need to do is **ftp** to **blandsworth.usnd.edu**, login as "anonymous", **cd pub/pencils**, and do a **dir**. Poke around a bit. It may contain good stuff, and it may not. It is a reasonable place to start.

Gopher

Gopher (Chapter 11) can be used to access other resource finders like Archie and WAIS. It can also be used by itself; Gopher menus are themselves pointers to resources. When looking for resources with Gopher, there are two particularly useful ways to start hunting: read the list of all the gopher servers in the world, or start searching for particular menus with Veronica.

There are getting to be more and more specialized Gopher servers around. Someone sees the power Gopher could bring to a community, so he or she builds a Gopher server tailored to that community. The person responsible for the server is on the lookout for more information sources in the area of interest. If you can find a Gopher server that has a collection you like, you can stay up-to-date by dropping into that server every now and then. To find a server that appears to have similar leanings to your own, just start from any server; find the list of "other Gopher servers"; and page through it. There are lots of them but, if you are lucky and patient, you might find the University of Minnesota Pencil Collection Gopher.

That might be pushing it a bit, but there are already specialized Gopher servers for soil science, history of science, birdwatching, and law. Pencil collecting can't be far behind.

If you can't find a specialized server to your liking, use Veronica to search for a couple of keywords that are relevant to your quest. Remember that if you find an interesting resource through a Gopher server, you can either continue to use that resource through Gopher (set a bookmark to come back again easily), or you can ask Gopher how to access the resource directly.* If Gopher accesses the resource through TELNET, you can just start **telnet** manually and skip the Gopher menus.

WAIS

The directory of servers makes it easy to find any WAIS service (Chapter 12). Some of the servers are actually indexes into other services. For example, the whole of the Archie database or the archives of many newsgroups can be searched through WAIS. This allows you to use the extended search capabilities of WAIS to look for things you might want.

The World Wide Web

The World Wide Web (Chapter 13) is also a great way to hunt for useful resources. Not only does it have resources of its own, but it allows you to use all the other search services. There are several subject-oriented menus, like CERN's "Virtual Library," and Yanoff's list of "Special Internet Connections." Resource lists like these are maintained by volunteers and are improving with time.

Make sure you check out lists of home pages when you find them. Lists of home pages are roughly equivalent to lists of Gopher servers. If you manage to find a home page with an interesting title, such as the "Pencil Institute of America Home Page," remember its URL or add it to your clients hotlist. Some Web clients come preconfigured with lists of good home pages in a pull-down menu.

A Few Special Resources

We tried to be selective in choosing resources for our catalog; we definitely didn't list every file that's available, or every site that has collections of files. It seems to have worked out very well, if we do say so ourselves. There are a few resources that are so exciting or important that we thought we would highlight them here.

---

*If you're using the ASCII ("curses") **gopher** client, use the = command.

The InterNIC

For a long time, no one has had the responsibility for providing network information services for the whole Internet. There have been any number of *NIC*s (Network Information Centers). Each has had a particular constituency; for example, the NYSERnet NIC would provide network information for customers of NYSERnet (an Internet service provider). So many global projects, like a unified white-pages directory, were never done. Everyone knew that these projects were good ideas, but no one was willing to step forward and volunteer—particularly if it was a big, unending job. The InterNIC, particularly funded by the National Science Foundation, was formed to solve this problem. In the parlance of sports advertising, it is the offical information provider of the Internet. InterNIC services are available to the entire Internet community, including users outside the U.S. Other NICs in the U.S. and abroad are working in cooperation with the InterNIC, and new NICs are being formed, such as the Asia-Pacific NIC (APNIC) and the Agriculture NIC (AgNIC).

The InterNIC has three parts:

- Registration Services
- Database Services
- Information Services

Each of these components is run by a different company with its own charter; but together they are providing a unified, useful service.

Registration Services

The InterNIC's registration services are responsible for assigning network addresses and top-level domain names. Important as this service is, it's not something you're likely to need, unless you're setting up a network at a new site—and even then, it's more common for your Internet service provider to deal with registration and related issues.

You might find Registration Services information useful if you need to get information about some remote domain or network. For example, the big boss comes down and says, "Find out if we can do email with Tunisia." The InterNIC might be able to tell you who to contact to find out more about computer networking in Tunisia; in particular, they would probably be able to put you in touch with their Tunisian counterparts (i.e., whatever organization is responsible for network registration and coordination).

Database Services

The Database Services component of the InterNIC has the task of creating databases in service to the Internet community. A big part of that is to coordinate the creation of a global White Pages directory. We showed you how to use the beginnings of this in Chapter 10, *Finding Someone*. This means that the traditional problem of finding someone on the Internet may be solved sometime soon.

The Database Services people are also trying to create an Internet equivalent to the "yellow pages." That is, they'd like to have a directory of services that's sorted by the service type, rather than alphabetically by name. Services could get a small listing for free, or they could pay something for a big listing, complete with pictures. It's not quite there yet, but will probably happen.

Information Services

The Information Services component of the InterNIC disseminates a wealth of information about the Internet by a variety of means. They are a reference desk where you can call, fax, or email questions. They run Gopher, WAIS, World Wide Web, and anonymous FTP servers to give free public access to this information. The Web server offered by the InterNIC includes an indexing service that allows easy searches for documents by topic and level of expertise. Much of it is user-oriented; it includes lists of resources, lists of network providers (including international providers), training courses, books, statistics, and archives of articles about the Internet. A lot of this information is available on a CD-ROM product called NICLink, intended for novice users and Internet trainers.

The InterNIC is known as the NIC of first and last resort. This means that they accept questions directly from users who are having trouble, but they are also a resource for other NICs to use when they encounter a question which stumps them.

Table 1: Accessing The InterNIC

Method	Address
Email	info@internic.net
Telnet	internic.net
FTP	ftp.internic.net
Archie	archie.internic.net
Gopher	gopher.internic.net
World Wide Web	http://www.internic.net/
Telephone	(800) 444-4345, (619) 455-4600
FAX	(619) 455-4640

U.S. Government Resources

The U.S. government (like many governments worldwide) issues tremendous amounts of information on just about every topic imaginable, ranging from economic statistics to hints on home maintenance. In the past, a lot of this information has been hard to get; often, it has been very expensive; even if it hasn't been expensive, it's been hard to find.

One of the Clinton administration's goals is to release as much of this information as possible through the Internet. One of the biggest conduits for releasing information is the Extension Service of the U.S. Department of Agriculture (**esusda.gov**), partnering with universities in every state and territory across the nation. Don't let the name fool you; it isn't just soybeans and hog bellies. How about:

- Distance education (education at remote locations, through correspondence, video, etc.)
- Problems of large cities
- Ethnic diversity
- Children and families
- Sustainable agriculture
- Economics of communities
- NAFTA accord
- National Performance Review
- National Health Care Reform Report
- National Water Quality Information Database
- National Family Life Database
- International Food and Nutrition Database
- White House press reports

There's a lot more; these are a few of the highlights. Some of these resources are listed in the *Resource Catalog*, but what's there is expanding all the time. If you are interested in information like this, your best bet is to get a catalog right from the source.

Most of these resources are provided by Almanac servers, which are like list-servers. (How to use them was explained in Chapter 7). There are any number of servers, each of which has its own collection of information. To get detailed information about how to use Almanac servers, send the one-line email message **send guide** to **almanac@esusda.gov**. For a catalog of what's available on any one server, send the one-line message **send catalog** to that server; for example, to find out what's available at the Extension Service's own server, send this message to **almanac@esusda.gov**. For an overall list of known servers, some hints on getting started, and a general survey of topics covered by Almanac servers, send the one-line message **send ces-docs explore-inet** to **almanac@esusda.gov**.

Here's a short—and, no doubt, already incomplete—list of Almanac servers.

Table 2: Almanac Servers

Location	Internet Address
Americans Communicating Electronically	almanac@ace.esusda.gov
Auburn University	almanac@acenet.auburn.edu
Cornell University	almanac@cce.cornell.edu
Extension Service-USDA	almanac@esusda.gov
National Ag Library	almanac@cyfer.esusda.gov
North Carolina State University	almanac@ces.ncsu.edu
Oregon State University	almanac@oes.orst.edu
Purdue University	almanac@ecn.purdue.edu
University of California	almanac@silo.ucdavis.edu
University of Missouri	almanac@ext.missouri.edu
University of Wisconsin	almanac@joe.uwex.edu
	almanac@wisplan.uwex.edu

The Global Network Navigator

The Global Network Navigator (GNN) is one of the first attempts to commercialize the World Wide Web technology. You might think of GNN as an online magazine, but it's probably better to think of it as an information service. Its news stories and features include links to the services being described, so you can think of it as a kind of "information interface" to the Net. The GNN editorial staff does the "Net surfing" for people who don't have the time or experience to do it themselves, researching special-interest areas of the Net, providing reviews of Internet resources, adding interesting editorial content, and clustering all this additional information around links to other Internet services.

GNN is a great place to start exploring the Net, especially if you have a direct (TCP/IP) connection.* In addition to the news magazine, GNN includes an expanded online version of the *Whole Internet Catalog* included in the back of this book. Instead of typing in a command to access the service being described, you can just click on a hypertext link to reach it. The online version of the catalog is updated regularly; you can check in at any time to find new resources. It's also a good way to track down resources that have changed or been reorganized since the last edition of the catalog.

GNN also includes "interest centers" that try to group all significant Internet services in a particular category, together with pointers to related commercial services. There is currently a travel center; other interest centers are being developed.

---

*Chapter 1 and Appendix A explain different types of Internet connections; Appendix A also discusses how to get an Internet connection.

The travel center includes travel book reviews and links to all the travel-related newsgroups, Gophers, FTP archives, and Web sites, plus a syndicated World Travel Watch column that describes trouble spots around the world, access to an up-to-date currency conversion program, dispatches and photos from travel writers, and advertising from travel publishers.

Advertising? On the Internet? Of course. Many commercial sites are now offering Gopher catalogs, or in some cases even Web servers, providing access to their information. This is non-intrusive advertising—making information available for people who want it. GNN goes one step further. Its developers argue that once the novelty factor has worn off, just throwing up a Gopher catalog won't do more than serve the customers you already have. In order to bring in new people, you need to create added value for specific audiences. Once people are visiting a travel center, links to travel-related catalogs and commercial services are providing an information service for the reader, rather than an additional nuisance.

The GNN Marketplace is another important innovation. The Marketplace contains pointers to various advertising documents—like an online version of the Yellow Pages. Unlike most advertising, GNN's advertisements are not thrust upon you; it's up to you to decide when (and whether) to read them. So, if you just had a huge lunch and are feeling fat, you can pop into the NordicTrack listing and see what you should be doing rather than eating.

You can get information about subscribing to GNN at the back of the book.

Domain Name Lookup

Throughout this book, we've talked in terms of these nice, memorable "domain names." Maybe you don't find them memorable, but they're certainly nicer than the alternative: addresses like 143.209.24.92. In Chapter 3, we described the Domain Name System, which translates names into addresses.

Unfortunately, there are a few sites that don't have access to the Domain Name System. This is a problem that really should be remedied by a system administrator or a service provider—but when things are broken, sometimes you don't have the option of waiting until they're fixed. If you're in this situation, take heart: there is a way out! There are a few services for looking up numeric addresses "by hand;" once you've done that, you can use the numeric address instead of the name. None of the tools we've discussed (except for email) care which you use—even the Web browsers! Just substitute a numeric address for the Internet name in the URL, and you can use it.

So—what are these magic resources? The easiest one to use is a **telnet** service run by the SWITCH (Swiss Academic and Research Network). Just **telnet** to the address 30.59.1.40, login as **lookup**, and enter the name you want to convert to an address. For example, you'd get an address for the FTP archive **ftp.uu.net** (an important source for software of all sorts) like this:

```
% telnet 30.59.1.40
login: lookup

SWITCH Internet Domain Name Service

Enter the full domain name or HELP:  ftp.uu.net

Non-authoritative answer:

Name: ftp.uu.net
Address: 192.48.96.9
```

You can type HELP to get a "help" screen. However, there isn't much help to give; you know just about all there is to know about this service.

Once you have the address, you can then use it in an **ftp** command:

```
% ftp 192.48.96.9
```

It's not convenient, but it works.

You can also get Internet addresses via electronic mail. The name server you use depends on where you are; it is best to use the server closest to you. In the U.S., use the address **resolve@cs.widener.edu** and include the message "site *internet-name*". Outside the U.S., use the address **dns@grasp.insa-lyon.fr** and include the message "ip *internet-name*". For example, to find out the address of **ftp.uu.net**, send the message **ip ftp.uu.net** to **dns@grasp.insa-lyon.fr**; equivalently, send the message **site ftp.uu.net** to **resolve@cs.widener.edu**. You'll get a message back looking like this:

```
Return-Path: <dns-request@grasp.insa-lyon.fr>
Date: Tue, 1 Mar 1994 20:17:33 GMT
From: dns@grasp.insa-lyon.fr (Mail Name Server)
Subject: Reply to your queries

you> ip ftp.uu.net

Officiel hostname: ftp.uu.net
Registered addresse(s):
        192.48.96.9
```

You may wonder why you can use an email address like **dns-request@grasp.insa-lyon.fr**, when you can't use other Internet addresses. Unlike the other services, electronic mail is a "store and forward" service. Your own computer doesn't necessarily need to look up domain names; it can send the mail on to a "smarter" computer that knows how to interrogate the Domain Name System. So you can often use email addresses even when you can't use domain names.

How We Did It

How did we create our resource catalog? What techniques did we use? We did all of the following:

- We listened to newsgroups and mailing lists looking for interesting announcements.

- We used what we learned to find other lists and used their information.

- We looked for sparse areas in the catalog and used Archie to perform subject searches (e.g., `archie -s music`). With that information, we then looked at the anonymous FTP servers to see if there was anything interesting in them.

- We visited a number of Gopher servers and tried to list any unique services we found.

- We included a summary of the most useful WAIS services from the directory of servers.

- We were happy to hear about neat resources other people have used, found or created. If you find a new one, mail us at **wic@ora.com**, and we'll take a look.

What Is a Resource?

What we included as a resource varies from subject to subject. There are subjects, like the Internet itself and computer science, where thousands of important files are scattered throughout the Internet, almost randomly. We chose not to include such resources; anyone can find these with Gopher or WAIS. There are other groups for which the sole motivation to be on the Internet might be to access one particular file; we tried to include these. In general, we included the most unique and interesting things we could find. Within each subject, resources were "graded on the curve." There was no absolute measure for what we considered interesting.

We biased our choices in favor of resources that anyone could use, or that could be used on the spur of the moment from the network. A prime example of this would be computational resources. We didn't list the NSF supercomputer centers, even though they were one of the prime reasons why the network became ubiquitous. Anyone who wants to do heavy-duty research computing can request time on a supercomputer, but they are not for everyone to use. If you are a valid user, each center will supply you with lots of documentation about how to use it. You can't just decide "I think I'll play on a Cray today."

On the other hand, there are a few sites that offer free UNIX computing. That is, anyone can **telnet** to them and run selected programs. With the emphasis on "anyone," we included such resources.

Finally, we tried to be broad rather than deep. In one respect, this book is an argument about why you should use the Internet. And the simplest argument for using the Net is that there are loads of resources interesting to all sorts of people, not just "geeks with pocket protectors." To prove this, we've tried to hit as many different and diverse topics as possible. If we've succeeded, even Internet veterans should be surprised at what we've found.

Accuracy and Permissions

We verified that every listed resource was working and available at some time when we were gathering information. That doesn't mean that these resources are still available, or that the usage information is still the same. There were times when the access information changed in the two weeks between the time we discovered the resource and the time we actually tried it. If we could figure out how to use a resource, we included it; if not, we chucked it.

For this reason, we included references to other resource directories and guides. They have the advantage of being online, hence easily updatable. This doesn't mean they actually are updated frequently. There's really no way to tell whether any online database is more or less up-to-date than this catalog. Online indexes are usually maintained by volunteer effort; you never know how much effort the volunteer has to expend.

Remember: a resource that is publicly accessible isn't necessarily a public resource. This caused me a bit of trouble. If I stumbled upon a good resource, how could I decide if it was intended to be public? The rule of thumb I used was that a public resource had to fall into one of these categories:

- Commonly known within the community (e.g., frequently mentioned and discussed in newsgroups)
- Listed in other resource guides or catalogs
- Easily found with public index utilities (e.g., Gopher, WAIS)

We ran across a few resources that didn't fall into these categories, were subject to restrictions, or seemed "dangerous" to the offerer. In these cases, we asked the owner if he or she would like to see the resource listed. Usually the answer was "yes." If the answer was "no," the resources are still available on the Internet. But you aren't hearing about them from me.

Using the Catalog

We tried to group the resources into the areas where they belonged, but then what do we know?* If you already know the name of a resource and would like to see if it's listed, you might start at the Index to the *Resource Catalog*. All the

---

*I'm not the only one who doesn't know about this. Cataloging of online resources is a really hot area of research in the library science community.

entries in the resource guide are listed there. So if you have a resource that you like, and you want to see where I put it, work backwards.

After a description of the resource, we tell you how to access the resource. We'll show you what kind of a resource is listed (FTP, Telnet, WAIS, Gopher, or World Wide Web), followed by the site's Internet address, followed by any other information you need: how to log in, what directory to **cd** to, what port to use (if it's non-standard). The command itself isn't that important; its main purpose is to tell you what kind of a service you're using. Use whatever command you have available that knows how to access that kind of service; use your FTP client to access an FTP resource, a Gopher client to access a Gopher resource, and so on.

The descriptions for WAIS, Gopher, and World Wide Web servers get a little more complicated. For WAIS servers, Internet addresses are irrelevant. Instead, we show the name of the WAIS database that you have to look up. This database should be in the list of databases your WAIS client knows about. If it isn't, you can find it in the master WAIS database, *directory-of-servers.src.*

For Gopher servers, the catalog shows which server to connect to, followed by the menu items to select. For the Flybase gopher server (which contains information about fruit flies), the catalog shows the following entry:

> *gopher ftp.bio.indiana.edu /Flybase*

This means to point your Gopher client at the server **ftp.bio.indiana.edu**, and then select the "Flybase" item from its root menu. To get to this server, you can either put its address on the command line, or search through a menu of Gopher servers until you find it.

A typical World Wide Web entry looks like this:

> *www http://www.nr.no/ordbok*

This resource is an online dictionary of Norwegian (listed under "Norway" in the "International Interest" section of the *Resource Catalog*). To access this resource, just type the command command **www http://www.nr.no/ordbok**. If you're using a public **www** client, give the command **go http://www.nr.no/ordbok**. That's a lot of typing—and this is a short URL. Unfortunately, there's really no other way to describe a Web resource.

Of course, you may not be using a program that's exactly equivalent to the one we list. Don't let that bother you. There are many World Wide Web clients besides **www**. You may be using Lynx, a version of Mosaic, or any of a number of other browsers. Don't let that confuse you; they should all work the same way. Similarly, if you're using **xgopher** or the Mac's TurboGopher, or another Gopher client, use the client you have—don't be confused because we list a different program name in the catalog.

Remember that the Internet is always changing. Servers get reorganized, so that the resources that are already there move around. If you can't find something, look around a bit; the server that provides the information may have undergone some "housecleaning," and you'll find what you want elsewhere.

By the way, we've included a handy "quick reference bookmark" in the back of the book. We hope to save you from leafing back and forth between the catalog and the chapters, looking up the syntax of commands you need to use.

AERONAUTICS & ASTRONAUTICS

Newsgroups:
sci.space, sci.astro, sci.aeronautics

NASA News

A short listing of current happenings at NASA. If you're interested in the space program, this is a great way to stay up-to-date. On a typical day, you'd find out about expected launches, or (perhaps) progress in a Space Shuttle mission.

Access via:
finger nasanews@space.mit.edu

NASA Spacelink

Entries about the history, current state, and future of NASA and space flight, provided by the NASA Marshall Space Flight Center. Also, some classroom materials and information on space technology transfer. This is a particularly valuable resource for educators.

Access via:
telnet spacelink.msfc.nasa.gov;
login *newuser;* password *newuser*

Information:
Telephone: (205) 544-6531

Shuttle and Satellite Images

The following FTP sites make available photographs and other images taken from the Space Shuttle, Magellan and Viking missions, and other good stuff. The data formats vary; check any README files, or other descriptive files that are available.

Access via:
telnet sanddunes.scd.ucar.edu
(Email: kelley@sanddunes.scd.ucar.edu for login, password, and manual.)

ftp sseop.jsc.nasa.gov; login *anonymous*
(Space shuttle images.)

ftp explorer.arc.nasa.gov;
login *anonymous;* cd *pub/SPACE/GIF*
(Images are in GIF and JPEG directories; lots of other information about all aspects of the U.S. space program in other directories. A gigantic archive.)

Space FAQs

Have you ever thought about becoming an astronaut? Here's where to find out what's required. Fifteen lists of "Frequently Asked Questions" are available. The lists are on topics ranging from "Astronomical Mnemonics" to "Orbital and Planetary Launch Services"—including "How to Become an Astronaut." Other files include a report on tidal bulges, information on interpreting satellite weather photos, and databases on constellations and nearby stars.

Other subdirectories under pub/SPACE contain detailed reports about individual space missions.

Access via:
ftp explorer.arc.nasa.gov;
cd *pub/SPACE/FAQ*

SpaceMet

A bulletin board system for exchanging information about space exploration from the view of science educators. Has information on past, current, and future NASA plans. Also contains information on curriculum planning. There is a section on events and meetings, but it is pretty local to the Northeastern U.S.

Access via:
telnet spacemet.phast.umass.edu

AGRICULTURE

Newsgroups:
alt.agriculture.[fruit, misc], misc.rural

See also: Forestry; Gardening; and Horticulture.

Advanced Technology Information Network

Any farmer knows that farming isn't a "mom and pop" business any more; it's high-tech, and it's important to keep up with the latest developments. This resource, and the others in this group, will help you stay up-to-date. A fairly complete agricultural information service offers market, news, events, weather, job listing, and safety information. Offered by the California Agricultural Technology Institute, so there is a "West Coast" bias to the information. Also contains information on trade, exports, and biotechnology.

Access via:
telnet caticsuf.csufresno.edu; login *super*

Commodity Market Reports

Commodity reports compiled by the U.S. Department of Agriculture Market News Service. Twelve hundred reports covering the U.S., updated daily.

Access via:
WAIS *agricultural-market-news.src*

Information:
Email: wais@oes.orst.edu

Not Just Cows

A guide to resources on the Internet and BITNET in agriculture and related subjects. Compiled by Wilfred (Bill) Drew.

Access via:
ftp ftp.sura.net; login *anonymous;* cd *pub/nic;* get *agricultural.list*

Information:
Email: drewwe@snymorva.bitnet

PEN Pages

A complete information server concerning all aspects of rural life. Sections on commodity prices, family farm life, seniors on the farm, news, and nutrition. Also, provides various announcements by the USDA including its CITExtension newsletter. Service provided by the Pennsylvania State University, so some information may be specific to that region.

Access via:
telnet psupen.psu.edu; login your two-letter state abbreviation

U.C. Davis Extension 4-H Project Catalog

Intended to help members of the 4-H youth project get started in areas ranging from bee-keeping to "poultry science," these files are available in PostScript and WordPerfect 5.1 formats.

Access via:
gopher gopher.ucdavis.edu /The Campus/ U. C. Cooperative Extension/4h-youth

ftp ftp.ucdavis.edu; login *anonymous;* cd *pub/extension/4h-youth*

USDA Extension Service Gopher

A "master gopher" for the U.S. Department of Agriculture's activities and extension service. This includes information about the extension service, policies of the USDA and extension

Excerpt from **PEN Pages**, *7/14/92:*

ADAPTING HOMES FOR ELDERLY

Since most information about a
person's surroundings comes
through eyesight, reduced
vision problems related to
aging are often compounded by
the interior design of a home.
The yellowing of the eye's
lens produces less contrast
between objects and makes it
harder to see colors in the
blue-violet range. Using warm
colors in the red and yellow
range are more comfortable for
elderly persons. The use of
contrasting colors helps to
make distinctions and judge-
ments easier for elderly persons. For example, the use of
contrasting colors can separate the floor from the base-
board. Also, using floor cov-
erings that are different in
color and texture could help
an elderly person identify
danger areas such as stair-
ways.

Source: Sarah Drummond,
Assistant Extension
Specialist, Oklahoma

Editor: J. Van Horn, Ph.D.,
CFLE, Professor, Rural
Sociology Dept. of Ag.
Economics and Rural Sociology,
Penn State May 1992
PENpages Number 085072114

Keywords: AGRICULTURAL-EC-RUR-
SOC, ELDERLY, HOME, HOUSING,
MAPP, NEWS, SAFETY, VANHORN-
JAMES

service, educational (and other) projects of the extension service, disaster relief informa-tion, and many pointers to other Government resources. The "About the Extension Service" file (on their main menu) is a helpful guide to the service they offer.

Access via:
gopher esusda.gov

A gopher server for CYFERnet, the Children Youth Family Education Research Network. The primary focus of this service is the sup-port of child, youth, and family development. There are pointers to resources on education, nutrition, the 4-H, etc. One interesting sec-tion of this server is ACE (Americans Communicating Electronically), a project for providing wider access to government infor-mation.

Access via:
gopher cyfer.esusda.gov

USDA Research Results

Summaries of recent research results from the USDA's agricultural and economic research services. Updated at least bimonthly.

Access via:
WAIS *usda-rrdb.src*

Information:
Email: wais@esusda.gov

ANTHROPOLOGY

Newsgroup:
sci.anthropology

Aboriginal Studies

A collection of records from the Aboriginal Studies Electronic Data Archive at the Australian Institute of Aboriginal Studies and the Australian National University.

Access via:
WAIS *ANU-Aboriginal-Studies.src*

Coombspapers Social Sciences Research Data Bank

An extensive archive of research information on the study of humans and their cultures. It is heavily laden with bibliographies, abstracts, books by Australian National University authors, and conference papers, rather like your library's old Vertical File, but you may be able to find more valuable information here, too.

Access via:
ftp coombs.anu.edu.au; login *anonymous*; cd *coombspapers*

Rice Anthropology Gopher

Mostly a set of pointers to other anthropology resources; nothing local as of November 1993.

Access via:
gopher riceinfo.rice.edu /Information by Subject Area/Anthropology and Culture

Thai Yunnan Project

Annotated bibliography and research notes collection of the Thai-Yunnan Project, Dept. of Anthropology, Australian National University, GPO Box 4, Canberra ACT 2601. Lots of data on ethnic groups of southeast Asia, including languages, religions, customs, etc.

Access via:
WAIS *ANU-Thai-Yunnan.src*

Information:
Telephone: +61 6 249-9262

Email: gew400@coombs.anu.edu.au

ARCHAEOLOGY

Newsgroup:
sci.archaeology

See also: Classical Languages & Literature

Ancient Near East—Cambridge

This site for Ancient Near East studies specializes in Egyptological material, and encourages scholarly contributions. Also contains a notice of an email list for the discussion of the Ancient Near East.

Access via:
ftp newton.newton.cam.ac.uk; login *anonymous*; cd *pub/ancient*

Information:
Email: Helen Strudwick (H.M.Strudwick@newton.cam.ac.uk) or Nigel Strudwick (ncs3@cus.cam.ac.uk)

Classics & Mediterranean Archaeology (U Mich)

A resource sponsored by the Department of Classical Studies, University of Michigan; many of the items pointed to here are to be found in this Catalog. See in particular the Pylos Regional Archaeological Project's 1993 *Preliminary Report,* a good example of the use of the Net for scholarly publication.

Access via:
www http://rome.classics.lsa.umich.edu/welcome.html

Dead Seas Scrolls Exhibition

An online version of the Library of Congress's exhibition titled "Scrolls from the Dead Sea: The Ancient Library of Qumran and Modern Scholarship." The exhibition covers the Jewish and Christian context of the scrolls and the Qumran community that deposited them, and includes images not only of selected pieces of the scrolls, but of other archaeological artifacts, such as pottery and coins.

Both FTP and WWW interfaces are available:

Access via:
ftp ftp.loc.gov; login *anonymous*;
cd *pub/exhibit.images/deadsea.scrolls.
exhibit*

*www http://sunsite.unc.edu/expo/
deadsea.scrolls.exhibit/intro.html*

New World Archaeology

ArchNet, at the University of Connecticut Dept. of Anthropology, covers archaeology in the Northeastern U.S. The home page also offers links to other archaeology sites.

Access via:
*www http://spirit.lib.uconn.edu/HTML/
archnet.html*

*gopher spirit.lib.uconn.edu /Academic
Subjects and Services/Information by Subject
Area (at Rice University)/Anthropology and
Culture/ArchNet - Archaeological Data at
UConn*

Oriental Institute

The FTP server of the Oriental Institute of the University of Chicago hosts announcements and the newsletter of the Archaeological Institute of America, the archives of the Ancient Near East email discussion list, announcements and the newsletter of the American Schools of Oriental Research, information about the Oriental Institute, its publications and holdings, along with some miscellaneous items of interest, and other research on the Ancient Near East. Encourages scholarly contributions.

Access via:
ftp oi.uchicago.edu; login *anonymous*;
cd *pub*

ASTRONOMY

Newsgroups:
sci.[astro, astro.fits,
astro.hubble,
astro.planetarium]

American Astronomical Society

Original material here is confined to information on the Society, meeting schedules, meeting abstracts, a staff directory and the AAS Job Register.

Access via:
*www http://blackhole.aas.org/
AAS-homepage.html*

Astronomical Databases

This FTP site includes several databases of astronomical objects, including the Yale Bright Star catalog, the Saguaro Astronomy Club databases, and an asteroid database. Some IBM PC software for using these databases is also available.

Access via:
ftp pomona.claremont.edu; login *anonymous*;
cd *yale_bsc.dir*

Astronomical Internet Resources

A hypertext roundup of worldwide Internet resources on astronomy and space, classed by method of access (WWW, Gopher, WAIS, FTP).

Access via:
www http://stsci.edu/net-resources.html

Astronomy at University of Massachusetts, Amherst

Both technical tools and astronomical images are available at this expanding site.

Access via:
*www http://donald.phast.umass.edu/
umasshome.html*

Centre de Donnés Astronomiques de Strasbourg

The Strasbourg Astronomical Data Center (CDS) is dedicated to the collection and worldwide distribution of astronomical data, and is located at the Observatoire de Strasbourg. The CDS hosts the SIMBAD astronomical database, a world reference database for the identification of astronomical objects, and other information and pointers of interest to stargazers.

Access via:
www http://cdsweb.u-strasbg.fr/CDS.html

Conservatoire National des Arts et Metiers (Images)

A bilingual French and English astronomy site, specializing in pictures. README files in all subdirectories give size and description of each image, and images added within the past 15 days are listed in README NEW. The FTP interface gives access to additional lists of images.

Access via:
www http://web.cnam.fr/astro.english.html (In English.)

www http://web.cnam.fr/astro.french.html (In French.)

ftp ftp.cnam.fr; login *anonymous;* cd *pub/Astro*

Lunar and Planetary Institute Information

Information about NASA's Lunar and Planetary Institute and its services. It includes a bibliographic database, and allows access to an electronic journal, "The Lunar & Planetary Information Bulletin." There is also a service called IRPS, which is the "Image Retrieval and Processing System." It is possible to order and (with the appropriate software) display digital images of the planets.

Primarily of use to researchers in lunar or planetary studies.

Access via:
telnet lpi.jsc.nasa.gov; login *lpi*

NASA/IPAC Extragalactic Database

The NED contains information about over 200,000 astronomical objects, as well as abstracts and bibliographies of astronomical publications.

Access via:
telnet denver.ipac.caltech.edu; login *ned*

NASA Langley Research Center

A WWW home page for this part of NASA. A link to "Other Government Labs" is interesting, too.

Access via:
www http://mosaic.larc.nasa.gov/larc.html

NASA Information Services via WWW

Gives access to all the NASA Center home pages.

Access via:
www http://hypatia.gsfc.nasa.gov/ NASA_homepage.html

National Space Science Data Center

The interface to many NASA data catalogs and centers. This system allows you to connect to facilities such as the Astronomical Data center, access the CANOPUS newsletter, and get data from and about various satellite sensors.

Access via:
telnet nssdca.gsfc.nasa.gov; login *nodis*

Project STELAR (Study of Electronic Literature for Astronomical Research)

A comprehensive home page for NASA's Goddard Space Flight Center's WWW server, highlighting the National Space Science Data Center's Project STELAR. Project STELAR itself is a pilot study of technical and practical issues in electronic access to astronomical literature; links are provided to relevant government and nongovernment resources, too.

Access via:
www http://hypatia.gsfc.nasa.gov/ STELAR_homepage.html

Space Images at Arizona

Maintained by the University of Arizona chapter of SEDS (Students for the Exploration and Development of Space), this site contains a considerable collection of images, along with other astronomical information.

Access via:
ftp seds.lpl.arizona.edu; login *anonymous*; cd *pub*

gopher bozo.lpl.arizona.edu/ ANONYMOUS FTP

Space Remote Sensing Center

The Institute for Technology Development/Space Remote Sensing Center, at NASA's Stennis Space Center in Mississippi, is a not-for-profit organization dedicated to the development and commercialization of remote sensing. It is also the North American Application Development Center for the pricey French SPOT Image Corporation. The contents are mostly data processing programs; there are also a few low-quality satellite images of the 1993 flood in the Midwest.

Access via:
www http://ma.itd.com:8000/welcome.html

ftp pa.itd.com; login *anonymous*; cd *pub*

Space Telescope Science Institute

Information about the Hubble Space Telescope and the Space Telescope Science Institute. Includes instrument reports, ample data, grant information, FAQ lists, long and short range plans, software, etc.

Access via:
www http://stsci.edu/top.html

gopher stsci.edu

ftp stsci.edu; login *anonymous*

AVIATION

Newsgroup:
rec.aviation

Aeronautics Archives

A group of aviation archives. Among other things, these archives include rec.aviation postings, aircraft specifications, FARs, and reviews of flight simulation software.

Access via:
WAIS *aeronautics.src*

ftp rascal.ics.utexas.edu; login *anonymous*; cd *misc/av*

DUAT

Pilot flight services via the Internet. It provides pilots with weather briefings and flight planning services. You must be a pilot (or a student pilot) to use this resource.

Access via:
telnet duat.gtefsd.com

telnet duats.gtefsd.com
(For students.)

BIOLOGY

Newsgroups:
sci.bio.[ecology,ethology,evolotion,herp,technology], bionet.[cellbiol, general, molbio]

Biology Overview

The revolution in biotechnology has provided a tremendous increase in the amount of information biologists are able to obtain about genetics and molecular biology. A worldwide increase in funding for genome research (the study of the information contained within the chromosomes of an organism), has caused the amount of new information to double yearly.

This increasing volume of information has created problems because the ability to distribute this genome information via traditional paper methods has been impossible for several years. The creation of the Internet protocols WAIS, Gopher, and WWW caused an explosion of biological information freely available on the Internet. Entries in this section represent Internet resources that specialize in information on one particular species, provide a specific type of information on all organisms, or distribute collections of general information. Most of these resources are Gopher servers, but many sites are rushing to convert their services into WWW.

Arabidopsis Information

Arabidopsis Thaliana is a small, rather unimpressive flowering plant used as a model system for research on plant biology. The Arabidopsis Research Companion supplies a Gopher interface to a WAIS database of the information in the Arabidopsis Thaliana Database. Highlights include known DNA sequences, genes, straines, and research literature citations; but there's much more available.

Access via:
gopher weeds.mgh.harvard.edu
/Arabidopsis Information (thale cress)

Australian National University Bioinformatics Hypermedia Service: Biodiversity, Taxonomy and Conservation

Plant biodiversity and conservation, including Australian and regional biodiversity information.

Access via:
www http://life.anu.edu.au/biodiversity.html

Australian National University Bioinformatics Hypermedia Service: Molecular Biology

A directory of links to molecular biology databases, bibliographies, and other information.

Access via:
www http://life.anu.edu.au/molbio.html

Biodiversity and Biological Collections Gopher

Run by Harvard University's Herbarium, "this Gopher contains information of interest to systematists and other biologists of the organismic kind." It also has information on Museum, Herbarium and Arboretum collection catalogs, Biodiversity information resources, and other directories, publications, and software.

Access via:
gopher huh.harvard.edu

Flybase

Information about Drosophila (fruit flies, to the uninitiated). The Gopher server has lots of other information for and about fly genetics. The entry for "stocks" is a searchable catalog of different genetic traits, and where to find flies with those traits. This is also an excellent site for pointers to other biology Gophers, software related to biology, news, and other material of interest.

Access via:
gopher fly.bio.indiana.edu /Flybase

EMBNET Bioinformation Resources

EMBnet (European Molecular Biology Network) is a computer network for European molecular biology and biotechnology researchers. To date this multinational collaboration has focused on DNA and protein sequence databases as well as analysis software.

Access via:
www http://shamrock.csc.fi/htbin/ imagerect/bank?64,314

GenBank & SwissProt

GenBank contains all published nucleic acid sequences. SwissProt, a European protein sequence database maintained by Amos Bairoch (Geneva) and the EMBL Data Library (Heidelberg) contains all published protein sequences. Searches of these databases may be based on accession number, description, locus name, keywords, source, organism, author, and title of journal article.

Access via:
gopher ftp.bio.indiana.edu /Genbank-Sequences

Geneva University Hospital Molecular Biology Server

This server is also known as the ExPASy Molecular Biology Server and is located in Geneva. ExPASy is focused on the analysis of protein and nucleic acid sequences. Links are provided to a variety of sequence databases: SWISS-PROT, SWISS-2DPAGE, PROSITE, REBASE, EMBL and OMIN, via Gopher, WAIS, and WWW.

Access via:
www http://expasy.hcuge.ch

GrainGenes, the Triticeae Genome Gopher

The GrainGenes Project is one of several genome database efforts funded by the United States Department of Agriculture and the National Agricultural Library. GrainGenes contains information on the genetics, biology, pathology, and seed resources of a variety of commercially important grain species, including wheat, barley, and oats. This information is provided as images, WAIS indexes, and text files.

Access via:
gopher greengenes.cit.cornell.edu

Johns Hopkins Bioinformatics Web Server

This creative WWW server provides a collection of interconnected protein sequence, structure, and enzyme function databases. These protein databases also include links to other information such as bibliographic citations from MEDLINE and pictures of three-dimensional crystal structures from the Brookhaven structural database (PDB). Electronic publications for biology include the *Primer on Molecular Genetics,* genomic information databases such as the Mouse Locus Catalog (with a fetching portrait of its subject), and links to other resources.

Access via:
www http://www.gdb.org/hopkins.html

Indiana Molecular Biology Archives

An extensive collection of information on genetics and molecular biology, including the Genbank collection of nucleic acid sequences.

Access via:
gopher fly.bio.indiana.edu / Molecular-Biology/Archive

www http://fly.bio.indiana.edu

Maize Genome Database Gopher

The Maize Genome Database Project is one of several genome database efforts funded by the United States Department of Agriculture and the National Agricultural Library. The Maize Genome Gopher provides access via WAIS indexes to information derived from the relational database MaizeDB, maintained by Prof. Ed Coe and his colleagues at the University of Missouri. MaizeDB includes a wealth of information on Maize including scientific literature, genetic maps, Maize researchers worldwide, and a catalog of available seed lines. The Gopher also provides access to the Maize Newsletter via text files or a WAIS index.

Access via:
gopher teosinte.agron.missouri.edu

Molecular Biology Sites

These links lead to a comprehensive Gopher site at Stanford that includes pointers to other Molecular Biology WWW, FTP, and Gopher sites.

Access via:
gopher genome-gopher.stanford.edu /FTP Archives for Molecular Biology
(Pointers to other sites.)

gopher genome-gopher.stanford.edu /Global Biological Information Servers by Topic
(Overview by topic.)

Molecular Biology WAIS Databases

These WAIS databases are relevant to the subject of Molecular Biology.

Access via:

WAIS *biosci.src*
(All messages posted to the BioSci electronic conferences, on a variety of biological research topics.)

WAIS *biology-journal-contents.src*
(A collection of bibliographic references from several journals made available to the BioSci system; updated weekly, Mondays 3 A.M. to

6 A.M. PST, and unavailable during this period.)

WAIS *prosite.src*
(PROSITE is a collection of protein sequence patterns that are characteristic of a particular function or type of protein. Included is a short descriptive summary of the patterns significance as well as appropriate references to the literature.)

WAIS *REBASE-enzyme.src*
(Keywords are strings of amino acids, such as CCCGGG.)

WAIS *REBASE_help.src*

WAIS *REBASE_news.src*

WAIS *REBASE_references.src*

National Genetic Resources Program Gopher

The NGRP Gopher server provides germplasm information about plants, animals, microbes, and insects within the National Genetic Resources Program of the U.S. Department of Agriculture's Agricultural Research Service (ARS). Links to the following topics are provided, along with links to other Gophers: National Plant Germplasm System (NPGS); National Animal Germplasm (including aquatics); National Microbial Germplasm; National Insect Genetic Resources; Plant Genome Database Gophers.

Access via:
gopher gopher.ars-grin.gov

Pacific Rim Biodiversity Catalog

A catalog, under construction, of the taxonomic, geographic, and temporal composition of the Pacific Rim zoological and paleontological holdings of scores of natural history institutions around the world. The catalog is searchable using keywords from a list provided. The project is a venture of the University of California Berkeley Museum of Paleontology and the Pacific Rim Research Program.

Access via:
www http://ucmp1.berkeley.edu/ pacrim.html

TAXACOM FTP Server

An information service for systematic biology. Data includes back issues of the journal Flora Online; Beanbag, a newsletter for legume researchers; Taxonomic standards; and many other resources for taxonomists. The README.TAX file serves as a table of contents.

Access via:
ftp huh.harvard.edu; login *anonymous*; cd *pub*

BOTANY

Botany at Georgia

The Botany Department at the University of Georgia maintains this WWW site, including departmental information, overviews of work currently being done on problems extending from molecular genetic regulatory mechanisms to the ecology of acid rain, and a Greenhouse Tour (takes some time to load).

Access via:
www http://dogwood.botany.uga.edu/

BUSINESS

Newsgroups:
biz.*, comp.newprod, misc.jobs.[offered, wanted]

See also: Economics

EDGAR

EDGAR is database of filings with the U.S. Securities and Exchange Commission (SEC). The file *full-index/company.idx* is an index (by company) of the files available.

Access via:
ftp town.hall.org; login *anonymous*; cd *edgar*

NASDAQ Financial Executive Journal

An electronic version of a quarterly sent free of charge to NASDAQ National Market company Chief Financial Officers and by subscription to others. As of January 1994 there were three issues available of this joint project of the Legal Information Institute at Cornell Law School and the NASDAQ Stock Market.

Access via:
www http://www.law.cornell.edu/nasdaq/ nasdtoc.html

North American Free Trade Agreement

NAFTA is complex; this resource provides an indexed view of the agreement and various ancillary documents. There is also currently an electronic conference on NAFTA sponsored by MexNET ("The Mexico Business Network"), for which a $25 registration fee is charged. For information on this conference send email to john.peake@mexnet.org.

Access via:
gopher wiretap.spies.com /North American Free Trade Agreement

Online Career Center

A resource for people who are recruiting employees or looking for jobs. It includes its own job listings and resumes, plus excerpts from other sources of job listings. There is also general corporate information, plus information about professional organizations, outplacement, and "employment events." You may post your resume in their database by mailing it (in ASCII form) to the address below; the message's "Subject:" line is the resume's title.

Access via:
gopher garnet.msen.com /The Online Career Center

Information:
Email: occ-resumes@msen.com;
occ-info@mail.msen.com

University of Minnesota Management Archive

Working papers, teaching materials, conference announcements, and the like, on the subject of business management. The archives of discussion lists sponsored by the Academy of Management are maintained here, too.

Access via:
gopher chimera.sph.umn.edu

U.S. Commerce Business Daily

A demo issue of the Commerce Business Daily. The entire publication is available by subscription.

Access via:
*gopher gopher.counterpoint.com
/Counterpoint Publishing/United States
Commerce Business Daily*

Stock Market Summary

A summary of the activity of the world's stock markets, including the New York Stock Exchange. This is part of the demo information of a2i, and while very cumbersome to get to, it is at least updated daily.

After logging in as "guest", select "n" ("NEW SCREEN-ORIENTED GUEST MENU"), specify your terminal type, select item 13 ("Current system information"), and finally select item 6 ("Market report").

Access via:
telnet a2i.rahul.net; login guest

Vienna Stock Exchange

Price and volume information for the Vienna Stock Exchange, covering the past day's trading and extending back a couple of months.

Access via:
telnet fiivs01.tu-graz.ac.at; login boerse

CHEMISTRY

Newsgroups:
sci.[chem, engr.chem, chem.organomet]

See also: Molecular Biology

American Chemical Society Gopher

Appears to cover journals and books published by the American Chemical Society, including a searchable index of ACS publications.

Access via:
gopher infx.infor.com

Periodic Table of Elements

What else can you say?

Access via:
*gopher gopher.tc.umn.edu
/Libraries/Reference Works/Periodic Table
of Elements*

Molecular Graphics Software

Contains various pieces of the raster3D application for molecular graphics, including several previewers.

Access via:
*ftp stanzi.bchem.washington.edu;
login anonymous; cd pub/raster3d*

Sheffield Chemistry Server

Run by the Department of Chemistry at the University of Sheffield, this site offers a periodic table database, interactive isotope pattern calculator, and more.

Access via:
www http://mac043025.shef.ac.uk/ chemistry/chemistry-home.html

CLASSICAL LANGUAGES & LITERATURE

Newsgroup:
sci.classics

See also: Archaeology; Literature

Bryn Mawr Classical Review

Mostly a review journal of Greek and Latin classics, this database also includes public interest articles on the classics.

Access via:
WAIS bryn-mawr-classical-review.src

gopher orion.lib.Virginia.EDU /Alphabetic Organization/Bryn Mawr Classical Review

Electronic Antiquity: Communicating the Classics

An Australian electronic journal inspired by the Bryn Mawr Classical Review and carrying academic articles on Greek and Roman Antiquity. The editors have maintained a monthly schedule since June 1993. There are both Gopher and FTP interfaces.

Please try to connect during off hours in Tasmania (Britain is more or less 10 hours behind Tasmanian time; California, 18 hours; Japan, 2 hours).

Access via:
gopher info.utas.edu.au /Publications/Electronic Antiquity: Communicating The Classics

ftp ftp.utas.edu.au; login *anonymous*; cd *departments/classics/antiquity*

Gesamtverzeichnis der griechischen Papyrusurkunden Aegyptens

This is an index of of dated Greek papyri from Egypt, arranged by century. The contents of the documents are not included, but standard papyrological abbreviations point to the printed literature. Entries span the dates 331 B.C.–A.D. 835.

Access via:
gopher sun3.urz.uni-heidelberg.de /Fakultaeten und Institute/Institut fuer Papyrologie

Project Libellus (Classics)

Classical texts formatted in the TEX typesetting language, with the TEX files necessary to format them if you have TEX on your system, and TEX-to-ASCII conversion programs. Works by Caesar, Catullus, Livy, and Virgil are available, along with at least one commentary.

Access via:
ftp ftp.u.washington.edu; login *anonymous*; cd *public/libellus*

Tables of Contents of Journals of Interest to Classicists

An extensive volunteer project to abstract the tables of contents of scholarly journals. You can search for the author or title of articles by topic (Archaeology, or Religion and Near Eastern Studies) but apparently not by field, although the files are marked up in such a way as to support such searching.

Access via:
gopher gopher.lib.Virginia.EDU /Alphabetic Organization/TOCS-IN: Tables of Contents of journals of interest to classicists

COMPUTING

Newsgroups:
comp.admin, comp.sys.[3b1, acorn, alliant, amiga.*, apollo, apple2, atari.*, att, cbm, cdc, concurrent, dec, encore, handhelds, hp48, hp, ibm.pc.*, ibm.ps2.*, intel, isis, laptops, m6809, m68k, m88k, mac.*, mentor, mips, misc, ncr, newton, next.*, northstar, novell, nsc, palmtops, pen, powerpc, prime, proteon, pyramid, ridge, sequent, sgi, sun.*, super, tahoe, tandy, ti, transputer, unisys, xerox, zenith], comp.[ai, arch, cogeng, compilers, compression, databases, dcom, editors, graphics, human-factors, lang, lsi, multimedia, music, parallel, programming, protocols, realtime, research, robotics, security, simulation, specification, terminals, theory, windows]

See also: Internet

CERT

CERT, the Computer Emergency Response Team, is a federally funded group charged with dealing with computer and network security problems. Their server has papers about security concerns, tools to evaluate security, and an archive of alerts about current break-in attempts.

Access via:
ftp *cert.sei.cmu.edu*; login *anonymous*; cd *pub*

CERT Security Advisories

Security has become a really hot topic in the last five years. Whether you're trying to protect your system from bright high school "crackers" or professional spies, it's certainly something you should keep informed about. CERT, the Computer Emergency Response Team, is a national focal point for security-related problems. When the CERT finds a security-related problem, it issues warnings to various mail lists. This is an indexed archive of those warnings. All system administrators should be aware of this archive!

To receive advisories as they are issued, send email to cert@cert.sei.cmu.edu.

Access via:
WAIS *cert-advisories.src*

Communications of the ACM

An experimental server offering the Communications of the ACM, from April 1989 to April 1992. It is unclear whether this will be offered in the future.

Access via:
WAIS *cacm.src*

Comprehensive TEX Archive Network

Contains tools, fonts, graphics, etc., for use with the TEX typesetting system, as well as the TEX software itself for various computers. The computer typesetting system, TEX, is the subject of CTAN, the Comprehensive TEX Archive Network.

Access via:
ftp *ftp.shsu.edu*; login *anonymous*; cd *tex-archive/*

Compression and Archival Software Summary

A table listing available software, by type of computer, to do and undo archiving and compression. For example: if you use an IBM PC running MS/DOS, and you want to read a UNIX compressed file, what software do you need? Where would you get the software? The more you use the Internet, the more this table will help you.

Access via:
ftp *ftp.cso.uiuc.edu*; login *anonymous*; cd *doc/pcnet*; get *compression*

Excerpt from **Computer Ethics Archive**, *7/1/85:*

```
COMPUTER CRIME AND UNLAWFUL
COMPUTER ACCESS

According to Section 21-3755 of
the Kansas Criminal Code, which
went into effect July 1, 1985,
computer crime is:

a) Willfully and without autho-
rization gaining or attempting to
gain access to and damaging, modi-
fying, altering, destroying, copy-
ing, disclosing, or taking posses-
sion of a computer, computer sys-
tem, computer network, or any
other property;

b) using a computer, computer sys-
tem, computer network, or any
other property for the purpose of
devising or executing a scheme or
artifice with the intent to
defraud or for the purpose of
obtaining money, property, ser-
vices, or any other thing of value
by means of false or fraudulent
pretense or representation; or

c) willfully exceeding the limits
of authorization and damaging,
modifying, altering, destroying,
copying, disclosing, or taking
possession of a computer, computer
system, computer network, or any
other property.
```

Computational Science Education Project

Electronic teaching materials for advanced undergraduates and beginning graduate students in computational sciences and engineering, from Vanderbilt University.

Access via:
www http://csep1.phy.ornl.gov/csep.html

Computer Ethics

Contains the computing ethics policies of over thirty universities. It also includes a bibliography, the BITNET abuse policy, and relevant laws covering computer crime from Canada and several states in the U.S.

Access via:
ftp ariel.unm.edu; login *anonymous;* cd *ethics*

Computer Science Archive Sites

This is a list of 210 sites that provide collections of computer science technical reports through anonymous FTP. This list is regularly posted to the news group comp.doc.techreports.

Access via:
WAIS *cs-techreport-archives.src*

Computer Science Paper Bibliography

The file is a list of journal articles from many computer journals. You can either get the entire list via FTP, or use WAIS to search for interesting articles.

Access via:
ftp cayuga.cs.rochester.edu;
login *anonymous;* cd *pub;*
get *papers.1st*

Computer Science Tech Reports

A collection of technical reports, abstracts, and papers in the field of Computer Science.

Access via:
WAIS *cs-techreport-abstracts.src*

WAIS *cs-techreport-archives.src*

Information:
Email: farrell@coral.cs.jcs.edu.au

Cryptography for Computers

The subject of cryptography grows more important to computing and the Internet with every passing day. Here are the leading resources we've located.

CipherText is newsletter in ASCII, new in November 1993, covering current cryptographic issues.

Access via:
ftp rsa.com; login *anonymous;*
cd *pub/ciphertext*

These sites offer a wide selection of documents and software pertaining to cryptography.

Access via:
ftp scss3.cl.msu.edu; login *anonymous;*
cd *pub/crypt*

ftp black.ox.ac.uk; login *anonymous;*
cd *DOCS/security/*

ftp ripem.msu.edu; login *anonymous;*
cd *pub/crypt/*

ftp ftp.dsi.unimi.it; login *anonymous;*
cd *pub/security/*

Free Software Foundation

The Free Software Foundation (FSF) is an organization devoted to the creation and dissemination of software that is free from licensing fees or restrictions. Software is distributed under the terms of the "General Public License," which also provides a good summary of the Foundation's goals and principles. The FSF has developed the GNU Emacs editor, in addition to replacements for many UNIX utilities and many other tools. A complete UNIX-like operating system (HURD) is in the works. FSF software is available from many places; the archive listed below is probably the most complete and up-to-date. In addition to the software itself, a number of position papers for the FSF are available. To read the GPL, look at the files whose names begin with COPYING.

Access via:
ftp prep.ai.mit.edu; login *anonymous;*
cd *pub/gnu*

High Performance Computing and Communications

The National Coordination Office for HPCC provides Internet users with access to material about the Federal HPPC Program.

Access via:
www http://www.hpcc.gov

Information System for Advanced Academic Computing

An information service for IBM customers to promote the use of their high-end computers in research and education.

Access via:
telnet isaac.engr.washington.edu
(Must apply for an account; can take a few weeks.)

Information:
Email: isaac@isaac.engr.washington.edu

INRIA Bibliography

The library catalog of the Institut National de la Recherche en Informatique et en Automatique (INRIA). The institute's mission is to provide for the management and knowledge transfer of scientific and technological information. The database, which is updated nightly, contains thousands of research reports, Ph.D. theses, and conference proceedings, along with hundreds of periodical subscriptions and videos. Keywords and catalogs are maintained in English and French.

Access via:
www http://zenon.inria.fr:8003

WAIS *bibs-zenon-inria-fr.src*

Information:
Email: doc@sophia.inria.fr

The Jargon File

This is a computing jargon dictionary. It was the basis for the book *The New Hacker's Dictionary*.

Access via:
www http://web.cnam.fr/bin.html/ By_Searchable_Index (Hypertext version.)

WAIS *jargon.src*

League for Programming Freedom

The League for Programming Freedom is an organization that opposes software patents and interface copyrights. They maintain an archive of position papers and legal information about important test cases.

Access via:
ftp prep.ai.mit.edu; login *anonymous*; cd *pub/lpf*

Information:
Email: lpf@uunet.uu.net

Multimedia

A substantial list of pointers to multimedia software, resources, and demos on the Internet.

Access via:
www http://cui_www.unige.ch/OSG/ MultimediaInfo/

Neural Networking Collection

A collection of literature, bibliographies, and indexes for the study of neural networks.

Access via:
WAIS *neuroprose.src*

ftp archive.cis.ohio-state.edu; login *anonymous*; cd *pub/neuroprose*

Excerpt from **The Jargon File**, *3/16/94*

```
kluge
/klooj/ [from the German
`klug', clever]   1. n. A Rube
Goldberg (or Heath Robinson)
device, whether in hardware or
software. (A long-ago
"Datamation" article by
Jackson Granholme said: "An
ill-assorted collection of
poorly matching parts, forming
a distressing whole.")

snarf
/snarf/ vt  1. To grab, esp.
to grab a large document or
file for the purpose of using
it with or without the
author's permission. See also
BLT

wetware
/wet'weir/ [prob. from the
novels of Rudy Rucker] n
1. The human nervous system,
as opposed to computer hard-
ware or software.
2. Human beings (programmers,
operators, administrators)
attached to a computer system,
as opposed to the system's
hardware or software. See
liveware, meatware.
```

NeXT.FAQ

A set of frequently asked questions about NeXT computers, dealing with hardware, software, specialized jargon, and configurations.

Access via:
WAIS *NeXT.FAQ.src*

Information:
Email: akers@next2.oit.unc.edu

Non-Latin Character Sets

Here we've gathered some resources that deal with fonts and character sets for languages that do not use the Latin alphabet.

Access via:
ftp *rama.poly.edu*; login *anonymous*; cd *pub/reader*
(For Arabic script — Arabic, Persian, Urdu, etc.)

ftp *ifcss.org*; login *anonymous*; cd *archive/act-info*; get *act.faq*
(For Chinese.)

ftp *ftp.uwtc.washington.edu*; login *anonymous*; cd *pub/Japanese/*
(For Japanese.)

ftp *mimsy.umd.edu*; login *anonymous*; cd *pub/cyrillic*
(For Russian.)

PC Magazine

Utility programs for IBM PC-compatibles, from PC Magazine, published by Ziff Davis.

This is just one of many places where this resource is available. Find others with "archie pcmag".

Access via:
ftp *ftp.wustl.edu*; login *anonymous*; cd *systems/ibmpc/msdos/pcmag*

Public UNIX Access

A few sites on the Internet are "freeish" public UNIX servers. The number of concurrent users is limited. On some servers, priority is given to "patrons" who make donations to keep the service alive.

Access via:
telnet *nyx.cs.du.edu*; login *new*

Repository of Machine Learning Databases and Domain Theories

The repository contains documented datasets and domain theories to evaluate machine learning algorithms in various areas. Some of the areas available are materials science, games, medicine, mechanical analysis, pattern recognition, and economics.

Access via:
ftp *ics.uci.edu*; login *anonymous*; cd *pub/machine-learning-databases*

Information:
Email: ml-repository@ics.uci.edu

San Diego Supercomputer Documentation

Primarily designed as a service to their own users; a lot of the information is not relevant to the average person. However, it is a free place to look at Cray documentation. If you want to find out what it's like to use a supercomputer, you can look here.

Access via:
WAIS *San_Diego_Super_Computer_Center_Docs.src*

SGML (Standard Generalized Markup Language)

SGML is a standard document markup language, increasingly used for marking up documents for interchange and for use with multiple document processing tools. The sites mentioned below all mirror each other to some degree.

Access via:
WAIS *SGML.src*

One of the best SGML information archives is maintained by the International SGML Users Group at the University of Oslo.

Access via:
ftp *ftp.ifi.uio.no*; login *anonymous*; cd *pub/SGML*; get *FAQ.0.0*
(A must for novice SGMLers.)

At Exeter, the SGML Project maintains a site that includes the archive of the Text Encoding Initiative (TEI), a major SGML effort aimed at representing historical literature, among other things.

Access via:
ftp sgml1.ex.ac.uk; login *anonymous*; cd *tei*

Documents produced by the SGML Users' Group's (SGML-UG) Special Interest Group on Hypertext and Multimedia (SIGhyper) may be searched by WAIS.

Access via:
WAIS *SIGHyper.src*

The University of Virginia Rare Book School maintains a set of documents explaining SGML and how to use it. There is also a very substantial archive of historical texts marked up in SGML, with plain text versions, and in some cases images of the documents. Access to texts restricted to University of Virginia users — which is frustrating because this would otherwise be the most significant collection of electronic text available.

Access via:
gopher orion.lib.Virginia.EDU /Electronic Text Center

Supernet

A bulletin board system for people doing supercomputing. General areas of postings include a research register, job bank, super-computing journal review, and software.

Access via:
telnet supernet.ans.net; login *hpcwire*

UNIX Booklist

A compilation of UNIX and C book titles, along with pertinent information for locating them (including ISBN, publisher, and order-ing information where available). Also includes short reviews and summaries of book contents. Maintained by Mitch Wright in his spare time. He encourages contribu-tions and corrections.

Access via:
ftp ftp.rahul.net; login *anonymous*;
cd *pub/mitch/YABL*; get *yabl*

Information:
Email: Mitch@yahoo.cirrus.com

UUNET FTP archives

One of the largest archives of free source code and USENET news available. The file ls-lR.Z is a compressed master list of every-thing that's available. You can also search the UUNET archives using WAIS.

Access via:
ftp ftp.uu.net; login *anonymous*

WAIS Software Search Sources

An extension of Archie, searchable through WAIS, using some of the same techniques as Netfind. Make sure you read the WAIS source file listed below to understand how to search it.

Access via:
WAIS *dynamic-archie.src*

COOKING

Newsgroups:
rec.food.[cooking, drink, recipes, restaurants, sourdough, veg], rec.crafts.brewing

Beer & Brewing

Spencer's Beer Page is a general-purpose all-round collection of resources on beer, ale, and brewing, from "kegging" to "wort chillers." It's maintained by Spencer W. Thomas, at the University of Michigan.

Access via:
*www http://guraldi.itn.
med.umich.edu/Beer*

This library contains a good collection of beer recipes and other information. Lots of information for home brewers, including software, recipe books, and archives of the Homebrew mailing list. Send subscription requests to homebrew-request.

Access via:
ftp mthvax.cs.miami.edu; login *anonymous;*
cd *homebrew*

Or search the relevant WAIS database:

Access via:
WAIS *homebrew.src*

Fat-Free FAQ

The "FAQ" is actually a directory of information about fat-free cooking; there is also a fat-free/vegetarian recipe archive.

Access via:
ftp rahul.net; login *anonymous;*
cd *pub/artemis/fatfree/FAQ*
(FAQ.)

ftp ftp.halcyon.com; login *anonymous;*
cd *pub/recipes*
(Recipe archive.)

Info and Softserver

A general information server at the University of Stuttgart. Has a collection of recipes and a cookbook online. Instructions are presented in German. Recipes are in both German and English.

Access via:
telnet rusmv1.rus.uni-stuttgart.de/cookbook;
login *info*

Recipe Archives

Recipe archives are proliferating; the largest are those containing recipes that have passed through the rec.food.cooking and rec.food.recipes newsgroups.

Access via:
WAIS *recipes.src*
(A set of recipes searchable by keyword and contents.)

WAIS *usenet-cookbook.src*

ftp gatekeeper.dec.com; login *anonymous;*
cd *pub/recipes*
(Organized by title.)

*www http://www.vuw.ac.nz/non-
local/recipes-archive/recipe-archive.html*
(Archives of the rec.food.recipes newsgroup, and the rec.food.cooking FAQ.)

Sourdough

Over half a dozen FAQs, on starters, bread, and sauerkraut.

Access via:
ftp microlib.cc.utexas.edu; login *anonymous;*
cd *pub/sourdough*

ECONOMICS

Newsgroup:
sci.econ

See also: Business

Economics Overview

There are many useful resources for economists and business users in general on the Internet. A comprehensive overview of many of these resources, "Resources for Economists on the Internet," by William L. Goffe, can be found at the Sam Houston State Gopher, and in other locations, too.

Among the best repositories of information (all of which have their own entries in this Catalog) are the U.S. Department of Commerce's Economic Bulletin Board, which lists a huge amount of current and historic U.S. macroeconomic data; the Rice Economics Gopher; and the Washington University Economics Working Paper Archive. These services are specifically designed to serve the needs of economists.

Cliometric Society

Contains searchable indexes of the membership lists of the Cliometric Society and the Economic History Association, along with the Cliometric Society's Newsletter and abstracts from ASSA meetings.

Access via:
gopher nextsrv.cas.muohio.edu /Cliometric Society

Economic Bulletin Board

Resources and pointers for both domestic and international trade.

Access via:
gopher una.hh.lib.umich.edu /ebb

Economic Data

Among tools for economists, much macroeconomic data is available in Clopper Almon's EconData package at the University of Maryland, which, when linked with its analysis and display package, is an especially useful tool for users of personal computers.

Access via:
gopher info.umd.edu /Educational Resources/Economic Data

Rice Economics Gopher

A compendium of Gopherable economics resources, updated weekly. Contains information from the 1990 census, lots of news about Asia and the Pacific Rim, plus access to several other resources covering economics and business. The latter group includes a TELNET-based bulletin board run by the U.S. commerce department. Also contains the electronic journal "Internet Business Journal: Commercial Opportunities in the Networking Age."

Access via:
gopher chico.rice.edu /Information by Subject Area/Economics and Business

Sam Houston State University Economics Gopher

This site displays an extensive array of economics resources, including many pointers to resources at other sites. It is maintained by the Network Access Initiative sponsored by the university's Department of Economics and Business Analysis. The site is organized and maintained by George D. Greenwade. Among the highlights is a particularly well organized and extensive bibliography of resources, written by Bill Goffe, "Resources for Economists on the Internet."

Access via:
gopher niord.shsu.edu /Economics (SHSU Network Access Initiative Project)

University of Manchester NetEc Gopher

A major source of economics papers in two parts: BibEc, an ASCII bibliography, and WoPEc, a collection of working papers in compressed PostScript format.

Access via:
gopher uts.mcc.ac.uk /Economics — NetEc

University of Michigan Economics Gopher

Includes bibliographies, data sets, and a section on the "Economics of the Internet."

Access via:
gopher alfred.econ.lsa.umich.edu

Washington University Economics Working Paper Archive

An extensive archive of economics working papers, catalogued by subject matter. Abstracts are available in ASCII, and most other papers are in TEX or PostScript. Both Gopher and WWW interfaces are available.

Access via:
gopher econwpa.wustl.edu

www http://econwpa.wustl.edu/ Welcome.html

EDUCATION

Newsgroups:
k12.ed.[art, business, comp.literacy, health-pe, life-skills, math, music, science, soc-studies, special, tag, tech] and k12.lang.[art, deutsch-eng, esp-eng, francais, russian]

Academe This Week

Excerpts from the Chronicle of Higher Education, the weekly tabloid that covers all aspects of the college and university business.

Access via:
gopher chronicle.merit.edu

Educator's Guide to Email Lists

A quite long collection of email lists that may be of interest to teachers.

Access via:
ftp nic.umass.edu; login anonymous; cd pub/ednet; get educatrs.lst

ERIC Digests Archive

Short reports of 1500 words or fewer, of interest to teachers, administrators, and others in the field of education. The reports are typically overviews of information on a given topic. Reports were produced by the ERIC Clearinghouses, funded by the U.S. Department of Education.

Access via:
WAIS *eric-archives.src*

WAIS *eric-digests.src*

WAIS *AskERIC-Helpsheets.src*

WAIS *AskERIC-infoguides.src*

WAIS *AskERIC-Lesson-Plans.src*

WAIS *AskERIC-Minisearches.src*

WAIS *AskERIC-Questions.src*

Federal Information Exchange

 An information liaison between various government agencies and the higher education community. Provides timely information on Federal education and research programs, scholarships and fellowships, surplus equipment, funding opportunities, and general information.

Access via:
telnet fedix.fie.com; login new

International Centre for Distance Learning

This database concentrates on "distance learning": correspondence courses, courses offered via television or audio tape, and other forms of "remote education." The database includes descriptions of "distance-learning" programs, and secondary literature about distance learning. The courses cover all academic disciplines (humanities, arts, sciences, engineering, agriculture, medicine, social sciences), all educational levels (from primary to post-graduate) and are taken from all parts of the world. This is normally a "for-pay" resource; the file *icdlinfo* describes how to register for an account. As of early 1994, this was being offered free, with a disclaimer that it may not remain so.

Access via:
telnet acsvax.open.ac.uk; login *ICDL*; give country name without spaces as account code; password *AAA*

telnet acsvax.open.ac.uk; login *ICDL* (For icdlinfo file.)

Information:
Email: n.ismail@vax.acs.open.ac.uk (comments on database); Email: l.r.a.melton@vax.acs.open.ac.uk (enquiries)

Telephone: +44.908.653537

Minority Online Information Service

Information about Black and Hispanic colleges and universities. Includes information on faculty, academic programs, degrees granted, and specialties. Part of the Federal Information Exchange.

Access via:
telnet fedix.fie.com; login *new*

National Center on Adult Literacy (NCAL)

NCAL's Gopher includes information on literacy programs in the U.S. and abroad.

Access via:
gopher litserver.literacy.upenn.edu

Software and Aids for Teaching of Mathematics

A collection of software to aid in the teaching of mathematics at the college and university

levels. Also includes newsletters, reprints, and other material of interest in the area. Most of the software is for IBM PC compatibles. Other computers may be supported in the future.

Access via:
ftp archives.math.utk.edu; login *anonymous*

Information:
Email: husch@math.utk.edu

SpaceMet

See: Aeronautics and Astronautics.

Teacher*Pages

A resource provided by Penn State University for educators at all levels. Information is available for many different school levels, academic areas, and subject areas.

Access via:
telnet psupen.psu.edu; login your two-letter state abbreviation

U.S. Department of Education Gopher

New in November 1993, this Gopher provides information about the Department of Education's programs and staff, along with announcements, press releases, and pointers to other resources.

Access via:
gopher gopher.ed.gov

ELECTRONIC MAGAZINES

Newsgroups:
alt.[authorware, etext, motherjones, wired, zines], rec.mag

Electronic Magazines Overview

Hundreds of electronic publications have been started in the last few years. Some of these are still in production; the static hulks of others litter many an Internet site.

Most are in ASCII text format, although a few are in proprietary or system-specific formats (i.e., Macintosh HyperCard). Distribution methods include email, USENET, FTP, Gopher, and World Wide Web.

The CICNet Electronic Journal Project

Intended to be a comprehensive archive of electronic journals and other publications. Possibly out of date; the index was last updated in July 1993.

Access via:
gopher gopher.cic.net /Electronic Serials

e-zine-list

A directory of electronically accessible zines, often personal and esoteric. Updated monthly.

Access via:
ftp ftp.netcom.com; login *anonymous*;
cd *pub/johnl/zines*; get *e-zine-list*
(In ASCII.)

www file://ftp.netcom.com/pub/johnl/
zines/e-zine-list.html
(In HTML.)

Electric Eclectic

A multimedia Internet journal based on the MIME standard, that's just getting started. The Eclectic is envisioned as a "meta-journal" or collection of "virtual magazines" on various topics, including literature, art, philosophy, current events, music, and almost anything else imaginable.

Information:
Email: ee-subscribe@eit.com
Email: ee-submit@eit.com
Email: ee-discuss-request@eit.com
Email: ee-volunteer@eit.com

Fine Art Forum

Fine Art Forum is a monthly magazine of arts announcements from persons and organizations in the U.S. and Europe. Although the magazine itself is still only ASCII text, a WWW front-end has been added, with pictures of the artists and their works, and links to other arts resources on the Net.

Access via:
www http://www.msstate.edu/
Fineart_Online/home.html

gopher gopher.msstate.edu /Resources
Maintained at MsState University/FineArt
Forum Online

ftp ftp.msstate.edu; login *anonymous*;
cd *pub/archives/fineart_online*

GRIST Online

A monthly, text-only magazine of poetry. Also has a few essays, letters to the editor, and calendars and announcements of readings, shows, and workshops. GRIST was originally published in print in the 1960s, and has been revived for the electronic medium (although print editions are still available).

Access via:
gopher etext.archive.umich.edu /Poetry/Grist

ftp etext.archive.umich.edu;
login *anonymous*; cd *pub/Poetry/Grist*

International Teletimes

A monthly general interest publication from Vancouver, Canada. Themes of past issues include history, the environment, and human rights. Regular departments feature a photography gallery and cuisine from around the world.

Access via:
www http://www.wimsey.com/
teletimes.root/teletimes_home_page.html

Mother Jones Magazine

Still carrying the torch of "progressive" politics, but now in hypertext.

Access via:
www http://www.mojones.com

Quanta Magazine

The science fiction and fantasy magazine Quanta, in ASCII and PostScript formats.

Access via:
gopher gopher.cic.net /Electronic Serials/Alphabetic List/Q/Quanta

ftp export.acs.cmu.edu; login anonymous; cd pub/quanta

ftp catless.newcastle.ac.uk; login anonymous; cd pub/Quanta

The University of Michigan Electronic Text Archive

A large and current archive of 'zines and other publications. The definitive source for current publications.

Access via:
gopher etext.archive.umich.edu

Whole Earth 'Lectronic Magazine

An electronic journal consisting mostly of fiction and book reviews. The server on which it sits contains areas on art, communications, cyberpunk, the Grateful Dead, the military and its practices, issues of the Whole Earth Review (successor to the Whole Earth Catalog). This magazine is published by the WELL (Whole Earth 'Lectronic Link), which was one of the early efforts at creating an electronic community, and was also spawned by the Whole Earth Catalog.

Access via:
gopher gopher.well.sf.ca.us /Whole Earth Review, the Magazine

ENGINEERING

Newsgroups:
sci.engr, sci.engr.[chem, biomed, civil, control, manufacturing, mech]

Cornell Theory Center Server

The Cornell Theory Center is one of four National Advanced Scientific Computing Centers supported by the National Science Foundation, and this is its home page. The site supports serious computer software and documentation only.

Access via:
www http://www.tc.cornell.edu/ctc.html

ENVIRONMENTAL STUDIES

Newsgroups:
sci.[environment, bio.ecology], talk.environment

BSIM Simulation Package

The Habitat Ecology Division of the Bedford Institute of Oceanography developed this simulation package, which is designed to help develop ecosystem models.

Access via:
gopher biome.bio.ns.ca /BSIM simulation package

ftp biome.bio.dfo.ca; login anonymous; cd pub/bsim

Carbon Dioxide Information Analysis Center

CDIAC is part of Oak Ridge National Laboratory. It provides information to researchers, policymakers, and educators about atmostpheric changes and climate change (in particular, "global warming"). Contains both data and scientific papers in this area. In addition to information about carbon dioxide levels, there is also information about CFCs (chlorinated fluorocarbons) and other gasses. Sponsored by the U.S. Department of Energy.

Access via:
ftp cdiac.esd.ornl.gov; login *anonymous*; cd *pub*

CIESIN Global Change Information Gateway

The Consortium for International Earth Science Information Network (CIESIN) provides information from the Socioeconomic Data and Application Center (SEDAC), CIESIN's gateway to the NASA Earth Observation System Data and Information System (EOSDIS), and the Global Change Research Information Office (GCRIO), CIESIN's gateway to the U.S. Global Change Research Program.

Access via:
gopher gopher.ciesin.org

Environmental Protection Agency Library

A catalog to the holdings of the EPA's national library. The database has subsections for material on hazardous waste, lake management and protection, and chemical agents. The library includes EPA reports and many other kinds of documents. Includes abstracts.

Access via:
telnet epaibm.rtpnc.epa.gov; select *PUBLIC*

Environmental Safety & Health Information Center

The Environmental Safety & Health Information Center (ESHIC) contains Department of Energy information relating to the environment.

Access via:
WAIS *eshic.src*

ERIN (Environmental Resources Information Network)

A World Wide Web cover page that collects information and newsletters about ecology-related programs, projects, and issues, primarily in Australia.

Access via:
www http://kaos.erin.gov.au/erin.html

Gopherable Environmental Studies Resources Index

A comprehensive index of Gopherable environmental resources.

Access via:
gopher gopher.unr.edu /Selected Information Resources by Discipline/Environmental Studies Resources

Oak Ridge National Laboratory (Environmental Science Division)

The Oak Ridge National Laboratory, now run by Martin Marietta Energy Systems for the U.S. Department of Energy, is emphasizing its environmental concerns:

"Whose `backyard' should we store hazardous wastes in? What would restore public confidence in nuclear power? What's the best way to encourage investments in energy efficiency? Over the past two decades, ORNL has developed social science theory and tools to tackle energy and environmental problems such as these. By teaming social scientists with physical scientists, analyses are conducted that reflect the complexity of real-world choices."

Access via:
www http://jupiter.esd.ornl.gov/

Pesticides

An agricultural extension bulletin written by Sue Snider and Mark Graustein. This bulletin explains what a pesticide is, the laws which regulate pesticides, and their uses, benefits, and detriments.

Access via:
gopher bluehen.ags.udel.edu /Search AGINFO/Pesticides

United Nations Rio Conference Agenda

See: Law, Columbia Online Legal Resources (JANUS)

Water Quality Education Materials

A set of educational materials on U.S. water quality assessment, maintenance, and improvement, provided by the Cooperative Extension System.

Access via:
WAIS *water-quality.src*

FORESTRY

Dendrome: Forest Tree Genome Mapping Database

Dendrome is a collection of specialized forest tree genome databases being developed by the Institute of Forest Genetics under the oversight of the National Agricultural Library.

Access via:
gopher s27w007.pswfs.gov

Social Sciences in Forestry

An annotated bibliography of the Forestry Library at the University of Minnesota, College of Natural Resources. The bibliography covers many areas of forestry, including the history, legislation, taxation, social and communal forestry, and agroforestry.

Access via:
gopher minerva.forestry.umn.edu /Social Sciences in Forestry Bibliography

Trees

Various kinds of information about trees including care and maintenance, planting, selection, and signs and symptoms of tree problems, thanks to the University of Delaware Agricultural Extension Service.

Access via:
gopher bluehen.ags.udel.edu /Info by type of publication/Fact Sheets/Ornamental Horticulture

FREE-NETS

Free-Net Overview

Free-Nets are grassroots efforts to provide networking services to an urban community, with access either at public libraries or by dialing in. It's also possible to access Free-Nets through the Internet. Free-Nets are usually organized around a model town that you "walk" through. You can stop at the "courthouse and government center" and discuss local issues with the mayor. Or you can stop by the "medical arts building" and discuss health issues with a health professional. Aside from discussions, there are usually bulletin boards, electronic mail, and other information services.

There are real hidden gem resources on some Free-Nets. These are indexed separately. Anyone can use a Free-Net as a guest, but guest privileges are limited; for example, you can't use email and a few other things. You can get further privileges by registering; registration is usually free to people within a certain district, and available at nominal charge to those outside. When you log in as a guest, you'll probably see a message telling you how to get registration information.

Free-Net software is menu-driven and designed for ease of use. So give them a try. If you think you'd like to organize a Free-Net for your town, contact Dr. T. M. Grundner at *tmg@nptn.org*

Buffalo Free-Net

Contains information about Western New York.

Access via:
telnet freenet.buffalo.edu; login *freeport*

CapAccess: The National Capital Area Public Access Network

A Free-Net for the Washington, D.C. metropolitan area. Concentrates on K-12 education, health and social services, library services, and government.

Access via:
telnet cap.gwu.edu; login *guest*;
password *visitor*

Cleveland Free-Net

The original Free-Net and still the hub of Free-Net development. Very heavily used, and therefore hard to log in to.

Access via:
telnet freenet-in-a.cwru.edu

Columbia Online Information Network

Community, education, and local government information for the Columbia, Missouri, area.

Access via:
telnet bigcat.missouri.edu; login *guest*

Denver Free-Net

Fairly strong on the fine arts.

Access via:
telnet freenet.hsc.colorado.edu; login *guest*

Erlangen-Nuernberg Free-Net

A Free-Net located in Germany, with topics including the European Community, film and video, education, and recreation. Menus are in German and English.

Access via:
telnet freenet-a.fim.uni-erlangen.de; login *gast*

Heartland Free-Net

A Free-Net centered in Peoria, Illinois. Contains information about recreation and jobs in the State of Illinois. Check the "home and garden center" for information about gardening.

Access via:
telnet heartland.bradley.edu; login *bbguest*

Lorain County Free-Net

A Free-Net centered in Elyria, Ohio. Pen pals, even some games.

Access via:
telnet freenet.lorain.oberlin.edu; login *guest*

National Capital Free-Net (Canada)

Some French-language menus; Canadian resources; Canadian politics.

Access via:
telnet freenet.carleton.ca; login *guest*

Tallahassee Free-Net

This Florida Free-Net includes information on business, religion, disabilities, and gardening.

Access via:
telnet freenet.fsu.edu; login *visitor*

Victoria (British Columbia) Free-Net

Contains sections on the environment and medicine.

Access via:
telnet freenet.victoria.bc.ca; login *guest*

Youngstown Free-Net

A Free-Net centered in Youngstown, Ohio. Very strong health section (see "hospital"), veterinarian (see "animal hospital"), and human services.

Access via:
telnet yfn.ysu.edu; login *visitor*

GARDENING

Newsgroup:
rec.gardens

The Gardener's Assistant

A shareware program for the personal computer (IBM-PC) that assists one in planning and planting a garden. You feed it a bunch of information, and it tells you what type of plants to grow, when to plant, and how to care for them. Registration information is available.

Access via:
ftp wuarchive.wustl.edu;
cd *systems/ibmpc/msdos/database*;
get *gardener.zip*

Master Gardener Information

Still under construction, this Gopher server (run by the Texas Agricultural Extension Service) offers information on fruits and nuts, flowering plants, annual and perennial ornamental trees and shrubs, turf grasses, and vegetables.

Access via:
gopher gopher.tamu.edu /Texas A&M Gophers/Texas Agricultural Extension Service Gopher (Linux)/Master Gardener Information

University of Missouri Horticulture Guides

Scores of articles, covering topics from "Armillaria root rot in fruit orchards" to "Vegetable harvest and storage." The emphasis is on the Missouri perspective, but much of the information is valuable wherever you garden.

Access via:
gopher bigcat.missouri.edu /Reference and Information Center/University of Missouri Horticulture Guides

GEOGRAPHY

CIA World Map

The CIA map database. The directory includes a map drawing program.

Access via:
ftp ftp.cs.toronto.edu; login *anonymous*;
cd *doc/geography/CIA_World_Map*

Geographic Information Server

An interface to data supplied by the U.S. Geodetic Survey and the U.S. Postal Service. Make requests by name (Sebastopol, or Sebastopol, CA); the server returns latitude, longitude, population, zipcode, elevation, etc.

Not all of this information is correct (zip code for Sebastopol, for example)!!!

Access via:
www http://sipb.mit.edu:8001/geo

telnet martini.eecs.umich.edu 3000

GEOLOGY

Newsgroup:
sci.geo.geology

Computer Oriented Geological Society (COGS)

The archives of the Computer Oriented Geological Society's bulletin board service. It contains lots of interesting material, including application forms for membership in the society. One file that's particularly worth having is internet.resources.earth.sci. This is a detailed list of many resources available, including many data archives, digitized maps, bibliographies and online publications. There's also a lot of software available, for disciplines such as Geophysics, Geochemistry, Hydrology, Mineralogy, Mining, oil exploration, etc. Landsat images are also available.

Access via:
ftp csn.org; login *anonymous*;
cd *COGS*

Information:
Email: cogs@flint.mines.colorado.edu

Telephone: (303) 751-8553

Earthquake Information

Information about recent earthquakes. Location, magnitude, and accuracy are given for each event.

Access via:
finger quake@geophys.washington.edu

Global Land Information System

GLIS is an interactive system supported by the U.S. Geological Survey, apparently providing access to or ordering information for all public computerized geographical information maintained by the USGS. It allows you to browse as a "guest" user, but you must register to obtain full functionality.

Access via:
telnet glis.cr.usgs.gov; press RETURN;
type *GUEST*

USGS Geological Fault Maps

A digital database of geological faults, covering the United States. Includes software to draw maps from the faults. The raw data isn't in any standard format (it appears to be latitude/longitude pairs), so you'll need the mapping software.

Access via:
ftp alum.wr.usgs.gov; login *anonymous*;
cd *pub/map*

USGS Weekly Seismicity Reports

Weekly reports of seismic activity (earthquakes, volcanos, etc.) and maps for Northern California, the U.S., and the World.

The weekmap.dos file is in ASCII format.

Access via:
ftp garlock.wr.usgs.gov; login *anonymous*;
cd *pub/WEEKREPS/*
(Including maps in GIF format.)

USGS Information

A service provided by the United States Geological Survey; information about the survey, resources they provide, software, and other services related to geology, hydrology, and cartography. Organized by topic, it includes audio and animated material as well as text and pictures.

Access via:
www http://info.er.usgs.gov/

GOVERNMENT, U.N. & INTERNATIONAL

International Treaties

The text of scores of treaties, both ratified and proposed.

Access via:
ftp wiretap.spies.com; login *anonymous*;
cd *Gov/Treaties/Hague*
(For information on the Hague Conventions.)

ftp wiretap.spies.com; login *anonymous*;
cd *Gov/Treaties/Geneva*
(For information on the Geneva Conventions.)

ftp wiretap.spies.com; login *anonymous*;
cd *Gov/Treaties/League*
(For information on protocols related to the League of Nations.)

ftp wiretap.spies.com; login *anonymous*;
cd *Gov/Treaties/Sea*
(For information on the U.N. Convention on the Law of the Sea, not yet in force.)

ftp wiretap.spies.com; login *anonymous*;
cd *Gov/Treaties/Treaties*
(For information on many other treaties.)

NATO

Press releases, speeches by the Secretary General (currently Manfred Woerner), a Fact Sheet, and electronic versions of the NATO Handbook and the NATO Review, all in ASCII.

Under "Allied" are press releases relating to current NATO operations, such as air flights over Bosnia.

Access via:
ftp info.umd.edu; login *anonymous*;
cd *info/Government/US/NATO*

United Nations Gopher

The U.N.'s very own Gopher, offering information on the United Nations, what it is and what it does, communications information pertaining to the U.N., and notably the World Health Organization Gopher.

Access via:
gopher nywork1.undp.org

World Constitutions

Over a dozen constitutions and similar documents from countries and would-be countries around the world.

Access via:
ftp wiretap.spies.com; login *anonymous*;
cd *Gov/World*

GOVERNMENT, U.S.

Americans with Disabilities Act Regulations

The Americans with Disabilities Act reaches into many aspects of life. This resource includes not only the text of regulations, subdivided by Federal agency, but also a wealth of supporting information and pointers to off-line resources.

Access via:
ftp info.umd.edu; login *anonymous*;
cd *inforM/Educational_Resources/United_States/Government/NationalIssues/ADARegulation*

Budget 1993

Summary of the budget as proposed by the President on April 8, 1993, subdivided by subject. The file modestly titled "totals-million" gives the big picture.

Access via:
ftp info.umd.edu; login anonymous; cd inforM/Educational_Resources/United_States/Government/NationalIssues/Budget-93

Budget 1994

The proposed 1994 Budget is available in several compressed forms and by section. You can select: Budget authority and Federal programs by agency; Federal programs by agency and account; Outlays by agency; Totals.

Access via:
ftp sunsite.unc.edu; login anonymous; cd pub/academic/political-science

Census 1990

A two-page summary of census results is available for each state.

Access via:
ftp info.umd.edu; login anonymous; cd inforM/Educational_Resources/United_States/Government/NationalIssues/Census-90

Congress Overview

A Democratic view of the Congress. Oddly, it also includes information on communicating with the Cabinet and other parts of the executive branch. There are biographical blurbs on Democrats (but no one else), and special files on women in the House and Senate.

Access via:
ftp info.umd.edu; login anonymous; cd info/Government/US/Congress

Copyright Information

The Library of Congress's information on works registered for copyright since 1978, including books, serials, films, music, maps, sound recordings, software, multimedia kits, drawings, posters, and sculpture.

Access via:
telnet locis.loc.gov

A Gopher interface is available through MARVEL.

Access via:
gopher marvel.loc.gov /Copyright

FDA Electronic Bulletin Board

See Medicine.

Federal Legislation

Access to information about Federal legislation.

Access via:
telnet locis.loc.gov

Federal Register

The Federal Register, categorized by agency, date of issue of regulation, and category, from July 1990. Published not by the government but by Counterpoint Publishing and the Internet Company. Full access is available only to subscribers (something to write your

Representative about!), and anything not typeset electronically is missing.

Access via:
gopher gopher.counterpoint.com 2002

Government Accounting Office

GAO reports on scores of topics.

Access via:
ftp info.umd.edu; login *anonymous;*
cd *inforM/Educational_Resources/
United_States/Government/NationalIssues/
GAO*

Library of Congress Services

More than just an online library catalog. LOCIS, the TELNET interface is pokey, but MARVEL, the Gopher interface is easy to use and has a lot of interesting material.

MARVEL is the Library of Congress's Machine-Assisted Realization of the Virtual Electronic Library, which combines the information available at and about the Library of Congress with other Internet resources. It aims to serve the staff of the Library of Congress, the U.S. Congress, and constituents throughout the world. Most files are plain ASCII text.

Access via:
telnet locis.loc.gov
gopher marvel.loc.gov

National Archives

The National Archive's Center for Electronic Records provides a historical repository for significant electronic records collected by the Federal government. Although the records are not available through the Internet, inquiries can be made through the email address noted in the "national.archives" file, which includes a write-up.

Access via:
ftp ftp.msstate.edu; login *anonymous;*
cd *pub/docs/history/USA/databases;*
get *national.archives*

Information:
Email: tif@nihcu.bitnet

Telephone: (202) 501-5579

National Information Infrastructure Proposal

The highly touted but rather vague proposal to network the country, released by the U.S. Government in September, 1993, in a hypertext version. To avoid the large graphics on the title page, you can go directly to the text of the proposal.

See also: Law, Columbia Online Legal Resources (JANUS)

Access via:
www http://sunsite.unc.edu/nii/NII-Table-of-Contents.html
(To start at the cover page.)

www http://sunsite.unc.edu/nii/NII-Agenda-for-Action.html
(For the text of the proposal.)

ftp sunsite.unc.edu; login *anonymous;*
cd *pub/academic/political-science/
internet-related/National-Information-Infrastructure*

gopher sunsite.unc.edu /What's New on SunSITE/National Information Infrastructure Information

National Performance Review

A hypertext version of Vice President Gore's proposal for "reinventing government," prepared by the Office for Information Technology at the University of North Carolina.

Access via:
www http://sunsite.unc.edu/npr/nptoc.html

ftp sunsite.unc.edu; login *anonymous;*
cd *pub/academic/political-science/National_Performance_Review*

gopher sunsite.unc.edu /What's New on
SunSITE/National Performance Review
(Reinventing Government)

WAIS National-performace-Review.src

National Referral Center

The National Referral Center Resources File
(NRCM) provides more than 12,000 descriptions of organizations qualified and willing to
answer questions and provide information on
many topics in science, technology, and the
social sciences. This file, updated weekly, is
based on a national inventory program
begun in 1962. Each description in the file
lists the name of the organization, mailing
address, location, telephone number, areas
of interest, holdings (special collections, databases, etc.), publications, and information
services. Additional information is often provided on an organization.

Access via:
telnet locis.loc.gov; Select 5. Organizations

NSF Awards

This is a subset of the STIS service. It consists
of the abstracts of the awards made by NSF
since 1990.

Access via:
WAIS nsf-awards.src

NSF Publications

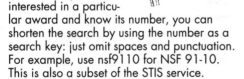

Publications of the
National Science
Foundation. They can
be searched.
However, if you are
interested in a particu-
lar award and know its number, you can
shorten the search by using the number as a
search key: just omit spaces and punctuation.
For example, use nsf9110 for NSF 91-10.
This is also a subset of the STIS service.

Access via:
WAIS nsf-pubs.src

Science and Technology Information Service

STIS provides information about programs
sponsored by the National Science
Foundation. The NSF Bulletin, Guide to
Programs, program announcements, press
releases, and a listing of awards are available.

Access via:
gopher stis.nsf.gov

telnet stis.nsf.gov; login public

Social Security Administration

Lots of documents about social security, as
you'd expect. You'll find listings of social
security publications, speeches and testimony
by members of the social security commission, press releases, etc. However, the
archive certainly isn't limited to social security
information; there are a lot of other government documents, along with random collections of information, such as an archive of
news postings on carpal tunnel syndrome.
Because there is so much information, of so
many types, you should look at the "index"
file before going anywhere else. (Skip the
first part, which talks about the
Administration's internal email system.)

Access via:
ftp soaf1.ssa.gov; login anonymous; cd pub

Supreme Court Rulings

See: Law

White House Overview

The FAQ file contains information on signing
up for daily electronic publications (press
releases), searching and retrieving speeches
and press releases, and sending email to the
White House.

Access via:
ftp info.umd.edu; login anonymous;
cd info/Government/US/WhiteHouse

HISTORY & CIVILIZATION

Newsgroups:
soc.history, sci.classics

See also: Literature; Classical Languages & Literature; History of Science

Bryn Mawr Medieval Review

A sister publication of the Bryn Mawr Classical Review; the first issue went out in late 1993.

Access via:
gopher orion.lib.Virginia.EDU /Electronic Journals/Bryn Mawr Medieval Review

EXPO: WWW Exhibit Organization

EXPO is the central point for a number of hypertext versions of exhibitions, including Library of Congress exhibitions, which are also listed individually in this Catalog. Much of the work behind EXPO has been done by Frans van Hoesel. For a quick look at EXPO's contents, see the "EXPO Overview" document.

Access via:
www http://sunsite.unc.edu/expo/ticket_office.html

www http://sunsite.unc.edu/expo/expo/overview.html

Middle East Studies Association

The Middle East Studies Association, a professional organization for scholars of the Middle East and related areas, maintains this site for certain parts of its *Bulletin* and other relevant information.

Access via:
gopher vmsgopher.cua.edu /The Catholic University of America Gopher service/Special Resources/Middle East Studies Association Bulletin

Mississippi State History Archives

This is an FTP site that contains many resources related to the study of history. It includes the National Council of History's Education newsletter (in the directory newsletters, files beginning with NCHE), materials on the Vietnam War, various bibliographies, and other material. Aside from the material on Vietnam and the NCHE newsletter, there doesn't appear to be any particular theme to what's available: there's material on medieval studies, French socialism, Andrew Jackson, the Native American movement, and other topics scattered around. If you're a historian, it's worth 10 minutes of your time to see what's available here.

Access via:
ftp ftp.msstate.edu; login *anonymous*; cd *docs/history*

Soviet Archives

The Library of Congress has an exhibit of materials from the newly opened Soviet archives. There is information about life under the Soviet system, Chernobyl, the Cold War, and Cuban missile crisis, and many other topics. Anyone interested in understanding recent history should know about this archive.

Both FTP and WWW interfaces are available:

Access via:
ftp ftp.loc.gov; login *anonymous*; cd *pub/exhibit.images/russian.archive.exhibit*

www http://sunsite.unc.edu/expo/soviet.exhibit/soviet.archive.html

U.S. Historical Documents

A selection of documents and secondary material relating to major events in U.S. history, such as the Mayflower Compact and the WWII Japanese Instrument of Surrender.

Access via:
ftp wiretap.spies.com; login *anonymous*; cd *Gov/US-History*

As part of Project Gutenberg:

Access via:
*gopher spinaltap.micro.umn.edu
/Gutenberg/Historical Documents*

The following resource also includes important U.S. historical documents, such as selections from the Federalist Papers.

Access via:
ftp ftp.eff.org; login *anonymous;* cd *pub/
academic/civics*

1492 Exhibition

An online version of the Library of Congress's 1992 exhibition titled "1492: An Ongoing Voyage," which concentrates on the New World and the Mediterranean world.

Both FTP and WWW interfaces are available:

Access via:
ftp ftp.loc.gov; login *anonymous;*
cd *pub/exhibit.images/1492.exhibit*

*www http://sunsite.unc.edu/expo/
1492.exhibit/Intro.html*

HISTORY OF ART

Newsgroups:
alt.architecture, rec.arts.fine

Architecture, etc.

ArchiGopher advertises itself as a server dedicated to the dissemination of architectural knowledge but actually covers more than that. There are links to a small archive of Kandinsky paintings; a small sample of drawings of Andrea Palladio's architectural projects, a collection of CAD computer models, and other possibly interesting items.

Access via:
gopher libra.arch.umich.edu

Included for some reason in the History of Science Gopher at Johns Hopkins University is a set of photographs of French "architectur-

al projects," which include fanciful design projects and sculpture.

Access via:
*gopher gopher.hs.jhu.edu /—>...Images/
Architecture*

Art History in Australia

The first resource below leads to a copy of the hypertext set of text and images, including a tutorial for learning about the history of prints and sample images from objects in the Australian National Gallery's collection, constructed by Michael Greenhalgh.

The second leads to Prof. Greenhalgh's expanded art history server at the Australian National University, which contains a good deal more material.

Access via:
*www http://www.ncsa.uiuc.edu/SDG/
Experimental/anu-art-history/home.html*

www http://rubens.anu.edu.au/

Black Artists at the National Museum of American Art

Half a dozen images by black artists, from the collection of the National Museum of American Art, along with a text file explaining the holdings of the museum in this area (more than 1,500 works of art in a variety of media, from portraiture of the early Republic to contemporary artists).

Access via:
*gopher gopher.upenn.edu /PennInfo via the
Gopher —>PennInfo Gateway/PennInfo/
Interdisciplinary Programs/African Studies*

Bodleian Library MSS

Announced as an experimental server, this Gopher site contains images of some of the many illustrated manuscripts in the collection of Oxford's most famous library.

Access via:
gopher rsl.ox.ac.uk /Bodleian Libraries (inc. Radcliffe Science Library)

Japanese Art

Here's a directory of GIFs of prints in the Ukiyo-e style (17th-19th centuries).

Access via:
ftp ftp.uwtc.washington.edu; login anonymous; cd pub/Japanese/Pictures/Ukiyo-e

Krannert Art Museum

A hypertext home page for the Krannert Art Museum (University of Illinois at Urbana-Champaign), including a Guide containing sample images of objects in the collection, each with commentary. The Guide is rather oddly divided into these sections: Sculpture, American and European painting, Twentieth-century art, [East and South] Asian art, Medieval and Near Eastern art.

While no author is mentioned, a glance at the exhibition calendar shows Eunice Maguire to be the principal curator.

Access via:
www http://www.ncsa.uiuc.edu/General/ UIUC/KrannertArtMuseum/KrannertArtHome. html

A Roman Palace in ex-Yugoslavia

An experiment in online art history presentation technique, this exhibit was constructed by Michael Greenhalgh, Department of Art History, Australian National University.

"Split—or Spalato—is one of the most extraordinary places of the later Roman world, being no less than the palace which the Emperor Diocletian began building in A.D.

293 in readiness for his retirement from politics in 305. On the Dalmatian coast, adjacent to the Roman city of Salonae, it takes the dual form of a legionary camp similar to those still to be seen on the frontiers of Syria (appropriately so, for Diocletian was of necessity a military emperor) but also, with its splendid loggias, of an Italian house."

EXPO also offers a version of this material.

Access via:
www http://www.ncsa.uiuc.edu/SDG/ Experimental/split/split1.html

www http://sunsite.unc.edu/expo/ palace.exhibit/intro.html
(EXPO.)

Vatican Library MSS Exhibit

Images and text from a recent exhibition at the Library of Congress, including manuscripts from the Vatican Library in all areas of historical interest. Images are in JPEG compression format and are *large* . A hypertext version is available through EXPO at the University of North Carolina.

Access via:
ftp ftp.loc.gov; login anonymous; cd pub/exhibit.images/vatican.exhibit
(Text in ASCII.)

www http://sunsite.unc.edu/expo/ vatican.exhibit/Vatican.exhibit.html
(Hypertext version, courtesy EXPO.)

HISTORY OF SCIENCE

History of Science Server

An attempt to collect and catalog the writings and papers of respected scientists in a single place.

Access via:
gopher gopher.hs.jhu.edu

HOST: An Electronic Bulletin for the History and Philosophy of Science and Technology

Published by the Institute for the History and Philosophy of Science, Toronto, this is a serious academic journal, dealing with the history of science from antiquity to the present, and includes book reviews and pointers to Internet resources. HOST is scheduled to appear semiannually, in Spring/Summer and Fall/Winter.

Access via:
gopher miles.library.arizona.edu /Resources By Discipline/History/History and Philosophy of Science and Technology

HOBBIES

Newsgroups:
alt.[aquaria, magic, sewing], rec.[antiques, aquaria, collecting, crafts.brewing, crafts.misc, crafts.textiles, folk-dancing, gambling, gardens, guns, juggling, models.railroad, models.rc, models.rockets, photo, radio.amateur.misc, radio.amateur.packet, radio.amateur.policy, radio.cb, railroad, roller-coaster, woodworking]

Ceramics Gopher

An experimental database of glazes, part of a project of the GlazeBase Working Group of the National Council for Education in the Ceramic Arts (NCECA). Includes information on and archives of a mailing list called ClayArt, articles on ceramics, a list of ceramics suppliers, GlazeBase (glaze database), and a material database.

Access via:
gopher gopher.sdsu.edu /SDSU Campus Topics/Departmental Information/Art Department/The Ceramics Gopher

Ham Radio

The national ham (amateur) radio call sign index allows you to look up hams by callsign, name, or area.

Access via:
www http://www.mit.edu:8001/callsign

telnet callsign.cs.buffalo.edu 2000

www http://www.mcc.ac.uk/OtherPages/AmateurRadio.html

This resource contains information on newsgroups related to amateur radio, excerpts from FCC rules, an FAQ, pointers to other sites, and a license exam quiz server.

Access via:
www http://www.acs.ncsu.edu/HamRadio

Hockey Cards Mailing List Archive

A mailing list dedicated to hockey card collectors. People to trade with and checklists are available. Subscribe with hockey-request@yahoo.cirrus.com.

Access via:
ftp ftp.rahul.net; login *anonymous*; cd *pub/mitch/hockey*

Information:
Email: mitch@cirrus.com

Horticultural Engineering Newsletter

Issues of the publication are available. Contains information on greenhouses, seeds, and other technical information about horticulture techniques. Accessed through the PEN Pages (see Agriculture).

Access via:
telnet psupen.psu.edu; login your two-letter **state abbreviation**

Tango

History of the tango, lyrics, notations, biographies, you name it, if it's about the tango it may very well be here.

Access via:
www http://litsun.epfl.ch/tango/ welcome.html

INTEREST GROUPS

Newsgroups:
soc.[answers, bi, college, couples, culture, feminism, men, motss, penpals, politics, religion, rights, roots, singles, veterans, women], talk.*

Columbia Index to Hispanic Legislation

Data provided by the Library of Congress to Columbia Law School concerning Hispanic oriented legislation.

Access via:
WAIS *columbia-spanish-law-catalog.src*

Information:
Email: willem@lawmail.law.columbia.edu

Deaf Gopher

This Gopher, at Michigan State University contains information about services for the deaf in Michigan, as well as "Deaf Alert," a collection of files containing information on the deaf in history and culture.

Access via:
gopher burrow.cl.msu.edu /Information for the MSU Community/MSU College & Departmental Information/Deaf-Gopher

Hispanic Interest

UCLA sponsors a Chicano-LatinoNet Gopher, with a WAIS index, lists of conferences, scholarships, and the like; there is also a directory with links to libraries containing material of Chicano-Latino interest.

Access via:
gopher latino.sscnet.ucla.edu

Feminism Information

Archive of information on feminism drawn from or related to the newsgroup soc.feminism, not including archives of that newsgroup.

Access via:
ftp rtfm.mit.edu; login *anonymous*;
cd *pub/usenet/news.answers/feminism*

Queer Resources Directory

A good resource for the gay, lesbian, and bisexual community. Has sections concerned with AIDS, facts and treatments; contact information for various support and activist groups; bibliography of publications of interest to the community; civil rights; and domestic partnerships. Also, has portions of the GLAAD Newsletter online.

Access via:
www file://vector.casti.com/pub/QRD/ .html/QRD-home-page.html
(WWW interface.)

gopher vector.casti.com /Queer Resources

ftp vector.casti.com; login *anonymous*;
cd *QRD*

Information:
Email: QRDstaff@vector.casti.com

INTERNATIONAL INTEREST

Newsgroup:
soc.culture.*

Algeria

A rather small archive, including travel information and contact information for the

Algerian government and Algerian universities (all in English).

Access via:
ftp ftp.cse.psu.edu; login *anonymous*;
cd *pub/mbarki/information/algeria*

Australia

Information compiled about computing, networking, and libraries in Australia.

Access via:
WAIS *aarnet-resource-guide.src*

A short hypertext "Guide to Australia," relying heavily on the Australian National University's Biodiversity Server.

Access via:
www http://life.anu.edu.au/education/ australia.html

Brazil

This server is run by the Rede Nacional de Pesquisa (National Research Network), which is apparently based in Rio de Janeiro. The information is in Portuguese.

Access via:
www http://www.rnp.br/

Chinese Community Information Center

This resource is run by the International Federation of Chinese Students and Scholars, that is, overseas Chinese, not the Chinese government. It offers information on immigration and tax law, Chinese studies, computing with Chinese characters, and related topics, and has a picture archive. There are both WWW and FTP interfaces.

Access via:
www http://ifcss.org:8001/index.html

ftp ifcss.org; login *anonymous*

gopher ifcss.org

Esperanto

Offers a course in Esperanto, a synthetic language invented by L. L. Zamenhof, a Pole, in 1887. The home page is in Dutch, but an English version is offered, too.

Access via:
www http://utis179.cs.utwente.nl:8001/ esperanto/hyperkursus/oficej.html

Europe

A home page for Europe, maintained in Portugal but including links to country-specific home pages in other countries.

Access via:
www http://s700.uminho.pt/europa.html

France & French Language

Le petit coin des francophones et autres grenouilles is a collection of pointers to French resources (in France and in French, both) of all types. This should be your first stop in exploring the French parts of the Internet.

Access via:
www http://cuisg13.unige.ch:8100/ franco.html

Germany

A small archive of information about Germany, Germans, and German culture. There is material in both German and English.

Access via:
ftp rascal.ics.utexas.edu; login *anonymous*;
cd *misc/germans*

Holland

A menu of information about Dutch Internet resources, including universities and libraries. This link is to the English version; there's a Dutch version, too.

Access via:
gopher rugcis.rug.nl /Informatiediensten buiten RUG/Nederland

Iran

A good collection of information and software relating to Iran and the Persian language. The Iran_Lib directory contains subdirectories including pictures (/Images/GIF), sounds, software for Persian, and much else.

Access via:
ftp tehran.stanford.edu; login *anonymous*

www http://tehran.stanford.edu/

Israel

The largest directory of information on Judaism, Hebrew, and Israel that we've found is in New York.

Access via:
ftp nysernet.org; login *anonymous*; cd *israel*

Japan Information

A multimedia site for information on Japan (want to hear the Japanese national anthem?). The link below leads to an English document that includes information on how to display the corresponding Japanese version.

Access via:
www http://www.ntt.jp/japan/

Lebanon

This commodious archive is a volunteer effort, established by Bertha Choueiry "as a repository of cultural material in the form of text, graphics and sounds pertaining to Lebanon and the Middle East, . . . [without] political,

religious, sectarian or ethnic affiliations." It includes everything from a list of Lebanese restaurants in London to GIFs of Lebanese musicians; there is also some material on Arabia and other parts of the Levant.

Access via:
ftp liasun3.epfl.ch; login *anonymous*; cd *users/choueiry*

Barre Ludvigsen has collected pointers to this and other Net resources relating to Lebanon.

Access via:
www http://www.ludvigsen.dhhalden.no/webdoc/levant_servers.html

Latin American Network Information Center

This Gopher is managed by the Institute of Latin American Studies (ILAS) at the University of Texas at Austin, to provide Latin American users with access to information services worldwide and to provide Latin Americanists around the world with access to information on and from Latin America.

Access via:
gopher lanic.utexas.edu

Mexico

New in November 1993, this Gopher is intended for both academic and commercial use.

Access via:
gopher telecom.mty.itesm.mx

New Zealand Information

A hypertext home page for New Zealand, with pointers to the Wellington City Council Gopher and the Victoria University at Wellington home page. Includes information

on the Maori language, New Zealand food, and the tuatara, a carnivorous reptile that has three eyes when young (it must be true—we read it on the Internet!).

Access via:
www http://www.cs.cmu.edu:8001/Web/ People/mjw/NZ/MainPage.html

Norway

New in September 1993, the Norwegian Televerkets Forskningsinstitutt has opened a WWW site, serving also the University of Oslo. Information is in Norwegian. There is a hypertext presentation of the Telemuseum Meny that includes pictures (small) and movies, among other items.

Access via:
www http://www.nta.no/uninett/ norweb.html

There's a Norwegian online dictionary at another site in Norway, run by Norsk Regnesentral.

Access via:
www http://www.nr.no/ordbok

Polish Journals

Collections of news analysis, press reviews, and humor from or about Poland and the Polish community abroad. The journal is in Polish.

Access via:
gopher gopher.cic.net /Electronic Serials/Alphabetic List/P/Pigulki/

If you're interested in Polish studies, also check out the Donosy journal. The journal is in Polish.
gopher gopher.cic.net /Electronic Serials/Alphabetic List/D/Donosy/

Portugal

Basic information, along with a clickable map that takes a long time to load.

Access via:
www http://s700.uminho.pt/Portugal/ portugal.html

The Project for American & French Research of the Treasury of the French Language

Also known as ARTFL, this is a searchable database of nearly 2000 texts, ranging from classic works of French literature to various kinds of non-fiction prose and technical writing. The eighteenth, nineteenth and twentieth centuries are about equally represented, with a smaller selection of seventeenth-century texts as well as some medieval and Renaissance texts. Genres include novels, verse, journalism, essays, correspondence, and treatises. Subjects include literary criticism, biology, history, economics, and philosophy. In most cases standard scholarly editions were used in converting the text into machine-readable form, and the data include page references to these editions.

Users access the database through the PhiloLogic system, "an easy to use full-text retrieval package."

This WWW site also includes pointers to other French language resources.

Access via:
www http://tuna.uchicago.edu/ARTFL.html

Russian

A collection of information and humor about Russia and the former Soviet Union, along with software (mostly fonts) for supporting the Cyrillic alphabet.

Access via:
ftp *mimsy.umd.edu;* login *anonymous;* cd *pub/cyrillic*

Turkey

Middle East Technical University, near Ankara, sponsors this WWW site, which provides information about the university and pointers to other resources in and relating to Turkey. Much of the information at this site is in Turkish.

Access via:
www *http://www.metu.edu.tr/*

INTERNET INFORMATION & RESOURCE DIRECTORIES

Acceptable Use Policies

Acceptable use policies for many networks. These define what kinds of network traffic are permitted on a particular network.

Access via:
ftp *nis.nsf.net;* login *anonymous;* cd *acceptable.use.policies*

Anonymous FTP Sites

A very long list of sites that allow anonymous FTP, formatted in ASCII.

Access via:
ftp *ftp.ucsc.edu;* login *anonymous;* cd *public;* get *ftpsites*

Archie Request Form

A neat forms-based WWW gateway to a multitude of Archie servers; makes Archie really easy. Be careful not to overdo it!

Access via:
www *http://hoohoo.ncsa.uiuc.edu/ archie.html*

BITNET and EARN Information

Everything you could want to know about BITNET and its European counterpart, EARN.

Access via:
ftp *lilac.berkeley.edu;* login *anonymous;* cd *netinfo/bitnet/*

Computers, Freedom, and Privacy

The proceedings of an ACM conference on these topics.

Access via:
WAIS *computers-freedom-and-privacy.src*

Computer usage policies, archives of old discussions, bibliographies.
WAIS *comp-acad-freedom.src*

Information:
Email: archivist@archive.orst.edu

December's Guide to Internet Resources

A lengthy list of pointers to information describing the Internet, computer networks, and issues related to computer-mediated communication, compiled by John December and updated regularly. Topics include the technical, social, cognitive, and psychological aspects of the Net.

The guide is available in plain ASCII, HTML (for WWW), and other formats.

Access via:
ftp *ftp.rpi.edu;* login *anonymous;* cd *pub/communications*

Directory of WAIS Servers

This is a list of all known servers for the WAIS system, offered as a WAIS database. The directory of servers is usually the first database you'll search when you start a WAIS search; it's where you'll find the databases that are relevant to the topic you're researching.

Access via:
WAIS *directory-of-servers.src*

WAIS *au-directory-of-servers.src* ("backup" copy, located in Australia; may have more info about Australian resources.)

Domain Name Lookup

Resources to turn domain names like wuarchive.wustl.edu into a numeric address. These are particularly useful if you find yourself on a computer that doesn't participate in the domain name system.

Access via:
telnet 130.59.1.40; login *lookup*

Information:
Email: resolve@cs.widener.edu; send message "site" followed by site name
Email: dns@grasp.insa-lyon.fr; send message "ip" followed by site name

Fidonet Node List

This is, essentially, a list of Fidonet addresses. Given the name of a person or organization on Fidonet, you can look up the relevant Fidonet node name; then convert the node name into an Internet address, as described in Chapter 7, *Electronic Mail*.

Access via:
WAIS *fidonet-nodelist.src*

Information:
Email:
David.Dodell@f15.n114.z1.fidonet.org

Gophers Worldwide

Some gopher servers, with especially complete lists of international gopher servers.

Access via:
gopher gopher.micro.umn.edu /Other Gopher and Information Servers (Indexed by continent and country.)

gopher gopher.rediris.es /Otros Gopher - Other Gophers /Otros servidores de Informacisn - Other Gopher and Information Servers

gopher sunic.sunet.se /Infoservers in European Countries

gopher sunic.sunet.se /Other Gopher and Information Servers

HYTELNET

HYTELNET is a menu-driven version of TELNET. It offers much of the functionality of Gopher's TELNET interface. This is an index of all the servers it knows about. You can use it to find library catalogs, bulletin boards, campus information servers, and other TELNET sites.

Access via:
WAIS *hytelnet.src*

IETF Documents

The IETF is the voluntary engineering group for the Internet. It produces various working group and planning reports. This service contains the text of those reports.

Access via:
WAIS *ietf-documents.src*

WAIS *ietf-docs.src*

WAIS *netinfo.src*

WAIS *netinfo-docs.src*

IETF Drafts

Whereas "IETF Documents" contains the official documents that have been received by the group, this resource contains the documents under construction. This is where you look if you want to find out where the Internet is heading.

Access via:
ftp *ds.internic.net*; login *anonymous*; cd *internet-drafts*

WAIS *internic-internet-drafts.src*

WAIS *ripe-internet-drafts.src*

Intenet Services

A voluntarily compiled list of Internet services, commonly referred to as the "Yanoff list." It gives a short description of each service and access.

Access via:
ftp *csd4.csd.uwm.edu*; login *anonymous*; cd *pub/inet.services.txt*

gopher *csd4.csd.uwm.edu /Remote Information Services/Special Internet Connections*

Information:
Email: yanoff@csd4.csd.uwm.edu

Internet Information Search

Many of the standard help texts and guides, such as the Hitchhikers Guide to the Internet,

Zen and the Art of the Internet, Netiquette, and others are indexed and contained here.

Access via:
WAIS *internet_info.src*

Internet Mail Guide

A detailed description of how to address electronic mail so that it will get from any network to any other network. This list includes lots of very small networks, special interest networks, and corporate networks, in addition to well known networks such as MCI, CompuServe, etc. Updated monthly.

Access via:
ftp *csd4.csd.uwm.edu*; login *anonymous*; cd *pub*; get *internetwork-mail-guide*

InterNIC Information Services

The InterNIC is the Internet's master information service. This resource includes gateways to major white pages services (X.500, whois, and netfind), plus lists of known FTP archives, Gopher servers, and pointers to other resources.

Access via:
gopher *is.internic.net*

List of Lists, Listservers, & Newsgroups

A compilation of news and mailing lists, both on BITNET and the Internet. There is a lot of overlap among the sources, so if you search you will likely find something multiple times. Most valuable as a "master list" of all known electronic mail discussion groups.

Access via:

ftp *ftp.sura.net*; cd */pub/nic*; get *interest-groups.txt*

(WARNING: This is a very long file.)

A long ASCII file, in alphabetical order, of listservers, written by Diane K. Kovacs.

Access via:
ftp class.org; login *anonymous*; cd *class*; get *kovacs_library_listservers*

Another large collection of mailing lists, maintained by Stephanie da Silva. For those with World Wide Web browsers, this is the most useable of all the lists of lists.

Access via;
www http://www.ii.uib.no/~magnus/ paml.html

Matrix News

Matrix News is a newsletter of the Matrix Information and Directory Services, Inc. The topics concern current and future network applications. Articles are copyrighted, but may be used freely with attribution. They may not be sold. Complete use of information can be found by searching for copyright.

Access via:
WAIS *matrix_news.src*

Information:
Email: mids@tic.com

Network Information Online

This service, formerly called NICOLAS, is now represented in the Godard Space Flight Center's Gopher site. The subdirectories contain much information on using the Internet (see in particular "Networking").

Access via:
gopher gopher.gsfc.nasa.gov

National Institute of Standards & Technology Gopher

The National Institute of Standards & Technology (NIST) deals with a wide range of topics; this Gopher is concerned with computers and networking.

Access via:
gopher gopher-server.nist.gov

NNSC Internet Resource Guide

The NSF Network Service Center asks people offering a service on the Internet to submit a description of the service. These are collected in this database.

Access via:
gopher ocf.berkeley.edu /OCF On-line Help/The Outside World

NorthWestNet User Services Internet Resource Guide

A book much like this one, which contains information on network use and resources available. Files are in PostScript and some are compressed.

Access via:
ftp ftphost.nwnet.net; login *anonymous*; cd *user-docs/nusirg*

RFC (Request for Comments)

RFCs are the documents that define the Internet. They talk about how it works, how to use it, and where it is going. Most RFCs are fairly technical. There are over 1200 RFCs. An index is in file rfc-index.txt. Some RFCs are distributed in text, and some in PostScript. The text documents have names of the form rfcnnnn.txt. PostScript RFCs are in files named rfcnnnn.ps. In either case, nnnn is the number of the RFC you want. Many computers only archive partial sets. The sources listed here are "official" servers with complete sets.

For more information on fetching RFCs, send an email message like:

mail rfc-info@isi.edu

Subject: getting rfcs

help: ways_to_get_rfcs

Access via:

WAIS *rfc.src*
(A search aid to the index of RFCs.)

ftp ftp.internic.net; login *anonymous;*
cd *rfc*

ftp nic.ddn.mil; login *anonymous;* cd *rfc*

ftp nis.nsf.net; login *anonymous;*
cd *internet/documents/rfc*
(A VM/CMS server — filenames are
different.)

ftp ftp.jvnc.net; login *anonymous;* cd *rfc*

ftp wuarchive.wustl.edu; login *anonymous;*
cd *doc/rfc*

ftp src.doc.ic.ac.uk; login *anonymous;* cd *rfc*

*gopher gopher.internic.net /Internic
Information/Internet Information/All About
Request for Comments/RFCs Directory*

Information:
E-mail mailserv@ds.internic.net. The message
body should contain any of:

document-by-name rfcnnnn (for plain text file)
file /ftp/rfc/rfcnnnn.txt (for a plain text file)
file /ftp/rfc/rfcnnnn.ps (for a postscript file)

Zen and the Art of the Internet

This is the well-received booklet by Brendan
Kehoe about using the Internet. It is a good
introduction to the topic, told in a readable
fashion. The work is available in several formats.

Access via:
ftp ftp.cs.widener.edu; login *anonymous;*
cd *pub/zen*

INTERNET
ORGANIZATIONS

Newsgroups:
news.[announce.important,
announce.newusers, newusers.questions,
answers, groups, future, lists, software.read-
ers, sysadmin, misc]

Electronic Frontier Foundation

The EFF exists to promote existing academic
and personal freedoms in the new worldwide
computer society. It fights against things such
as network censorship and for things such as
freely available information. Included on this
server is information about the foundation (in
the EFF directory), the Computer and
Academic Freedom Archives, and many
electronic journals and magazines, such as
Effector, Athene, and DragonZine.

Access via:
WAIS *eff-documents.src*

WAIS *eff-talk.src*

ftp ftp.eff.org; login *anonymous;*
cd */pub/EFF*

Internet Society

The Internet Society is an international professional organization established to encourage
the evolution, standardization, and dissemination of techniques and technologies which
allow diverse information systems to communicate. The Society publishes newsletters,
organizes conferences, and manages email
distribution lists to educate a worldwide community about the global network of networks
known as the Internet which links more than
four million users and one million computers.
The Society sponsors the Internet Architecture
Board and its Internet Engineering and
Research Task Forces, and maintains liaisons
with other international organizations and
standards bodies as part of its effort to assist
in the evolution and growth of the critically
important infrastructure represented by the
Internet.

Access via:
ftp cnri.reston.va.us; login *anonymous;*
cd *isoc*

Information:
Email: isoc@nri.reston.va.us

Telephone: (703) 620-8990

INTERNET SERVICES

Newsgroups:
news.[announce.important,
announce.newusers, newusers.questions,
answers, groups, future, lists, software.read-
ers, sysadmin, misc]

Internet Service Providers

Listings, variously organized, of organizations that provide commercial and noncom-
mercial access to the Internet, drawn from the
book *Internet: Getting Started.*

Access via:
ftp nis.nsf.net; login *anonymous;*
cd *internet/providers*

Prototype WAIS FTP Server

Sort of "Archie meets FTP," with a WAIS
interface. Here is the description from the
directory of servers:

This server searches README files throughout
the entire FTP directory tree. When an interesting file is found, it should be used as a relevance feedback document. When the search
is re-done, the user will get a listing of the FTP
directory in which the README file resides.
The user can then retrieve files from that
directory. Text files are returned as type TEXT,
all other files are returned as type FTP.

Access via:
WAIS *quake.think.com-ftp.src*

LAW

Newsgroup:
misc.legal

Columbia Online Legal Resources (JANUS)

A specialized WAIS server and public-access
client for the legal community. Databases
available include the Columbia law catalog,

the law of the seas, legal emplyers (index of
U.S. and overseas firms), U.S. Supreme Court
Decisions, and U.S. court clerkship require-
ments. Also includes the Agenda of the
United Nations Rio Conference (on the envi-
ronment), other databases about the U.N.,
and WAIS-searchable sources for the
National Information Infrastructure and
National Performance Review proposals.

Access via;
telnet lawnet.law.columbia.edu; login *lawnet;*
select *"Project JANUS"*

WAIS *JANUS-dir-of-servers.src*

www http://www.janus.columbia.edu

Information:
Email: willem@futureinfo.com

Declaration of Independence

The most subversive document in the history
of the world, in ASCII (signers's names
omitted).

Access via:
ftp ftp.eff.org; login *anonymous;*
cd *pub/academic/civics;* get *dec_of_ind*

Cornell Legal Information Institute

The leading Internet site for law, part of the
Cornell Law School. Gopher and WWW
interfaces exist.

The Gopher interface
includes an index of
legal academia, an
archive of the "law-lib"
mailing list, the
"teknoids" mailing list
(which has lots of arti-
cles about computer
applications used in
law), and other ser-
vices of
interest.

The WWW interface
includes directories
dealing with the U.S.

Copyright Act, the U.S. Patent Act, the U.S. Lanham Act (Trademarks), and the Nasdaq Financial Executive Journal; the site is expanding actively.

Access via:
gopher fatty.law.cornell.edu

www http://www.law.cornell.edu/ lii.table.html

Corporation for Research and Educational Networking (CREN)

CREN is the corporation that runs BITNET. It has asked its attorneys to research their liability in using the network to access foreign countries. These files are specific to BITNET, but are probably applicable to the Internet as well.

mail listserv@bitnic.bitnet; body of message should contain 3 lines:

get legal commerce

get legal gtda

get legal counsel

Indiana University Law School

This server includes two legal journals (Global Legal Studies, Federal Communications Law), information on feminist law resources, plus pointers to other legal resources on the Internet.

Access via:
www http://www.law.indiana.edu/law/ lawsch.html

Supreme Court Rulings

Project HERMES is a project to make the Supreme Court's opinions and rulings publicly available via the Internet. Opinions and decisions from the 1989 term on are available. It helps to know the number of the document you are looking for.

See also: Columbia Online Legal Resource (JANUS)

Access via:
ftp ftp.cwru.edu; login *anonymous*; cd *hermes*

ftp info.umd.edu; login *anonymous*; cd *info/Government/US/SupremeCt*

Sydney University Law School FTP Archive

Contains an interesting collection of various U.S. laws. The laws are both state and Federal. Organized both by state and topic.

Access via:
ftp sulaw.law.su.oz.au; login *anonymous*; cd *pub/law*

U.S. Constitution

The text of the Constitution in full or divided by Article and Amendment.

Access via:
ftp info.umd.edu; login *anonymous*; cd *info/Government/US/Constitution*

Washington and Lee Law Library

A mixed collection of legal data. Text of some laws can be found, along with some information on conferences and meetings.

Access via:
ftp liberty.uc.wlu.edu; login *anonymous*; cd *pub/lawlib*

LITERATURE

Newsgroups:
rec.arts[books, sf, theatre, poems, prose]

See also: Classical Languages & Literature

See: Classical Languages & Literature

L'Association des Bibliophiles Universels

ABU is a library of public domain French literature, with pointers to other resources. The group was founded in April 1993 to develop and promote "numerical techniques enabling the free manipulation of information, the use of these techniques for the diffusion of the research work of members of the society and public domain information."

Access via:
www http://www.cnam.fr/ABU/principal/ABU.v2.html

Chinese Literature

This resource offers novels, poetry, and classics of Chinese literature, in Chinese characters. These are the archives of the alt.chinese.text newsgroup. If you want to learn how to ftp or read Chinese files, send a message to ftp-info@ifcss.org, or get the act/chinese-text-faq file.

Access via:
ftp ifcss.org; login *anonymous*;
cd *act/archive*

gopher ifcss.org /act/archive

CURIA Irish Manuscript Project

Also known as the *Thesaurus Linguarum Hiberniae,* this project is dedicated to collecting and generating machine-readable copies of Irish manuscript texts from 600 to 1600 A.D., some of which may be browsed online.

Access via:
www http://curia.ucc.ie/curia/menu.html

Dante Project

Contains reviews of Dante's Divine Comedy by various historical authors. A useful service for Dante scholars, but the user interface is very confusing.

Access via:
telnet lib.dartmouth.edu; connect *dante*

Dracula

Bram Stoker's 1897 horror novel, lightly hypertexted.

Access via:
www http://www.cs.cmu.edu:8001/Web/People/rgs/drac-table.html

Indexes of Online Books

Hypertext indexes of books available online, recently updated.

Access via:
www http://www.cs.cmu.edu:8001/Web/bookauthors.html
(Indexed by author.)

www http://www.cs.cmu.edu:8001/Web/booktitles.html
(Indexed by title.)

Internet Wiretap Book Collection

A rather large collection of electronic texts, including religious texts, fiction, nonfiction, and electronic texts available from other sources.

Access via:

gopher wiretap.Spies.COM /Wiretap Online Library

Lewis Carroll

Slightly hypertexted versions of Project Gutenberg's original electronic versions of *Alice's Adventures in Wonderland* and *Alice Through the Looking Glass* . Easier to read than ASCII.

Access via:

www http://cs.indiana.edu/metastuff/ dir.html

Online Book Initiative

Electronic texts by many authors, from Emily Bronte to Karl Marx, along with electronic journals, excerpts from newsgroups, and pointers to other sources of electronic texts and other Internet resources. A major resource for literature—and all texts are freely redistributable.

The FTP interface provides a long menu, not well organized (a good point at which to use your browser's search facility). The Gopher interface includes links to the OBI FAQ, an explanatory file, and a long but properly alphabetized menu of the same contents.

Access via:

ftp world.std.com; login *anonymous*; cd *obi*

gopher world.std.com/OBI The Online Book Initiative/

Online Books FAQ

One of the best hypertext directories of electronic books available through the Internet, along with other pertinent information.

Access via:

www http://cs.indiana.edu/metastuff/ bookfaq.html

Poetry

A collection of poems by Emily Bronte, Burns, Byron, T.S. Eliot, Frost, Yeats, and others. The WAIS index poetry.src, which is a different resource, provides the poems of Shakespeare, Yeats, Elizabeth Sawyer, and others.

Access via:

gopher ocf.berkeley.edu /OCF On-line Library/Poetry

WAIS *poetry.src*

Excerpt from **Shakespeare***, 3/20/94, (http://the-tech.mit.edu/Shakespeare.html)*

```
HAMLET
Now I am alone.
O, what a rogue and peasant slave
    am I!
Is it not monstrous that this
    player here,
But in a fiction, in a dream of
    passion,
Could force his soul so to his
    own conceit
That from her working all his
    visage wann'd,
Tears in his eyes, distraction
    in's aspect,
A broken voice, and his whole
    function suiting
With forms to his conceit? and
    all for nothing!
For Hecuba!
What's Hecuba to him, or he to
    Hecuba,
That he should weep for her?
    What would he do,
Had he the motive and the cue for
    passion
That I have? He would drown the
    stage with tears
And cleave the general ear with
    horrid speech,
Make mad the guilty and appal
    the free,
Confound the ignorant, and amaze
    indeed
The very faculties of eyes and
    ears.
```

Project Gutenberg

Project Gutenberg is an ambitious nonprofit and volunteer effort to get as much literature as possible into machine readable form. Their holdings include the works of Shakespeare, lots of Lewis Carroll, Moby Dick, and a rapidly growing number of classic texts, speeches, and reference materials. Manuscripts are in text only, with no special formatting. Filenames vary from server to server, but usually will have a mnemonic name followed by a version number (e.g. alice28.txt). The higher the version number, the more verification of the electronic text has been done. Since the text takes up a lot of disk space, some servers don't store the entire archive, and some compress the texts. Newsletters of the society, an index, and a README file are available on the mrcnext.cso.uiuc.edu source.

Access via:
www http://med-amsa.bu.edu/Gutenberg/
Welcome.html
(A WWW interface to the mrcnext.cso.uiuc.edu files.)

gopher gopher.tc.umn.edu
/Libraries/Electronic Books

ftp mrcnext.cso.uiuc.edu; login *anonymous*;
cd *etext*

Information:
Email: hart@vmd.cso.uiuc.edu

Project Runeberg (Scandinavian Literature)

A Project Gutenberg for Scandinavian languages, complete with support for Scandinavian character sets.

Access via:
gopher gopher.lysator.liu.se
/Projects...Project Runeberg, Scandinavian
e-texts

ftp ftp.lysator.liu.se; login *anonymous*;
cd *pub/runeberg*

www http://www.lysator.liu.se/
runeberg.html

Science Fiction News Group Archive

The archives of rec.arts.sf.reviews. The archives are available in "raw form," through anonymous FTP. The README file explains how the archive is organized. You can also search the archive through WAIS. This is another great place to look for spontaneous reviews or discussions of science fiction.

Access via:
WAIS sf-reviews.src

Shakespeare

A complete corpus of Shakespeare online, in ASCII.

In England, ftp to the Imperial College, London:

Access via:
ftp src.doc.ic.ac.uk; login *anonymous*;
cd *pub/literary/authors/shakespeare*

In the U.S., gopher to the University of Minnesota:

Access via:
gopher joeboy.micro.umn.edu /Ebooks/ By Title/Complete Works of Shakespeare

All of Shakespeare's plays, lightly hypertexted but with built-in links to a glossary:

Access via:
www http://the-tech.mit.edu/ Shakespeare.html

MATHEMATICS

Newsgroups:
sci.[math, math.num-analysis, math.stat, math.symbolic, math.research], k12.ed.math

Centre International de Rencontres Mathematiques Bibliography

The bibliography of the CIRM in Marseille. Index words are in French.

Access via:
WAIS *cirm-books.src.src*

WAIS *cirm-papers.src*

Information:
Email: rolland@cirm.univ-mrs.fr

e-MATH

e-MATH is an Internet node that provides mathematicians with an expanding list of services that can be accessed electronically. e-MATH is intended as an electronic clearing house for timely professional and research information in the mathematical sciences. Some of the current services are the AMS (American Mathematical Society) membership database, employment opportunities, publication ordering, author lists, meeting notices, and a directory of journals and newsletters.

Access via:
telnet e-math.ams.com; login e-math; password e-math

Information:
Email: support@e-math.ams.com

Fractals

Both static and animated (MPEG) fractal images are available from Rennes University, France. Note that MPEG files are long and take some time to retrieve.

Access via:
www http://www.cnam.fr/fractals.html

MEDICINE

Newsgroups:
sci.med, sci.med.[aids, dentistry, physics, pharmacy, nutrition, occupational, psychobiology, telemedicine]

See:
Agriculture - PEN Pages

Alcoholism Research Data Base

A database of articles and other information related to alcoholism and other forms of substance abuse.

Access via:
telnet lib.dartmouth.edu

Information:
Once you're in, type "Select file cork"

AIDS Information

The National Institute of Allergy and Infectious Disease maintains a special section of its Gopher for AIDS information.

Access via:
gopher odie.niaid.nih.gov /AIDS Related Information

Here's an online newsletter on the treatment of AIDS.

Access via:
gopher gopher.cic.net /Electronic Serials/Alphabetic List/A/AIDS News Service

CancerNet (NCI International Cancer Information Center)

The National Cancer Institute's Gopher and WWW server, with information for physicians and patients both.

Access via:
www http://biomed.nus.sg/Cancer/ welcome.html

gopher biomed.nus.sg /NUS-NCI CancerNet Gopher

Cholesterol

An explanation of what cholesterol is, where it comes from, and how it affects the body.

Access via:
gopher bluehen.ags.udel.edu /Cooperative Extension/Cooperative Extension Bulletins/Food, Health and Nutrition/Cholesterol

Clinical Alerts

Clinical Alerts are distributed by the National Institutes of Health and the National Library of Medicine for the purpose of getting important findings out to health professionals as quickly as possible.

Access via:
gopher uicvm.uic.edu /The Library/Clinical Alerts

Conversational Hypertext

A "natural language information system." We don't know if this is more interesting as an example of a hypertext application, or as a

source of information. At any rate, information on AIDS and Epilepsy is currently available, along with the Canadian Department of Communications.

Access via:
telnet debra.dgbt.doc.ca 3000

Family Medicine Discussion Archives

A growing collection of material relating to family medicine, including archived mailings from the FAM-MED listserv. These are discussions about uses of computers and networking to help in the teaching and practice of family medicine. Also included are pointers to other relevant Internet resources.

Access via:
ftp ftp.gac.edu; login anonymous; cd pub/fam-med/

FDA Electronic Bulletin Board

A bulletin board containing information on FDA (Food and Drug Administration) actions, congressional testimony, news releases, consumer information, AIDS, and veterinary medicine. You can use this database to find out, for example, what drugs have been approved recently.

Access via:
telnet fdabbs.fda.gov; login bbs

Great Beginnings

A newsletter on the care and feeding of infants and young toddlers. It includes information about parental expectations, typical behavior, home-made toys, language games, and so on.

Access via:
gopher bluehen.ags.udel.edu /Information By Topic/Families/Great Beginnings Newsletters

Handicap News BBS Archive

A collection of information and sources for and about the disabled. The archive includes legal and medical data, in addition to information about social services.

Access via:
ftp handicap.shel.isc-br.com; login anonymous

ftp handicap.shel.isc-br.com; login anonymous; cd pub

Internet/BITNET Health Science Resources

A very large file of email discussion lists, USENET newsgroups, Free-Nets, and other Internet resources relating to health and medicine, compiled by Lee Hancock of the University of Kansas Medical Center.

Access via:
ftp ftp.sura.net; login anonymous; cd pub/nic; get medical.resources.9-93

MEDLINE

The MEDLINE database contains article citations and abstracts, indexed from over 4000 journals in medicine and related health sciences. Some university libraries, especially medical school libraries, provide access to MEDLINE; however, access is normally limited to students, faculty, and staff. We've listed several libraries that provide MEDLINE. If you don't have ties to one of these institutions, check with your own library.

Access via:
telnet melvyl.ucop.edu

telnet lib.dartmouth.edu

telnet library.umdnj.edu; login *LIBRARY*

telnet utmem1.utmem.edu; login *HARVEY*

National Health Security Plan

The proposal formally announced in September 1993 by President Clinton to overhaul the practice of medicine and medical insurance in the U.S., in a hypertext version.

Access via:
www http://sunsite.unc.edu/nhs/NHS-T-o-C

National Institute of Allergy and Infectious Disease Gopher

Notable for its AIDS directory, but includes much administrative information also.

Access via:
gopher gopher.niaid.nih.gov

National Institutes of Health (NIH)

This is the former Gopher server, with a WWW front end now available, too. The site includes information on and links to biomedical data, activities and grants of the NIH, and the NIH Library (via TELNET).

Access via:
www http://www.nih.gov/

gopher gopher.nh.gov

National Library of Medicine

The National Library of Medicine (NLM) holds over 4.5 million records, including books, journals, reports, manuscripts, and audio-visual items, and offers online information on a variety of medical topics.

Access via:
www http://www.nlm.nih.gov/

telnet etnet.nlm.nih.govi; login *etnet*

Palo Alto Medical Foundation

A symposium on managed health care: is it capable of maintaining quality while reducing costs? It includes representatives from the government, business, industry, and academia. A very interesting set of presentations.

Access via:
www http://www.service.com/PAMF/ home.html

World Health Organization

A Gopher service offering information on the WHO's major health programs, as well as press releases, email/phone contacts, and general information about the organization.

Access via:
gopher gopher.who.ch

The WHO's FTP site offers some of the same information, particularly under the directories "programme" and "subject", but is less easy to navigate.

Access via:
ftp ftp.who.ch; login anonymous

MISCELLANEOUS

Genealogy

Genealogical information of all types, including database programs, lists of genealogical societies, and newsletters, as well as cemetery information. There is also information on the National Genealogical Society and a list of tips for beginners.

Access via:
ftp ftp.cac.psu.edu; login anonymous; cd genealogy

Note: All files which are not programs have a .zip extension.

Wedding Planner

Weddings are complicated affairs, particularly if you want to observe all the proper protocols. This resource may help you: it's a shareware Wedding Planner program for a personal computer.

Access via:
*ftp wuarchive.wustl.edu;
cd /systems/ibmpc/msdos/database;
get wedplan.zip*

MOVIES

Newsgroups:
rec.arts.[animation, cinema, movies]

Film Database

An indexed database of synopses, cast lists, etc., for over 6500 films. All films were released prior to 1986.

Access via:
gopher info.mcc.ac.uk /Miscellaneous items/Film database

Hypertext Movie Database Browser

New in August 1993, this interface promises eventually to provide sound and video clips (but doesn't yet).

Access via:
www http://www.cm.cf.ac.uk/Movies/moviequery.html

USENET Movie Review Archive

An archive of movie reviews that have appeared in the news group rec.arts.movies organized by year and month; can be rather slow.

Access via:
gopher ashpool.micro.umn.edu /fun/Movies

MUSIC

Newsgroups:
alt.[emusic, exotic-music], k12.ed.music, rec.music.[afro-latin, a-cappela, beatles, bluenote, cd, celtic, christian, classical, compose, country, dementia, dylan, early, folk, funky, gaffa, gdead, indian, industrial, info, makers, marketplace, misc, newage, reggae, reviews, synth, video]

Acoustic Guitar Digest

An electronic magazine for the acoustic guitar enthusiast.

Access via:
www http://www.acns.nwu.edu/guitar

ftp casbah.acns.nwu.edu; login *anonymous*; cd *pub/acoustic-guitar*

Banjo Tablature Archive

Includes original and transcribed tablature for the five-string banjo; all styles are represented, from bluegrass to jazz and classical.

Access via:
www http://www.vuw.ac.nz/who/Nathan.Torkington/banjo/tab/home.html

The Bottom Line Archive (Bass)

An electronic magazine for acoustic and electric bass enthusiasts. Contains album and equipment reviews, lots of good information from other bass players, and our favorite picture of Carol Kaye, grandmother of all electric bassists.

Access via:
www http://syy.oulu.fi/tbl.html

ftp ftp.uwp.edu; login *anonymous*; cd *pub/music/lists/bass*

Digital Tradition Folk Song Database

Allows users to search for and display lyrics, and can even provide audio of the song tunes for some systems.

Access via:
www http://web2.xerox.com/digitrad

ftp parcftp.xerox.com; login *anonymous*; cd *pub/music/digital_tradition*

Ethnomusicology Research Digest

Serious information about tools and techniques for recording music in the real world, formatted in ASCII.

Access via:
gopher gopher.cic.net /Electronic Serials/Alphabetic List/E/Ethnomusicology Research Digest

Folk Music

Sources for folk music lyrics, discographies, clubs, and so on.

Access via:
ftp nysernet.org; login *anonymous*; cd *folk_music*

Guitar Chords and Tablature

Guitar tablature and chords for songs of many popular artists from current to old, electric to acoustic. Entries are submitted by the people on the Net who have worked out the tab or chords. Submissions copied from books are not allowed. Organized by artist/group.

Access via:
ftp *ftp.nevada.edu*; login *anonymous*;
cd *pub/guitar*

Indian Classical Music

A database of Indian CDs. Coverage is best for Hindustani music, but it also includes some Karnatic CDs. Try searching for Shankar to get a flavor for what is there.

Access via:
WAIS *indian-classical-music.src*

MIDI Information

MIDI (Musical Instrument Digital Interface) is a common interface for computer-assisted music. The NetJam resource at Berkeley is meant to stimulate musical collaboration through organized exchange of MIDI and other related information. The WAIS database points to archives of technical documents and discussions about MIDI.

Access via:
ftp *xcf.berkeley.edu*; login *anonymous*;
cd *pub/misc/netjam*
(NetJam.)

WAIS *midi.src*

MTV.COM

Adam Curry's mtv.com site offers information on pop music, interviews with musicians, and even some short videos. Choose your method of connection!

Access via:
gopher *mtv.com*

ftp *mtv.com*; login *anonymous*

www *http://mtv.com/*

University of Wisconsin-Parkside Music Archive

A general source for many types of music information, both recorded and home-made. Items include information on building classical CD collections, lyrics, guitar chords, and pictures of artists.

Access via:
ftp *ftp.uwp.edu*; login *anonymous*;
cd *pub/music*

WNUR-FM Jazz Information Server

A hypertext resource on jazz, including discographies, lists of jazz music stores, hotlines, clubs, radio stations, and pictures of jazz musicians. This Web site is maintained by the staff of WNUR-FM of Evanston, Illinois.

Access via:
www *http://www.acns.nwu.edu/jazz*

OCEANOGRAPHY

Bedford Institute of Oceanography

Existing for the purpose of exchanging scientific data and programs with other marine scientists, the Habitat Ecology Division of the Bedford Institute of Oceanography developed the BSIM simulation, and has files of the Uniforum Atlantic minutes. This server also has information on fishery science.

Access via:

gopher biome.bio.dfo.ca

ftp biome.bio.dfo.ca; login *anonymous*

OCEANIC (Ocean Information Center)

The Ocean Information Center Bulletin Board provided by the University of Delaware. Has very technical and organizational material about various oceanographic experiments, field trials, and meetings.

Access via:

telnet delocn.udel.edu; login *info*

USGS, Branch of Atlantic Marine Geology

Located in Woods Hole, Mass. Contains abstracts and preprints of several geological journals, marine geology data sets, and information about what goes on in Woods Hole.

Access via:

gopher bramble.er.usgs.gov

PALAEONTOLOGY

Newsgroup:
sci.archaeology

Honolulu Community College Dinosaur Exhibit

A fun, well-designed tour of the permanent dinosaur exhibit at Honolulu Community College, complete with photographs, illustrations, movies, and even audio narration. The exhibits themselves are actually replicas from the originals at the American Museum of Natural History in New York City.

Access via:

www http://www.hcc.hawaii.edu/dinos/dinos.1.html

U.C. Berkeley Museum of Paleontology Gopher

Includes information on the U.C. Berkeley Museum of Paleontology and its holdings. This is an obvious resource if you're interested in fossils, but it has a lot of resources for other naturalists. The library of images includes a large collection of shark pictures, plus pictures of animals, plants, birds, and a library of animal sounds (including whale sounds).

Access via:

gopher ucmp1.berkeley.edu

U.C. Berkeley Museum of Paleontology Public Exhibits

The Museum's own WWW site features exhibits on Fossil Life, Sharks of the California Coast, and the Palaeontological Institute of Russia. The Fossil Life exhibition is also accessible through EXPO.

Access via:
www http://ucmp1.berkeley.edu/ welcome.html
(At Berkeley, all exhibits.)

www http://sunsite.unc.edu/expo/ paleo.exhibit/paleo.html
(EXPO, Fossil Life only.)

Paleontological Society Gopher

A Gopher server providing skeletal information about the Kentucky Paleontological Society. Contains information about the Society, notices of meetings and conferences, job postings, grant availability, book notices, etc.

Access via:
gopher uicvm.uic.edu /The Researcher/Paleontology/Paleontological Society

Palynology & Palaeoclimatology (ANU Bioinformatics Hypermedia Service)

Mainly links to Australian National University or other Internet resources relating to the Quaternary period (that's the past two million years or so). Palynology is the study of pollen.

Access via:
www http://life.anu.edu.au/ landscape_ecology/pollen.html

PETS

Newsgroups:
rec.pets, rec.pets.[birds, cats, dogs, herp]

See:
Free-Nets - Youngstown Free-Net; Medicine & Health - FDA Electronic Bulletin Board

AVES: Bird Related Information

An archive of images of birds, with very basic information about various species, keyed to the images. Also includes sounds. Some of the images are of only moderate quality.

Access via:
gopher vitruvius.cecer.army.mil

Llamas

A small directory including information about organizations of llama enthusiasts, a Llama.FAQ file, and some small black-and-white images

Access via:
gopher gopher.hs.jhu.edu /—>...Images/ Miscellaneous/Llamas

Pet FAQs

News group FAQs, mostly about dogs, but there are also FAQs on aquariums and fleas (for those of you thinking of starting a circus).

Access via:
ftp quartz.rutgers.edu;
login anonymous; cd pub/pets

PHILOSOPHY

Newsgroup:
sci.philosophy

American Philosophical Association Gopher

Serious information on serious subjects. Contains addresses, information on upcoming events, grants, fellowships and academic positions, bibliographies, and calls for papers.

Access via:
gopher apa.oxy.edu

PHYSICS

Newsgroups:
sci.physics.[accelerators, fusion, particle, research], sci.space

High Energy Physics (CERN)

Physics resources are a bit hard to come by, on the Internet: physicists have their own network, called HEPnet, which uses a different set of protocols. However, the World Wide Web provides access to many resources through a gateway—which you'd expect, since it was spawned at CERN, the European high energy physics laboratory. WWW currently provides access to information from CERN, DESY (a German physics lab), NIKHEF (Dutch physics center), SLAC (Stanford Linear Accelerator), and Fermilab.

Access via:
www http://info.cern.ch/hypertext/ DataSources/bySubject/Physics/HEP.html

Los Alamos Physics Information Service

Both nuclear and particle physics are represented on these Gopher and WWW servers, which are maintained by the Los Alamos National Laboratory (LANL). Primarily devoted to preprints on nuclear and high-energy physics. Abstracts and the papers themselves are available, as well as text searching of abstracts, authors, and titles.

Access via:
www http://mentor.lanl.gov/Welcome.html

Nonlinear Dynamics Archive

Contains preprints of papers, abstracts, software, and other material related to nonlinear dynamics. Apparently organized according to the institution that the software or paper came from, so you'll need to look at the README file to figure out what's available.

Access via:
ftp lyapunov.ucsd.edu; login *anonymous*; cd *pub*

Information:
Email: mbk@inls1.ucsd.edu (Matt Kennel)

Physics News

News and information related to physics, including links to other science news resources and updates on Congressional action on science funding.

Access via:
www http://www.het.brown.edu/news/ index.html

POLITICS & POLITICAL ACTIVISM

Newsgroups:
alt.activism, misc.activism.progressive, soc.politics

Congressional Contact Information

Contains the names, addresses and phone numbers of members of Congress. It can be searched by name, city, state, or postal code.

Access via:
WAIS *US-Congress-Phone-Fax.src*

Environmental Activism Server

What's your favorite cause? This server carries information on all sorts of causes, ranging from "Agran for President '92," to "Earth First!" to the Gulf War, to U.S.–Japan trade. It also includes lists of government telephone numbers, articles, and judicial decisions on the environmental movement.

Access via:
ftp pencil.cs.missouri.edu; login *anonymous;* cd *pub/map*

Political Contact Information

Addresses, telephone and fax numbers, and other contact information for government and media people, mixed with historical documents.

Access via:
ftp ftp.eff.org; login *anonymous;* cd *pub/academic/civics*

Presidential Election 1992

History is written by the victors, so this resource largely reflects the Democratic Party's view of the election, and a subdirectory is devoted to the "Year of the Woman." There is a subdirectory titled "Republican," though.

The "IssueBriefs" subdirectory includes positions by both parties. There is no trace anywhere of Ross Perot.

Access via:
ftp info.umd.edu; login *anonymous;* cd *info/Government/US/Election92*

Privacy Forum

The Internet Privacy Forum is a moderated digest for the discussion and analysis of issues relating to the general topic of privacy.

Access via:
gopher vortex.com /*** PRIVACY Forum ***

Ross Perot

Ross' book *United We Stand,* broken up into chapters formatted in ASCII.

Access via:
gopher joeboy.micro.umn.edu /EBooks/ By Title/United We Stand

PSYCHOLOGY

Newsgroup:
sci.psychology

Princeton Psychology Archive

A large repository, apparently mostly for the American Psychological Association's electronic journal *Psycoloquy.*

Access via:
ftp princeton.edu; login *anonymous;* cd *pub/harnad*

Psycoloquy

An online academic journal about psychology, published by the American Psychological Association.

Access via:
www http://info.cern.ch./hypertext/ DataSources/bySubject/Psychology/ Psycoloquy.html

RECREATION

Newsgroups:
alt.[aquaria, magic, sewing], rec.[antiques, aquaria, collecting, crafts.brewing, crafts.misc, crafts.textiles, folk-dancing, gambling, gardens, guns, juggling, models.railroad, models.rc, models.rockets, photo, radio.amateur.misc, radio.amateur.packet, radio.amateur.policy, radio.cb, railroad, roller-coaster, woodworking]

Biking Information (Norway)

A program called Bike Manager, instructions for making your own brake booster, and the "Great Trail of Strength Report" for 1991 through 1993 can be found here.

Access via:
ftp ugle.unit.no; login *anonymous*;
cd *local/biking*

Chess

The FTP site listed below contains a lot of material, including chess programs for various computer platforms and an FAQ.

At Assumption College there is a server that allows you to meet and play chess with other people. If you prefer, you can just "watch." Players must register with the server, allowing them to save games and participate in a rating system.

Access via:
ftp remus.ucs.uoknor.edu; login *anonymous*;
cd *pub/chess*

telnet eve.assumption.edu

Internet Go Server

A computer that allows you to meet other people and play "go" with them. Watching and kibitzing on other games is allowed.

Access via:
telnet hellspark.wharton.upenn.edu 6969;
login *guest*

Juggling FTP Archives

A set of resources for the juggling enthusiast. Has such resources as Jugglers World Newsletter, lists of vendors, festivals, clubs. Also, some information on the International Jugglers Association.

Access via:
ftp cogsci.indiana.edu; login *anonymous*;
cd *pub/juggling*

Information:
Email: moocow@piggy.cogsci.indiana.edu

Martial Arts

A martial arts archive in Israel includes information on several of the martial arts, including "Stretching."

Access via:
*www http://archie.ac.il:8001/papers/rma/
rma.html*

More specifically, here are lists of known Aikido dojos by continent. Affiliation is flagged in the list as well. Other information includes listings of events, books, and videos.

Access via:
ftp cs.ucsd.edu; login *anonymous*;
cd *pub/aikido*

Additional Aikido information may also be found in this Gopher resource:

Access via:
*gopher somalia.earth.nwu.edu /Aikido
Resources*

Scuba Diving Information

Lots of information about scuba diving, including reviews of different places to go, condition reports, news about equipment. A lot of the stuff has been collected from rec.scuba, but there's other material available, too. Anyone want to go to Vanuatu?

Access via:
ftp ames.arc.nasa.gov; login *anonymous*;
cd *pub/SCUBA*

Information:
Email: yee@ames.arc.nasa.gov

Skiing FAQ

A list of frequently asked questions about skiing, as well as ski information for Utah, Idaho, and Wyoming. The Utah information is the most complete.

Access via:
ftp *ski.utah.edu*; login *anonymous*; cd *skiing*

Skydiving

Includes pictures, an FAQ, the archive of rec.skydiving, and pointers to other skydiving resources on the Internet.

"If piloting an airplane is flying, then piloting a boat is swimming. To get the full experience, you have to *get out* into the element."

Access via:
www *http://www.cis.ufl.edu/skydive/*

Simulated Conversations

The Conversational Hypertext server offers some simulated conversations, some of which are similar in flavor to fantasy games. They are a big improvment over the time-honored (but rather worn) psychoanalysis simulations.

Access via:
telnet *debra.doc.ca*

Windsurfing

You want to windsurf in Corpus Christi, TX, or down the Columbia River Gorge? How about information on windsurfing shops and launch sites in the San Francisco Bay area? This, along with phone numbers for various wind reporting stations, windsurfing bitmaps, and hot topics of discussion are located here.

Access via:
ftp *lemming.uvm.edu*; login *anonymous*; cd *rec.windsurfing*

REFERENCE

Acronym Dictionary

A searchable Gopher index of 6,000 acronyms.

Access via:
www *http://curia.ucc.ie/info/net/ acronyms/acro.html*

CIA World Factbook

The CIA maintains a dossier on every country in the world. This is the 1993 version of that dossier, describing 249 nations. Each entry contains information about population, economic condition, trade, conflicts and politics. There's lots of stuff you won't find here—such as the number of nuclear warheads aimed at the Pentagon. But you will find lots of basic information about almost any country you can think of.

Access via:
WAIS *world-factbook93.src*

Online Dictionary

An online English dictionary; type the word, you get the definition.

Access via:
telnet *chem.ucsd.edu*; login *webster*

Reader's Guide to Periodical Literature

Yes, that old workhorse, the Reader's Guide to Periodical Literature, is available on the Internet. In case you've forgotten, it's a topic-oriented index to virtually all general-interest magazines published in the U.S.: Time, Popular Mechanics, etc. You can search it electronically, by author, title, subject, keyword, and so on.

Access via:
telnet *lib.uwstout.edu*; login *library*

Roget's Thesaurus

See: Literature - Project Gutenberg

Zipcode Guide 1991

A list of postal zipcodes for the U.S. from 1991. The format is:

00401:Pleasantville, NY

00501:Holtsville, NY

Access via:
WAIS *zipcodes.src*

RELIGION & BELIEF

Newsgroups:
soc.religion.[bahai, christian, christian.bible-study, eastern, islam, quaker], alt.atheism, alt.atheism.moderated, alt.hindu, alt.religion, talk.religion

ANU Asian Religions Bibliography

A collection (450Kb) of bibliographic references to selected (mainly Buddhist) Asian religions. From documents deposited with the Coombspapers Social Sciences Research Data Bank, Research Schools of Social Sciences and Pacific Studies, Australian National University, GPO Box 4, Canberra ACT 2601.

Access via:
WAIS *ANU-Asian-Religions.src*

Information:
Email: wais@coombs.anu.edu.au

Telephone: +61 6 249-4600

Astrology

This astrology resource resides under the Southern Cross, in Australia. It includes lessons, a bibliography, and lists of resources about astrology, in addition to newsgroup archives and relevant software.

Access via:
ftp *hilbert.maths.utas.edu.au*;
login *anonymous*; cd *pub/astrology*

Atheism

Mostly composed of material from alt.atheism and alt.atheism.moderated, including FAQs.

Access via:
ftp *ftp.mantis.co.uk*; login *anonymous*;
cd *pub/alt.atheism*

Bible

A complete King James Bible, with cross references and lexicon.

Access via:
WAIS *bible.src*
(Available 9 A.M.—9 P.M. EST.)

The King James Bible in compressed format for the PC or the Mac.

Access via:
ftp wuarchive.wustl.edu; login *anonymous*;
cd *doc/bible*

The Bible can be found in many languages (English, Finnish, German, Greek, Hebrew, Latin, Swahili, Turkish) in Finland.

Access via:
ftp nic.funet.fi; login *anonymous*;
cd *pub/doc/bible/texts*

The Bible in two English translations, plus Greek (including the Septuagint) and Latin, all keyword searchable. Also includes material on the Church Fathers. Even if you're not interested in Biblical studies, this resource shows you how good a well-constructed server can be. This site also has information on Islam and Mormon, and many other electronic texts. (Access to some electronic texts is limited to the campus.)

Access via:
gopher ccat.sas.upenn.edu /CCAT Text Archives and Related Material from Elsewhere/Religion/Biblical

Book of Mormon

The Book of Mormon, searchable through WAIS; also available through Project Gutenberg in text form.

See also: Literature, Project Gutenberg

Access via:
WAIS *Book_of_Mormon.src*

Catholicism

A Gopher resource at American University provides a rich mine of material on Catholicism, including recent Papal encyclicals.

Access via:
gopher auvm.american.edu /Catholic Files

John Ockerbloom maintains a fine set of pointers to "Catholic Resources on the Net."

Access via:
www http://www.cs.cmu.edu:8001/Web/ People/spok/catholic.html

Coptic Christianity

Copt Net is a group serving the emigrant Coptic (Egyptian) Orthodox. The FTP archive includes contents of the group's newsletter, articles on the Coptic church, a directory of Coptic churches worldwide outside Egypt, a GIF archive of religious images, the King James Bible, texts of hymns, a selection of lections, and more.

Access via:
ftp pharos.bu.edu; login *anonymous*; cd *CN*

Ecumenical efforts to heal the schism that developed in A.D. 451 at the Council of Chalcedon are discussed from the Coptic point of view in a long article, "Recent Efforts for Unity Between the Two Families of the Orthodox Church."

Access via:
gopher wiretap.Spies.COM /Wiretap Online Library/Articles/Religion and Philosophy/orthodox.cop

Electric Mystic's Guide to the Internet

A rather long and thorough bibliography of Internet resources on religion (not just mysticism), by Michael Strangelove. It's available in various but nonhypertext formats; you'll have to retrieve the document in parts, whichever format you prefer. Many of the resources are at the Australian National University.

In the same directory as Strangelove's guide there are other bibliographies on religion, referring to Internet and print sources.

Access via:
ftp panda1.uottawa.ca; login *anonymous*; cd *pub/religion*

Hinduism

Archives of *Hindu Digest*, an electronic publication distributed on the news group alt.hindu.

Access via:
gopher gopher.cic.net /Electronic Serials/Alphabetic List/H/Hindu Digest

Islam

The Qur'an is available in English translation via Gopher and WAIS:

Access via:
WAIS *Quran.src*

gopher latif.com/The Quran (In English only)

gophercs1.presby.edu /Religion Resources/Quran (Koran) - full text/

A large archive is maintained by the American Arab Scientific Society, Boston Chapter; despite the nonsectarian name of this group, the archive is largely of interest to Muslims, including information on sightings of the hilal, prayer timing software, and a list of bookstores that sell books on Islam or the Middle East, or books in Arabic or Persian.

Access via:
ftp cs.bu.edu; login *anonymous*; cd *amass*

A new "Guide to Islamic Resources on the Internet".

Access via:
ftp aql.gatech.edu; login *anonymous*; cd *pub/NetInfo/Documents*; get *Guide_to_Islamic_Resources_on_ The_Internet.gz*

ftp ftp.netcom.com; login *anonymous*; cd *pub/amcgee/african/islam/ cybermuslim.guide*

An evangelistic group called the Organization for New Muslims maintains a collection of resources mainly useful to American Muslims, including some of those cited above.

Access via:
gopher latif.com

Jainism

An Indian religion dating from the 6th century B.C. and related to Hinduism. This resource offers explanatory material, bibliography, and documents comparing Jainism with certain other religions.

Access via:
gopher wiretap.Spies.COM /Wiretap Online Library/Religion/Jainism

Judaism

The largest directory of information on Judaism, Hebrew, and Israel that we've found is in New York.

Access via:
ftp nysernet.org; login *anonymous*; cd *israel*

Mystical & Occult

These resources were collected on Friday the 13th before moonrise. Novices will have to grope around a bit; initiates may be able to divine which directories are the ones they seek.

Access via:
ftp quartz.rutgers.edu; login *anonymous*; cd *pub/occult*

*ftp ftp.netcom.com; login anonymous;
cd pub/alamut/mageguide*

*ftp slopoke.mlb.semi.harris.com;
login anonymous; cd pub/magick*

Presbyterianism

The *Westminster Confession of Faith* is
available in ASCII.

Access via:
*gopher cs1.presby.edu /Religion
Resources/Westminster Confession of Faith*

Religious Studies Publication Journal

This journal is designed to facilitate the dissemination of Religious Studies publications
and resource information.

Access via:
*gopher gopher.usak.ca /Library/
E—Journals/Humanities & Social
Sciences/Religious Studies Publications
Journal - CONTENTS*

Satanism Enthusiasts

Archives of a newsletter called *The Watcher:
New Zealand Voice of the Left Hand Path*,
which is an occult print and electronic publication. These people appear to be having a
lot of fun with their religious opinions.

Access via:
*gopher gopher.cic.net /Electronic
Serials/Alphabetic List/W/watcher*

Urantia Book

An anonymous spiritualist and Christian reve-
lation, ca. 1920—35, actually written by
Wilfred C. Kellogg (d. 1956) and edited by
William Samuel Sadler (1975—1969), both
former Seventh-Day Adventists, and published

in 1955. Kellogg was an informally adopted
son of the founder of the corn flake company.

This archive contains an index, in several formats, and commentary.

Access via:
*ftp wuarchive.wustl.edu; login anonymous;
cd pub/urantia; get ubpapers.txt*

TECHNOLOGY

Newsgroups:
sci.engr, sci.engr.[chem, biomed, civil,
control, manufacturing, mech]

NASA Mid-Continent Technology Transfer Center

As part of the National Technology Transfer
Network, six Regional Technology Transfer
Centers were established in 1991 by the
United States Government and NASA. The
14 state mid-continent region is served by the
Mid-Continent Technology Transfer Center
(MCTTC). The 14 states in the region are:
Arkansas, Colorado, Iowa, Kansas, Missouri,
Montana, Nebraska, New Mexico, North
Dakota, Oklahoma, South Dakota, Texas,
Utah, and Wyoming.

The mission of the Mid-Continent Technology
Transfer Center is to serve the national interest by providing business, engineering, scientific, information, and educational services for
the mid-continent region enabling public and
private enterprises to acquire, develop and
apply technologies from or with NASA, federal laboratories and other sources to expand
the use of technology, promote commercialization and improve competitiveness.

This is a good site for reaching other technol-
ogy-related Gopher servers.

Access via:
gopher technology.com

TELEVISION

Newsgroups:
alt.fan.*, alt.tv.*, rec.arts.*, rec.music.*, rec.arts.startrek

Monty Python

A large collection of Monty Python sketches.

Access via:
gopher ocf.berkeley.edu /OCF On-line Library/Monty_Python

Satellite TV

Pointers to useful information on the net relating to satellite TV and radio, assembled by Jay Novello.

Access via:
www http://itre.uncecs.edu/misc/sat.html

The Simpsons Archive

Everything you wanted to know about the Simpsons. Play dates, credits, bibliographies, episode summaries, etc.

Access via:
ftp ftp.cs.widener.edu; login *anonymous*; cd *pub/simpsons*

TRAVEL

Newsgroups:
rec.travel, rec.travel.[air, marketplace]

See also: International Interest

SPIRES Guide to Restaurants

A database of restaurant information, searchable by name, cuisine, city, state, and average price per meal. Listings are thin: only two restaurants are listed for Los Angeles, for example.

Access via:
gopher isumvs.iastate.edu /Serendipity/Restaurants: SPIRES Guide to Restaurants/

State Department Travel Advisories

These advisories from the U.S. State Department warn about some of the areas in which travel is dangerous. If you like to travel to out-of-the-way places, this resource is invaluable!

St. Olaf College in Northfield, Minnesota, is the Internet and BITNET distribution point for this information and has made it part of their WWW and Gopher sites; the FTP directory maintained by the University of Maryland mirrors the same information.

Access via:
www http://www.stolaf.edu/network/travel-advisories.html

gopher gopher.stolaf.edu /Internet Resources/US-State-Department-Travel-Advisories

ftp info.umd.edu; login *anonymous*; cd *inforM/Educational_Resources/United States/Government/TravelAdvisories*

Travel Information Library

Includes information about travel modalities, destinations, and the like, along with pointers to other travel information resources; much of the contents seems to be derived from the newsgroup rec.travel.

Access via:
ftp ftp.cc.umanitoba.ca; login *anonymous*; cd *rec-travel/README.html*

www ftp://ftp.cc.umanitoba.ca/rec.travel/README.html

Virtual Tourist

Connections to tourist guides for a number of locations, including Australia, Japan, New Zealand, many European countries, and many points in the United States. The Japanese tourist guide contains a number of maps, several audio files (including the national anthem), plus weather information, cultural information, etc.

Access via:
www http://wings.buffalo.edu/world

GNN Travelers' Tales Resource Center

O'Reilly's own online travel center, with articles on using the Internet to prepare for a trip, travel information for destinations around the world, pointers to other travel resources, and a marketplace.

Access via:
www http://nearnet.gnn.com/mkt/travel/center.html

USENET NEWS

Newsgroups:
news.answers, news.newusers.questions, news.software, news.groups

All the FAQs

"Frequently Asked Questions" files for all newsgroups are archived at rtfm.mit.edu. An index file lists every file in the directory with full title and a list of newsgroups, which may be useful for searching. There is also a "periodic-postings" directory containing files that discuss other helpful files posted periodically to newsgroups.

Access via:
ftp rtfm.mit.edu; login *anonymous*;
cd *pub/usenet/news.answers*

News Posting Service via Email

These servers allow you to post to USENET newsgroups even if you aren't part of the USENET system. Use dashes in the group-name rather than periods: for example, rec-music-folk rather than rec.music.folk. Remember to include your email address in your posting so you can get replies.

Information:
Email: groupname@cs.utexas.edu, or
Email: groupname@pws.bull.com

USENET Software: History and Sources

A frequently updated list and comparison of news reading software. A good place to start if you are unhappy with the newsreader you are currently using, and want to see what alternatives are available.

Access via:
ftp rtfm.mit.edu; login *anonymous*;
cd *pub/usenet/news.answers/usenet-software*; get *part1*

USENET Periodic Posting Archives

A repository of the periodic informational postings of the newsgroups. There is a directory corresponding to each newsgroup name. The directory contains all regular postings to the newsgroups (including FAQ lists), as well as many other "general interest" postings that have sprung out of the newsgroups.

Access via:
ftp rtfm.mit.edu; login *anonymous*;
cd *pub/usenet-by-group*

What is USENET?

A long explanation trying to explain what the USENET news system is, how it is managed, a

Access via:
ftp rtfm.mit.edu; cd pub/usenet-by group/news.ansers/what_is_usenet?; get part1

WEATHER & METEOROLOGY

Newsgroup:
sci.geo.meteorology

Australian National University (ANU); Bioinformatics Hypermedia Service: Weather

Satellite images, forecasts, and links to other weather resources. Best used for weather information you can't find closer to your own site.

Access via:
www http://life.anu.edu.au/weather.html

Minnesota Climatology Working Group

The University of Minnesota Climatology Working Group exists to provide climatological information to public agencies in the State of Minnesota. Information such as insect degree days (an important piece of information for campers!), crop degree days, and almost any type of climatological information pertaining to Minnesota that you'd want to know.

Access via:
gopher gopher.soils.umn.edu /MN Climatology Working Group

NCAR Data Support Section Server

The National Center for Atmospheric Research has a wide variety of data and programs available to aid meteorological research. Some of these are available for free through this server. Some are offline, but can be "mounted" (i.e., placed online for tempo-rary access) for a fee. And some are so big they can only be ordered on tape.

Access via:
www http://www.ucar.edu/metapage.html

ftp ncardata.ucar.edu; login anonymous; cd pub/weather

Network Sources for Meteorology and Weather

A regularly updated compilation by Ilana Stern of the National Center for Atmospheric Research, describing weather and meteorological data sources for the Internet, as well as on CD-ROM and tape.

Access via:
www http://www.cis.ohio-state.edu/hyper-text/faq/usenet/weather/top.html

ftp rtfm.mit.edu; login anonymous; cd pub/usenet/news.answers/weather/data/

Weather Maps

Many sites make various different collections of weather maps available. The data available and their formats vary, so you'll have to look carefully at what you find. It's important to look at any README files, or other descriptions, that are in these archives.

Access via:
ftp unidata.ucar.edu; login anonymous; cd images
(Weather radar maps, GOES HUGO images.)

ftp aurelie.soest.hawaii.edu;
login *anonymous; cd pub/avhrr/images*
(Sea surface temperature data for Hawaii
and vicinity.)

Weather Underground

What's the weather in Butte, Montana? This
is where to find out; it's one of the most interesting (and, if you're a skier, useful) services
on the Internet. The Weather Underground
provides a menu-driven server giving current
weather information and forecasts for non-
commercial use. The weather reports are
taken from the National Weather Service;
reports are available for the entire United
States and Canada. As we said, ski conditions are available in the winter. Several
weather advisories and earthquake reports
are also available.

Access via:
WAIS *weather.src*

telnet *madlab.sprl.umich.edu 3000*

WHITE PAGES

Knowbot Information Service

The Knowbot Information Service is a "white
pages" service that will search for a name
through a large number of Internet databases. It's a great way to look up friends and
acquaintances. It's not yet as convenient as it
might be, but Knowbots are among the
newest and most advanced services on the
Internet; it's worth knowing about them.

Access via:
telnet *info.cnri.reston.va.us 185*; enter email
address

Knowbot Information Service Documentation

Documentation describing the philosophy and
use of the Knowbot Information white pages

service. Files are available in PostScript and
ASCII format.

Access via:
ftp nri.reston.va.us; login *anonymous;*
cd *rdroms*

List of Internet Whois Servers

Lists of all of the known whois-style white
pages servers on the Internet, and related
information.

Access via:
ftp rtfm.mit.edu; login *anonymous;*
cd *pub/whois*

Information:
Email: mhpower@athena.mit.edu

Netfind

A very persistent program that searches a
variety of databases to help you find someone. Not very easy to use, but it may be easier than looking through several different
white pages servers to find someone.

Access via:
telnet *bruno.cs.colorado.edu;* login *netfind*

telnet *archie.au;* login *netfind*

telnet *dino.conicit.ve;* login *netfind*

telnet *ds.internic.net;* login *netfind*

telnet *mudhoney.micro.umn.edu;* login *netfind*

telnet *netfind.oc.com;* login *netfind*

PSI White Pages Pilot Project: User's Handbook

In PostScript format; many files.

Access via:
ftp ftp.psi.com; login *anonymous;* cd *wp/ps*

USENET Addresses

This contains a list of all people who have posted to USENET newsgroups passing through MIT. This is an excellent way to find out a reasonably up-to-date address for many users of the Net.

For information by email send mail to mail-server@pit-manager.mit.edu; place "help" in the message body.

The filenames begin with "addresses", one for each month back into 1992 and for occasional months before that. They are very large.

Access via:
ftp rtfm.mit.edu; login anonymous;
cd pub/usenet-addresses/lists

GETTING CONNECTED TO THE INTERNET

Grades of Service
Service Providers

No matter who you are, you get access to the Internet via a *service provider*. Service providers sell several different kinds of service, each with its own advantages and disadvantages. As with buying a car, you have to decide what features you want, how much you're willing to pay, and then go comparison-shopping.

But before you even read the list of providers, there's one thing you should do. In Chapter 1, *What Is This Book About*, we said that many, many people have access to the Internet and don't know it. Are you one of these? Find out. If your company or school is on the Internet, it almost certainly has better service than you can afford as an individual.

In other words, you may *already* have an Internet connection available to you. You don't need to go out and find a service provider, you don't need to pay any extra bills; you just need to use what you already have. If you're a student at a four-year college or university, you can almost assume that your school is on the Internet, and you can probably get access as a student. Many junior colleges and a growing number of secondary schools are on the Net. Go to your computer center or computer science department and ask around. Ask a number of places before giving up—many times the only people who are aware of the Internet are those people who actually use it. If you're no longer part of academia, the problem is a little more difficult.

How do you find out if your company has Internet access? Anyone who is responsible for managing computer systems or taking care of your corporate network should be able to tell you. If most of your computer systems run UNIX, there's a good chance that you're on the Internet or at least can exchange email and USENET news with the Internet. For historical reasons, if your computers are mostly running DOS, you probably aren't connected to the Internet—but there's no reason you couldn't be. Don't hesitate to dig some; if you're in marketing or accounting, you may not be aware of the nice Internet connection that the research or engineering group has been keeping to itself. If your company has a connection, but it's not in your department, your job is to ask "why?" Write a proposal and get it into next year's budget. Do whatever's necessary. If the resource already exists, it won't cost your company much more to give it to you. And even if your company doesn't have a connection, they're still the best place to start. Find some other people who need Internet access, figure out how to justify it economically, and make a proposal.

If your company doesn't have a connection, and you're not a student, there are still two ways of coming by Internet access inexpensively. The first thing to do is check out the public library. Some libraries offer a service called a *Free-Net*. It is a community-based information and email system which allows Internet access. You can either use the Free-Net from the library or dial in to it. Although only a few libraries provide this service at the moment, the number is growing. The Free-Nets we knew about when we compiled the catalog are listed under Free-Net.

The second is to become a student. Find out whether or not your community college has an Internet connection. If it does, sign up for a course or two. At many community colleges it is cheaper to take a course than it would be to arrange Internet services with a service provider as an individual. Learn basketweaving, and you can have something to do when you go crazy because the network is down. Once you are enrolled, ask for Internet access. There's a need for a public archive of significant basket designs—isn't there?

Grades of Service

Well, you're still reading. So you probably didn't find any "free" Internet access points. Or, perhaps, someone said, "Sounds like a good idea. Why don't you do some research about what it will cost?" As we said, there are many different ways of connecting to the Internet. So, before you start your research, here's a summary of some types of connections that are available.

Dedicated Internet Access

Corporations and large institutions that want Internet access should look into dedicated network access. This gives you complete access to all of the Internet's facilities. A service provider leases a dedicated telephone line at a speed of your choosing (the faster the line speed, the more it costs), and places a special routing computer at your location. That router is responsible for taking communications from your site destined for somewhere else and sending them on their way (and vice versa). This is all quite expensive, running at least $2000 initially and several thousand dollars a year in monthly fees. However, once you've set up the connection, you can let as many computers as you like connect to the Internet—perhaps one computer in every classroom in your high school. To do so, you only need to place the computers on a local area network, along with the router.

Dedicated access offers the most flexible connection. Each computer is a full-fledged Internet member, capable of performing any network function. If there is some really neat new application you want to try, you only need to load the software and give it a whirl. However, since a dedicated connection is costly, it is most appropriate for a group setting, and impractical for home users.

Dedicated Internet access usually requires some support structure for your local network. The service provider will help you in the beginning, but once you get running, he is only responsible for the router and the phone line. What happens on your local network is your business. If you are responsible for the care and feeding of the LAN, this book won't be enough. The Nutshell Handbook *TCP/IP Network Administration*, by Craig Hunt, will help you to set up and run your local network. A class or two wouldn't hurt. And keep this book in mind; you may want to give it to users who keep bothering you with simple questions.

SLIP and PPP

In the past few years, some less expensive techniques for "almost-dedicated access" have appeared. These are called SLIP and PPP; they are versions of the Internet software that run over normal phone lines, using standard high-speed modems. You may have to buy the SLIP or PPP software and a more expensive modem, but you won't have the very high connection costs.* You don't even have to use a "dedicated" phone line; you can use SLIP or PPP to dial in to your network when you want access, leaving the phone line free for other use when you don't need it. The real advantage of SLIP or PPP is that it allows a full-fledged connection to the Internet. You're not using someone else's system as an "access point" to the Net; you're on the Net yourself.

SLIP and PPP are very appropriate for connecting a home computer to a larger local network, which is in turn connected to the Internet. For example, you might use SLIP to connect your home computer to your company or campus network; then your home computer will have full Internet access, just as if it were on your company's Ethernet. SLIP and PPP are also appropriate for connecting a home computer (or perhaps a very small local network) to a service provider, who can give you full Internet access. They aren't appropriate for connecting a medium-sized or large network to the Internet; they can't talk fast enough to support many users at once. So if you have a medium or large network (or if you might have one in a few years), it's best to look into "real" dedicated access.

SLIP is a moderate-cost option: it provides very good service and isn't terribly expensive—but you'd wish it were cheaper. A service provider, like UUNET or PSI, would typically charge something like $250/month for unlimited SLIP or PPP service; alternatively, there may be a lower monthly charge, with an additional hourly fee. You also have to worry about the telephone bill. Many service providers provide 800 numbers or local access numbers in major urban areas to minimize this cost.

---

*By high-speed, we mean at least 9600 baud. A V.32bis or V.42bis modem is ideal. You could probably make SLIP work with a cheaper 2400-baud modem, but it would be painful. In any case, your service provider will be able to make recommendations about what to buy. Some service providers even sell modems; that's a good way to avoid problems. You will usually get a good price, and if you run into trouble, your provider can't tell you "Your modem isn't a type we support."

Installing SLIP or PPP, configuring them, and getting them running are not covered in this book. See the Nutshell Handbook *TCP/IP Network Administration* for more information about them. If you use Microsoft Windows, look into O'Reilly & Associates "Internet in a Box" product; that's a nicely packaged Internet kit, including newsreaders, mailers, Web browsers, and support for PPP.

ISDN Access

ISDN stands for "Integrated Services Digital Network." In essence, it means using a digital telephone line between your home or office and the telephone company's switching office (or "central office"). This might sound like a new technology, but it actually isn't. Although it's only now coming into common use in the United States, ISDN has been widely used in Europe for a number of years. ISDN access can be either dial-up (intermittent access, as needed), or dedicated (a permanent connection to the Internet).

The big advantage of ISDN is that it provides very high-speed access at relatively low cost. One ISDN channel includes two 56 or 64Kb digital channels (depending on the implementation your phone company uses). With access speeds like this, multimedia services really zip! You won't have to wait ten minutes to download someone's graphics-filled WWW home page.

Pricing is a big variable. It is almost certainly a lot less than a traditional dedicated line of the same speed would have cost a few years ago. Typical ISDN line charges are in the $20 to $50 per month range. Rates depend entirely on how the service is tariffed with the local public utilities commission. You may be able to save some money by using your ISDN line for your regular phone service, in addition to Internet access, but be careful. You can't use regular phones over an ISDN line, and ISDN phones cost hundreds of dollars. And sometimes, ISDN voice calls are billed at business rates, so your cost per call might be higher.

The disadvantage of ISDN that its availability in the U.S. is spotty. If you're in a big city, there's a good change you can get it; if you're in a suburb, you probably can't; if you're in a rural area, forget it. You may need to spend a week trying to find the one person at your local phone company who knows what ISDN is (and getting past the two hundred who don't and try to sell you something else).

Since there hasn't been a lot of ISDN service around, many Internet providers don't have the equipment to handle incoming ISDN calls. ISDN equipment used to be pretty scarce, but it is getting cheaper and more available as demand increases. You may need to shop around to find service, but you should eventually find it.

Dial-up Access

What if you can't afford dedicated access, and you don't want to experiment with SLIP or PPP? Is there any easy way to get network access? Yes—just get a timesharing account on a computer that already has dedicated access. Then use your home computer to log in to this remote system, and do your network work there. Timesharing access is almost (but not quite) as good as having your own connection, and it's considerably easier to set up. Your computer doesn't actually become part of the Internet; it's just accessing a service computer that's permanently connected to the network. Many organizations provide this kind of service. Since you are sharing the connection with others, the cost of these services is greatly reduced (typically around $20 to $40 per month—possibly with some additional per-hour access fee). The cheapest rates apply if you contract for "off peak" service only (i.e., nights and weekends). If you can find a Free-Net in your area, it will be even more economical; as the name implies, the service will be free.

This type of connection has its pros and cons. On the good side, you probably have all the hardware and software you need (i.e., a modem and a terminal emulation package). Even if you have to buy them, you can come by them for less than $200. On the bad side, you can only do what the service provider allows. You may not be able to use all the services that the Internet has. There is probably no way to load a random nifty software application and use it; you have to appeal to the provider to add that service. You can't run fancy X-based applications, like Mosaic. Some access providers may limit the amount of disk space you can use. And again, you're responsible for phone bills, though (as we said above) some providers have 800 numbers or local access numbers.

By the way, it's worth mentioning one new kind of dial-up service. PSI (one of the major service providers) is distributing a free software package called PSIlink. It allows a PC running DOS to connect to their system and use the Internet's electronic mail, bulletin board, and file transfer services. They've managed to hide most of the problems that dial-up access entails; the files you want are automatically transferred to your home system, for example. The cost of this service is roughly $30/month. The drawback is that you're limited to what one service provider gives you. As you might expect, the software companies like PSI give away won't work with their competitors' systems. If this strikes you as a fair trade, look into it.

UUCP Access

We'll mention, in passing, a subclass of dial-up access. All UNIX systems support a set of services called UUCP, which transfer data over standard phone lines. If you find a cooperating service provider (like UUNET, an employer, or a friend), you can arrange to use UUCP to pick up Internet mail and USENET news. Your system uses UUCP to dial into a remote system at regular intervals and transfer news and mail back home. You can therefore read your mail on your own system, rather than someone else's. You can't do much more than read mail and news, since you're really not connected to the Internet at all. Your computer just dials up an Internet computer periodically and transfers files.

UUCP is common, and (if you have UNIX and a modem) you won't need to spend anything on software or equipment. Any UNIX system has all the software you need. And it's easy to find someone to give you a UUCP connection for free, or at least cheap. If all you want is electronic mail on your home system, it will do the job. Setting up UUCP is not trivial, but not terribly difficult, either. See the Nutshell handbooks *Managing UUCP and USENET* and *Using UUCP and USENET* for more information.

Access Via Other Networks

Most networking services, like BITNET and CompuServe, have set up *gateways* that allow you to exchange electronic mail with systems on the Internet. Some have set up gateways that let you read the Internet's bulletin boards (USENET news). And there are a few services scattered around that let you request a file via an electronic mail message; such services fetch the file and mail it to you automatically. This isn't as good as getting the file directly, but it works.

This may be all you need. But it's definitely not an Internet connection; you only have access to a few services. What you can do is fairly limited; there's a lot more out there waiting for you.

There is another way you might use other networks to get to the Internet. If you are using one of the "UNIX for the masses" services, like the Well, to provide you with Internet dial-up services, you usually have to pay for your own long distance calls to the host computer. It might be more economical to use other networks, like CompuServe, to get from your home to the Internet computer. Then, you can get to wherever on the Internet you like.

Telephone Connections

Whatever alternative you choose, you're going to have some kind of telephone connection—whether it's a very expensive T3 line or a standard voice line. Here's a summary of the most common service grades:

Table A-1: Telephone Line Options

Service Grade	Speed	Notes
Standard voice line	0 to 19.2Kb	No extra cost; SLIP or dial-up connections
ISDN	56Kb	Digital phone line; availability spotty; dedicated or dial-up
Leased line	56-64Kb	Small dedicated link to a service provider
T1	1.544Mb	Dedicated link with heavy use
T2	6Mb	Not commonly used in networking
T3	45Mb	Major networking artery for a large corporation or university

Service Providers

Internet service providers are participating in a competitive market. For any given kind of service, there are usually several providers available—and several different price structures. In the tables coming up, we've listed as many service providers as we could find. There are probably others. I can't tell you which ones are better than others; like the evolution of species, each has its own niche in the market. As you investigate, you'll certainly find different trade-offs you can make: quality of service versus price; initial cost versus monthly cost; 800-number access versus long-distance phone charges; and so on. However, I can give you some hints about how to shop.

POPs and 800 Numbers

One of the largest expenses in getting an Internet connection may be your phone bill. Service providers have come up with two approaches to this problem. One is to install 800 numbers that you can dial "for free." The other is to install local access numbers (called *points of presence*, or *POPs*), in major metropolitan areas. Providers like PSI and Netcom take the POP approach; AlterNet takes the 800-number approach. (These options are irrelevant to leased-line connections, which are negotiated separately with your phone company.)

Both approaches have obvious advantages and disadvantages. Dialing into a service provider can get very expensive, if it isn't a local phone call. The 800 number seems to be cheaper, but—realize that someone still has to pay the bill, and that's going to be you. The provider may be able to get a better "bulk rate" for 800 service than you can for regular long-distance calls, but the difference won't be that substantial. You can expect service providers with 800 access to charge significantly higher monthly fees, or to have some kind of surcharge based on your connection time. Make sure to take that into account when doing a cost comparison. Estimate the amount of time you're going to spend on the Net;* figure out how much this would cost in long-distance charges to a provider; and compare that with the charges for the equivalent 800-number service.

Getting access through a local POP is ideal—if you can find one. You'll only have local phone calls to deal with. Even if your Internet time rivals the time your teenage kids spend on the phone, there won't be any extra charges to surprise you. However, that's only an option if there really is a local POP. If you live just one town outside of a provider's local calling area, tough. (And if you live out in in the sticks, good luck!)

You should also consider how you will use your connection. If you are a traveling salesman driving from small town to small town, 800 service will probably be better, because you can call it from anywhere. If you travel between large cities, any national or international service provider with POPs will work, too. There will be a POP in every reasonable-sized city (populations above about 500,000, it appears). If you are looking for a cheap connection only to be used from home, you might check out the rash of local service providers. (In this case, you might try joining one of the "Internet Coops" that are starting up—particularly if you have some technical skills.)

---

*Be careful not to underestimate; networking often becomes addicting.

There's No Such Thing as a Cheap Lunch

Since the first edition of this book, service providers have sprouted like weeds. And still there aren't enough of them. It's becoming clear, though, that there are wide differences in the quality of service that the providers offer. Some hold your hand while you get started, answer your questions, fix things quickly when they break, and so on. Others don't. That's not surprising—auto dealers, insurance agencies, and other businesses are the same. Most Internet service providers are extremely helpful (unlike insurance companies). Their biggest problem is that as a rule, they're too busy. But there are some service providers who will pocket your check and walk away. Some careful shopping will keep you out of trouble.

Here's one particular aspect of service you should think about. Lately, we've seen some very low-priced offers for true Internet connectivity (i.e., SLIP or PPP connections): in the range for $20 per month for unlimited access. That's certainly a good deal. If it really works—which it may. But it may not.

What's the problem? I suspect that these service providers are working on a "health club" model. For every person who buys a health club membership and works out faithfully, there are four or five who buy memberships and show up once or twice. If all the members worked out three times a week, the health club couldn't stay in business without drastically raising its prices and alienating its members . . . in which case, it would go out of business anyway. The same thing may be going on here. To offer unlimited access with very low monthly fees, the service provider must have a huge number of users and a relatively small number of phone lines and modems. The more users are sharing a limited bank of phones, the more likely you are to get a busy signal when you try to dial in. $20 per month is not a good price if all you're buying is a busy signal.

Keep in mind, though, that you might not have this problem. Nobody really knows how the service provider business will shake out. And getting people who use the Net for an hour every other month to subsidize your networking habit is great; but there's the risk that more people will actually make use of the service than you (and the service provider) are counting on. Just keep your eyes open and realize that there may be some drawbacks to offers that sound too good to be true.

Internet Coops

One exciting development in the service provider arena has been the development of Internet cooperatives: groups of individuals and companies who buy a high-speed dedicated line from another service provider and then share it. As a result, the members get better service for less money than they could afford individually. Coops range from a few individuals sharing a PPP connection to elaborate arrangements for sharing leased T1 lines.

Since labor for running the coop (system administration, network administration, dealing with service providers and phone companies, billing) is often donated, members with technical skills are particularly valuable. You're particularly valuable if you have any technical expertise. Don't count yourself out if you're not a UNIX guru; other kinds of expertise are needed, too. Someone with a solid telecommunications background, or someone who can help support clients using Windows, would be very valuable to most coops. For that matter, few coops would sneer at a lawyer who could file incorporation papers or an accountant who could prepare financial statements.

A few of the providers we've listed are cooperatives. The more important question, though, is whether a cooperative is forming in your area—and there's no way we can tell you about that. Talk to your friends who are interested in the Internet; listen for rumors and investigate them; if you have access to USENET news, watch the newsgroups *alt.internet.access.wanted* and *alt.internet.services.* The first group consists mostly of people trying to find out how to get Internet access in a particular area. Don't just listen; get things started yourself by asking "Does anyone know how to get an Internet connection in Fargo, North Dakota?" You may find out about an active service provider in your neighborhood, a coop that's forming in your area, or other people who would like access with whom you can form a coop of your own.

Regional Versus National

Service providers within the U.S. and Canada tend to group themselves into two categories: national and regional. National providers market their services to anyone in their nation. Regional providers have staked out an area of their country and only market their services within that area. Of course, once you're connected to the Internet, you have access to the entire world. So the difference between national and regional providers depends on what you like. Regional providers would claim that they give better ("more personal" service), and that they can adapt more quickly to their clients' needs. (One regional provider helps its clients do teleconferencing, for example.) Nationwide providers would counter that claim by saying that they can bring more resources to bear to solve a particular client's problems.

International providers (providers that offer Internet connections in more than one country) are more difficult to categorize. One would assume that the national providers are ones who do international connections, too. This is true, but a number of regionals also do this. Many U.S. regional providers got dragged into providing international connections early in the Internet game, before most of the national providers existed, and they still have them today. So, if you are looking to connect from another country, you need to look at both national and regional provider tables.

Who you call depends on how and where you want to connect. How you should connect depends on the size of your connection. If you are an individual or really small business, you will probably be looking for providers of dial-up or SLIP/PPP services. Medium to large businesses should look to SLIP/PPP or dedicated services. Here are a few guidelines to help you in looking for a provider:

- If you want to connect a single site in one country to the Internet, or if you want to connect several sites in the same geographical area to the Internet, call either national or regional providers that offer suitable services. For example, if you want to connect several offices in New England to the Internet, you can contact either Northeast regional providers or national providers. Obviously, if you're only interested in connecting one site to the Internet, regional and national providers can serve you equally well; your choice will be based on price and the services that are available.

- If you want to connect several widely distributed sites within the same country to the Internet (e.g., offices in Washington D.C., Los Angles, and Chicago), talk to suitable national providers. If you try to do this with regional providers, you will probably end up dealing with multiple contracts, operations centers, etc. It's probably not worth the effort.

- If you want to connect sites in the U.S. and sites in other countries to the Internet (e.g., offices in Washington D.C. and London), talk to either a national provider or a regional provider with international connections on the coast closest to where you want to reach. It may be very hard to deal with a foreign bureaucracy; an experienced provider who is currently serving the country in question is valuable.

- If you are a lone researcher outside of the U.S., would like an Internet connection for yourself or your institution, and don't know where to start, try contacting:

  Robert D. Collet
  Principal Investigator,
  NSFnet International Connections Manager (ICM)
  Program Manager, SprintLink
  Sprint Communications Company
  Government Systems Division -- Mail Stop: VAHRNA611
  13221 Woodland Park Road
  Herndon, Virginia, 22071 U.S.A.

  Tel: +1-703-904-2230
  FAX: +1-703-904-2119
  Pager: +1-800-SKY-PAGE   PIN: 45469

  email: rcollet@icm1.icp.net, rcollet@sprint.com, or
      PN=ROBERT.D.COLLET/O=US.SPRINT/ADMD=TELEMAIL/C=US/@sprint.com

He is the person responsible for international connections for the NSFnet portion of the Internet.

In Europe, you might also try:

  RIPE NCC
  Kruislaan 409
  NL-1098 SJ Amsterdam
  The Netherlands

  Tel: +31 20 592 5065
  Email: ncc@ripe.net

The Providers Themselves

Now we're through the preliminaries. Below, we'll give you a table of providers offering nationwide and international service, followed by a table of providers offering regional service within the U.S. and Canada. But first, we'll tell you how to get your own information.

Much of the information in our tables was gathered from a file called the PDIAL list. To get your own copy of this list, send the one-line email message **send PDIAL** to **info-deli-server@netcom.com**. It's updated frequently (every few months). The PDIAL list is also available at many anonymous FTP sites, though finding the most recent version can be tricky; getting the file through email is the best way to be sure you have something up-to-date. Another major source was the newsgroup *alt.internet.services*; this and *alt.internet.access.wanted* are well worth watching if you want to find out about Internet access opportunities.

Here are the providers themselves:

Table A-2: Nationwide and International Service Providers

Provider	Coverage	Services
AlterNet		
AlterNet, operated by UUNET Technologies, Inc. 3110 Fairview Park Drive Suite 570 Falls Church, VA 22042 (703) 204-8000 (703) 204-8001 (FAX) (800) 4-UUNET-3 info@uunet.uu.net	Worldwide	Dedicated (9.6Kb - 10Mb) Dial-up SLIP/PPP UUCP
ANS (Advanced Networks and Services)		
100 Clearbrook Road Elmsford, NY 10523 (703) 758-7700 (800) 456-8276 info@ans.net	Worldwide	Dedicated (56Kb - 45Mb) Dial-up SLIP/PPP
CLASS (Cooperative Library Agency for Systems and Services)		
1415 Koll Circle, Suite 101 San Jose, CA 95112-4698 (800) 488-4559 (408) 453-0444 class@class.org, nanfito@class.org	National (member libraries only)	Dial-up

Table A.2: Nationwide and International Service Providers (continued)

Provider	Coverage	Services
commercial link systems		
Internet Service Center Sternstr. 2 24116 Kiel Germany +49 431 9790161 +49 431 978126 info@cls.net	Schleswig Holstein (N. Germany, North of Hamburg)	ISDN Dial-up SLIP/PPP UUCP
CNS (Community News Service)		
1155 Kelly Johnson Blvd. Suite 400 Colorado Springs, CO 80920 (800) 592-1240 (719) 592-1240 service@cscns.com	U.S., including Hawaii, Alaska, Puerto Rico, and U.S. Virgin Islands	Dedicated (56Kb - 1.5Mb) Dial-up SLIP UUCP
Connect.com.au		
Connect.com.au Pty Ltd. 29 Fitzgibbon Crescent Caulfield Vic 3161 Australia 1800 818 262 or 03 528-2239 connect@connect.com.au	Australia	Dedicated Dial-up SLIP/PPP UUCP
CONNECT		
UK PC User's Group PO Box 360 Harrow HA1 4LQ England +44 (0)81 863 1191 +44 (0)81 863 6095 (FAX) +44 (0)81 863 6646 (data) info@ibmpcug.co.uk	UK	Dial-up UUCP
Demon Internet Ltd.		
Demon Systems Ltd. 42 Hendon Lane London N3 1TT England +44 81 349 0063 internet@demon.co.uk	UK	Dedicated (14.4Kb - 64Kb) Dial-up SLIP/PPP

Table A.2: Nationwide and International Service Providers (continued)

Provider	Coverage	Services
The Direct Connection		
PO Box 931 London SE18 3PW England 081 317 0100 081 317 2222 (data) helpdesk@dircon.co.uk	UK (England)	Dial-up SLIP/PPP UUCP
EUnet Limited		
EUnet Support +31 20 592 5109 +31 20 592 5163 (FAX) info@eu.net	Europe, Northern Africa, CIS (former Soviet Union)	Dedicated ISDN Dial-up UUCP
EUnet GB		
EUnet GB Support +44 227 475497 sales@Britain.EU.net	UK	Dedicated (64Kb ISDN Dial-up UUCP, SLIP/PPP
HoloNet		
Information Access Technologies, Inc. 46 Shattuck Square Suite 11 Berkeley, CA 94704-1152 (510) 704-0160 (510) 704-8019 (FAX) info@holonet.net, support@holonet.net	U.S.	Dedicated (64Kb - 1.5Mb) Dial-up SLIP/PPP UUCP
HookUp Communications		
1075 North Service Road West Oakville, Ontario Canada M2L 2G2 (905) 847-8000 (800) 363-0400 info@hookup.net	Canada	Dedicated Dial-up SLIP/PPP/CSLIP UUCP

Table A.2: Nationwide and International Service Providers (continued)

Provider	Coverage	Services
Institute for Global Communications/IGC Networks		
18 De Boom Street San Francisco, CA 94107 +1 (415) 442-0220 +1 (415) 546-1794 (FAX) support@igc.apc.org	Worldwide	Dial-up
Individual Network e.V.		
c/o Thomas Neugebauer Neusser Gasse 93 50259 Pulheim Germany (02238) 15071 (data) +49 2238 15071 (data) IN-Info@Individual.net	Germany	ISDN-IP SLIP/PPP UUCP
Individual Network e.V. – Rhein-Main		
Oliver Boehmer Linkstr. 15 65933 Frankfurt Germany 069/39048413 info@rhein-main.de	Rhein-Main-Area (Frankfurt), Germany	ISDN SLIP/PPP UUCP
Interconnect Australia Pty Ltd.		
29 Fitzgibbon Crescent Caulfield, Victoria Australia, 3161 +61 3 528 2239 +61 3 528 5887 (FAX) info@interconnect.com.au, sales@interconnect.com.au	Australia (all capitals except Darwin & Hobart) 1-900 number for rural Australia	Dial-up
Inter Networking Systems		
Gaswerkstrasse 11 Postfach 101312 44543 Castrop-Rauxel Germany +49 2305 356505 +49 2305 25411 (FAX) info@ins.net	Ruhrgebiet Area, Northrhine Westfalia (Germany)	Dedicated ISDN Dial-up SLIP/PPP UUCP

Table A.2: Nationwide and International Service Providers (continued)

Provider	Coverage	Services
MAZ Internet Services		
Karnapp 20 D-21079 Hamburg Germany +49 40 766 29 1623 maz-isc@maz-hh.de	Germany	Dedicated ISDN Dial-up SLIP/PPP
Millenium Online		
One Corporate Drive Clearwater, FL 34622 (800) 736-0122 (800) 774-0122 info@mill.com, jjablow@mill.com	Worldwide	Dial-up Dedicated
MUC.DE e.V.		
Frankfurter Ring 193a D-80807 Muenchen Germany +49-89-324683-11 postmaster@muc.de, vorstand@muc.de	Grossraum Muenchen (Munich/Bavaria)	Dial-up SLIP/PPP UUCP-Polling
OARnet		
Ohio Supercomputer Center 1224 Kinnear Road Columbus, OH 43085 (614) 292-9248 alison@osc.edu	U.S.	Dedicated ISDN Frame Relay Dial-up SLIP/PPP
PSI (Performance Systems International)		
510 Huntmar Park Drive Herndon, VA 22070 (703) 709-0300 (800) 82PSI82 (US only) (703) 904-1207 (FAX) (800) FAXPSI1 (FAXBACK info) info@psi.com	Worldwide	Dedicated (19.2Kb - 1.5Mb) ISDN Dial-up SLIP/PPP PSILink, UUCP

Table A.2: Nationwide and International Service Providers (continued)

Provider	Coverage	Services
SpaceNet GmbH		
Frankfurter Ring 193a D-80807 Muenchen Germany +49-89-324683-0 info@spacenet.de	Europe	
UUNET		
See AlterNet		
UUNorth Inc.		
3555 Don Mills Road Unit 6-304 Willowdale, Ontario Canada M2H 3N3 (416) 225-8649 c.smith@uunorth.north.net	Canada	Dedicated Dial-up SLIP/PPP UUCP
The WELL		
1750 Bridgeway Suite A-200 Sausalito, CA 94965 (415) 332-4335 info@well.sf.ca.us	Access through X.25 and direct dial	Dial-up
WinNET (UK)		
PO Box 360 Harrow HA1 4LQ England +44 (0)81 863 1191 +44 (0)81 863 6095 (FAX) +44 (0)81 863 6646 (data) info@win-uk.net	UK	Dial-up UUCP

Table A.2: Nationwide and International Service Providers (continued)

Provider	Coverage	Services
The World		
Software Tool & Die 1330 Beacon Street Brookline, MA 02146 (617) 739-0202 (617) 739-0914 (FAX) (617) 739-WRLD (data) info@world.std.com	U.S.	Dial-up
XLink		
NTG Netzwerk und Telematic GmbH Vincenz-Priessnitz-Str. 3 D-76131 Karlsuhe, FRG +49 721 9652 0 +49 721 9652 210 (FAX) info@xlink.net	Germany	Dedicated Dial-up SLIP/PPP UUCP

Table A-3: Regional Service Providers

Provider	Coverage	Services
agora.rain.com		
(503) 293-1772 info@agora.rain.com	Metro Portland OR	Dial-up
APK - Public Access UNI* Site		
19709 Mohican Ave Cleveland, OH 44119 (216) 481-9436 (data) (216) 481-1960 (data) info@wariat.org, zbig@wariat.org	Cleveland and neighborhoods (area code 216)	Dial-up
ARnet		
Walter Neilson (403) 450-5188 neilson@arc.ab.ca	Alberta, Canada	

Table A.3: Regional Service Providers (continued)

Provider	Coverage	Services
a2i Communications		
1211 Park Avenue #202 San Jose, CA 95126-2924 info@rahul.net	San Francisco Bay	Dial-up
BCnet		
BCnet Headquarters 515 West Hastings Street Vancouver, BC Canada V6B 5K3 (604) 291-5209 Mike@BC.net	British Columbia	Dedicated (4800 - 10Mb)
The Black Box		
P.O. Box 591822 Houston, TX 77259-1822 (713) 480-2684 (713) 480-2686 (data) info@blkbox.com	713 area code	Dial-up
CAPCON Connect		
CAPCON Library Network 1320 19th St. N.W. Suite 400 Washington, D.C. 20036 (202) 331-5771 (800) 543-4599 (MD and VA) capcon@capcon.net	Washington D.C., suburban MD and northern VA	Dedicated Dial-up
CENTnet, Inc.		
90 Sherman Street Cambridge, MA 02140 (617) 868-1198 (617) 661-1116 (FAX) sales@cent.net	**MA and adjacent areas**	**Dedicated (56Kb - 1.5Mb) Frame Relay SLIP/PPP**

Table A.3: Regional Service Providers (continued)

Provider	Coverage	Services
CERFnet		
PO Box 85608 San Diego, CA 92186-9784 (800) 876-2373 (619) 455-3990 sales@cerf.net	California International (Korea, Mexico, Brazil)	Dedicated (14.4Kb - 45Mb) Dial-up SLIP/PPP
CICnet		
ITI Building 2901 Hubbard Drive, Pod G Ann Arbor, MI 48105 (313) 998-6103 info@cic.net	Midwest U.S. (IL IA MN WI MI OH IN)	Dedicated (56Kb - 1.5Mb) SLIP/PPP
ClarkNet		
Clark Internet Services, Inc. 10600 Route 108 Ellicott City, MD 21042 (301) 854-0446 (410) 730-9765 (FAX) info@clark.net, all-info@clark.net	Metro Baltimore, Metro Washington DC, N. Virginia	Dedicated (56k - 1.5Mb) ISDN, SMDS Dial-up SLIP/PPP/CSLIP UUCP
Colorado SuperNet		
Colorado SuperNet, Inc. Colorado School of Mines 1500 Illinois Golden, CO 80401 (303) 273-3471 (303) 273-3475 (FAX) info@csn.org	Colorado	Dedicated (9.6Kb - 1.5Mb) Dial-up SLIP/PPP UUCP
Communications Accessibles Montreal		
2665 Ste-Cunegonde #002 Montreal, QC Canada H3J 2X3 (514) 931-0749 (514) 931-2250 (data) info@cam.org	Montreal (514 area code)	Dial-up SLIP/CSLIP/PPP UUCP

Table A.3: Regional Service Providers (continued)

Provider	Coverage	Services
CONCERT/NCREN		
PO Box 12889	North Carolina	Dedicated
3021 Cornwallis Road		(56Kb - 1.5Mb)
Research Triangle Park, NC 27709		SLIP/PPP
(919) 248-1999		UUCP
info@concert.net, info@ncren.net		
The Coop		
Colorado Internet Cooperative	Metro Denver	Dedicated
Association		(56Kb - 1.5Mb)
2525 Arapahoe Ave., Bldg. E4		SLIP/PPP
Boulder, CO 80302		
(303) 443-3786		
coop@coop.net		
CRL Network Services		
Box 326	California, AZ (Phoenix,	Dedicated
Larkspur, CA 94977	Tempe), Atlanta metro	(56Kb - 1.5Mb)
Larkspur, CA 94977	Chicago, Boston metro,	Dial-up
(415) 837-5300	Denver, Detroit,	SLIP/PPP
(415) 392-9000 (FAX)	New York City, St. Louis	UUCP
(415) 705-6060 (data)	metro, TX (Dallas,	
info@crl.com, sales@crl.com	Austin, San Antonio,	
	Houston)	
CTSNET		
CTS Network Services	San Diego County	Dedicated
4444 Convoy Street		(56Kb - 1.5Mb)
Suite 300		ISDN, Dial-up
San Diego, CA 92111-3708		SLIP/PPP
(619) 637-3637		UUCP
(619) 637-3630 (FAX)		
(619) 637-3660 (data)		
support@ctsnet.cts.com		
CyberGate, Inc.		
662 S. Military Trail	Florida and	Dedicated
Deerfield Beach, FL 33442	SE U.S.	Dial-up
(305) 428-GATE (4283)		SLIP/PPP
(305) 428-7977 (FAX)		UUCP
sales@gate.net		

Table A.3: Regional Service Providers (continued)

Provider	Coverage	Services
The Cyberspace Station		
204 N. El Camino Real Suite E626 Encinitas, CA 92024 (619) 944-9498 x626 (Ans. Svc.) (619) 634-1376 (data) info@cyber.net	San Diego County (619 area code)	Dial-up PPP UUCP
Echo		
97 Perry Street Suite 13 New York, NY 10014 (212) 255-3839 (212) 989-8411 (data) horn@echonyc.com	New York City	Dial-up SLIP/PPP
Eskimo North		
P.O. Box 75284 Seattle, WA 98125-0284 (206) 367-7457 nanook@eskimo.com	Seattle/Tacoma area (most of Snohomish, King, and Pierce counties)	Dial-up
ESNET		
2817 Falvy Ave. San Diego, CA 92111 (619) 278-3905 (data)	S. California	Dial-up
Evergreen Internet Express		
5333 N. 7th Street Suite B-220 Phoenix, AZ 85014 (602) 230-9330 (702) 831-2500 evergreen@libre.com	Southwest (AZ, NV, NM, CA, Mexico, NAFTA ports)	Dedicated (56Kb - 1.5Mb) Frame Relay Dial-up, SLIP/PPP

Table A.3: Regional Service Providers (continued)

Provider	Coverage	Services
Express Access		
Digital Express Group, Inc. 6006 Greenbelt Road Suite 228 Greenbelt, MD 20770 (301) 220-2020 (800) 969-9090 info@digex.com	Washington DC, Baltimore MD, Gaithersburg/ Damascus MD, New Brunswick NJ, Orange County CA, Atlantic City NJ	Dedicated (56Kb - 1.5Mb) Dial-up SLIP/PPP
fsp (Freelance Systems Programming)		
807 Saint Nicholas Avenue Dayton, OH 45410 (513) 258-7246 (513) 254-7745 (data) fsp@Dayton.fsp.com	Dayton OH and Montgomery County OH	Dial-up
Global Enterprise Services, Inc.		
JvNCnet. Sergio Heker 3 Independence Way Princeton, NJ 08540 (609) 897-7300 (800) 35-TIGER market@jvnc.net	New York, New Jersey, Connecticut, Philadelphia	Dedicated (19.2Kb - 1.5Mb) Dial-up SLIP
IDS World Network		
3 Franklin Road East Greenwich, RI 02818 (401) 884-7856 (401) 884-9002 (data) (305) 534-0321 (data, Miami) info@ids.net	Rhode Island, Miami FL	Dial-up SLIP/PPP UUCP
InfiNet, L.C.		
801 Boush Street Suite 203 Norfolk, VA 32510 (800) 849-7214 (804) 622-4289 (804) 622-7158 (FAX) system@infi.net	Hampton Roads, the Virginia Peninsula, and Richmond	Dial-up UUCP

Table A.3: Regional Service Providers (continued)

Provider	Coverage	Services
InterAccess		
9400 W. Foster Ave. Suite 111 Chicago, IL 60656 (800) 967-1580 (708) 671-0112 info@interaccess.com	Chicagoland	Dedicated (14.4Kb - 28.8Kb) Dial-up SLIP/PPP UUCP
Interpath		
PO Box 12800 Raleigh, NC 27605 (919) 890-6300 info@interpath.net	North Carolina	Dedicated (56Kb - 1.5Mb) Dial-up SLIP/PPP, UUCP
Maestro		
Maestro Technologies, Inc. 29 John Street Suite 1601 New York, NY 10038 (212) 240-9600	New York	Dial-up SLIP/PPP UUCP
MBnet		
Bill Reid (204) 474-9727 info@MBnet.MB.CA	Manitoba, Canada	Dedicated Dial-up SLIP/PPP, UUCP
MCSNet		
Macro Computer Solutions, Inc. 1300 W. Belmont Suite 4 Chicago, IL 60657 (312) BIT-UNIX (248-8649) info@mcs.net, info@mcs.com	Greater Chicagoland	Dedicated Dial-up SLIP/PPP
Merit/MichNet		
2200 Bonisteel Boulevard Ann Arbor, MI 48109-2112 (313) 764-9430 (313) 747-3185 (FAX) info@merit.edu	Michigan	Dedicated Dial-up

Table A.3: Regional Service Providers (continued)

Provider	Coverage	Services
MRNet (Minnesota Regional Network)		
511 11th Avenue So, Box 212 Minneapolis, MN 55415 (612) 342-2570 (612) 344-1716 (FAX) info@mr.net	Minnesota	Dedicated (56Kb - 1.5Mb) SLIP
MSEN		
320 Miller Street Ann Arbor, MI 48103 (313) 998-4562 info@msen.com	Michigan, Ohio, Indiana, Illinois	Dedicated (64Kb - 1.5Mb) Dial-up SLIP/PPP, UUCP
MV Communications, Inc.		
PO Box 4963 Manchester, NH 03108-4963 (603) 429-2223 (603) 424-7428 (data) info@mv.mv.com, mv-admin@mv.mv.com	New Hampshire	Dial-up SLIP/PPP UUCP
NEARNET(sm)		
BBN Technology Services Inc. 10 Moulton Street Cambridge, MA 02138 (617) 873-8730 nearnet-join@nic.near.net	Northeastern U.S. (New England, NY, NJ)	Dedicated (9.6Kb - 10Mb) SLIP/PPP
NeoSoft		
3408 Mangum Houston, TX 77092 (713) 684-5969 (713) 684-5936 (FAX) (713) 684-5900 (data) info@NeoSoft.com	Houston TX, Clear Lake TX area, New Orleans LA	Dedicated (56Kb - 1.5Mb) Frame Relay Dial-up SLIP/PPP
Netcom Online Communication Services		
4000 Moorepark Avenue #209 San Jose, CA 95117 (408) 554-8649 info@netcom.com	California	Dedicated (56Kb - 1.5Mb) Frame Relay Dial-up SLIP, UUCP

Table A.3: Regional Service Providers (continued)

Provider	Coverage	Services
netILLINOIS		
Peter Roll netILLINOIS 1840 Oak Avenue Evanston, IL 60201 (708) 866-1825 (708) 866-1857 (FAX) p-roll@nwu.edu	Illinois (area codes 312 and 708)	Dedicated (56Kb - 1.5Mb) SLIP/PPP
NevadaNet		
University of Nevada System Computing Services 4505 Maryland Parkway Las Vegas, NV 89154 (702) 739-3557	Nevada	Dedicated
New York Net		
Bob Tinkelman (718) 776-6811 sales@new-york.net	New York State, New Jersey, Connecticut	Dedicated (56Kb - 1.5Mb) Frame Relay Dial-up, SLIP/PPP
North Shore Access		
Eco Software, Inc. 145 Munroe Street, Suite 405 Lynn, MA 01901 (617) 593-3110 (voice/FAX) (617) 593-4557 (data) info@northshore.ecosoft.com	Eastern MA	Dial-up SLIP/PPP UUCP
NorthWestNet		
2435 233rd Place NE Redmond, WA 98053 (206) 562-3000 ehood@nwnet.net	Northwestern U.S. (OR WA WY AK ID MT ND)	Dedicated (56Kb - 1.5Mb)

Table A.3: Regional Service Providers (continued)

Provider	Coverage	Services
NSTN		
201 Brownlow Ave. Dartmouth, NS Canada B3B 1W2 (902) 468-NSTN (6786) (902) 468-3679 (FAX) info@nstn.ns.ca, info-request@nstn.ns.ca	Nova Scotia, Ottowa, Toronto	Dedicated (9.6Kb - 56Kb) Dial-up SLIP
Nuance Network Services		
904 Bob Wallace Avenue Suite 119 Huntsville, AL 35801 (205) 533-4296 staff@nuance.com	Huntsville AL area	Dial-up SLIP/PPP ISDN
NYSERNet		
200 Elwood Davis Rd. Suite 103 Liverpool, NY 13088-6147 (315) 453-2912 info@nysernet.org	New York State	Dedicated (19.2Kb - 1.5Mb) Dial-up SLIP/PPP
Nyx		
Prof. Andrew Burt Dept. of Math & Computer Science University of Denver Denver, CO 80208 (303) 871-3324 (data) support@nyx.cs.du.edu	Denver/Boulder CO	Dial-up
Old Colorado City Communications		
2502 W. Colorado Ave., Suite 203 Colorado Springs, CO 80904 (719) 636-2040 (719) 593-7575 (719) 593-7521 (FAX) dave@oldcolo.com, thefox@oldcolo.com	Colorado Springs area	SLIP Dial-up

Table A.3: Regional Service Providers (continued)

Provider	Coverage	Services
Olympus		
(206) 385-0464 info@olympus.net	WA (Olympic Peninsula, E. Jefferson County)	Dedicated Dial-up PPP
Onet		
4 Bancroft Avenue Rm 118 University of Toronto Toronto, Ontario Canada M5S 1A1 (416) 978-8948 Warren.Jackson@UToronto.ca	Ontario, Canada	Institutional connections only
Panix		
162 W13 St. #31 New York, NY 10011 (212) 787-6160 (212) 787-3100 (data) info@panix.com, staff@panix.com	New York City and Long Island	Dedicated (1.5Mb) Dial-up SLIP/PPP UUCP
PEINet Inc.		
Berni Gardiner (902) 892-7346 gardiner@peinet.pe.ca	Prince Edward Island, Canada	Dedicated Dial-up SLIP
The Pipeline		
150 Broadway Suite 1710 New York, NY 10038 (212) 267-3636 (212) 267-9112 (data) infobot@pipeline.com	Metro New York	Dial-up SLIP/PPP
Portal Communications		
20863 Stevens Creek Boulevard Suite #200 Cupertino, CA 95014 (408) 973-9111 info@portal.com	San Francisco Bay	Dialup SLIP/PPP UUCP

Table A.3: Regional Service Providers (continued)

Provider	Coverage	Services
PREPnet		
305 S. Craig, 2nd Floor Pittsburgh, PA 15213 (412) 268-7870 twb+@andrew.cmu.edu	Pennsylvania, Delaware	Dedicated (9.6Kb - 1.5Mb) Frame Relay/SMDS Dial-up SLIP/PPP
PSCnet		
Pittsburgh Supercomputing Center 4400 5th Avenue Pittsburgh, PA 15213 (412) 268-4960 pscnet-admin@psc.edu	Eastern U.S.	Dedicated (Affiliated projects only)
Real/Time Communications		
6721 N. Lamar #103 Austin, TX 78752 (512) 451-0046 (512) 459-3858 (FAX) (512) 459-4391 (data) (512) 459-0604 (data) hosts@bga.com	Austin TX	Dedicated Dial-up SLIP/PPP UUCP
RISQ		
1801 Avenue McGill College Bureau 800 Montreal, Quebec Canada H3A 2N4 (514) 398-1234 turcotte@clouso.crim.ca	Quebec, Canada	Dedicated (19.2Kb - 10Mb) SLIP/PPP
Santa Cruz Community Internet		
903 Pacific Ave. #203A Santa Cruz, CA 95060 (408) 457-5050 info@scruz.net	Santa Cruz and San Jose CA	Dedicated (56Kb - 1.5Mb) ISDN SLIP/PPP

Table A.3: Regional Service Providers (continued)

Provider	Coverage	Services
SASK#net		
William Maes (306) 585-4132 wmaes@max.cc.uregina.ca	Saskatchewan	
Sesquinet		
Office of Networking Services Rice University Houston, TX 77251-1892 (713) 527-4988 farrell@rice.edu	Texas	Dedicated (9.6Kb - 1.5Mb)
South Coast Computing Services, Inc.		
P.O. Box 270355 Houston, TX 77277 (713) 661-3301 (713) 661-8593 (data) info@sccsi.com	Houston metro	Dedicated (56k) Dial-up SLIP/PPP
SSNet		
1254 Lorewood Grove Road Middletown, DE 19709 (302) 378-1386 (800) 331-1386 (302) 378-3871 (FAX) (302) 378-1881 (data) info@ssnet.com, sharris@ssnet.com	Delaware, Lower PA	Dial-up SLIP/PPP UUCP
SURAnet		
8400 Baltimore Boulevard Suite 101 College Park, MD 20740-2496 (301) 982-4600 (301) 982-4605 (FAX) info@sura.net	Southeastern U.S., Caribbean basin, and South America	Dedicated (56Kb - 45Mb) SMDS Dial-up, SLIP/PPP

Table A.3: Regional Service Providers (continued)

Provider	Coverage	Services
Teleport		
319 SW Washington #803 Portland, OR 97204 (503) 223-4245 (503) 223-4372 (FAX) (503) 220-1016 (data) info@teleport.com	Portland OR	Dial-up SLIP/PPP UUCP
Telerama		
P.O. Box 60024 Pittsburgh, PA 15211 (412) 481-3505 (412) 481-8568 (FAX) sysop@telerama.lm.com	Pittsburgh	Dial-up SLIP UUCP
Texas Metronet		
860 Kinwest Parkway Suite 179 Irving, TX 75063-3440 (214) 705-2900 (214) 705-2901 (data) info@metronet.com	Dallas (214) and Fort Worth (817)	Dial-up SLIP/PPP UUCP
The Little Garden		
(415) 487-1902 info@tlg.org	San Francisco Bay	Dedicated (56Kb - 1.5Mb) Full-time SLIP/PPP
THEnet		
Texas Higher Education Network Information Center c/o University of Texas System Office of Telecomm. Services Service Building, Room 319 Austin, TX 78712-1024 (512) 471-2400 info@nic.the.net	Texas (Education, research, and governmental communities only)	Dedicated (1.5Mb) Dial-up SLIP

Table A.3: Regional Service Providers (continued)

Provider	Coverage	Services
VERnet		
Academic Computing Center Gilmer Hall University of Virginia Charlottesville, VA 22903 net-info@ver.net (804) 924-0616	Virginia	Dedicated
Vnet		
Vnet Internet Access, Inc. PO Box 31474 Charlotte, NC 28231 (800) 377-3282 (Sales) (704) 334-3282 (Support) (704) 334-6880 (FAX) info@vnet.net	North Carolina, Atlanta	Dedicated Dial-up SLIP/PPP UUCP
Westnet		
c/o Pat Burns 601 S. Howes, 6th Floor Colorado State University Fort Collins, CO 80523 (303) 491-7260 pburns@westnet.net	Southwestern U.S. (AZ CO ID NM UT WY)	Dedicated
WiscNet		
1210 W. Dayton Street Madison, WI 53706 (608) 262-8874 dorl@macc.wisc.edu	Wisconsin	Dedicated (56Kb - 1.5Mb)
XNet		
XNet Information Systems P.O. Box 1511 Lisle, IL 60532 (708) 983-6064 (708) 983-6879 (FAX) (708) 983-6435 (data) info@xnet.com	Chicago area, DuPage County, Cook County	Dedicated Dial-up SLIP/PPP UUCP

Table A.3: Regional Service Providers (continued)

Provider	Coverage	Services
Zilker Internet Park		
1106 Clayton Lane Suite 500W Austin, TX 78623 (512) 206-3854 (512) 206-3852 (FAX) info@zilker.net	Austin, TX	Dedicated ISDN Dial-up SLIP/PPP

INTERNATIONAL NETWORK CONNECTIVITY

Summary of International Connectivity
Country Codes and Connectivity

Outside of the United States, the top-level domains used in Internet addresses are two-letter country codes. The country codes (and their names) are defined in an International standards document called ISO 3166. The bulk of this appendix is a table, distributed by Lawrence Landweber and the Internet Society, that shows all of these codes.* The table also shows what kind of network connectivity each country has. They aren't all connected to the Internet, so services like FTP and TELNET may not be available; but well over half have some kind of international network connectivity (whether BITNET, UUCP, Fidonet, or something else), so you can at least send email.

Summary of International Connectivity

The total number of entities with international network connectivity is 146. Figure B-1 summarizes the countries that have network connectivity, and the kind of connectivity they have.

Country Codes and Connectivity

Entries in the connectivity table look like this:

```
BIUFO AT        Austria
```

This entry means that AT is the top-level domain name for Austria; a domain name like **ffr.syh.at** is probably from an Internet site in Austria. The notation in the left column shows the kind of connectivity each country has, as shown in Table B-1.

---

*The official and up-to-date version of this information may be found on the Internet Society Gopher: *gopher.isoc.org/Internet Information/Charts & Graphs*. The name will be something like *Connectivi-tyChart*; the actual name varies with the version.

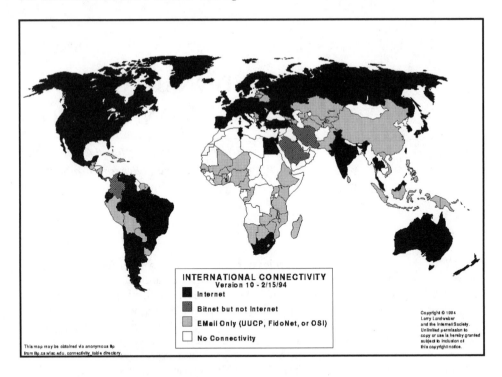

Figure B-1: International connectivity summary

Table B-1: Key to Connectivity Table

Key	Type of connectivity
- - - - -	No verified connectivity
B	Bitnet connectivity
I	Internet connectivity
U	UUCP connectivity
F	Fidonet connectivity
O	OSI connectivity

Lowercase letters indicate minimal connectivity; uppercase indicates widespread connectivity. This entry indicates that Austria has BITNET, Internet, UUCP, Fidonet, and OSI connectivity—i.e., every kind of connectivity that's currently possible.

The information in this list is available from the anonymous FTP site **ftp.wisc.edu**, in the directory *connectivity_table*. It's updated several times a year. We've made a number of modifications to the list to bring it closer to actual usage. For example, Great Britain uses the country code UK, rather than its assigned ISO code (GB). When the Soviet Union was dissolved, the SU code was deleted from the list; we put it back in, because it's still being used, along with the new country codes for the former Soviet states. We deleted Puerto Rico, even though it has its own country code (PR); as far as we know, Puerto Rican sites use the US codes. In the future, this can only get more complicated: when the Virgin Islands get on the Net, will they use their own country codes, or the US and UK domains?

-----	AF	Afghanistan		--u--	CG	Congo
-----	AL	Albania		--u--	CK	Cook Islands
-----	DZ	Algeria		bIuf-	CR	Costa Rica
-----	AS	American Samoa		--uf-	CI	Cote d'Ivoire
-----	AD	Andorra		-IuFo	HR	Croatia
-----	AO	Angola		--U--	CU	Cuba
-----	AI	Anguilla		bI---	CY	Cyprus
-I---	AQ	Antarctica		BIUF-	CZ	Czech Republic
-----	AG	Antigua and Barbuda		bIuFO	DK	Denmark
BIUF-	AR	Argentina		-----	DJ	Djibouti
--U--	AM	Armenia		-----	DM	Dominica
---f-	AW	Aruba		--Uf-	DO	Dominican Republic
-IUFo	AU	Australia		-----	TP	East Timor
BIUFO	AT	Austria		bIu--	EC	Ecuador
--U--	AZ	Azerbaijan		bIU--	EG	Egypt
-----	BS	Bahamas		-----	SV	El Salvador
b----	BH	Bahrain		-----	GQ	Equatorial Guinea
-----	BD	Bangladesh		-IUF-	EE	Estonia
--u--	BB	Barbados		---f-	ET	Ethiopia
--UF-	BY	Belarus		-----	FK	Falkland Islands
BIUFO	BE	Belgium		--u--	FO	Faroe Islands
--u--	BZ	Belize		-Iu--	FJ	Fiji
-----	BJ	Benin		BIUFO	FI	Finland
--Uf-	BM	Bermuda		BIUFO	FR	France
-----	BT	Bhutan		--u--	GF	French Guiana
--U--	BO	Bolivia		--u--	PF	French Polynesia
-----	BA	Bosnia-Herzegovina		-----	TF	French Southern Territories
--uf-	BW	Botswana		-----	GA	Gabon
-----	BV	Bouvet Island		-----	GM	Gambia
BIUFO	BR	Brazil		--UF-	GE	Georgia
-----	IO	British Indian Ocean Territory		BIUFO	DE	Germany
-----	BN	Brunei Darussalam		--uF-	GH	Ghana
bIUF-	BG	Bulgaria		-----	GI	Gibraltar
--U--	BF	Burkina Faso		BIUFO	GR	Greece
-----	BI	Burundi		-I-f-	GL	Greenland
-----	KH	Cambodia		--u--	GD	Grenada
--u--	CM	Cameroon		b-uf-	GP	Guadeloupe
BIUFO	CA	Canada		-I-F-	GU	Guam
-----	CV	Cape Verde		--u--	GT	Guatemala
-----	KY	Cayman Islands		-----	GN	Guinea
-----	CF	Central African Republic		-----	GW	Guinea-Bissau
-----	TD	Chad		-----	GY	Guyana
BIUF-	CL	Chile		-----	HT	Haiti
--u-O	CN	China		-----	HM	Heard and McDonald
-----	CX	Christmas Island		-----	HN	Honduras
-----	CC	Cocos (Keeling) Islands		BI-F-	HK	Hong Kong
B-u--	CO	Colombia		BIUFo	HU	Hungary
-----	KM	Comoros		-IUFo	IS	Iceland

bIUfO	IN	India
--u--	ID	Indonesia
b----	IR	Iran
-----	IQ	Iraq
BIUFO	IE	Ireland
BIUF-	IL	Israel
BIUFO	IT	Italy
--u--	JM	Jamaica
BIUF-	JP	Japan
-----	JO	Jordan
--Uf-	KZ	Kazakhstan
---f-	KE	Kenya
--u--	KI	Kiribati
-----	KP	Korea (People's Republic)
BIUFO	KR	Korea (Republic)
-I---	KW	Kuwait
--U--	KG	Kyrgyz Republic
-----	LA	Laos
-IUF-	LV	Latvia
-----	LB	Lebanon
--u--	LS	Lesotho
-----	LR	Liberia
-----	LY	Libya
-I-f-	LI	Liechtenstein
--UFo	LT	Lithuania
bIUFo	LU	Luxembourg
---F-	MO	Macau
--u--	MK	Macedonia
--u--	MG	Madagascar
---f-	MW	Malawi
bIUF-	MY	Malaysia
-----	MV	Maldives
--U--	ML	Mali
--u--	MT	Malta
-----	MH	Marshall Islands
-----	MQ	Martinique
-----	MR	Mauritania
--uf-	MU	Mauritius
-----	YT	Mayotte
BIuF-	MX	Mexico
-----	FM	Micronesia
--uF-	MD	Moldova
-----	MC	Monaco
-----	MN	Mongolia
-----	MS	Montserrat
-----	MA	Morocco
--Uf-	MZ	Mozambique
-----	MM	Myanmar
--Uf-	NA	Namibia
-----	NR	Nauru
-----	NP	Nepal
BIUFo	NL	Netherlands
--u--	AN	Netherlands Antilles
-----	NT	Neutral Zone (Saudia Arabia/Iraq)
--U--	NC	New Caledonia
-IUF-	NZ	New Zealand
--u--	NI	Nicaragua
--u--	NE	Niger
---f-	NG	Nigeria
--u--	NU	Niue
-----	NF	Norfolk Island
-----	MP	Northern Mariana Islands
BIUFO	NO	Norway
-----	OM	Oman
--U--	PK	Pakistan
-----	PW	Palau
b-uF-	PA	Panama
--u--	PG	Papua New Guinea
--u--	PY	Paraguay
--Uf-	PE	Peru
--uF-	PH	Philippines
-----	PN	Pitcairn
BIUF-	PL	Poland
bIUFO	PT	Portugal
-----	QA	Qatar
--u--	RE	Re'union
BIuf-	RO	Romania
BIUF-	RU	Russian Federation
-----	RW	Rwanda
-----	SH	Saint Helena
-----	KN	Saint Kitts and Nevis
--u--	LC	Saint Lucia
-----	PM	Saint Pierre and Miquelon
-----	VC	Saint Vincent and the Grenadines
--u--	WS	Samoa
-----	SM	San Marino
-----	ST	Sao Tome and Principe
B----	SA	Saudi Arabia
--Uf-	SN	Senegal
--u--	SC	Seychelles
-----	SL	Sierra Leone
bIuF-	SG	Singapore
bIuF-	SK	Slovakia
-IUFO	SI	Slovenia
--u--	SB	Solomon Islands
-----	SO	Somalia
-IUFO	ZA	South Africa
bIuF-	SU	Soviet Union (former)
BIUFO	ES	Spain
--U--	LK	Sri Lanka
-----	SD	Sudan
--u--	SR	Suriname
-----	SJ	Svalbard and Jan Mayen
--u--	SZ	Swaziland
BIUFo	SE	Sweden
BIUFO	CH	Switzerland
-----	SY	Syria
BIuF-	TW	Taiwan, Province of China
--uf-	TJ	Tajikistan
---f-	TZ	Tanzania

```
-IUF- TH   Thailand
--u-- TG   Togo
----- TK   Tokelau
--u-- TO   Tonga
--u-- TT   Trinidad and Tobago
bIUfo TN   Tunisia
BI-F- TR   Turkey
--u-- TM   Turkmenistan
----- TC   Turks and Caicos Islands
----- TV   Tuvalu
---f- UG   Uganda
-IUF- UA   Ukraine
----- AE   United Arab Emirates
bIUFO UK   United Kingdom
BIUFO US   United States
--UF- UY   Uruguay
--UF- UZ   Uzbekistan
--u-- VU   Vanuatu
----- VA   Vatican City State
-IU-- VE   Venezuela
--u-- VN   Vietnam
----- VG   Virgin Islands (British)
---f- VI   Virgin Islands (U.S.)
----- WF   Wallis and Futuna Islands
----- EH   Western Sahara
----- YE   Yemen
--uf- YU   Yugoslavia
----- ZR   Zaire
---f- ZM   Zambia
--uf- ZW   Zimbabwe
```

ACCEPTABLE USE

This is the official "acceptable use" policy for the NSFNET, dated June 1992. As of publication, this is the most recent version of this policy. You can get an up-to-date version of the policy via anonymous FTP from **nic.merit.edu**, in the file */nsfnet/acceptable.use.policies/nsfnet.txt*. This directory also contains the policies of several other networks.

Though the first paragraph of this policy sounds scary, don't be put off by it. As we said in Chapter 3, "support" of research and education is interpreted fairly loosely. And remember that the NSFNET is not the Internet. It's only a part of the Internet, and it has one of the strictest acceptable use policies. As time goes on, the NSFNET's policy is becoming less and less important. A primary goal of the recent efforts towards privatization is to create an Internet without acceptable use policies: i.e., a network where there are no restrictions on commercial use, hobbyist use, or otherwise.

Therefore, the network to which you connect may have a significantly different policy; some branches of the Internet actively encourage commercial use. Take up any questions with your service provider—your provider determines what's acceptable for your connection. If you want an Internet connection for strictly commercial or personal use, it's easy to find a provider who will serve you.

The NSFNET Backbone Services Acceptable Use Policy

General Principle:

- NSFNET Backbone services are provided to support open research and education in and among US research and instructional institutions, plus research arms of for-profit firms when engaged in open scholarly communication and research. Use for other purposes is not acceptable.

Specifically Acceptable Uses:

- Communication with foreign researchers and educators in connection with research or instruction, as long as any network that the foreign user employs for such communication provides reciprocal access to US researchers and educators.

- Communication and exchange for professional development, to maintain currency, or to debate issues in a field or subfield of knowledge.

- Use for disciplinary-society, university-association, government-advisory, or standards activities related to the user's research and instructional activities.

- Use in applying for or administering grants or contracts for research or instruction, but not for other fundraising or public relations activities.

- Any other administrative communications or activities in direct support of research and instruction.

- Announcements of new products or services for use in research or instruction, but not advertising of any kind.

- Any traffic originating from a network of another member agency of the Federal Networking Council if the traffic meets the acceptable use policy of that agency.

- Communication incidental to otherwise acceptable use, except for illegal or specifically unacceptable use.

Unacceptable Uses:

- Use for for-profit activities, unless covered by the General Principle or as a specifically acceptable use.

- Extensive use for private or personal business.

This statement applies to use of the NSFNET Backbone only. NSF expects that connecting networks will formulate their own use policies. The NSF Division of Networking and Communications Research and Infrastructure will resolve any questions about this Policy or its interpretation.

A UNIX PRIMER

Logging In
Command Basics
Directory Structure
Other Books

While you don't need to know UNIX to use the Internet, it can help—particularly if you access the Internet through a public-access UNIX system. Fortunately, though, you really only need to know a dozen or so simple commands. Here's a five-minute UNIX primer.

Logging In

UNIX is, by nature, a multi-user timesharing system. Whenever you start a UNIX session, you have to start by telling UNIX who you are. This is true whether you are at a terminal in your office or dialing into a huge public-access site. It's not like DOS, Windows, or the Macintosh, which are operating systems with no concept of multiple users. UNIX needs to know who you are to keep you and your property separate from the tens, hundreds, or maybe even thousands of other people who might be using the system.

We've already seen the UNIX login dialog in Chapter 5, *Remote Login*. Here's a brief recap:

```
SunOS UNIX (sonne)

login: krol        type your user name
Password:          type the password given to you by the sysadmin
Last login: Sat Sep  7 17:16:35 from ux1.uiuc.edu
SunOS Release 4.1(GENERIC) #1:Tue Mar 6 17:27:17 PST 1990
%                  now you're ready to go
```

The username is the name your account is known by; your system administrator will assign it when setting up your account. The password proves that you are who you say you are and prevents someone else from getting access to your account illegitimately. The system doesn't "echo" your password when you type it, to prevent other people from seeing it. Your system administrator will probably assign you an initial password and then tell you how to pick (and change) your password. Some hints about passwords are given in Chapter 4, *What's Allowed on the Internet.* The % is a prompt telling you that UNIX is ready to accept commands. The prompt may not be the same on the system you use; often, the UNIX prompt includes the computer's name.

On some systems, you may need to give a "dial-up password" when you log in through a phone line. The system administrator will give you the dial-up password to use, if you need one.

You may also be asked what kind of terminal you are using. Again, because UNIX is a time-sharing operating system, people can connect all kinds of hardware to it. The way you tell UNIX your terminal type varies, but it usually looks something like this:

```
Last login: Sat Sep  7 17:16:35 from ux1.uiuc.edu
SunOS Release 4.1(GENERIC) #1:Tue Mar 6 17:27:17 PST 1990
TERM=(vt100)?             prompt for terminal type
sonne%                    now you're ready to go
```

The line `(vt100)?` is saying "I think you're using a VT100 terminal. If that's true, type RETURN and you can go on. If it's not, tell me your terminal type." VT100 is a good guess, since most commonly used communications package support *VT100 emulation*—i.e., they know how to make your computer work like a VT100.

If UNIX is confused about your terminal type, all sorts of things will work incorrectly: you might find that carriage returns don't work, or that characters appear in reverse video, and all sorts of things. If you have problems, contact your system administrator.

To end your UNIX session, give the command **logout**.

Command Basics

We'll start by showing how UNIX commands work and then go on to list the most commonly used and necessary commands.

How Commands Look

Most UNIX commands look like this:

```
% command options arguments
```

That is, there's a command, followed by some options to the command, followed by some arguments. Arguments are usually names of files. The options all begin with a dash. For example, the command below says "execute the command **ls** with the option –l on the file *a.out*":

```
% ls -l a.out
```

That's 90 percent of what you need to know. Command names are almost always lowercase; options are usually single letters (either uppercase or lowercase). Unlike many other operating systems, UNIX cares about the difference between uppercase and lowercase.

If you use two or more single-letter options, most commands let you stick the options together. For example, these two commands are identical:

```
% ls -lg a.out
% ls -l -g a.out
```

Some options require arguments of their own. In that case, the option's argument follows the option, and the option can't be stuck together with others. This primer doesn't describe any of these commands.

There are a few commands that don't fit the rules very well, and one of these is important: that's **tar**. (The others you'll never need.) In the list of commands, I just give a "cookbook" for the three ways you'll need to use **tar**. Follow the cookbook, and you'll be OK.

Essential Commands

Here's the list of basic commands that I promised. I've shown MS-DOS equivalents in capital letters. Some of these commands are explained further below.

logout
> Terminate your UNIX session.

ls List the files in your current directory. It's the equivalent of DIR in many other operating systems. **ls -l** gives you more detailed information, including file size, ownership, and creation date. **ls** has many, many options, but –l is the one you'll use most often.

rm *files*
> DELETE (remove) one or more files. For example, **rm file1 file2 file3** deletes three files named *file1*, *file2*, and *file3*. The command **rm –i** asks you for confirmation before deleting each file.

mv *oldname newname*
> RENAME (move) a file from *oldname* to *newname*. Lots of people complain about the **mv** command—they have trouble remembering it, because it really means RENAME. They have a good point. However, UNIX users like to think about "moving files around" rather than renaming them. If you think in terms of moving files around, UNIX will make more sense.

cp *file1 file2*
> COPY *file1* into a new file, called *file2*.

more *file*
> Display an ASCII file on your screen, a page at a time. Type SPACE to see the next page. Many people use a command called **cat** for this purpose—and they complain, because the name is completely misleading. Well, that's their fault. **cat** wasn't designed to display files; it just happens to

work (though not very well). **more** is really a better tool; don't bother with **cat**.* Now, the name **more** isn't exactly intuitive either; it might help to remember the phrase "show me more of this file."

grep *pattern file*

Show all occurrences of *pattern* in a file. (I admit: this is about as unintuitive as command names get.) The search is case-sensitive. **grep** is used to find particular text strings in files. For example, if *phones* is a list of telephone numbers and names, the command

```
% grep "John Johnson" phones
```

finds John's entry in the phone list. Notice that we put quotes around the search pattern; the quotes *never* hurt, and they're necessary whenever you're searching for something with a space or an asterisk in it.

grep –i *pattern file*

Same as the previous command, except that it's not case-sensitive: upper-case and lowercase letters are the same.

pwd Show your current working directory.

cd *dir*

Change your working directory.

mkdir *dir*

Create a new directory called *dir*, with no files in it.

rmdir *dir*

Delete (remove) the directory called *dir*. *dir* must be empty—that is, it may not have any files in it.

man *command*

Display the UNIX on-line documentation about the given *command*.

uuencode *final-name* < *file* > *output*

Create an ASCII version of a binary file, suitable for shipping in a mail message. *final-name* is the name the file should have when it's unpacked; *file* is the name of the file you're encoding; and *output* is the encoded file that you'll mail off to someone else. The > and < symbols are for *standard input* and *standard output*, which we'll discuss briefly below.

uudecode *encoded-file*

The opposite of **uuencode**

---

*There is one time **cat** is useful for displaying files. It's a quick-and-dirty way to download a file; just turn on screen capture on your PC and then **cat** the file you want. But be careful: don't **cat** a binary file!

compress file

> Compress a file so that it takes up less storage. The result is a binary file with the same name as the original, with .Z added to the end. The original file is deleted. You can't mail a compressed file, because it's binary; however, you can **uuencode** it. A similar common UNIX program is **gzip**.

uncompress file

> Given a compressed file, get the original back. A similar common UNIX program is **gunzip**.

tar   tar was designed for making tapes (the name stands for "tape archive"), but it's also used to create file archives (conglomerates that include several files), like the ones you find on the Internet. Its command structure is weird. Rather than explain how **tar** works, I'll just give you the three commands that do everything you'll need. In these examples, *file.tar* is a tar archive. In the first two, we'll work with an archive you got from somewhere else. In the last, we'll create an archive.

```
% tar tf file.tar          --list files in the archive
% tar xf file.tar          --extract files from the archive
% tar cf file.tar list     --create a new archive, including
                                the files in list
```

Standard Input and Output

Historically, one of UNIX's strengths has been the flexibility of its input and output system. Most commands send their output to your terminal. However, you can save the output of any command in a file by *redirecting* it. Similarly, many commands take their input from your keyboard; however, you can redirect the input from a file. (The secret behind this is that UNIX treats all I/O operations the same way—everything "looks like" a file. You don't have to understand what that means to use UNIX, though.)

> *file* Standard output; put the output into a file, instead of sending it to the screen. Anything already in the file is destroyed. For example, if you want to list the files in your directory, but you want to save the list in a file rather than viewing it, you can give the command:

```
% ls -l > filelist.
```

>> *file* Standard output, append; put the output into a file, following whatever is already there.

< *file* Standard input; take the input from a file, instead of sending it to the screen. The **uuencode** command listed earlier uses standard input and output; for an example, look back at that.

| *another-command*

> Pipe; take the standard output of one program and use it as the standard input of another. This is really one of UNIX's best features; you

can use it to create your own commands. Let's say you want a list of all the files that belong to **edk**. You can't do this with any of the **ls** command's many options. However, you can use a pipe to combine **ls -l** and **grep**:

```
% ls -l | grep "edk"
```

ls -l lists all the files, including ownership information, and **grep** extracts the entries that contain the string **edk**. If you only use UNIX occasionally, you can get by without pipes. If you start doing anything substantial with pipes, you'll quickly realize how useful they are.

Standard input and output redirectors are generally put at the end of the command, following all the options and arguments.

Directory Structure

Like MS-DOS and the Macintosh, UNIX has a hierarchical (or "tree-structured") filesystem. This means that every file is in a *directory*; directories can include other directories. The Macintosh calls directories "folders"; DOS and Windows systems use the same language as UNIX for talking about files and directories.

UNIX uses a slash (/) to separate the directory names.* For example, */home/john/letters/mom.txt* means "the file *mom.txt*, in the directory *letters*, in the directory *john*, in the directory *home*. We could also say that *john* is a subdirectory of the directory *home*, and so on.

You should notice a few other things about this example:

- The name begins with a /. The initial / means "the root directory," which is essentially the point at which all of the system's disk drives are glued together. In UNIX, you never refer to a disk drive itself; you always refer to subdirectories under the root.

- UNIX systems are, by nature, multi-user systems. Every user is assigned a "home directory" to keep his or her own files, even if the system only has one user. */home/john* is probably the home directory for the user "john."

- Users can also create their own directories, just as John has created a *letters* directory.

Our sample filename, */home/john/letters/mom.txt*, is called an *absolute pathname*, because it shows an entire "path" for locating the file, starting from the root, or /. However, you don't need to use absolute pathnames all the time. Here are a few abbreviations:

- At any time, you have a *working directory*. You can give paths that are relative to your working directory, rather than absolute paths from the root. For example, if your working directory is */home/john*, you can use *letters/mom.txt*;

---

*Note that MS-DOS uses a backwards slash, or backslash (\) for the same purpose. Folklore has it that the developers of DOS were trying to make it look like UNIX, but got it wrong.

if your working directory is */home/john/letters*, you can just use the filename, *mom.txt*. (In fact, that's what you'll do most of the time: refer to a file within your current working directory.)

The command **pwd** prints the name of your working directory; **cd** *dir* changes your working directory. So, if your working directory is */home/john*, **cd letters** moves you into the *letters* directory. **mkdir** *dir* creates a new directory; and **rmdir** *dir* deletes a directory—provided that it doesn't contain any files.

- You can use the abbreviation ~ to mean your home directory, or *~name* to mean "the home directory of user *name*." For example, *~john/letters/mom.txt* is another way of referring to John's letter to his mother. The command **cd** (with no argument) always takes you back to your home directory, regardless of your starting point.

- The abbreviation .. means "the parent directory." It's most often used with **cd** commands; for example, if your current directory is *~john/letters*, the command **cd ..** moves you back to *~john*.

You should become familiar with the way UNIX organizes files. Unlike personal computers, which typically have relatively small disks, UNIX systems usually have large disks, and many of them. Gigabyte disk drives are common, and most systems have several disk drives. A large system may have dozens. (By the way, that's why it's good that you never refer to the disk drives themselves. All the information UNIX needs is contained in the directory structure.) The more storage there is, the more important it is to organize it well; and the more important directories become.

Legal Filenames

UNIX doesn't have very many rules about filenames. On most modern UNIX systems, filenames can have any length. Filenames can also include just about any character—except for the slash (/), which is used to separate directories. However, you're best off limiting yourself to upper- and lowercase letters, numbers, periods (.) and commas (,). Spaces and other special characters can be made to work, but they require special handling. Rather than explaining how, my advice is "just say no."

Don't put a period at the beginning of a filename; the UNIX **ls** command won't list it, unless you give the special command **ls -a**. This is actually a nice feature—it lets you "hide" certain files so they won't clutter up your directory listings. However, if you're new to UNIX, you'll find it confusing.

Filename Wildcards

The standard UNIX filename wildcards are *, ?, and [ ]. * is by far the most frequently used. Their meanings are:

- *: match anything. For example: * by itself matches any file in your directory; *.**txt** matches any filename ending in .**txt**; and **gorilla.*** matches any filename begining with **gorilla**.

- ?: match any single character. For example: **source.?** matches **source.h**, **source.c**, **source.y**, and any other single letter.

- [. . .]: match any single character that's given inside the brackets. You can list individual characters: for example, **[chyf]** matches c, h, y, or f. You can also list ranges: for example, **[a-z]** matches any lowercase letter, and **[a-z0-9A-Z]** matches any alphabetic character or numeral. Note that any single range should not mix upper- and lowercase letters, or letters and numbers. **[a-Z]** or **[A-9]** would have surprising results—they might do what you intended, but only if you're lucky.

You can count on the wildcards listed above no matter what version of UNIX you're using.

Unfortunately, you can't use the filename wildcards in the "pattern" part of a **grep** command. Instead, **grep** uses a more complex feature called "regular expressions," which I won't describe.* You can, of course, use wildcards in the *file* part of a **grep** command: for example,

```
% grep "John Johnson" *
```

searches for John's name in all files in your current directory.

Other Books

There are many introductory books about UNIX. Here are a few that might help you:

- *Learning the UNIX Operating System*, by Grace Todino, John Strang, and Jerry Peek (O'Reilly & Associates): A good general introduction. It's short and to the point, but very accessible to new users.

- *Life with UNIX*, by Don Libes (Prentice-Hall, 1989). Another general introduction that has helped many people.

- *UNIX in a Nutshell* (O'Reilly & Associates) provides a brief summary of all the UNIX commands. There are different versions of this book for different versions of the UNIX operating system.

- *Learning the Vi Editor*, by Linda Lamb and *Learning Emacs*, by Deb Cameron and Bill Rosenblatt (both published by O'Reilly & Associates). You can't do much with an operating system if you can't edit files. The most commonly used editors for UNIX are **vi** and **emacs**. They are too complicated to describe here, but these books provide excellent introductions.

---

*I've refused to talk about regular expressions elsewhere, and I'm not going to change my mind here! Seriously, they can be complicated; the best detailed discussion available is in the Nutshell Handbook *sed and awk*, by Dale Dougherty. They are also discussed in most UNIX handbooks, including most of the books listed in the following section.

GLOSSARY

AFS

A set of protocols that allows you to use files on other network machines *as if* they were local. So, rather than using FTP to transfer a file to your local computer, you can read it, write it, or edit it on the remote computer—using the same commands that you'd use locally. Very similar in concept to NFS (q.v.), though it provides better performance. Not yet in widespread use, though a commercial version is currently available from a company called Transarc.

Application

(a) Software that performs a particular useful function for you. ("Do you have an electronic mail application installed on your computer?")

(b) The useful function itself (e.g., transferring files is a useful application of the Internet.)

Archie

A system for locating files that are publicly available by anonymous FTP. Archie is described in Chapter 9, *Finding Software*.

ARPAnet

An experimental network established in the 70's where the theories and software on which the Internet is based were tested. No longer in existence.

baud

When transmitting data, the number of times the medium's "state" changes per second. For example: a 2400-baud modem changes the signal it sends on the phone line 2400 times per second. Since each change in state can correspond to multiple bits of data, the actual bit rate of data transfer may exceed the baud rate. Also, see "bits per second."

BIND

The UNIX implementation of DNS (q.v.). It stands for "Berkeley Internet Name Domain."

bits per second (bps)

The speed at which bits are transmitted over a communications medium.

BTW

Common abbreviation in mail and news, meaning "by the way."

Chat

See "IRC chat."

CIX

Commercial Internet Exchange; an agreement among network providers that allows them to do accounting for commercial traffic. Although it has been discussed a lot in the press, it's primarily a concern for network providers.

client

A software application (q.v.) that works on your behalf to extract a service from a server somewhere on the network. Think of your telephone as a client and the telephone company as a server to get the idea.

datagram

A packet (q.v.) of information that is sent to the receiving computer without any prior warning. Conceptually, a "datagram" is somewhat like a telegram: it's a self-contained message that can arrive at any time, without notice. Datagraphs are usually used in applications where the amount of information transfer is occasional and small.

DDN

Defense Data Network; a portion of the Internet which connects to U.S. military bases and contractors; used for non-secure communications. MILNET is one of the DDN networks. The DDN used to run "the NIC," which coordinated the Internet as a whole. However, the InterNIC (q.v.) has taken over that function; now the DDN NIC is only responsible for the DDN.

DECnet

A set of proprietary networking protocols used by Digital Equipment Corporation operating systems, instead of TCP/IP. These protocols are not compatible with the Internet.

dedicated line

See "leased line."

DFS

For all practical purposes, another name for AFS. More specifically, DFS refers to the AFS implementation that's part of the Open Software Foundation's DCE (Distributed Computing Environment). Enough letters for you?

dial-up

(a) A connection to a computer made by calling the computer up on the telephone. Often, dial-up only refers to the kind of connection you make when using a terminal emulator and a regular modem. For the technoids: switched character-oriented asynchronous communication.

(b) A port (q.v.) that accepts dial-up connections. ("How many dial-up ports on your computer?")

DNS

The Domain Name System; a distributed database system for translating computer names (like **ruby.ora.com**) into numeric Internet addresses (like **194.56.78.2**), and vice-versa. DNS allows you to use the Internet without remembering long lists of numbers.

DoD

The (U.S.) Department of Defense, whose Advanced Research Projects Agency got the Internet started by funding the ARPAnet.

Ethernet

A kind of "local area network." It's pretty confusing because there are several different kinds of wiring, which support different communication speeds, ranging from 2 to 10 million bits per second. What makes an Ethernet an Ethernet is the way the computers on the network decide whose turn it is to talk. Computers using TCP/IP are frequently connected to the Internet over an Ethernet.

FAQ

Either a frequently asked question, or a list of frequently asked questions and their answers. Many USENET newsgroups, and some non-USENET mailing lists, maintain FAQ lists (FAQs) so that participants don't spend lots of time answering the same set of questions.

Flame

A virulent and (often) largely personal attack against the author of a USENET posting. "Flames" are unfortunately common. People who frequently write flames are known as "flamers."

followup

A response to a USENET posting (q.v.).

Frame Relay

A data communication technology which is sometimes used to provide higher speed (above 56Kb and less than 1.5Mb) for Internet connections. Its usual application is in connecting work groups rather than individuals.

Free-net

An organization to provide free Internet access to people in a certain area, usually through public libraries.

FTP

(a) The File Transfer Protocol; a protocol that defines how to transfer files from one computer to another.

(b) An application program which moves files using the File Transfer Protocol. FTP is described in detail in Chapter 6, *Moving Files: FTP.*

FYI

(a) A common abbreviation in mail and news, meaning "for your information."

(b) A series of informative papers about the Internet; they're similar to RFCs (q.v.), but don't define new standards.

gateway

A computer system that transfers data between normally incompatible applications or networks. It reformats the data so that it is acceptable for the new network (or application) before passing it on. A gateway might connect two dissimilar networks, like DECnet and the Internet; or it might allow two incompatible applications to communicate over the same network (like mail systems with different message formats). The term is often used interchangeably with router (q.v.), but this usage is incorrect.

Gopher

A menu-based system for exploring Internet resources. Gopher is described in detail in Chapter 11, *Tunneling Through the Internet: Gopher.*

html

Hypertext markup language; the language in which World Wide Web documents are written.

hypermedia

A combination of hypertext (q.v.) and multimedia (q.v.).

hypertext

Documents that contain links to other documents; selecting a link automatically displays the second document.

IAB

The Internet Architecture Board; the "ruling council" that makes decisions about standards and other important issues.

IETF

The Internet Engineering Task Force; a volunteer group that investigates and solves technical problems and makes recommendations to the IAB (q.v.).

IMHO

Common abbreviation in mail and news, meaning "in my humble opinion."

Internet

(a) Generally (not capitalized), any collection of distinct networks working together as one.

(b) Specifically (capitalized), the world-wide "network of networks" that are connected to each other, using the IP protocol and other similar protocols. The Internet provides file transfer, remote login, electronic mail, news, and other services.

InterNIC

The combined name for the providers of registration, information, and database services to the Internet. The InterNIC is discussed in the "Introduction" to the *Resource Catalog*. It provides many network resources of its own.

IP

The Internet Protocol; the most important of the protocols on which the Internet is based. It allows a packet to traverse multiple networks on the way to its final destination.

IRC chat

A service that allows large group conversations over the Internet.

ISDN

Integrated Services Digital Network; a digital telephone service. Essentially, with ISDN service, the phone lines to your house are carrying digital signals, rather than analog signals. If you have the appropriate hardware and software, if your local central office provides ISDN service, and if your service provider supports it (a lot of ifs), ISDN allows high-speed home access to the Internet (56Kb).

ISO

The International Organization for Standardization; an organization that has defined a different set of network protocols, called the ISO/OSI protocols. In theory, the ISO/OSI protocols will eventually replace the Internet Protocol. When and if this will actually happen is a hotly debated topic.

ISOC

The Internet Society: an organization whose members support a worldwide information network. It is also the governing body to which the IAB (q.v.) reports.

Knowbot

An experimental information-retrieval tool; a "robotic librarian." There isn't much to say about them yet, but they're something to watch for.

Leased line

A permanently connected private telephone line between two locations.

Leased lines are typically used to connect a moderate-sized local network to an Internet service provider.

mail reflector

A special mail address; electronic mail sent to this address is automatically forwarded to a set of other addresses. Typically, used to implement a mail discussion group.

MILNET

One of the DDN networks that make up the Internet; devoted to non-classified military (U.S.) communications. It was built using the same technology as the ARPAnet, and remained in production when the ARPAnet was decommissioned.

modem

A piece of equipment that connects a computer to a data transmission line (typically a telephone line of some sort). Most people use modems that transfer data at speeds ranging from 1200 bits per second (bps) to 19.2 Kbps. There are also modems providing higher speeds and supporting other media. These are used for special purposes—for example, to connect a large local network to its network provider over a leased line.

Mosaic

One particular browser for the World Wide Web that supports hypermedia. Mosaic is often used (incorrectly) as a synonym for the World Wide Web.

MUD

Multi-User Dungeon; a group of role-playing games modelled on the original "Dungeons and Dragons" games. MUDs have also been used in other contexts; they have been used as conferencing tools and educational aids.

Multimedia

Documents that include different kinds of data; for example, plain text and audio, or text in several different languages, or plain text and a spreadsheet.

NIC

(a) Network Information Center; any organization that's responsible for supplying information about any network.

(b) The DDN's NIC, which plays an important role in overall Internet coordination.

NFS

The Network File System; a set of protocols that allows you to use files on other network machines *as if* they were local. So, rather than using FTP to transfer a file to your local computer, you can read it, write it, or edit it on the remote computer—using the same commands that you'd use locally. NFS was originally developed by Sun Microsystems, Inc. and is currently in widespread use.

NNTP

Network News Transfer Protocol: the protocol used to transfer USENET news articles between computers on the Internet.

NOC

Network Operations Center; a group which is responsible for the day-to-day care and feeding of a network. Each service provider usually has a separate NOC, so you need to know which one to call when you have problems.

NREN

The National Research and Education Network; a U.S. effort to combine networks operated by different federal agencies into a single high-speed network. While this transition will be of significant technical and historical importance, it should have no effect on the typical Internet user.

NSFNET

The National Science Foundation Network; the NSFNET is *not* the Internet. It's just one of the networks that make up the Internet.

NTP

Network Time Protocol: a protocol used to synchronize time between computers on the Internet.

octet

Internet standards-monger's lingo for a set of eight bits, i.e., a *byte*.

OSI

Open Systems Interconnect; another set of network protocols. See "ISO."

packet

A bundle of data. On the Internet, data is broken up into small chunks, called *packets*; each packet traverses the network independently. Packet sizes can vary from roughly 40 to 32,000 bytes, depending on network hardware and media, but packets are normally less than 1500 bytes long.

port

(a) A number that identifies a particular Internet application. When your computer sends a packet to another computer, that packet contains information about what protocol it's using (e.g., TCP or UDP), and what application it's trying to communicate with. The port number identifies the application.

(b) One of a computer's physical input/output channels (i.e., a plug on the back).

Unfortunately, these two meanings are completely unrelated. The first is more common when you're talking about the Internet (as in "**telnet** to port 1000"); the second is more common when you're talking about hardware ("connect your modem to the serial port on the back of your computer.")

posting

An individual article sent to a USENET (q.v.) newsgroup; or the act of sending an article to a USENET newsgroup.

PPP

Point-to-Point Protocol; a protocol that allows a computer to use the TCP/IP (Internet) protocols (and become a full-fledged Internet member) with a standard telephone line and a high-speed modem. PPP is a new standard, which replaces SLIP (q.v.). Although PPP is less common than SLIP, it's quickly increasing in popularity.

protocol

A protocol is just a definition of how computers will act when talking to each other. Protocol definitions range from how bits are placed on a wire to the format of an electronic mail message. Standard protocols allow computers from different manufacturers to communicate; the computers can use completely different software, providing that the programs running on both ends agree on what the data means.

Relevance feedback

The process of using a document that you retrieved in a search to further refine your search. WAIS supports relevance feedback, though (currently) only through WAIS clients (and at that, not all WAIS clients). Advanced World Wide Web browsers like Mosaic may support relevance feedback for WAIS servers in the future.

RFC

Request for Comments; a set of papers in which the Internet's standards, proposed standards, and generally agreed-upon ideas are documented and published.

router

A system that transfers data between two networks that use the same protocols. The networks may differ in physical characteristics (e.g., a router may transfer data between an Ethernet and a leased telephone line).

RTFM

Common abbreviation in mail and news, meaning "read the ... manual."

server

(a) Software that allows a computer to offer a service to another computer. Other computers contact the server program by means of matching client (q.v.) software.

(b) The computer on which the server software runs.

service provider

An organization that provides connections to a part of the Internet. If you want to connect your company's network, or even your personal computer, to the Internet, you have to talk to a service provider.

shell

On a UNIX system, software that accepts and processes command lines from your terminal. UNIX has multiple shells available (e.g., C shell, Bourne shell, Korn shell), each with slightly different command formats and facilities.

signature

A file, typically five lines long or so, that people often insert at the end of electronic mail messages or USENET news articles. A signature contains, minimally, a name and an email address. Signatures usually also contain postal addresses, and often contain silly quotes, pictures, and other things. Some are very elaborate, though signatures more than five or six lines long are in questionable taste.

SLIP

Serial Line IP; a protocol that allows a computer to use the Internet protocols (and become a full-fledged Internet member) with a standard telephone line and a high-speed modem. SLIP is being superseded by PPP (q.v.), but is still in common use.

smiley

Smiling faces used in mail and news to indicate humor and irony. The most common smiley is :-). You'll also see :-(, meaning disappointment, and lots of other variations. Since the variations are so, er, "variant," it's not worth going into detail. You'll pick up their connotations with time.

SRI

A California-based research institute that runs the Network Information Systems Center (NISC). The SRI has played an important role in coordinating the Internet.

switched access

A network connection that can be created and destroyed as needed. Dial-up connections are the simplest form of switched connections. SLIP or PPP also are commonly run over switched connections.

TCP

The Transmission Control Protocol. One of the protocols on which the Internet is based. For the technoids, TCP is a connection-oriented reliable protocol.

TELNET

(a) A "terminal emulation" protocol that allows you to log in to other computer systems on the Internet.

(b) An application program that allows you to log in to another computer system using the TELNET protocol. **telnet** is described in detail in Chapter 5, *Remote Login*.

timeout

A timeout is what happens when two computers are "talking" and one computer—for any reason—fails to respond. The other computer will keep on trying for a certain amount of time, but will eventually "give up."

tn3270

A special version of the **telnet** program that interacts properly with IBM mainframes.

Token ring

A technology for creating a local area network that may then be connected to the Internet. Token ring networks often use the TCP/IP protocols. See also "Ethernet."

UDP

The User Datagram Protocol. Another of the protocols on which the Internet is based. For the technoids, UDP is a connectionless unreliable protocol. If you're not a technoid, don't let the word "unreliable" worry you.

UNIX

A popular operating system that was very important in the development of the Internet. Contrary to rumor, though, you do NOT have to use UNIX to use the Internet. There are various flavors of UNIX. Two common ones are BSD and System V.

USENET

The USENET is an informal, rather anarchic, group of systems that exchange "news." News is essentially similar to "bulletin boards" on other networks. USENET actually predates the Internet, but these days, the Internet is used to transfer much of the USENET's traffic. USENET is described in detail in Chapter 8, *Network News*.

UUCP

UNIX-to-UNIX copy; a facility for copying files between UNIX systems, on which mail and USENET news services were built. While UUCP is still useful, the Internet provides a better way to do the same job.

Veronica

A service, very similar to Archie, that's built into Gopher. Just as Archie allows you to search all FTP sites for files, Veronica allows you to search all Gopher sites for menu items (files, directories, and other resources). Veronica is described in Chapter 11, *Tunneling Through the Internet: Gopher.*

WAIS

Wide Area Information Service; a very powerful system for looking up information in databases (or libraries) across the Internet. WAIS is described in detail in Chapter 12, *Searching Indexed Databases: WAIS.*

White Pages

Lists of Internet users that are accessible through the Internet. There are several different kinds of white-pages servers and services, described in Chapter 10, *Finding Someone.*

World Wide Web

A hypertext-based system for finding and accessing Internet resources. WWW is described in Chapter 13, *Hypertext Spanning the Internet: WWW.*

WWW

See "World Wide Web."

TECHNICAL INDEX

10baseT Ethernet, troubleshooting, 360
= (equals sign) command, 259

A

"acceptable use" policy, 495
account command (in ftp), 79
addresses, aliases for, 116
America Online, 107
Applelink, 107
ATTmail, 107
Bix, 107
Compuserve, 108
Delphi, 107
email, 106-110;
acquiring, 110;
format, 110
eWorld, 107
Fidonet, 108
MCImail, 109
Prodigy, 107
Sprintmail, 108
UUCP, 109
Advanced Networks and Services
(ANS), 37, 467
advertising, 376
AFS, 336, 505
AgNIC, 373
agricultural extension service,
374
aliases, and mailing lists, 119
for addresses, 116
almanac, 139, 143, 375
file retrieval, 145-146
Alternative Newsgroup (alt
news) Hierarchies, 155
AlterNet, 467

American Online addresses, 107
Andrew Filesystem (AFS), 336
anonymous ftp, 81-83
and bypassing passwords, 45
list of servers, 199
ANS, 37, 467
APNIC, 373
Applelink addresses, 107
application gateways, 106
application protocols, 52
applications, 29, **505**
Archie, 187-205, 371, 378, **505**
access through gopher, 188
and Telnet, 191-201
and X Windows, 205
bugs in, 199
commands, 198-202
compressing files, 201
contacting, 189-191
directing responses of, 201
getting description of, 199
getting list of anonymous
FTP servers, 199, 201
getting variable values, 200
getting version of, 200
help in, 199, 201
limiting output of, 200
list of servers, 190
listing files that match keyword, 202
look for specific files, 201
paging in, 200
quitting, 202
search results via email, 199
searches, 257
setting default email address,
200
setting parameters, 199
setting terminal type, 200

Archie (cont'd)
    sorting output, 200
    unsetting variables, 200
    using by electronic mail,
      201-203
    (see also files, searching
      for.)
Archie command, 203
archival utilities, BACKUP
    (VMS), 89
    shell, 88-89
    ZIP, 89
ARPAnet, 13, **505**
articles, (see News articles)
ASCII command, 74
    in ftp, 79
ASCII files, sending as binary,
    124
    transferring, 74
askcc, 121
ATTmail addresses, 107
audio on the Internet, 349-350
AUI, 363
auto-selecting News articles, 167

B

BACKUP (VMS), 89
baud, **505**
binary command (in ftp), 79
binary files, and Gopher, 258
    sending as ASCII, 124
    transferring, 74
BIND, 505
bionet newsgroup, 155
bit newsgroup, 155
BITFTP, 148
BITNET, 15, 139
bits per second (bps), 505
Bix addresses, 107
biz newsgroups, 155
bookmarks, in gopher, 260-262
Boolean variables, and Archie,
    200
bounced email, 132
browsers, 287
BTW, 506

bugs, in Archie, 199
bugs command, Archie, 199
bus, Ethernet cable, 363

C

cable, Ethernet, 363
cancelling, messages, 123
carbon copies, 121-122
    blind, 122
carriage returns, telnet, 55
case-sensitive, commands, 177
    searches, 247
Cc, 121
cd command, 73
    in ftp, 79-80
censorship on the Internet, 157
CERT, 44
CIX, 506
Clarinet, 156
    newsgroup, 156
clients, 51, **506**
    mimicking alternate, 58
close command, ftp, 79
    telnet, 53
coaxial Ethernets, 363-365
.COM files, 91
command mode, telnet, 52-55
commands, Archie, 203
    ftp, 79-81
    nn Newsreader, 176-180
    R, 325
    rcp, 325, 329-331
    rdist, 331-333
    rlogin, 325, 327-329
    telnet, 53-55
    Web, 293
commercial information ser-
    vices, 156
commercial use of the Internet,
    37
comp newsgroups, 154
compressing files, 83-84
    Archie, 201
Compuserve addresses, 108
Computer Emergency Response
    Team (CERT), 44
computer newsgroups, 154
connecting to, ftp site, 80

connecting to (cont'd)
Internet, 7-10, 457-488;
international connections,
18
"connection closed by foreign
host" error message, 60
consultant.micro.umn.edu,
Gopher client, 237
conversations on the Net,
339-346
talk program, 340-341
Ytalk program, 342
copying, files and directories via
the network, 325
files from the Internet, 65-99
cpio utility, 89
CSO, directories, 212
name servers, 251
cursor positioning, 62

D

daemons, 51
data, compression, 83
sending binary as ASCII, 124
transferring, 74
datagram, 506
DDN, 506
DECnet, 15, **506**
decompressing files, 84
decrypting News articles, 171
dedicated Internet access, 458
delete command (in ftp), 80
deleting files, 80
Delphi addresses, 107
Department of Defense, 507
destination files, 67
DFS, 506
dial-up connections, 506
Internet access, 460
troubleshooting, 361-362
Digital Equipment VMS systems,
and ftp, 90
filename wildcards, 70
dir command, 69
ftp, 80
directories, and ftp, 73
copying, 331
listing, 80

moving, 85-89
printing name of current
remote, 80
directory services, 373
.DIR files, 91
disk sharing, 335-336
display command, telnet, 53
distribution of News articles,
174
DNS, 30-34, **507**
DoD (Department of Defense),
507
domain name lookup, 32
Domain Name System (DNS),
30-34
domains, 30-34
high-level, 32
DOS systems, and ftp, 93

E

echoing, turning on/off, 53
editors, using in email, 115
education (using Internet for),
36
electronic mail, (see email)
email, 101-146
addresses, 106-110;
acquiring, 110;
format, 110;
setting default, 200
and file retrieval, 143
and using Archie, 201-203
bouncing, 132
cancelling, 123
carbon copies, 121-122
choosing packages, 110-111
editing, 115
etiquette, 104
features, 115
forwarding, 117
how it works, 105-106
multimedia, 126-132
multiple recipients, 137
reading, 112, 123
receiving, 123
replying to, 120

email (cont'd)
    replying to News articles
      with, 175
    returned, 132
    saving, 117
    sending, 114
    undeliverable, 136
    unknown hosts, 133
    unknown recipients, 135
    using editors in, 115
    writing hints, 104
    (see also messages.)
encrypting News articles, 171
error messages, 356-357
    "connection closed by for-
      eign host", 60
    "host not responding", 68
    "host timed out", 68
    "host unreachable", 68
    "login incorrect", 68
    "no such file or directory",
      68
    "returned mail", 136
    "service unavailable", 136
    "unknown hosts", 133
    "unknown recipients", 135
    "user unknown", 137
escape character, and telnet, 52,
    54
escape key, versus escape char-
    acter, 52
escape sequences, in rlogin, 329
/etc/hosts.equiv, 326
Ethernet, 507
    cable, 363
    coaxial, 363-365
    terminator caps, 363
    transceiver cable, 363
ethics and the Internet, 40-43
etiquette, in email, 104
eWorld addresses, 107
executable (.EXE) files, 76, 91
export laws, 37

F

FAQs (Frequently Asked Ques-
    tions), 175, 239, 370, **507**
FAX (over the Internet), 338-339
Fidonet addresses, 108
file command, 76
files, compressed, 83
    copying from the Internet,
      65-99
    decompressing, 84
    deleting, 80
    destination of, 67
    distributing, 331-333
    finding on the Internet, 187
    including in email, 119, 123
    listing, 69
    moving, 65-99;
      between systems, 329-331
    retrieving, 143
    searching for, 187;
      by directory, 196;
      by filename, 192, 195;
      within a domain, 196
    sharing, 335-336
    signature, 122
    source, 67
    suffixes for, 84
    tar, 87
    transferring, 72;
      ASCII, 74;
      binary, 74;
      large, 83;
      multiple, 77, 83;
      with ftp, 65-99
find command, Archie, 199
finding resources (on your own),
    370
finding things on the Internet,
    233-264
    (see also Gopher.)
finger command, 212-215
flames, 176, **507**
folders, 116
    appending to, 117
    creating, 117
follow-up, 507
    articles, 171, 184
.FOR files, 91
.forward file, 117

forwarding email, 117
Frame Relay, 507
fred, 223
Free Software Foundation (FSF), 88, 156, 309
  newsgroup, 156
Free-net, 507
Frequently Asked Questions (FAQs), 370
From field, in email, 120
ftp, 65-99, **508**
  and directories, 73
  and Gopher, 256-259
  anonymous; (see anonymous ftp)
  changing directories in, 79-80
  closing connection in, 79
  commands, 79-81
  confirmation prompting before transfer, 80
  connecting to site, 80
  deleting files, 80
  directory listing, 80
  documentation for, 80
  ending session in, 80
  entering ASCII mode, 79
  entering binary mode, 79
  exiting, 80
  getting multiple files, 80
  information about accounting, 79
  information about data transfer, 80
  on different systems, 89-97
  sending multiple files, 80
  sending username to remote machine, 81
  showing current remote directory, 80
  using, 66-81
ftpmail, 143, 146-148
FYI, 508

G

games, Multi-User Dungeon (MUD), 347-349
  playing on the Internet, 346-349
gatewayed newsgroups, 156
gateways, 508
  application, 106
German newsgroup, 155
GNN, 376
  interest centers, 376
  marketplace, 377
GNU, newsgroup, 156
  project, 156
Gopher, 234-242, 371, 378, 380, **508**
  accessing, 236
  and ftp, 256-259, 308-310
  and telnet, 259-260
  and the Web, 291-293
  bookmarks, 260-262
  development of, 263
  history of, 236
  how it works, 238
  index searches in, 244-247
  jughead searches in, 251
  licensing restrictions, 235
  looking at text files, 240-242
  moving between servers, 242-243
  paging in, 241
  saving items, 242
  searches, 247
  using, 238-242
  Veronica searches in, 247-251
  what it is doing while you wait, 259
  (see also Gopher clients.)
Gopher clients, 236-238
  for different computers, 236
  public, 237
  starting, 238-242
  (see also Gopher.)
gopher.uiuc.edu, gopher client, 237
Government, U.S., agricultural extension service, 374

grep command, 72
.gz, file suffix, 84

H

hardware, troubleshooting, 354
hash command (in ftp), 80
help command, Archie, 199, 201
    ftp, 80
help information, telnet, 53
hepnet newsgroup, 156
high-level domains, 32
home page (setting up), 317-318
"host not responding" error message, 68
"host timed out" error message, 68
"host unreachable" error message, 68
hosts, and bypassing passwords, 45
    file, 33
html, 508
    editors, 322
hypermedia, 508
hypertext, 233, 287-288, **508**
    editors, 288

I

IAB, 16, **508**
IBM mainframes, telnetting to, 58
IBM VM systems, and ftp, 94
IBM/PC, and Gopher clients, 236
ieee newsgroup, 156
IETF, 16, 350, **508**
IEUnet, 148
IMHO, 176, **508**
index resources, 244
index searches, 229
    in Gopher, 244-247
    in WAIS, 265
    in Web, 306-308
    (see also searches.)

indexes, building in WAIS from files, 285
info newsgroup, 156
information services, commercial, 156
international connections, 18, 489-493
Internet, 509
    access, 457-488;
        dedicated, 458;
        dialup, 460;
        ISDN, 460
    addressing rules, 106
    censorship, 157
    commercial use of, 37, 42-43
    composition, 15
    connection, 7-10
    ethics and, 40-43
    finding things on, 233-264, 287-323;
        (see also Gopher.)
    funding of, 17, 20, 36
    future of, 18
    getting connected to, 457-488
    history, 13
    how it works, 23-34
    legal implications, 35-39
    locating people on, 209-231
    News, 151-185;
        (see also News.)
    overview, 13-21
    political support for, 39
    privatization, 42-43
    security issues, 43-48
    troubleshooting, 351-366
Internet Architecture Board, 16
Internet Engineering Task Force, 16, 350
Internet Gopher, (see Gopher)
Internet Relay Chat (IRC), 342-346
Internet Society, 16
Internet Talk Radio, 349
InterNIC, 372, **509**
    database services, 373
    information services, 374
    registration services, 373
IP (Internet Protocol), 24, **509**
    addresses, 26

IP (Internet Protocol) (cont'd)
IRC (Internet Relay Chat),
    342-346, **509**
ISDN, 460, **509**
ISO, 509
ISOC, 16, **509**

J

Japanese newsgroup, 156
jughead searches, in Gopher,
    251

K

k12 newsgroup, 156
key mapping (3270), 61
killing News articles, 167
Knowbot Information Service
    (KIS), 227
Knowbots, 350, **509**

L

LAN (Local Area Network), 14,
    362
lcd command, 73
leased line, 509
legalities and the Internet, 35-39
    export laws, 37
    liability on the Net, 38
    property rights, 38
liability (legal), 38
librarians (robotic), 350
libraries, adding with WAIS, 283
    WAIS, 266
licensing restrictions, Gopher,
    235
list command, Archie, 199, 201
listing files, 69
listserv, 139-141, 143
    file retrieval, 144-146
Live Audio, 349-350
Live Video, 349-350
local servers, and addresses, 33

locating things on the Internet,
    233-264
    (see also Gopher.)
logging in without a password,
    81
login, remote, 327-329
"login incorrect" error message,
    68
ls command, 69
    ftp, 80

M

Macintosh, and ftp, 96
    and Gopher clients, 236
mail, (see email)
mail command, 111-115
    and sending messages, 114
    Archie, 199
mail reflector, 138, **510**
mailing lists, 119, 138, 370
    moderated, 142
mailserv, 139
mailto command, Archie, 200
Majordomo, 139, 143
    file retrieval, 144-146
Malamud, Carl, 349
manpage command, Archie, 199
map3270 file, 62
maxhits command, Archie, 200
mbox file, 117
MCImail addresses, 109
messages, 114
    cancelling, 123
    editing, 115
    incorrectly placed by ftp, 98
    reading, 112
    replying to, 120
    saving in folders, 116
    sending, 114
    (see also email.)
mget command, 77
    ftp, 80
MILNET, **510**
MIME, 123, 126-132
misc newsgroups, 154
mobile Internet users, 210
mode command, telnet, 53
modem, **510**

moderated mailing lists, 142
more command, 72
Mosaic, 306, 381, 510
    and telnet, 310
    creating hypertext docu-
        ments, 322
    hints for using, 318-321
    making your own links in,
        321
    (see also xmosaic.)
moving, directories, 85-89
    files, 65-99
mput command, 77
    ftp, 80
MSDOS systems, and ftp, 93
MUD (Multi-User Dungeon),
        347-349, 510
multicasting, 349-350
multimedia, 510
    mail, 123, 126-132
multiple files, transferring, 77
multiple names, 34
Multi-purpose Internet Mail
        Extensions (MIME), 126-132
Multi-User Dungeon (MUD),
        347-349

N

n command (News), 162
name servers, 251
names, domain, 30-34
    multiple, 34
National Information Infrastruc-
        ture, 36
net, (see Internet)
net articles, replying via email,
        175
Netfind, 229-231
network, future of, 18
    operations center, 17
    packet switch, 24
    schematic, 354
    time protocol, 337
Network Information Centers,
        372
network news, 370, 378
News, 151-185

articles; (see News articles)
categories, 154
choosing programs, 152
groups, 153-157
implementation of, 155
n command, 162
newsgroups, 154
reading, 160-171
starting a new discussion,
        173, 184
threads, 160
(see also newsgroups.)
News articles, catching up on,
        169, 177
distribution of, 174
encrypting/decrypting, 170
expiring, 156
killing, 167
locating, 178
marking as read, 177
posting, 171-176
replying to, 171
rereading, 156
saving, 165
searching for strings in, 177
selecting, 167
news newsgroups, 154
newsgroups, 153-157
    alt, 155
    bionet, 155
    bit, 155
    biz, 155
    comp, 154
    gatewayed, 156
    German, 155
    gnu, 156
    hepnet, 156
    ieee, 156
    info, 156
    Japanese, 156
    k12, 156
    listing subscription status of,
        179
    locally creating, 154
    misc, 154
    moving to next newsgroup,
        179
    navigating, 163
    news, 154
    rec, 154

newsgroups (cont'd)
    relcom, 156
    sci, 154
    soc, 154
    subscribing to, 166
    talk, 154
    u3b, 156
    unsubscribing from, 166
    VAX/VMS, 156
    vmsnet, 156
.newsrc file, 158
newsreading programs, nn, 152
    rn, 152
    tin, 152, 180-185
    trn, 152
    Web browers as, 314
NFS, 336, 510
NIC, 510
NII, 36
nn Newsreader, 152
    command-line options,
        177-178
    commands, 176-180
    invoking, 177
    mail facility, 175
    quitting, 179
    reading mode commands,
        179
    selection mode commands,
        178
    setting up, 158
    (see also News.)
.nn/init, 158
NNTP, 511
no such file or directory, error
        message, 68
NOC, 17, **511**
non-standard ports, and telnet,
        56
non-standard servers, and telnet,
        55
NREN, 36, **511**
NSFNET, 14, **511**
NTP, 337, **511**

O

octet, 511
open command, ftp, 80
    telnet, 53
OSI, 511

P

packet switch networks, 24
packets, 26, **511**
PAGER environment variable, in
        Gopher, 241
paging, in Gopher, 241
passwords, 45-46
    bypassing, 45
patent laws, 38
path command, Archie, 201
people, locating on the Internet,
        209-231
    locating with Gopher, 251
**Performance Systems Interna-
        tional**, 37
PF keys, 59
Pine, 129-132
.pit, file suffix, 84
politics and the Internet, 39
ports, 511
    telnet and non-standard, 56
posting news articles, 171-176,
        184, **512**
PPP connections, 459, **512**
    troubleshooting, 362
privacy-enhanced mail, 103
privatization, 19
Prodigy addresses, 107
prog command, Archie, 198, 201
programmed function keys, 59
prompt command (in ftp), 80
property rights, 38
protocols, 28, **512**
    application, 52
    definition, 52
    (see also transmission proto-
        cols.)
**PSI (Performance Systems Inter-
        national)**, 37
PSIlink, 461

public files, and property rights, 39
pwd command (in ftp), 80

Q

quit command, Archie, 202
  ftp, 80
  telnet, 53

R

R command (mail), 120
r command (mail), 120
R commands, 325-333
  rcp, 325, 329-331
  rdist, 331-333
  rlogin, 325
  security, 326
rcp command, 325, 329-331
rdist command, 331-333
reading, email, 112
  News, 160-171
rec newsgroups, 154
recreational newsgroups, 154
recursive file listings, 71
reflectors (mail), 138
regular expressions, 167
relcom newsgroup, 156
relevance feedback, 512
remote computers, browsing on, 69
remote logins, 49-63, 327-329
  aborting, 329
  suspending, 329
remote systems, security, 326
replying, to email, 120
  to News articles, 171, 175, 184
research (using Internet for), 36
resource catalog, how to use, 380
resources, accessing through the Internet, 233-264, 287-323
  finding on your own, 370
  index, 244

retrieval of files, via email, 143-148
  via ftp, 65-99
"returned mail" error message, 136
RFC, 512
.rhosts, 326
rlogin command, 325, 327-329
  escape sequences, 329
rn newsreader, 152
robotic librarians, 350
root servers, and addresses, 33
rot13, 170
routers, 24, **512**
RTFM, 512

S

saving, email, 117
  Gopher items, 242
  messages in folders, 116
  News articles, 165
schematic, network, 354
science newsgroups, 154
searches, Archie, 200, 257
  Gopher, 247
  WAIS, 245, 265-286;
    refining, 275-277;
    saving, 276;
    unsuccessful, 276-277
  Web, 306-308
security, and R (remote) commands, 326-327
  and the Internet, 43-48
  CERT, 44
  importing software, 46
  passwords, 45-46
  system software flaws, 47
selecting News articles, 167
send command, telnet, 53
sending email, 114
servers, 51, **513**
  Archie, 190, 200, 202
  building your own, 285-286
  moving between, 242-243
  telnet and non-standard, 55
service providers, 462-488, **513**
  international, 465
  national, 465, 467

service providers (cont'd)
   regional, 465, 473
"service unavailable" error message, 136
set command, Archie, 199
   telnet, 53
set match_domain command, 196
set match_path command, 196
shell, **513**
   archives, 88
shopping, 377
show command, Archie, 200
signature files, 122, **513**
.Sit, file suffix, 84
site, connecting to, 80
SLIP connections, 459, **513**
   troubleshooting, 362
smileys, 104, **513**
soc newsgroup, 154
software, Free Software Foundation (FSF), 46, 156
   looking for via Archie, 196
   misconfigured, 47
   obtaining from FTP site info.cern.ch, 287
   security risks of importing, 46
sort command, Archie, 200
source files, 67
   adding to WAIS, 282-285
   building your own, 285-286
Sprintmail addresses, 108
SRI, **513**
status command, telnet, 53
strings, searching for, 177
subscribing to newsgroups, 151, 157, 166
   with nn, 158, 166
   with tin, 181
subscription status of newsgroups, 179
swais, 268, 277-282
switched access, 513

T

talk newsgroups, 154
talk program, 340-341
talking to others on the Net, 340-341
   (see also conversations on the Net.)
tar files, 87
TCP (Transmission Control Protocol), 27, **514**
telephone connections, 462
telnet, 49-63, **514**
   and Archie, 191-201
   and Gopher, 259-260
   and non-standard servers, 55
   and the escape character, 52
   and the whois database, 219
   carriage returns, 55
   closing the connection, 53
   command mode, 52-55
   commands, 53-55
   echoing on or off, 53
   exiting, 53
   getting help information, 53
   how to use, 50-51
   listing available commands, 53
   opening the connection, 53
   printing status information, 53
   suspending, 53-54
   to IBM mainframes, 58
   to non-standard ports, 56
telnet command, 327
   (see also rlogin command.)
term command, Archie, 200
terminator caps, Ethernet, 363
text files, including in email, 119
threads, 152, 160, 181, 183-184
tilde escape commands, 115, 329
   ~., 329
   ~b, 122
   ~CTRL-z, 329
   ~e, 115
   ~f, 118
   ~m, 118
   ~r, 119

time, synchronizing on computers, 337
timed daemon, 337
timeout, **514**
tin newsreader, 152, 180-185
tn3270, 59-63, **514**
To field, mail, 121
toggle command, telnet, 53
token ring net, 514
 troubleshooting, 360, 365
transceiver cable, 363
transferring, data, 74
 files, 72
 large files, 83
 multiple files, 77
transmission protocols, 28
 Transmission Control Protocol (TCP), 27
 User Datagram Protocol
 (UDP), 28
trn newsreader, 152
trojan horse programs, 46
troubleshooting, 351-366
 10baseT Ethernet, 360
 dial-up connections, 361-362
 error messages, 356-357
 LAN connections, 362
 network schematic, 354
 PPP connections, 362
 SLIP connections, 362
 token ring net, 360
.TXT files, 91

U

u3b newsgroup, 156
UDP, 28, **514**
uncompress command, 84
UNIX, 514
 BSD (Berkeley) UNIX, 325
 curses version, 237
 file permissions, 330
 Gopher clients, 237
 mail, 111-115
 R commands, 325
 regular expressions, 167
 talk program, 340-341
 tar files, 87
 wais, 268

"unknown hosts" error message,
 133
"unknown recipients" error message, 135
unset command, Archie, 200
unsubscribing to newsgroups,
 159, 166, 181
USENET, 153, **514**
 user list, 219
user command (in ftp), 81
user datagram protocol, 28
"user unknown" error message,
 137
UUCP, 515
 access, 461
 addresses, 109
UUNET, 37

V

Vacation (the program), 148-150
variables, Archie, 200-201
VAX/VMS newsgroup, 156
Veronica, **515**
 searches in Gopher, 247-251
version command, Archie, 200
vi, using in email, 115
video on the Internet, 349-350
VMS systems, and ftp, 90
 filename wildcards, 70
vmsnet newsgroup, 156

W

WAIS, 233, 378, 380, **515**
 accessing, 268
 adding sources to, 282-285
 and the Web, 310
 how it works, 266-267
 libraries, 266
 public clients, 277-282
 searches, 245, 265-286
 servers, 313
 swais, 277-282
 UNIX interface, 268
 using, 269-275
 X version, 268
waisindex, 285

Weather Underground, example, 57

Web, 233, 287-323, 372, 381
and Gopher, 291-293
and reading network news, 314
and WAIS, 310
and xmosaic, 294-306
commands, 293
future of, 321-323
getting started, 289-291
going outside, 314-317
using, 293-317

whatis command, Archie, 198, 202

white pages, 209, 227, 373, **515**
servers, 251-255

whois command, 216

Whois directory, 215

Wide Area Information Service, (see WAIS)

wildcards, 77

World Wide Web, **515**
(see Web)

WWW, (see Web)

X

X Window System, 333-335
and Archie, 205
and Gopher clients, 236
setting display, 333-335
xhost command, 335

X.500, addresses, 108
directory service, 221
standard, 211

xhost command, 335

xmosaic, 294-306
(see also Mosaic.)

xwais, 268

Y

yellow pages, 373

Ytalk, 342

Z

z command, telnet, 53-54

Z39.50 standard, 266

.Z, file suffix, 84

.z, file suffix, 84

ZIP (program), 89

.ZIP, file suffix, 84

.zoo, file suffix, 84

CATALOG INDEX

1492 Exhibition 418

A

Aboriginal studies 385
Academe This Week 404
"acceptable use" policies 425
Acoustic Guitar Digest 439
Acronym Dictionary 446
Advanced Technology Information
    Network 384
Advertising on the Internet 377
Aeronautics 383
Aeronautics Archives 389
AgNIC 373
Agriculture 384
    Advanced Technology Information
        Network 384
    Agricultural extension service 375
    Commodity Market Reports 384
    Maize Genome Database Gopher 392
    Not Just Cows 384
    PEN Pages 384
    U.C. Davis Extension 4-H Project
        Catalog 384
    USDA
        Extension Service Gopher 384
        research results 385
AIDS 435
Alcoholism 435
Algeria 421
Almanac 375-376
American Astronomical Society 387

American Chemical Society Gopher 394
American Philosophical Association
    Gopher 443
"Americans with Disabilities" Act 413
Anonymous FTP sites 425
Anthropology 385
    aboriginal studies 385
    Coombspapers Social Sciences Research
        Data Bank 386
    Rice Anthropology Gopher 386
    Thai Yunnan Project 386
APNIC 373
Arabidopsis 390
Archaeology 386
    Classics And Mediterranean Archaeology
        (U Mich) 386
    Dead Seas Scrolls Exhibition 386
    Near East 386
    New World archaeology 387
Archie 371, 379, 425
Architecture 418
Archival software 396
Art history
    architecture 418
    Australian 418
    Black Artists at the National Museum of
        American Art 418
    Bodleian Library MSS 419
    Japanese 419
    Krannert Art Museum 419
    Roman palace in ex-Yugoslavia 419
    Vatican Library MSS Exhibit 419
Astrology 447

Astronautics 383
  NASA News 383
  NASA Spacelink 383
  satellite images 383
  shuttle images 383
  space FAQs 383
  SpaceMet 383
Astronomy 387
  American Astronomical Society 387
  Centre De Donnés Astronomiques De
    Strasbourg 388
  databases 387
  images 387-389
  internet resources on 387
  Lunar And Planetary Institute 388
  NASA Information Services Via WWW
    388
  NASA Langley Research Center 388
  NASA/IPAC Extragalactic Database 388
  National Space Science Data Center 388
  Project STELAR (Study Of Electronic
    Literature For Astronomical Research)
    389
  Space Remote Sensing Center 389
  Space Telescope Science Institute 389
  University of Arizona space images 389
  University of Massachusetts, Amherst
    387
Atheism 447
Australia 422
Australian National University (ANU)
  Bioinformatics Hypermedia Service
    weather and global monitoring 453
  Asian religions bibliography 447
  Bioinformatics Hypermedia Service 390,
    442
    molecular biology 390
AVES 442
Aviation 389
  Aeronautics Archives 389
  DUAT 389

B

Banjo Tablature Archive 439
Bass playing 439

Bedford Institute of Oceanography 441
Beer 401
Belief systems 447
  see also Religion
Bible 447
Biking (Norway) 445
Biodiversity And Biological Collections
  Gopher 390
Biology 390
  Arabidopsis 390
  Australian National University
    Bioinformatics Hypermedia Service
    390
  Biodiversity And Biological Collections
    Gopher 390
  Flybase 390
  GenBank 391
  GrainGenes 391
  images 391
  Johns Hopkins Bioinformatics Web
    Server 391
  overview 390
  Pacific Rim Biodiversity Catalog 392
  SwissProt 391
  TAXACOM FTP Server 393
  Triticeae Genome Gopher 391
  see also molecular biology
Birds 442
BITNET 425
Black artists 418
Bodleian Library MSS 419
Book of Mormon 448
Botany 393
  at University of Georgia 393
Bottom Line Archive 439
Brazil 422
Bryn Mawr
  Classical Review 395
  Medieval Review 417
BSIM Simulation Package 407
Budget (U.S.) 414
Buffalo Free-Net 410
Business 393
  NAFTA (North American Free Trade
    Agreement) 393
  NASDAQ Financial Executive Journal
    393

Business *(continued)*
    stock market 394
    U.S. Commerce Business Daily 394
    University of Minnesota Management
        Archive 394
    Vienna Stock Exchange 394

C

Canada National Capital Free-Net 410
CancerNet (NCI International Cancer
    Information Center) 436
CapAccess (National Capital Area Public
    Access Network) 410
Carbon Dioxide Information Analysis
    Center 408
Catholicism 448
Census 1990 414
Centre De Donnés Astronomiques De
    Strasbourg 388
Centre International de Rencontres
    Mathematiques Bibliography 435
Ceramics Gopher 420
CERN 443
CERT 396
Character sets (non-Latin) 400
Chemistry 394
    American Chemical Society Gopher 394
    molecular graphics software 394
    Periodic Table of Elements 394
    Sheffield Chemistry Server 395
Chess 445
Chinese Community Information Center
    422
Chinese literature 432
Cholesterol 436
CIA World Factbook 446
CIA World Map 411
CICNet Electronic Journal Project 406
CIESIN Global Change Information
    Gateway 408
Civilization 417
    see also History
Classical languages 395
Classical literature 395
    Bryn Mawr Classical Review 395

Egyptian 395
electronic journals 395
Classics And Mediterranean Archaeology
    (U Mich) 386
Cleveland Free-Net 410
Clinical alerts 436
Cliometric Society 403
COGS (Computer Oriented Geological
    Society) 412
Columbia Index to Hispanic Legislation
    421
Columbia Online Information Network 410
Columbia Online Legal Resources (JANUS)
    430
Com-priv Mailing List Archive 425
Commodity Market Reports 384
Communications of the ACM 396
Compression software 396
Computational Science Education Project
    397
Computer ethics 397
Computer Oriented Geological Society
    (COGS) 412
Computer science
    archive sites 397
    paper bibliography 397
    technical reports 397
Computing 396
Congress Overview 414
Congressional Contact Information 443
Conservatoire National des Arts et Metiers
    388
Conversational hypertext 436
Cooking 401
Coombspapers Social Sciences Research
    Data Bank 386
Coptic Christianity 448
Copyrights 414
Cornell Legal Information Institute 430
Cornell Theory Center Server 407
CREN (Corporation for Research and
    Educational Networking) 431
Cryptography (computer) 398
CURIA Irish Manuscript Project 432
Cyrillic 425

D

Dante Project 432
Dead Seas Scrolls Exhibition 386
Deaf Gopher 421
December's Guide to Internet Resources 425
Declaration of Independence 430
Dendrome (Forest Tree Genome Mapping Database) 409
Denver Free-Net 410
Dictionary (online) 447
Digital Tradition Folk Song Database 439
Directory services 374
Domain Name Lookup 377-378, 426
Dracula 432
DUAT 389

E

E-MATH 435
E-zine-list 406
EARN 425
Earthquakes 412
Economics 402
    Cliometric Society 403
    Economic Bulletin Board 403
    economic data 403
    overview 402
    Rice Economics Gopher 403
    Sam Houston State University Economics Gopher 403
    University of Manchester NetEc Gopher 403
    University of Michigan Economics Gopher 404
    Washington University Economics Working Paper Archive 404
EDGAR 393
Education 404
    Academe This Week 404
    ERIC Digests Archive 404
    Federal Information Exchange 404
    International Centre For Distance Learning 404
    Minority Online Information Service 405
    National Center on Adult Literacy (NCAL) 405
    software for teaching mathematics 405
    SpaceMet 405
    Teacher*Pages 405
    U.S. Department Of Education Gopher 405
"Electronic Antiquity: Communicating the Classics" 395
Electric Eclectic 406
Electronic Frontier Foundation 429
Electronic magazines 405, 433
EMBNET Bioinformation Resources 391
Engineering 407
    Cornell Theory Center Server 407
Environmental Activism Server 444
Environmental Protection Agency Library 408
Environmental Resources Information Network (ERIN) 408
Environmental Safety And Health Information Center 408
Environmental studies 407
    BSIM Simulation Package 407
    Carbon Dioxide Information Analysis Center 408
    CIESIN Global Change Information Gateway 408
    Environmental Protection Agency Library 408
    Environmental Safety and Health Information Center 408
    Gopherable Environmental Studies Resources Index 408
    Oak Ridge National Laboratory (Environmental Sci Division) 408
    pesticides 409
    United Nations Rio Summit Agenda 409
    water quality education materials 409
ERIC Digests Archive 404
ERIN (Environmental Resources Information Network) 408
Erlangen-Nuernberg Free-Net 410
Esperanto 422
Ethnomusicology Research Digest 439
Europe 422
EXPO (WWW Exhibit Organization) 417

F

Family Medicine Discussion Archives 436
FAQs 370, 452
    fat-free cooking 402
    NeXT.FAQ 399
    online books 433
    pets 442
    skiing 446
    sourdough 402
    space 383
FDA Electronic Bulletin Board 414, 436
Federal Information Exchange 404
Federal legislation 414
Federal Register 414
Feminism 421
Fidonet Node List 426
Film Database 438
Finding resources (on your own) 370
Fine Art Forum 406
Flybase 390
Folk music 439
Forestry 409
    Dendrome (Forest Tree Genome
        Mapping Database) 409
    social sciences in 409
    trees 409
Fractals 435
France 422
Free Software Foundation 398
Free-nets 409
    Buffalo Free-Net 410
    CapAccess (National Capital Area Public
        Access Network) 410
    Cleveland Free-Net 410
    Columbia Online Information Network
        410
    Denver Free-Net 410
    Erlangen-Nuernberg Free-Net 410
    Heartland Free-Net 410
    Lorain County Free-Net 410
    National Capital Free-Net (Canada) 410
    Tallahassee Free-Net 411
    Victoria (British Columbia) Free-Net 411
    Youngstown Free-Net 411
French 422

L'Association des Bibliophiles Universels
    432
Project for American and French
    Research of the Treasury of the
    French Language 424
Frequently Asked Questions (*see also*
    FAQs) 370
FTP (anonymous sites) 425

G

Gardening 411
    Gardener's Assistant 411
    Master Gardener Information 411
    University of Missouri Horticulture
        Guides 411
GenBank 391
Genealogy 438
Geneva University Hospital Molecular
    Biology Server 391
Geographic Information Server 412
Geography 411
    CIA World Map 411
Geology 412
    Computer Oriented Geological Society
        (COGS) 412
    earthquakes 412
    Global Land Information System 412
    USGS 413
    USGS Geological Fault Maps 412
Germany 422
Gesamtverzeichnis der griechischen
    Papyrusurkunden Aegyptens 395
Global Land Information System 412
GNN 376-377
    interest centers 376
    marketplace 377
    Travelers' Tales Resource Center 452
Gopher 371, 379, 381
    American Chemical Society 394
    American Philosophical Association 443
    Biodiversity and Biological Collections
        390
    ceramics 420
    Deaf 421
    Extension Service 384

Gopher *(continued)*
    list of gophers worldwide 426
    Maize Genome Database 392
    National Genetic Resources Program
      392
    National Institute of Allergy and
      Infectious Disease 437
    National Institute Of Standards And
      Technology 428
    Paleontological Society 442
    Rice Anthropology 386
    Rice Economics 403
    Sam Houston State University 403
    Triticeae Genome 391
    U.C. Berkeley Museum of Paleontology
      441
    U.N. 413
    U.S. Department of Education 405
    University of Manchester NetEc 403
    University of Michigan Economics 404
Gopherable Environmental Studies
    Resources Index 408
Government
    international 413
    NATO 413
    U.N. 413
    U.N. Gopher 413
    U.S. 413
      Agricultural extension service 375

      Americans with Disabilities Act 413
      Regulations 413
      Budget 1993 414
      Budget 1994 414
      Census 1990 414
      Congress Overview 414
      copyrights 414
      FDA Electronic Bulletin Board 414
      federal legislation 414
      Federal Register 414
      Government Accounting Office 415
      Library of Congress services 415
      National Archives 415
      National Information Infrastructure
      Proposal 415
      National Performance Review 415
      National Referral Center 416

      NSF Awards 416
      NSF Publications 416
      Science and Technology Information
      Service 416
      Social Security Administration 416
      Supreme Court rulings 416
      White House 416
    World Constitutions 413
Government Accounting Office 415
GrainGenes 391
"Great Beginnings" newsletter 437
GRIST Online 406
Guitar 440

H

Ham radio 420
Hancock's Health Sciences Resources 437
Handicap News BBS Archive 437
Heartland Free-Net 410
High energy physics 443
High Performance Computing and
    Communications (HPCC) 398
Hinduism 449
Hispanic interest 421
History 417
    1492 Exhibition 418
    Bryn Mawr Medieval Review 417
    EXPO (WWW Exhibit Organization) 417
    Middle East Studies Association 417
    Mississippi State History Archives 417
    of art 418
      see also Art history
    of science 419
      HOST Electronic Bulletin 420
      Server 419
    Soviet Archives 417
    U.S. historical documents 417
Hobbies 420
    Ceramics Gopher 420
    Ham Radio 420
    Hockey Cards Mailing List Archive 420
    Horticultural Engineering Newsletter
      420
    tango 421
Hockey Cards Mailing List Archive 420

Holland 423
Honolulu Community College Dinosaur
    Exhibit 441
Horticultural Engineering Newsletter 420
HOST 420
Hypertext (conversational) 436
Hypertext Movie Database Browser 439
HYTELNET 426

I

IETF
    documents 426
    drafts 427
Images
    archaeological 386
    architectural 418
    art 406, 418-419
    artists 406
    astronomical 387-389
    biological 391, 441
    birds 442
    Carol Keye 439
    Chinese 422
    crystal structure 391
    dinosaur 441
    fractal 435
    geological 413
    Iran 423
    llamas 442
    musicians 440
    Norwegian 424
    photograph gallery 406
    religious 448
    satellite 383, 412, 453
    SGML documents 400
    skydiving 446
Indian classical music 440
Indiana Molecular Biology Archives 391
Indiana University Law School 431
Information System for Advanced
    Academic Computing 398
INRIA bibliography 398
Interest groups 421
    Columbia Index to Hispanic Legislation
      421

Deaf Gopher 421
    Feminism 421
    Hispanic Interest 421
    Queer Resources Directory 421
International Centre For Distance Learning
    404
International interest 421
"International Teletimes" magazine 406
International treaties 413
Internet Go Server 445
Internet information 425
    "acceptable use" policies 425
    anonymous FTP sites 425
    Archie 425
    BITNET 425
    Com-priv Mailing List Archive 425
    December's Guide to Internet Resources
      425
    Domain Name Lookup 426
    EARN 425
    Fidonet Node List 426
    Gophers Worldwide 426
    HYTELNET 426
    IETF documents 426
    IETF drafts 427
    Inet Services 427
    Internet Information Search 427
    Internet Mail Guide 427
    InterNIC Information Services 427
    List of Lists, Listservers, and
      Newsgroups 427
    Matrix News 428
    National Institute of Standards and
      Technology Gopher 428
    Network Information Online 428
    NNSC Internet Resource Guide 428
    NorthWestNet User Services Internet
      Resource Guide 428
    RFC (Request for Comments) 428
    WAIS servers 426
    "Zen and the Art of the Internet" 429
Internet Information Search 427
Internet Mail Guide 427
Internet organizations 429
    Electronic Frontier Foundation 429
    Internet Society 429
Internet resource directories 425

Internet services 430
   prototype WAIS FTP Server 430
   providers of 430
Internet Society 429
Internet Wiretap Book Collection 432
InterNIC 373-374
   database services 373
   InterNIC Information Services 374, 427
   registration services 373
Iran 423
Islam 449
Israel 423

J

Jainism 449
JANUS 430
Japan 423
   art 419
Jargon File 399
Job-hunting (Online Career Center) 393
Johns Hopkins Bioinformatics Web Server 391
Journals *see* Online magazines
Judaism 449
Juggling FTP Archives 445

K

Knowbot Information Service 454
Krannert Art Museum 419

L

L'Association des Bibliophiles Universels 432
Latin American Network Information Center 423
Law 430
   Columbia Online Legal Resources (JANUS) 430
   Cornell Legal Information Institute 430
   Declaration of Independence 430
   Indiana University Law School 431
   Supreme Court Rulings 431

   Sydney University Law School FTP Archive 431
   U.S. Constitution 431
   Washington and Lee Law Library 431
League for Programming Freedom 399
Lebanon 423
Lewis Carroll 433
Library of Congress Services 415
List
   of Internet Whois Servers 454
   of Lists, Listservers, And Newsgroups 427
Literature 432
   Chinese 432
   CURIA Irish Manuscript Project 432
   Dante Project 432
   Dracula 432
   indexes of online books 432
   Internet Wiretap Book Collection 432
   L'Association des Bibliophiles Universels 432
   Lewis Carroll 433
   online books
      FAQs 433
      Online Book Initiative 433
   poetry 433
   Project Gutenberg 434
   Project Runeberg (Scandinavian Literature) 434
   Science Fiction News Group Archive 434
   Shakespeare 434
Llamas 442
Lorain County Free-Net 410
Los Alamos Physics Information Service 443
Lunar And Planetary Institute 388

M

Machine learning 400
Mailing lists 370
Maize Genome Database Gopher 392
Martial arts 445
Master Gardener Information 411

Mathematics 435
  Centre International de Rencontres
    Mathematiques Bibliography 435
  e-MATH 435
  fractals 435
Matrix News 428
Medicine 435
  "Great Beginnings" 437
  AIDS 435
  alcoholism 435
  CancerNet (NCI International Cancer
    Information Center) 436
  cholesterol 436
  clinical alerts 436
  conversational hypertext 436
  Family Medicine Discussion Archives
    436
  FDA Electronic Bulletin Board 436
  Handicap News BBS Archive 437
  Internet/BITNET Health Science
    Resources 437
  MEDLINE 437
  National Health Security Plan 437
  National Institute of Allergy and
    Infectious Disease Gopher 437
  National Institutes of Health (NIH) 437
  National Library of Medicine 437
  Palo Alto Medical Foundation 438
  World Health Organization 438
MEDLINE 437
Meteorology *see* Weather
Mexico 423
Middle East Studies Association 417
MIDI 440
Minnesota Climatology Working Group
  453
Minority Online Information Service 405
Mississippi State History Archives 417
Molecular biology
  Australian National University
    Bioinformatics Hypermedia Service
    390
  EMBNET Bioinformation Resources 391
  Geneva University Hospital Molecular
    Biology Server 391
  Internet sites 392

National Genetic Resources Program
    Gopher 392
  WAIS databases 392
  see also Biology
Molecular Biology Sites 392
Molecular Graphics software 394
Monty Python 451
Mosaic 381
Mother Jones Magazine 407
Movies 438
  Film Database 438
  Hypertext Movie Database Browser 439
  USENET Movie Review Archive 439
MTV 440
Multimedia 399
Music 439
  Acoustic Guitar Digest 439
  Banjo Tablature Archive 439
  bass playing 439
  Bottom Line Archive 439
  Digital Tradition Folk Song Database
    439
  Ethnomusicology Research Digest 439
  folk music 439
  guitar 440
  Indian classical music 440
  MIDI 440
  MTV 440
  University of Wisconsin-Parkside Music
    Archive 440
  WNUR-FM Jazz Information Server 440
Mystical 449

N

NAFTA (North American Free Trade
    Agreement) 393
NASA Information Services Via WWW 388
NASA Langley Research Center 388
NASA Mid-Continent Technology Transfer
    Center 450
NASA News 383
NASA Spacelink 383
NASA/IPAC Extragalactic Database 388
NASDAQ Financial Executive Journal 393
National Archives 415

National Capital Free-Net (Canada) 410
National Center on Adult Literacy (NCAL)
    405
National Genetic Resources Program
    Gopher 392
National Health Security Plan 437
National Information Infrastructure
    Proposal 415
National Institute of Allergy and Infectious
    Disease Gopher 437
National Institute of Standards and
    Technology Gopher 428
National Institutes of Health (NIH) 437
National Library of Medicine 437
National Performance Review 415
National Referral Center 416
National Space Science Data Center 388
NATO 413
NCAL (National Center on Adult Literacy)
    405
NCAR Data Support Section Server 453
NCI International Cancer Information
    Center 436
Near East 386
    ancient 386
Netfind 454
Network Information Centers 373-374
Network Information Online 428
Network news 370, 379
Neural networking 399
New World archaeology 387
New Zealand 423
News posting via email 452
Newsgroups 427
NeXT.FAQ 399
NIH (National Institutes of Health) 437
NNSC Internet Resource Guide 428
Nonlinear Dynamics Archive 443
NorthWestNet User Services Internet
    Resource Guide 428
Norway 424
    biking 445
Not Just Cows 384
NSF Awards 416
NSF Publications 416

O

Oak Ridge National Laboratory
    Environmental Sciences Division 408
Occult 449
Oceanography 441
    Bedford Institute of Oceanography 441
    OCEANIC (Ocean Information Center)
    441
    USGS, Branch of Atlantic Marine
    Geology 441
Online books
    FAQs 433
    index 432
    Online Book Initiative 433
Online Career Center 393
Online magazines
    Athene 429
    Beanbag 393
    Bryn Mawr Classical Review 395
    CICNet Electronic Journal Project 406
    classics journals 395
    DragonZine 429
    e-zine-list 406
    Effector 429
    "Electronic Antiquity: Communicating
    the Classics" 395
    Electric Eclectic 406
    Fine Art Forum 406
    Flora Online 393
    GRIST Online 406
    HOST (History and Philosophy of
    Science and Technology) 420
    International Teletimes 406
    Internet Business Journal: Commercial
    Opportunities in the Networking
    Age" 403
    Lunar and Planetary Information
    Bulletin 388
    Mother Jones Magazine 407
    NASDAQ Financial Executive Journal
    393, 430
    overview 405
    Polish Journal 424
    Psycoloquy 444
    Quanta Magazine 407

Online magazines *(continued)*
  The University of Michigan electronic
    text archive 407
  Whole Earth 'Lectronic Magazine 407
Oriental Institute 387

P

Pacific Rim Biodiversity Catalog 392
Palaeoclimatology 442
Palaeontology 441
Paleontology
  Honolulu Community College Dinosaur
    Exhibit 441
  Paleontological Society Gopher 442
  Palynology and Palaeoclimatology (ANU
    Bioinformatics Hypermedia Service)
    442
  U.C. Berkeley Museum of Paleontology
    Gopher 441
  public exhibits 442
Palo Alto Medical Foundation 438
Palynology 442
PC Magazine 400
PEN Pages 384
Periodic Table of Elements 394
Pesticides 409
Pets 442
  AVES 442
  birds 442
  FAQs about 442
  llamas 442
Philosophy 443
  American Philosophical Association
    Gopher 443
Photographs *see* Images
Physics 443
  High Energy Physics (CERN) 443
  Los Alamos Physics Information Service
    443
  Nonlinear Dynamics Archive 443
Pictures *see* Images
Poetry 433
Poland 424
Political activism 443

Politics 443
  Environmental Activism Server 444
  making congressional contacts 443
  making political contacts 444
  Presidential Election 1992 444
  Privacy Forum 444
  Ross Perot 444
Portugal 424
Presbyterianism 450
Presidential election (1992) 444
Princeton Psychology Archive 444
Privacy Forum 444
Project for American and French Research
    of the Treasury of the French
    Language 424
Project Gutenberg 434
Project Libellus 395
Project Runeberg (Scandinavian Literature)
    434
Project STELAR (Study Of Electronic
    Literature For Astronomical Research)
    389
PSI White Pages Pilot Project 454
Psychology 444
  Princeton Psychology Archive 444
  Psycoloquy journal 444
Psycoloquy journal 444

Q

Quanta Magazine 407
Queer Resources Directory 421

R

Reader's Guide to Periodical Literature 447
Recipes
  archives for 402
  fat-free 402
  Info and Softserver (University of
    Stuttgart) 402
Recreation 444
  biking (Norway) 445
  chess 445
  Internet Go Server 445
  Juggling FTP Archives 445

Recreation *(continued)*
    martial arts 445
    scuba diving 445
    simulated conversations 446
    skiing 446
    skydiving 446
    windsurfing 446
Reference guides 446
    Acronym Dictionary 446
    CIA World Factbook 446
    Online Dictionary 447
    Reader's Guide to Periodical Literature
        447
    Roget's Thesaurus 447
    Zipcode Guide 1991 447
Religion 447
    ANU Asian Religions Bibliography 447
    astrology 447
    atheism 447
    Bible 447
    Book of Mormon 448
    Catholicism 448
    Coptic Christianity 448
    Hinduism 449
    Islam 449
    Jainism 449
    Judaism 449
    mysticism and occult 449
    Presbyterianism 450
    Religious Studies Publication Journal
        450
    Satanism 450
    Urantia Book 450
Resource catalog (how to use) 380-382
Resources 379
    finding on your own 370
Restaurants (SPIRES Guide) 451
RFC (Request for Comments) 428
Rice Anthropology Gopher 386
Rice Economics Gopher 403
Roget's Thesaurus 447
Roman palace in ex-Yugoslavia 419
Ross Perot 444
Russian 425

S

Sam Houston State University Economics
    Gopher 403
Satanism 450
Satellite images 383
Satellite TV 451
Scandinavian literature 434
Science and Technology Information
    Service 416
Science Fiction News Group Archive 434
Scuba diving 445
SEC 393
SGML (Standard Generalized Markup
    Language) 400
Shakespeare 434
Sheffield Chemistry Server 395
Shopping on the Internet 377
Shuttle images 383
Simpsons Archive 451
Simulated conversations 446
Skiing FAQ 446
Skydiving 446
Social sciences in forestry 409
Social Security Administration 416
Software
    Archie 425
    for teaching mathematics 405
    Free Software Foundation 398
Sourdough FAQs 402
Soviet Archives 417
Space FAQs 383
Space images (University of Arizona) 389
Space Remote Sensing Center 389
Space Telescope Science Institute 389
SpaceMet 383, 405
SPIRES Guide to Restaurants 451
State Department Travel Advisories 451
Stock market 394
Supercomputers
    San Diego Supercomputer 400
    Supernet 401
Supreme Court rulings 416, 431
SwissProt 391
Sydney University Law School FTP
    Archive 431

T

Tallahassee Free-Net 411
Tango 421
TAXACOM FTP Server 393
Teacher*Pages 405
Technology 450
   transfer 450
Television 451
   Monty Python 451
   Satellite TV 451
   Simpsons Archive 451
TEX 396
Thai Yunnan Project 386
Travel 451
   GNN Travelers' Tales Resource Center 452
   State Department Travel Advisories 451
   Travel Information Library 451
   Virtual Tourist 452
Trees 409
Triticeae Genome Gopher 391
Turkey 425
Typesetting 396

U

U.C. Berkeley Museum of Paleontology Gopher 441
   public exhibits 442
U.C. Davis Extension 4-H Project Catalog 384
U.S. Commerce Business Daily 394
U.S. Constitution 431
U.S. Department Of Education Gopher 405
U.S. historical documents 417
U.S. Securities and Exchange Commission (SEC) 393
United Nations
   Gopher 413
   Rio Conference Agenda 409
United States *see* U.S.
University of Manchester NetEc Gopher 403
University of Michigan Economics Gopher 404

University of Michigan electronic text archive 407
University of Minnesota Management Archive 394
University of Missouri Horticulture Guides 411
University of Wisconsin-Parkside Music Archive 440
UNIX
   booklist 401
   public access 400
Urantia Book 450
USDA
   Extension Service Gopher 384
   research results 385
USENET
   addresses 455
   FAQs 452
   Movie Review Archive 439
   news 452
   news posting via email 452
   Periodic Posting Archives 452
   software 452
   what is 452
USGS 413
   Branch of Atlantic Marine Geology 441
   geological fault maps 412
   Weekly Seismicity Report 412
UUNET FTP archives 401

V

Vatican Library MSS Exhibit 419
Victoria Free-Net (British Columbia) 411
Vienna Stock Exchange 394
Virtual Tourist 452

W

WAIS 372, 379, 381
   prototype FTP Server 430
   servers directory 426
   software search sources 401
Washington and Lee Law Library 431
Washington University Economics Working Paper Archive 404

Water quality education materials 409
Weather 453
    Australian National University
        Bioinformatics Hypermedia Service
        453
    maps 453
    Minnesota Climatology Working Group
        453
    NCAR Data Support Section Server 453
    network sources for 453
Web 372, 381
Wedding planning 438
White House 416
White pages 373, 454
    Internet Whois Servers 454
    Knowbot Information Service 454
    Netfind 454
    PSI White Pages Pilot Project 454
    USENET addresses 455
Whole Earth 'Lectronic Magazine 407
Windsurfing 446
WNUR-FM Jazz Information Server 440
Womens' studies 421
World Constitutions 413
World Health Organization 438
WWW *see* Web

Y

Yellow pages 374
Youngstown Free-Net 411

Z

"Zen and the Art of the Internet" 429
Zipcode Guide (1991) 447

About the Author

Raised in the Chicago area, Ed Krol went to the University of Illinois, got a degree in Computer Science, and never left.

In 1985, Krol became part of a networking group at the University of Illinois, where he became the network manager at the time the National Center for Supercomputer Applications was formed. It was there that he managed the installation of the original NSFnet. During the same period, he also wrote the "Hitchhiker's Guide to the Internet," because he had so much trouble getting information and was sick of telling the same story to everyone.

In 1989, Krol opted to leave the fast lane and returned to pastoral life on campus, where he remains to this day, Assistant Director for Network Information Services, Computing and Communications Service Office, University of Illinois, Urbana. He also writes a monthly column for *Network World*.

He has a wife and daughter (who is in the hacker's dictionary as the toddler responsible for "Molly-guards"). In his spare time Krol is a pilot and plays hockey.

Colophon

Our look is the result of reader comments, our own experimentation, and feedback from distribution channels.

Distinctive covers complement our distinctive approach to technical topics, breathing personality and life into potentially dry subjects.

The image featured on the cover of *The Whole Internet User's Guide & Catalog* is an alchemist. Alchemy, the precursor of modern chemistry, first appeared around 100 AD in Alexandria, Egypt—a product of the fusion of Greek and Oriental culture. The goal of this philosophic science was to achieve the transmutation of base metals into gold, regarded as the most perfect of metals.

Alchemy was based on three key precepts. The first was Aristotle's teachings that the basis for all material objects could be found in the four elements: fire, water, air, and earth. By altering the proportions in which the qualities were combined, elements could be changed into one another. The second precept arose from the philosophic thought of the time: metals, like all other substances, could be converted into one another. The third precept was taken from astrology: metals, like plants and animals, could be born, nourished, and caused to grow through imperfect stages into a final, perfect form.

Early alchemists were generally from artisan classes. As alchemy gained adherents, philosophers became more involved, and the cryptic language used by the early artisan-alchemists to protect trade secrets became virtually its own language, with symbols and fanciful terms. Over the centuries, the language of alchemy became ever more complex, reaching its height in Medieval Europe in the fourteenth and fifteenth centuries. Alchemy was superseded by the advent of modern chemistry at the end of the eighteenth century.

Edie Freedman designed this cover and the entire UNIX bestiary that appears on other Nutshell Handbooks. The cover image is adapted from a 19th-century engraving from the Dover Pictorial Archive. The cover layout was produced with Quark XPress 3.1 using the ITC Garamond font.

The inside formats were implemented in sqtroff by Lenny Muellner. The text and heading fonts are ITC Garamond Light and Garamond Book Italic. The illustrations that appear in the book are a combination of figures created by Chris Reilley, and wood engravings from the Dover Pictorial Archive and the Ron Yablon Graphic Archives, and were created in Adobe PhotoShop and Aldus Freehand.